WORLD TOURISM ORGANIZATION
ORGANISATION MONDIALE DU TOURISME
ORGANIZACIÓN MUNDIAL DEL TURISMO
ВСЕМИРНАЯ ТУРИСТСКАЯ ОРГАНИЗАЦИЯ
منظمة السياحة العالمية

Yearbook of Tourism Statistics

Data 1999-2003

M - Z

2005 Edition

Yearbook of Tourism Statistics 2005 Edition

ISBN: 92-844-0775-3
ISBN: 92-844-0776-1Vol. I
ISBN: 92-844-0777-X Vol. II

Published by the World Tourism Organization

Disclaimer

Printed by the World Tourism Organization
Madrid, Spain

TABLE OF CONTENTS

	Pages
INTRODUCTION / INTRODUCCION	ix
COUNTRY TABLES BY ALPHABETICAL ORDER	
VOLUME I (from A to L)	3-528
Albania/Albanie	3
Algeria/Algérie/Argelia	6
American Samoa/Samoa américaines/ Samoa Americana	8
Andorra/Andorre	10
Angola	11
Anguilla/Anguila	24
Argentina/Argentine	26
Armenia/Arménie	27
Aruba	30
Australia/Australie	38
Austria/Autriche	44
Azerbaijan/Azerbaïdjan/Azerbaiyán	52
Bahamas	56
Bahrain/Bahreïn/Bahrein	66
Bangladesh	71
Barbados/Barbade	75
Belarus/Bélarus/Belarús	80
Belgium/Belgique/Bélgica	83
Belize/Belice	103
Benin/Bénin	106
Bermuda/Bermudes/Bermudas	112
Bhutan/Bhoutan/Bhután	114
Bolivia/Bolivie	116
Bonaire	120
Bosnia and Herzegovina/Bosnie-Herzégovine Bosnia y Herzegovina	123
Botswana	127
Brazil/Brésil/Brasil	130
British Virgin Islands/Iles Vierges britanniques/ Islas Vírgenes Británicas	132
Brunei Darussalam/Brunéi Darussalam	133
Bulgaria/Bulgarie	135
Burkina Faso	142
Burundi	146
Cambodia/Cambodge/Camboya	147
Cameroon/Cameroun/Camerún	149
Canada/Canadá	151
Cape Verde/Cap-Vert/Cabo Verde	161
Cayman Islands/Iles Caïmanes/Islas Caimán	164
Chad/Tchad	169
Chile/Chili	173
China/Chine	177
Colombia/Colombie	187
Comoros/Comores/Comoras	189
Congo	190
Cook Islands/Iles Cook/Islas Cook	192
Costa Rica	193
Croatia/Croatie/Croacia	195
Cuba	203
Curaçao	207
Cyprus/Chypre/Chipre	210
Czech Republic/République Tchèque/ República Checa	212
Democratic Republic of the Congo/République démocratique du Congo/República Democrática del Congo	221
Denmark/Danemark/Dinamarca	222
Dominica/Dominique	226
Dominican Republic/République dominicaine/ República Dominicana	228
Ecuador/Equateur	230
Egypt/Egypte/Egipto	232
El Salvador	240
Eritrea/Erythrée	245
Estonia/Estonie	247
Ethiopia/Ethiopie/Etiopía	255
Fiji/Fidji	257
Finland/Finlande/Finlandia	259
France/Francia	276
French Guiana/Guyana française/Guyana Francesa	284
French Polynesia/Polynésie française/ Polinesia Francesa	285
Gabon/Gabón	293
Gambia/Gambie	294
Georgia/Géorgie	295
Germany/Allemagne/Alemania	301
Ghana	309
Greece/Grèce/Grecia	311
Grenada/Grenade/Granada	313
Guadeloupe/Guadalupe	318
Guam	320
Guatemala	321
Guinea/Guinée	324
Guinea-Bissau/Guinée-Bissau	337
Guyana/Guyane	339
Haiti/Haïti/Haití	340
Honduras	341
Hong Kong, China/Hong-Kong, Chine	345
Hungary/Hongrie/Hungría	352
Iceland/Islande/Islandia	365
India/Inde	369
Indonesia/Indonésie	375
Iran, Islamic Republic of/Iran, République islamique d'/Iran, República Islámica del	381
Iraq	384
Ireland/Irlande/Irlanda	386
Israel/Israël	388
Italy/Italie/Italia	400
Jamaica/Jamaïque	414
Japan/Japon/Japón	421
Jordan/Jordanie/Jordania	424
Kazakhstan/Kazajstán	430

TABLE OF CONTENTS

	Pages
Kenya	434
Kiribati	438
Korea, Republic of/Corée, République de/ Corea, República de	439
Kuwait/Koweït	444
Kyrgyzstan/Kirghizistan/Kirguistán	449
Lao People's Democratic Republic/ République démocratique populaire lao/ República Democrática Popular Lao	451
Latvia/Lettonie/Letonia	453
Lebanon/Liban/Líbano	465
Lesotho	470
Libyan Arab Jamahiriya/Jamahiriya arabe libyenne/Jamahiriya Arabe Libia	471
Liechtenstein	475
Lithuania/Lituanie/Lituania	479
Luxembourg/Luxemburgo	489
Notes to tables (from A to L)	
English	493
French	505
Spanish	517
VOLUME II (from M to Z)	531-993
Macau, China/Macao, Chine/Macao, China	531
Madagascar	540
Malawi	542
Malaysia/Malaisie/Malasia	544
Maldives/Maldivas	551
Mali/Malí	556
Malta/Malte	558
Marshall Islands/Iles Marshall/Islas Marshall	566
Martinique/Martinica	567
Mauritius/Maurice/Mauricio	572
Mexico/Mexique/México	579
Micronesia (Federated States of)/Micronésie (Etats fédérés de)/Micronesia (Estados Federados de)	580
Monaco/Mónaco	581
Mongolia/Mongolie	585
Montserrat	593
Morocco/Maroc/Marruecos	594
Mozambique	603
Myanmar	604
Namibia/Namibie	608
Nepal/Népal	610
Netherlands/Pays-Bas/Países Bajos	614
New Caledonia/Nouvelle-Calédonie/ Nueva Caledonia	620
New Zealand/Nouvelle-Zélande/ Nueva Zelandia	625
Nicaragua	630
Niger/Níger	634
Nigeria	635
Niue/Nioue	639
Northern Mariana Islands/Iles Mariannes du Nord/Islas Marianas Septentrionales	640

	Pages
Norway/Norvège/Noruega	642
Oman/Omán	645
Pakistan/Pakistán	650
Palau/Palaos	653
Palestine/Palestina	654
Panama/Panamá	656
Papua New Guinea/Papouasie-Nouvelle-Guinée/Papua Nueva Guinea	658
Paraguay	660
Peru/Pérou/Perú	665
Philippines/Filipinas	670
Poland/Pologne/Polonia	678
Portugal	703
Puerto Rico/Porto Rico	719
Qatar	723
Republic of Moldova/République de Moldova/ República de Moldova	725
Reunion/Réunion/Reunión	729
Romania/Roumanie/Rumania	730
Russian Federation/Fédération de Russie/ Federación de Rusia	743
Rwanda	748
Saba	752
Saint Eustatius/Saint-Eustache/ San Eustaquio	754
Saint Kitts and Nevis/Saint-Kitts-et-Nevis/ Saint Kitts y Nevis	756
Saint Lucia/Sainte-Lucie/Santa Lucía	758
Saint Maarten/Saint-Martin/San Martín	760
Saint Vincent and the Grenadines/ Saint-Vincent-et-les Grenadines/ San Vicente y las Granadinas	761
Samoa	763
Sao Tome and Principe/Sao Tomé-et-Principe/Santo Tomé y Príncipe	764
Saudi Arabia/Arabie saoudite/Arabia Saudita	766
Senegal/Sénégal	771
Serbia and Montenegro/ Serbie-et-Monténégro/Serbia y Montenegro	775
Seychelles	783
Sierra Leone/Sierra Leona	786
Singapore/Singapour/Singapur	788
Slovakia/Slovaquie/Eslovaquia	794
Slovenia/Slovénie/Eslovenia	800
South Africa/Afrique du Sud/Sudáfrica	808
Spain/Espagne/España	816
Sri Lanka	823
Sudan/Soudan/Sudán	829
Swaziland/Swazilandia	830
Sweden/Suède/Suecia	831
Switzerland/Suisse/Suiza	836
Syrian Arab Republic/République arabe syrienne/República Arabe Siria	842

Pages

Taiwan (Province of China)/Taiwan (Province de Chine)/Taiwan (Provincia de China) 848
Tajikistan/Tadjikistan/Tayikistán 854
Thailand/Thaïlande/Tailandia 856
The former Yugoslav Republic of Macedonia/ L'ex République yougoslave de Macédoine/ La Ex República Yugoslava de Macedonia 864
Togo 872
Tonga 876
Trinidad and Tobago/Trinité-et-Tobago/ Trinidad y Tabago 878
Tunisia/Tunisie/Túnez 883
Turkey/Turquie/Turquía 889
Turks and Caicos Islands/Iles Turques et Caïques/Islas Turcas y Caicos 907
Tuvalu 909

Uganda/Ouganda 910
Ukraine/Ucrania 912
United Arab Emirates/Emirats arabes unis/ Emiratos Árabes Unidos 917
United Kingdom/Royaume-Uni/Reino Unido..... 921
United Republic of Tanzania/République-Unie de Tanzanie/República Unida de Tanzania 926
United States/Etats-Unis/Estados Unidos 930
United States Virgin Islands/Iles Vierges américaines/Islas Vírgenes Americanas........ 935
Uruguay 937
Uzbekistan/Ouzbékistan/Uzbekistán 939

Vanuatu 940
Venezuela 941
Viet Nam 945

Yemen/Yémen 949

Zambia/Zambie 951
Zimbabwe 953

Notes to tables (from M to Z)
English 956
French 968
Spanish 981

Pages

COUNTRY TABLES BY GEOGRAPHICAL ORDER

AFRICA – AFRIQUE

East Africa – Afrique orientale – Africa Oriental
Burundi 146
Comoros 189
Djibouti
Eritrea 245
Ethiopia 255
Kenya 434
Madagascar 540
Malawi 542
Mauritius 572
Mozambique 603
Reunion 729
Rwanda 748
Seychelles 783
Somalia
Uganda 910
United Republic of Tanzania 926
Zambia 951
Zimbabwe 953

Central Africa – Afrique centrale – Africa Central
Angola 11
Cameroon 149
Central African Republic
Chad 169
Congo 190
Democratic Republic of the Congo 221
Equatorial Guinea
Gabon 293
Sao Tome and Principe 764

North Africa – Afrique du Nord – Africa del Norte
Algeria 6
Morocco 594
Sudan 829
Tunisia 883

Southern Africa – Afrique australe – Africa Austral
Botswana 127
Lesotho 470
Namibia 608
South Africa 808
Swaziland 830

West Africa – Afrique occidentale – Africa Occidental
Benin 106
Burkina Faso 142
Cape Verde 161
Côte d'Ivoire
Gambia 294
Ghana 309

Pages

West Africa – Afrique occidentale – Africa Occidental (cont.)
Guinea ... 324
Guinea-Bissau ... 337
Liberia
Mali ... 556
Mauritania
Niger ... 634
Nigeria ... 635
Saint Helena
Senegal ... 771
Sierra Leone ... 786
Togo ... 872

AMERICAS – AMERIQUES

Caribbean – Caraïbes – El Caribe
Anguilla ... 24
Antigua and Barbuda
Aruba ... 30
Bahamas ... 56
Barbados ... 75
Bermuda ... 112
Bonaire ... 120
British Virgin Islands ... 132
Cayman Islands ... 164
Cuba ... 203
Curaçao ... 207
Dominica ... 226
Dominican Republic ... 228
Grenada ... 313
Guadeloupe ... 318
Haiti ... 340
Jamaica ... 414
Martinique ... 567
Montserrat ... 593
Puerto Rico ... 719
Saba ... 752
Saint Eustatius ... 754
Saint Kitts and Nevis ... 756
Saint Lucia ... 758
Saint Maarten ... 760
Saint Vincent and the Grenadines ... 761
Trinidad and Tobago ... 878
Turks and Caicos Islands ... 907
United States Virgin Islands ... 935

Central America – Amérique centrale – América Central
Belize ... 103
Costa Rica ... 193
El Salvador ... 240
Guatemala ... 321
Honduras ... 341
Nicaragua ... 630
Panama ... 656

North America – Amérique septentrionale – América del Norte
Canada ... 151
Greenland
Mexico ... 579
Saint Pierre and Miquelon
United States ... 930

South America – Amérique du Sud – América del Sur
Argentina ... 26
Bolivia ... 116
Brazil ... 130
Chile ... 173
Colombia ... 187
Ecuador ... 230
Falkland Islands
French Guiana ... 284
Guyana ... 339
Paraguay ... 660
Peru ... 665
Suriname
Uruguay ... 937
Venezuela ... 941

EAST ASIA AND THE PACIFIC – ASIE DE L'EST ET LE PACIFIQUE – ASIA ORIENTAL Y EL PACIFICO

North-East Asia – Asie du Nord-Est – Asia del Nordeste
China ... 177
Hong Kong, China ... 345
Japan ... 421
Korea, Democratic People's Republic of
Korea, Republic of ... 439
Macau, China ... 531
Mongolia ... 585
Taiwan (Province of China) ... 848

South-East Asia – Asie du Sud-Est – Asia del Sudeste
Brunei Darussalam ... 133
Cambodia ... 147
Indonesia ... 375
Lao People's Democratic Republic ... 451
Malaysia ... 544
Myanmar ... 604
Philippines ... 670
Singapore ... 788
Thailand ... 856
Timor-Leste
Viet Nam ... 945

Australasia – Australasie
Australia ... 38
New Zealand ... 625

Pages

Melanesia – Mélanésie
Fiji .. 257
New Caledonia 620
Papua New Guinea 658
Solomon Islands
Vanuatu 940

Micronesia – Micronésie
Guam 320
Kiribati 438
Marshall Islands 566
Micronesia (Federated States of) 580
Nauru
Northern Mariana Islands 640
Palau 653

Polynesia – Polynésie – Polinesia
American Samoa 8
Cook Islands 192
French Polynesia 285
Niue 639
Pitcairn
Samoa 763
Tokelau
Tonga 876
Tuvalu 909
Wallis and Futuna Islands

SOUTH ASIA – ASIE DU SUD – ASIA MERIDIONAL

Afghanistan
Bangladesh 71
Bhutan 114
India 369
Iran, Islamic Republic of 381
Maldives 551
Nepal 610
Pakistan 650
Sri Lanka 823

EUROPE – EUROPA

Central/Eastern Europe – Europe Centrale/orientale – Europa Central/Oriental
Armenia 27
Azerbaijan 52
Belarus 80
Bulgaria 135
Czech Republic 212
Estonia 247
Georgia 295
Hungary 352
Kazakhstan 430
Kyrgyzstan 449
Latvia 453
Lithuania 479
Poland 678
Republic of Moldova 725

Pages

Central/Eastern Europe – Europe Centrale/orientale – Europa Central/Oriental (cont.)
Romania 730
Russian Federation 743
Slovakia 794
Tajikistan 854
Turkmenistan
Ukraine 912
Uzbekistan 939

Northern Europe – Europe du Nord – Europa del Norte
Denmark 222
Finland 259
Iceland 365
Ireland 386
Norway 642
Sweden 831
United Kingdom 921

Southern Europe – Europe du Sud – Europa Meridional
Albania 3
Andorra 10
Bosnia and Herzegovina 123
Croatia 195
Greece 311
Holy See
Italy 400
Malta 558
Portugal 703
San Marino
Serbia and Montenegro 775
Slovenia 800
Spain 816
The Former Yugoslav Republic of Macedonia (TFYROM) 864

Western Europe – Europe occidentale – Europa Occidental
Austria 44
Belgium 83
France 276
Germany 301
Liechtenstein 475
Luxembourg 489
Monaco 581
Netherlands 614
Switzerland 836

East Mediterranean Europe – Europe méditerranéenne orientale – Europa Mediterránea Oriental
Cyprus 210
Israel 388
Turkey 889

Pages

MIDDLE EAST – MOYEN-ORIENT – ORIENTE MEDIO

Bahrain 66
Egypt 232
Iraq 384
Jordan 424
Kuwait 444
Lebanon 465
Libyan Arab Jamahiriya 471
Oman 645
Palestine 654
Qatar 723
Saudi Arabia 766
Syrian Arab Republic 842
United Arab Emirates 917
Yemen 949

INTRODUCTION

The present Yearbook of Tourism Statistics, published in two volumes, has been prepared by the WTO Department of Statistics and Economic Measurement of Tourism. It is the 57 edition in a series initiated in 1947. It presents for 204 countries and territories data on total arrivals and overnight stays associated to inbound tourism with breakdown by country of origin.

In the present Yearbook, the titles of the tables are in English only. Notes are given in English, French and Spanish. Names of countries, regions and sub-regions as well as the classification included on the tables are in English only.

The statistical data published are those officially received from national tourism administrations and national statistical offices.

All the data received are subject to different kind of controls:

- Comparison with the data provided at a previous moment, but referred to the same period;
- Comparison of the total figures with the corresponding breakdown;
- Comparison of the same figures with the corresponding breakdown by concepts;
- Control for logic consistency between data;
- Control for exchange rate variation to remain acceptable.

Any discrepancies observed are consulted with the informing unit that confirms or rectifies, if necessary, the data previously sent.

Due to the rounding in the partial figures, the totals shown in the different tables of the Yearbook of Tourism Statistics may not coincide with the totals shown in the basic indicators of the Compendium of Tourism Statistics.

Consequently, **the data included in this Yearbook have an official character and have been entered in the WTO database as of 31 March 2005**. Therefore, any corrections or changes in the tables received after this date will be included in the next edition of the Yearbook.

Volumes I and II contain data of total arrivals and overnight stays of international inbound tourism with breakdown by country of origin. Countries are classified in accordance with English alphabetical order. Volume I covers countries from A to L (Albania to Luxembourg) and Volume II covers countries from M to Z (Macau, China to Zimbabwe).

Volumes I and II cover information on:

➢ Arrivals

A. Border statistics
- Table 1. Arrivals of non-resident tourists at national borders
- Table 2. Arrivals of non-resident visitors at national borders

B. Statistics on accommodation establishments
- Table 3. Arrivals of non-resident tourists in hotels and similar establishments
- Table 4. Arrivals of non-resident tourists in all types of accommodation establishments.

When a person visits the same country several times a year, each visit by the same person is counted as a separate arrival. If a person visits several countries during the course of a single trip, his/her arrival in each country is recorded separately. Consequently, *arrivals* are not necessarily equal to the number of different persons travelling.

Arrivals data correspond to international visitors to the economic territory of the country of reference and include both tourists and same-day non-resident visitors.

Data may be obtained from different sources: border statistics derived from administrative records (police, immigration, traffic counts, and other types of controls), border surveys and registrations at accommodation establishments.

➢ Overnight stays

- Table 5. Overnight stays of non-resident tourists in hotels and similar establishments
- Table 6. Overnight stays of non-resident tourists in all types of accommodation establishments.

Overnight stays refers to the number of nights spent by non-resident tourists in accommodation establishments (*guests*). If one person travels to a country and spends five nights there, that makes five tourist overnight stays (or person-nights).

The World Tourism Organization wishes to express its gratitude to the national tourism administrations and national statistical offices of the various countries and territories for their valuable co-operation.

Madrid, April 2005

INTRODUCTION

La Section Statistiques et mesure économique du tourisme de l'OMT est chargée d'élaborer l'Annuaire des Statistiques du Tourisme. Le présent Annuaire, qui est publié en deux volumes, constitue la 57e édition d'une qui a débuté en 1947. Il contient pour 204 pays et territoires des données détaillées sur la ventilation par pays d'origine des totaux des arrivées et des nuitées associées au tourisme récepteur.

Dans le présent Annuaire les titres des tableaux sont publiés en anglais uniquement. Les notes sont fournies en anglais, français et espagnol. Le nom des pays, régions et sous-régions ainsi que les classifications incluses dans les divers tableaux des arrivées et des nuitées sont publiés uniquement en anglais.

Les données publiées sont celles officiellement reçues des administrations nationales du tourisme et des instituts nationaux de la statistique.

Toutes les données reçues sont soumises à différents types de contrôle:

- comparaison avec les données fournies précédemment pour la même période,
- comparaison des totaux et de leur ventilation,
- comparaison des mêmes chiffres avec la ventilation correspondante par concepts,
- contrôle de la cohérence logique des données,
- contrôle de l'acceptabilité, compte tenu du pourcentage de variation.

Les anomalies éventuellement relevées sont consultées avec l'unité chargée de l'information qui confirme ou, au besoin, rectifie les données envoyées.

Etant donné l'arrondissement des données partielles, les totaux qui apparaissent dans les différents tableaux de l'Annuaire des statistiques du tourisme peuvent ne pas correspondre aux totaux des Indicateurs de base du Compendium des statistiques du tourisme.

En conséquence, **les données figurant dans le présent Annuaire ont un caractère officiel et ont été introduites dans la base de données de l'OMT jusqu'à la date limite du 31 mars 2005.** Toute correction ou modification reçue après cette date sera incorporée à la prochaine édition de l'Annuaire.

Les volumes I et II contiennent des données détaillées sur la ventilation par pays d'origine des totaux des arrivées et des nuitées du tourisme international récepteur. Les pays ont été classés par ordre alphabétique anglais. Le Volume I inclut les pays qui se trouvent entre les lettres A et L (de l'Albanie au Luxembourg) et le Volume II inclus les pays qui se trouvent entre les lettres M et Z (de Macao, Chine au Zimbabwe).

Les Volumes I et II de l'Annuaire portent sur:

➢ Arrivées

A. Statistiques de frontière
- Tableau 1. Arrivées de touristes non résidents aux frontières nationales
- Tableau 2. Arrivées de visiteurs non résidents aux frontières nationales

B. Statistiques dans les établissements d'hébergement
- Tableau 3. Arrivées de touristes non résidents dans les hôtels et établissements assimilés
- Tableau 4. Arrivées de touristes non résidents dans tous les types d'établissements d'hébergement

Lorsqu'une personne visite le même pays plusieurs fois dans l'année, chacune de ses visites est comptée séparément comme une arrivée. Si une personne visite plusieurs pays au cours d'un seul et même voyage, son arrivée dans chaque pays est enregistrée séparément. Par conséquent, le nombre d'arrivées n'est pas forcément égal au nombre de personnes qui voyagent.

Les données des arrivées correspondent aux visiteurs internationaux du territoire économique du pays dont il s'agit, visiteurs qui comprennent à la fois les touristes et les visiteurs de la journée (excursionnistes) non résidents.

Ces données peuvent être obtenues de différentes sources : statistiques des frontières tirées des registres administratifs (police, immigration, comptages de véhicules et autre types de contrôle), enquêtes aux frontières et registres des établissements d'hébergement.

➢ Nuitées

- Tableau 5. Nuitées de touristes non résidents dans les hôtels et établissements assimilés
- Tableau 6. Nuitées de touristes non résidents dans tous les types d'établissements d'hébergement

Nuitées indique le nombre de nuits que les touristes non résidents ont passées dans les établissements d'hébergement (en qualité de clients). Si une personne se rend dans un pays et y passe cinq nuits, on enregistre cinq nuitées de touriste (ou nuits-personne).

L'Organisation mondiale du tourisme tient à exprimer sa gratitude aux administrations nationales du tourisme et aux instituts nationaux de la statistique des divers pays et territoires pour leur précieuse coopération.

Madrid, avril 2005

INTRODUCCION

La Sección de Estadísticas y Evaluación Económica del Turismo de la OMT es la encargada de elaborar el Anuario de Estadísticas de Turismo. La presente edición del Anuario, que se publica en dos volúmenes, constituye la 57 edición de una serie que comenzó en 1947. Contiene para 204 países y territorios, datos detallados sobre el desglose por país de origen de los totales de llegadas y pernoctaciones asociadas al turismo receptor.

En el presente Anuario los títulos de los cuadros aparecen en inglés únicamente. Las notas figuran en inglés, francés y español. Se publica únicamente en inglés el nombre de los países, las regiones y subregiones así como las clasificaciones incluidas en los diversos cuadros.

Los datos publicados son los remitidos oficialmente por las administraciones nacionales de turismo y los institutos nacionales de estadística.

Todos los datos recibidos están sujetos a diversos controles:

- comparación con los datos facilitados con anterioridad y referidos al mismo periodo;
- comparación de los totales con el desglose correspondiente;
- comparación de las mismas cifras con el desglose correspondiente por conceptos;
- control de coherencia lógica entre diferentes datos;
- control de mantenimiento de aceptabilidad, cuenta habida del porcentaje de variación.

Se consultan todas las discrepancias con la unidad informante, la cual confirma o rectifica, si es necesario, los datos remitidos.

Debido al redondeo de las cifras parciales, los totales que aparecen en los distintos cuadros del Anuario de Estadísticas de Turismo, pueden no coincidir con los totales que aparecen en los Indicadores Básicos del Compendio de Estadísticas de Turismo.

Así pues, **las cifras incluidas en este Anuario tienen carácter oficial y han sido introducidas en la base de datos de la OMT al 31 de marzo de 2005.** Por consiguiente, cualquier corrección o cambio recibido después de esta fecha aparecerá en la próxima edición del Anuario.

Los volúmenes I y II contienen datos detallados sobre el desglose por país de origen de las tablas de llegadas y pernoctaciones del turismo internacional receptor. Se han clasificado los países por orden alfabético. El volumen I contiene los países incluidos entre las letras A y L (de Albania a Luxemburgo) y el volumen II contiene los países incluidos de la M a la Z (de Macao, China a Zimbabwe).

Los volúmenes I y II del Anuario incluyen la siguiente información:

➢ Llegadas

A. Estadísticas de fronteras
- Cuadro 1. Llegadas de turistas no residentes en las fronteras nacionales
- Cuadro 2. Llegadas de visitantes no residentes en las fronteras nacionales

B. Estadísticas en establecimientos de alojamiento
- Cuadro 3. Llegadas de turistas no residentes a los hoteles y establecimientos asimilados
- Cuadro 4. Llegadas de turistas no residentes en todo tipo de establecimientos de alojamiento

Cuando una persona visita un mismo país varias veces en un año, cada una de esas visitas se cuenta como una llegada. Si una persona visita varios países en el transcurso de un mismo viaje, cada llegada a uno de esos países se registra por separado. Por lo tanto, el número de llegadas no tiene que ser igual al número de personas que viajan.

Los datos de llegadas se refieren a las llegadas de visitantes internacionales en el territorio económico del país de referencia, sean turistas o visitantes del día no residentes.

Los datos pueden proceder de diversas fuentes: estadísticas de fronteras basadas en registros administrativos (policía, inmigración, recuentos de circulación y otros tipos de controles), encuestas en las fronteras e inscripciones en establecimientos de alojamiento.

- Pernoctaciones

  - Cuadro 5. Pernoctaciones de turistas no residentes en hoteles y establecimientos asimilados
  - Cuadro 6. Pernoctaciones de turistas no residentes en todo tipo de establecimientos de alojamiento

Las *pernoctaciones* se refieren al número de noches que pasan los turistas no residentes en establecimientos de alojamiento. Si una persona viaja a un país y pasa en él cinco noches, se contarán cinco pernoctaciones turísticas (o pernoctaciones/persona).

La Organización Mundial del Turismo desea expresar su agradecimiento a las administraciones nacionales de turismo y a los institutos nacionales de estadística de los diversos países y territorios por su valiosa cooperación.

Madrid, abril de 2005

COUNTRY TABLES M - Z

➢ Arrivals

A. Border statistics

- Table 1. Arrivals of non-resident tourists at national borders
- Table 2. Arrivals of non-resident visitors at national borders

B. Statistics on accommodation establishments

- Table 3. Arrivals of non-resident tourists in hotels and similar establishments
- Table 4. Arrivals of non-resident tourists in all types of accommodation establishments

➢ Overnight stays

- Table 5. Overnight stays of non-resident tourists in hotels and similar establishments
- Table 6. Overnight stays of non-resident tourists in all types of accommodation establishments

1999 - 2003

MACAU, CHINA

2. ARRIVALS OF NON-RESIDENT VISITORS AT NATIONAL BORDERS, BY NATIONALITY

		1999	2000	2001	2002	2003	Market share 03	% change 03-02
TOTAL	(*)	**7,443,924**	**9,162,212**	**10,278,973**	**11,530,841**	**11,887,876**	**100.00**	**3.10**
AFRICA		**4,114**	**4,334**	**4,092**	**4,407**	**4,657**	**0.04**	**5.67**
EAST AFRICA		**685**	**697**	**788**	**886**	**857**	**0.01**	**-3.27**
BURUNDI		4	7	5	9	4		-55.56
ETHIOPIA		19	7	16	15	18		20.00
KENYA		52	83	47	56	64		14.29
MADAGASCAR			52	78	68	45		-33.82
MALAWI		4	17	9	6	2		-66.67
MAURITIUS		219	227	273	263	174		-33.84
MOZAMBIQUE		148	126	146	127	151		18.90
RWANDA		2	2	3	3	4		33.33
SEYCHELLES		102	68	85	188	273		45.21
SOMALIA		4	3	3	5	16		220.00
ZIMBABWE		58	56	46	74	48		-35.14
UGANDA		25	19	18	25	19		-24.00
TANZANIA		33	21	53	40	30		-25.00
ZAMBIA		15	9	6	7	9		28.57
CENTRAL AFR		**262**	**192**	**124**	**120**	**248**		**106.67**
ANGOLA		98	49	51	38	114		200.00
CAMEROON		66	46	32	39	58		48.72
CONGO		11	25	10	10	25		150.00
EQ.GUINEA		36	42	15	22	40		81.82
GABON		20	4	4	1	1		
SAO TOME PRN		31	26	12	10	10		
NORTH AFRICA		**175**	**223**	**227**	**257**	**156**		**-39.30**
ALGERIA		40	27	33	37	34		-8.11
MOROCCO		51	119	94	106	52		-50.94
SUDAN		44	36	61	65	55		-15.38
TUNISIA		40	41	39	49	15		-69.39
SOUTHERN AFR		**1,746**	**2,100**	**1,879**	**1,923**	**1,866**	**0.02**	**-2.96**
BOTSWANA			8	3	1	1		
LESOTHO			4	9	2			
NAMIBIA		6	15	8	2	1		-50.00
SOUTH AFRICA		1,732	2,069	1,857	1,913	1,862	0.02	-2.67
SWAZILAND		8	4	2	5	2		-60.00
WEST AFRICA		**1,246**	**1,122**	**1,074**	**1,221**	**1,530**	**0.01**	**25.31**
CAPE VERDE		303	185	192	183	203		10.93
BENIN		13	13	11	6	7		16.67
GAMBIA		100	151	74	34	25		-26.47
GHANA		56	54	59	23	51		121.74
GUINEA		81	13	22	16	13		-18.75
COTE IVOIRE		22	25	12	15	11		-26.67
LIBERIA		24	25	28	30	17		-43.33
MALI		17	4	37	45	66		46.67
MAURITANIA		37	6	6	20	14		-30.00
NIGER		6	9	9	9	8		-11.11
NIGERIA		433	460	408	671	864	0.01	28.76
GUINEABISSAU		12	47	56	44	85		93.18
ST.HELENA		1	1		1			
SENEGAL		14	28	13	17	36		111.76
SIERRA LEONE		115	91	137	84	63		-25.00

2. ARRIVALS OF NON-RESIDENT VISITORS AT NATIONAL BORDERS, BY NATIONALITY

	1999	2000	2001	2002	2003	Market share 03	% change 03-02
TOGO	9	9	10	16	24		50.00
BURKINA FASO	3	1		7	43		514.29
AMERICAS	**105,715**	**117,989**	**118,817**	**128,219**	**95,502**	**0.80**	**-25.52**
CARIBBEAN	**409**	**651**	**721**	**711**	**403**		**-43.32**
ANTIGUA,BARB	9	29	20	24	13		-45.83
BAHAMAS	4	13	31	23	30		30.43
BARBADOS	12	25	5	12	7		-41.67
BERMUDA	4	3	3	1	2		100.00
CAYMAN IS	9	9	7	3	5		66.67
CUBA	34	27	39	71	24		-66.20
DOMINICAN RP	123	340	404	320	128		-60.00
GUADELOUPE		1		1			
HAITI	3	6	3	2	2		
JAMAICA	30	50	53	88	124		40.91
MARTINIQUE	22	3	3	2	3		50.00
NETH.ANTILES	1	2			1		
ARUBA	25	14	10	3	2		-33.33
CURACAO	2	5	2	1	1		
PUERTO RICO	2						
ST.LUCIA	10	16	2	2	3		50.00
ST.VINCENT,G	4	4	3	3	2		-33.33
TRINIDAD TBG	115	104	136	155	56		-63.87
CENTRAL AMER	**1,438**	**1,614**	**1,722**	**1,924**	**1,305**	**0.01**	**-32.17**
BELIZE	450	481	691	572	439		-23.25
COSTA RICA	323	363	330	452	339		-25.00
EL SALVADOR	38	64	25	29	19		-34.48
GUATEMALA	77	111	96	123	62		-49.59
HONDURAS	187	194	224	300	90		-70.00
NICARAGUA	10	5	1	12	8		-33.33
PANAMA	353	396	355	436	348		-20.18
NORTH AMER	**98,314**	**110,305**	**110,836**	**119,723**	**89,693**	**0.75**	**-25.08**
CANADA	24,084	28,256	28,613	31,152	24,842	0.21	-20.26
MEXICO	1,197	1,585	1,483	1,923	942	0.01	-51.01
USA	73,033	80,464	80,740	86,648	63,909	0.54	-26.24
SOUTH AMER	**5,554**	**5,419**	**5,538**	**5,861**	**4,101**	**0.03**	**-30.03**
ARGENTINA	602	667	568	336	263		-21.73
BOLIVIA	161	101	281	231	75		-67.53
BRAZIL	2,660	2,301	2,453	2,657	1,968	0.02	-25.93
CHILE	310	372	312	383	221		-42.30
COLOMBIA	301	434	381	465	283		-39.14
ECUADOR	132	165	233	223	126		-43.50
FALKLAND IS	10	12	10	3	1		-66.67
FR.GUIANA		1	2		1		
GUYANA	25	9	23	27	9		-66.67
PARAGUAY	49	61	46	37	29		-21.62
PERU	660	567	567	647	480		-25.81
SURINAME	28	39	73	128	59		-53.91
URUGUAY	117	88	81	73	36		-50.68
VENEZUELA	499	602	508	651	550		-15.51
EAST AS/PACI	**7,154,937**	**8,871,880**	**10,005,009**	**11,249,556**	**11,672,634**	**98.19**	**3.76**

2. ARRIVALS OF NON-RESIDENT VISITORS AT NATIONAL BORDERS, BY NATIONALITY

	1999	2000	2001	2002	2003	Market share 03	% change 03-02
N/EAST ASIA	**6,994,466**	**8,681,084**	**9,806,950**	**11,029,879**	**11,487,853**	**96.64**	**4.15**
CHINA	1,630,643	2,285,471	2,981,409	4,183,725	5,681,102	47.79	35.79
TAIWAN(P.C.)	1,000,151	1,334,376	1,476,342	1,557,611	1,045,755	8.80	-32.86
HK,CHINA	4,167,404	4,851,901	5,141,176	5,070,850	4,621,203	38.87	-8.87
JAPAN	160,963	161,541	159,012	164,429	97,051	0.82	-40.98
KOREA D P RP	1,502	1,502	1,339	1,511	1,219	0.01	-19.32
KOREA REP.	33,501	45,827	47,235	50,657	40,092	0.34	-20.86
MONGOLIA	302	466	437	1,096	1,431	0.01	30.57
S/EAST ASIA	**122,111**	**149,961**	**155,888**	**175,910**	**149,282**	**1.26**	**-15.14**
BRUNEI DARSM	127	200	188	122	125		2.46
MYANMAR	991	1,359	1,123	1,167	810	0.01	-30.59
CAMBODIA	646	514	663	990	283		-71.41
INDONESIA	9,535	17,272	17,989	20,035	18,130	0.15	-9.51
LAO P.DEM.R.	24	76	36	68	28		-58.82
MALAYSIA	20,871	27,338	28,678	33,153	26,086	0.22	-21.32
PHILIPPINES	38,213	44,487	51,085	55,343	51,101	0.43	-7.66
TIMOR-LESTE	10	7	13	9	94		944.44
SINGAPORE	20,109	27,035	26,544	32,424	26,821	0.23	-17.28
VIET NAM	3,761	4,706	5,887	6,537	6,337	0.05	-3.06
THAILAND	27,824	26,967	23,682	26,062	19,467	0.16	-25.31
AUSTRALASIA	**37,236**	**39,013**	**40,704**	**42,559**	**34,603**	**0.29**	**-18.69**
AUSTRALIA	31,379	33,161	34,227	36,282	29,607	0.25	-18.40
NEW ZEALAND	5,857	5,852	6,477	6,277	4,996	0.04	-20.41
MELANESIA	**160**	**149**	**164**	**205**	**192**		**-6.34**
SOLOMON IS	4	10	9	2	10		400.00
FIJI	87	86	97	130	149		14.62
NEW CALEDŃIA	7		3	2	2		
VANUATU	40	31	11	13	8		-38.46
PAPUA N.GUIN	22	22	44	58	23		-60.34
MICRONESIA	**604**	**1,389**	**1,002**	**757**	**595**	**0.01**	**-21.40**
NAURU	420	1,147	890	702	536		-23.65
MARSHALL IS	184	242	112	55	59		7.27
POLYNESIA	**360**	**284**	**301**	**246**	**109**		**-55.69**
TONGA	331	245	270	229	93		-59.39
SAMOA	29	39	31	17	16		-5.88
EUROPE	**163,427**	**148,361**	**130,265**	**127,614**	**94,078**	**0.79**	**-26.28**
C/E EUROPE	**3,281**	**4,158**	**4,471**	**5,674**	**4,329**	**0.04**	**-23.70**
BULGARIA	96	151	63	47	78		65.96
CZECH RP/SVK	260	289	358	501	498		-0.60
HUNGARY	190	330	367	601	411		-31.61
POLAND	893	831	1,184	1,340	774	0.01	-42.24
ROMANIA	156	103	140	216	210		-2.78
USSR(former)	1,686	2,454	2,359	2,969	2,358	0.02	-20.58
NORTHERN EUR	**71,975**	**73,525**	**62,496**	**59,258**	**45,503**	**0.38**	**-23.21**
DENMARK	1,972	1,580	1,475	1,568	1,409	0.01	-10.14
FINLAND	1,154	883	1,012	1,765	954	0.01	-45.95
ICELAND	243	100	86	140	55		-60.71
IRELAND	2,183	1,965	1,764	1,877	1,361	0.01	-27.49
NORWAY	1,013	927	987	1,096	797	0.01	-27.28
SWEDEN	2,603	2,684	2,550	2,857	2,093	0.02	-26.74

MACAU, CHINA

2. ARRIVALS OF NON-RESIDENT VISITORS AT NATIONAL BORDERS, BY NATIONALITY

	1999	2000	2001	2002	2003	Market share 03	% change 03-02
UK	62,807	65,386	54,622	49,955	38,834	0.33	-22.26
SOUTHERN EUR	**38,898**	**23,467**	**19,237**	**18,920**	**12,620**	**0.11**	**-33.30**
ALBANIA	8	13	19	7	11		57.14
ANDORRA	5	3	3	1	4		300.00
GREECE	407	389	275	339	211		-37.76
HOLY SEE	2	2	8		2		
ITALY	4,933	4,614	4,671	4,847	3,249	0.03	-32.97
MALTA	97	112	83	84	45		-46.43
PORTUGAL	30,914	16,092	11,804	11,170	7,666	0.06	-31.37
SAN MARINO					3		
SPAIN	2,214	2,179	2,132	2,429	1,380	0.01	-43.19
YUGOSLAV SFR	318	63	242	43	49		13.95
WESTERN EUR	**47,454**	**45,298**	**42,144**	**41,434**	**29,593**	**0.25**	**-28.58**
AUSTRIA	2,075	1,745	1,693	1,660	1,035	0.01	-37.65
BELGIUM	1,712	1,769	1,625	1,660	1,451	0.01	-12.59
FRANCE	16,761	16,842	16,517	16,809	11,925	0.10	-29.06
GERMANY	18,219	16,232	13,983	12,694	9,479	0.08	-25.33
LIECHTENSTEN	12	4	13	3	8		166.67
LUXEMBOURG	123	80	81	128	69		-46.09
MONACO	30	10	14	19	18		-5.26
NETHERLANDS	5,193	5,072	5,110	5,292	3,761	0.03	-28.93
SWITZERLAND	3,329	3,544	3,108	3,169	1,847	0.02	-41.72
EAST/MED EUR	**1,819**	**1,913**	**1,917**	**2,328**	**2,033**	**0.02**	**-12.67**
CYPRUS	51	36	32	45	41		-8.89
ISRAEL	1,148	1,215	1,397	1,638	1,427	0.01	-12.88
TURKEY	620	662	488	645	565		-12.40
MIDDLE EAST	**682**	**773**	**938**	**899**	**1,147**	**0.01**	**27.59**
MIDDLE EAST	**682**	**773**	**938**	**899**	**1,147**	**0.01**	**27.59**
BAHRAIN	29	30	19	23	18		-21.74
IRAQ	48	44	28	32	17		-46.88
JORDAN	86	115	70	188	173		-7.98
KUWAIT	28	80	41	79	54		-31.65
LEBANON	56	73	72	132	251		90.15
LIBYA	3	3	3	4	7		75.00
OMAN	35	17	11	5	10		100.00
QATAR	10	7	10	15	22		46.67
SAUDI ARABIA	143	119	164	113	126		11.50
SYRIA	58	76	90	85	259		204.71
EGYPT	147	166	397	156	150		-3.85
YEMEN	39	43	33	67	60		-10.45
SOUTH ASIA	**14,010**	**17,008**	**17,731**	**17,719**	**17,324**	**0.15**	**-2.23**
SOUTH ASIA	**14,010**	**17,008**	**17,731**	**17,719**	**17,324**	**0.15**	**-2.23**
AFGHANISTAN	66	13	18	13	7		-46.15
BANGLADESH	2,165	3,477	2,309	1,398	1,048	0.01	-25.04
BHUTAN	48	52	59	85	50		-41.18
SRI LANKA	592	564	637	707	567		-19.80
INDIA	7,158	8,111	9,229	10,460	9,847	0.08	-5.86
IRAN	55	69	68	351	529		50.71
MALDIVES	13	4	2	66	10		-84.85
NEPAL	880	1,093	1,739	2,168	2,655	0.02	22.46

2. ARRIVALS OF NON-RESIDENT VISITORS AT NATIONAL BORDERS, BY NATIONALITY

	1999	2000	2001	2002	2003	Market share 03	% change 03-02
PAKISTAN	3,033	3,625	3,670	2,471	2,611	0.02	5.67
REG.NOT SPEC	**1,039**	**1,867**	**2,121**	**2,427**	**2,534**	**0.02**	**4.41**
NOT SPECIFIE	**1,039**	**1,867**	**2,121**	**2,427**	**2,534**	**0.02**	**4.41**
OTH.WORLD	1,039	1,867	2,121	2,427	2,534	0.02	4.41

Source: World Tourism Organization (WTO)

MACAU, CHINA

2. ARRIVALS OF NON-RESIDENT VISITORS AT NATIONAL BORDERS, BY COUNTRY OF RESIDENCE

	1999	2000	2001	2002	2003	Market share 03	% change 03-02
TOTAL	**7,443,924**	**9,162,212**	**10,278,973**	**11,530,841**	**11,887,876**	**100.00**	**3.10**
AFRICA	**4,121**	**4,182**	**3,823**	**6,765**	**7,116**	**0.06**	**5.19**
SOUTHERN AFR				**1,658**	**1,598**	**0.01**	**-3.62**
SOUTH AFRICA				1,658	1,598	0.01	-3.62
OTHER AFRICA	**4,121**	**4,182**	**3,823**	**5,107**	**5,518**	**0.05**	**8.05**
OTHER AFRICA				5,107	5,518	0.05	8.05
ALL AFRICA	4,121	4,182	3,823				
AMERICAS	**96,968**	**108,626**	**109,044**	**115,383**	**86,674**	**0.73**	**-24.88**
NORTH AMER	**88,687**	**99,835**	**100,055**	**107,079**	**80,653**	**0.68**	**-24.68**
CANADA	21,135	25,482	26,448	28,552	23,202	0.20	-18.74
MEXICO				1,623	809	0.01	-50.15
USA	67,552	74,353	73,607	76,904	56,642	0.48	-26.35
SOUTH AMER				**2,485**	**1,899**	**0.02**	**-23.58**
BRAZIL				2,485	1,899	0.02	-23.58
OTHER AMERIC	**8,281**	**8,791**	**8,989**	**5,819**	**4,122**	**0.03**	**-29.16**
OTH AMERICA	8,281	8,791	8,989	5,819	4,122	0.03	-29.16
EAST AS/PACI	**7,190,754**	**8,910,805**	**10,032,388**	**11,280,134**	**11,693,497**	**98.36**	**3.66**
N/EAST ASIA	**7,040,474**	**8,732,612**	**9,844,786**	**11,070,558**	**11,514,601**	**96.86**	**4.01**
CHINA	1,645,193	2,274,713	3,005,722	4,240,446	5,742,036	48.30	35.41
TAIWAN(P.C.)	984,820	1,311,035	1,451,826	1,532,929	1,022,830	8.60	-33.28
HK,CHINA	4,229,833	4,954,619	5,196,136	5,101,437	4,623,162	38.89	-9.38
JAPAN	145,284	144,888	140,937	142,588	85,613	0.72	-39.96
KOREA D P RP				1,528	1,237	0.01	-19.04
KOREA REP.	33,483	45,365	48,274	50,447	38,281	0.32	-24.12
OT NORTH AS	1,861	1,992	1,891	1,183	1,442	0.01	21.89
S/EAST ASIA	**116,312**	**141,846**	**150,025**	**171,176**	**147,829**	**1.24**	**-13.64**
INDONESIA	8,905	16,920	16,771	19,423	17,705	0.15	-8.85
MALAYSIA	20,025	25,753	27,254	31,323	24,555	0.21	-21.61
PHILIPPINES	36,614	42,111	50,705	54,739	52,162	0.44	-4.71
SINGAPORE	19,596	26,026	25,702	30,940	25,767	0.22	-16.72
THAILAND	25,706	24,396	21,572	24,625	18,096	0.15	-26.51
OTH S/E ASIA	5,466	6,640	8,021	10,126	9,544	0.08	-5.75
AUSTRALASIA	**32,384**	**33,931**	**35,395**	**36,517**	**29,743**	**0.25**	**-18.55**
AUSTRALIA	27,161	28,809	29,334	31,028	25,385	0.21	-18.19
NEW ZEALAND	5,223	5,122	6,061	5,489	4,358	0.04	-20.60
OT.EAST AS/P	**1,584**	**2,416**	**2,182**	**1,883**	**1,324**	**0.01**	**-29.69**
OTH OCEANIA	1,584	2,416	2,182	1,883	1,324	0.01	-29.69
EUROPE	**137,443**	**120,907**	**114,595**	**111,526**	**83,592**	**0.70**	**-25.05**
NORTHERN EUR	**47,449**	**45,558**	**44,666**	**44,692**	**36,737**	**0.31**	**-17.80**
IRELAND				1,651	1,208	0.01	-26.83
SWEDEN				2,524	1,701	0.01	-32.61
UK	47,449	45,558	44,666	40,517	33,828	0.28	-16.51

2. ARRIVALS OF NON-RESIDENT VISITORS AT NATIONAL BORDERS, BY COUNTRY OF RESIDENCE

	1999	2000	2001	2002	2003	Market share 03	% change 03-02
SOUTHERN EUR	**29,882**	**16,877**	**14,139**	**16,494**	**11,043**	**0.09**	**-33.05**
ITALY	4,703	4,513	4,315	4,327	3,240	0.03	-25.12
PORTUGAL	25,179	12,364	9,824	10,057	6,576	0.06	-34.61
SPAIN				2,110	1,227	0.01	-41.85
WESTERN EUR	**32,732**	**30,582**	**28,162**	**36,029**	**25,372**	**0.21**	**-29.58**
AUSTRIA				1,452	941	0.01	-35.19
FRANCE	16,082	16,186	15,986	16,304	11,676	0.10	-28.39
GERMANY	16,650	14,396	12,176	10,721	7,643	0.06	-28.71
NETHERLANDS				4,781	3,554	0.03	-25.66
SWITZERLAND				2,771	1,558	0.01	-43.77
OTHER EUROPE	**27,380**	**27,890**	**27,628**	**14,311**	**10,440**	**0.09**	**-27.05**
OTHER EUROPE	27,380	27,890	27,628	14,311	10,440	0.09	-27.05
MIDDLE EAST	**746**	**871**	**1,059**				
MIDDLE EAST	**746**	**871**	**1,059**				
ALL MID EAST	746	871	1,059				
SOUTH ASIA	**13,592**	**16,636**	**17,838**	**16,832**	**16,763**	**0.14**	**-0.41**
SOUTH ASIA	**13,592**	**16,636**	**17,838**	**16,832**	**16,763**	**0.14**	**-0.41**
BANGLADESH				1,564	1,604	0.01	2.56
INDIA	7,094	7,530	8,659	10,574	9,820	0.08	-7.13
NEPAL				2,248	2,749	0.02	22.29
PAKISTAN				2,446	2,590	0.02	5.89
OTH STH ASIA	6,498	9,106	9,179				
REG.NOT SPEC	**300**	**185**	**226**	**201**	**234**		**16.42**
NOT SPECIFIE	**300**	**185**	**226**	**201**	**234**		**16.42**
OTH.WORLD	300	185	226	201	234		16.42

Source: World Tourism Organization (WTO)

MACAU, CHINA

3. ARRIVALS OF NON-RESIDENT TOURISTS IN HOTELS AND SIMILAR ESTABLISHMENTS, BY COUNTRY OF RESIDENCE

	1999	2000	2001	2002	2003	Market share 03	% change 03-02
TOTAL	**2,138,386**	**2,551,843**	**2,624,522**	**2,996,079**	**2,870,465**	**100.00**	**-4.19**
AMERICAS	**15,721**	**15,090**	**16,433**	**16,900**	**15,000**	**0.52**	**-11.24**
NORTH AMER	**15,721**	**15,090**	**16,433**	**16,900**	**15,000**	**0.52**	**-11.24**
CANADA	3,206	3,573	3,805	3,970	3,813	0.13	-3.95
USA	12,515	11,517	12,628	12,930	11,187	0.39	-13.48
EAST AS/PACI	**2,073,369**	**2,491,726**	**2,571,823**	**2,947,196**	**2,823,542**	**98.37**	**-4.20**
N/EAST ASIA	**2,047,280**	**2,463,834**	**2,541,332**	**2,919,454**	**2,797,618**	**97.46**	**-4.17**
CHINA	816,825	1,038,075	1,076,439	1,451,250	1,431,294	49.86	-1.38
TAIWAN(P.C.)	221,072	233,581	188,989	166,332	111,410	3.88	-33.02
HK,CHINA	963,014	1,133,540	1,207,938	1,249,155	1,218,648	42.45	-2.44
JAPAN	36,838	46,463	56,021	39,718	25,230	0.88	-36.48
KOREA REP.	9,531	12,175	11,945	12,999	11,036	0.38	-15.10
S/EAST ASIA	**19,744**	**22,556**	**25,003**	**22,181**	**20,637**	**0.72**	**-6.96**
INDONESIA	1,231	3,001	3,516	3,121	4,402	0.15	41.04
MALAYSIA	2,861	3,541	4,416	4,871	3,971	0.14	-18.48
PHILIPPINES	1,982	3,245	5,017	3,434	2,265	0.08	-34.04
SINGAPORE	5,496	5,445	5,860	6,193	6,339	0.22	2.36
THAILAND	8,174	7,324	6,194	4,562	3,660	0.13	-19.77
AUSTRALASIA	**6,345**	**5,336**	**5,488**	**5,561**	**5,287**	**0.18**	**-4.93**
AUSTRALIA	5,189	4,315	4,502	4,489	4,234	0.15	-5.68
NEW ZEALAND	1,156	1,021	986	1,072	1,053	0.04	-1.77
EUROPE	**40,449**	**27,971**	**21,929**	**20,310**	**19,843**	**0.69**	**-2.30**
NORTHERN EUR	**9,363**	**9,805**	**7,551**	**6,958**	**8,725**	**0.30**	**25.40**
UK	9,363	9,805	7,551	6,958	8,725	0.30	25.40
SOUTHERN EUR	**17,466**	**4,101**	**2,977**	**3,705**	**2,952**	**0.10**	**-20.32**
ITALY	1,042	707	824	1,048	708	0.02	-32.44
PORTUGAL	16,424	3,394	2,153	2,657	2,244	0.08	-15.54
WESTERN EUR	**6,463**	**5,667**	**5,362**	**4,971**	**3,629**	**0.13**	**-27.00**
FRANCE	3,772	3,343	2,706	2,579	1,765	0.06	-31.56
GERMANY	2,691	2,324	2,656	2,392	1,864	0.06	-22.07
OTHER EUROPE	**7,157**	**8,398**	**6,039**	**4,676**	**4,537**	**0.16**	**-2.97**
OTHER EUROPE	7,157	8,398	6,039	4,676	4,537	0.16	-2.97
SOUTH ASIA	**894**	**1,114**	**1,769**	**1,892**	**2,068**	**0.07**	**9.30**
SOUTH ASIA	**894**	**1,114**	**1,769**	**1,892**	**2,068**	**0.07**	**9.30**
INDIA	894	1,114	1,769	1,892	2,068	0.07	9.30
REG.NOT SPEC	**7,953**	**15,942**	**12,568**	**9,781**	**10,012**	**0.35**	**2.36**
NOT SPECIFIE	**7,953**	**15,942**	**12,568**	**9,781**	**10,012**	**0.35**	**2.36**
OTH.WORLD	7,953	15,942	12,568	9,781	10,012	0.35	2.36

Source: World Tourism Organization (WTO)

5. OVERNIGHT STAYS OF NON-RESIDENT TOURISTS IN HOTELS AND SIMILAR ESTABLISHMENTS, BY COUNTRY OF RESIDENCE

	1999	2000	2001	2002	2003	Market share 03	% change 03-02
TOTAL	**2,885,173**	**3,219,037**	**3,344,070**	**3,656,239**	**3,456,057**	**100.00**	**-5.48**
AMERICAS	**41,655**	**42,871**	**29,682**	**33,536**	**36,662**	**1.06**	**9.32**
NORTH AMER	**41,655**	**42,871**	**29,682**	**33,536**	**36,662**	**1.06**	**9.32**
CANADA	10,982	12,163	7,930	10,976	15,182	0.44	38.32
USA	30,673	30,708	21,752	22,560	21,480	0.62	-4.79
EAST AS/PACI	**2,723,950**	**3,098,712**	**3,249,088**	**3,563,783**	**3,359,285**	**97.20**	**-5.74**
N/EAST ASIA	**2,667,027**	**3,048,857**	**3,204,277**	**3,515,708**	**3,292,564**	**95.27**	**-6.35**
CHINA	962,780	1,199,402	1,308,556	1,726,084	1,655,341	47.90	-4.10
TAIWAN(P.C.)	307,020	311,105	269,037	201,253	133,004	3.85	-33.91
HK,CHINA	1,319,558	1,458,748	1,533,688	1,513,772	1,449,451	41.94	-4.25
JAPAN	62,821	62,288	72,301	54,443	38,706	1.12	-28.91
KOREA REP.	14,848	17,314	20,695	20,156	16,062	0.46	-20.31
S/EAST ASIA	**45,689**	**41,131**	**35,766**	**37,284**	**55,446**	**1.60**	**48.71**
INDONESIA	2,935	5,424	4,590	3,915	5,730	0.17	46.36
MALAYSIA	6,038	5,511	6,489	7,585	6,787	0.20	-10.52
PHILIPPINES	4,089	6,035	7,352	4,654	3,428	0.10	-26.34
SINGAPORE	15,495	8,930	8,333	13,206	31,312	0.91	137.10
THAILAND	17,132	15,231	9,002	7,924	8,189	0.24	3.34
AUSTRALASIA	**11,234**	**8,724**	**9,045**	**10,791**	**11,275**	**0.33**	**4.49**
AUSTRALIA	9,227	7,327	7,392	8,903	8,492	0.25	-4.62
NEW ZEALAND	2,007	1,397	1,653	1,888	2,783	0.08	47.40
EUROPE	**102,132**	**50,575**	**41,861**	**41,501**	**39,001**	**1.13**	**-6.02**
NORTHERN EUR	**15,444**	**15,573**	**11,674**	**11,312**	**13,610**	**0.39**	**20.31**
UK	15,444	15,573	11,674	11,312	13,610	0.39	20.31
SOUTHERN EUR	**57,678**	**10,030**	**7,856**	**10,854**	**8,822**	**0.26**	**-18.72**
ITALY	2,162	1,055	1,827	2,346	1,967	0.06	-16.16
PORTUGAL	55,516	8,975	6,029	8,508	6,855	0.20	-19.43
WESTERN EUR	**15,161**	**12,036**	**12,759**	**11,495**	**9,115**	**0.26**	**-20.70**
FRANCE	10,224	8,106	7,298	7,422	5,666	0.16	-23.66
GERMANY	4,937	3,930	5,461	4,073	3,449	0.10	-15.32
OTHER EUROPE	**13,849**	**12,936**	**9,572**	**7,840**	**7,454**	**0.22**	**-4.92**
OTHER EUROPE	13,849	12,936	9,572	7,840	7,454	0.22	-4.92
SOUTH ASIA	**2,197**	**1,868**	**2,614**	**2,528**	**3,065**	**0.09**	**21.24**
SOUTH ASIA	**2,197**	**1,868**	**2,614**	**2,528**	**3,065**	**0.09**	**21.24**
INDIA	2,197	1,868	2,614	2,528	3,065	0.09	21.24
REG.NOT SPEC	**15,239**	**25,011**	**20,825**	**14,891**	**18,044**	**0.52**	**21.17**
NOT SPECIFIE	**15,239**	**25,011**	**20,825**	**14,891**	**18,044**	**0.52**	**21.17**
OTH.WORLD	15,239	25,011	20,825	14,891	18,044	0.52	21.17

Source: World Tourism Organization (WTO)

MADAGASCAR

1. ARRIVALS OF NON-RESIDENT TOURISTS AT NATIONAL BORDERS, BY NATIONALITY

	1999	2000	2001	2002	2003	Market share 03	% change 03-02
TOTAL	**138,253**	**160,071**	**170,208**	**61,674**	**139,000**	**100.00**	**125.38**
AFRICA	**20,461**	**24,534**	**31,488**	**6,218**	**17,000**	**12.23**	**173.40**
EAST AFRICA	**14,931**	**18,932**	**25,531**	**6,218**			
MAURITIUS	3,871	4,526	8,510	3,134			
REUNION	11,060	14,406	17,021	3,084			
OTHER AFRICA	**5,530**	**5,602**	**5,957**		**17,000**	**12.23**	
OTHER AFRICA	5,530	5,602	5,957				
ALL AFRICA					17,000	12.23	
AMERICAS	**6,913**	**6,402**	**6,808**	**1,880**	**4,000**	**2.88**	**112.77**
NORTH AMER	**6,913**	**6,402**	**6,808**	**1,880**			
CANADA,USA	6,913	6,402	6,808	1,880			
OTHER AMERIC					**4,000**	**2.88**	
ALL AMERICAS					4,000	2.88	
EAST AS/PACI	**2,489**	**2,055**	**3,404**	**617**	**2,000**	**1.44**	**224.15**
N/EAST ASIA	**2,489**	**2,055**	**3,404**	**617**			
JAPAN	2,489	2,055	3,404	617			
OT.EAST AS/P					**2,000**	**1.44**	
AEAP					2,000	1.44	
EUROPE	**95,395**	**110,449**	**119,144**	**43,172**	**100,000**	**71.94**	**131.63**
NORTHERN EUR	**4,148**	**4,802**	**5,106**	**2,467**			
UK	4,148	4,802	5,106	2,467			
SOUTHERN EUR	**8,295**	**8,004**	**8,510**	**3,084**			
ITALY	8,295	8,004	8,510	3,084			
WESTERN EUR	**82,952**	**97,643**	**105,528**	**37,621**			
FRANCE	74,657	88,039	95,316	32,070			
GERMANY	5,530	6,403	6,808	3,084			
SWITZERLAND	2,765	3,201	3,404	2,467			
OTHER EUROPE					**100,000**	**71.94**	
ALL EUROPE					100,000	71.94	
REG.NOT SPEC	**12,995**	**16,631**	**9,364**	**9,787**	**16,000**	**11.51**	**63.48**
NOT SPECIFIE	**12,995**	**16,631**	**9,364**	**9,787**	**16,000**	**11.51**	**63.48**
OTH.WORLD	12,995	16,631	9,364	9,787	16,000	11.51	63.48

Source: World Tourism Organization (WTO)

MADAGASCAR

5. OVERNIGHT STAYS OF NON-RESIDENT TOURISTS IN HOTELS AND SIMILAR ESTABLISHMENTS, BY NATIONALITY

	1999	2000	2001	2002	2003	Market share 03	% change 03-02
TOTAL (*)	**2,626,807**	**3,041,349**	**3,233,952**	**555,066**	**1,970,000**	**100.00**	**254.91**
AFRICA	**388,759**	**466,146**	**598,272**	**55,962**			
EAST AFRICA	**283,689**	**359,708**	**485,089**	**55,962**			
MAURITIUS	73,549	85,994	161,690	28,206			
REUNION	210,140	273,714	323,399	27,756			
OTHER AFRICA	**105,070**	**106,438**	**113,183**				
OTHER AFRICA	105,070	106,438	113,183				
AMERICAS	**131,347**	**121,638**	**129,352**	**16,920**			
NORTH AMER	**131,347**	**121,638**	**129,352**	**16,920**			
CANADA,USA	131,347	121,638	129,352	16,920			
EAST AS/PACI	**47,291**	**39,045**	**64,676**	**5,556**			
N/EAST ASIA	**47,291**	**39,045**	**64,676**	**5,556**			
JAPAN	47,291	39,045	64,676	5,556			
EUROPE	**1,812,505**	**2,098,531**	**2,253,736**	**388,548**			
NORTHERN EUR	**78,812**	**91,238**	**87,014**	**22,203**			
UK	78,812	91,238	87,014	22,203			
SOUTHERN EUR	**157,605**	**152,076**	**161,690**	**27,756**			
ITALY	157,605	152,076	161,690	27,756			
WESTERN EUR	**1,576,088**	**1,855,217**	**2,005,032**	**338,589**			
FRANCE	1,418,483	1,672,741	1,811,004	288,630			
GERMANY	105,070	121,657	129,352	27,756			
SWITZERLAND	52,535	60,819	64,676	22,203			
REG.NOT SPEC	**246,905**	**315,989**	**187,916**	**88,080**	**1,970,000**	**100.00**	**2,136.60**
NOT SPECIFIE	**246,905**	**315,989**	**187,916**	**88,080**	**1,970,000**	**100.00**	**2,136.60**
OTH.WORLD	246,905	315,989	187,916	88,080	1,970,000	100.00	2.136.60

Source: World Tourism Organization (WTO)

MALAWI

1. ARRIVALS OF NON-RESIDENT TOURISTS AT NATIONAL BORDERS, BY COUNTRY OF RESIDENCE

	1999	2000	2001	2002	2003	Market share 03	% change 03-02
TOTAL (*)	**254,352**	**228,106**	**266,300**	**382,647**	**420,911**	**100.00**	**10.00**
AFRICA	**187,610**	**179,000**	**184,900**	**299,485**	**329,435**	**78.27**	**10.00**
EAST AFRICA	**79,469**	**91,200**	**140,000**	**247,435**	**272,179**	**64.66**	**10.00**
MOZAMBIQUE	20,924	18,300	36,500	83,064	91,370	21.71	10.00
ZIMBABWE	20,350	18,700	28,500	54,075	59,483	14.13	10.00
ZAMBIA	38,195	34,200	39,600	39,189	43,108	10.24	10.00
OTH.EAST.AFR		20,000	35,400	71,107	78,218	18.58	10.00
SOUTHERN AFR	**16,680**	**15,000**	**28,500**	**46,755**	**51,431**	**12.22**	**10.00**
ALL STH AFRI	16,680	15,000	28,500	46,755	51,431	12.22	10.00
OTHER AFRICA	**91,461**	**72,800**	**16,400**	**5,295**	**5,825**	**1.38**	**10.01**
OTHER AFRICA	91,461	72,800	16,400	5,295	5,825	1.38	10.01
AMERICAS	**12,718**	**10,000**	**23,000**	**15,251**	**16,774**	**3.99**	**9.99**
NORTH AMER	**6,995**	**3,000**	**14,500**	**14,885**	**16,371**	**3.89**	**9.98**
CANADA,USA	6,995	3,000	14,500	14,885	16,371	3.89	9.98
OTHER AMERIC	**5,723**	**7,000**	**8,500**	**366**	**403**	**0.10**	**10.11**
OTH AMERICA	5,723	7,000	8,500	366	403	0.10	10.11
EAST AS/PACI	**10,174**	**10,000**	**7,300**	**5,542**	**6,096**	**1.45**	**10.00**
OT.EAST AS/P	**10,174**	**10,000**	**7,300**	**5,542**	**6,096**	**1.45**	**10.00**
ALL ASIA	10,174	10,000	7,300	5,542	6,096	1.45	10.00
EUROPE	**40,696**	**26,106**	**51,100**	**55,710**	**61,281**	**14.56**	**10.00**
NORTHERN EUR	**22,383**	**17,200**	**27,500**	**20,693**	**22,762**	**5.41**	**10.00**
UK/IRELAND	22,383	17,200	27,500	20,693	22,762	5.41	10.00
OTHER EUROPE	**18,313**	**8,906**	**23,600**	**35,017**	**38,519**	**9.15**	**10.00**
OTHER EUROPE	18,313	8,906	23,600	35,017	38,519	9.15	10.00
MIDDLE EAST	**280**			**5,000**	**5,500**	**1.31**	**10.00**
MIDDLE EAST	**280**			**5,000**	**5,500**	**1.31**	**10.00**
ALL MID EAST	280			5,000	5,500	1.31	10.00
SOUTH ASIA	**2,874**	**3,000**		**1,659**	**1,825**	**0.43**	**10.01**
SOUTH ASIA	**2,874**	**3,000**		**1,659**	**1,825**	**0.43**	**10.01**
ALL STH ASIA	2,874	3,000		1,659	1,825	0.43	10.01

Source: World Tourism Organization (WTO)

MALAWI

6. OVERNIGHT STAYS OF NON-RESIDENT TOURISTS IN ALL TYPES OF ACCOMMODATION ESTABLISHMENTS, BY COUNTRY OF RESIDENCE

		1999	2000	2001	2002	2003	Market share 03	% change 03-02
TOTAL	(*)	**1,013,257**	**1,325,000**	**2,029,050**	**2,892,726**	**3,258,728**	**100.00**	**12.65**
AFRICA		**809,086**	**860,000**	**1,497,690**	**2,276,085**	**2,668,424**	**81.89**	**17.24**
EAST AFRICA		**686,525**	**729,600**	**1,134,000**	**1,880,505**	**2,204,650**	**67.65**	**17.24**
MOZAMBIQUE		141,301	149,600	295,650	631,286	740,097	22.71	17.24
ZIMBABWE		137,418	146,400	230,850	410,970	481,812	14.79	17.24
ZAMBIA		257,924	273,600	320,760	297,836	349,175	10.72	17.24
OTH.EAST.AFR		149,882	160,000	286,740	540,413	633,566	19.44	17.24
SOUTHERN AFR		**112,719**	**120,000**	**230,850**	**355,338**	**416,591**	**12.78**	**17.24**
ALL STH AFRI		112,719	120,000	230,850	355,338	416,591	12.78	17.24
OTHER AFRICA		**9,842**	**10,400**	**132,840**	**40,242**	**47,183**	**1.45**	**17.25**
OTHER AFRICA		9,842	10,400	132,840	40,242	47,183	1.45	17.25
AMERICAS		**29,538**	**24,000**	**117,450**	**113,126**			
NORTH AMER		**29,538**	**24,000**	**117,450**	**113,126**			
CANADA,USA		29,538	24,000	117,450	113,126			
EUROPE		**129,449**	**195,200**	**413,910**	**423,396**	**496,376**	**15.23**	**17.24**
NORTHERN EUR		**74,622**	**137,600**	**222,750**	**157,267**	**184,372**	**5.66**	**17.24**
UK/IRELAND		74,622	137,600	222,750	157,267	184,372	5.66	17.24
OTHER EUROPE		**54,827**	**57,600**	**191,160**	**266,129**	**312,004**	**9.57**	**17.24**
OTHER EUROPE		54,827	57,600	191,160	266,129	312,004	9.57	17.24
REG.NOT SPEC		**45,184**	**245,800**		**80,119**	**93,928**	**2.88**	**17.24**
NOT SPECIFIE		**45,184**	**245,800**		**80,119**	**93,928**	**2.88**	**17.24**
OTH.WORLD		45,184	245,800		80,119	93,928	2.88	17.24

Source: World Tourism Organization (WTO)

MALAYSIA

1. ARRIVALS OF NON-RESIDENT TOURISTS AT NATIONAL BORDERS, BY COUNTRY OF RESIDENCE

	1999	2000	2001	2002	2003	Market share 03	% change 03-02
TOTAL (*)	**7,931,149**	**10,221,582**	**12,775,073**	**13,292,010**	**10,576,915**	**100.00**	**-20.43**
AFRICA	**29,863**	**74,314**	**161,926**	**148,102**	**137,061**	**1.30**	**-7.45**
EAST AFRICA	**7,944**	**21,114**	**66,438**	**60,275**	**53,558**	**0.51**	**-11.14**
MAURITIUS	644	2,121	7,959	7,814	5,300	0.05	-32.17
OTH.EAST.AFR	7,300	18,993	58,479	52,461	48,258	0.46	-8.01
CENTRAL AFR	**583**	**1,940**	**11,021**	**11,627**	**12,641**	**0.12**	**8.72**
ALL MID AFRI	583	1,940	11,021	11,627	12,641	0.12	8.72
NORTH AFRICA	**1,969**	**8,151**	**18,418**	**17,332**	**16,654**	**0.16**	**-3.91**
ALL NORT AFR	1,969	8,151	18,418	17,332	16,654	0.16	-3.91
SOUTHERN AFR	**12,357**	**17,134**	**52,081**	**47,699**	**43,863**	**0.41**	**-8.04**
SOUTH AFRICA	11,523	11,540	20,766	13,720	12,577	0.12	-8.33
OTH.SOUTH.AF	834	5,594	31,315	33,979	31,286	0.30	-7.93
WEST AFRICA	**7,010**	**25,975**	**13,968**	**11,169**	**10,345**	**0.10**	**-7.38**
ALL.WEST.AFR	7,010	25,975	13,968	11,169	10,345	0.10	-7.38
AMERICAS	**122,079**	**307,692**	**321,841**	**283,216**	**270,157**	**2.55**	**-4.61**
CARIBBEAN	**3,619**	**33,994**	**57,492**	**52,193**	**50,969**	**0.48**	**-2.35**
ALL CO CARIB	3,619	33,994	57,492	52,193	50,969	0.48	-2.35
CENTRAL AMER	**1,829**	**7,761**	**19,005**	**17,771**	**15,724**	**0.15**	**-11.52**
ALL CENT AME	1,829	7,761	19,005	17,771	15,724	0.15	-11.52
NORTH AMER	**110,031**	**242,940**	**187,524**	**166,349**	**161,410**	**1.53**	**-2.97**
CANADA	25,987	55,799	38,935	34,996	26,978	0.26	-22.91
MEXICO	742	2,846	1,770	2,284	1,491	0.01	-34.72
USA	83,260	184,100	145,827	127,920	131,071	1.24	2.46
OT.NORTH.AME	42	195	992	1,149	1,870	0.02	62.75
SOUTH AMER	**6,600**	**22,997**	**57,820**	**46,903**	**42,054**	**0.40**	**-10.34**
ARGENTINA	1,579	4,984	4,891	1,211	2,030	0.02	67.63
BRAZIL	870	2,423	2,255	2,560	2,184	0.02	-14.69
VENEZUELA	836	3,258	8,044	6,636	7,748	0.07	16.76
OTH SOUTH AM	3,315	12,332	42,630	36,496	30,092	0.28	-17.55
EAST AS/PACI	**6,826,835**	**8,716,429**	**10,832,535**	**11,456,003**	**9,076,881**	**85.82**	**-20.77**
N/EAST ASIA	**723,922**	**1,248,861**	**1,325,421**	**1,314,707**	**833,787**	**7.88**	**-36.58**
CHINA	190,851	425,246	453,246	557,647	350,597	3.31	-37.13
TAIWAN(P.C.)	136,863	213,016	249,811	209,706	137,419	1.30	-34.47
HK,CHINA	66,981	76,344	144,611	116,409	72,027	0.68	-38.13
JAPAN	286,940	455,981	397,639	354,563	213,527	2.02	-39.78
KOREA REP.	41,650	72,443	66,343	64,301	46,246	0.44	-28.08
OT NORTH AS	637	5,831	13,771	12,081	13,971	0.13	15.64
S/EAST ASIA	**5,948,835**	**7,199,942**	**9,217,496**	**9,887,122**	**8,044,033**	**76.05**	**-18.64**
BRUNEI DARSM	187,704	195,059	309,529	256,952	215,634	2.04	-16.08
MYANMAR	2,027	3,762	7,219	6,962	7,112	0.07	2.15
INDONESIA	307,373	545,051	777,449	769,128	621,651	5.88	-19.17
LAO P.DEM.R.	178	782	2,391	1,808	2,372	0.02	31.19
PHILIPPINES	47,238	81,927	122,428	107,527	90,430	0.85	-15.90
SINGAPORE	4,900,084	5,420,200	6,951,594	7,547,761	5,922,306	55.99	-21.54

MALAYSIA

1. ARRIVALS OF NON-RESIDENT TOURISTS AT NATIONAL BORDERS, BY COUNTRY OF RESIDENCE

	1999	2000	2001	2002	2003	Market share 03	% change 03-02
VIET NAM	3,827	7,969	18,729	21,158	21,663	0.20	2.39
THAILAND	498,578	940,215	1,018,797	1,166,937	1,152,296	10.89	-1.25
OTH S/E ASIA	1,826	4,977	9,360	8,889	10,569	0.10	18.90
AUSTRALASIA	**152,039**	**256,126**	**252,233**	**218,951**	**163,489**	**1.55**	**-25.33**
AUSTRALIA	134,311	236,775	222,340	193,794	144,507	1.37	-25.43
NEW ZEALAND	17,728	19,351	29,893	25,157	18,982	0.18	-24.55
OT.EAST AS/P	**2,039**	**11,500**	**37,385**	**35,223**	**35,572**	**0.34**	**0.99**
OTH OCEANIA	2,039	11,500	37,385	35,223	35,572	0.34	0.99
EUROPE	**308,713**	**590,304**	**703,724**	**636,972**	**456,351**	**4.31**	**-28.36**
C/E EUROPE	**5,699**	**19,708**	**63,130**	**77,395**	**68,294**	**0.65**	**-11.76**
OTH C/E EUR	4,253	13,909	58,854	72,328	63,059	0.60	-12.82
CIS	1,446	5,799	4,276	5,067	5,235	0.05	3.32
NORTHERN EUR	**180,672**	**343,495**	**362,571**	**324,203**	**193,909**	**1.83**	**-40.19**
DENMARK	4,286	10,599	19,770	17,297	13,434	0.13	-22.33
FINLAND	7,711	22,667	15,284	12,908	11,041	0.10	-14.46
IRELAND	5,728	7,439	14,175	11,182	9,391	0.09	-16.02
NORWAY	5,558	15,866	12,530	11,589	7,856	0.07	-32.21
SWEDEN	20,778	48,739	35,053	29,044	23,560	0.22	-18.88
UK	136,398	237,757	262,423	239,294	125,569	1.19	-47.53
OTH NORT EUR	213	428	3,336	2,889	3,058	0.03	5.85
SOUTHERN EUR	**19,137**	**45,758**	**74,153**	**74,824**	**64,316**	**0.61**	**-14.04**
ITALY	14,470	34,548	20,636	16,805	12,872	0.12	-23.40
SPAIN	2,772	5,706	31,733	34,477	29,432	0.28	-14.63
OT SOUTH EUR	1,895	5,504	21,784	23,542	22,012	0.21	-6.50
WESTERN EUR	**100,602**	**172,638**	**197,478**	**154,808**	**124,641**	**1.18**	**-19.49**
AUSTRIA	6,171	7,003	9,400	7,543	6,599	0.06	-12.51
BELGIUM	5,130	12,518	9,465	7,812	6,387	0.06	-18.24
FRANCE	21,208	31,785	32,922	27,434	23,845	0.23	-13.08
GERMANY	43,316	74,556	70,401	54,645	41,145	0.39	-24.70
LUXEMBOURG	236	755	576	579	492		-15.03
NETHERLANDS	17,955	35,400	52,034	39,303	28,822	0.27	-26.67
SWITZERLAND	6,534	10,213	20,429	15,614	14,475	0.14	-7.29
OTH WEST EUR	52	408	2,251	1,878	2,876	0.03	53.14
EAST/MED EUR	**2,603**	**8,705**	**6,392**	**5,742**	**5,191**	**0.05**	**-9.60**
TURKEY	2,603	8,705	6,392	5,742	5,191	0.05	-9.60
MIDDLE EAST	**19,128**	**44,665**	**108,384**	**126,037**	**75,025**	**0.71**	**-40.47**
MIDDLE EAST	**19,128**	**44,665**	**108,384**	**126,037**	**75,025**	**0.71**	**-40.47**
JORDAN		2,888	3,688	3,611	2,143	0.02	-40.65
KUWAIT		1,095	7,428	10,470	3,599	0.03	-65.63
LEBANON		899	4,443	5,336	7,787	0.07	45.93
OMAN		1,223	7,284	8,432	5,703	0.05	-32.36
SAUDI ARABIA	11,564	27,808	39,957	45,007	20,077	0.19	-55.39
SYRIA		2,784	18,205	21,109	16,776	0.16	-20.53
UNTD ARAB EM	2,909	2,391	13,762	14,124	6,047	0.06	-57.19
OT MIDD EAST	4,655	5,577	13,617	17,948	12,893	0.12	-28.16
SOUTH ASIA	**68,992**	**180,016**	**212,083**	**244,351**	**209,120**	**1.98**	**-14.42**

MALAYSIA

1. ARRIVALS OF NON-RESIDENT TOURISTS AT NATIONAL BORDERS, BY COUNTRY OF RESIDENCE

	1999	2000	2001	2002	2003	Market share 03	% change 03-02
SOUTH ASIA	**68,992**	**180,016**	**212,083**	**244,351**	**209,120**	**1.98**	**-14.42**
BANGLADESH	3,251	6,241	13,552	17,450	21,005	0.20	20.37
SRI LANKA	7,948	16,500	13,171	12,882	13,268	0.13	3.00
INDIA	46,537	132,127	143,513	183,360	145,153	1.37	-20.84
IRAN	4,297	4,514	15,015	9,414	10,412	0.10	10.60
PAKISTAN	4,105	14,402	16,158	11,723	9,484	0.09	-19.10
OTH STH ASIA	2,854	6,232	10,674	9,522	9,798	0.09	2.90
REG.NOT SPEC	**555,539**	**308,162**	**434,580**	**397,329**	**352,320**	**3.33**	**-11.33**
NOT SPECIFIE	**555,539**	**308,162**	**434,580**	**397,329**	**352,320**	**3.33**	**-11.33**
OTH.WORLD	555,539	308,162	434,580	397,329	352,320	3.33	-11.33

Source: World Tourism Organization (WTO)

3. ARRIVALS OF NON-RESIDENT TOURISTS IN HOTELS AND SIMILAR ESTABLISHMENTS, BY COUNTRY OF RESIDENCE

	1999	2000	2001	2002	2003	Market share 03	% change 03-02
TOTAL	**10,339,913**	**12,392,736**	**13,114,590**	**15,615,497**	**13,239,227**	**100.00**	**-15.22**
AFRICA		**81,205**	**91,591**	**104,526**	**103,847**	**0.78**	**-0.65**
SOUTHERN AFR		**61,938**	**68,449**	**70,635**	**65,441**	**0.49**	**-7.35**
SOUTH AFRICA		61,938	68,449	70,635	65,441	0.49	-7.35
OTHER AFRICA		**19,267**	**23,142**	**33,891**	**38,406**	**0.29**	**13.32**
OTHER AFRICA		19,267	23,142	33,891	38,406	0.29	13.32
AMERICAS	**411,410**	**470,537**	**449,847**	**574,832**	**480,022**	**3.63**	**-16.49**
NORTH AMER	**411,410**	**428,524**	**405,921**	**497,890**	**420,687**	**3.18**	**-15.51**
CANADA	71,674	77,154	83,219	101,826	80,029	0.60	-21.41
USA	339,736	351,370	322,702	396,064	340,658	2.57	-13.99
OTHER AMERIC		**42,013**	**43,926**	**76,942**	**59,335**	**0.45**	**-22.88**
OTH AMERICA		42,013	43,926	76,942	59,335	0.45	-22.88
EAST AS/PACI	**6,803,341**	**8,112,183**	**8,453,345**	**10,180,318**	**8,668,586**	**65.48**	**-14.85**
N/EAST ASIA	**3,042,470**	**3,544,522**	**3,526,790**	**4,513,080**	**3,268,111**	**24.69**	**-27.59**
CHINA	825,950	894,022	974,148	1,421,768	1,007,679	7.61	-29.12
TAIWAN(P.C.)	626,457	696,583	594,885	713,402	479,765	3.62	-32.75
HK,CHINA	530,746	699,591	711,886	739,686	576,062	4.35	-22.12
JAPAN	960,459	1,151,974	1,058,237	1,432,142	1,059,415	8.00	-26.03
KOREA REP.	98,858	102,352	187,634	206,082	145,190	1.10	-29.55
S/EAST ASIA	**3,001,401**	**3,485,395**	**3,932,005**	**4,469,553**	**4,398,609**	**33.22**	**-1.59**
BRUNEI DARSM	249,190	222,386	267,388	247,137	231,530	1.75	-6.32
INDONESIA	361,606	462,188	558,517	735,788	811,353	6.13	10.27
PHILIPPINES	124,576	178,253	163,675	166,429	189,329	1.43	13.76
SINGAPORE	2,075,283	2,350,892	2,533,803	2,956,297	2,692,035	20.33	-8.94
VIET NAM		25,475	111,792	34,147	75,587	0.57	121.36
THAILAND	190,746	246,201	296,830	329,755	398,775	3.01	20.93
AUSTRALASIA	**759,470**	**944,831**	**846,560**	**971,191**	**754,994**	**5.70**	**-22.26**
AUSTRALIA	676,738	855,807	754,097	844,400	660,302	4.99	-21.80
NEW ZEALAND	82,732	89,024	92,463	126,791	94,692	0.72	-25.32
OT.EAST AS/P		**137,435**	**147,990**	**226,494**	**246,872**	**1.86**	**9.00**
OTHER ASIA		137,435	147,990	226,494	246,872	1.86	9.00
EUROPE	**1,815,058**	**2,902,497**	**2,902,090**	**3,186,049**	**2,701,960**	**20.41**	**-15.19**
C/E EUROPE		**20,696**	**30,585**	**44,161**	**48,415**	**0.37**	**9.63**
CIS		20,696	30,585	44,161	48,415	0.37	9.63
NORTHERN EUR	**1,221,553**	**1,443,642**	**1,236,226**	**1,659,536**	**1,449,465**	**10.95**	**-12.66**
DENMARK	41,655	43,612	42,156	60,355	47,500	0.36	-21.30
FINLAND	31,325	35,783	30,384	44,663	29,847	0.23	-33.17
IRELAND	13,675	15,159	26,144	42,885	26,996	0.20	-37.05
NORWAY	28,793	30,692	41,002	39,502	49,569	0.37	25.48
SWEDEN	75,745	83,066	69,993	108,659	92,239	0.70	-15.11
UK	1,030,360	1,235,330	1,026,547	1,363,472	1,203,314	9.09	-11.75

MALAYSIA

3. ARRIVALS OF NON-RESIDENT TOURISTS IN HOTELS AND SIMILAR ESTABLISHMENTS, BY COUNTRY OF RESIDENCE

	1999	2000	2001	2002	2003	Market share 03	% change 03-02
SOUTHERN EUR		**126,067**	**129,317**	**131,234**	**116,188**	**0.88**	**-11.47**
ITALY		105,693	101,523	105,679	84,551	0.64	-19.99
SPAIN		20,374	27,794	25,555	31,637	0.24	23.80
WESTERN EUR	**593,505**	**1,119,353**	**1,339,700**	**1,091,462**	**885,577**	**6.69**	**-18.86**
AUSTRIA		86,780	84,816	104,601	84,262	0.64	-19.44
BELGIUM	25,504	37,655	33,398	62,890	37,977	0.29	-39.61
FRANCE	107,143	111,642	102,278	139,051	106,976	0.81	-23.07
GERMANY	313,125	377,248	292,406	357,656	303,290	2.29	-15.20
LUXEMBOURG	2,586	9,877	120,318	8,380	8,640	0.07	3.10
NETHERLANDS	145,147	399,458	315,502	297,036	253,443	1.91	-14.68
SWITZERLAND		93,996	100,735	121,848	90,989	0.69	-25.33
OTH WEST EUR		2,697	290,247				
OTHER EUROPE		**192,739**	**166,262**	**259,656**	**202,315**	**1.53**	**-22.08**
OTHER EUROPE		192,739	166,262	259,656	202,315	1.53	-22.08
MIDDLE EAST	**235,140**	**365,358**	**619,009**	**825,684**	**554,881**	**4.19**	**-32.80**
MIDDLE EAST	**235,140**	**365,358**	**619,009**	**825,684**	**554,881**	**4.19**	**-32.80**
ALL MID EAST	235,140	365,358	619,009	825,684	554,881	4.19	-32.80
SOUTH ASIA	**97,733**	**221,308**	**370,820**	**448,417**	**518,427**	**3.92**	**15.61**
SOUTH ASIA	**97,733**	**221,308**	**370,820**	**448,417**	**518,427**	**3.92**	**15.61**
BANGLADESH		26,756	115,444	47,344	46,624	0.35	-1.52
SRI LANKA		13,786	36,759	23,463	33,809	0.26	44.09
INDIA	97,733	159,440	190,598	324,818	356,378	2.69	9.72
PAKISTAN		21,326	28,019	52,792	81,616	0.62	54.60
REG.NOT SPEC	**977,231**	**239,648**	**227,888**	**295,671**	**211,504**	**1.60**	**-28.47**
NOT SPECIFIE	**977,231**	**239,648**	**227,888**	**295,671**	**211,504**	**1.60**	**-28.47**
OTH.WORLD	977,231	239,648	227,888	295,671	211,504	1.60	-28.47

Source: World Tourism Organization (WTO)

MALAYSIA

5. OVERNIGHT STAYS OF NON-RESIDENT TOURISTS IN HOTELS AND SIMILAR ESTABLISHMENTS, BY COUNTRY OF RESIDENCE

	1999	2000	2001	2002	2003	Market share 03	% change 03-02
TOTAL	**17,410,073**	**21,295,679**	**20,450,452**	**25,140,393**			
AFRICA		**163,534**	**151,496**	**174,081**			
SOUTHERN AFR		**129,813**	**112,958**	**116,646**			
SOUTH AFRICA		129,813	112,958	116,646			
OTHER AFRICA		**33,721**	**38,538**	**57,435**			
OTHER AFRICA		33,721	38,538	57,435			
AMERICAS	**560,782**	**836,296**	**743,306**	**970,425**			
NORTH AMER	**560,782**	**764,766**	**672,639**	**854,566**			
CANADA		134,952	145,620	187,413			
USA	560,782	629,814	527,019	667,153			
OTHER AMERIC		**71,530**	**70,667**	**115,859**			
OTH AMERICA		71,530	70,667	115,859			
EAST AS/PACI	**9,688,152**	**12,992,273**	**12,535,982**	**15,871,935**			
N/EAST ASIA	**4,406,457**	**5,559,383**	**5,096,253**	**7,016,406**			
CHINA	1,070,741	1,252,308	1,250,812	2,038,839			
TAIWAN(P.C.)	835,971	1,084,451	850,215	1,109,190			
HK,CHINA	826,321	1,068,251	1,008,066	1,126,402			
JAPAN	1,673,424	1,976,115	1,675,966	2,381,264			
KOREA REP.		178,258	311,194	360,711			
S/EAST ASIA	**4,031,022**	**5,494,924**	**5,829,796**	**6,948,661**			
BRUNEI DARSM		358,430	382,183	373,837			
INDONESIA	580,253	794,950	847,587	1,167,069			
PHILIPPINES		312,426	273,277	290,107			
SINGAPORE	3,149,319	3,602,965	3,710,450	4,562,563			
VIET NAM		37,838	168,052	57,634			
THAILAND	301,450	388,315	448,247	497,451			
AUSTRALASIA	**1,250,673**	**1,700,841**	**1,382,693**	**1,532,072**			
AUSTRALIA	1,167,941	1,541,954	1,234,651	1,318,591			
NEW ZEALAND	82,732	158,887	148,042	213,481			
OT.EAST AS/P		**237,125**	**227,240**	**374,796**			
OTHER ASIA		237,125	227,240	374,796			
EUROPE	**2,960,506**	**5,899,478**	**5,161,067**	**5,622,759**			
C/E EUROPE		**48,034**	**60,041**	**96,192**			
CIS		48,034	60,041	96,192			
NORTHERN EUR	**2,378,094**	**3,314,859**	**2,225,722**	**3,007,476**			
DENMARK		78,166	74,621	119,866			
FINLAND		81,656	61,424	91,859			
IRELAND		27,351	41,153	70,733			
NORWAY		56,429	73,910	76,228			
SWEDEN		159,755	130,177	190,512			
UK	2,378,094	2,911,502	1,844,437	2,458,278			

5. OVERNIGHT STAYS OF NON-RESIDENT TOURISTS IN HOTELS AND SIMILAR ESTABLISHMENTS, BY COUNTRY OF RESIDENCE

	1999	2000	2001	2002	2003	Market share 03	% change 03-02
SOUTHERN EUR		**221,067**	**203,374**	**238,595**			
ITALY		181,565	158,403	187,581			
SPAIN		39,502	44,971	51,014			
WESTERN EUR	**582,412**	**1,988,291**	**2,404,348**	**1,843,306**			
AUSTRIA		131,434	131,294	166,673			
BELGIUM		78,902	66,945	114,379			
FRANCE		221,130	175,553	245,311			
GERMANY	582,412	582,683	501,160	575,969			
LUXEMBOURG		15,911	240,405	15,973			
NETHERLANDS		739,921	532,125	506,660			
SWITZERLAND		213,225	175,509	217,694			
OTH WEST EUR		5,085	581,357	647			
OTHER EUROPE		**327,227**	**267,582**	**437,190**			
OTHER EUROPE		327,227	267,582	437,190			
MIDDLE EAST		**643,833**	**921,602**	**1,205,533**			
MIDDLE EAST		**643,833**	**921,602**	**1,205,533**			
ALL MID EAST		643,833	921,602	1,205,533			
SOUTH ASIA		**373,656**	**609,698**	**834,237**			
SOUTH ASIA		**373,656**	**609,698**	**834,237**			
BANGLADESH		39,777	161,486	81,892			
SRI LANKA		33,476	66,045	44,701			
INDIA		265,943	339,001	621,577			
PAKISTAN		34,460	43,166	86,067			
REG.NOT SPEC	**4,200,633**	**386,609**	**327,301**	**461,423**			
NOT SPECIFIE	**4,200,633**	**386,609**	**327,301**	**461,423**			
OTH.WORLD	4,200,633	386,609	327,301	461,423			

Source: World Tourism Organization (WTO)

MALDIVES

1. ARRIVALS OF NON-RESIDENT TOURISTS AT NATIONAL BORDERS, BY NATIONALITY

	1999	2000	2001	2002	2003	Market share 03	% change 03-02
TOTAL (*)	429,666	467,154	460,984	484,680	563,593	100.00	16.28
AFRICA	1,846	2,311	2,060	3,002	3,984	0.71	32.71
EAST AFRICA	172	307	285	418	442	0.08	5.74
COMOROS			1		1		
ETHIOPIA	4	8	13	20	4		-80.00
ERITREA	5	3	12	9	38	0.01	322.22
DJIBOUTI	4		1				
KENYA	47	77	85	120	79	0.01	-34.17
MADAGASCAR	1	11	4	7	4		-42.86
MALAWI	3	2	31	10			
MAURITIUS	17	31	6	18	48	0.01	166.67
MOZAMBIQUE	8	6	15	10	9		-10.00
SEYCHELLES	14	26	41	125	146	0.03	16.80
SOMALIA	1	1	2	5	10		100.00
ZIMBABWE	35	126	40	53	57	0.01	7.55
UGANDA	4	1	3	6	23		283.33
TANZANIA	18	14	20	27	16		-40.74
ZAMBIA	10	1	11	8	7		-12.50
OTH.EAST.AFR	1						
CENTRAL AFR	22	15	17	13	24		84.62
ANGOLA	5	5	2	1	9		800.00
CAMEROON	13	5	11	7	10		42.86
CONGO	3	5	3	5	5		
DEM.R.CONGO	1		1				
NORTH AFRICA	135	151	216	517	386	0.07	-25.34
ALGERIA	34	19	41	200	70	0.01	-65.00
MOROCCO	55	76	109	218	186	0.03	-14.68
SUDAN	8	10	17	19	57	0.01	200.00
TUNISIA	38	46	49	80	73	0.01	-8.75
SOUTHERN AFR	1,464	1,784	1,387	1,934	2,954	0.52	52.74
BOTSWANA	3	1	3	7	3		-57.14
LESOTHO			3	3	2		-33.33
NAMIBIA	22	16	11	9	17		88.89
SOUTH AFRICA	1,437	1,767	1,368	1,914	2,929	0.52	53.03
SWAZILAND	2		2	1	3		200.00
WEST AFRICA	53	52	126	101	139	0.02	37.62
CAPE VERDE		2		1	1		
GAMBIA	7	6	2	1	1		
GHANA		4	8	5	15		200.00
GUINEA	3	1	2				
COTE IVOIRE	3	4	3	8	28		250.00
LIBERIA	1	3	16	16	17		6.25
MALI	3	1	3	4	3		-25.00
MAURITANIA	5	3	46	26	27		3.85
NIGERIA	22	23	36	19	26		36.84
SENEGAL	4	3	4	4	18		350.00
SIERRA LEONE	2	1	2	17	2		-88.24
TOGO	2	1	2		1		
BURKINA FASO			2				
OTH.WEST.AFR	1						
OTHER AFRICA		2	29	19	39	0.01	105.26

MALDIVES

1. ARRIVALS OF NON-RESIDENT TOURISTS AT NATIONAL BORDERS, BY NATIONALITY

	1999	2000	2001	2002	2003	Market share 03	% change 03-02
OTHER AFRICA		2	29	19	39	0.01	105.26
AMERICAS	**6,082**	**7,108**	**6,814**	**7,487**	**7,660**	**1.36**	**2.31**
CARIBBEAN	**46**	**96**	**79**	**66**	**86**	**0.02**	**30.30**
ANTIGUA,BARB	1		3				
BAHAMAS		3	4	6	4		-33.33
BARBADOS		4	4	2	3		50.00
CUBA	18	37	23	28	39	0.01	39.29
DOMINICA	12	7	4	10	10		
GRENADA	1	32	1		1		
HAITI			8	1	2		100.00
JAMAICA	4	3	10	9	8		-11.11
ST.LUCIA		2	4	1	1		
TRINIDAD TBG	10	8	18	9	18		100.00
CENTRAL AMER	**21**	**115**	**24**	**47**	**33**	**0.01**	**-29.79**
BELIZE	4	5	1	27	6		-77.78
COSTA RICA	8	7	3	10	7		-30.00
EL SALVADOR	4	1	9	4	8		100.00
GUATEMALA	2	6	6	3	7		133.33
HONDURAS		88		1	1		
NICARAGUA		1	3	1	4		300.00
PANAMA	3	7	2	1			
NORTH AMER	**5,318**	**6,156**	**5,971**	**6,706**	**6,783**	**1.20**	**1.15**
CANADA	1,165	1,316	1,442	1,569	1,649	0.29	5.10
MEXICO	50	45	94	107	129	0.02	20.56
USA	4,103	4,795	4,435	5,030	5,005	0.89	-0.50
SOUTH AMER	**697**	**741**	**718**	**665**	**756**	**0.13**	**13.68**
ARGENTINA	199	176	148	93	113	0.02	21.51
BOLIVIA	4	5	2	6	3		-50.00
BRAZIL	374	318	338	381	447	0.08	17.32
CHILE	24	41	95	34	32	0.01	-5.88
COLOMBIA	35	29	52	59	62	0.01	5.08
ECUADOR	15	16	8	14	7		-50.00
PARAGUAY		4	2	7			
PERU	16	20	38	21	43	0.01	104.76
SURINAME	4		1	1			
URUGUAY	9	105	11	8	11		37.50
VENEZUELA	17	27	23	41	38	0.01	-7.32
OTHER AMERIC			**22**	**3**	**2**		**-33.33**
OTH AMERICA			22	3	2		-33.33
EAST AS/PACI	**60,598**	**73,411**	**68,967**	**77,289**	**83,640**	**14.84**	**8.22**
N/EAST ASIA	**48,477**	**58,334**	**55,954**	**63,803**	**65,542**	**11.63**	**2.73**
CHINA	3,973	5,380	7,342	12,092	15,021	2.67	24.22
TAIWAN(P.C.)			1	17			
HK,CHINA		1		291			
JAPAN	40,230	47,180	41,895	43,705	42,081	7.47	-3.72
KOREA REP.	4,272	5,771	6,708	7,696	8,417	1.49	9.37
MONGOLIA	2	2	8	2	23		1,050.00
S/EAST ASIA	**5,787**	**6,062**	**5,827**	**7,709**	**11,048**	**1.96**	**43.31**
BRUNEI DARSM	9	5	22	26	87	0.02	234.62

MALDIVES

1. ARRIVALS OF NON-RESIDENT TOURISTS AT NATIONAL BORDERS, BY NATIONALITY

	1999	2000	2001	2002	2003	Market share 03	% change 03-02
MYANMAR	16	22	26	21	59	0.01	180.95
CAMBODIA	5		23	3	4		33.33
INDONESIA	255	325	328	460	566	0.10	23.04
LAO P.DEM.R.	1	1	5	1	2		100.00
MALAYSIA	1,716	1,829	1,478	2,240	2,251	0.40	0.49
PHILIPPINES	291	317	346	405	376	0.07	-7.16
SINGAPORE	2,383	2,530	2,227	2,520	4,653	0.83	84.64
VIET NAM	28	26	22	31	41	0.01	32.26
THAILAND	1,083	1,007	1,350	2,002	3,009	0.53	50.30
AUSTRALASIA	**6,325**	**9,000**	**7,107**	**5,696**	**6,864**	**1.22**	**20.51**
AUSTRALIA	5,784	8,090	6,435	5,063	6,110	1.08	20.68
NEW ZEALAND	541	910	672	633	754	0.13	19.12
MELANESIA	**4**	**10**	**18**	**9**	**11**		**22.22**
FIJI	2	10	7	5	11		120.00
VANUATU			2				
NORFOLK IS	2		9	4			
MICRONESIA	**4**		**4**	**6**	**4**		**-33.33**
KIRIBATI	1		3	3	2		-33.33
MIDWAY IS	3						
MICRONESIA			1				
MARSHALL IS				3	2		-33.33
POLYNESIA	**1**		**24**	**2**	**7**		**250.00**
TONGA	1		5		2		
SAMOA			19	2	5		150.00
OT.EAST AS/P		**5**	**33**	**64**	**164**	**0.03**	**156.25**
OTHER ASIA			6				
OTH OCEANIA		5	27	64	164	0.03	156.25
EUROPE	**340,469**	**362,196**	**364,105**	**373,428**	**443,093**	**78.62**	**18.66**
C/E EUROPE	**7,986**	**8,883**	**9,551**	**14,259**	**21,935**	**3.89**	**53.83**
AZERBAIJAN	10	2	12	23	39	0.01	69.57
ARMENIA	4	5	10	13	12		-7.69
BULGARIA	391	210	116	190	342	0.06	80.00
CZECH RP/SVK	62						
CZECH REP	841	1,091	1,054	1,493	1,936	0.34	29.67
ESTONIA	40	43	28	80	83	0.01	3.75
GEORGIA	4	6	27	26	111	0.02	326.92
HUNGARY	977	1,120	1,281	1,589	2,543	0.45	60.04
KAZAKHSTAN	55	47	72	99	362	0.06	265.66
KYRGYZSTAN	4	6		3	23		666.67
LATVIA	114	129	138	147	172	0.03	17.01
LITHUANIA	49	55	104	144	164	0.03	13.89
REP MOLDOVA	20	15	34	39	70	0.01	79.49
POLAND	1,029	1,264	1,311	1,116	982	0.17	-12.01
ROMANIA	117	149	193	256	363	0.06	41.80
RUSSIAN FED	3,428	3,608	3,983	7,550	12,108	2.15	60.37
SLOVAKIA	498	662	630	707	1,552	0.28	119.52
TAJIKISTAN	1	3	6	1			
TURKMENISTAN	5		76	37	37	0.01	
UKRAINE	331	442	456	720	995	0.18	38.19
USSR(former)	6						
UZBEKISTAN		26	20	26	41	0.01	57.69

MALDIVES

1. ARRIVALS OF NON-RESIDENT TOURISTS AT NATIONAL BORDERS, BY NATIONALITY

	1999	2000	2001	2002	2003	Market share 03	% change 03-02
NORTHERN EUR	**69,198**	**77,236**	**82,263**	**85,560**	**100,310**	**17.80**	**17.24**
DENMARK	715	772	891	938	1,073	0.19	14.39
FINLAND	526	350	304	388	614	0.11	58.25
ICELAND	17	7	17	33	23		-30.30
IRELAND	1,045	1,486	1,211	1,303	1,684	0.30	29.24
NORWAY	750	945	577	772	987	0.18	27.85
SWEDEN	2,226	2,236	2,112	1,749	1,940	0.34	10.92
UK	63,919	71,440	77,151	80,377	93,989	16.68	16.94
SOUTHERN EUR	**102,063**	**119,217**	**126,724**	**126,647**	**153,503**	**27.24**	**21.21**
ALBANIA	8	16	15	29	44	0.01	51.72
ANDORRA	12	6	4	18	6		-66.67
BOSNIA HERZG	63	74	67	78	96	0.02	23.08
CROATIA	264	294	313	316	304	0.05	-3.80
GREECE	2,128	1,776	1,775	2,446	2,287	0.41	-6.50
ITALY	88,697	106,323	115,740	114,955	140,304	24.89	22.05
MALTA	40	57	99	157	99	0.02	-36.94
PORTUGAL	4,117	4,276	3,526	2,785	3,379	0.60	21.33
SLOVENIA	705	733	674	703	661	0.12	-5.97
SPAIN	5,634	5,322	4,203	5,160	6,323	1.12	22.54
TFYROM	49						
SERBIA,MTNEG	346	340	308				
WESTERN EUR	**159,538**	**154,200**	**143,694**	**144,363**	**163,356**	**28.98**	**13.16**
AUSTRIA	13,550	11,725	10,494	10,480	12,391	2.20	18.23
BELGIUM	3,114	5,071	3,719	2,606	2,795	0.50	7.25
FRANCE	23,832	27,517	30,542	31,228	41,055	7.28	31.47
GERMANY	86,497	77,642	66,149	63,212	70,762	12.56	11.94
LIECHTENSTEN	83	75	107	91	88	0.02	-3.30
LUXEMBOURG	253	348	242	344	404	0.07	17.44
MONACO	38	19	31	33	27		-18.18
NETHERLANDS	9,315	7,275	4,097	4,662	5,047	0.90	8.26
SWITZERLAND	22,856	24,528	28,313	31,707	30,787	5.46	-2.90
EAST/MED EUR	**1,684**	**2,022**	**1,714**	**1,986**	**3,233**	**0.57**	**62.79**
CYPRUS	244	257	263	274	243	0.04	-11.31
ISRAEL	155	346	453	391	548	0.10	40.15
TURKEY	1,285	1,419	998	1,321	2,442	0.43	84.86
OTHER EUROPE		**638**	**159**	**613**	**756**	**0.13**	**23.33**
OTHER EUROPE		638	159	613	756	0.13	23.33
MIDDLE EAST	**1,278**	**1,480**	**2,031**	**2,941**	**3,636**	**0.65**	**23.63**
MIDDLE EAST	**1,278**	**1,480**	**2,031**	**2,941**	**3,636**	**0.65**	**23.63**
BAHRAIN	33	49	53	80	101	0.02	26.25
PALESTINE	16	8	10	18	27		50.00
IRAQ	7	24	13	22	23		4.55
JORDAN	97	74	142	202	204	0.04	0.99
KUWAIT	262	256	373	492	533	0.09	8.33
LEBANON	188	264	235	314	342	0.06	8.92
LIBYA	31	15	35	33	60	0.01	81.82
OMAN	29	34	57	63	115	0.02	82.54
QATAR	14	23	26	75	87	0.02	16.00
SAUDI ARABIA	307	413	542	975	1,296	0.23	32.92
SYRIA	37	42	76	74	105	0.02	41.89
UNTD ARAB EM	142	163	287	348	360	0.06	3.45

MALDIVES

1. ARRIVALS OF NON-RESIDENT TOURISTS AT NATIONAL BORDERS, BY NATIONALITY

	1999	2000	2001	2002	2003	Market share 03	% change 03-02
EGYPT	105	104	154	221	358	0.06	61.99
YEMEN	10	11	28	24	25		4.17
SOUTH ASIA	**19,393**	**20,648**	**17,007**	**20,533**	**21,580**	**3.83**	**5.10**
SOUTH ASIA	**19,393**	**20,648**	**17,007**	**20,533**	**21,580**	**3.83**	**5.10**
AFGHANISTAN	4	8	6	5	7		40.00
BANGLADESH	237	321	321	241	313	0.06	29.88
BHUTAN	8	17	9	24	41	0.01	70.83
SRI LANKA	6,375	8,413	6,902	6,909	7,296	1.29	5.60
INDIA	11,621	10,616	8,511	11,377	11,502	2.04	1.10
IRAN	89	101	142	556	345	0.06	-37.95
NEPAL	77	123	99	92	134	0.02	45.65
PAKISTAN	982	1,049	1,017	1,329	1,942	0.34	46.12

Source: World Tourism Organization (WTO)

3. ARRIVALS OF NON-RESIDENT TOURISTS IN HOTELS AND SIMILAR ESTABLISHMENTS, BY NATIONALITY

	1999	2000	2001	2002	2003	Market share 03	% change 03-02
TOTAL	**82,159**	**86,469**	**88,639**	**95,851**	**69,691**	**100.00**	**-27.29**
AFRICA	**15,852**	**18,962**	**19,241**	**21,165**	**21,579**	**30.96**	**1.96**
WEST AFRICA	**14,026**	**16,312**	**16,478**	**18,125**	**14,232**	**20.42**	**-21.48**
ALL.WEST.AFR	14,026	16,312	16,478	18,125	14,232	20.42	-21.48
OTHER AFRICA	**1,826**	**2,650**	**2,763**	**3,040**	**7,347**	**10.54**	**141.68**
OTHER AFRICA	1,826	2,650	2,763	3,040	7,347	10.54	141.68
AMERICAS	**8,671**	**9,306**	**8,393**	**9,232**	**3,379**	**4.85**	**-63.40**
NORTH AMER	**8,671**	**9,306**	**8,393**	**9,232**	**3,379**	**4.85**	**-63.40**
CANADA	2,645	2,465	2,512	3,217	1,562	2.24	-51.45
USA	6,026	6,841	5,881	6,015	1,817	2.61	-69.79
EAST AS/PACI	**782**	**1,020**	**1,081**	**1,189**	**1,287**	**1.85**	**8.24**
N/EAST ASIA	**782**	**1,020**	**1,081**	**1,189**	**1,287**	**1.85**	**8.24**
JAPAN	782	1,020	1,081	1,189	583	0.84	-50.97
OT NORTH AS					704	1.01	
EUROPE	**49,733**	**48,304**	**50,694**	**55,763**	**37,922**	**54.41**	**-31.99**
C/E EUROPE	**1,428**	**1,447**	**1,497**	**1,572**	**186**	**0.27**	**-88.17**
USSR(former)	531	615	648	681	120	0.17	-82.38
OTH C/E EUR	897	832	849	891	66	0.09	-92.59
NORTHERN EUR	**2,156**	**3,527**	**3,701**	**4,071**	**1,926**	**2.76**	**-52.69**
UK	1,063	1,211	1,269	1,395	1,460	2.09	4.66
SCANDINAVIA	1,093	2,316	2,432	2,676	466	0.67	-82.59
SOUTHERN EUR	**11,493**	**12,698**	**12,941**	**14,235**	**6,113**	**8.77**	**-57.06**
ITALY	8,321	9,638	9,852	10,676	3,476	4.99	-67.44
SPAIN	3,172	3,060	3,089	3,559	2,637	3.78	-25.91
WESTERN EUR	**34,656**	**30,632**	**32,555**	**35,885**	**29,697**	**42.61**	**-17.24**
AUSTRIA	78	73	192	201	530	0.76	163.68
FRANCE	22,213	19,008	20,418	22,325	22,539	32.34	0.96
GERMANY	3,651	2,776	2,821	3,103	2,412	3.46	-22.27
SWITZERLAND	802	917	931	1,285	954	1.37	-25.76
BENELUX	7,912	7,858	8,193	8,971	3,262	4.68	-63.64
MIDDLE EAST	**1,369**	**2,206**	**2,445**	**2,567**	**707**	**1.01**	**-72.46**
MIDDLE EAST	**1,369**	**2,206**	**2,445**	**2,567**	**707**	**1.01**	**-72.46**
ALL MID EAST	1,369	2,206	2,445	2,567	707	1.01	-72.46
REG.NOT SPEC	**5,752**	**6,671**	**6,785**	**5,935**	**4,817**	**6.91**	**-18.84**
NOT SPECIFIE	**5,752**	**6,671**	**6,785**	**5,935**	**4,817**	**6.91**	**-18.84**
OTH.WORLD	5,752	6,671	6,785	5,935	4,817	6.91	-18.84

Source: World Tourism Organization (WTO)

5. OVERNIGHT STAYS OF NON-RESIDENT TOURISTS IN HOTELS AND SIMILAR ESTABLISHMENTS, BY NATIONALITY

	1999	2000	2001	2002	2003	Market share 03	% change 03-02
TOTAL	**165,117**	**173,560**	**177,917**	**193,167**	**228,663**	**100.00**	**18.38**
AFRICA	**49,077**	**51,548**	**54,340**	**58,178**	**74,291**	**32.49**	**27.70**
WEST AFRICA	**45,826**	**47,236**	**49,414**	**52,360**	**43,830**	**19.17**	**-16.29**
ALL.WEST.AFR	45,826	47,236	49,414	52,360	43,830	19.17	-16.29
OTHER AFRICA	**3,251**	**4,312**	**4,926**	**5,818**	**30,461**	**13.32**	**423.56**
OTHER AFRICA	3,251	4,312	4,926	5,818	30,461	13.32	423.56
AMERICAS	**10,373**	**11,744**	**12,330**	**13,575**	**22,213**	**9.71**	**63.63**
NORTH AMER	**10,373**	**11,744**	**12,330**	**13,575**	**22,213**	**9.71**	**63.63**
CANADA	4,192	4,644	4,768	5,430	8,094	3.54	49.06
USA	6,181	7,100	7,562	8,145	14,119	6.17	73.35
EAST AS/PACI	**6,478**	**1,413**	**1,575**	**1,645**	**2,421**	**1.06**	**47.17**
N/EAST ASIA	**6,478**	**1,413**	**1,575**	**1,645**	**2,421**	**1.06**	**47.17**
JAPAN	6,478	1,413	1,575	1,645	2,421	1.06	47.17
EUROPE	**91,893**	**99,216**	**99,663**	**108,600**	**114,300**	**49.99**	**5.25**
C/E EUROPE	**1,978**	**2,248**	**2,442**	**2,715**	**2,650**	**1.16**	**-2.39**
USSR(former)	968	801	897	1,005	1,580	0.69	57.21
OTH C/E EUR	1,010	1,447	1,545	1,710	1,070	0.47	-37.43
NORTHERN EUR	**3,710**	**5,647**	**5,749**	**6,516**	**7,767**	**3.40**	**19.20**
UK	1,872	2,136	2,174	2,477	2,480	1.08	0.12
SCANDINAVIA	1,838	3,511	3,575	4,039	5,287	2.31	30.90
SOUTHERN EUR	**16,638**	**19,308**	**19,590**	**20,634**	**23,912**	**10.46**	**15.89**
ITALY	10,212	11,687	11,791	12,380	15,525	6.79	25.40
SPAIN	6,426	7,621	7,799	8,254	8,387	3.67	1.61
WESTERN EUR	**69,567**	**72,013**	**71,882**	**78,735**	**79,971**	**34.97**	**1.57**
AUSTRIA	299	207	291	362	1,048	0.46	189.50
FRANCE	48,832	50,995	51,231	56,000	54,335	23.76	-2.97
GERMANY	7,026	4,817	5,042	5,604	6,406	2.80	14.31
SWITZERLAND	949	1,026	1,064	1,810	2,736	1.20	51.16
BENELUX	12,461	14,968	14,254	14,959	15,446	6.75	3.26
MIDDLE EAST	**1,369**	**2,822**	**2,912**	**3,412**	**4,322**	**1.89**	**26.67**
MIDDLE EAST	**1,369**	**2,822**	**2,912**	**3,412**	**4,322**	**1.89**	**26.67**
ALL MID EAST	1,369	2,822	2,912	3,412	4,322	1.89	26.67
REG.NOT SPEC	**5,927**	**6,817**	**7,097**	**7,757**	**11,116**	**4.86**	**43.30**
NOT SPECIFIE	**5,927**	**6,817**	**7,097**	**7,757**	**11,116**	**4.86**	**43.30**
OTH.WORLD	5,927	6,817	7,097	7,757	11,116	4.86	43.30

Source: World Tourism Organization (WTO)

MALTA

1. ARRIVALS OF NON-RESIDENT TOURISTS AT NATIONAL BORDERS, BY NATIONALITY

	1999	2000	2001	2002	2003	Market share 03	% change 03-02
TOTAL	**1,214,230**	**1,215,712**	**1,180,145**	**1,133,814**	**1,126,601**	**100.00**	**-0.64**
AFRICA	**7,387**	**9,691**	**8,694**	**9,086**			
EAST AFRICA	**395**	**621**	**337**	**460**			
BURUNDI	4		2	4			
ETHIOPIA	20	34	18	6			
DJIBOUTI	2	6	16	32			
KENYA	111	98	80	124			
MADAGASCAR	22	16	9	6			
MALAWI	15	34	12	6			
MAURITIUS	51	46	37	35			
MOZAMBIQUE	3	14	2	4			
RWANDA	2			2			
SEYCHELLES	16	38	18	26			
SOMALIA	7	16	12	10			
ZIMBABWE	62	116	34	73			
UGANDA	24	81	24	52			
TANZANIA	34	78	43	44			
ZAMBIA	22	44	30	36			
CENTRAL AFR	**40**	**66**	**76**	**66**			
ANGOLA	2	4	12	12			
CAMEROON	19	24	38	28			
CONGO	12	30	16	20			
EQ.GUINEA	7	8	4	4			
GABON				2			
SAO TOME PRN			6				
NORTH AFRICA	**5,750**	**7,375**	**6,729**	**7,047**			
ALGERIA	305	289	369	791			
MOROCCO	1,212	1,647	1,278	1,210			
SUDAN	89	109	79	86			
TUNISIA	4,144	5,330	5,003	4,960			
SOUTHERN AFR	**815**	**1,190**	**1,078**	**1,004**			
BOTSWANA	11	20	12	4			
NAMIBIA	3	16	6	8			
SOUTH AFRICA	798	1,136	1,050	988			
SWAZILAND	3	18	10	4			
WEST AFRICA	**387**	**439**	**474**	**509**			
CAPE VERDE	5		6	4			
BENIN	2	4	2	8			
GAMBIA	16	25	16	24			
GHANA	90	65	66	100			
GUINEA	7	8	4	4			
COTE IVOIRE	4	10		36			
LIBERIA	5	8	2	4			
MALI	3	8	10	6			
MAURITANIA	21	20	28	38			
NIGERIA	196	217	296	227			
GUINEABISSAU	3						
SENEGAL	17	14	16	18			
SIERRA LEONE	16	46	22	32			
TOGO	2	14	6	8			

MALTA

1. ARRIVALS OF NON-RESIDENT TOURISTS AT NATIONAL BORDERS, BY NATIONALITY

	1999	2000	2001	2002	2003	Market share 03	% change 03-02
AMERICAS	**25,951**	**26,934**	**27,945**	**27,005**	**20,657**	**1.83**	**-23.51**
NORTH AMER	**25,575**	**26,523**	**27,545**	**26,738**	**20,657**	**1.83**	**-22.74**
CANADA	7,017	7,256	7,559	6,658			
USA	18,558	19,267	19,986	20,080	20,657	1.83	2.87
SOUTH AMER	**376**	**411**	**400**	**267**			
ARGENTINA	376	411	400	267			
EAST AS/PACI	**17,620**	**21,162**	**22,246**	**25,020**			
N/EAST ASIA	**7,095**	**9,351**	**11,650**	**14,327**			
CHINA	699	882	995	1,446			
JAPAN	6,396	8,469	10,655	12,881			
AUSTRALASIA	**10,525**	**11,811**	**10,596**	**10,693**			
AUSTRALIA	9,656	10,841	9,595	9,542			
NEW ZEALAND	869	970	1,001	1,151			
EUROPE	**1,107,725**	**1,103,945**	**1,079,862**	**1,039,904**	**939,793**	**83.42**	**-9.63**
C/E EUROPE	**47,211**	**49,207**	**52,474**	**54,542**	**21,096**	**1.87**	**-61.32**
AZERBAIJAN	91	65	34	64			
ARMENIA	177	173	183	180			
BULGARIA	1,285	1,252	1,422	2,113			
CZECH REP	6,225	6,368	4,685	5,816			
ESTONIA	1,356	254	218	211			
GEORGIA	88	84	185	112			
HUNGARY	8,250	8,615	7,736	8,245			
KAZAKHSTAN	148	138	191	200			
LATVIA	131	647	904	272			
LITHUANIA	199	192	267	367			
REP MOLDOVA	33	85	54	186			
POLAND	6,766	7,792	7,956	6,856			
ROMANIA	1,732	955	1,152	1,421			
RUSSIAN FED	16,223	18,781	22,054	22,919	21,096	1.87	-7.95
SLOVAKIA	1,701	1,363	1,851	1,820			
TAJIKISTAN	11	2	6	3			
UKRAINE	2,768	2,409	3,447	3,617			
UZBEKISTAN	27	32	129	140			
NORTHERN EUR	**493,269**	**500,918**	**526,036**	**509,377**	**507,267**	**45.03**	**-0.41**
DENMARK	17,276	17,086	18,194	17,427	17,747	1.58	1.84
FAEROE IS	12	38	8	50			
FINLAND	4,242	5,802	5,939	4,306	6,113	0.54	41.96
ICELAND	200	182	309	419			
IRELAND	20,082	19,848	21,855	21,316			
NORWAY	10,024	9,133	10,777	9,786	11,825	1.05	20.84
SWEDEN	19,065	20,050	17,424	11,738	12,017	1.07	2.38
UK	422,368	428,779	451,530	444,335	459,565	40.79	3.43
SOUTHERN EUR	**123,103**	**117,844**	**122,153**	**131,901**	**94,175**	**8.36**	**-28.60**
ALBANIA	207	201	230	355			
ANDORRA	8	72	30	64			
BOSNIA HERZG	382	368	266	270			
CROATIA	2,657	1,940	1,404	1,061			

MALTA

1. ARRIVALS OF NON-RESIDENT TOURISTS AT NATIONAL BORDERS, BY NATIONALITY

	1999	2000	2001	2002	2003	Market share 03	% change 03-02
GREECE	10,705	8,325	8,131	6,982			
ITALY	92,726	92,522	93,564	100,875	94,175	8.36	-6.64
PORTUGAL	4,921	4,169	4,699	3,964			
SAN MARINO	31	82	46	78			
SLOVENIA	4,096	2,743	1,593	2,473			
SPAIN	5,597	5,563	9,091	12,883			
TFYROM			216	323			
SERBIA,MTNEG	1,773	1,859	2,883	2,573			
WESTERN EUR	**432,533**	**422,979**	**370,671**	**336,512**	**317,255**	**28.16**	**-5.72**
AUSTRIA	29,027	28,119	27,670	24,448	28,416	2.52	16.23
BELGIUM	28,349	26,713	23,695	24,018	23,724	2.11	-1.22
FRANCE	73,264	75,809	82,669	80,101	76,384	6.78	-4.64
GERMANY	212,430	204,747	160,262	142,106	125,811	11.17	-11.47
LIECHTENSTEN	78	118	80	74			
LUXEMBOURG	584	1,294	1,158	977			
MONACO	8	28	16	18			
NETHERLANDS	65,345	64,168	50,756	44,395	40,810	3.62	-8.08
SWITZERLAND	23,448	21,983	24,365	20,375	22,110	1.96	8.52
EAST/MED EUR	**11,609**	**12,997**	**8,528**	**7,572**			
CYPRUS	2,368	1,949	1,640	2,524			
ISRAEL	4,248	3,973	3,559	1,310			
TURKEY	4,993	7,075	3,329	3,738			
MIDDLE EAST	**48,480**	**46,287**	**33,771**	**25,484**	**20,218**	**1.79**	**-20.66**
MIDDLE EAST	**48,480**	**46,287**	**33,771**	**25,484**	**20,218**	**1.79**	**-20.66**
LEBANON	881	780	648	329			
LIBYA	44,968	43,267	31,017	22,783	20,218	1.79	-11.26
OMAN	17	17	30	8			
QATAR	8	32	18	4			
SAUDI ARABIA	151	153	108	116			
SYRIA	359	287	307	260			
UNTD ARAB EM	188	114	143	52			
EGYPT	1,908	1,637	1,500	1,932			
SOUTH ASIA	**2,054**	**1,944**	**1,613**	**1,549**			
SOUTH ASIA	**2,054**	**1,944**	**1,613**	**1,549**			
AFGHANISTAN	8	17	11	9			
BANGLADESH	107	78	34	55			
INDIA	1,319	1,206	1,027	1,048			
IRAN	177	177	182	138			
MALDIVES	30	38	24	42			
NEPAL	7	4	10	6			
PAKISTAN	406	424	325	251			
REG.NOT SPEC	**5,013**	**5,749**	**6,014**	**5,766**	**145,933**	**12.95**	**2,430.92**
NOT SPECIFIE	**5,013**	**5,749**	**6,014**	**5,766**	**145,933**	**12.95**	**2,430.92**
OTH.WORLD	5,013	5,749	6,014	5,766	145,933	12.95	2,430.92

Source: World Tourism Organization (WTO)

MALTA

3. ARRIVALS OF NON-RESIDENT TOURISTS IN HOTELS AND SIMILAR ESTABLISHMENTS, BY NATIONALITY

	1999	2000	2001	2002	2003	Market share 03	% change 03-02
TOTAL (*)	**891,614**	**845,456**	**832,620**	**796,508**	**905,994**	**100.00**	**13.75**
AMERICAS	**15,366**	**14,986**	**15,533**	**15,899**	**10,354**	**1.14**	**-34.88**
NORTH AMER	**15,366**	**14,986**	**15,533**	**15,899**	**10,354**	**1.14**	**-34.88**
CANADA	3,474	3,199	3,491	2,944			
USA	11,892	11,787	12,042	12,955	10,354	1.14	-20.08
EUROPE	**785,290**	**738,897**	**727,385**	**692,068**	**758,999**	**83.78**	**9.67**
NORTHERN EUR	**383,485**	**354,920**	**381,841**	**368,747**	**427,136**	**47.15**	**15.83**
DENMARK	15,692	15,023	15,810	15,480	18,722	2.07	20.94
IRELAND	15,739	15,099	17,636	16,750			
NORWAY	7,691	6,877	7,895	6,896	9,577	1.06	38.88
SWEDEN	14,811	14,346	11,767	7,136	8,617	0.95	20.75
UK	329,552	303,575	328,733	322,485	390,220	43.07	21.00
SOUTHERN EUR	**61,418**	**62,058**	**65,959**	**72,703**	**62,631**	**6.91**	**-13.85**
ITALY	53,125	54,611	55,100	59,354	62,631	6.91	5.52
PORTUGAL	3,935	3,383	3,906	3,357			
SPAIN	4,358	4,064	6,953	9,992			
WESTERN EUR	**333,416**	**313,580**	**274,905**	**247,215**	**269,232**	**29.72**	**8.91**
AUSTRIA	21,484	19,479	17,045	15,395	20,168	2.23	31.00
BELGIUM	22,512	20,124	19,283	19,574	24,206	2.67	23.66
FRANCE	58,088	58,755	65,789	62,256	67,728	7.48	8.79
GERMANY	163,120	150,524	116,381	102,219	104,931	11.58	2.65
NETHERLANDS	50,088	48,163	38,309	32,942	34,179	3.77	3.76
SWITZERLAND	18,124	16,535	18,098	14,829	18,020	1.99	21.52
EAST/MED EUR	**6,971**	**8,339**	**4,680**	**3,403**			
ISRAEL	3,096	3,007	2,456	970			
TURKEY	3,875	5,332	2,224	2,433			
MIDDLE EAST	**16,985**	**19,107**	**15,004**	**11,168**	**14,323**	**1.58**	**28.25**
MIDDLE EAST	**16,985**	**19,107**	**15,004**	**11,168**	**14,323**	**1.58**	**28.25**
LIBYA	16,985	19,107	15,004	11,168	14,323	1.58	28.25
REG.NOT SPEC	**73,973**	**72,466**	**74,698**	**77,373**	**122,318**	**13.50**	**58.09**
NOT SPECIFIE	**73,973**	**72,466**	**74,698**	**77,373**	**122,318**	**13.50**	**58.09**
OTH.WORLD	73,973	72,466	74,698	77,373	122,318	13.50	58.09

Source: World Tourism Organization (WTO)

MALTA

4. ARRIVALS OF NON-RESIDENT TOURISTS IN ALL TYPES OF ACCOMMODATION ESTABLISHMENTS, BY NATIONALITY

	1999	2000	2001	2002	2003	Market share 03	% change 03-02
TOTAL (*)	**1,214,230**	**1,215,713**	**1,180,145**	**1,133,814**	**1,089,089**	**100.00**	**-3.94**
AMERICAS	**25,575**	**26,521**	**27,545**	**26,738**	**13,896**	**1.28**	**-48.03**
NORTH AMER	**25,575**	**26,521**	**27,545**	**26,738**	**13,896**	**1.28**	**-48.03**
CANADA	7,017	7,254	7,559	6,658			
USA	18,558	19,267	19,986	20,080	13,896	1.28	-30.80
EAST AS/PACI	**10,525**	**11,811**	**10,596**	**10,693**			
AUSTRALASIA	**10,525**	**11,811**	**10,596**	**10,693**			
AUSTRALIA	9,656	10,841	9,595	9,542			
NEW ZEALAND	869	970	1,001	1,151			
EUROPE	**1,003,380**	**999,824**	**971,984**	**931,134**	**894,575**	**82.14**	**-3.93**
NORTHERN EUR	**478,791**	**485,760**	**509,003**	**494,816**	**502,240**	**46.12**	**1.50**
DENMARK	17,276	17,085	18,194	17,427	19,909	1.83	14.24
IRELAND	20,082	19,846	21,855	21,316			
SWEDEN	19,065	20,050	17,424	11,738	10,433	0.96	-11.12
UK	422,368	428,779	451,530	444,335	471,898	43.33	6.20
SOUTHERN EUR	**92,726**	**92,522**	**93,564**	**100,875**	**78,366**	**7.20**	**-22.31**
ITALY	92,726	92,522	93,564	100,875	78,366	7.20	-22.31
WESTERN EUR	**431,863**	**421,542**	**369,417**	**335,443**	**313,969**	**28.83**	**-6.40**
AUSTRIA	29,027	28,119	27,670	24,448	24,423	2.24	-0.10
BELGIUM	28,349	26,713	23,695	24,018	26,268	2.41	9.37
FRANCE	73,264	75,814	82,669	80,101	77,029	7.07	-3.84
GERMANY	212,430	204,747	160,262	142,106	124,773	11.46	-12.20
NETHERLANDS	65,345	64,166	50,756	44,395	39,807	3.66	-10.33
SWITZERLAND	23,448	21,983	24,365	20,375	21,669	1.99	6.35
MIDDLE EAST	**44,968**	**43,267**	**31,017**	**22,783**	**17,455**	**1.60**	**-23.39**
MIDDLE EAST	**44,968**	**43,267**	**31,017**	**22,783**	**17,455**	**1.60**	**-23.39**
LIBYA	44,968	43,267	31,017	22,783	17,455	1.60	-23.39
REG.NOT SPEC	**129,782**	**134,290**	**139,003**	**142,466**	**163,163**	**14.98**	**14.53**
NOT SPECIFIE	**129,782**	**134,290**	**139,003**	**142,466**	**163,163**	**14.98**	**14.53**
OTH.WORLD	129,782	134,290	139,003	142,466	163,163	14.98	14.53

Source: World Tourism Organization (WTO)

MALTA

5. OVERNIGHT STAYS OF NON-RESIDENT TOURISTS IN HOTELS AND SIMILAR ESTABLISHMENTS, BY NATIONALITY

	1999	2000	2001	2002	2003	Market share 03	% change 03-02
TOTAL (*)	**8,150,489**	**6,977,942**	**7,474,880**	**7,020,619**	**8,155,499**	**100.00**	**16.16**
AFRICA	**15,464**	**25,171**	**24,321**	**22,436**			
NORTH AFRICA	**15,464**	**25,171**	**24,321**	**22,436**			
TUNISIA	15,464	25,171	24,321	22,436			
AMERICAS	**127,066**	**121,210**	**133,106**	**127,275**	**72,156**	**0.88**	**-43.31**
NORTH AMER	**127,066**	**121,210**	**133,106**	**127,275**	**72,156**	**0.88**	**-43.31**
CANADA	29,502	26,417	30,402	25,417			
USA	97,564	94,793	102,704	101,858	72,156	0.88	-29.16
EAST AS/PACI	**51,226**	**69,258**	**76,899**	**88,299**			
N/EAST ASIA	**30,051**	**47,898**	**53,818**	**63,512**			
JAPAN	30,051	47,898	53,818	63,512			
AUSTRALASIA	**21,175**	**21,360**	**23,081**	**24,787**			
AUSTRALIA	21,175	21,360	23,081	24,787			
EUROPE	**7,739,474**	**6,488,512**	**7,006,247**	**6,585,137**	**7,109,082**	**87.17**	**7.96**
C/E EUROPE	**302,986**	**266,985**	**303,881**	**319,468**	**143,351**	**1.76**	**-55.13**
CZECH REP	46,101	30,881	23,704	28,031			
HUNGARY	52,339	46,309	43,126	47,317			
POLAND	38,133	37,719	41,697	29,118			
OTH C/E EUR	166,413	152,076	195,354	215,002	143,351	1.76	-33.33
NORTHERN EUR	**3,925,042**	**3,154,577**	**3,844,632**	**3,720,930**	**4,364,032**	**53.51**	**17.28**
DENMARK	142,003	116,654	130,082	117,415	159,319	1.95	35.69
FINLAND	30,231	36,322	35,513	25,778			
IRELAND	147,384	126,290	165,265	165,422			
NORWAY	76,087	59,254	77,115	66,249	90,603	1.11	36.76
SWEDEN	124,469	111,039	94,632	60,451	76,091	0.93	25.87
UK	3,404,868	2,705,018	3,342,025	3,285,615	4,038,019	49.51	22.90
SOUTHERN EUR	**533,354**	**474,955**	**505,878**	**516,645**	**436,386**	**5.35**	**-15.53**
GREECE	42,380	38,563	34,898	24,535			
ITALY	430,494	381,284	394,539	409,092	436,386	5.35	6.67
PORTUGAL	29,388	25,256	25,435	20,493			
SPAIN	31,092	29,852	51,006	62,525			
WESTERN EUR	**2,936,584**	**2,540,351**	**2,320,904**	**2,007,461**	**2,165,313**	**26.55**	**7.86**
AUSTRIA	159,913	146,690	127,250	106,463	147,654	1.81	38.69
BELGIUM	208,583	163,950	159,750	167,384	203,339	2.49	21.48
FRANCE	462,225	444,916	491,997	445,511	492,752	6.04	10.60
GERMANY	1,522,694	1,270,897	1,061,388	900,404	891,821	10.94	-0.95
NETHERLANDS	437,842	389,156	338,026	272,462	292,673	3.59	7.42
SWITZERLAND	145,327	124,742	142,493	115,237	137,074	1.68	18.95
EAST/MED EUR	**41,508**	**51,644**	**30,952**	**20,633**			
ISRAEL	20,465	19,584	15,957	5,999			
TURKEY	21,043	32,060	14,995	14,634			

5. OVERNIGHT STAYS OF NON-RESIDENT TOURISTS IN HOTELS AND SIMILAR ESTABLISHMENTS, BY NATIONALITY

	1999	2000	2001	2002	2003	Market share 03	% change 03-02
MIDDLE EAST	**90,125**	**140,479**	**118,805**	**79,348**	**88,640**	**1.09**	**11.71**
MIDDLE EAST	**90,125**	**140,479**	**118,805**	**79,348**	**88,640**	**1.09**	**11.71**
LIBYA	90,125	140,479	118,805	79,348	88,640	1.09	11.71
REG.NOT SPEC	**127,134**	**133,312**	**115,502**	**118,124**	**885,621**	**10.86**	**649.74**
NOT SPECIFIE	**127,134**	**133,312**	**115,502**	**118,124**	**885,621**	**10.86**	**649.74**
OTH.WORLD	127,134	133,312	115,502	118,124	885,621	10.86	649.74

Source: World Tourism Organization (WTO)

MALTA

6. OVERNIGHT STAYS OF NON-RESIDENT TOURISTS IN ALL TYPES OF ACCOMMODATION ESTABLISHMENTS, BY NATIONALITY

	1999	2000	2001	2002	2003	Market share 03	% change 03-02
TOTAL (*)	**11,658,245**	**10,266,188**	**11,066,813**	**10,599,206**	**11,115,204**	**100.00**	**4.87**
AMERICAS	**267,121**	**237,913**	**283,660**	**274,690**	**172,611**	**1.55**	**-37.16**
NORTH AMER	**267,121**	**237,913**	**283,660**	**274,690**	**172,611**	**1.55**	**-37.16**
CANADA	86,621	72,931	86,908	79,279			
USA	180,500	164,982	196,752	195,411	172,611	1.55	-11.67
EAST AS/PACI	**161,719**	**114,841**	**154,313**	**154,269**			
AUSTRALASIA	**161,719**	**114,841**	**154,313**	**154,269**			
AUSTRALIA	161,719	114,841	154,313	154,269			
EUROPE	**9,824,858**	**8,461,103**	**9,147,536**	**8,715,429**	**8,865,678**	**79.76**	**1.72**
NORTHERN EUR	**5,073,513**	**4,300,155**	**5,159,031**	**5,049,974**	**5,458,200**	**49.11**	**8.08**
DENMARK	161,535	134,608	151,218	130,173	170,311	1.53	30.83
IRELAND	197,129	164,196	208,852	204,650			
SWEDEN	185,502	160,910	162,683	115,072	123,021	1.11	6.91
UK	4,529,347	3,840,441	4,636,278	4,600,079	5,164,868	46.47	12.28
SOUTHERN EUR	**766,635**	**670,500**	**708,878**	**739,117**	**627,109**	**5.64**	**-15.15**
ITALY	766,635	670,500	708,878	739,117	627,109	5.64	-15.15
WESTERN EUR	**3,984,710**	**3,490,448**	**3,279,627**	**2,926,338**	**2,780,369**	**25.01**	**-4.99**
AUSTRIA	242,947	220,304	228,072	188,663	198,408	1.79	5.17
BELGIUM	264,345	221,597	202,299	211,708	224,381	2.02	5.99
FRANCE	614,184	588,978	659,602	629,473	624,119	5.62	-0.85
GERMANY	2,074,610	1,756,246	1,512,683	1,323,534	1,182,857	10.64	-10.63
NETHERLANDS	587,574	523,466	459,379	379,662	357,293	3.21	-5.89
SWITZERLAND	201,050	179,857	217,592	193,298	193,311	1.74	0.01
MIDDLE EAST	**294,574**	**336,493**	**261,430**	**177,002**	**144,391**	**1.30**	**-18.42**
MIDDLE EAST	**294,574**	**336,493**	**261,430**	**177,002**	**144,391**	**1.30**	**-18.42**
LIBYA	294,574	336,493	261,430	177,002	144,391	1.30	-18.42
REG.NOT SPEC	**1,109,973**	**1,115,838**	**1,219,874**	**1,277,816**	**1,932,524**	**17.39**	**51.24**
NOT SPECIFIE	**1,109,973**	**1,115,838**	**1,219,874**	**1,277,816**	**1,932,524**	**17.39**	**51.24**
OTH.WORLD	1,109,973	1,115,838	1,219,874	1,277,816	1,932,524	17.39	51.24

Source: World Tourism Organization (WTO)

MARSHALL ISLANDS

1. ARRIVALS OF NON-RESIDENT TOURISTS AT NATIONAL BORDERS, BY NATIONALITY

	1999	2000	2001	2002	2003	Market share 03	% chan 03-02
TOTAL (*)	**4,622**	**5,246**	**5,444**	**6,002**	**7,195**	**100.00**	**19**
AMERICAS	**2,064**	**2,022**	**2,107**	**2,127**	**2,281**	**31.70**	**7**
NORTH AMER	**2,062**	**2,019**	**2,100**	**2,124**	**2,273**	**31.59**	**7**
CANADA	45	20	61	59	80	1.11	35
USA	2,017	1,999	2,039	2,065	2,193	30.48	6
OTHER AMERIC	**2**	**3**	**7**	**3**	**8**	**0.11**	**166**
OTH AMERICA	2	3	7	3	8	0.11	166
EAST AS/PACI	**2,234**	**2,673**	**3,076**	**3,569**	**4,518**	**62.79**	**26**
N/EAST ASIA	**876**	**1,011**	**1,613**	**1,654**	**1,431**	**19.89**	**-13**
CHINA	150	83	114	189	96	1.33	-49
TAIWAN(P.C.)			412	402	224	3.11	-44
JAPAN	610	856	996	892	1,024	14.23	14
KOREA REP.	116	72	91	171	87	1.21	-49
S/EAST ASIA	**197**	**170**	**222**	**258**	**258**	**3.59**	
PHILIPPINES	197	170	222	258	258	3.59	
AUSTRALASIA	**264**	**202**	**291**	**325**	**350**	**4.86**	**7**
AUSTRALIA	146	140	190	191	208	2.89	8
NEW ZEALAND	118	62	101	134	142	1.97	5
MELANESIA	**58**	**148**	**94**	**103**	**136**	**1.89**	**32**
FIJI	58	148	94	103	136	1.89	32
MICRONESIA	**563**	**824**	**599**	**689**	**1,159**	**16.11**	**68**
KIRIBATI	289	321	283	269	582	8.09	116
NAURU	5	18	66	130	153	2.13	17
MICRONESIA	221	420	203	245	353	4.91	44
PALAU	48	65	47	45	71	0.99	57
POLYNESIA	**15**	**17**	**21**	**17**	**27**	**0.38**	**58**
TUVALU	15	17	21	17	27	0.38	58
OT.EAST AS/P	**261**	**301**	**236**	**523**	**1,157**	**16.08**	**121**
OTHER ASIA	213	109	165	414	1,039	14.44	150
OTH OCEANIA	48	192	71	109	118	1.64	8
EUROPE	**220**	**129**	**221**	**261**	**325**	**4.52**	**24**
NORTHERN EUR	**106**	**31**	**102**	**133**	**167**	**2.32**	**25**
UK	106	31	102	133	167	2.32	25
WESTERN EUR	**40**	**25**	**27**	**34**	**36**	**0.50**	**5**
GERMANY	40	25	27	34	36	0.50	5
OTHER EUROPE	**74**	**73**	**92**	**94**	**122**	**1.70**	**29**
OTHER EUROPE	74	73	92	94	122	1.70	29
REG.NOT SPEC	**104**	**422**	**40**	**45**	**71**	**0.99**	**57**
NOT SPECIFIE	**104**	**422**	**40**	**45**	**71**	**0.99**	**57**
OTH.WORLD	104	241	40	45	71	0.99	57
N RESID ABRO		181					

MARTINIQUE

1. ARRIVALS OF NON-RESIDENT TOURISTS AT NATIONAL BORDERS, BY COUNTRY OF RESIDENCE

	1999	2000	2001	2002	2003	Market share 03	% change 03-02
TOTAL (*)	**564,304**	**526,291**	**460,382**	**446,689**	**453,159**	**100.00**	**1.45**
AMERICAS	**85,291**	**80,168**	**54,744**	**70,378**	**71,559**	**15.79**	**1.68**
CARIBBEAN	**51,983**	**52,992**	**34,854**	**47,129**	**53,495**	**11.80**	**13.51**
BARBADOS	1,455	1,463	1,509	3,475	1,976	0.44	-43.14
DOMINICA	1,606	1,855	1,516	3,363	3,033	0.67	-9.81
GUADELOUPE	42,872	41,102	27,476	31,713	40,668	8.97	28.24
ST.LUCIA	4,994	5,771	2,953	5,168	5,842	1.29	13.04
OTH CARIBBE	1,056	2,801	1,400	3,410	1,976	0.44	-42.05
NORTH AMER	**20,291**	**10,499**	**4,161**	**8,712**	**5,141**	**1.13**	**-40.99**
CANADA	5,244	5,425	1,945	4,474	2,584	0.57	-42.24
USA	15,047	5,074	2,216	4,238	2,557	0.56	-39.66
SOUTH AMER	**13,017**	**16,677**	**15,729**	**14,537**	**12,923**	**2.85**	**-11.10**
FR.GUIANA	11,837	13,860	14,171	11,247	10,619	2.34	-5.58
VENEZUELA	1,180	2,817	1,558	3,290	2,304	0.51	-29.97
EUROPE	**474,475**	**443,046**	**403,316**	**371,978**	**379,922**	**83.84**	**2.14**
NORTHERN EUR	**4,871**	**4,330**	**3,433**	**3,206**	**3,802**	**0.84**	**18.59**
UK/IRELAND	3,010	2,501	2,747	2,158	1,945	0.43	-9.87
SCANDINAVIA	1,861	1,829	686	1,048	1,857	0.41	77.19
SOUTHERN EUR	**5,221**	**3,541**	**2,226**	**4,111**	**2,788**	**0.62**	**-32.18**
ITALY	5,221	3,541	2,226	4,111	2,788	0.62	-32.18
WESTERN EUR	**461,275**	**431,135**	**396,394**	**363,066**	**371,287**	**81.93**	**2.26**
FRANCE	447,730	418,536	384,355	349,212	357,726	78.94	2.44
GERMANY	3,736	2,504	3,618	1,588	2,767	0.61	74.24
SWITZERLAND	4,217	4,006	2,982	5,728	2,963	0.65	-48.27
BENELUX	5,592	6,089	5,439	6,538	7,831	1.73	19.78
OTHER EUROPE	**3,108**	**4,040**	**1,263**	**1,595**	**2,045**	**0.45**	**28.21**
OTHER EUROPE	3,108	4,040	1,263	1,595	2,045	0.45	28.21
REG.NOT SPEC	**4,538**	**3,077**	**2,322**	**4,333**	**1,678**	**0.37**	**-61.27**
NOT SPECIFIE	**4,538**	**3,077**	**2,322**	**4,333**	**1,678**	**0.37**	**-61.27**
OTH.WORLD	4,538	3,077	2,322	4,333	1,678	0.37	-61.27

Source: World Tourism Organization (WTO)

MARTINIQUE

3. ARRIVALS OF NON-RESIDENT TOURISTS IN HOTELS AND SIMILAR ESTABLISHMENTS, BY NATIONALITY

	1999	2000	2001	2002	2003	Market share 03	% change 03-02
TOTAL	**286,641**	**266,727**	**233,708**	**197,529**	**186,547**	**100.00**	**-5.56**
AMERICAS	**30,303**	**31,303**	**20,876**	**28,738**	**22,788**	**12.22**	**-20.70**
CARIBBEAN	**18,133**	**25,590**	**18,790**	**23,882**	**20,138**	**10.80**	**-15.68**
ALL CO CARIB	18,133	25,590	18,790	23,882	20,138	10.80	-15.68
NORTH AMER	**12,170**	**5,713**	**2,086**	**4,856**	**2,650**	**1.42**	**-45.43**
CANADA	2,112	2,494	804	2,280	1,301	0.70	-42.94
USA	10,058	3,219	1,282	2,576	1,349	0.72	-47.63
EUROPE	**253,185**	**234,056**	**211,597**	**166,653**	**162,944**	**87.35**	**-2.23**
WESTERN EUR	**236,629**	**218,854**	**201,755**	**153,210**	**150,746**	**80.81**	**-1.61**
FRANCE	236,629	218,854	201,755	153,210	150,746	80.81	-1.61
OTHER EUROPE	**16,556**	**15,202**	**9,842**	**13,443**	**12,198**	**6.54**	**-9.26**
OTHER EUROPE	16,556	15,202	9,842	13,443	12,198	6.54	-9.26
REG.NOT SPEC	**3,153**	**1,368**	**1,235**	**2,138**	**815**	**0.44**	**-61.88**
NOT SPECIFIE	**3,153**	**1,368**	**1,235**	**2,138**	**815**	**0.44**	**-61.88**
OTH.WORLD	3,153	1,368	1,235	2,138	815	0.44	-61.88

Source: World Tourism Organization (WTO)

MARTINIQUE

4. ARRIVALS OF NON-RESIDENT TOURISTS IN ALL TYPES OF ACCOMMODATION ESTABLISHMENTS, BY NATIONALITY

	1999	2000	2001	2002	2003	Market share 03	% change 03-02
TOTAL	**564,303**	**526,290**	**460,384**	**446,688**	**453,162**	**100.00**	**1.45**
AMERICAS	**85,291**	**80,167**	**54,745**	**70,378**	**71,560**	**15.79**	**1.68**
CARIBBEAN	**65,000**	**69,668**	**50,584**	**61,666**	**66,418**	**14.66**	**7.71**
ALL CO CARIB	65,000	69,668	50,584	61,666	66,418	14.66	7.71
NORTH AMER	**20,291**	**10,499**	**4,161**	**8,712**	**5,142**	**1.13**	**-40.98**
CANADA	5,244	5,425	1,945	4,474	2,584	0.57	-42.24
USA	15,047	5,074	2,216	4,238	2,558	0.56	-39.64
EUROPE	**474,474**	**443,046**	**403,317**	**371,977**	**379,924**	**83.84**	**2.14**
WESTERN EUR	**447,730**	**418,535**	**384,355**	**349,212**	**357,726**	**78.94**	**2.44**
FRANCE	447,730	418,535	384,355	349,212	357,726	78.94	2.44
OTHER EUROPE	**26,744**	**24,511**	**18,962**	**22,765**	**22,198**	**4.90**	**-2.49**
OTHER EUROPE	26,744	24,511	18,962	22,765	22,198	4.90	-2.49
REG.NOT SPEC	**4,538**	**3,077**	**2,322**	**4,333**	**1,678**	**0.37**	**-61.27**
NOT SPECIFIE	**4,538**	**3,077**	**2,322**	**4,333**	**1,678**	**0.37**	**-61.27**
OTH.WORLD	4,538	3,077	2,322	4,333	1,678	0.37	-61.27

Source: World Tourism Organization (WTO)

MARTINIQUE

5. OVERNIGHT STAYS OF NON-RESIDENT TOURISTS IN HOTELS AND SIMILAR ESTABLISHMENTS, BY COUNTRY OF RESIDENCE

	1999	2000	2001	2002	2003	Market share 03	% change 03-02
TOTAL	**2,572,586**	**2,440,576**	**2,029,631**	**1,991,313**	**1,693,378**	**100.00**	**-14.96**
AMERICAS	**261,420**	**286,428**	**181,455**	**197,522**	**215,410**	**12.72**	**9.06**
CARIBBEAN	**154,003**	**234,148**	**163,323**	**157,350**	**198,843**	**11.74**	**26.37**
ALL CO CARIB	154,003	234,148	163,323	157,350	198,843	11.74	26.37
NORTH AMER	**107,417**	**52,280**	**18,132**	**40,172**	**16,567**	**0.98**	**-58.76**
CANADA	18,788	22,823	6,989	21,850	10,114	0.60	-53.71
USA	88,629	29,457	11,143	18,322	6,453	0.38	-64.78
EUROPE	**2,275,580**	**2,141,628**	**1,839,177**	**1,776,015**	**1,472,678**	**86.97**	**-17.08**
WESTERN EUR	**2,134,904**	**2,002,529**	**1,753,629**	**1,663,288**	**1,407,028**	**83.09**	**-15.41**
FRANCE	2,134,904	2,002,529	1,753,629	1,663,288	1,407,028	83.09	-15.41
OTHER EUROPE	**140,676**	**139,099**	**85,548**	**112,727**	**65,650**	**3.88**	**-41.76**
OTHER EUROPE	140,676	139,099	85,548	112,727	65,650	3.88	-41.76
REG.NOT SPEC	**35,586**	**12,520**	**8,999**	**17,776**	**5,290**	**0.31**	**-70.24**
NOT SPECIFIE	**35,586**	**12,520**	**8,999**	**17,776**	**5,290**	**0.31**	**-70.24**
OTH.WORLD	35,586	12,520	8,999	17,776	5,290	0.31	-70.24

Source: World Tourism Organization (WTO)

MARTINIQUE

6. OVERNIGHT STAYS OF NON-RESIDENT TOURISTS IN ALL TYPES OF ACCOMMODATION ESTABLISHMENTS, BY NATIONALITY

	1999	2000	2001	2002	2003	Market share 03	% change 03-02
TOTAL	7,497,439	6,955,717	5,556,473	6,022,276	6,135,774	100.00	1.88
AMERICAS	**791,728**	**775,817**	**441,896**	**640,173**	**780,515**	**12.72**	**21.92**
CARIBBEAN	**587,514**	**678,054**	**398,282**	**542,623**	**720,487**	**11.74**	**32.78**
ALL CO CARIB	587,514	678,054	398,282	542,623	720,487	11.74	32.78
NORTH AMER	**204,214**	**97,763**	**43,614**	**97,550**	**60,028**	**0.98**	**-38.46**
CANADA	79,327	56,216	28,759	57,329	36,647	0.60	-36.08
USA	124,887	41,547	14,855	40,221	23,381	0.38	-41.87
EUROPE	**6,656,257**	**6,145,019**	**5,096,094**	**5,333,802**	**5,336,093**	**86.97**	**0.04**
WESTERN EUR	**6,420,933**	**5,870,772**	**4,901,852**	**5,079,663**	**5,098,216**	**83.09**	**0.37**
FRANCE	6,420,933	5,870,772	4,901,852	5,079,663	5,098,216	83.09	0.37
OTHER EUROPE	**235,324**	**274,247**	**194,242**	**254,139**	**237,877**	**3.88**	**-6.40**
OTHER EUROPE	235,324	274,247	194,242	254,139	237,877	3.88	-6.40
REG.NOT SPEC	**49,454**	**34,881**	**18,483**	**48,301**	**19,166**	**0.31**	**-60.32**
NOT SPECIFIE	**49,454**	**34,881**	**18,483**	**48,301**	**19,166**	**0.31**	**-60.32**
OTH.WORLD	49,454	34,881	18,483	48,301	19,166	0.31	-60.32

Source: World Tourism Organization (WTO)

MAURITIUS

1. ARRIVALS OF NON-RESIDENT TOURISTS AT NATIONAL BORDERS, BY COUNTRY OF RESIDENCE

	1999	2000	2001	2002	2003	Market share 03	% change 03-02
TOTAL	**578,085**	**656,453**	**660,318**	**681,648**	**702,018**	**100.00**	**2.99**
AFRICA	**156,228**	**163,763**	**168,319**	**172,351**	**173,996**	**24.79**	**0.95**
EAST AFRICA	**106,176**	**111,987**	**116,993**	**126,443**	**123,814**	**17.64**	**-2.08**
BURUNDI	29	27	53	51	60	0.01	17.65
COMOROS	728	945	860	945	1,437	0.20	52.06
ETHIOPIA	79	81	64	49	142	0.02	189.80
ERITREA	2	11	20	14	8		-42.86
DJIBOUTI	13	33	19	16	49	0.01	206.25
KENYA	1,655	1,801	1,734	1,507	1,510	0.22	0.20
MADAGASCAR	7,880	7,057	6,674	9,417	11,044	1.57	17.28
MALAWI	205	230	176	121	181	0.03	49.59
MOZAMBIQUE	569	434	518	440	394	0.06	-10.45
REUNION	83,749	86,945	91,140	96,375	95,679	13.63	-0.72
RWANDA	25	80	95	40	92	0.01	130.00
SEYCHELLES	7,893	9,229	10,687	13,468	9,869	1.41	-26.72
SOMALIA	1	19	10	8	3		-62.50
ZIMBABWE	2,606	3,435	3,860	3,185	2,343	0.33	-26.44
UGANDA	128	183	148	176	205	0.03	16.48
TANZANIA	293	1,032	513	277	342	0.05	23.47
ZAMBIA	321	445	422	354	456	0.06	28.81
CENTRAL AFR	**625**	**319**	**417**	**301**	**438**	**0.06**	**45.51**
ANGOLA	210	111	156	129	119	0.02	-7.75
CAMEROON	117	44	65	51	110	0.02	115.69
CENT.AFR.REP	1	1	4	5	10		100.00
CHAD	14	5	10	4	8		100.00
CONGO	93	86	86	56	92	0.01	64.29
DEM.R.CONGO	12	34	16	9	12		33.33
EQ.GUINEA				2	3		50.00
GABON	174	38	76	43	83	0.01	93.02
SAO TOME PRN	4		4	2	1		-50.00
NORTH AFRICA	**268**	**339**	**301**	**352**	**607**	**0.09**	**72.44**
ALGERIA	73	84	65	48	196	0.03	308.33
MOROCCO	79	91	120	157	149	0.02	-5.10
SUDAN	17	60	27	34	81	0.01	138.24
TUNISIA	99	104	89	113	181	0.03	60.18
SOUTHERN AFR	**47,797**	**49,834**	**49,067**	**43,708**	**46,960**	**6.69**	**7.44**
BOTSWANA	406	400	442	463	445	0.06	-3.89
LESOTHO	124	95	119	94	97	0.01	3.19
NAMIBIA	521	503	486	366	550	0.08	50.27
SOUTH AFRICA	46,583	48,683	47,882	42,685	45,756	6.52	7.19
SWAZILAND	163	153	138	100	112	0.02	12.00
WEST AFRICA	**608**	**555**	**717**	**685**	**1,220**	**0.17**	**78.10**
CAPE VERDE	13	2		15	24		60.00
BENIN	25	9	17	14	56	0.01	300.00
GAMBIA	25	40	68	52	50	0.01	-3.85
GHANA	104	81	78	70	178	0.03	154.29
GUINEA	41	75	110	99	148	0.02	49.49
COTE IVOIRE	104	92	63	111	134	0.02	20.72
LIBERIA	5	3	36	2	2		
MALI	39	24	40	25	90	0.01	260.00
MAURITANIA	4	3	6	7	19		171.43

MAURITIUS

1. ARRIVALS OF NON-RESIDENT TOURISTS AT NATIONAL BORDERS, BY COUNTRY OF RESIDENCE

	1999	2000	2001	2002	2003	Market share 03	% change 03-02
NIGER	7	4	3	3	13		333.33
NIGERIA	89	131	156	123	231	0.03	87.80
GUINEABISSAU	6	4	1	1	1		
SENEGAL	105	58	88	121	183	0.03	51.24
SIERRA LEONE	8	8	10	12	18		50.00
TOGO	15	11	9	16	27		68.75
BURKINA FASO	18	10	32	14	46	0.01	228.57
OTHER AFRICA	**754**	**729**	**824**	**862**	**957**	**0.14**	**11.02**
OTHER AFRICA	754	729	824	862	957	0.14	11.02
AMERICAS	**5,820**	**7,643**	**8,055**	**7,451**	**8,106**	**1.15**	**8.79**
CARIBBEAN	**96**	**129**	**99**	**131**	**110**	**0.02**	**-16.03**
ANTIGUA,BARB	1			4	2		-50.00
BAHAMAS	11	2	5	9	6		-33.33
BARBADOS	1	3	2	11	8		-27.27
BERMUDA	3	1	5		1		
CUBA	6	8	17	7	20		185.71
DOMINICA	1	2					
DOMINICAN RP	5	3	2	2	1		-50.00
GRENADA		6	2	2	1		-50.00
GUADELOUPE	24	17	20	33	9		-72.73
HAITI	3	9	5	4	11		175.00
JAMAICA	7	16	6	8	6		-25.00
MARTINIQUE	27	49	23	37	31		-16.22
ANGUILLA	1		1		1		
TRINIDAD TBG	6	12	11	14	13		-7.14
TURKS,CAICOS		1					
CENTRAL AMER	**9**	**7**	**15**	**23**	**31**		**34.78**
BELIZE	2	2	1	3			
COSTA RICA	2		3	11	11		
EL SALVADOR	4		5	3	13		333.33
GUATEMALA		3	3	1	4		300.00
HONDURAS	1		1	2	1		-50.00
NICARAGUA		2	2	3	2		-33.33
NORTH AMER	**4,888**	**5,559**	**5,801**	**5,988**	**6,424**	**0.92**	**7.28**
CANADA	1,506	1,812	1,845	1,842	1,845	0.26	0.16
GREENLAND	1	1	1		1		
MEXICO	36	42	32	30	73	0.01	143.33
USA	3,345	3,704	3,923	4,116	4,505	0.64	9.45
SOUTH AMER	**826**	**1,946**	**2,136**	**1,297**	**1,518**	**0.22**	**17.04**
ARGENTINA	214	406	698	191	264	0.04	38.22
BOLIVIA		7		2	3		50.00
BRAZIL	283	716	644	505	482	0.07	-4.55
CHILE	262	580	603	337	469	0.07	39.17
COLOMBIA	10	21	17	25	25		
ECUADOR	2	4	4	5	5		
GUYANA	11	12	8	13	14		7.69
PARAGUAY		9	3	13	3		-76.92
PERU	24	48	33	132	149	0.02	12.88
SURINAME	3	9	8	7	22		214.29
URUGUAY	14	116	107	58	76	0.01	31.03
VENEZUELA	3	18	11	9	6		-33.33

MAURITIUS

1. ARRIVALS OF NON-RESIDENT TOURISTS AT NATIONAL BORDERS, BY COUNTRY OF RESIDENCE

	1999	2000	2001	2002	2003	Market share 03	% change 03-02
OTHER AMERIC	**1**	**2**	**4**	**12**	**23**		**91.67**
OTH AMERICA	1	2	4	12	23		91.67
EAST AS/PACI	**21,531**	**24,083**	**24,534**	**24,694**	**21,934**	**3.12**	**-11.18**
N/EAST ASIA	**6,823**	**7,493**	**8,113**	**8,908**	**7,046**	**1.00**	**-20.90**
CHINA	2,189	2,459	3,615	4,248	3,738	0.53	-12.01
TAIWAN(P.C.)	1,110	1,113	1,081	1,159	790	0.11	-31.84
HK,CHINA	859	1,227	1,488	1,201	676	0.10	-43.71
JAPAN	2,324	2,389	1,589	1,958	1,572	0.22	-19.71
KOREA REP.	328	292	331	333	259	0.04	-22.22
MACAU, CHINA	7	7	4	6	8		33.33
MONGOLIA	6	6	5	3	3		
S/EAST ASIA	**6,194**	**7,095**	**6,959**	**6,735**	**5,074**	**0.72**	**-24.66**
BRUNEI DARSM	10	8	10	12	8		-33.33
MYANMAR	10	15	9	4	5		25.00
CAMBODIA	13	3	3	1	3		200.00
INDONESIA	296	610	422	285	295	0.04	3.51
LAO P.DEM.R.	2		1				
MALAYSIA	1,529	1,616	2,215	1,944	1,586	0.23	-18.42
PHILIPPINES	459	508	536	670	562	0.08	-16.12
SINGAPORE	3,661	4,104	3,431	3,114	2,102	0.30	-32.50
VIET NAM	33	37	40	175	133	0.02	-24.00
THAILAND	181	194	292	530	380	0.05	-28.30
AUSTRALASIA	**8,442**	**9,385**	**9,314**	**8,930**	**9,674**	**1.38**	**8.33**
AUSTRALIA	8,076	8,771	8,790	8,387	9,103	1.30	8.54
NEW ZEALAND	366	614	524	543	571	0.08	5.16
MELANESIA	**60**	**71**	**123**	**100**	**72**	**0.01**	**-28.00**
SOLOMON IS			3		1		
FIJI	13	16	12	35	19		-45.71
NEW CALEDNIA	40	51	99	63	49	0.01	-22.22
VANUATU	6	2	6	2	2		
PAPUA N.GUIN	1	2	3		1		
MICRONESIA	**2**	**24**	**7**		**1**		
KIRIBATI	2	21	7				
NAURU		3			1		
POLYNESIA	**10**	**14**	**14**	**19**	**53**	**0.01**	**178.95**
AMER SAMOA	1	3	2	6	42	0.01	600.00
COOK IS	1						
FR.POLYNESIA	8	11	12	13	11		-15.38
OT.EAST AS/P		**1**	**4**	**2**	**14**		**600.00**
OTHER ASIA			3	2	2		
OTH OCEANIA		1	1		12		
EUROPE	**379,051**	**440,279**	**437,615**	**451,791**	**465,620**	**66.33**	**3.06**
C/E EUROPE	**4,720**	**5,643**	**6,643**	**8,051**	**8,795**	**1.25**	**9.24**
AZERBAIJAN	3	2	1	8	10		25.00
ARMENIA	5		3	5	14		180.00
BULGARIA	105	140	110	131	201	0.03	53.44
BELARUS	29	15	45	32	40	0.01	25.00
CZECH REP	847	894	1,037	1,469	1,359	0.19	-7.49

MAURITIUS

1. ARRIVALS OF NON-RESIDENT TOURISTS AT NATIONAL BORDERS, BY COUNTRY OF RESIDENCE

	1999	2000	2001	2002	2003	Market share 03	% change 03-02
ESTONIA	31	44	54	123	181	0.03	47.15
GEORGIA	3	2	4	4	4		
HUNGARY	563	631	700	980	932	0.13	-4.90
KAZAKHSTAN	4	13	19	23	82	0.01	256.52
LATVIA	67	53	61	165	86	0.01	-47.88
LITHUANIA	11	50	62	78	119	0.02	52.56
REP MOLDOVA	3	3	3	2	6		200.00
POLAND	1,248	1,308	1,716	1,499	1,329	0.19	-11.34
ROMANIA	75	97	126	156	419	0.06	168.59
RUSSIAN FED	1,038	1,400	1,772	2,172	2,908	0.41	33.89
SLOVAKIA	261	282	324	563	457	0.07	-18.83
TAJIKISTAN	2						
UKRAINE	284	501	437	510	506	0.07	-0.78
USSR(former)	118	163	144	82	116	0.02	41.46
UZBEKISTAN	1		1	11	9		-18.18
OTH C/E EUR	22	45	24	38	17		-55.26
NORTHERN EUR	**69,325**	**88,100**	**91,395**	**94,573**	**105,899**	**15.08**	**11.98**
DENMARK	1,140	1,225	1,509	1,521	1,836	0.26	20.71
FAEROE IS	1	3		1	1		
FINLAND	1,225	1,413	1,522	1,948	1,914	0.27	-1.75
ICELAND	15	23	7	39	26		-33.33
IRELAND	1,329	1,979	2,535	3,032	3,414	0.49	12.60
NORWAY	2,380	3,275	2,748	2,718	2,641	0.38	-2.83
SWEDEN	4,552	5,694	5,186	4,647	4,857	0.69	4.52
UK	58,683	74,488	77,888	80,667	91,210	12.99	13.07
SOUTHERN EUR	**44,976**	**48,379**	**47,307**	**49,422**	**53,004**	**7.55**	**7.25**
ALBANIA	1	4	6	4	8		100.00
ANDORRA	27	13	14	21	34		61.90
BOSNIA HERZG	5	2	11	6	13		116.67
CROATIA	80	47	103	74	99	0.01	33.78
GIBRALTAR	1	8	4		6		
GREECE	675	506	960	1,180	1,910	0.27	61.86
ITALY	36,675	39,000	37,343	38,263	39,774	5.67	3.95
MALTA	24	39	33	47	81	0.01	72.34
PORTUGAL	1,109	1,333	1,538	1,733	1,616	0.23	-6.75
SAN MARINO	20	24	5	18	18		
SLOVENIA	99	106	126	185	250	0.04	35.14
SPAIN	6,204	7,226	7,058	7,770	9,081	1.29	16.87
TFYROM	6	13	19	9	4		-55.56
SERBIA,MTNEG	50	58	87	112	110	0.02	-1.79
WESTERN EUR	**259,455**	**297,531**	**291,707**	**298,968**	**296,561**	**42.24**	**-0.81**
AUSTRIA	8,095	8,874	8,696	8,782	8,893	1.27	1.26
BELGIUM	9,586	10,998	10,398	10,579	10,170	1.45	-3.87
FRANCE	175,431	198,423	197,595	202,869	200,229	28.52	-1.30
GERMANY	45,206	52,869	50,866	53,762	53,970	7.69	0.39
LIECHTENSTEN	14	20	22	27	37	0.01	37.04
LUXEMBOURG	593	753	613	726	758	0.11	4.41
MONACO	139	196	177	227	172	0.02	-24.23
NETHERLANDS	4,110	4,925	4,913	4,625	4,403	0.63	-4.80
SWITZERLAND	16,281	20,473	18,427	17,371	17,929	2.55	3.21
EAST/MED EUR	**575**	**626**	**563**	**777**	**1,358**	**0.19**	**74.77**
CYPRUS	55	39	64	101	439	0.06	334.65
ISRAEL	289	280	307	286	235	0.03	-17.83
TURKEY	231	307	192	390	684	0.10	75.38

MAURITIUS

1. ARRIVALS OF NON-RESIDENT TOURISTS AT NATIONAL BORDERS, BY COUNTRY OF RESIDENCE

	1999	2000	2001	2002	2003	Market share 03	% change 03-02
OTHER EUROPE					**3**		
OTHER EUROPE					3		
MIDDLE EAST	**527**	**591**	**729**	**2,287**	**4,800**	**0.68**	**109.88**
MIDDLE EAST	**527**	**591**	**729**	**2,287**	**4,800**	**0.68**	**109.88**
BAHRAIN	28	28	27	40	113	0.02	182.50
PALESTINE	1			4	9		125.00
IRAQ	8	2	2	5	3		-40.00
JORDAN	6	6	12	47	76	0.01	61.70
KUWAIT	47	50	48	130	319	0.05	145.38
LEBANON	37	50	44	77	274	0.04	255.84
LIBYA	7	12	12	20	38	0.01	90.00
OMAN	23	4	20	36	101	0.01	180.56
QATAR	3	3	22	32	55	0.01	71.88
SAUDI ARABIA	134	131	232	365	709	0.10	94.25
SYRIA	3	3	9	59	145	0.02	145.76
UNTD ARAB EM	147	162	110	1,192	2,559	0.36	114.68
EGYPT	78	138	187	270	390	0.06	44.44
YEMEN	5	2	4	10	9		-10.00
SOUTH ASIA	**14,694**	**19,598**	**20,946**	**22,869**	**27,277**	**3.89**	**19.28**
SOUTH ASIA	**14,694**	**19,598**	**20,946**	**22,869**	**27,277**	**3.89**	**19.28**
BANGLADESH	65	70	141	117	122	0.02	4.27
BHUTAN	2			1	4		300.00
SRI LANKA	662	1,828	1,556	1,185	812	0.12	-31.48
INDIA	13,583	17,241	18,890	20,898	25,367	3.61	21.38
IRAN	38	71	22	47	68	0.01	44.68
MALDIVES	14	10	9	15	29		93.33
NEPAL	22	56	39	22	45	0.01	104.55
PAKISTAN	308	322	289	584	830	0.12	42.12
REG.NOT SPEC	**234**	**496**	**120**	**205**	**285**	**0.04**	**39.02**
NOT SPECIFIE	**234**	**496**	**120**	**205**	**285**	**0.04**	**39.02**
OTH.WORLD	234	496	120	205	285	0.04	39.02

Source: World Tourism Organization (WTO)

5. OVERNIGHT STAYS OF NON-RESIDENT TOURISTS IN HOTELS AND SIMILAR ESTABLISHMENTS, BY COUNTRY OF RESIDENCE

	1999	2000	2001	2002	2003	Market share 03	% change 03-02
TOTAL	**5,729,464**	**6,412,876**	**6,527,800**	**6,768,870**	**6,952,313**	**100.00**	**2.71**
AFRICA	**1,223,781**	**1,278,549**	**1,311,737**	**1,351,988**	**1,446,983**	**20.81**	**7.03**
EAST AFRICA	**771,350**	**807,086**	**863,329**	**930,497**	**1,013,685**	**14.58**	**8.94**
COMOROS	9,612	12,394	9,965	11,026	15,971	0.23	44.85
KENYA	12,904	12,585	10,780	8,784	11,347	0.16	29.18
MADAGASCAR	74,643	65,526	66,177	81,758	128,437	1.85	57.09
REUNION	576,423	596,449	632,970	675,483	738,968	10.63	9.40
SEYCHELLES	67,271	82,577	96,303	113,942	92,493	1.33	-18.82
ZIMBABWE	28,106	37,555	47,134	39,504	26,469	0.38	-33.00
ZAMBIA	2,391						
SOUTHERN AFR	**412,869**	**422,300**	**400,656**	**376,588**	**379,561**	**5.46**	**0.79**
SOUTH AFRICA	412,869	422,300	400,656	376,588	379,561	5.46	0.79
OTHER AFRICA	**39,562**	**49,163**	**47,752**	**44,903**	**53,737**	**0.77**	**19.67**
OTHER AFRICA	39,562	49,163	47,752	44,903	53,737	0.77	19.67
AMERICAS	**67,168**	**78,749**	**83,242**	**83,650**	**83,594**	**1.20**	**-0.07**
NORTH AMER	**58,732**	**61,639**	**66,198**	**68,326**	**66,063**	**0.95**	**-3.31**
CANADA	26,779	28,920	29,131	29,848	27,268	0.39	-8.64
USA	31,953	32,719	37,067	38,478	38,795	0.56	0.82
OTHER AMERIC	**8,436**	**17,110**	**17,044**	**15,324**	**17,531**	**0.25**	**14.40**
OTH AMERICA	8,436	17,110	17,044	15,324	17,531	0.25	14.40
EAST AS/PACI	**235,682**	**247,128**	**272,994**	**290,767**	**273,016**	**3.93**	**-6.10**
N/EAST ASIA	**64,656**	**53,765**	**67,885**	**68,924**	**60,175**	**0.87**	**-12.69**
CHINA	29,302	30,110	45,769	46,813	44,106	0.63	-5.78
TAIWAN(P.C.)	13,394						
HK,CHINA	9,367	9,601	11,955	10,941	6,767	0.10	-38.15
JAPAN	12,593	14,054	10,161	11,170	9,302	0.13	-16.72
S/EAST ASIA	**36,324**	**34,748**	**39,948**	**37,541**	**27,129**	**0.39**	**-27.74**
MALAYSIA	14,399	12,750	16,528	17,138	12,258	0.18	-28.47
SINGAPORE	21,925	21,998	23,420	20,403	14,871	0.21	-27.11
AUSTRALASIA	**91,655**	**96,932**	**104,232**	**98,869**	**100,332**	**1.44**	**1.48**
AUSTRALIA	91,655	96,932	104,232	98,869	100,332	1.44	1.48
OT.EAST AS/P	**43,047**	**61,683**	**60,929**	**85,433**	**85,380**	**1.23**	**-0.06**
OTHER ASIA	38,864	54,850	55,401	79,944	79,386	1.14	-0.70
OTH OCEANIA	4,183	6,833	5,528	5,489	5,994	0.09	9.20
EUROPE	**4,043,898**	**4,617,513**	**4,650,685**	**4,786,630**	**4,858,369**	**69.88**	**1.50**
NORTHERN EUR	**770,021**	**940,180**	**994,001**	**1,023,085**	**1,090,213**	**15.68**	**6.56**
SWEDEN	49,730	55,381	51,906	45,368	47,100	0.68	3.82
UK	720,291	884,799	942,095	977,717	1,043,113	15.00	6.69
SOUTHERN EUR	**385,939**	**405,136**	**378,852**	**384,938**	**411,350**	**5.92**	**6.86**
ITALY	336,271	349,267	326,100	329,809	346,865	4.99	5.17
SPAIN	49,668	55,869	52,752	55,129	64,485	0.93	16.97

5. OVERNIGHT STAYS OF NON-RESIDENT TOURISTS IN HOTELS AND SIMILAR ESTABLISHMENTS, BY COUNTRY OF RESIDENCE

	1999	2000	2001	2002	2003	Market share 03	% change 03-02
WESTERN EUR	**2,743,301**	**3,100,334**	**3,083,035**	**3,156,636**	**3,119,525**	**44.87**	**-1.18**
AUSTRIA	92,886	96,998	94,102	96,686	96,299	1.39	-0.40
BELGIUM	126,221	132,571	125,752	124,586	121,687	1.75	-2.33
FRANCE	1,719,893	1,934,683	1,966,911	2,020,850	1,996,305	28.71	-1.21
GERMANY	553,112	635,600	612,881	651,913	636,435	9.15	-2.37
NETHERLANDS	44,797	52,137	54,162	52,091	48,417	0.70	-7.05
SWITZERLAND	206,392	248,345	229,227	210,510	220,382	3.17	4.69
OTHER EUROPE	**144,637**	**171,863**	**194,797**	**221,971**	**237,281**	**3.41**	**6.90**
OTHER EUROPE	144,637	171,863	194,797	221,971	237,281	3.41	6.90
SOUTH ASIA	**157,110**	**188,008**	**207,965**	**253,340**	**287,741**	**4.14**	**13.58**
SOUTH ASIA	**157,110**	**188,008**	**207,965**	**253,340**	**287,741**	**4.14**	**13.58**
INDIA	157,110	188,008	207,965	253,340	287,741	4.14	13.58
REG.NOT SPEC	**1,825**	**2,929**	**1,177**	**2,495**	**2,610**	**0.04**	**4.61**
NOT SPECIFIE	**1,825**	**2,929**	**1,177**	**2,495**	**2,610**	**0.04**	**4.61**
OTH.WORLD	1,825	2,929	1,177	2,495	2,610	0.04	4.61

Source: World Tourism Organization (WTO)

MEXICO

1. ARRIVALS OF NON-RESIDENT TOURISTS AT NATIONAL BORDERS, BY COUNTRY OF RESIDENCE

	1999	2000	2001	2002	2003	Market share 03	% change 03-02
TOTAL (*)	**19,042,726**	**20,641,358**	**19,810,459**	**19,666,677**	**18,665,384**	**100.00**	**-5.09**
AMERICAS	**18,182,563**	**19,949,917**	**19,172,090**	**19,133,397**	**18,155,315**	**97.27**	**-5.11**
NORTH AMER	**17,965,031**	**19,762,670**	**18,997,697**	**18,861,872**	**17,858,021**	**95.67**	**-5.32**
CANADA	501,996	477,191	374,577	360,854	292,222	1.57	-19.02
USA	17,463,035	19,285,479	18,623,120	18,501,018	17,565,799	94.11	-5.05
OTHER AMERIC	**217,532**	**187,247**	**174,393**	**271,525**	**297,294**	**1.59**	**9.49**
OTH AMERICA	217,532	187,247	174,393	271,525	297,294	1.59	9.49
EUROPE	**562,790**	**400,566**	**362,480**	**479,174**	**443,366**	**2.38**	**-7.47**
OTHER EUROPE	**562,790**	**400,566**	**362,480**	**479,174**	**443,366**	**2.38**	**-7.47**
ALL EUROPE	562,790	400,566	362,480	479,174	443,366	2.38	-7.47
REG.NOT SPEC	**297,373**	**290,875**	**275,889**	**54,106**	**66,703**	**0.36**	**23.28**
NOT SPECIFIE	**297,373**	**290,875**	**275,889**	**54,106**	**66,703**	**0.36**	**23.28**
OTH.WORLD	297,373	290,875	275,889	54,106	66,703	0.36	23.28

Source: World Tourism Organization (WTO)

MICRONESIA (FEDERATED STATES OF)

1. ARRIVALS OF NON-RESIDENT TOURISTS AT NATIONAL BORDERS, BY COUNTRY OF RESIDENCE

	1999	2000	2001	2002	2003	Market share 03	% change 03-02
TOTAL (*)	**16,140**	**20,501**	**15,265**	**19,046**	**18,168**	**100.00**	**-4.61**
AMERICAS	**7,449**	**8,991**	**7,074**	**8,435**	**7,673**	**42.23**	**-9.03**
NORTH AMER	**7,449**	**8,991**	**7,074**	**8,435**	**7,673**	**42.23**	**-9.03**
CANADA	192	212	171	220	214	1.18	-2.73
USA	7,257	8,779	6,903	8,215	7,459	41.06	-9.20
EAST AS/PACI	**7,242**	**9,925**	**6,936**	**9,062**	**8,933**	**49.17**	**-1.42**
N/EAST ASIA	**3,309**	**4,871**	**3,118**	**4,057**	**3,901**	**21.47**	**-3.85**
JAPAN	3,309	4,871	3,118	4,057	3,901	21.47	-3.85
AUSTRALASIA	**730**	**918**	**610**	**741**	**803**	**4.42**	**8.37**
AUSTRALIA	584	817	516	572	652	3.59	13.99
NEW ZEALAND	146	101	94	169	151	0.83	-10.65
OT.EAST AS/P	**3,203**	**4,136**	**3,208**	**4,264**	**4,229**	**23.28**	**-0.82**
OTHER ASIA	2,258	2,928	2,247	2,827	2,878	15.84	1.80
OTH OCEANIA	945	1,208	961	1,437	1,351	7.44	-5.98
EUROPE	**1,379**	**1,461**	**1,188**	**1,474**	**1,493**	**8.22**	**1.29**
OTHER EUROPE	**1,379**	**1,461**	**1,188**	**1,474**	**1,493**	**8.22**	**1.29**
ALL EUROPE	1,379	1,461	1,188	1,474	1,493	8.22	1.29
REG.NOT SPEC	**70**	**124**	**67**	**75**	**69**	**0.38**	**-8.00**
NOT SPECIFIE	**70**	**124**	**67**	**75**	**69**	**0.38**	**-8.00**
OTH.WORLD	70	124	67	75	69	0.38	-8.00

Source: World Tourism Organization (WTO)

MONACO

3. ARRIVALS OF NON-RESIDENT TOURISTS IN HOTELS AND SIMILAR ESTABLISHMENTS, BY NATIONALITY

	1999	2000	2001	2002	2003	Market share 03	% change 03-02
TOTAL	**278,448**	**300,185**	**269,925**	**262,520**	**234,638**	**100.00**	**-10.62**
AFRICA	**2,326**	**2,459**	**2,372**	**2,440**	**2,228**	**0.95**	**-8.69**
OTHER AFRICA	**2,326**	**2,459**	**2,372**	**2,440**	**2,228**	**0.95**	**-8.69**
ALL AFRICA	2,326	2,459	2,372	2,440	2,228	0.95	-8.69
AMERICAS	**41,660**	**43,622**	**35,991**	**31,096**	**22,660**	**9.66**	**-27.13**
NORTH AMER	**39,461**	**41,016**	**34,102**	**29,576**	**21,025**	**8.96**	**-28.91**
CANADA	3,086	3,360	3,043	3,127	2,462	1.05	-21.27
MEXICO	1,284	1,197	1,064	1,019	776	0.33	-23.85
USA	35,091	36,459	29,995	25,430	17,787	7.58	-30.06
SOUTH AMER	**2,199**	**2,606**	**1,889**	**1,520**	**1,635**	**0.70**	**7.57**
ARGENTINA	889	995	732	409	624	0.27	52.57
BRAZIL	1,310	1,611	1,157	1,111	1,011	0.43	-9.00
EAST AS/PACI	**11,689**	**19,311**	**13,473**	**12,143**	**9,781**	**4.17**	**-19.45**
N/EAST ASIA	**9,081**	**16,403**	**11,304**	**9,950**	**7,681**	**3.27**	**-22.80**
CHINA	1,189	1,651	1,304	1,698	1,306	0.56	-23.09
JAPAN	7,892	14,752	10,000	8,252	6,375	2.72	-22.75
AUSTRALASIA	**2,608**	**2,908**	**2,169**	**2,193**	**2,100**	**0.89**	**-4.24**
AUSTRALIA	2,608	2,908	2,169	2,193	2,100	0.89	-4.24
EUROPE	**202,394**	**210,506**	**195,531**	**194,244**	**177,922**	**75.83**	**-8.40**
C/E EUROPE	**2,718**	**3,113**	**3,464**	**3,748**	**3,047**	**1.30**	**-18.70**
RUSSIAN FED	2,718	3,113	3,464	3,748	3,047	1.30	-18.70
NORTHERN EUR	**35,682**	**40,111**	**40,479**	**43,857**	**37,243**	**15.87**	**-15.08**
DENMARK	1,513	1,865	1,575	1,532	1,822	0.78	18.93
NORWAY	1,692	1,777	1,500	1,594	1,064	0.45	-33.25
SWEDEN	2,957	3,476	2,967	2,660	1,775	0.76	-33.27
UK	29,520	32,993	34,437	38,071	32,582	13.89	-14.42
SOUTHERN EUR	**82,763**	**79,510**	**71,157**	**68,541**	**65,795**	**28.04**	**-4.01**
ITALY	75,840	70,795	63,643	60,822	58,797	25.06	-3.33
PORTUGAL	1,036	1,947	1,244	1,272	888	0.38	-30.19
SPAIN	5,887	6,768	6,270	6,447	6,110	2.60	-5.23
WESTERN EUR	**80,092**	**86,231**	**78,830**	**76,659**	**70,733**	**30.15**	**-7.73**
AUSTRIA	2,476	2,683	2,464	2,198	2,687	1.15	22.25
BELGIUM	4,297	4,613	4,648	4,525	3,906	1.66	-13.68
FRANCE	45,539	48,335	44,474	41,392	40,643	17.32	-1.81
GERMANY	14,125	15,566	13,985	14,983	12,455	5.31	-16.87
NETHERLANDS	4,979	6,015	4,638	5,319	4,486	1.91	-15.66
SWITZERLAND	8,676	9,019	8,621	8,242	6,556	2.79	-20.46
EAST/MED EUR	**1,139**	**1,541**	**1,601**	**1,439**	**1,104**	**0.47**	**-23.28**
ISRAEL	1,139	1,541	1,601	1,439	1,104	0.47	-23.28
MIDDLE EAST	**3,717**	**4,173**	**3,325**	**4,024**	**3,320**	**1.41**	**-17.50**

MONACO

3. ARRIVALS OF NON-RESIDENT TOURISTS IN HOTELS AND SIMILAR ESTABLISHMENTS, BY NATIONALITY

	1999	2000	2001	2002	2003	Market share 03	% change 03-02
MIDDLE EAST	**3,717**	**4,173**	**3,325**	**4,024**	**3,320**	**1.41**	**-17.50**
ALL MID EAST	3,717	4,173	3,325	4,024	3,320	1.41	-17.50
REG.NOT SPEC	**16,662**	**20,114**	**19,233**	**18,573**	**18,727**	**7.98**	**0.83**
NOT SPECIFIE	**16,662**	**20,114**	**19,233**	**18,573**	**18,727**	**7.98**	**0.83**
OTH.WORLD	16,662	20,114	19,233	18,573	18,727	7.98	0.83

Source: World Tourism Organization (WTO)

MONACO

5. OVERNIGHT STAYS OF NON-RESIDENT TOURISTS IN HOTELS AND SIMILAR ESTABLISHMENTS, BY NATIONALITY

	1999	2000	2001	2002	2003	Market share 03	% change 03-02
TOTAL	**813,919**	**860,842**	**797,842**	**764,712**	**674,312**	**100.00**	**-11.82**
AFRICA	**6,768**	**8,792**	**7,867**	**9,061**	**9,493**	**1.41**	**4.77**
OTHER AFRICA	**6,768**	**8,792**	**7,867**	**9,061**	**9,493**	**1.41**	**4.77**
ALL AFRICA	6,768	8,792	7,867	9,061	9,493	1.41	4.77
AMERICAS	**136,764**	**138,156**	**114,258**	**104,098**	**75,323**	**11.17**	**-27.64**
NORTH AMER	**129,458**	**129,817**	**108,829**	**99,122**	**68,049**	**10.09**	**-31.35**
CANADA	10,268	9,713	11,322	12,021	9,724	1.44	-19.11
MEXICO	3,213	2,500	2,013	2,656	2,553	0.38	-3.88
USA	115,977	117,604	95,494	84,445	55,772	8.27	-33.95
SOUTH AMER	**7,306**	**8,339**	**5,429**	**4,976**	**7,274**	**1.08**	**46.18**
ARGENTINA	2,862	3,360	1,775	1,244	2,891	0.43	132.40
BRAZIL	4,444	4,979	3,654	3,732	4,383	0.65	17.44
EAST AS/PACI	**31,545**	**50,296**	**34,361**	**32,709**	**26,837**	**3.98**	**-17.95**
N/EAST ASIA	**23,702**	**42,206**	**28,025**	**26,151**	**20,395**	**3.02**	**-22.01**
CHINA	2,942	5,418	3,380	4,313	3,109	0.46	-27.92
JAPAN	20,760	36,788	24,645	21,838	17,286	2.56	-20.84
AUSTRALASIA	**7,843**	**8,090**	**6,336**	**6,558**	**6,442**	**0.96**	**-1.77**
AUSTRALIA	7,843	8,090	6,336	6,558	6,442	0.96	-1.77
EUROPE	**562,248**	**580,133**	**555,423**	**534,594**	**487,282**	**72.26**	**-8.85**
C/E EUROPE	**14,837**	**13,948**	**15,257**	**17,658**	**15,744**	**2.33**	**-10.84**
RUSSIAN FED	14,837	13,948	15,257	17,658	15,744	2.33	-10.84
NORTHERN EUR	**105,704**	**118,812**	**123,761**	**130,696**	**108,061**	**16.03**	**-17.32**
DENMARK	4,516	5,974	4,737	5,783	6,115	0.91	5.74
NORWAY	5,657	5,835	5,497	5,950	3,267	0.48	-45.09
SWEDEN	8,246	11,118	9,221	9,214	5,810	0.86	-36.94
UK	87,285	95,885	104,306	109,749	92,869	13.77	-15.38
SOUTHERN EUR	**211,160**	**202,290**	**185,631**	**174,651**	**165,765**	**24.58**	**-5.09**
ITALY	191,364	177,271	162,961	149,398	142,266	21.10	-4.77
PORTUGAL	2,684	6,364	3,903	5,813	4,793	0.71	-17.55
SPAIN	17,112	18,655	18,767	19,440	18,706	2.77	-3.78
WESTERN EUR	**225,546**	**239,076**	**224,739**	**205,319**	**193,141**	**28.64**	**-5.93**
AUSTRIA	9,187	8,112	11,053	9,255	11,238	1.67	21.43
BELGIUM	14,524	14,656	17,449	14,220	13,156	1.95	-7.48
FRANCE	116,693	123,698	109,372	97,673	94,866	14.07	-2.87
GERMANY	41,196	44,578	44,721	38,806	34,459	5.11	-11.20
NETHERLANDS	15,331	19,355	15,265	17,567	14,297	2.12	-18.61
SWITZERLAND	28,615	28,677	26,879	27,798	25,125	3.73	-9.62
EAST/MED EUR	**5,001**	**6,007**	**6,035**	**6,270**	**4,571**	**0.68**	**-27.10**
ISRAEL	5,001	6,007	6,035	6,270	4,571	0.68	-27.10
MIDDLE EAST	**19,795**	**19,592**	**17,020**	**21,120**	**14,809**	**2.20**	**-29.88**

MONACO

5. OVERNIGHT STAYS OF NON-RESIDENT TOURISTS IN HOTELS AND SIMILAR ESTABLISHMENTS, BY NATIONALITY

	1999	2000	2001	2002	2003	Market share 03	% change 03-02
MIDDLE EAST	**19,795**	**19,592**	**17,020**	**21,120**	**14,809**	**2.20**	**-29.88**
ALL MID EAST	19,795	19,592	17,020	21,120	14,809	2.20	-29.88
REG.NOT SPEC	**56,799**	**63,873**	**68,913**	**63,130**	**60,568**	**8.98**	**-4.06**
NOT SPECIFIE	**56,799**	**63,873**	**68,913**	**63,130**	**60,568**	**8.98**	**-4.06**
OTH.WORLD	56,799	63,873	68,913	63,130	60,568	8.98	-4.06

Source: World Tourism Organization (WTO)

MONGOLIA

1. ARRIVALS OF NON-RESIDENT TOURISTS AT NATIONAL BORDERS, BY NATIONALITY

	1999	2000	2001	2002	2003	Market share 03	% change 03-02
TOTAL	**137,961**	**137,374**	**165,899**	**228,719**	**201,153**	**100.00**	**-12.05**
AFRICA	**89**	**154**	**180**	**143**	**207**	**0.10**	**44.76**
EAST AFRICA	**16**	**7**	**11**	**14**	**27**	**0.01**	**92.86**
ETHIOPIA	8	1		3	5		66.67
KENYA	1			5	8		60.00
SEYCHELLES			1				
SOMALIA	4		3	3			
ZIMBABWE	3	6	1	1	2		100.00
UGANDA			2	2	7		250.00
ZAMBIA			4		5		
CENTRAL AFR	**17**	**21**	**17**	**26**	**32**	**0.02**	**23.08**
ANGOLA			8	6			
CAMEROON	15	9	7	11	6		-45.45
CONGO	2	12	1	9	12	0.01	33.33
OTH MID.AFRI			1		14	0.01	
NORTH AFRICA	**3**	**4**	**5**	**6**	**5**		**-16.67**
ALGERIA			1	4	1		-75.00
MOROCCO	2	2	3	1	3		200.00
TUNISIA	1	2	1	1	1		
SOUTHERN AFR	**40**	**110**	**135**	**78**	**78**	**0.04**	
NAMIBIA		1	4		6		
SOUTH AFRICA	40	109	131	78	72	0.04	-7.69
WEST AFRICA	**7**	**12**	**11**	**4**	**21**	**0.01**	**425.00**
GHANA		3		1	5		400.00
LIBERIA	2		2		3		
MAURITANIA	2	6	2	1	2		100.00
NIGER	3	3	7		11	0.01	
NIGERIA				2			
OTHER AFRICA	**6**		**1**	**15**	**44**	**0.02**	**193.33**
OTHER AFRICA	6		1	15	44	0.02	193.33
AMERICAS	**4,969**	**5,831**	**6,296**	**7,973**	**6,863**	**3.41**	**-13.92**
CARIBBEAN	**6**	**1**	**6**	**14**	**38**	**0.02**	**171.43**
CUBA	6	1	5	14	37	0.02	164.29
DOMINICAN RP			1		1		
CENTRAL AMER	**13**	**18**	**26**	**10**	**13**	**0.01**	**30.00**
BELIZE	7	1	1				
COSTA RICA		1	19	5	5		
GUATEMALA	1		1		3		
HONDURAS	3	10	1	3	1		-66.67
NICARAGUA		6	2	2	4		100.00
PANAMA	2		2				
NORTH AMER	**4,871**	**5,734**	**6,155**	**7,807**	**6,701**	**3.33**	**-14.17**
CANADA	417	484	691	1,057	1,149	0.57	8.70
MEXICO	21	16	18	25	19	0.01	-24.00
USA	4,433	5,234	5,446	6,725	5,533	2.75	-17.72
SOUTH AMER	**79**	**77**	**105**	**135**	**90**	**0.04**	**-33.33**

MONGOLIA

1. ARRIVALS OF NON-RESIDENT TOURISTS AT NATIONAL BORDERS, BY NATIONALITY

	1999	2000	2001	2002	2003	Market share 03	% change 03-02
ARGENTINA	20	17	50	30	18	0.01	-40.00
BOLIVIA	11	1	1	1	1		
BRAZIL	27	39	24	45	37	0.02	-17.78
CHILE	5	2	7	19	14	0.01	-26.32
COLOMBIA	8	7	7	23	9		-60.87
ECUADOR			1	4	2		-50.00
GUYANA			2	6			
PERU	4	8	5	6	4		-33.33
URUGUAY	2		7				
VENEZUELA	2	3	1	1	5		400.00
OTHER AMERIC		**1**	**4**	**7**	**21**	**0.01**	**200.00**
OTH AMERICA		1	4	7	21	0.01	200.00
EAST AS/PACI	**66,649**	**69,257**	**79,492**	**122,106**	**120,716**	**60.01**	**-1.14**
N/EAST ASIA	**64,069**	**67,120**	**76,914**	**117,977**	**116,465**	**57.90**	**-1.28**
CHINA	48,257	49,341	57,440	89,041	90,337	44.91	1.46
TAIWAN(P.C.)	440	456	488	589	438	0.22	-25.64
HK,CHINA	146	118	187	366	380	0.19	3.83
JAPAN	10,900	10,283	10,247	13,262	7,717	3.84	-41.81
KOREA D P RP	295	286	179	239	420	0.21	75.73
KOREA REP.	4,015	6,635	8,372	14,474	17,166	8.53	18.60
MACAU, CHINA	16	1	1	6	7		16.67
S/EAST ASIA	**1,313**	**904**	**1,013**	**1,724**	**1,508**	**0.75**	**-12.53**
MYANMAR	10	4		8	5		-37.50
CAMBODIA	20	5	7	14	12	0.01	-14.29
INDONESIA	29	47	35	88	236	0.12	168.18
LAO P.DEM.R.	5		2	20	19	0.01	-5.00
MALAYSIA	215	157	217	363	266	0.13	-26.72
PHILIPPINES	122	248	149	239	219	0.11	-8.37
SINGAPORE	822	275	433	729	386	0.19	-47.05
VIET NAM	53	74	118	135	189	0.09	40.00
THAILAND	37	94	52	128	176	0.09	37.50
AUSTRALASIA	**1,267**	**1,232**	**1,562**	**2,387**	**2,694**	**1.34**	**12.86**
AUSTRALIA	951	854	1,139	1,754	2,244	1.12	27.94
NEW ZEALAND	316	378	423	633	450	0.22	-28.91
MELANESIA		**1**		**7**	**14**	**0.01**	**100.00**
FIJI		1		7	14	0.01	100.00
POLYNESIA			**2**	**4**	**2**		**-50.00**
TONGA			2	4	2		-50.00
OT.EAST AS/P			**1**	**7**	**33**	**0.02**	**371.43**
OTHER ASIA			1	7	33	0.02	371.43
EUROPE	**65,764**	**61,593**	**79,368**	**97,673**	**72,345**	**35.97**	**-25.93**
C/E EUROPE	**54,152**	**48,179**	**62,049**	**74,881**	**55,980**	**27.83**	**-25.24**
AZERBAIJAN	35	50	65	57	55	0.03	-3.51
ARMENIA	40	60	54	102	99	0.05	-2.94
BULGARIA	54	36	27	87	71	0.04	-18.39
BELARUS	101	127	125	185	139	0.07	-24.86
CZECH REP	277	301	416	519	419	0.21	-19.27
ESTONIA	5	8	10	19	21	0.01	10.53

MONGOLIA

1. ARRIVALS OF NON-RESIDENT TOURISTS AT NATIONAL BORDERS, BY NATIONALITY

	1999	2000	2001	2002	2003	Market share 03	% change 03-02
GEORGIA	8	7	11	9	4		-55.56
HUNGARY	97	74	103	119	128	0.06	7.56
KAZAKHSTAN	632	1,208	1,291	1,820	1,782	0.89	-2.09
KYRGYZSTAN	23	61	103	229	236	0.12	3.06
LATVIA	4	16	15	26	33	0.02	26.92
LITHUANIA	4	14	7	13	6		-53.85
REP MOLDOVA	68	67	50	124	90	0.04	-27.42
POLAND	170	295	460	731	205	0.10	-71.96
ROMANIA	19	11	18	19	30	0.01	57.89
RUSSIAN FED	51,755	45,204	58,534	69,778	51,438	25.57	-26.28
SLOVAKIA	44	47	32	57	76	0.04	33.33
TAJIKISTAN	4	10	16	47	30	0.01	-36.17
TURKMENISTAN	27	14	14		61	0.03	
UKRAINE	757	553	643	879	994	0.49	13.08
UZBEKISTAN	28	16	55	61	63	0.03	3.28
NORTHERN EUR	**3,615**	**4,215**	**5,274**	**6,874**	**5,081**	**2.53**	**-26.08**
DENMARK	524	468	558	763	436	0.22	-42.86
FINLAND	185	204	304	480	264	0.13	-45.00
ICELAND					20	0.01	
IRELAND	109	73	84	206	220	0.11	6.80
NORWAY	314	345	505	674	296	0.15	-56.08
SWEDEN	696	792	1,274	1,277	991	0.49	-22.40
UK	1,787	2,333	2,549	3,474	2,854	1.42	-17.85
SOUTHERN EUR	**883**	**973**	**1,331**	**1,539**	**1,043**	**0.52**	**-32.23**
CROATIA	3	7	2	22	13	0.01	-40.91
GREECE	16	61	89	87	153	0.08	75.86
ITALY	570	629	921	987	565	0.28	-42.76
MALTA	1	1	2				
PORTUGAL	37	47	24	51	28	0.01	-45.10
SLOVENIA	8	5	16	9	19	0.01	111.11
SPAIN	248	223	226	290	220	0.11	-24.14
TFYROM					43	0.02	
SERBIA,MTNEG			51	93	2		-97.85
WESTERN EUR	**6,777**	**7,802**	**10,181**	**13,559**	**9,786**	**4.86**	**-27.83**
AUSTRIA	250	441	573	664	319	0.16	-51.96
BELGIUM	273	350	456	708	405	0.20	-42.80
FRANCE	1,773	1,638	2,600	2,845	2,744	1.36	-3.55
GERMANY	2,967	3,515	4,661	6,780	4,973	2.47	-26.65
LIECHTENSTEN			3	1			
LUXEMBOURG	8	18	3	19	10		-47.37
NETHERLANDS	1,068	1,268	1,273	1,679	697	0.35	-58.49
SWITZERLAND	438	572	612	863	638	0.32	-26.07
EAST/MED EUR	**337**	**424**	**533**	**820**	**445**	**0.22**	**-45.73**
ISRAEL	122	162	299	478	231	0.11	-51.67
TURKEY	215	262	234	342	214	0.11	-37.43
OTHER EUROPE					**10**		
OTHER EUROPE					10		
MIDDLE EAST	**66**	**78**	**93**	**155**	**229**	**0.11**	**47.74**
MIDDLE EAST	**66**	**78**	**93**	**155**	**229**	**0.11**	**47.74**
IRAQ	4	4	5	3	29	0.01	866.67
JORDAN	2	2	2	7	2		-71.43

MONGOLIA

1. ARRIVALS OF NON-RESIDENT TOURISTS AT NATIONAL BORDERS, BY NATIONALITY

	1999	2000	2001	2002	2003	Market share 03	% change 03-02
KUWAIT		7	33	69	64	0.03	-7.25
LEBANON	22	6	3	8	6		-25.00
OMAN		2		2	1		-50.00
SAUDI ARABIA	18	29	11	13	12	0.01	-7.69
SYRIA	7	21	20	39	93	0.05	138.46
UNTD ARAB EM	5	3	3	3	3		
EGYPT	8	2	4	11	2		-81.82
YEMEN		2	2		5		
OT MIDD EAST			10		12	0.01	
SOUTH ASIA	**332**	**412**	**462**	**655**	**778**	**0.39**	**18.78**
SOUTH ASIA	**332**	**412**	**462**	**655**	**778**	**0.39**	**18.78**
AFGHANISTAN	6	2	1		5		
BANGLADESH	11	10	13	44	53	0.03	20.45
BHUTAN		4	1	4	38	0.02	850.00
SRI LANKA	37	35	27	43	55	0.03	27.91
INDIA	214	197	270	340	402	0.20	18.24
IRAN	12	6	73	43	12	0.01	-72.09
NEPAL	22	18	15	77	72	0.04	-6.49
PAKISTAN	30	140	62	104	141	0.07	35.58
REG.NOT SPEC	**92**	**49**	**8**	**14**	**15**	**0.01**	**7.14**
NOT SPECIFIE	**92**	**49**	**8**	**14**	**15**	**0.01**	**7.14**
OTH.WORLD	92	49	8	14	15	0.01	7.14

Source: World Tourism Organization (WTO)

MONGOLIA

2. ARRIVALS OF NON-RESIDENT VISITORS AT NATIONAL BORDERS, BY NATIONALITY

	1999	2000	2001	2002	2003	Market share 03	% change 03-02
TOTAL	158,734	158,205	192,050	235,165	204,845	100.00	-12.89
AFRICA	115	183	249	143	209	0.10	46.15
EAST AFRICA	26	9	26	17	32	0.02	88.24
ETHIOPIA	10	1	5	3	5		66.67
KENYA	1	2	2	5	8		60.00
MOZAMBIQUE	2		2				
SEYCHELLES	1						
SOMALIA	4		3	3			
ZIMBABWE	3	6	3	1	2		100.00
UGANDA			2	2	7		250.00
TANZANIA	3		1	3	5		66.67
ZAMBIA	2		8		5		
CENTRAL AFR	21	30	20	26	32	0.02	23.08
ANGOLA			8	6			
CAMEROON	17	17	11	11	6		-45.45
CONGO	4	13	1	9	12	0.01	33.33
OTH MID.AFRI					14	0.01	
NORTH AFRICA	9	4	12	8	8		
ALGERIA			5	4	1		-75.00
MOROCCO	2	2	3	1	3		200.00
SUDAN	3		3	2	3		50.00
TUNISIA	4	2	1	1	1		
SOUTHERN AFR	44	118	163	78	83	0.04	6.41
BOTSWANA					2		
LESOTHO	1		1		1		
NAMIBIA		1	5		6		
SOUTH AFRICA	43	117	157	78	74	0.04	-5.13
WEST AFRICA	15	16	23	13	22	0.01	69.23
GHANA		3	5	6	5		-16.67
GUINEA	1		1				
LIBERIA	2		2	3	3		
MAURITANIA	4	6	4	2	2		
NIGER	6		11		11	0.01	
NIGERIA		6		2			
SIERRA LEONE	2	1			1		
OTHER AFRICA		6	5	1	32	0.02	3,100.00
OTHER AFRICA		6	5	1	32	0.02	3.100.00
AMERICAS	6,059	7,217	7,701	8,115	6,900	3.37	-14.97
CARIBBEAN	10	12	10	15	38	0.02	153.33
BARBADOS				1			
CUBA	10	11	8	14	37	0.02	164.29
DOMINICAN RP			2		1		
HAITI		1					
CENTRAL AMER	26	24	29	14	30	0.01	114.29
BELIZE	15	1	1				
COSTA RICA		2	19	5	5		
EL SALVADOR				4	17	0.01	325.00
GUATEMALA	1		1		3		

MONGOLIA

2. ARRIVALS OF NON-RESIDENT VISITORS AT NATIONAL BORDERS, BY NATIONALITY

	1999	2000	2001	2002	2003	Market share 03	% change 03-02
HONDURAS	6	11	1	3	1		-66.67
NICARAGUA	1	10	3	2	4		100.00
PANAMA	3		4				
NORTH AMER	**5,913**	**7,079**	**7,506**	**7,949**	**6,738**	**3.29**	**-15.23**
CANADA	516	611	825	1,062	1,149	0.56	8.19
MEXICO	16	17	28	27	19	0.01	-29.63
USA	5,381	6,451	6,653	6,860	5,570	2.72	-18.80
SOUTH AMER	**110**	**102**	**152**	**135**	**90**	**0.04**	**-33.33**
ARGENTINA	23	18	60	30	18	0.01	-40.00
BOLIVIA	18	9	3	1	1		
BRAZIL	33	42	33	45	37	0.02	-17.78
CHILE	10	9	10	19	14	0.01	-26.32
COLOMBIA	9	11	14	23	9		-60.87
ECUADOR	1	1	3	4	2		-50.00
GUYANA			12	6			
PERU	10	9	8	6	4		-33.33
URUGUAY	2		7				
VENEZUELA	4	3	2	1	5		400.00
OTHER AMERIC			**4**	**2**	**4**		**100.00**
OTH AMERICA			4	2	4		100.00
EAST AS/PACI	**79,421**	**80,720**	**93,080**	**126,238**	**122,403**	**59.75**	**-3.04**
N/EAST ASIA	**76,324**	**78,035**	**90,011**	**122,103**	**118,142**	**57.67**	**-3.24**
CHINA	58,346	57,546	67,360	92,657	91,934	44.88	-0.78
TAIWAN(P.C.)	504	578	627	589	439	0.21	-25.47
HK,CHINA	174	184	252	366	380	0.19	3.83
JAPAN	11,775	11,392	11,473	13,708	7,757	3.79	-43.41
KOREA D P RP	333	295	200	240	420	0.21	75.00
KOREA REP.	5,171	8,039	10,098	14,536	17,205	8.40	18.36
MACAU, CHINA	21	1	1	7	7		
S/EAST ASIA	**1,652**	**1,197**	**1,304**	**1,724**	**1,542**	**0.75**	**-10.56**
BRUNEI DARSM		1			3		
MYANMAR	11	5	3	8	5		-37.50
CAMBODIA	20	12	11	14	12	0.01	-14.29
INDONESIA	34	73	49	88	238	0.12	170.45
LAO P.DEM.R.	7	16	8	20	19	0.01	-5.00
MALAYSIA	242	203	235	363	267	0.13	-26.45
PHILIPPINES	175	249	208	239	221	0.11	-7.53
SINGAPORE	968	383	526	729	386	0.19	-47.05
VIET NAM	137	114	165	135	190	0.09	40.74
THAILAND	58	141	99	128	176	0.09	37.50
OTH S/E ASIA					25	0.01	
AUSTRALASIA	**1,444**	**1,446**	**1,750**	**2,394**	**2,698**	**1.32**	**12.70**
AUSTRALIA	1,066	1,008	1,262	1,761	2,247	1.10	27.60
NEW ZEALAND	378	438	488	633	451	0.22	-28.75
MELANESIA	**1**	**8**	**3**	**7**	**14**	**0.01**	**100.00**
FIJI	1	6	1	7	14	0.01	100.00
PAPUA N.GUIN		2	2				
MICRONESIA		**1**			**1**		
GUAM		1			1		

MONGOLIA

2. ARRIVALS OF NON-RESIDENT VISITORS AT NATIONAL BORDERS, BY NATIONALITY

	1999	2000	2001	2002	2003	Market share 03	% change 03-02
POLYNESIA		**33**	**11**	**4**	**2**		**-50.00**
TONGA		33	11	4	2		-50.00
OT.EAST AS/P			**1**	**6**	**4**		**-33.33**
OTHER ASIA			1	6	4		-33.33
EUROPE	**72,430**	**69,354**	**90,164**	**99,839**	**74,308**	**36.28**	**-25.57**
C/E EUROPE	**58,824**	**53,522**	**70,641**	**76,648**	**57,885**	**28.26**	**-24.48**
AZERBAIJAN	35	83	71	57	55	0.03	-3.51
ARMENIA	41	70	79	102	99	0.05	-2.94
BULGARIA	75	64	42	89	71	0.03	-20.22
BELARUS	104	152	161	185	139	0.07	-24.86
CZECH REP	401	415	494	520	424	0.21	-18.46
ESTONIA	9	9	16	19	21	0.01	10.53
GEORGIA	9	8	11	9	4		-55.56
HUNGARY	131	133	125	119	128	0.06	7.56
KAZAKHSTAN	905	1,677	1,569	1,976	1,785	0.87	-9.67
KYRGYZSTAN	25	74	113	229	238	0.12	3.93
LATVIA	8	29	29	29	33	0.02	13.79
LITHUANIA	13	18	8	13	6		-53.85
REP MOLDOVA	76	79	53	124	90	0.04	-27.42
POLAND	189	325	490	731	205	0.10	-71.96
ROMANIA	27	24	26	19	30	0.01	57.89
RUSSIAN FED	55,782	49,456	66,415	71,368	53,330	26.03	-25.27
SLOVAKIA	53	76	57	57	76	0.04	33.33
TAJIKISTAN	4	16	24	47	30	0.01	-36.17
TURKMENISTAN	27	14	14		61	0.03	
UKRAINE	877	781	765	894	997	0.49	11.52
UZBEKISTAN	33	19	79	61	63	0.03	3.28
NORTHERN EUR	**4,282**	**5,042**	**6,017**	**7,049**	**5,093**	**2.49**	**-27.75**
DENMARK	586	602	617	763	438	0.21	-42.60
FINLAND	230	283	323	480	264	0.13	-45.00
ICELAND	3	4	3		20	0.01	
IRELAND	120	76	95	206	221	0.11	7.28
NORWAY	350	373	526	674	298	0.15	-55.79
SWEDEN	772	904	1,331	1,388	993	0.48	-28.46
UK	2,221	2,800	3,122	3,538	2,859	1.40	-19.19
SOUTHERN EUR	**1,128**	**1,227**	**1,526**	**1,539**	**1,034**	**0.50**	**-32.81**
ALBANIA		5	1		4		
BOSNIA HERZG	3	1		5			
CROATIA	4	17	7	22			
GREECE	26	69	118	87	153	0.07	75.86
HOLY SEE	3						
ITALY	664	743	971	987	566	0.28	-42.65
MALTA	1	1	2				
PORTUGAL	48	56	33	51	28	0.01	-45.10
SLOVENIA	9	11	18	9	19	0.01	111.11
SPAIN	281	245	269	290	221	0.11	-23.79
TFYROM	7	2			43	0.02	
SERBIA,MTNEG	82	77	107	88			
WESTERN EUR	**7,791**	**8,984**	**11,337**	**13,754**	**9,825**	**4.80**	**-28.57**
AUSTRIA	313	502	633	665	321	0.16	-51.73
BELGIUM	325	383	523	708	405	0.20	-42.80

MONGOLIA

2. ARRIVALS OF NON-RESIDENT VISITORS AT NATIONAL BORDERS, BY NATIONALITY

	1999	2000	2001	2002	2003	Market share 03	% change 03-02
FRANCE	1,983	1,841	2,762	2,891	2,751	1.34	-4.84
GERMANY	3,506	4,206	5,388	6,856	4,999	2.44	-27.09
LIECHTENSTEN			3	1			
LUXEMBOURG	10	24	10	19	10		-47.37
NETHERLANDS	1,146	1,391	1,352	1,739	697	0.34	-59.92
SWITZERLAND	508	637	666	875	642	0.31	-26.63
EAST/MED EUR	**405**	**579**	**641**	**848**	**451**	**0.22**	**-46.82**
CYPRUS			1		1		
ISRAEL	143	208	337	478	232	0.11	-51.46
TURKEY	262	371	303	370	218	0.11	-41.08
OTHER EUROPE			**2**	**1**	**20**	**0.01**	**1,900.00**
OTHER EUROPE			2	1	20	0.01	1.900.00
MIDDLE EAST	**115**	**106**	**141**	**155**	**229**	**0.11**	**47.74**
MIDDLE EAST	**115**	**106**	**141**	**155**	**229**	**0.11**	**47.74**
BAHRAIN		1			3		
IRAQ	7	9	9	3	29	0.01	866.67
JORDAN	3	6	9	7	2		-71.43
KUWAIT	18	10	34	69	64	0.03	-7.25
LEBANON	28	9	9	8	6		-25.00
OMAN		2	1	2	1		-50.00
SAUDI ARABIA	23	32	11	13	12	0.01	-7.69
SYRIA	11	22	26	39	93	0.05	138.46
UNTD ARAB EM	5	3	13	3	3		
EGYPT	17	10	16	11	2		-81.82
YEMEN	3	2	3		5		
OT MIDD EAST			10		9		
SOUTH ASIA	**584**	**625**	**705**	**662**	**781**	**0.38**	**17.98**
SOUTH ASIA	**584**	**625**	**705**	**662**	**781**	**0.38**	**17.98**
AFGHANISTAN	6	2	1		5		
BANGLADESH	20	16	22	44	53	0.03	20.45
BHUTAN	1	6	4	4	38	0.02	850.00
SRI LANKA	51	45	49	43	57	0.03	32.56
INDIA	366	337	406	347	403	0.20	16.14
IRAN	24	10	95	43	12	0.01	-72.09
NEPAL	40	37	38	77	72	0.04	-6.49
PAKISTAN	76	172	90	104	141	0.07	35.58
REG.NOT SPEC	**10**		**10**	**13**	**15**	**0.01**	**15.38**
NOT SPECIFIE	**10**		**10**	**13**	**15**	**0.01**	**15.38**
OTH.WORLD	10		10	13	15	0.01	15.38

Source: World Tourism Organization (WTO)

MONTSERRAT

1. ARRIVALS OF NON-RESIDENT TOURISTS AT NATIONAL BORDERS, BY COUNTRY OF RESIDENCE

	1999	2000	2001	2002	2003	Market share 03	% change 03-02
TOTAL (*)	**9,785**	**10,337**	**9,800**	**9,623**	**8,414**	**100.00**	**-12.56**
AMERICAS	**6,790**	**7,231**	**7,143**	**6,778**	**5,938**	**70.57**	**-12.39**
CARIBBEAN	**5,233**	**5,324**	**5,123**	**4,453**	**4,035**	**47.96**	**-9.39**
ALL CO CARIB	5,233	5,324	5,123	4,453	4,035	47.96	-9.39
NORTH AMER	**1,557**	**1,907**	**2,020**	**2,325**	**1,903**	**22.62**	**-18.15**
CANADA	307	346	368	375	302	3.59	-19.47
USA	1,250	1,561	1,652	1,950	1,601	19.03	-17.90
EUROPE	**2,178**	**2,592**	**2,419**	**2,581**	**2,271**	**26.99**	**-12.01**
NORTHERN EUR	**2,178**	**2,592**	**2,419**	**2,581**	**2,271**	**26.99**	**-12.01**
UK	2,178	2,592	2,419	2,581	2,271	26.99	-12.01
REG.NOT SPEC	**817**	**514**	**238**	**264**	**205**	**2.44**	**-22.35**
NOT SPECIFIE	**817**	**514**	**238**	**264**	**205**	**2.44**	**-22.35**
OTH.WORLD	817	514	238	264	205	2.44	-22.35

Source: World Tourism Organization (WTO)

MOROCCO

1. ARRIVALS OF NON-RESIDENT TOURISTS AT NATIONAL BORDERS, BY NATIONALITY

	1999	2000	2001	2002	2003	Market share 03	% change 03-02
TOTAL	3,816,641	4,239,962	4,342,150	4,303,446	4,551,684	100.00	5.77
AFRICA	87,888	88,689	96,694	91,698	103,194	2.27	12.54
EAST AFRICA	1,389	1,464	1,614	1,854	1,837	0.04	-0.92
BURUNDI	31	10	54	37	42		13.51
COMOROS	120	199	264	397	410	0.01	3.27
ETHIOPIA	144	163	143	149	155		4.03
ERITREA	40	83	30	24	25		4.17
DJIBOUTI	115	93	114	96	170		77.08
KENYA	248	212	251	471	346	0.01	-26.54
MADAGASCAR	101	77	85	71	71		
MALAWI	76	12	10	33	15		-54.55
MAURITIUS	133	146	190	145	152		4.83
MOZAMBIQUE	17	20	19	16	30		87.50
RWANDA	56	175	177	126	101		-19.84
SEYCHELLES	3	10	4	6	6		
SOMALIA	70	63	73	61	58		-4.92
ZIMBABWE	80	53	54	117	105		-10.26
UGANDA	55	59	44	36	67		86.11
TANZANIA	72	69	69	57	37		-35.09
ZAMBIA	28	20	33	12	47		291.67
CENTRAL AFR	3,176	3,824	4,282	3,675	3,802	0.08	3.46
ANGOLA	175	181	195	245	315	0.01	28.57
CAMEROON	586	611	813	598	696	0.02	16.39
CENT.AFR.REP	109	116	140	129	140		8.53
CHAD	162	218	179	208	175		-15.87
CONGO	690	1,350	1,487	1,427	1,346	0.03	-5.68
DEM.R.CONGO	91	60	12	7	32		357.14
EQ.GUINEA	39	85	45	85	82		-3.53
GABON	1,324	1,203	1,411	976	1,016	0.02	4.10
NORTH AFRICA	47,025	47,585	52,281	48,346	48,578	1.07	0.48
ALGERIA	17,965	20,251	21,928	22,527	23,095	0.51	2.52
SUDAN	867	839	787	807	838	0.02	3.84
TUNISIA	28,193	26,495	29,566	25,012	24,645	0.54	-1.47
SOUTHERN AFR	2,750	3,176	3,319	2,344	1,996	0.04	-14.85
BOTSWANA	19	10	16	32	11		-65.63
LESOTHO	3	3	5	6			
NAMIBIA	16	30	99	31	31		
SOUTH AFRICA	2,693	3,072	3,112	2,236	1,950	0.04	-12.79
SWAZILAND	19	61	87	39	4		-89.74
WEST AFRICA	33,548	32,640	35,198	35,479	46,981	1.03	32.42
CAPE VERDE	88	67	51	87	80		-8.05
BENIN	269	355	283	216	236	0.01	9.26
GAMBIA	271	148	180	199	179		-10.05
GHANA	363	607	168	250	297	0.01	18.80
GUINEA	5,182	5,926	7,161	7,270	8,907	0.20	22.52
COTE IVOIRE	2,231	1,969	2,451	3,240	3,314	0.07	2.28
LIBERIA	117	88	131	67	74		10.45
MALI	6,028	6,145	4,297	3,522	4,507	0.10	27.97
MAURITANIA	4,975	5,886	6,734	8,017	15,913	0.35	98.49
NIGER	1,805	1,887	1,827	1,479	1,366	0.03	-7.64
NIGERIA	2,077	986	789	569	491	0.01	-13.71

MOROCCO

1. ARRIVALS OF NON-RESIDENT TOURISTS AT NATIONAL BORDERS, BY NATIONALITY

	1999	2000	2001	2002	2003	Market share 03	% change 03-02
GUINEABISSAU	72	94	151	63	51		-19.05
SENEGAL	9,214	7,775	10,025	9,670	10,674	0.23	10.38
SIERRA LEONE	144	167	125	167	158		-5.39
TOGO	216	113	268	140	154		10.00
BURKINA FASO	496	427	557	523	580	0.01	10.90
AMERICAS	**178,642**	**178,625**	**149,103**	**119,229**	**107,877**	**2.37**	**-9.52**
CARIBBEAN	**429**	**2,668**	**2,290**	**465**	**366**	**0.01**	**-21.29**
BAHAMAS	24	5	8	2	5		150.00
BARBADOS	29	45	10	10	5		-50.00
BERMUDA	9	2	6	11	3		-72.73
CUBA	62	177	86	77	108		40.26
DOMINICA	56	56	143	126	98		-22.22
HAITI	64	63	68	47	54		14.89
JAMAICA	92	48	37	55	40		-27.27
PUERTO RICO	18	2,153	1,888	12	32		166.67
TRINIDAD TBG	75	119	44	125	21		-83.20
CENTRAL AMER	**440**	**527**	**501**	**541**	**626**	**0.01**	**15.71**
BELIZE	4	3	2	10	3		-70.00
COSTA RICA	125	160	151	155	207		33.55
EL SALVADOR	67	48	42	49	103		110.20
GUATEMALA	95	86	91	140	118		-15.71
HONDURAS	66	132	145	100	111		11.00
NICARAGUA	27	32	27	40	55		37.50
PANAMA	56	66	43	47	29		-38.30
NORTH AMER	**163,362**	**159,020**	**132,165**	**105,035**	**95,766**	**2.10**	**-8.82**
CANADA	30,686	34,320	31,633	28,503	27,606	0.61	-3.15
MEXICO	2,969	3,632	3,460	3,687	3,715	0.08	0.76
USA	129,707	121,068	97,072	72,845	64,445	1.42	-11.53
SOUTH AMER	**14,411**	**16,410**	**14,146**	**13,177**	**11,065**	**0.24**	**-16.03**
ARGENTINA	5,887	6,876	5,693	2,697	3,433	0.08	27.29
BOLIVIA	28	47	56	113	78		-30.97
BRAZIL	4,511	5,139	4,310	6,335	3,650	0.08	-42.38
CHILE	1,485	1,605	1,464	1,592	1,390	0.03	-12.69
COLOMBIA	655	759	867	505	533	0.01	5.54
ECUADOR	124	134	170	163	150		-7.98
GUYANA	31	14	12	37	12		-67.57
PARAGUAY	29	30	29	19	46		142.11
PERU	389	469	376	442	522	0.01	18.10
SURINAME	6	4	11	9	3		-66.67
URUGUAY	455	431	432	276	342	0.01	23.91
VENEZUELA	811	902	726	989	906	0.02	-8.39
OTHER AMERIC			**1**	**11**	**54**		**390.91**
OTH AMERICA			1	11	54		390.91
EAST AS/PACI	**45,397**	**49,486**	**43,459**	**44,242**	**41,651**	**0.92**	**-5.86**
N/EAST ASIA	**28,738**	**29,753**	**21,869**	**23,078**	**22,194**	**0.49**	**-3.83**
CHINA	2,124	1,972	2,595	2,986	2,579	0.06	-13.63
TAIWAN(P.C.)	901	878	532	601	535	0.01	-10.98
HK,CHINA	46	13	20	28	26		-7.14
JAPAN	23,466	23,643	15,278	14,262	13,982	0.31	-1.96

MOROCCO

1. ARRIVALS OF NON-RESIDENT TOURISTS AT NATIONAL BORDERS, BY NATIONALITY

	1999	2000	2001	2002	2003	Market share 03	% change 03-02
KOREA D P RP				259	224		-13.51
KOREA REP.	2,201	3,247	3,444	4,942	4,848	0.11	-1.90
S/EAST ASIA	**4,997**	**5,216**	**5,558**	**6,285**	**7,022**	**0.15**	**11.73**
BRUNEI DARSM	70	18	26	11	47		327.27
MYANMAR	48	56	46	20	18		-10.00
CAMBODIA	5	11	9	16	21		31.25
INDONESIA	733	898	877	956	1,241	0.03	29.81
MALAYSIA	643	722	736	1,431	1,194	0.03	-16.56
PHILIPPINES	2,666	2,657	3,081	2,669	3,068	0.07	14.95
SINGAPORE	314	388	350	561	800	0.02	42.60
VIET NAM	63	54	54	69	70		1.45
THAILAND	455	412	379	552	563	0.01	1.99
AUSTRALASIA	**11,662**	**14,517**	**16,032**	**14,879**	**12,433**	**0.27**	**-16.44**
AUSTRALIA	9,483	11,636	13,321	12,164	10,047	0.22	-17.40
NEW ZEALAND	2,179	2,881	2,711	2,715	2,386	0.05	-12.12
MICRONESIA					**2**		
KIRIBATI					2		
EUROPE	**1,753,652**	**1,918,545**	**1,864,450**	**1,868,540**	**1,880,177**	**41.31**	**0.62**
C/E EUROPE	**31,136**	**32,545**	**29,968**	**27,278**	**32,213**	**0.71**	**18.09**
AZERBAIJAN	24	23	22	20	20		
ARMENIA	17	40	22	13	26		100.00
BULGARIA	1,172	1,052	1,043	936	1,525	0.03	62.93
BELARUS	37	28	79	150	104		-30.67
CZECH REP	4,076	4,728	4,166	3,292	5,031	0.11	52.83
ESTONIA	2,728	1,602	231	203	135		-33.50
HUNGARY	3,019	2,792	2,446	2,275	4,982	0.11	118.99
KAZAKHSTAN	55	17	63	87	73		-16.09
LITHUANIA	414	194	241	235	906	0.02	285.53
POLAND	8,679	8,628	8,796	6,972	5,457	0.12	-21.73
ROMANIA	2,071	2,071	2,024	2,174	2,773	0.06	27.55
RUSSIAN FED	4,530	8,089	8,476	8,234	8,039	0.18	-2.37
SLOVAKIA	2,298	1,690	1,110	1,253	1,133	0.02	-9.58
UKRAINE	2,008	1,590	1,240	1,413	1,988	0.04	40.69
UZBEKISTAN	8	1	9	21	21		
NORTHERN EUR	**223,344**	**226,754**	**219,672**	**213,161**	**216,554**	**4.76**	**1.59**
DENMARK	15,896	14,619	16,094	11,185	15,593	0.34	39.41
FINLAND	12,957	11,765	10,544	9,197	9,661	0.21	5.05
ICELAND	347	629	321	233	330	0.01	41.63
IRELAND	11,354	10,943	11,816	14,263	15,166	0.33	6.33
NORWAY	19,794	21,826	15,699	12,057	17,651	0.39	46.40
SWEDEN	30,661	29,725	29,464	19,650	24,094	0.53	22.62
UK	132,335	137,247	135,734	146,576	134,059	2.95	-8.54
SOUTHERN EUR	**380,139**	**413,978**	**367,188**	**363,414**	**374,962**	**8.24**	**3.18**
ALBANIA	60	55	45	57	45		-21.05
ANDORRA	74	140	217	143	129		-9.79
BOSNIA HERZG	138	306	143	156	144		-7.69
CROATIA	546	767	1,033	654	599	0.01	-8.41
GREECE	6,536	5,381	5,198	5,212	5,337	0.12	2.40
ITALY	121,759	142,426	123,628	112,518	100,001	2.20	-11.12
MALTA	321	386	420	378	282	0.01	-25.40
PORTUGAL	25,018	31,302	35,103	42,022	36,389	0.80	-13.40

MOROCCO

1. ARRIVALS OF NON-RESIDENT TOURISTS AT NATIONAL BORDERS, BY NATIONALITY

	1999	2000	2001	2002	2003	Market share 03	% change 03-02
SAN MARINO	148	10	15	31	27		-12.90
SLOVENIA	573	497	502	522	532	0.01	1.92
SPAIN	224,565	232,245	200,519	201,258	231,156	5.08	14.86
TFYROM	76	82	64	109	68		-37.61
SERBIA,MTNEG	325	381	301	354	253	0.01	-28.53
WESTERN EUR	**1,110,106**	**1,234,127**	**1,243,385**	**1,259,230**	**1,248,186**	**27.42**	**-0.88**
AUSTRIA	19,493	23,297	21,235	15,928	12,798	0.28	-19.65
BELGIUM	78,271	79,918	84,011	83,966	80,062	1.76	-4.65
FRANCE	697,771	813,865	840,230	877,465	916,147	20.13	4.41
GERMANY	220,488	211,039	196,700	172,860	129,391	2.84	-25.15
LIECHTENSTEN	31	35	30	56	37		-33.93
LUXEMBOURG	1,816	1,895	1,692	1,596	1,000	0.02	-37.34
MONACO	75	86	97	88	92		4.55
NETHERLANDS	54,168	59,436	60,489	65,085	66,486	1.46	2.15
SWITZERLAND	37,993	44,556	38,901	42,186	42,173	0.93	-0.03
EAST/MED EUR	**8,927**	**11,141**	**4,237**	**5,457**	**8,262**	**0.18**	**51.40**
CYPRUS	184	160	210	202	150		-25.74
ISRAEL	4,523	6,365	129	102	100		-1.96
TURKEY	4,220	4,616	3,898	5,153	8,012	0.18	55.48
MIDDLE EAST	**78,271**	**78,514**	**85,391**	**85,996**	**78,639**	**1.73**	**-8.56**
MIDDLE EAST	**78,271**	**78,514**	**85,391**	**85,996**	**78,639**	**1.73**	**-8.56**
BAHRAIN	1,949	1,700	2,157	2,624	2,779	0.06	5.91
PALESTINE	1,239	1,534	1,039	971	950	0.02	-2.16
IRAQ	1,210	1,319	1,428	1,351	821	0.02	-39.23
JORDAN	3,567	3,634	3,759	3,796	3,829	0.08	0.87
KUWAIT	2,617	3,328	3,672	4,632	4,276	0.09	-7.69
LEBANON	2,819	3,366	3,796	4,223	3,754	0.08	-11.11
LIBYA	9,235	11,357	13,226	11,723	9,572	0.21	-18.35
OMAN	1,415	1,264	1,735	2,084	2,174	0.05	4.32
QATAR	1,155	1,110	1,074	1,231	1,388	0.03	12.75
SAUDI ARABIA	32,891	31,749	32,955	32,305	28,921	0.64	-10.48
SYRIA	1,850	2,811	4,028	3,708	3,688	0.08	-0.54
UNTD ARAB EM	5,186	5,021	5,551	6,298	5,908	0.13	-6.19
EGYPT	12,277	9,427	10,044	10,209	9,648	0.21	-5.50
YEMEN	861	894	927	841	931	0.02	10.70
SOUTH ASIA	**5,256**	**5,107**	**5,548**	**6,053**	**5,383**	**0.12**	**-11.07**
SOUTH ASIA	**5,256**	**5,107**	**5,548**	**6,053**	**5,383**	**0.12**	**-11.07**
AFGHANISTAN	30	56	56	74	77		4.05
BANGLADESH	272	415	239	264	149		-43.56
SRI LANKA	163	193	317	215	163		-24.19
INDIA	2,637	2,568	2,873	3,450	3,145	0.07	-8.84
IRAN	617	461	696	576	790	0.02	37.15
MALDIVES	188	111	104	53	19		-64.15
NEPAL	24	35	15	68	56		-17.65
PAKISTAN	1,325	1,268	1,248	1,353	984	0.02	-27.27
REG.NOT SPEC	**1,667,535**	**1,920,996**	**2,097,505**	**2,087,688**	**2,334,763**	**51.29**	**11.83**
NOT SPECIFIE	**1,667,535**	**1,920,996**	**2,097,505**	**2,087,688**	**2,334,763**	**51.29**	**11.83**
OTH.WORLD	3,663	6,539	5,017	6,509	6,954	0.15	6.84

MOROCCO

1. ARRIVALS OF NON-RESIDENT TOURISTS AT NATIONAL BORDERS, BY NATIONALITY

	1999	2000	2001	2002	2003	Market share 03	% change 03-02
N RESID ABRO	1,663,872	1,914,457	2,092,488	2,081,179	2,327,809	51.14	11.85

Source: World Tourism Organization (WTO)

3. ARRIVALS OF NON-RESIDENT TOURISTS IN HOTELS AND SIMILAR ESTABLISHMENTS, BY NATIONALITY

	1999	2000	2001	2002	2003	Market share 03	% change 03-02
TOTAL (*)	**3,216,948**	**3,387,719**	**3,083,299**	**2,632,507**	**2,446,496**	**100.00**	**-7.07**
AFRICA	**49,798**	**48,548**	**52,302**	**55,774**	**64,477**	**2.64**	**15.60**
NORTH AFRICA	**22,549**	**21,201**	**23,664**	**23,077**	**25,207**	**1.03**	**9.23**
ALGERIA	8,010	9,103	9,894	10,099	11,521	0.47	14.08
TUNISIA	14,539	12,098	13,770	12,978	13,686	0.56	5.46
WEST AFRICA	**2,941**	**4,042**	**3,376**	**4,447**	**4,722**	**0.19**	**6.18**
MAURITANIA	2,941	4,042	3,376	4,447	4,722	0.19	6.18
OTHER AFRICA	**24,308**	**23,305**	**25,262**	**28,250**	**34,548**	**1.41**	**22.29**
OTHER AFRICA	24,308	23,305	25,262	28,250	34,548	1.41	22.29
AMERICAS	**158,983**	**176,729**	**138,798**	**97,304**	**74,268**	**3.04**	**-23.67**
NORTH AMER	**158,983**	**176,729**	**138,798**	**97,304**	**74,268**	**3.04**	**-23.67**
CANADA	24,883	26,985	22,054	16,330	16,145	0.66	-1.13
USA	134,100	149,744	116,744	80,974	58,123	2.38	-28.22
EAST AS/PACI	**74,613**	**67,157**	**43,079**	**38,723**	**36,417**	**1.49**	**-5.96**
N/EAST ASIA	**74,613**	**67,157**	**43,079**	**38,723**	**36,417**	**1.49**	**-5.96**
JAPAN	74,613	67,157	43,079	38,723	36,417	1.49	-5.96
EUROPE	**2,675,261**	**2,829,667**	**2,612,667**	**2,202,994**	**2,038,916**	**83.34**	**-7.45**
C/E EUROPE	**4,602**	**3,273**	**3,084**	**2,552**	**4,522**	**0.18**	**77.19**
CIS	4,602	3,273	3,084	2,552	4,522	0.18	77.19
NORTHERN EUR	**185,138**	**201,775**	**202,284**	**159,808**	**148,732**	**6.08**	**-6.93**
DENMARK	12,284	10,954	10,924	5,584	6,224	0.25	11.46
FINLAND	8,419	7,625	6,053	6,273	6,366	0.26	1.48
NORWAY	13,917	15,789	14,717	5,393	6,766	0.28	25.46
SWEDEN	33,433	31,548	24,890	12,899	16,969	0.69	31.55
UK	117,085	135,859	145,700	129,659	112,407	4.59	-13.31
SOUTHERN EUR	**540,975**	**557,936**	**486,881**	**407,294**	**357,095**	**14.60**	**-12.33**
ITALY	250,831	249,701	227,850	197,718	153,681	6.28	-22.27
PORTUGAL	27,658	32,911	31,504	39,920	30,789	1.26	-22.87
SPAIN	262,486	275,324	227,527	169,656	172,625	7.06	1.75
WESTERN EUR	**1,944,546**	**2,066,683**	**1,920,418**	**1,633,340**	**1,528,567**	**62.48**	**-6.41**
AUSTRIA	20,430	21,247	19,322	17,926	18,555	0.76	3.51
BELGIUM	100,594	87,238	84,851	77,446	69,580	2.84	-10.16
FRANCE	1,280,461	1,453,581	1,370,469	1,202,764	1,206,656	49.32	0.32
GERMANY	442,446	407,570	354,436	234,322	149,131	6.10	-36.36
NETHERLANDS	44,567	46,089	43,815	53,622	46,376	1.90	-13.51
SWITZERLAND	56,048	50,958	47,525	47,260	38,269	1.56	-19.02
MIDDLE EAST	**80,831**	**81,741**	**80,735**	**81,658**	**74,432**	**3.04**	**-8.85**
MIDDLE EAST	**80,831**	**81,741**	**80,735**	**81,658**	**74,432**	**3.04**	**-8.85**
LIBYA	6,606	7,578	8,810	7,788	5,877	0.24	-24.54
SAUDI ARABIA	34,580	34,986	35,383	34,696	28,931	1.18	-16.62

3. ARRIVALS OF NON-RESIDENT TOURISTS IN HOTELS AND SIMILAR ESTABLISHMENTS, BY NATIONALITY

	1999	2000	2001	2002	2003	Market share 03	% change 03-02
SYRIA	1,559	2,010	2,266	2,674	2,359	0.10	-11.78
UNTD ARAB EM	3,290	2,897	4,022	5,473	5,571	0.23	1.79
EGYPT	7,789	6,746	7,749	7,527	8,176	0.33	8.62
OT MIDD EAST	27,007	27,524	22,505	23,500	23,518	0.96	0.08
REG.NOT SPEC	**177,462**	**183,877**	**155,718**	**156,054**	**157,986**	**6.46**	**1.24**
NOT SPECIFIE	**177,462**	**183,877**	**155,718**	**156,054**	**157,986**	**6.46**	**1.24**
OTH.WORLD	169,231	177,879	144,492	142,284	143,400	5.86	0.78
N RESID ABRO	8,231	5,998	11,226	13,770	14,586	0.60	5.93

Source: World Tourism Organization (WTO)

5. OVERNIGHT STAYS OF NON-RESIDENT TOURISTS IN HOTELS AND SIMILAR ESTABLISHMENTS, BY NATIONALITY

	1999	2000	2001	2002	2003	Market share 03	% change 03-02
TOTAL (*)	**11,891,058**	**13,251,700**	**12,308,803**	**10,851,497**	**10,399,693**	**100.00**	**-4.16**
AFRICA	**236,779**	**261,058**	**369,089**	**365,084**	**312,921**	**3.01**	**-14.29**
NORTH AFRICA	**99,829**	**87,866**	**138,346**	**133,159**	**172,145**	**1.66**	**29.28**
ALGERIA	35,005	37,243	54,063	52,242	71,267	0.69	36.42
TUNISIA	64,824	50,623	84,283	80,917	100,878	0.97	24.67
WEST AFRICA	**31,600**	**88,713**	**102,231**	**94,878**	**36,385**	**0.35**	**-61.65**
MAURITANIA	31,600	88,713	102,231	94,878	36,385	0.35	-61.65
OTHER AFRICA	**105,350**	**84,479**	**128,512**	**137,047**	**104,391**	**1.00**	**-23.83**
OTHER AFRICA	105,350	84,479	128,512	137,047	104,391	1.00	-23.83
AMERICAS	**440,742**	**492,555**	**426,762**	**317,968**	**289,419**	**2.78**	**-8.98**
NORTH AMER	**440,742**	**492,555**	**426,762**	**317,968**	**289,419**	**2.78**	**-8.98**
CANADA	92,637	101,731	88,797	69,984	89,023	0.86	27.20
USA	348,105	390,824	337,965	247,984	200,396	1.93	-19.19
EAST AS/PACI	**138,332**	**130,139**	**95,464**	**81,688**	**97,627**	**0.94**	**19.51**
N/EAST ASIA	**138,332**	**130,139**	**95,464**	**81,688**	**97,627**	**0.94**	**19.51**
JAPAN	138,332	130,139	95,464	81,688	97,627	0.94	19.51
EUROPE	**10,175,682**	**11,358,377**	**10,441,623**	**9,130,254**	**8,686,810**	**83.53**	**-4.86**
C/E EUROPE	**20,573**	**19,191**	**16,399**	**14,216**	**51,312**	**0.49**	**260.95**
CIS	20,573	19,191	16,399	14,216	51,312	0.49	260.95
NORTHERN EUR	**1,035,824**	**1,176,447**	**1,191,679**	**873,040**	**857,595**	**8.25**	**-1.77**
DENMARK	86,327	68,370	73,570	40,586	42,677	0.41	5.15
FINLAND	71,373	67,994	48,035	49,392	53,608	0.52	8.54
NORWAY	101,684	120,124	96,364	37,667	44,844	0.43	19.05
SWEDEN	235,039	240,368	177,229	86,474	127,460	1.23	47.40
UK	541,401	679,591	796,481	658,921	589,006	5.66	-10.61
SOUTHERN EUR	**1,596,259**	**1,717,908**	**1,497,946**	**1,277,246**	**1,261,496**	**12.13**	**-1.23**
ITALY	815,823	867,381	780,187	673,386	537,170	5.17	-20.23
PORTUGAL	85,750	121,641	107,296	129,959	123,274	1.19	-5.14
SPAIN	694,686	728,886	610,463	473,901	601,052	5.78	26.83
WESTERN EUR	**7,523,026**	**8,444,831**	**7,735,599**	**6,965,752**	**6,516,407**	**62.66**	**-6.45**
AUSTRIA	64,309	72,425	61,663	54,955	51,982	0.50	-5.41
BELGIUM	542,284	514,864	491,533	451,728	407,999	3.92	-9.68
FRANCE	4,274,787	5,400,395	5,091,513	4,794,802	4,838,695	46.53	0.92
GERMANY	2,211,619	2,048,457	1,692,078	1,209,449	849,627	8.17	-29.75
NETHERLANDS	196,474	194,897	196,268	250,447	197,103	1.90	-21.30
SWITZERLAND	233,553	213,793	202,544	204,371	171,001	1.64	-16.33
MIDDLE EAST	**318,504**	**363,140**	**384,692**	**374,326**	**321,837**	**3.09**	**-14.02**
MIDDLE EAST	**318,504**	**363,140**	**384,692**	**374,326**	**321,837**	**3.09**	**-14.02**
LIBYA	28,915	37,447	59,669	48,448	35,551	0.34	-26.62
SAUDI ARABIA	149,533	175,708	180,044	167,318	134,250	1.29	-19.76

5. OVERNIGHT STAYS OF NON-RESIDENT TOURISTS IN HOTELS AND SIMILAR ESTABLISHMENTS, BY NATIONALITY

	1999	2000	2001	2002	2003	Market share 03	% change 03-02
SYRIA	5,629	9,323	10,494	13,519	10,759	0.10	-20.42
UNTD ARAB EM	11,046	10,609	14,261	16,536	16,488	0.16	-0.29
EGYPT	35,238	29,027	29,938	33,199	33,159	0.32	-0.12
OT MIDD EAST	88,143	101,026	90,286	95,306	91,630	0.88	-3.86
REG.NOT SPEC	**581,019**	**646,431**	**591,173**	**582,177**	**691,079**	**6.65**	**18.71**
NOT SPECIFIE	**581,019**	**646,431**	**591,173**	**582,177**	**691,079**	**6.65**	**18.71**
OTH.WORLD	560,848	616,057	538,274	509,203	567,197	5.45	11.39
N RESID ABRO	20,171	30,374	52,899	72,974	123,882	1.19	69.76

Source: World Tourism Organization (WTO)

MOZAMBIQUE

2. ARRIVALS OF NON-RESIDENT VISITORS AT NATIONAL BORDERS, BY COUNTRY OF RESIDENCE

	1999	2000	2001	2002	2003	Market share 03	% change 03-02
TOTAL			404,093	942,885	726,099	100.00	-22.99
AFRICA			367,593	848,259	591,647	81.48	-30.25
EAST AFRICA				463,440	236,203	32.53	-49.03
MALAWI				224,274	121,267	16.70	-45.93
ZIMBABWE				233,496	114,936	15.83	-50.78
ZAMBIA				5,670			
SOUTHERN AFR			299,900	374,238	355,444	48.95	-5.02
SOUTH AFRICA			276,100	336,657	335,426	46.20	-0.37
SWAZILAND			23,800	37,581	20,018	2.76	-46.73
OTHER AFRICA			67,693	10,581			
OTHER AFRICA			67,693	10,581			
AMERICAS				10,401	5,035	0.69	-51.59
NORTH AMER				6,627	5,035	0.69	-24.02
USA				6,627	5,035	0.69	-24.02
OTHER AMERIC				3,774			
OTH AMERICA				3,774			
EAST AS/PACI				5,721			
OT.EAST AS/P				5,721			
ALL ASIA				5,721			
EUROPE			36,500	53,691	42,698	5.88	-20.47
NORTHERN EUR			5,900	13,638	5,798	0.80	-57.49
UK			5,900	13,638	5,798	0.80	-57.49
SOUTHERN EUR			30,600	19,089	25,392	3.50	33.02
PORTUGAL			30,600	19,089	25,392	3.50	33.02
OTHER EUROPE				20,964	11,508	1.58	-45.11
OTHER EUROPE				20,964	11,508	1.58	-45.11
REG.NOT SPEC				24,813	86,719	11.94	249.49
NOT SPECIFIE				24,813	86,719	11.94	249.49
OTH.WORLD				24,813	86,719	11.94	249.49

Source: World Tourism Organization (WTO)

MYANMAR

1. ARRIVALS OF NON-RESIDENT TOURISTS AT NATIONAL BORDERS, BY NATIONALITY

	1999	2000	2001	2002	2003	Market share 03	% change 03-02
TOTAL (*)	**198,210**	**207,665**	**204,862**	**217,212**	**205,610**	**100.00**	**-5.34**
AFRICA	**316**	**304**	**312**	**430**	**390**	**0.19**	**-9.30**
OTHER AFRICA	**316**	**304**	**312**	**430**	**390**	**0.19**	**-9.30**
ALL AFRICA	316	304	312	430	390	0.19	-9.30
AMERICAS	**12,748**	**15,312**	**16,671**	**17,824**	**16,426**	**7.99**	**-7.84**
NORTH AMER	**12,149**	**14,691**	**15,864**	**16,953**	**15,775**	**7.67**	**-6.95**
CANADA	1,879	2,022	2,340	2,476	2,519	1.23	1.74
USA	10,270	12,669	13,524	14,477	13,256	6.45	-8.43
OTHER AMERIC	**599**	**621**	**807**	**871**	**651**	**0.32**	**-25.26**
OTH AMERICA	599	621	807	871	651	0.32	-25.26
EAST AS/PACI	**126,136**	**129,347**	**122,327**	**124,280**	**115,614**	**56.23**	**-6.97**
N/EAST ASIA	**77,927**	**77,529**	**71,915**	**70,492**	**64,074**	**31.16**	**-9.10**
CHINA	12,148	14,336	16,788	17,732	15,564	7.57	-12.23
TAIWAN(P.C.)	32,977	32,098	26,020	22,849	19,645	9.55	-14.02
HK,CHINA	1,598	1,742	1,408	1,277	1,667	0.81	30.54
JAPAN	25,319	21,930	20,118	20,744	18,799	9.14	-9.38
KOREA REP.	5,885	7,423	7,581	7,890	8,399	4.08	6.45
S/EAST ASIA	**38,049**	**40,653**	**38,358**	**40,778**	**42,590**	**20.71**	**4.44**
MALAYSIA	7,583	9,938	11,296	12,532	10,003	4.87	-20.18
SINGAPORE	11,074	11,645	9,939	11,310	10,373	5.04	-8.28
THAILAND	19,392	19,070	17,123	16,936	22,214	10.80	31.16
AUSTRALASIA	**4,204**	**4,716**	**5,069**	**5,912**	**5,721**	**2.78**	**-3.23**
AUSTRALIA	3,642	4,120	4,442	5,194	4,950	2.41	-4.70
NEW ZEALAND	562	596	627	718	771	0.37	7.38
OT.EAST AS/P	**5,956**	**6,449**	**6,985**	**7,098**	**3,229**	**1.57**	**-54.51**
OTHER ASIA	5,956	6,449	6,985	7,098	3,229	1.57	-54.51
EUROPE	**51,627**	**54,905**	**57,490**	**65,477**	**60,364**	**29.36**	**-7.81**
C/E EUROPE	**750**	**308**	**1,542**	**2,077**	**2,203**	**1.07**	**6.07**
RUSSIAN FED	253	308	434	556	551	0.27	-0.90
OTH C/E EUR	497		1,108	1,521	1,652	0.80	8.61
NORTHERN EUR	**9,267**	**9,020**	**8,424**	**8,620**	**7,848**	**3.82**	**-8.96**
UK	9,267	9,020	8,424	8,620	7,848	3.82	-8.96
SOUTHERN EUR	**8,868**	**9,330**	**9,895**	**11,764**	**8,300**	**4.04**	**-29.45**
ITALY	6,925	6,852	6,618	7,908	6,129	2.98	-22.50
SPAIN	1,943	2,478	3,277	3,856	2,171	1.06	-43.70
WESTERN EUR	**28,741**	**30,422**	**32,047**	**37,735**	**37,639**	**18.31**	**-0.25**
AUSTRIA	1,380	1,727	2,126	3,616	4,756	2.31	31.53
BELGIUM	2,106	2,334	2,408	2,364	2,159	1.05	-8.67
FRANCE	13,594	13,313	12,461	14,108	13,125	6.38	-6.97
GERMANY	9,039	9,920	11,450	12,952	13,341	6.49	3.00
SWITZERLAND	2,622	3,128	3,602	4,695	4,258	2.07	-9.31

MYANMAR

1. ARRIVALS OF NON-RESIDENT TOURISTS AT NATIONAL BORDERS, BY NATIONALITY

	1999	2000	2001	2002	2003	Market share 03	% change 03-02
OTHER EUROPE	**4,001**	**5,825**	**5,582**	**5,281**	**4,374**	**2.13**	**-17.17**
OTHER EUROPE	4,001	5,825	5,582	5,281	4,374	2.13	-17.17
MIDDLE EAST	**1,416**	**1,263**	**1,416**	**2,022**	**1,148**	**0.56**	**-43.22**
MIDDLE EAST	**1,416**	**1,263**	**1,416**	**2,022**	**1,148**	**0.56**	**-43.22**
ALL MID EAST	1,416	1,263	1,416	2,022	1,148	0.56	-43.22
SOUTH ASIA	**5,967**	**6,534**	**6,646**	**7,179**	**11,668**	**5.67**	**62.53**
SOUTH ASIA	**5,967**	**6,534**	**6,646**	**7,179**	**11,668**	**5.67**	**62.53**
BANGLADESH	884	929	1,074	1,488	1,999	0.97	34.34
INDIA	5,083	5,605	5,572	5,691	6,291	3.06	10.54
PAKISTAN					742	0.36	
OTH STH ASIA					2,636	1.28	

Source: World Tourism Organization (WTO)

5. OVERNIGHT STAYS OF NON-RESIDENT TOURISTS IN HOTELS AND SIMILAR ESTABLISHMENTS, BY NATIONALITY

	1999	2000	2001	2002	2003	Market share 03	% change 03-02
TOTAL	**1,387,563**	**1,443,671**	**1,434,034**	**1,520,505**	**1,415,624**	**100.00**	**-6.90**
AFRICA	**2,212**	**2,128**	**2,184**	**3,010**	**2,730**	**0.19**	**-9.30**
OTHER AFRICA	**2,212**	**2,128**	**2,184**	**3,010**	**2,730**	**0.19**	**-9.30**
ALL AFRICA	2,212	2,128	2,184	3,010	2,730	0.19	-9.30
AMERICAS	**89,236**	**99,379**	**116,697**	**124,768**	**114,982**	**8.12**	**-7.84**
NORTH AMER	**85,043**	**95,032**	**111,048**	**118,671**	**110,425**	**7.80**	**-6.95**
CANADA	13,153	14,154	16,380	17,332	17,633	1.25	1.74
USA	71,890	80,878	94,668	101,339	92,792	6.55	-8.43
OTHER AMERIC	**4,193**	**4,347**	**5,649**	**6,097**	**4,557**	**0.32**	**-25.26**
OTH AMERICA	4,193	4,347	5,649	6,097	4,557	0.32	-25.26
EAST AS/PACI	**883,052**	**903,250**	**856,289**	**869,960**	**809,298**	**57.17**	**-6.97**
N/EAST ASIA	**545,589**	**540,554**	**503,405**	**493,444**	**448,518**	**31.68**	**-9.10**
CHINA	85,086	100,352	117,516	124,124	108,948	7.70	-12.23
TAIWAN(P.C.)	230,889	224,686	182,140	159,943	137,515	9.71	-14.02
HK,CHINA	11,186	12,194	9,856	8,939	11,669	0.82	30.54
JAPAN	177,233	151,361	140,826	145,208	131,593	9.30	-9.38
KOREA REP.	41,195	51,961	53,067	55,230	58,793	4.15	6.45
S/EAST ASIA	**266,343**	**284,571**	**268,506**	**285,446**	**298,130**	**21.06**	**4.44**
MALAYSIA	53,081	69,566	79,072	87,724	70,021	4.95	-20.18
SINGAPORE	77,518	81,515	69,573	79,170	72,611	5.13	-8.28
THAILAND	135,744	133,490	119,861	118,552	155,498	10.98	31.16
AUSTRALASIA	**29,428**	**32,982**	**35,483**	**41,384**	**40,047**	**2.83**	**-3.23**
AUSTRALIA	25,494	28,840	31,094	36,358	34,650	2.45	-4.70
NEW ZEALAND	3,934	4,142	4,389	5,026	5,397	0.38	7.38
OT.EAST AS/P	**41,692**	**45,143**	**48,895**	**49,686**	**22,603**	**1.60**	**-54.51**
OTHER ASIA	41,692	45,143	48,895	49,686	22,603	1.60	-54.51
EUROPE	**361,382**	**384,335**	**402,430**	**458,360**	**422,548**	**29.85**	**-7.81**
C/E EUROPE	**5,250**	**2,156**	**10,794**	**14,560**	**15,421**	**1.09**	**5.91**
RUSSIAN FED	1,771	2,156	3,038	3,892	3,857	0.27	-0.90
OTH C/E EUR	3,479		7,756	10,668	11,564	0.82	8.40
NORTHERN EUR	**64,869**	**63,140**	**58,968**	**60,340**	**54,936**	**3.88**	**-8.96**
UK	64,869	63,140	58,968	60,340	54,936	3.88	-8.96
SOUTHERN EUR	**62,074**	**65,310**	**69,265**	**82,348**	**58,100**	**4.10**	**-29.45**
ITALY	48,473	47,964	46,326	55,356	42,903	3.03	-22.50
SPAIN	13,601	17,346	22,939	26,992	15,197	1.07	-43.70
WESTERN EUR	**201,182**	**212,954**	**224,329**	**264,145**	**263,473**	**18.61**	**-0.25**
AUSTRIA	9,660	12,089	14,882	25,312	33,292	2.35	31.53
BELGIUM	14,742	16,338	16,856	16,548	15,113	1.07	-8.67
FRANCE	95,153	93,191	87,227	98,756	91,875	6.49	-6.97
GERMANY	63,273	69,440	80,150	90,664	93,387	6.60	3.00
SWITZERLAND	18,354	21,896	25,214	32,865	29,806	2.11	-9.31

MYANMAR

5. OVERNIGHT STAYS OF NON-RESIDENT TOURISTS IN HOTELS AND SIMILAR ESTABLISHMENTS, BY NATIONALITY

	1999	2000	2001	2002	2003	Market share 03	% change 03-02
OTHER EUROPE	**28,007**	**40,775**	**39,074**	**36,967**	**30,618**	**2.16**	**-17.17**
OTHER EUROPE	28,007	40,775	39,074	36,967	30,618	2.16	-17.17
MIDDLE EAST	**9,912**	**8,841**	**9,912**	**14,154**	**8,036**	**0.57**	**-43.22**
MIDDLE EAST	**9,912**	**8,841**	**9,912**	**14,154**	**8,036**	**0.57**	**-43.22**
ALL MID EAST	9,912	8,841	9,912	14,154	8,036	0.57	-43.22
SOUTH ASIA	**41,769**	**45,738**	**46,522**	**50,253**	**58,030**	**4.10**	**15.48**
SOUTH ASIA	**41,769**	**45,738**	**46,522**	**50,253**	**58,030**	**4.10**	**15.48**
BANGLADESH	6,188	6,503	7,518	10,416	13,993	0.99	34.34
INDIA	35,581	39,235	39,004	39,837	44,037	3.11	10.54

Source: World Tourism Organization (WTO)

NAMIBIA

1. ARRIVALS OF NON-RESIDENT TOURISTS AT NATIONAL BORDERS, BY COUNTRY OF RESIDENCE

	1999	2000	2001	2002	2003	Market share 03	% change 03-02
TOTAL			**670,497**	**757,201**	**695,221**	**100.00**	**-8.19**
AFRICA			**536,203**	**591,612**	**525,885**	**75.64**	**-11.11**
EAST AFRICA			**21,280**	**32,737**	**51,429**	**7.40**	**57.10**
ZIMBABWE			12,970	19,145	17,795	2.56	-7.05
ZAMBIA			8,310	13,592	33,634	4.84	147.45
CENTRAL AFR			**237,691**	**278,816**	**222,752**	**32.04**	**-20.11**
ANGOLA			237,691	278,816	222,752	32.04	-20.11
SOUTHERN AFR			**271,508**	**273,222**	**244,688**	**35.20**	**-10.44**
BOTSWANA			29,699	29,328	22,679	3.26	-22.67
SOUTH AFRICA			241,809	243,894	222,009	31.93	-8.97
OTHER AFRICA			**5,724**	**6,837**	**7,016**	**1.01**	**2.62**
OTHER AFRICA			5,724	6,837	7,016	1.01	2.62
AMERICAS			**9,056**	**9,625**	**11,775**	**1.69**	**22.34**
NORTH AMER			**9,056**	**9,625**	**11,775**	**1.69**	**22.34**
USA			9,056	9,625	11,775	1.69	22.34
EAST AS/PACI				**3,430**	**4,280**	**0.62**	**24.78**
AUSTRALASIA				**3,430**	**4,280**	**0.62**	**24.78**
AUSTRALIA				3,430	4,280	0.62	24.78
EUROPE			**112,182**	**140,781**	**141,834**	**20.40**	**0.75**
NORTHERN EUR			**17,692**	**25,272**	**24,607**	**3.54**	**-2.63**
UK			13,941	19,560	19,291	2.77	-1.38
SCANDINAVIA			3,751	5,712	5,316	0.76	-6.93
SOUTHERN EUR			**6,661**	**16,714**	**16,792**	**2.42**	**0.47**
ITALY			6,661	9,059	8,809	1.27	-2.76
PORTUGAL				3,244	3,535	0.51	8.97
SPAIN				4,411	4,448	0.64	0.84
WESTERN EUR			**59,898**	**94,786**	**95,717**	**13.77**	**0.98**
AUSTRIA				4,983	5,023	0.72	0.80
BELGIUM				3,444	4,197	0.60	21.86
FRANCE			6,922	9,194	9,364	1.35	1.85
GERMANY			52,976	61,236	58,036	8.35	-5.23
NETHERLANDS				9,654	11,778	1.69	22.00
SWITZERLAND				6,275	7,319	1.05	16.64
OTHER EUROPE			**27,931**	**4,009**	**4,718**	**0.68**	**17.69**
OTHER EUROPE			27,931	4,009	4,718	0.68	17.69
REG.NOT SPEC			**13,056**	**11,753**	**11,447**	**1.65**	**-2.60**
NOT SPECIFIE			**13,056**	**11,753**	**11,447**	**1.65**	**-2.60**
OTH.WORLD			13,056	11,753	11,447	1.65	-2.60

Source: World Tourism Organization (WTO)

NAMIBIA

2. ARRIVALS OF NON-RESIDENT VISITORS AT NATIONAL BORDERS, BY COUNTRY OF RESIDENCE

	1999	2000	2001	2002	2003	Market share 03	% change 03-02
TOTAL			861,184	947,778			
AFRICA			669,639	745,709			
EAST AFRICA			28,527	49,172			
ZIMBABWE			15,604	22,796			
ZAMBIA			12,923	26,376			
CENTRAL AFR			284,853	330,764			
ANGOLA			284,853	330,764			
SOUTHERN AFR			347,922	354,499			
BOTSWANA			39,398	39,784			
SOUTH AFRICA			308,524	314,715			
OTHER AFRICA			8,337	11,274			
OTHER AFRICA			8,337	11,274			
AMERICAS			10,334	12,050			
NORTH AMER			10,334	12,050			
ALL NORTH AM			10,334	12,050			
EUROPE			123,622	169,689			
NORTHERN EUR			20,241	31,041			
UK			15,853	23,945			
SCANDINAVIA			4,388	7,096			
SOUTHERN EUR			7,098	10,161			
ITALY			7,098	10,161			
WESTERN EUR			65,414	84,202			
FRANCE			7,572	10,716			
GERMANY			57,842	73,486			
OTHER EUROPE			30,869	44,285			
OTHER EUROPE			30,869	44,285			
REG.NOT SPEC			57,589	20,330			
NOT SPECIFIE			57,589	20,330			
OTH.WORLD			57,589	20,330			

Source: World Tourism Organization (WTO)

NEPAL

1. ARRIVALS OF NON-RESIDENT TOURISTS AT NATIONAL BORDERS, BY NATIONALITY

	1999	2000	2001	2002	2003	Market share 03	% change 03-02
TOTAL	**491,504**	**463,646**	**361,237**	**275,468**	**338,132**	**100.00**	**22.75**
AFRICA	**1,857**	**2,040**	**1,596**	**1,132**	**1,612**	**0.48**	**42.40**
OTHER AFRICA	**1,857**	**2,040**	**1,596**	**1,132**	**1,612**	**0.48**	**42.40**
ALL AFRICA	1,857	2,040	1,596	1,132	1,612	0.48	42.40
AMERICAS	**53,006**	**55,108**	**43,754**	**24,058**	**25,254**	**7.47**	**4.97**
NORTH AMER	**48,374**	**50,485**	**40,399**	**22,255**	**23,887**	**7.06**	**7.33**
CANADA	7,578	8,590	7,068	3,747	4,154	1.23	10.86
MEXICO	1,464	1,453	1,279	990	895	0.26	-9.60
USA	39,332	40,442	32,052	17,518	18,838	5.57	7.54
SOUTH AMER	**2,501**	**2,551**	**1,799**	**610**	**866**	**0.26**	**41.97**
ARGENTINA	1,102	1,130	1,102	233	227	0.07	-2.58
BRAZIL	1,399	1,421	697	377	639	0.19	69.50
OTHER AMERIC	**2,131**	**2,072**	**1,556**	**1,193**	**501**	**0.15**	**-58.01**
OTH AMERICA	2,131	2,072	1,556	1,193	501	0.15	-58.01
EAST AS/PACI	**89,754**	**106,313**	**84,473**	**65,697**	**91,314**	**27.01**	**38.99**
N/EAST ASIA	**49,901**	**57,089**	**49,136**	**40,736**	**48,174**	**14.25**	**18.26**
CHINA	5,638	7,139	8,738	8,715	7,562	2.24	-13.23
JAPAN	38,893	41,070	28,830	23,223	27,412	8.11	18.04
KOREA REP.	5,370	8,880	11,568	8,798	13,200	3.90	50.03
S/EAST ASIA	**14,112**	**19,602**	**12,975**	**10,191**	**23,783**	**7.03**	**133.37**
INDONESIA	538	979	532	514	824	0.24	60.31
MALAYSIA	2,953	3,486	3,787	2,777	8,197	2.42	195.17
PHILIPPINES	609	685	411	388	468	0.14	20.62
SINGAPORE	5,140	5,743	2,933	1,818	3,165	0.94	74.09
THAILAND	4,872	8,709	5,312	4,694	11,129	3.29	137.09
AUSTRALASIA	**15,178**	**15,544**	**12,992**	**8,404**	**9,583**	**2.83**	**14.03**
AUSTRALIA	11,873	12,189	10,455	7,159	7,916	2.34	10.57
NEW ZEALAND	3,305	3,355	2,537	1,245	1,667	0.49	33.90
OT.EAST AS/P	**10,563**	**14,078**	**9,370**	**6,366**	**9,774**	**2.89**	**53.53**
OTHER ASIA	10,534	13,981	9,326	6,350	9,749	2.88	53.53
OTH OCEANIA	29	97	44	16	25	0.01	56.25
EUROPE	**179,048**	**174,390**	**145,273**	**99,474**	**112,346**	**33.23**	**12.94**
C/E EUROPE	**6,723**	**6,992**	**6,201**	**5,276**	**6,451**	**1.91**	**22.27**
CZECH REP	1,216	1,152	926	929	989	0.29	6.46
HUNGARY	580	634	407	338	356	0.11	5.33
POLAND	1,708	1,820	1,504	1,117	1,817	0.54	62.67
RUSSIAN FED	1,608	1,795	1,827	1,563	1,989	0.59	27.26
OTH C/E EUR	1,611	1,591	1,537	1,329	1,300	0.38	-2.18
NORTHERN EUR	**51,116**	**52,079**	**43,876**	**26,504**	**28,812**	**8.52**	**8.71**
DENMARK	4,577	4,847	3,854	2,040	2,178	0.64	6.76
FINLAND	1,412	1,460	893	714	813	0.24	13.87
IRELAND	2,313	2,435	1,400	874	1,112	0.33	27.23
NORWAY	2,195	2,212	1,768	1,043	1,365	0.40	30.87

NEPAL

1. ARRIVALS OF NON-RESIDENT TOURISTS AT NATIONAL BORDERS, BY NATIONALITY

	1999	2000	2001	2002	2003	Market share 03	% change 03-02
SWEDEN	3,767	3,360	2,428	826	1,243	0.37	50.48
UK	36,852	37,765	33,533	21,007	22,101	6.54	5.21
SOUTHERN EUR	**23,460**	**21,572**	**15,691**	**13,819**	**16,901**	**5.00**	**22.30**
GREECE (*)	1,220	1,207	1,049	495	393	0.12	-20.61
ITALY	12,870	11,491	8,745	8,057	8,243	2.44	2.31
SPAIN	9,370	8,874	5,897	5,267	8,265	2.44	56.92
WESTERN EUR	**88,370**	**83,837**	**71,042**	**46,795**	**48,027**	**14.20**	**2.63**
AUSTRIA	6,377	5,221	4,164	3,140	3,025	0.89	-3.66
BELGIUM	5,496	5,406	4,803	2,847	2,582	0.76	-9.31
FRANCE	24,490	24,506	21,187	13,376	15,865	4.69	18.61
GERMANY	26,378	26,263	21,577	15,774	14,866	4.40	-5.76
NETHERLANDS	17,198	16,211	13,662	8,306	8,443	2.50	1.65
SWITZERLAND	8,431	6,230	5,649	3,352	3,246	0.96	-3.16
EAST/MED EUR	**7,412**	**8,073**	**7,411**	**6,286**	**10,733**	**3.17**	**70.74**
ISRAEL	7,412	8,073	7,411	6,286	10,733	3.17	70.74
OTHER EUROPE	**1,967**	**1,837**	**1,052**	**794**	**1,422**	**0.42**	**79.09**
OTHER EUROPE	1,967	1,837	1,052	794	1,422	0.42	79.09
SOUTH ASIA	**167,834**	**125,787**	**86,141**	**85,107**	**107,606**	**31.82**	**26.44**
SOUTH ASIA	**167,834**	**125,787**	**86,141**	**85,107**	**107,606**	**31.82**	**26.44**
BANGLADESH	9,262	8,731	7,742	5,507	5,031	1.49	-8.64
BHUTAN	1,564	1,426	1,523	1,426	1,307	0.39	-8.35
SRI LANKA	12,432	16,649	9,844	9,805	13,930	4.12	42.07
INDIA	140,661	95,915	64,320	66,777	86,363	25.54	29.33
IRAN	233	269	179	121	49	0.01	-59.50
MALDIVES	148	177	214	230	165	0.05	-28.26
PAKISTAN	3,534	2,620	2,319	1,241	761	0.23	-38.68
REG.NOT SPEC	**5**	**8**					
NOT SPECIFIE	**5**	**8**					
OTH.WORLD	5	8					

Source: World Tourism Organization (WTO)

NEPAL

1. ARRIVALS OF NON-RESIDENT TOURISTS AT NATIONAL BORDERS, BY COUNTRY OF RESIDENCE

	1999	2000	2001	2002	2003	Market share 03	% change 03-02
TOTAL	**491,504**	**463,646**	**361,237**	**275,468**	**338,132**	**100.00**	**22.75**
AFRICA	**1,891**	**2,038**	**2,038**	**1,117**	**1,501**	**0.44**	**34.38**
OTHER AFRICA	**1,891**	**2,038**	**2,038**	**1,117**	**1,501**	**0.44**	**34.38**
ALL AFRICA	1,891	2,038	2,038	1,117	1,501	0.44	34.38
AMERICAS	**51,422**	**52,964**	**42,751**	**25,110**	**25,156**	**7.44**	**0.18**
NORTH AMER	**46,901**	**48,511**	**39,213**	**21,403**	**23,751**	**7.02**	**10.97**
CANADA	6,834	7,764	6,373	3,366	3,984	1.18	18.36
MEXICO	1,386	1,370	1,400	961	896	0.26	-6.76
USA	38,681	39,377	31,440	17,076	18,871	5.58	10.51
SOUTH AMER	**2,399**	**2,449**	**1,995**	**518**	**902**	**0.27**	**74.13**
ARGENTINA	1,039	1,068	1,297	137	280	0.08	104.38
BRAZIL	1,360	1,381	698	381	622	0.18	63.25
OTHER AMERIC	**2,122**	**2,004**	**1,543**	**3,189**	**503**	**0.15**	**-84.23**
OTH AMERICA	2,122	2,004	1,543	3,189	503	0.15	-84.23
EAST AS/PACI	**95,565**	**111,667**	**88,005**	**67,985**	**91,582**	**27.08**	**34.71**
N/EAST ASIA	**52,205**	**59,773**	**51,404**	**41,712**	**48,277**	**14.28**	**15.74**
CHINA	5,160	6,627	8,564	8,026	5,677	1.68	-29.27
HK,CHINA	3,381	3,724	2,906	2,113	1,564	0.46	-25.98
JAPAN	38,566	40,841	28,554	22,941	27,267	8.06	18.86
KOREA REP.	5,098	8,581	11,380	8,632	13,769	4.07	59.51
S/EAST ASIA	**16,637**	**21,779**	**14,221**	**11,134**	**24,094**	**7.13**	**116.40**
INDONESIA	660	1,032	543	544	557	0.16	2.39
MALAYSIA	2,835	3,310	3,734	2,762	8,191	2.42	196.56
PHILIPPINES	725	829	576	469	505	0.15	7.68
SINGAPORE	6,500	7,021	3,600	2,193	3,449	1.02	57.27
THAILAND	5,917	9,587	5,768	5,166	11,392	3.37	120.52
AUSTRALASIA	**15,036**	**15,136**	**13,119**	**8,335**	**9,519**	**2.82**	**14.21**
AUSTRALIA	11,997	12,138	10,711	7,179	7,916	2.34	10.27
NEW ZEALAND	3,039	2,998	2,408	1,156	1,603	0.47	38.67
OT.EAST AS/P	**11,687**	**14,979**	**9,261**	**6,804**	**9,692**	**2.87**	**42.45**
OTHER ASIA	11,653	14,882	9,208	6,781	9,663	2.86	42.50
OTH OCEANIA	34	97	53	23	29	0.01	26.09
EUROPE	**173,976**	**169,367**	**142,483**	**97,026**	**111,822**	**33.07**	**15.25**
C/E EUROPE	**6,504**	**6,760**	**6,684**	**5,082**	**6,418**	**1.90**	**26.29**
CZECH REP	1,197	1,123	867	893	1,016	0.30	13.77
HUNGARY	548	619	373	350	362	0.11	3.43
POLAND	1,620	1,738	1,486	1,104	1,780	0.53	61.23
RUSSIAN FED	1,583	1,770	1,745	1,531	1,958	0.58	27.89
OTH C/E EUR	1,556	1,510	2,213	1,204	1,302	0.39	8.14
NORTHERN EUR	**47,720**	**48,569**	**41,707**	**24,911**	**28,113**	**8.31**	**12.85**
DENMARK	4,447	4,721	3,642	1,913	2,165	0.64	13.17
FINLAND	1,280	1,354	763	676	790	0.23	16.86
IRELAND	1,922	2,035	1,298	839	987	0.29	17.64

NEPAL

1. ARRIVALS OF NON-RESIDENT TOURISTS AT NATIONAL BORDERS, BY COUNTRY OF RESIDENCE

	1999	2000	2001	2002	2003	Market share 03	% change 03-02
NORWAY	2,183	2,171	1,766	1,036	1,388	0.41	33.98
SWEDEN	3,607	3,208	2,341	768	1,233	0.36	60.55
UK	34,281	35,080	31,897	19,679	21,550	6.37	9.51
SOUTHERN EUR	**23,251**	**21,489**	**15,417**	**13,805**	**16,838**	**4.98**	**21.97**
GREECE (*)	1,194	1,156	1,057	506	391	0.12	-22.73
ITALY	12,656	11,384	8,503	8,002	8,201	2.43	2.49
SPAIN	9,401	8,949	5,857	5,297	8,246	2.44	55.67
WESTERN EUR	**87,286**	**82,840**	**70,181**	**46,192**	**48,165**	**14.24**	**4.27**
AUSTRIA	6,303	5,074	3,964	3,080	3,199	0.95	3.86
BELGIUM	5,513	5,427	4,824	2,825	2,581	0.76	-8.64
FRANCE	23,942	24,028	20,788	13,135	15,730	4.65	19.76
GERMANY	25,990	25,907	21,809	15,570	14,875	4.40	-4.46
NETHERLANDS	16,872	15,878	13,049	8,049	8,339	2.47	3.60
SWITZERLAND	8,666	6,526	5,747	3,533	3,441	1.02	-2.60
EAST/MED EUR	**7,335**	**7,933**	**7,343**	**6,266**	**10,921**	**3.23**	**74.29**
ISRAEL	7,335	7,933	7,343	6,266	10,921	3.23	74.29
OTHER EUROPE	**1,880**	**1,776**	**1,151**	**770**	**1,367**	**0.40**	**77.53**
OTHER EUROPE	1,880	1,776	1,151	770	1,367	0.40	77.53
SOUTH ASIA	**168,649**	**127,602**	**85,960**	**84,230**	**108,071**	**31.96**	**28.30**
SOUTH ASIA	**168,649**	**127,602**	**85,960**	**84,230**	**108,071**	**31.96**	**28.30**
BANGLADESH	10,003	9,365	8,108	5,756	5,215	1.54	-9.40
BHUTAN	1,608	1,454	1,527	1,418	1,295	0.38	-8.67
SRI LANKA	12,413	16,628	9,874	9,756	13,960	4.13	43.09
INDIA	140,672	96,995	63,722	65,743	86,578	25.60	31.69
IRAN	169	200	142	105	97	0.03	-7.62
MALDIVES	159	181	232	221	163	0.05	-26.24
PAKISTAN	3,625	2,779	2,355	1,231	763	0.23	-38.02
REG.NOT SPEC	**1**	**8**					
NOT SPECIFIE	**1**	**8**					
OTH.WORLD	1	8					

Source: World Tourism Organization (WTO)

3. ARRIVALS OF NON-RESIDENT TOURISTS IN HOTELS AND SIMILAR ESTABLISHMENTS, BY COUNTRY OF RESIDENCE

	1999	2000	2001	2002	2003	Market share 03	% change 03-02
TOTAL (*)	**7,551,000**	**7,736,000**	**7,445,000**	**7,432,800**	**6,930,500**	**100.00**	**-6.76**
AFRICA	**105,000**	**106,000**	**138,700**	**171,600**	**129,400**	**1.87**	**-24.59**
OTHER AFRICA	**105,000**	**106,000**	**138,700**	**171,600**	**129,400**	**1.87**	**-24.59**
ALL AFRICA	105,000	106,000	138,700	171,600	129,400	1.87	-24.59
AMERICAS	**1,151,000**	**1,203,000**	**1,192,400**	**1,091,600**	**988,200**	**14.26**	**-9.47**
NORTH AMER	**1,024,000**	**1,085,000**	**1,077,000**	**974,500**	**903,500**	**13.04**	**-7.29**
CANADA	96,000	96,000	92,500	95,600	87,300	1.26	-8.68
USA	928,000	989,000	984,500	878,900	816,200	11.78	-7.13
OTHER AMERIC	**127,000**	**118,000**	**115,400**	**117,100**	**84,700**	**1.22**	**-27.67**
OTH AMERICA	127,000	118,000	115,400	117,100	84,700	1.22	-27.67
EAST AS/PACI	**680,000**	**705,000**	**661,100**	**720,000**	**608,800**	**8.78**	**-15.44**
N/EAST ASIA	**202,000**	**192,000**	**180,800**	**185,100**	**136,900**	**1.98**	**-26.04**
JAPAN	202,000	192,000	180,800	185,100	136,900	1.98	-26.04
S/EAST ASIA	**28,000**	**27,000**	**23,100**	**21,800**	**10,900**	**0.16**	**-50.00**
INDONESIA	20,000	20,000	15,000	21,800	10,900	0.16	-50.00
THAILAND	8,000	7,000	8,100				
AUSTRALASIA	**94,000**	**80,000**	**83,200**	**83,000**	**64,100**	**0.92**	**-22.77**
AUSTRALIA	79,000	70,000	70,700	70,400	55,200	0.80	-21.59
NEW ZEALAND	15,000	10,000	12,500	12,600	8,900	0.13	-29.37
OT.EAST AS/P	**356,000**	**406,000**	**374,000**	**430,100**	**396,900**	**5.73**	**-7.72**
OTHER ASIA	326,000	369,000	352,900	411,400	377,400	5.45	-8.26
OTH OCEANIA	30,000	37,000	21,100	18,700	19,500	0.28	4.28
EUROPE	**5,615,000**	**5,722,000**	**5,452,800**	**5,449,600**	**5,204,100**	**75.09**	**-4.50**
C/E EUROPE	**147,000**	**138,000**	**146,100**	**135,100**	**133,200**	**1.92**	**-1.41**
CZECH REP	28,000	24,000	21,900	23,100	20,800	0.30	-9.96
HUNGARY	16,000	16,000	16,200	17,100	15,200	0.22	-11.11
POLAND	50,000	47,000	46,900	41,100	41,800	0.60	1.70
RUSSIAN FED	44,000	41,000	53,800	45,300	48,600	0.70	7.28
SLOVAKIA	9,000	10,000	7,300	8,500	6,800	0.10	-20.00
NORTHERN EUR	**2,017,000**	**2,152,000**	**2,223,300**	**2,136,800**	**1,935,800**	**27.93**	**-9.41**
DENMARK	88,000	97,000	83,400	85,100	93,800	1.35	10.22
FINLAND	36,000	41,000	37,800	41,700	40,500	0.58	-2.88
ICELAND	9,000	5,000	5,300	4,400	5,000	0.07	13.64
IRELAND	65,000	73,000	76,500	91,600	86,700	1.25	-5.35
NORWAY	68,000	84,000	73,900	66,600	62,300	0.90	-6.46
SWEDEN	125,000	127,000	111,700	103,800	92,800	1.34	-10.60
UK	1,626,000	1,725,000	1,834,700	1,743,600	1,554,700	22.43	-10.83
SOUTHERN EUR	**552,000**	**567,000**	**550,600**	**583,700**	**576,000**	**8.31**	**-1.32**
GREECE	23,000	29,000	27,800	28,100	26,200	0.38	-6.76
ITALY	285,000	286,000	270,400	277,100	276,900	4.00	-0.07
PORTUGAL	36,000	38,000	31,300	36,600	33,400	0.48	-8.74
SPAIN	208,000	214,000	221,100	241,900	239,500	3.46	-0.99

NETHERLANDS

3. ARRIVALS OF NON-RESIDENT TOURISTS IN HOTELS AND SIMILAR ESTABLISHMENTS, BY COUNTRY OF RESIDENCE

	1999	2000	2001	2002	2003	Market share 03	% change 03-02
WESTERN EUR	**2,360,000**	**2,382,000**	**2,196,100**	**2,335,300**	**2,297,500**	**33.15**	**-1.62**
AUSTRIA	54,000	53,000	53,000	56,500	50,400	0.73	-10.80
BELGIUM	401,000	416,000	413,700	441,200	465,000	6.71	5.39
FRANCE	417,000	437,000	399,200	448,800	389,900	5.63	-13.12
GERMANY	1,328,000	1,325,000	1,198,200	1,247,000	1,259,800	18.18	1.03
LUXEMBOURG	21,000	23,000	21,400	34,900	32,200	0.46	-7.74
SWITZERLAND	139,000	128,000	110,600	106,900	100,200	1.45	-6.27
EAST/MED EUR	**20,000**	**25,000**	**19,300**	**19,700**	**22,300**	**0.32**	**13.20**
TURKEY	20,000	25,000	19,300	19,700	22,300	0.32	13.20
OTHER EUROPE	**519,000**	**458,000**	**317,400**	**239,000**	**239,300**	**3.45**	**0.13**
OTHER EUROPE	519,000	458,000	317,400	239,000	239,300	3.45	0.13

Source: World Tourism Organization (WTO)

NETHERLANDS

4. ARRIVALS OF NON-RESIDENT TOURISTS IN ALL TYPES OF ACCOMMODATION ESTABLISHMENTS, BY COUNTRY OF RESIDENCE

	1999	2000	2001	2002	2003	Market share 03	% change 03-02
TOTAL	**9,874,000**	**10,003,000**	**9,499,900**	**9,595,300**	**9,180,700**	**100.00**	**-4.32**
AFRICA	**107,000**	**108,000**	**140,500**	**172,800**	**130,600**	**1.42**	**-24.42**
OTHER AFRICA	**107,000**	**108,000**	**140,500**	**172,800**	**130,600**	**1.42**	**-24.42**
ALL AFRICA	107,000	108,000	140,500	172,800	130,600	1.42	-24.42
AMERICAS	**1,162,000**	**1,216,000**	**1,202,900**	**1,099,700**	**996,100**	**10.85**	**-9.42**
OTHER AMERIC	**1,162,000**	**1,216,000**	**1,202,900**	**1,099,700**	**996,100**	**10.85**	**-9.42**
ALL AMERICAS	1,162,000	1,216,000	1,202,900	1,099,700	996,100	10.85	-9.42
EAST AS/PACI	**700,000**	**723,000**	**677,600**	**731,200**	**622,100**	**6.78**	**-14.92**
OT.EAST AS/P	**700,000**	**723,000**	**677,600**	**731,200**	**622,100**	**6.78**	**-14.92**
ALL ASIA	562,000	595,000	563,500	624,400	530,600	5.78	-15.02
ALL OCEANIA	138,000	128,000	114,100	106,800	91,500	1.00	-14.33
EUROPE	**7,905,000**	**7,956,000**	**7,478,900**	**7,591,600**	**7,431,900**	**80.95**	**-2.10**
NORTHERN EUR	**1,834,000**	**1,957,000**	**2,043,700**	**2,065,400**	**1,867,800**	**20.34**	**-9.57**
DENMARK	108,000	119,000	104,500	102,600	116,000	1.26	13.06
SWEDEN				111,600	105,800	1.15	-5.20
UK	1,726,000	1,838,000	1,939,200	1,851,200	1,646,000	17.93	-11.08
SOUTHERN EUR	**579,000**	**624,000**	**601,200**	**621,500**	**613,600**	**6.68**	**-1.27**
ITALY	350,000	374,000	342,600	345,700	338,900	3.69	-1.97
SPAIN	229,000	250,000	258,600	275,800	274,700	2.99	-0.40
WESTERN EUR	**4,318,000**	**4,217,000**	**3,862,500**	**4,097,900**	**4,162,300**	**45.34**	**1.57**
BELGIUM	647,000	677,000	628,800	704,800	779,300	8.49	10.57
FRANCE	472,000	512,000	455,400	511,200	465,300	5.07	-8.98
GERMANY	3,046,000	2,884,000	2,656,800	2,754,500	2,803,000	30.53	1.76
SWITZERLAND	153,000	144,000	121,500	127,400	114,700	1.25	-9.97
OTHER EUROPE	**1,174,000**	**1,158,000**	**971,500**	**806,800**	**788,200**	**8.59**	**-2.31**
OTHER EUROPE	1,174,000	1,158,000	971,500	806,800	788,200	8.59	-2.31

Source: World Tourism Organization (WTO)

NETHERLANDS

5. OVERNIGHT STAYS OF NON-RESIDENT TOURISTS IN HOTELS AND SIMILAR ESTABLISHMENTS, BY COUNTRY OF RESIDENCE

	1999	2000	2001	2002	2003	Market share 03	% change 03-02
TOTAL (*)	**15,218,000**	**15,695,000**	**14,954,800**	**14,921,600**	**13,798,300**	**100.00**	**-7.53**
AFRICA	**242,000**	**242,000**	**287,600**	**358,400**	**268,400**	**1.95**	**-25.11**
OTHER AFRICA	**242,000**	**242,000**	**287,600**	**358,400**	**268,400**	**1.95**	**-25.11**
ALL AFRICA	242,000	242,000	287,600	358,400	268,400	1.95	-25.11
AMERICAS	**2,358,000**	**2,401,000**	**2,372,600**	**2,127,700**	**1,892,900**	**13.72**	**-11.04**
NORTH AMER	**2,088,000**	**2,157,000**	**2,133,300**	**1,895,300**	**1,713,400**	**12.42**	**-9.60**
CANADA	192,000	193,000	191,400	195,700	173,900	1.26	-11.14
USA	1,896,000	1,964,000	1,941,900	1,699,600	1,539,500	11.16	-9.42
OTHER AMERIC	**270,000**	**244,000**	**239,300**	**232,400**	**179,500**	**1.30**	**-22.76**
OTH AMERICA	270,000	244,000	239,300	232,400	179,500	1.30	-22.76
EAST AS/PACI	**1,307,000**	**1,364,000**	**1,248,100**	**1,354,800**	**1,144,700**	**8.30**	**-15.51**
N/EAST ASIA	**379,000**	**365,000**	**338,300**	**340,500**	**257,700**	**1.87**	**-24.32**
JAPAN	379,000	365,000	338,300	340,500	257,700	1.87	-24.32
S/EAST ASIA	**60,000**	**53,000**	**48,900**	**28,000**	**24,300**	**0.18**	**-13.21**
INDONESIA	42,000	39,000	33,600	28,000	24,300	0.18	-13.21
THAILAND	18,000	14,000	15,300				
AUSTRALASIA	**184,000**	**162,000**	**161,500**	**157,800**	**129,900**	**0.94**	**-17.68**
AUSTRALIA	155,000	142,000	137,300	135,200	112,700	0.82	-16.64
NEW ZEALAND	29,000	20,000	24,200	22,600	17,200	0.12	-23.89
OT.EAST AS/P	**684,000**	**784,000**	**699,400**	**828,500**	**732,800**	**5.31**	**-11.55**
OTHER ASIA	628,000	712,000	664,300	792,100	701,100	5.08	-11.49
OTH OCEANIA	56,000	72,000	35,100	36,400	31,700	0.23	-12.91
EUROPE	**11,311,000**	**11,688,000**	**11,046,500**	**11,080,700**	**10,492,300**	**76.04**	**-5.31**
C/E EUROPE	**303,000**	**312,000**	**322,700**	**306,300**	**279,000**	**2.02**	**-8.91**
CZECH REP	55,000	54,000	47,500	52,500	43,400	0.31	-17.33
HUNGARY	35,000	38,000	34,100	35,900	32,300	0.23	-10.03
POLAND	97,000	106,000	108,000	99,800	89,700	0.65	-10.12
RUSSIAN FED	97,000	89,000	113,600	98,700	100,100	0.73	1.42
SLOVAKIA	19,000	25,000	19,500	19,400	13,500	0.10	-30.41
NORTHERN EUR	**4,007,000**	**4,299,000**	**4,426,100**	**4,274,200**	**3,733,100**	**27.05**	**-12.66**
DENMARK	169,000	200,000	155,000	166,700	178,100	1.29	6.84
FINLAND	73,000	80,000	76,500	81,900	74,700	0.54	-8.79
ICELAND	17,000	11,000	11,000	9,600	10,900	0.08	13.54
IRELAND	143,000	157,000	171,500	197,000	173,900	1.26	-11.73
NORWAY	128,000	161,000	140,600	130,800	118,600	0.86	-9.33
SWEDEN	236,000	243,000	215,900	199,000	178,600	1.29	-10.25
UK	3,241,000	3,447,000	3,655,600	3,489,200	2,998,300	21.73	-14.07
SOUTHERN EUR	**1,182,000**	**1,210,000**	**1,186,000**	**1,231,900**	**1,218,000**	**8.83**	**-1.13**
GREECE	54,000	67,000	69,300	61,500	56,000	0.41	-8.94
ITALY	603,000	606,000	581,000	591,400	589,200	4.27	-0.37
PORTUGAL	94,000	94,000	72,200	77,800	66,800	0.48	-14.14
SPAIN	431,000	443,000	463,500	501,200	506,000	3.67	0.96

NETHERLANDS

5. OVERNIGHT STAYS OF NON-RESIDENT TOURISTS IN HOTELS AND SIMILAR ESTABLISHMENTS, BY COUNTRY OF RESIDENCE

	1999	2000	2001	2002	2003	Market share 03	% change 03-02
WESTERN EUR	**4,758,000**	**4,905,000**	**4,461,300**	**4,755,400**	**4,735,800**	**34.32**	**-0.41**
AUSTRIA	111,000	110,000	111,900	112,300	102,400	0.74	-8.82
BELGIUM	713,000	741,000	714,600	767,100	819,600	5.94	6.84
FRANCE	759,000	788,000	718,000	793,200	698,600	5.06	-11.93
GERMANY	2,863,000	2,960,000	2,660,800	2,802,200	2,843,700	20.61	1.48
LUXEMBOURG	41,000	49,000	43,400	66,800	71,900	0.52	7.63
SWITZERLAND	271,000	257,000	212,600	213,800	199,600	1.45	-6.64
EAST/MED EUR	**42,000**	**52,000**	**41,400**	**40,600**	**46,000**	**0.33**	**13.30**
TURKEY	42,000	52,000	41,400	40,600	46,000	0.33	13.30
OTHER EUROPE	**1,019,000**	**910,000**	**609,000**	**472,300**	**480,400**	**3.48**	**1.72**
OTHER EUROPE	1,019,000	910,000	609,000	472,300	480,400	3.48	·1.72

Source: World Tourism Organization (WTO)

6. OVERNIGHT STAYS OF NON-RESIDENT TOURISTS IN ALL TYPES OF ACCOMMODATION ESTABLISHMENTS, BY COUNTRY OF RESIDENCE

		1999	2000	2001	2002	2003	Market share 03	% change 03-02
TOTAL	(*)	**27,433,000**	**27,261,000**	**25,501,700**	**26,367,700**	**25,341,400**	**100.00**	**-3.89**
AFRICA		**262,000**	**251,000**	**296,800**	**367,900**	**273,800**	**1.08**	**-25.58**
OTHER AFRICA		**262,000**	**251,000**	**296,800**	**367,900**	**273,800**	**1.08**	**-25.58**
ALL AFRICA		262,000	251,000	296,800	367,900	273,800	1.08	-25.58
AMERICAS		**2,427,000**	**2,453,000**	**2,418,000**	**2,167,500**	**1,937,000**	**7.64**	**-10.63**
OTHER AMERIC		**2,427,000**	**2,453,000**	**2,418,000**	**2,167,500**	**1,937,000**	**7.64**	**-10.63**
ALL AMERICAS		2,427,000	2,453,000	2,418,000	2,167,500	1,937,000	7.64	-10.63
EAST AS/PACI		**1,397,000**	**1,434,000**	**1,314,200**	**1,405,300**	**1,206,900**	**4.76**	**-14.12**
OT.EAST AS/P		**1,397,000**	**1,434,000**	**1,314,200**	**1,405,300**	**1,206,900**	**4.76**	**-14.12**
ALL ASIA		1,115,000	1,166,000	1,087,900	1,196,600	1,017,300	4.01	-14.98
ALL OCEANIA		282,000	268,000	226,300	208,700	189,600	0.75	-9.15
EUROPE		**23,347,000**	**23,123,000**	**21,472,700**	**22,427,000**	**21,923,700**	**86.51**	**-2.24**
NORTHERN EUR		**3,983,000**	**4,253,000**	**4,403,500**	**4,464,900**	**3,974,500**	**15.68**	**-10.98**
DENMARK		239,000	271,000	235,100	226,100	265,500	1.05	17.43
SWEDEN					222,600	224,600	0.89	0.90
UK		3,744,000	3,982,000	4,168,400	4,016,200	3,484,400	13.75	-13.24
SOUTHERN EUR		**1,265,000**	**1,370,000**	**1,349,800**	**1,382,400**	**1,416,100**	**5.59**	**2.44**
ITALY		758,000	809,000	767,700	775,400	786,200	3.10	1.39
SPAIN		507,000	561,000	582,100	607,000	629,900	2.49	3.77
WESTERN EUR		**15,587,000**	**14,948,000**	**13,540,700**	**14,708,600**	**14,706,800**	**58.03**	**-0.01**
BELGIUM		1,772,000	1,882,000	1,683,600	1,941,400	2,137,000	8.43	10.08
FRANCE		942,000	1,030,000	892,600	997,900	954,900	3.77	-4.31
GERMANY		12,538,000	11,716,000	10,706,900	11,481,500	11,350,300	44.79	-1.14
SWITZERLAND		335,000	320,000	257,600	287,800	264,600	1.04	-8.06
OTHER EUROPE		**2,512,000**	**2,552,000**	**2,178,700**	**1,871,100**	**1,826,300**	**7.21**	**-2.39**
OTHER EUROPE		2,512,000	2,552,000	2,178,700	1,871,100	1,826,300	7.21	-2.39

Source: World Tourism Organization (WTO)

NEW CALEDONIA

1. ARRIVALS OF NON-RESIDENT TOURISTS AT NATIONAL BORDERS, BY NATIONALITY

	1999	2000	2001	2002	2003	Market share 03	% change 03-02
TOTAL	**99,735**	**109,587**	**100,515**	**103,933**	**101,983**	**100.00**	**-1.88**
AFRICA	**270**	**208**	**188**	**137**	**132**	**0.13**	**-3.65**
SOUTHERN AFR	**93**						
SOUTH AFRICA	93						
OTHER AFRICA	**177**	**208**	**188**	**137**	**132**	**0.13**	**-3.65**
OTHER AFRICA	177						
ALL AFRICA		208	188	137	132	0.13	-3.65
AMERICAS	**2,115**	**2,660**	**1,916**	**2,304**	**2,008**	**1.97**	**-12.85**
NORTH AMER	**1,940**	**2,465**	**1,785**	**2,114**	**1,735**	**1.70**	**-17.93**
CANADA	397	540	570	741	541	0.53	-26.99
USA	1,543	1,925	1,215	1,373	1,194	1.17	-13.04
SOUTH AMER	**50**	**20**	**13**	**17**	**12**	**0.01**	**-29.41**
ARGENTINA	50	20	13	17	12	0.01	-29.41
OTHER AMERIC	**125**	**175**	**118**	**173**	**261**	**0.26**	**50.87**
OTH AMERICA	125	175	118	173	261	0.26	50.87
EAST AS/PACI	**52,757**	**59,014**	**55,234**	**52,906**	**52,125**	**51.11**	**-1.48**
N/EAST ASIA	**31,041**	**31,120**	**28,209**	**27,439**	**28,768**	**28.21**	**4.84**
TAIWAN(P.C.)	24	18	71	24	10	0.01	-58.33
HK,CHINA	7	4	7	1	10	0.01	900.00
JAPAN	31,010	30,970	27,951	27,234	28,560	28.00	4.87
KOREA REP.		128	180	180	188	0.18	4.44
AUSTRALASIA	**19,263**	**24,642**	**24,193**	**22,364**	**20,499**	**20.10**	**-8.34**
AUSTRALIA	12,797	15,839	16,686	16,683	14,667	14.38	-12.08
NEW ZEALAND	6,466	8,803	7,507	5,681	5,832	5.72	2.66
MELANESIA	**1,121**	**1,463**	**1,345**	**1,567**	**1,614**	**1.58**	**3.00**
VANUATU	1,121	1,463	1,345	1,567	1,614	1.58	3.00
OT.EAST AS/P	**1,332**	**1,789**	**1,487**	**1,536**	**1,244**	**1.22**	**-19.01**
OTHER ASIA	866	731	834	1,017	842	0.83	-17.21
OTH OCEANIA	466	1,058	653	519	402	0.39	-22.54
EUROPE	**44,525**	**47,597**	**43,069**	**48,527**	**47,616**	**46.69**	**-1.88**
NORTHERN EUR	**1,148**	**1,310**	**1,355**	**1,501**	**1,204**	**1.18**	**-19.79**
UK	1,148	1,310	1,355	1,501	1,204	1.18	-19.79
SOUTHERN EUR	**533**	**571**	**654**	**563**	**538**	**0.53**	**-4.44**
ITALY	533	571	654	563	538	0.53	-4.44
WESTERN EUR	**41,591**	**44,209**	**39,985**	**45,189**	**44,433**	**43.57**	**-1.67**
FRANCE	40,632	43,158	39,146	44,481	43,384	42.54	-2.47
GERMANY	503	597	469	320	545	0.53	70.31
SWITZERLAND	456	454	370	388	504	0.49	29.90
OTHER EUROPE	**1,253**	**1,507**	**1,075**	**1,274**	**1,441**	**1.41**	**13.11**
OTHER EUROPE	1,253	1,507	1,075	1,274	1,441	1.41	13.11

NEW CALEDONIA

1. ARRIVALS OF NON-RESIDENT TOURISTS AT NATIONAL BORDERS, BY NATIONALITY

	1999	2000	2001	2002	2003	Market share 03	% change 03-02
REG.NOT SPEC	**68**	**108**	**108**	**59**	**102**	**0.10**	**72.88**
NOT SPECIFIE	**68**	**108**	**108**	**59**	**102**	**0.10**	**72.88**
OTH.WORLD	68	108	108	59	102	0.10	72.88

Source: World Tourism Organization (WTO)

NEW CALEDONIA

1. ARRIVALS OF NON-RESIDENT TOURISTS AT NATIONAL BORDERS, BY COUNTRY OF RESIDENCE

		1999	2000	2001	2002	2003	Market share 03	% change 03-02
TOTAL	(*)	**99,735**	**109,587**	**100,515**	**103,933**	**101,983**	**100.00**	**-1.88**
AFRICA		**597**	**583**	**592**	**520**	**489**	**0.48**	**-5.96**
EAST AFRICA		**348**	**367**	**392**	**363**	**343**	**0.34**	**-5.51**
REUNION	(*)	348	367	392	363	343	0.34	-5.51
OTHER AFRICA		**249**	**216**	**200**	**157**	**146**	**0.14**	**-7.01**
OTHER AFRICA		249	216	200	157	146	0.14	-7.01
AMERICAS		**1,738**	**2,523**	**1,870**	**2,141**	**1,753**	**1.72**	**-18.12**
CARIBBEAN		**188**	**168**	**191**	**226**	**152**	**0.15**	**-32.74**
ALL CO CARIB	(*)	188	168	191	226	152	0.15	-32.74
NORTH AMER		**1,403**	**2,175**	**1,538**	**1,724**	**1,381**	**1.35**	**-19.90**
CANADA		337	453	424	522	387	0.38	-25.86
ST.PIERRE,MQ		2						
USA		1,064	1,722	1,114	1,202	994	0.97	-17.30
SOUTH AMER		**49**	**27**	**15**	**20**	**15**	**0.01**	**-25.00**
ARGENTINA		49	27	15	20	15	0.01	-25.00
OTHER AMERIC		**98**	**153**	**126**	**171**	**205**	**0.20**	**19.88**
OTH AMERICA		98	153	126	171	205	0.20	19.88
EAST AS/PACI		**64,749**	**72,129**	**69,980**	**67,998**	**65,382**	**64.11**	**-3.85**
N/EAST ASIA		**31,160**	**31,169**	**28,197**	**27,354**	**28,644**	**28.09**	**4.72**
TAIWAN(P.C.)		35	17	73	42	8	0.01	-80.95
HK,CHINA		70	44	80	59	57	0.06	-3.39
JAPAN		31,017	31,051	27,954	27,202	28,490	27.94	4.73
KOREA REP.		38	57	90	51	89	0.09	74.51
AUSTRALASIA		**21,657**	**27,588**	**27,249**	**25,151**	**21,987**	**21.56**	**-12.58**
AUSTRALIA		14,567	18,012	19,200	19,216	15,957	15.65	-16.96
NEW ZEALAND		7,090	9,576	8,049	5,935	6,030	5.91	1.60
MELANESIA		**2,480**	**2,606**	**2,492**	**2,538**	**2,373**	**2.33**	**-6.50**
VANUATU		2,480	2,606	2,492	2,538	2,373	2.33	-6.50
POLYNESIA		**7,488**	**8,096**	**10,422**	**11,265**	**11,009**	**10.79**	**-2.27**
FR.POLYNESIA		3,267	3,676	3,840	3,706	3,866	3.79	4.32
WALLIS FUT.I		4,221	4,420	6,582	7,559	7,143	7.00	-5.50
OT.EAST AS/P		**1,964**	**2,670**	**1,620**	**1,690**	**1,369**	**1.34**	**-18.99**
OTHER ASIA		914	945	824	1,081	851	0.83	-21.28
OTH OCEANIA		1,050	1,725	796	609	518	0.51	-14.94
EUROPE		**32,111**	**33,651**	**27,652**	**32,683**	**32,492**	**31.86**	**-0.58**
NORTHERN EUR		**374**	**527**	**376**	**551**	**473**	**0.46**	**-14.16**
UK		374	527	376	551	473	0.46	-14.16
SOUTHERN EUR		**456**	**473**	**562**	**461**	**486**	**0.48**	**5.42**
ITALY		456	473	562	461	486	0.48	5.42
WESTERN EUR		**30,322**	**31,554**	**25,955**	**30,677**	**30,398**	**29.81**	**-0.91**

NEW CALEDONIA

1. ARRIVALS OF NON-RESIDENT TOURISTS AT NATIONAL BORDERS, BY COUNTRY OF RESIDENCE

	1999	2000	2001	2002	2003	Market share 03	% change 03-02
FRANCE	29,500	30,702	25,202	29,964	29,440	28.87	-1.75
GERMANY	369	408	363	318	453	0.44	42.45
SWITZERLAND	453	444	390	395	505	0.50	27.85
OTHER EUROPE	**959**	**1,097**	**759**	**994**	**1,135**	**1.11**	**14.19**
OTHER EUROPE	959	1,097	759	994	1,135	1.11	14.19
REG.NOT SPEC	**540**	**701**	**421**	**591**	**1,867**	**1.83**	**215.91**
NOT SPECIFIE	**540**	**701**	**421**	**591**	**1,867**	**1.83**	**215.91**
OTH.WORLD	540	701	421	591	1,867	1.83	215.91

Source: World Tourism Organization (WTO)

NEW CALEDONIA

5. OVERNIGHT STAYS OF NON-RESIDENT TOURISTS IN HOTELS AND SIMILAR ESTABLISHMENTS, BY COUNTRY OF RESIDENCE

	1999	2000	2001	2002	2003	Market share 03	% change 03-02
TOTAL (*)	**349,995**	**371,904**	**399,668**	**351,765**	**343,490**	**100.00**	**-2.35**
EAST AS/PACI	**229,995**	**248,701**	**276,813**	**223,328**	**199,026**	**57.94**	**-10.88**
N/EAST ASIA	**115,870**	**113,421**	**123,594**	**109,490**	**99,072**	**28.84**	**-9.52**
JAPAN	115,870	113,421	123,594	109,490	99,072	28.84	-9.52
AUSTRALASIA	**114,125**	**135,280**	**153,219**	**113,838**	**99,954**	**29.10**	**-12.20**
AUSTRALIA	76,417	88,613	112,273	93,744	79,590	23.17	-15.10
NEW ZEALAND	37,708	46,667	40,946	20,094	20,364	5.93	1.34
EUROPE	**93,842**	**95,129**	**94,428**	**100,296**	**117,642**	**34.25**	**17.29**
WESTERN EUR	**93,842**	**95,129**	**94,428**	**100,296**	**117,642**	**34.25**	**17.29**
FRANCE	93,842	95,129	94,428	100,296	117,642	34.25	17.29
REG.NOT SPEC	**26,158**	**28,074**	**28,427**	**28,141**	**26,822**	**7.81**	**-4.69**
NOT SPECIFIE	**26,158**	**28,074**	**28,427**	**28,141**	**26,822**	**7.81**	**-4.69**
OTH.WORLD	26,158	28,074	28,427	28,141	26,822	7.81	-4.69

Source: World Tourism Organization (WTO)

NEW ZEALAND

2. ARRIVALS OF NON-RESIDENT VISITORS AT NATIONAL BORDERS, BY COUNTRY OF RESIDENCE

		1999	2000	2001	2002	2003	Market share 03	% change 03-02
TOTAL	(*)	**1,607,241**	**1,786,765**	**1,909,381**	**2,045,064**	**2,104,420**	**100.00**	**2.90**
AFRICA		**17,233**	**19,268**	**21,331**	**20,679**	**19,395**	**0.92**	**-6.21**
EAST AFRICA		**1,503**	**2,317**	**3,268**	**3,970**	**2,876**	**0.14**	**-27.56**
BURUNDI		13						
ETHIOPIA		86	15	15	55	47		-14.55
ERITREA			15	34	35			
DJIBOUTI				15				
KENYA		248	193	259	267	243	0.01	-8.99
MADAGASCAR				13	13			
MALAWI		97	32	66	51	49		-3.92
MAURITIUS		84	125	111	152	176	0.01	15.79
MOZAMBIQUE		29	17	69	56			
REUNION		64	99	34	161	173	0.01	7.45
RWANDA		13			18			
SEYCHELLES		41		49		35		
SOMALIA			15	32	36			
ZIMBABWE		574	1,521	2,231	2,808	1,789	0.09	-36.29
UGANDA		23	45	49	55			
TANZANIA		91	117	148	91	204	0.01	124.18
ZAMBIA		140	123	143	172	160	0.01	-6.98
CENTRAL AFR		**96**	**106**	**79**	**104**	**81**		**-22.12**
ANGOLA		66	43	34	53	81		52.83
CAMEROON		14	15	32				
CHAD					18			
CONGO			32		18			
DEM.R.CONGO				13	15			
EQ.GUINEA			16					
GABON		16						
NORTH AFRICA		**125**	**63**	**34**	**137**	**31**		**-77.37**
ALGERIA			15		69			
MOROCCO		30	15	17				
WESTN.SAHARA		43			14			
SUDAN			16	17	36			
TUNISIA		52	17		18	31		72.22
SOUTHERN AFR		**15,176**	**16,537**	**17,652**	**16,185**	**16,190**	**0.77**	**0.03**
BOTSWANA		113	135	211	219	246	0.01	12.33
LESOTHO		27	46	15	13	34		161.54
NAMIBIA		124	125	184	110	92		-16.36
SOUTH AFRICA		14,896	16,200	17,229	15,790	15,818	0.75	0.18
SWAZILAND		16	31	13	53			
WEST AFRICA		**333**	**245**	**298**	**283**	**217**	**0.01**	**-23.32**
CAPE VERDE			15					
BENIN		13	12					
GHANA		110	110	129	66			
GUINEA			15					
COTE IVOIRE		16			33			
MALI		28		17	33			
NIGER			14	15				
NIGERIA		111	79	107	118	217	0.01	83.90
ST.HELENA					15			
SENEGAL		13		13				

NEW ZEALAND

2. ARRIVALS OF NON-RESIDENT VISITORS AT NATIONAL BORDERS, BY COUNTRY OF RESIDENCE

	1999	2000	2001	2002	2003	Market share 03	% change 03-02
SIERRA LEONE			17	18			
BURKINA FASO	42						
AMERICAS	**228,654**	**245,000**	**240,296**	**261,273**	**266,245**	**12.65**	**1.90**
CARIBBEAN	**1,068**	**1,247**	**940**	**1,349**	**908**	**0.04**	**-32.69**
ANTIGUA,BARB	30	11	20	73			
BAHAMAS	92	130	143	84	122	0.01	45.24
BARBADOS	83	47	34	78			
BERMUDA	266	385	281	304	289	0.01	-4.93
BR.VIRGIN IS	24	71	32	55			
CAYMAN IS	149	80	139	183	289	0.01	57.92
CUBA				74			
DOMINICA		16					
DOMINICAN RP	72	138	17	70	19		-72.86
GUADELOUPE				13			
HAITI				17			
JAMAICA	185	91	49	86	90		4.65
MARTINIQUE			30				
NETH.ANTILES	14	15		20			
ARUBA	14		17				
PUERTO RICO	41	130	43	142			
ST.KITTS NEV			17				
ST.LUCIA				33			
ST.VINCENT,G				13			
TRINIDAD TBG	82	104	118	72	99		37.50
TURKS,CAICOS	16			17			
US.VIRGIN IS		29		15			
CENTRAL AMER	**386**	**436**	**293**	**352**	**206**	**0.01**	**-41.48**
BELIZE	29	15	15				
COSTA RICA	175	152	101	73	69		-5.48
EL SALVADOR	23	32	17				
GUATEMALA	50	92	94	138	100		-27.54
HONDURAS		73	34	53			
NICARAGUA	27	15		17			
PANAMA	82	57	32	71	37		-47.89
NORTH AMER	**216,029**	**230,848**	**226,095**	**248,013**	**254,284**	**12.08**	**2.53**
CANADA	33,296	32,971	36,694	39,669	39,940	1.90	0.68
GREENLAND	42	30		20	23		15.00
MEXICO	1,810	2,066	2,020	3,035	2,697	0.13	-11.14
USA	180,881	195,781	187,381	205,289	211,624	10.06	3.09
SOUTH AMER	**11,171**	**12,469**	**12,968**	**11,559**	**10,847**	**0.52**	**-6.16**
ARGENTINA	5,001	5,271	4,680	2,603	2,252	0.11	-13.48
BOLIVIA	97	56	30	66	43		-34.85
BRAZIL	3,484	4,632	5,664	5,735	5,325	0.25	-7.15
CHILE	1,016	1,078	1,123	1,438	1,765	0.08	22.74
COLOMBIA	587	449	424	510	442	0.02	-13.33
ECUADOR	110	61	133	131	83		-36.64
FALKLAND IS	36	45		63	104		65.08
FR.GUIANA		16					
GUYANA			17				
PARAGUAY	85	86	88	126	129	0.01	2.38
PERU	222	236	171	273	228	0.01	-16.48
SURINAME			17				

NEW ZEALAND

2. ARRIVALS OF NON-RESIDENT VISITORS AT NATIONAL BORDERS, BY COUNTRY OF RESIDENCE

	1999	2000	2001	2002	2003	Market share 03	% change 03-02
URUGUAY	285	287	345	312	317	0.02	1.60
VENEZUELA	248	252	276	302	159	0.01	-47.35
EAST AS/PACI	**958,462**	**1,068,991**	**1,158,944**	**1,240,381**	**1,271,657**	**60.43**	**2.52**
N/EAST ASIA	**284,564**	**322,794**	**356,540**	**427,742**	**381,169**	**18.11**	**-10.89**
CHINA	23,241	33,502	53,174	76,534	65,989	3.14	-13.78
TAIWAN(P.C.)	40,228	40,848	36,188	38,358	25,008	1.19	-34.80
HK,CHINA	29,694	29,942	30,439	28,873	26,347	1.25	-8.75
JAPAN	147,345	151,373	149,085	173,567	150,851	7.17	-13.09
KOREA D P RP	249	93	15	17	19		11.76
KOREA REP.	43,234	66,581	87,167	109,936	112,658	5.35	2.48
MACAU, CHINA	518	382	356	331	297	0.01	-10.27
MONGOLIA	55	73	116	126			
S/EAST ASIA	**88,647**	**99,640**	**91,990**	**97,349**	**91,077**	**4.33**	**-6.44**
BRUNEI DARSM	1,401	872	938	882	1,228	0.06	39.23
MYANMAR	131	106	135	95	159	0.01	67.37
CAMBODIA	387	406	447	441	359	0.02	-18.59
INDONESIA	6,207	9,047	9,654	8,248	8,557	0.41	3.75
LAO P.DEM.R.	123	168	144	103	135	0.01	31.07
MALAYSIA	17,174	20,531	21,074	22,195	23,002	1.09	3.64
PHILIPPINES	5,148	5,066	4,788	5,150	4,825	0.23	-6.31
TIMOR-LESTE	32	122	173	206			
SINGAPORE	33,903	35,725	32,808	34,019	32,603	1.55	-4.16
VIET NAM	895	904	1,015	1,178	1,458	0.07	23.77
THAILAND	23,246	26,693	20,814	24,832	18,751	0.89	-24.49
AUSTRALASIA	**523,428**	**573,862**	**630,549**	**632,470**	**702,162**	**33.37**	**11.02**
AUSTRALIA	523,428	573,862	630,549	632,470	702,162	33.37	11.02
MELANESIA	**25,181**	**26,119**	**28,851**	**29,475**	**29,897**	**1.42**	**1.43**
SOLOMON IS	560	720	520	408	408	0.02	
FIJI	14,234	13,656	16,386	15,633	15,999	0.76	2.34
NEW CALEDNIA	6,171	7,282	7,401	8,584	9,254	0.44	7.81
VANUATU	1,186	1,471	1,573	1,586	1,433	0.07	-9.65
NORFOLK IS	693	944	1,020	1,125	947	0.05	-15.82
PAPUA N.GUIN	2,337	2,046	1,951	2,139	1,856	0.09	-13.23
MICRONESIA	**824**	**1,235**	**974**	**1,158**	**935**	**0.04**	**-19.26**
KIRIBATI	329	544	597	660	576	0.03	-12.73
GUAM	200	203	109	199	154	0.01	-22.61
NAURU	179	294	129	136	91		-33.09
N.MARIANA IS	16	12	32	35			
MICRONESIA	11	59	47	70			
MARSHALL IS	63	85	60	37	114	0.01	208.11
PALAU	26	38		21			
POLYNESIA	**35,818**	**45,341**	**50,040**	**52,187**	**54,162**	**2.57**	**3.78**
AMER SAMOA	1,141	1,260	1,202	1,463	1,599	0.08	9.30
COOK IS	5,950	6,641	7,309	7,972	8,163	0.39	2.40
FR.POLYNESIA	8,102	11,792	15,799	17,046	17,436	0.83	2.29
NIUE	958	1,389	1,048	892	1,097	0.05	22.98
PITCAIRN	26	14	30	36			
TOKELAU	104	166	155	176	195	0.01	10.80
TONGA	7,326	8,515	9,507	9,854	10,131	0.48	2.81
TUVALU	407	613	600	719	594	0.03	-17.39
WALLIS FUT.I	65	124	132	152			

NEW ZEALAND

2. ARRIVALS OF NON-RESIDENT VISITORS AT NATIONAL BORDERS, BY COUNTRY OF RESIDENCE

	1999	2000	2001	2002	2003	Market share 03	% change 03-02
SAMOA	11,739	14,827	14,258	13,877	14,947	0.71	7.71
OT.EAST AS/P					**12,255**	**0.58**	
OTHER ASIA					240	0.01	
OTH OCEANIA					12,015	0.57	
EUROPE	**317,810**	**371,684**	**387,222**	**423,200**	**460,938**	**21.90**	**8.92**
C/E EUROPE	**7,362**	**7,803**	**7,450**	**9,258**	**10,682**	**0.51**	**15.38**
AZERBAIJAN	69	14	30	36			
ARMENIA	16	17	15				
BULGARIA	67	32	60	140	134	0.01	-4.29
BELARUS	37		34	33	53		60.61
CZECH REP	1,567	1,985	1,540	2,116	3,498	0.17	65.31
ESTONIA	70	30	54	139	42		-69.78
GEORGIA	90	17		17			
HUNGARY	578	717	748	1,188	1,228	0.06	3.37
KAZAKHSTAN	45	68	77	45	127	0.01	182.22
KYRGYZSTAN	16	32	13	35	18		-48.57
LATVIA	103	78	100	74			
LITHUANIA	52	50	84	49	65		32.65
REP MOLDOVA		11	17				
POLAND	1,156	1,317	1,099	1,413	1,456	0.07	3.04
ROMANIA	121	251	316	412	281	0.01	-31.80
RUSSIAN FED	1,378	1,336	1,294	1,648	1,852	0.09	12.38
SLOVAKIA	255	261	385	422	349	0.02	-17.30
TAJIKISTAN	14						
UKRAINE	1,702	1,572	1,541	1,491	1,579	0.08	5.90
UZBEKISTAN	26	15	43				
NORTHERN EUR	**197,626**	**234,444**	**247,088**	**277,157**	**308,140**	**14.64**	**11.18**
DENMARK	7,265	7,371	7,426	8,001	8,752	0.42	9.39
FAEROE IS	27		17	57			
FINLAND	2,008	1,940	2,062	2,091	2,107	0.10	0.77
ICELAND	136	174	77	138	200	0.01	44.93
IRELAND	7,011	9,559	11,252	13,489	15,282	0.73	13.29
NORWAY	3,293	3,863	4,033	4,086	4,352	0.21	6.51
SWEDEN	9,615	11,287	10,575	12,309	12,628	0.60	2.59
UK	168,271	200,250	211,646	236,986	264,819	12.58	11.74
SOUTHERN EUR	**13,263**	**14,678**	**13,322**	**15,874**	**15,617**	**0.74**	**-1.62**
ALBANIA	14	17	28	20			
ANDORRA	41	30	100	105	54		-48.57
BOSNIA HERZG	54	32	103	58	51		-12.07
CROATIA	254	233	257	294	354	0.02	20.41
GIBRALTAR	30	31	17	31			
GREECE	489	659	509	469	517	0.02	10.23
HOLY SEE	14		17	16			
ITALY	7,173	7,885	6,632	8,379	7,487	0.36	-10.65
MALTA	89	105	146	139	137	0.01	-1.44
PORTUGAL	619	770	600	617	806	0.04	30.63
SAN MARINO		17					
SLOVENIA	388	534	487	478	710	0.03	48.54
SPAIN	3,834	4,157	4,200	5,030	5,247	0.25	4.31
TFYROM	56	61	30	30	41		36.67
SERBIA,MTNEG	208	147	196	208	213	0.01	2.40
WESTERN EUR	**94,690**	**108,606**	**111,640**	**112,775**	**119,108**	**5.66**	**5.62**

2. ARRIVALS OF NON-RESIDENT VISITORS AT NATIONAL BORDERS, BY COUNTRY OF RESIDENCE

	1999	2000	2001	2002	2003	Market share 03	% change 03-02
AUSTRIA	4,234	5,001	4,804	4,824	5,171	0.25	7.19
BELGIUM	2,912	3,688	3,623	3,962	3,953	0.19	-0.23
FRANCE	9,300	10,716	10,934	13,239	14,800	0.70	11.79
GERMANY	46,243	51,451	52,482	48,951	52,534	2.50	7.32
LIECHTENSTEN	16	49	32	83	22		-73.49
LUXEMBOURG	240	295	360	324	357	0.02	10.19
MONACO	99	92	86	122	108	0.01	-11.48
NETHERLANDS	19,553	23,873	25,164	26,037	26,388	1.25	1.35
SWITZERLAND	12,093	13,441	14,155	15,233	15,775	0.75	3.56
EAST/MED EUR	**4,869**	**6,153**	**7,722**	**8,136**	**7,110**	**0.34**	**-12.61**
CYPRUS	206	226	227	191	197	0.01	3.14
ISRAEL	4,125	5,430	7,149	7,481	6,454	0.31	-13.73
TURKEY	538	497	346	464	459	0.02	-1.08
OTHER EUROPE					**281**	**0.01**	
OTHER EUROPE					281	0.01	
MIDDLE EAST	**4,574**	**4,741**	**5,474**	**5,922**	**7,048**	**0.33**	**19.01**
MIDDLE EAST	**4,574**	**4,741**	**5,474**	**5,922**	**7,048**	**0.33**	**19.01**
BAHRAIN	292	306	326	291	300	0.01	3.09
PALESTINE	16	15	17				
IRAQ	96	178	156	117			
JORDAN	83	92	109	139	140	0.01	0.72
KUWAIT	294	304	237	181	314	0.01	73.48
LEBANON	98	59	112	15	75		400.00
LIBYA	53	15	47	39			
OMAN	320	317	375	463	510	0.02	10.15
QATAR	183	152	178	191	254	0.01	32.98
SAUDI ARABIA	1,180	1,171	1,289	1,503	1,723	0.08	14.64
SYRIA	36	15	32	52	54		3.85
UNTD ARAB EM	1,622	1,814	2,184	2,574	3,305	0.16	28.40
EGYPT	271	271	358	323	373	0.02	15.48
YEMEN	30	32	54	34			
SOUTH ASIA	**8,307**	**10,494**	**14,988**	**19,410**	**17,028**	**0.81**	**-12.27**
SOUTH ASIA	**8,307**	**10,494**	**14,988**	**19,410**	**17,028**	**0.81**	**-12.27**
AFGHANISTAN	13		13				
BANGLADESH	240	361	511	534	623	0.03	16.67
BHUTAN	23	15	51		19		
SRI LANKA	806	914	893	884	945	0.04	6.90
INDIA	6,602	8,327	12,665	17,270	14,790	0.70	-14.36
IRAN	200	290	177	160	323	0.02	101.88
MALDIVES	38	32	110	70			
NEPAL	91	117	158	152			
PAKISTAN	294	438	410	340	328	0.02	-3.53
REG.NOT SPEC	**72,201**	**66,587**	**81,126**	**74,199**	**62,109**	**2.95**	**-16.29**
NOT SPECIFIE	**72,201**	**66,587**	**81,126**	**74,199**	**62,109**	**2.95**	**-16.29**
OTH.WORLD	56,866	48,053	59,112	59,025	62,109	2.95	5.22
N RESID ABRO	15,335	18,534	22,014	15,174			

Source: World Tourism Organization (WTO)

NICARAGUA

1. ARRIVALS OF NON-RESIDENT TOURISTS AT NATIONAL BORDERS, BY NATIONALITY

	1999	2000	2001	2002	2003	Market share 03	% change 03-02
TOTAL	**468,159**	**485,909**	**482,869**	**471,622**	**525,775**	**100.00**	**11.48**
AFRICA	**192**	**563**	**560**	**287**	**378**	**0.07**	**31.71**
EAST AFRICA	**58**	**85**	**106**	**39**	**47**	**0.01**	**20.51**
BURUNDI		1	1				
ETHIOPIA	9	8	11	12	13		8.33
KENYA	9	32	26	5	9		80.00
MADAGASCAR	1		6		1		
MALAWI		1		1	2		100.00
MAURITIUS	1	20	11	9			
MOZAMBIQUE	3	3	12	1	6		500.00
RWANDA			1	1	1		
ZIMBABWE	25	7	6	3	5		66.67
UGANDA	5	6	13	5	6		20.00
TANZANIA	3	7	11	2	2		
ZAMBIA	2		8		2		
CENTRAL AFR	**8**	**55**	**82**	**16**	**9**		**-43.75**
ANGOLA	3	9	14	6	2		-66.67
CAMEROON	4	44	60	6	5		-16.67
CENT.AFR.REP		1	2		1		
CONGO		1	6	4	1		-75.00
DEM.R.CONGO	1						
NORTH AFRICA	**19**	**13**	**37**	**24**	**35**	**0.01**	**45.83**
ALGERIA	3	5	5	7	5		-28.57
MOROCCO	14	8	9	10	30	0.01	200.00
SUDAN			20				
TUNISIA	2		3	7			
SOUTHERN AFR	**71**	**83**	**92**	**98**	**109**	**0.02**	**11.22**
LESOTHO	1		1				
SOUTH AFRICA	70	83	91	98	109	0.02	11.22
WEST AFRICA	**36**	**300**	**165**	**34**	**26**		**-23.53**
CAPE VERDE		3	2		2		
BENIN		4	6	3			
GAMBIA		1	1	4			
GHANA	11	38	36	5	3		-40.00
GUINEA		1	5	5	2		-60.00
MALI		3	3	5	2		-60.00
MAURITANIA	3	13	3	1	2		100.00
NIGERIA	2	220	89	6	7		16.67
ST.HELENA				1			
SENEGAL	18	9	14	1	7		600.00
SIERRA LEONE	2	6	5	2	1		-50.00
BURKINA FASO		2	1	1			
OTHER AFRICA		**27**	**78**	**76**	**152**	**0.03**	**100.00**
OTHER AFRICA		27	78	76	152	0.03	100.00
AMERICAS	**424,072**	**437,062**	**432,474**	**417,226**	**464,176**	**88.28**	**11.25**
CARIBBEAN	**2,889**	**3,859**	**3,911**	**2,306**	**2,363**	**0.45**	**2.47**
ANTIGUA,BARB				1	3		200.00
BAHAMAS	10	10	11	17	39	0.01	129.41

NICARAGUA

1. ARRIVALS OF NON-RESIDENT TOURISTS AT NATIONAL BORDERS, BY NATIONALITY

	1999	2000	2001	2002	2003	Market share 03	% change 03-02
BARBADOS	9	17	16	8	20		150.00
BERMUDA			1		3		
CAYMAN IS	93	99	93	92	72	0.01	-21.74
CUBA	1,648	1,572	1,550	1,114	1,179	0.22	5.83
DOMINICA	11	6	1	3	9		200.00
DOMINICAN RP	832	1,880	1,960	773	667	0.13	-13.71
GRENADA	2	3	5	8	15		87.50
GUADELOUPE			1				
HAITI	63	65	80	68	54	0.01	-20.59
JAMAICA	83	93	104	113	161	0.03	42.48
MARTINIQUE			1				
ARUBA	1						
PUERTO RICO	86	59	41	62	83	0.02	33.87
ANGUILLA				1			
ST.LUCIA	21	11	4	3	6		100.00
ST.VINCENT,G	1	3	6	8	7		-12.50
TRINIDAD TBG	29	41	37	35	45	0.01	28.57
CENTRAL AMER	**316,568**	**307,226**	**301,584**	**287,245**	**310,239**	**59.01**	**8.01**
BELIZE	265	369	330	274	289	0.05	5.47
COSTA RICA	71,476	67,189	62,055	57,824	76,659	14.58	32.57
EL SALVADOR	61,603	69,283	71,886	69,691	73,806	14.04	5.90
GUATEMALA	37,202	36,146	38,311	36,964	40,132	7.63	8.57
HONDURAS	133,745	122,631	118,282	111,947	107,365	20.42	-4.09
PANAMA	12,277	11,608	10,720	10,545	11,988	2.28	13.68
NORTH AMER	**92,680**	**104,320**	**107,255**	**115,536**	**139,137**	**26.46**	**20.43**
CANADA	8,063	10,515	11,138	9,800	13,124	2.50	33.92
MEXICO	7,860	9,406	7,742	7,873	117,156	22.28	1,388.07
USA	76,757	84,399	88,375	97,863	8,857	1.68	-90.95
SOUTH AMER	**11,935**	**21,657**	**19,724**	**12,139**	**12,437**	**2.37**	**2.45**
ARGENTINA	1,577	1,979	2,034	2,247	2,672	0.51	18.91
BOLIVIA	436	537	555	516	591	0.11	14.53
BRAZIL	1,002	1,105	1,129	1,171	1,311	0.25	11.96
CHILE	1,294	1,364	1,436	1,431	1,407	0.27	-1.68
COLOMBIA	2,617	2,194	2,706	2,715	2,269	0.43	-16.43
ECUADOR	1,028	8,461	6,439	838	767	0.15	-8.47
GUYANA	39	40	20	20	33	0.01	65.00
PARAGUAY	63	89	115	117	117	0.02	
PERU	2,371	4,135	3,356	1,194	1,001	0.19	-16.16
SURINAME	2	3	4	4	16		300.00
URUGUAY	235	320	311	381	437	0.08	14.70
VENEZUELA	1,271	1,430	1,619	1,505	1,816	0.35	20.66
EAST AS/PACI	**7,763**	**9,189**	**8,940**	**8,732**	**10,674**	**2.03**	**22.24**
N/EAST ASIA	**4,404**	**5,905**	**5,290**	**4,920**	**5,865**	**1.12**	**19.21**
CHINA	981	1,805	916	716	1,418	0.27	98.04
TAIWAN(P.C.)	843	1,245	1,356	1,118	905	0.17	-19.05
HK,CHINA	3	10	15	9	85	0.02	844.44
JAPAN	1,759	1,734	1,709	1,799	1,908	0.36	6.06
KOREA REP.	818	1,110	1,294	1,278	1,547	0.29	21.05
MONGOLIA		1			2		
S/EAST ASIA	**2,549**	**2,362**	**2,682**	**2,478**	**2,929**	**0.56**	**18.20**
MYANMAR	134	183	234	126	42	0.01	-66.67
INDONESIA	31	91	101	115	713	0.14	520.00

NICARAGUA

1. ARRIVALS OF NON-RESIDENT TOURISTS AT NATIONAL BORDERS, BY NATIONALITY

	1999	2000	2001	2002	2003	Market share 03	% change 03-02
LAO P.DEM.R.			10	23	1		-95.65
MALAYSIA	23	18	36	32	35	0.01	9.38
PHILIPPINES	2,314	2,032	2,219	2,115	2,074	0.39	-1.94
SINGAPORE	30	16	31	31	33	0.01	6.45
VIET NAM	4	11	13	3	7		133.33
THAILAND	13	11	38	33	24		-27.27
AUSTRALASIA	**809**	**914**	**962**	**1,325**	**1,868**	**0.36**	**40.98**
AUSTRALIA	577	676	700	1,046	1,573	0.30	50.38
NEW ZEALAND	232	238	262	279	295	0.06	5.73
MELANESIA			**2**				
FIJI			2				
MICRONESIA		**7**	**2**		**5**		
KIRIBATI		7	2		5		
POLYNESIA	**1**	**1**	**2**	**9**	**7**		**-22.22**
TONGA			2	3	1		-66.67
TUVALU	1	1		6	6		
EUROPE	**35,521**	**38,357**	**40,153**	**44,730**	**49,147**	**9.35**	**9.87**
C/E EUROPE	**1,790**	**1,439**	**1,497**	**1,972**	**1,593**	**0.30**	**-19.22**
ARMENIA			38	1	1		
BULGARIA	123	63	60	71	256	0.05	260.56
BELARUS		3	10		3		
CZECH RP/SVK	170	189	213	156	252	0.05	61.54
ESTONIA		8	20	26	23		-11.54
GEORGIA		1		41	3		-92.68
HUNGARY	33	48	43	25	91	0.02	264.00
LATVIA	33	7	14	75	4		-94.67
LITHUANIA	65	31	16	74	24		-67.57
POLAND	316	217	203	304	276	0.05	-9.21
ROMANIA	85	107	60	72	62	0.01	-13.89
RUSSIAN FED	487	511	529	628	404	0.08	-35.67
UKRAINE	478	254	291	486	188	0.04	-61.32
USSR(former)				13	6		-53.85
NORTHERN EUR	**6,980**	**7,968**	**8,707**	**9,849**	**11,947**	**2.27**	**21.30**
DENMARK	1,064	1,101	1,241	1,142	1,395	0.27	22.15
FINLAND	627	420	399	434	465	0.09	7.14
ICELAND	10	20	15	25	47	0.01	88.00
IRELAND	244	399	417	413	566	0.11	37.05
NORWAY	724	886	818	897	995	0.19	10.93
SWEDEN	1,458	1,662	1,777	1,765	1,879	0.36	6.46
UK	2,853	3,480	4,040	5,173	6,600	1.26	27.59
SOUTHERN EUR	**12,748**	**12,562**	**13,208**	**13,584**	**14,004**	**2.66**	**3.09**
ALBANIA	9	1	3	2	2		
ANDORRA	6	3	3	5	7		40.00
CROATIA	98	48	109	95	63	0.01	-33.68
GREECE	297	279	265	268	222	0.04	-17.16
ITALY	3,330	3,919	3,803	4,098	4,363	0.83	6.47
MALTA	2	6	9	6	2		-66.67
PORTUGAL	102	104	135	144	206	0.04	43.06
SAN MARINO	1	7	7	24	10		-58.33
SLOVENIA	23	20	19	44	88	0.02	100.00
SPAIN	8,863	8,162	8,837	8,884	9,039	1.72	1.74

NICARAGUA

1. ARRIVALS OF NON-RESIDENT TOURISTS AT NATIONAL BORDERS, BY NATIONALITY

	1999	2000	2001	2002	2003	Market share 03	% change 03-02
YUGOSLAV SFR					2		
SERBIA,MTNEG	17	13	18	14			
WESTERN EUR	**13,578**	**15,761**	**16,063**	**18,427**	**20,522**	**3.90**	**11.37**
AUSTRIA	621	688	852	793	576	0.11	-27.36
BELGIUM	961	1,085	1,017	1,236	1,326	0.25	7.28
FRANCE	2,575	2,985	3,073	3,519	3,886	0.74	10.43
GERMANY	4,611	5,582	5,694	6,500	6,886	1.31	5.94
LIECHTENSTEN	2		2		7		
LUXEMBOURG	29	39	56	22	53	0.01	140.91
NETHERLANDS	2,861	3,227	3,206	4,236	5,417	1.03	27.88
SWITZERLAND	1,918	2,155	2,163	2,121	2,371	0.45	11.79
EAST/MED EUR	**425**	**627**	**678**	**898**	**1,081**	**0.21**	**20.38**
CYPRUS	6	6	3	9	3		-66.67
ISRAEL	374	535	553	855	971	0.18	13.57
TURKEY	45	86	122	34	107	0.02	214.71
MIDDLE EAST	**97**	**128**	**131**	**64**	**89**	**0.02**	**39.06**
MIDDLE EAST	**97**	**128**	**131**	**64**	**89**	**0.02**	**39.06**
PALESTINE	11	6	8	6	13		116.67
IRAQ	6	6	2				
JORDAN	14	26	17	21	15		-28.57
KUWAIT	1	2	10	1			
LEBANON	6	6	2	2	11		450.00
LIBYA	29	33	30	28	36	0.01	28.57
QATAR		1	1	1			
SAUDI ARABIA	19	16	7	1	2		100.00
UNTD ARAB EM				1	10		900.00
EGYPT	11	30	54	3	2		-33.33
YEMEN		2					
SOUTH ASIA	**461**	**531**	**590**	**549**	**1,254**	**0.24**	**128.42**
SOUTH ASIA	**461**	**531**	**590**	**549**	**1,254**	**0.24**	**128.42**
AFGHANISTAN		1					
BANGLADESH	28	26	46	53	35	0.01	-33.96
SRI LANKA	17	13	33	11	2		-81.82
INDIA	364	432	414	423	1,153	0.22	172.58
IRAN	20	11	49	27	6		-77.78
MALDIVES		8	10	3	1		-66.67
NEPAL	2		2	1	8		700.00
PAKISTAN	30	40	36	31	49	0.01	58.06
REG.NOT SPEC	**53**	**79**	**21**	**34**	**57**	**0.01**	**67.65**
NOT SPECIFIE	**53**	**79**	**21**	**34**	**57**	**0.01**	**67.65**
OTH.WORLD	53	79	21	34	57	0.01	67.65

Source: World Tourism Organization (WTO)

NIGER

1. ARRIVALS OF NON-RESIDENT TOURISTS AT NATIONAL BORDERS, BY NATIONALITY

	1999	2000	2001	2002	2003	Market share 03	% change 03-02
TOTAL (*)	**38,900**	**45,700**	**52,000**	**39,000**			
AFRICA	**27,000**	**28,000**	**37,000**	**26,000**			
OTHER AFRICA	**27,000**	**28,000**	**37,000**	**26,000**			
ALL AFRICA	27,000	28,000	37,000	26,000			
AMERICAS	**1,900**	**2,700**	**2,000**	**2,000**			
NORTH AMER	**1,500**	**2,200**	**2,000**	**2,000**			
CANADA	500	700	1,000	1,000			
USA	1,000	1,500	1,000	1,000			
OTHER AMERIC	**400**	**500**					
OTH AMERICA	400	500					
EAST AS/PACI	**1,000**	**1,000**	**1,000**	**2,000**			
OT.EAST AS/P	**1,000**	**1,000**	**1,000**	**2,000**			
ALL ASIA	1,000	1,000	1,000	2,000			
EUROPE	**9,000**	**14,000**	**11,000**	**9,000**			
WESTERN EUR	**8,000**		**9,000**	**8,000**			
FRANCE	6,000		7,000	6,000			
GERMANY	1,000		1,000	1,000			
BENELUX	1,000		1,000	1,000			
OTHER EUROPE	**1,000**	**14,000**	**2,000**	**1,000**			
OTHER EUROPE	1,000		2,000	1,000			
ALL EUROPE		14,000					
MIDDLE EAST			**1,000**				
MIDDLE EAST			**1,000**				
ALL MID EAST			1,000				

Source: World Tourism Organization (WTO)

NIGERIA

2. ARRIVALS OF NON-RESIDENT VISITORS AT NATIONAL BORDERS, BY NATIONALITY

	1999	2000	2001	2002	2003	Market share 03	% change 03-02
TOTAL	**1,424,840**	**1,491,767**	**1,752,948**	**2,045,543**	**2,253,115**	**100.00**	**10.15**
AFRICA	**1,003,133**	**1,050,993**	**1,234,733**	**1,450,814**	**1,554,308**	**68.98**	**7.13**
EAST AFRICA	**42,510**	**44,533**	**52,326**	**61,483**	**72,244**	**3.21**	**17.50**
ETHIOPIA	17,703	18,546	21,791	25,604	30,085	1.34	17.50
KENYA	9,655	10,115	11,885	13,965	16,409	0.73	17.50
MOZAMBIQUE	4,747	4,973	5,843	6,866	8,068	0.36	17.51
RWANDA	59	61	72	85	100		17.65
SOMALIA	124	130	153	180	212	0.01	17.78
ZIMBABWE	5,002	5,240	6,157	7,234	8,500	0.38	17.50
UGANDA	845	885	1,040	1,222	1,436	0.06	17.51
TANZANIA	3,843	4,026	4,731	5,559	6,532	0.29	17.50
ZAMBIA	532	557	654	768	902	0.04	17.45
CENTRAL AFR	**111,713**	**117,034**	**137,513**	**161,580**	**189,857**	**8.43**	**17.50**
ANGOLA	2,914	3,053	3,587	4,215	4,953	0.22	17.51
CAMEROON	51,083	53,516	62,881	73,885	86,815	3.85	17.50
CENT.AFR.REP	3,494	3,660	4,300	5,053	5,937	0.26	17.49
CHAD	40,576	42,508	49,947	58,688	68,958	3.06	17.50
CONGO	3,689	3,865	4,541	5,336	6,270	0.28	17.50
DEM.R.CONGO	3,665	3,840	4,512	5,302	6,230	0.28	17.50
EQ.GUINEA	241	253	297	349	410	0.02	17.48
GABON	5,918	6,200	7,285	8,560	10,058	0.45	17.50
SAO TOME PRN	133	139	163	192	226	0.01	17.71
NORTH AFRICA	**87,188**	**91,430**	**107,430**	**126,230**	**148,321**	**6.58**	**17.50**
ALGERIA	17,264	18,276	21,474	25,232	29,648	1.32	17.50
MOROCCO	27,577	28,790	33,828	39,748	46,704	2.07	17.50
SUDAN	30,068	31,500	37,013	43,490	51,101	2.27	17.50
TUNISIA	12,279	12,864	15,115	17,760	20,868	0.93	17.50
SOUTHERN AFR	**18,575**	**19,460**	**22,686**	**26,657**	**31,322**	**1.39**	**17.50**
BOTSWANA	3,091	3,238	3,805	4,471	5,253	0.23	17.49
LESOTHO	3,139	3,289	3,685	4,330	5,088	0.23	17.51
NAMIBIA	7,969	8,349	9,810	11,527	13,544	0.60	17.50
SOUTH AFRICA	4,376	4,584	5,386	6,329	7,437	0.33	17.51
WEST AFRICA	**743,147**	**778,536**	**914,778**	**1,074,864**	**1,112,564**	**49.38**	**3.51**
CAPE VERDE	125	131	154	181	213	0.01	17.68
BENIN	187,538	196,468	230,849	271,248	318,716	14.15	17.50
GAMBIA	8,594	9,003	10,579	12,430	14,605	0.65	17.50
GHANA	98,364	103,048	121,081	142,270	16,767	0.74	-88.21
GUINEA	9,346	9,791	11,504	13,517	15,882	0.70	17.50
COTE IVOIRE	24,165	25,316	29,746	34,952	41,069	1.82	17.50
LIBERIA	51,224	53,663	63,054	74,088	87,053	3.86	17.50
MALI	17,640	18,480	21,714	25,514	29,979	1.33	17.50
MAURITANIA	405	424	498	585	687	0.03	17.44
NIGER	296,010	310,106	364,375	428,141	503,066	22.33	17.50
SENEGAL	10,427	10,924	12,836	15,082	17,721	0.79	17.50
SIERRA LEONE	7,889	8,266	9,712	11,412	13,409	0.60	17.50
TOGO	16,233	17,006	19,982	23,479	27,588	1.22	17.50
BURKINA FASO	15,187	15,910	18,694	21,965	25,809	1.15	17.50
AMERICAS	**55,593**	**58,242**	**68,435**	**80,412**	**94,486**	**4.19**	**17.50**
CARIBBEAN	**6,887**	**7,215**	**8,478**	**9,961**	**11,705**	**0.52**	**17.51**

NIGERIA

2. ARRIVALS OF NON-RESIDENT VISITORS AT NATIONAL BORDERS, BY NATIONALITY

	1999	2000	2001	2002	2003	Market share 03	% change 03-02
BARBADOS	871	913	1,073	1,261	1,482	0.07	17.53
CUBA	993	1,040	1,222	1,436	1,687	0.07	17.48
DOMINICAN RP	279	292	343	403	474	0.02	17.62
HAITI	122	128	150	176	207	0.01	17.61
JAMAICA	2,202	2,307	2,711	3,185	3,742	0.17	17.49
TRINIDAD TBG	2,420	2,535	2,979	3,500	4,113	0.18	17.51
CENTRAL AMER	**271**	**284**	**334**	**392**	**461**	**0.02**	**17.60**
COSTA RICA	154	161	189	222	261	0.01	17.57
NICARAGUA	117	123	145	170	200	0.01	17.65
NORTH AMER	**33,532**	**35,129**	**41,276**	**48,500**	**56,987**	**2.53**	**17.50**
CANADA	4,938	5,173	6,078	7,142	8,392	0.37	17.50
MEXICO	19,910	20,858	24,508	28,797	33,836	1.50	17.50
USA	8,684	9,098	10,690	12,561	14,759	0.66	17.50
SOUTH AMER	**14,903**	**15,614**	**18,347**	**21,559**	**25,333**	**1.12**	**17.51**
ARGENTINA	3,147	3,297	3,874	4,552	5,349	0.24	17.51
BOLIVIA	180	189	222	261	307	0.01	17.62
BRAZIL	5,179	5,426	6,376	7,492	8,803	0.39	17.50
CHILE	2,785	2,918	3,429	4,029	4,734	0.21	17.50
COLOMBIA	2,310	2,420	2,844	3,342	3,927	0.17	17.50
GUYANA	176	184	216	254	298	0.01	17.32
PARAGUAY	370	388	456	536	630	0.03	17.54
PERU	465	487	572	672	790	0.04	17.56
VENEZUELA	291	305	358	421	495	0.02	17.58
EAST AS/PACI	**87,815**	**91,997**	**108,097**	**110,832**	**130,228**	**5.78**	**17.50**
N/EAST ASIA	**53,007**	**55,531**	**65,250**	**60,486**	**71,071**	**3.15**	**17.50**
CHINA	15,877	16,633	19,544	22,964	26,983	1.20	17.50
TAIWAN(P.C.)	10,786	11,300	13,278	15,602	18,332	0.81	17.50
HK,CHINA	7,984	8,364	9,828	11,548	13,569	0.60	17.50
JAPAN	5,928	6,210	7,297	8,574	10,074	0.45	17.49
KOREA REP.	12,432	13,024	15,303	1,798	2,113	0.09	17.52
S/EAST ASIA	**33,056**	**34,630**	**40,690**	**47,811**	**56,178**	**2.49**	**17.50**
MYANMAR	37	39	46	54	63		16.67
INDONESIA	8,122	8,509	9,998	11,748	13,804	0.61	17.50
MALAYSIA	8,350	8,748	10,279	12,078	14,192	0.63	17.50
PHILIPPINES	6,874	7,201	8,461	9,942	11,682	0.52	17.50
SINGAPORE	5,572	5,837	6,858	8,058	9,468	0.42	17.50
THAILAND	4,101	4,296	5,048	5,931	6,969	0.31	17.50
AUSTRALASIA	**1,752**	**1,836**	**2,157**	**2,535**	**2,979**	**0.13**	**17.51**
AUSTRALIA	1,172	1,228	1,443	1,696	1,993	0.09	17.51
NEW ZEALAND	580	608	714	839	986	0.04	17.52
EUROPE	**220,817**	**230,316**	**270,056**	**317,317**	**372,846**	**16.55**	**17.50**
C/E EUROPE	**42,571**	**44,601**	**52,404**	**61,576**	**72,351**	**3.21**	**17.50**
BULGARIA	6,739	7,060	8,296	9,748	11,454	0.51	17.50
CZECH RP/SVK	5,452	5,712	6,712	7,887	9,267	0.41	17.50
HUNGARY	8,129	8,516	10,006	11,757	13,814	0.61	17.50
POLAND	6,105	6,398	7,515	8,830	10,375	0.46	17.50
ROMANIA	10,420	10,916	12,826	15,071	17,708	0.79	17.50
USSR(former)	5,726	5,999	7,049	8,283	9,733	0.43	17.51

NIGERIA

2. ARRIVALS OF NON-RESIDENT VISITORS AT NATIONAL BORDERS, BY NATIONALITY

	1999	2000	2001	2002	2003	Market share 03	% change 03-02
NORTHERN EUR	**51,842**	**54,311**	**63,230**	**74,295**	**87,297**	**3.87**	**17.50**
DENMARK	7,792	8,163	9,592	11,271	13,243	0.59	17.50
FINLAND	8,698	9,112	10,707	12,581	14,783	0.66	17.50
IRELAND	4,885	5,118	6,014	7,066	8,303	0.37	17.51
NORWAY	6,041	6,329	7,437	8,738	10,267	0.46	17.50
SWEDEN	5,526	5,789	6,802	7,992	9,391	0.42	17.51
UK	18,900	19,800	22,678	26,647	31,310	1.39	17.50
SOUTHERN EUR	**47,548**	**48,794**	**57,356**	**67,393**	**79,186**	**3.51**	**17.50**
GREECE	1,923	1,015	1,193	1,402	1,647	0.07	17.48
ITALY	31,284	32,770	38,509	45,248	53,166	2.36	17.50
PORTUGAL	3,795	3,970	4,672	5,490	6,451	0.29	17.50
SPAIN	9,936	10,400	12,231	14,371	16,886	0.75	17.50
YUGOSLAV SFR	610	639	751	882	1,036	0.05	17.46
WESTERN EUR	**66,995**	**70,184**	**82,466**	**96,898**	**113,855**	**5.05**	**17.50**
AUSTRIA	2,026	2,121	2,492	2,928	3,440	0.15	17.49
BELGIUM	3,258	3,413	4,010	4,712	5,537	0.25	17.51
FRANCE	29,508	30,913	36,323	42,680	50,149	2.23	17.50
GERMANY	28,782	30,153	35,430	41,630	48,915	2.17	17.50
LUXEMBOURG	529	554	651	765	899	0.04	17.52
NETHERLANDS	2,559	2,681	3,150	3,701	4,349	0.19	17.51
SWITZERLAND	333	349	410	482	566	0.03	17.43
EAST/MED EUR	**11,861**	**12,426**	**14,600**	**17,155**	**20,157**	**0.89**	**17.50**
CYPRUS	1,356	1,421	1,669	1,961	2,304	0.10	17.49
ISRAEL	7,205	7,548	8,869	10,421	12,245	0.54	17.50
TURKEY	3,300	3,457	4,062	4,773	5,608	0.25	17.49
MIDDLE EAST	**23,895**	**25,034**	**29,414**	**34,560**	**40,608**	**1.80**	**17.50**
MIDDLE EAST	**23,895**	**25,034**	**29,414**	**34,560**	**40,608**	**1.80**	**17.50**
IRAQ	1,813	1,899	2,231	2,621	3,080	0.14	17.51
JORDAN	917	961	1,129	1,327	1,559	0.07	17.48
KUWAIT	349	366	430	505	593	0.03	17.43
LEBANON	9,071	9,503	11,166	13,120	15,416	0.68	17.50
LIBYA	2,284	2,393	2,812	3,304	3,882	0.17	17.49
SAUDI ARABIA	908	951	1,117	1,312	1,542	0.07	17.53
SYRIA	431	452	531	624	733	0.03	17.47
EGYPT	7,768	8,138	9,562	11,235	13,201	0.59	17.50
YEMEN	354	371	436	512	602	0.03	17.58
SOUTH ASIA	**32,435**	**33,978**	**36,335**	**44,701**	**52,523**	**2.33**	**17.50**
SOUTH ASIA	**32,435**	**33,978**	**36,335**	**44,701**	**52,523**	**2.33**	**17.50**
AFGHANISTAN	178	187	220	259	304	0.01	17.37
BANGLADESH	210	220	259	304	357	0.02	17.43
SRI LANKA	438	457	537	631	741	0.03	17.43
INDIA	13,999	14,666	15,233	17,899	21,031	0.93	17.50
IRAN	4,376	4,584	5,796	6,467	7,599	0.34	17.50
NEPAL	22	23	27	32	38		18.75
PAKISTAN	13,212	13,841	14,263	19,109	22,453	1.00	17.50
REG.NOT SPEC	**1,152**	**1,207**	**5,878**	**6,907**	**8,116**	**0.36**	**17.50**
NOT SPECIFIE	**1,152**	**1,207**	**5,878**	**6,907**	**8,116**	**0.36**	**17.50**

NIGERIA

2. ARRIVALS OF NON-RESIDENT VISITORS AT NATIONAL BORDERS, BY NATIONALITY

	1999	2000	2001	2002	2003	Market share 03	% change 03-02
OTH.WORLD	1,152	1,207	5,878	6,907	8,116	0.36	17.50

Source: World Tourism Organization (WTO)

NIUE

1. ARRIVALS OF NON-RESIDENT TOURISTS AT NATIONAL BORDERS, BY COUNTRY OF RESIDENCE

	1999	2000	2001	2002	2003	Market share 03	% change 03-02
TOTAL (*)	**1,870**	**1,647**	**1,407**	**2,084**	**2,707**	**100.00**	**29.89**
AMERICAS	**86**	**155**	**193**	**252**	**178**	**6.58**	**-29.37**
NORTH AMER	**86**	**155**	**193**	**252**	**178**	**6.58**	**-29.37**
CANADA	8	12		31	25	0.92	-19.35
USA	78	143	193	221	153	5.65	-30.77
EAST AS/PACI	**1,635**	**1,370**	**1,023**	**1,387**	**2,247**	**83.01**	**62.00**
N/EAST ASIA	**21**	**14**		**9**	**18**	**0.66**	**100.00**
JAPAN	21	14		9	18	0.66	100.00
AUSTRALASIA	**1,289**	**1,123**	**817**	**1,106**	**1,719**	**63.50**	**55.42**
AUSTRALIA	215	175	142	180	325	12.01	80.56
NEW ZEALAND	1,074	948	675	926	1,394	51.50	50.54
OT.EAST AS/P	**325**	**233**	**206**	**272**	**510**	**18.84**	**87.50**
OTHER ASIA	7	10	30	17	20	0.74	17.65
OTH OCEANIA	318	223	176	255	490	18.10	92.16
EUROPE	**112**	**104**	**174**	**275**	**235**	**8.68**	**-14.55**
NORTHERN EUR	**49**	**32**		**93**	**82**	**3.03**	**-11.83**
UK	49	32		93	82	3.03	-11.83
WESTERN EUR	**37**	**25**		**72**	**80**	**2.96**	**11.11**
FRANCE	6	4		30	17	0.63	-43.33
GERMANY	31	21		42	63	2.33	50.00
OTHER EUROPE	**26**	**47**	**174**	**110**	**73**	**2.70**	**-33.64**
OTHER EUROPE	26	47	174	110	73	2.70	-33.64
REG.NOT SPEC	**37**	**18**	**17**	**170**	**47**	**1.74**	**-72.35**
NOT SPECIFIE	**37**	**18**	**17**	**170**	**47**	**1.74**	**-72.35**
OTH.WORLD	37	18	17	170	47	1.74	-72.35

Source: World Tourism Organization (WTO)

NORTHERN MARIANA ISLANDS

2. ARRIVALS OF NON-RESIDENT VISITORS AT NATIONAL BORDERS, BY NATIONALITY

	1999	2000	2001	2002	2003	Market share 03	% change 03-02
TOTAL	**501,788**	**528,608**	**444,284**	**475,547**	**459,458**	**100.00**	**-3.38**
AFRICA	**15**	**36**					
SOUTHERN AFR	**6**	**22**					
SOUTH AFRICA	6	22					
OTHER AFRICA	**9**	**14**					
OTHER AFRICA	9	14					
AMERICAS	**49,892**	**52,331**	**35,460**	**36,451**	**34,670**	**7.55**	**-4.89**
CENTRAL AMER	**23**	**18**					
ALL CENT AME	23	18					
NORTH AMER	**49,559**	**52,001**	**35,449**	**36,451**	**34,670**	**7.55**	**-4.89**
CANADA	652	721	307	593	206	0.04	-65.26
MEXICO	16	40					
USA	48,891	51,240	35,142	35,858	34,464	7.50	-3.89
SOUTH AMER	**299**	**299**					
ALL SOUTH AM	299	299					
OTHER AMERIC	**11**	**13**	**11**				
OTH AMERICA	11	13	11				
EAST AS/PACI	**449,339**	**473,883**	**407,104**	**437,322**	**422,811**	**92.02**	**-3.32**
N/EAST ASIA	**441,722**	**466,524**	**401,473**	**432,173**	**415,912**	**90.52**	**-3.76**
CHINA	1,828	1,698	2,101	10,470	15,213	3.31	45.30
TAIWAN(P.C.)	2,890	9,960	4,507	1,228	711	0.15	-42.10
HK,CHINA	5,379	5,009	4,327	3,416	2,271	0.49	-33.52
JAPAN	380,473	377,899	333,911	326,735	328,075	71.40	0.41
KOREA REP.	51,150	71,936	56,627	90,324	69,642	15.16	-22.90
MACAU, CHINA	2	22					
S/EAST ASIA	**2,775**	**3,151**	**3,010**	**3,024**	**4,688**	**1.02**	**55.03**
INDONESIA	42	49					
MALAYSIA	83	72					
PHILIPPINES	2,327	2,665	2,625	2,906	4,570	0.99	57.26
SINGAPORE	117	97					
VIET NAM	14	11					
THAILAND	189	249	385	118	118	0.03	
OTH S/E ASIA	3	8					
AUSTRALASIA	**1,116**	**765**	**384**	**316**	**372**	**0.08**	**17.72**
AUSTRALIA	997	643	384	316	372	0.08	17.72
NEW ZEALAND	119	122					
MELANESIA	**64**	**50**					
SOLOMON IS	2						
FIJI	41	41					
NEW CALEDNIA	3	2					
PAPUA N.GUIN	18	7					
MICRONESIA	**3,627**	**3,352**	**2,237**	**1,809**	**1,839**	**0.40**	**1.66**
KIRIBATI		4					
MICRONESIA	2,482	2,337	1,498	1,061	1,100	0.24	3.68

NORTHERN MARIANA ISLANDS

2. ARRIVALS OF NON-RESIDENT VISITORS AT NATIONAL BORDERS, BY NATIONALITY

	1999	2000	2001	2002	2003	Market share 03	% change 03-02
PALAU	1,145	1,011	739	748	739	0.16	-1.20
POLYNESIA	**30**	**34**					
AMER SAMOA		5					
TONGA	7	8					
SAMOA	23	21					
OT.EAST AS/P	**5**	**7**					
OTH OCEANIA	5	7					
EUROPE	**2,374**	**2,166**	**566**	**598**	**439**	**0.10**	**-26.59**
C/E EUROPE	**411**	**220**					
USSR(former)	411	220					
NORTHERN EUR	**750**	**965**					
DENMARK	99	63					
FINLAND	23	4					
NORWAY	20	21					
SWEDEN	65	66					
UK	543	811					
SOUTHERN EUR	**228**	**154**					
ITALY	84	68					
PORTUGAL	119	57					
SPAIN	25	29					
WESTERN EUR	**864**	**656**					
AUSTRIA	26	11					
BELGIUM	21	11					
FRANCE	367	279					
GERMANY	336	269					
NETHERLANDS	37	30					
SWITZERLAND	77	56					
OTHER EUROPE	**121**	**171**	**566**	**598**	**439**	**0.10**	**-26.59**
OTHER EUROPE	121	171					
ALL EUROPE			566	598	439	0.10	-26.59
MIDDLE EAST	**74**	**49**					
MIDDLE EAST	**74**	**49**					
ALL MID EAST	74	49					
SOUTH ASIA	**66**	**93**					
SOUTH ASIA	**66**	**93**					
BANGLADESH	4	3					
INDIA	55	80					
NEPAL		4					
PAKISTAN	6	5					
OTH STH ASIA	1	1					
REG.NOT SPEC	**28**	**50**	**1,154**	**1,176**	**1,538**	**0.33**	**30.78**
NOT SPECIFIE	**28**	**50**	**1,154**	**1,176**	**1,538**	**0.33**	**30.78**
OTH.WORLD	28	50	1,154	1,176	1,538	0.33	30.78

NORWAY

1. ARRIVALS OF NON-RESIDENT TOURISTS AT NATIONAL BORDERS, BY NATIONALITY

	1999	2000	2001	2002	2003	Market share 03	% change 03-02
TOTAL (*)	**3,223,000**	**3,104,000**	**3,073,000**	**3,111,000**	**3,146,000**	**100.00**	**1.13**
AMERICAS	**159,000**	**141,000**	**141,000**	**126,000**	**127,000**	**4.04**	**0.79**
NORTH AMER	**159,000**	**141,000**	**141,000**	**126,000**	**127,000**	**4.04**	**0.79**
USA	159,000	141,000	141,000	126,000	127,000	4.04	0.79
EUROPE	**2,965,000**	**2,855,000**	**2,817,000**	**2,868,000**	**2,915,000**	**92.66**	**1.64**
NORTHERN EUR	**1,915,000**	**1,859,000**	**1,850,000**	**1,878,000**	**1,828,000**	**58.11**	**-2.66**
DENMARK	573,000	556,000	545,000	554,000	556,000	17.67	0.36
FINLAND	229,000	212,000	190,000	215,000	185,000	5.88	-13.95
SWEDEN	894,000	863,000	884,000	860,000	844,000	26.83	-1.86
UK	219,000	228,000	231,000	249,000	243,000	7.72	-2.41
SOUTHERN EUR	**79,000**	**64,000**	**70,000**	**76,000**	**89,000**	**2.83**	**17.11**
ITALY	42,000	39,000	41,000	44,000	53,000	1.68	20.45
SPAIN	37,000	25,000	29,000	32,000	36,000	1.14	12.50
WESTERN EUR	**843,000**	**825,000**	**778,000**	**798,000**	**852,000**	**27.08**	**6.77**
AUSTRIA	24,000	27,000	22,000	22,000	22,000	0.70	
BELGIUM	27,000	36,000	25,000	28,000	33,000	1.05	17.86
FRANCE	84,000	86,000	79,000	83,000	90,000	2.86	8.43
GERMANY	521,000	505,000	492,000	507,000	543,000	17.26	7.10
NETHERLANDS	133,000	127,000	121,000	120,000	126,000	4.01	5.00
SWITZERLAND	54,000	44,000	39,000	38,000	38,000	1.21	
OTHER EUROPE	**128,000**	**107,000**	**119,000**	**116,000**	**146,000**	**4.64**	**25.86**
OTHER EUROPE	128,000	107,000	119,000	116,000	146,000	4.64	25.86
REG.NOT SPEC	**99,000**	**108,000**	**115,000**	**117,000**	**104,000**	**3.31**	**-11.11**
NOT SPECIFIE	**99,000**	**108,000**	**115,000**	**117,000**	**104,000**	**3.31**	**-11.11**
OTH.WORLD	99,000	108,000	115,000	117,000	104,000	3.31	-11.11

Source: World Tourism Organization (WTO)

NORWAY

5. OVERNIGHT STAYS OF NON-RESIDENT TOURISTS IN HOTELS AND SIMILAR ESTABLISHMENTS, BY NATIONALITY

		1999	2000	2001	2002	2003	Market share 03	% change 03-02
TOTAL	(*)	**5,207,568**	**4,966,857**	**4,815,439**	**4,705,537**	**4,374,657**	**100.00**	**-7.03**
AFRICA		**10,537**	**10,431**	**9,979**	**13,867**	**13,181**	**0.30**	**-4.95**
OTHER AFRICA		**10,537**	**10,431**	**9,979**	**13,867**	**13,181**	**0.30**	**-4.95**
ALL AFRICA		10,537	10,431	9,979	13,867	13,181	0.30	-4.95
AMERICAS		**461,454**	**437,338**	**413,567**	**386,755**	**326,508**	**7.46**	**-15.58**
NORTH AMER		**448,291**	**423,935**	**397,466**	**373,589**	**315,405**	**7.21**	**-15.57**
CANADA		17,616	14,756	13,786	14,724	14,575	0.33	-1.01
MEXICO		1,955	1,753	1,843	2,638	2,749	0.06	4.21
USA		428,720	407,426	381,837	356,227	298,081	6.81	-16.32
OTHER AMERIC		**13,163**	**13,403**	**16,101**	**13,166**	**11,103**	**0.25**	**-15.67**
OTH AMERICA		13,163	13,403	16,101	13,166	11,103	0.25	-15.67
EAST AS/PACI		**290,264**	**320,613**	**316,563**	**297,561**	**234,066**	**5.35**	**-21.34**
N/EAST ASIA		**173,171**	**180,824**	**167,483**	**147,048**	**112,559**	**2.57**	**-23.45**
JAPAN		173,171	180,824	167,483	147,048	112,559	2.57	-23.45
AUSTRALASIA		**16,778**	**14,835**	**16,588**	**19,967**	**17,016**	**0.39**	**-14.78**
AUSTRALIA		14,743	13,329	14,550	18,045	14,527	0.33	-19.50
NEW ZEALAND		2,035	1,506	2,038	1,922	2,489	0.06	29.50
OT.EAST AS/P		**100,315**	**124,954**	**132,492**	**130,546**	**104,491**	**2.39**	**-19.96**
OTHER ASIA		100,315	124,954	132,492	130,546	104,491	2.39	-19.96
EUROPE		**4,277,458**	**4,032,738**	**3,886,613**	**3,827,537**	**3,613,793**	**82.61**	**-5.58**
C/E EUROPE		**47,886**	**41,340**	**40,142**	**40,681**	**44,511**	**1.02**	**9.41**
CZECH REP		18,606	13,603	12,470	11,139	11,756	0.27	5.54
HUNGARY		6,120	6,205	5,266	6,024	7,649	0.17	26.98
POLAND		19,533	19,479	18,724	20,507	21,904	0.50	6.81
SLOVAKIA		3,627	2,053	3,682	3,011	3,202	0.07	6.34
NORTHERN EUR		**2,174,218**	**1,993,535**	**1,967,807**	**1,920,697**	**1,688,138**	**38.59**	**-12.11**
DENMARK		840,109	813,482	776,811	736,430	617,141	14.11	-16.20
FINLAND		87,618	72,769	69,286	69,899	60,315	1.38	-13.71
ICELAND		14,586	14,141	12,318	11,811	11,658	0.27	-1.30
IRELAND		5,380	6,550	7,334	7,934	7,435	0.17	-6.29
SWEDEN		684,323	614,172	585,433	549,930	475,234	10.86	-13.58
UK		542,202	472,421	516,625	544,693	516,355	11.80	-5.20
SOUTHERN EUR		**348,928**	**339,191**	**318,654**	**333,158**	**350,888**	**8.02**	**5.32**
GREECE		13,109	15,217	11,508	12,884	14,265	0.33	10.72
ITALY		144,463	143,778	122,126	130,396	142,275	3.25	9.11
PORTUGAL		13,858	11,921	13,408	14,075	13,872	0.32	-1.44
SPAIN		177,498	168,275	171,612	175,803	180,476	4.13	2.66
WESTERN EUR		**1,592,146**	**1,543,575**	**1,431,690**	**1,396,009**	**1,396,725**	**31.93**	**0.05**
AUSTRIA		29,449	26,887	27,770	24,497	25,296	0.58	3.26
BELGIUM		34,134	33,263	26,042	26,762	31,908	0.73	19.23
FRANCE		274,986	257,424	230,055	229,600	220,013	5.03	-4.18
GERMANY		882,931	838,595	814,352	767,787	773,724	17.69	0.77

NORWAY

5. OVERNIGHT STAYS OF NON-RESIDENT TOURISTS IN HOTELS AND SIMILAR ESTABLISHMENTS, BY NATIONALITY

	1999	2000	2001	2002	2003	Market share 03	% change 03-02
LUXEMBOURG	2,094	2,199	1,989	2,456	2,634	0.06	7.25
NETHERLANDS	296,998	317,572	270,452	280,081	283,355	6.48	1.17
SWITZERLAND	71,554	67,635	61,030	64,826	59,795	1.37	-7.76
EAST/MED EUR	**4,806**	**4,880**	**2,669**	**3,899**	**3,361**	**0.08**	**-13.80**
TURKEY	4,806	4,880	2,669	3,899	3,361	0.08	-13.80
OTHER EUROPE	**109,474**	**110,217**	**125,651**	**133,093**	**130,170**	**2.98**	**-2.20**
OTHER EUROPE	109,474	110,217	125,651	133,093	130,170	2.98	-2.20
REG.NOT SPEC	**167,855**	**165,737**	**188,717**	**179,817**	**187,109**	**4.28**	**4.06**
NOT SPECIFIE	**167,855**	**165,737**	**188,717**	**179,817**	**187,109**	**4.28**	**4.06**
OTH.WORLD	167,855	165,737	188,717	179,817	187,109	4.28	4.06

Source: World Tourism Organization (WTO)

OMAN

3. ARRIVALS OF NON-RESIDENT TOURISTS IN HOTELS AND SIMILAR ESTABLISHMENTS, BY NATIONALITY

	1999	2000	2001	2002	2003	Market share 03	% change 03-02
TOTAL	**502,788**	**571,110**	**562,119**	**602,109**	**629,986**	**100.00**	**4.63**
AFRICA	**22,402**	**18,352**	**20,191**	**15,527**	**19,035**	**3.02**	**22.59**
EAST AFRICA	**4,923**	**6,368**	**12,145**	**4,789**	**6,202**	**0.98**	**29.51**
KENYA			536				
UGANDA			110				
TANZANIA	4,923	6,368	11,499	4,789	6,202	0.98	29.51
NORTH AFRICA	**2,930**	**2,851**	**4,420**	**4,632**	**6,287**	**1.00**	**35.73**
ALGERIA	32	76	91				
MOROCCO	1,007	613	960	1,556	1,892	0.30	21.59
SUDAN	1,394	1,635	2,211	2,128	2,639	0.42	24.01
TUNISIA	497	527	1,158	948	1,756	0.28	85.23
SOUTHERN AFR			**1,398**	**3,691**	**3,246**	**0.52**	**-12.06**
SOUTH AFRICA			1,398	3,691	3,246	0.52	-12.06
WEST AFRICA	**126**	**81**	**323**				
GHANA	126	81	47				
NIGERIA			276				
OTHER AFRICA	**14,423**	**9,052**	**1,905**	**2,415**	**3,300**	**0.52**	**36.65**
OTHER AFRICA	14,423	9,052	1,905	2,415	3,300	0.52	36.65
AMERICAS	**22,484**	**34,089**	**48,574**	**36,717**	**36,356**	**5.77**	**-0.98**
NORTH AMER	**22,058**	**33,548**	**33,469**	**32,450**	**29,866**	**4.74**	**-7.96**
CANADA	3,602	6,759	6,444	6,803	5,246	0.83	-22.89
USA	18,456	26,789	27,025	25,647	24,620	3.91	-4.00
SOUTH AMER	**426**	**541**	**87**	**870**	**390**	**0.06**	**-55.17**
ARGENTINA	224	132	15				
BRAZIL	202	409	72	870	390	0.06	-55.17
OTHER AMERIC			**15,018**	**3,397**	**6,100**	**0.97**	**79.57**
OTH AMERICA			15,018	3,397	6,100	0.97	79.57
EAST AS/PACI	**120,834**	**98,295**	**36,913**	**47,012**	**51,026**	**8.10**	**8.54**
N/EAST ASIA	**6,047**	**10,259**	**7,189**	**9,152**	**10,923**	**1.73**	**19.35**
CHINA	1,274	1,456	1,666	6,761	4,351	0.69	-35.65
JAPAN	4,773	8,803	5,523	2,391	6,572	1.04	174.86
S/EAST ASIA	**4,752**	**12,704**	**10,799**	**6,593**	**5,609**	**0.89**	**-14.92**
INDONESIA			388				
PHILIPPINES	4,752	12,704	9,885	6,593	5,609	0.89	-14.92
THAILAND			526				
AUSTRALASIA	**4,172**	**6,176**	**5,379**	**8,595**	**7,926**	**1.26**	**-7.78**
AUSTRALIA	3,518	4,742	4,562	6,496	6,379	1.01	-1.80
NEW ZEALAND	654	1,434	817	2,099	1,547	0.25	-26.30
OT.EAST AS/P	**105,863**	**69,156**	**13,546**	**22,672**	**26,568**	**4.22**	**17.18**
OTHER ASIA	66,173	29,015	13,546	11,052	20,903	3.32	89.13
OTH OCEANIA	39,690	40,141		11,620	5,665	0.90	-51.25

OMAN

3. ARRIVALS OF NON-RESIDENT TOURISTS IN HOTELS AND SIMILAR ESTABLISHMENTS, BY NATIONALITY

	1999	2000	2001	2002	2003	Market share 03	% change 03-02
EUROPE	**172,022**	**227,143**	**197,279**	**186,320**	**163,855**	**26.01**	**-12.06**
C/E EUROPE			**2,094**				
CZECH REP			100				
RUSSIAN FED			1,994				
NORTHERN EUR	**58,598**	**71,315**	**90,912**	**80,739**	**64,359**	**10.22**	**-20.29**
DENMARK	1,511	1,910	1,684	2,249	1,766	0.28	-21.48
FINLAND			503				
IRELAND			429				
NORWAY			1,590				
SWEDEN	2,199	2,850	1,677	1,629	2,061	0.33	26.52
UK	54,888	66,555	85,029	76,861	60,532	9.61	-21.24
SOUTHERN EUR	**6,343**	**8,832**	**8,212**	**10,486**	**10,597**	**1.68**	**1.06**
ITALY	5,703	7,663	6,930	9,032	8,901	1.41	-1.45
PORTUGAL			442				
SPAIN	640	1,169	840	1,454	1,696	0.27	16.64
WESTERN EUR	**91,711**	**110,832**	**85,355**	**76,566**	**67,862**	**10.77**	**-11.37**
AUSTRIA	5,784	5,201	4,473	5,149	3,139	0.50	-39.04
BELGIUM			3,523				
FRANCE	14,843	16,718	11,522	15,770	14,803	2.35	-6.13
GERMANY	45,063	58,357	46,128	33,300	31,133	4.94	-6.51
NETHERLANDS	9,624	11,746	10,095	10,053	9,052	1.44	-9.96
SWITZERLAND	16,397	18,810	9,614	12,294	9,735	1.55	-20.82
EAST/MED EUR			**654**				
CYPRUS			263				
TURKEY			391				
OTHER EUROPE	**15,370**	**36,164**	**10,052**	**18,529**	**21,037**	**3.34**	**13.54**
OTHER EUROPE	15,370	36,164	10,052	18,529	21,037	3.34	13.54
MIDDLE EAST	**111,159**	**127,676**	**154,554**	**165,879**	**204,586**	**32.47**	**23.33**
MIDDLE EAST	**111,159**	**127,676**	**154,554**	**165,879**	**204,586**	**32.47**	**23.33**
BAHRAIN	8,642	15,827	18,538	17,609	29,881	4.74	69.69
PALESTINE			326				
IRAQ			1,527				
JORDAN	3,741	3,954	5,337	6,610	9,167	1.46	38.68
KUWAIT	8,705	10,196	11,378	10,052	11,218	1.78	11.60
LEBANON	3,188	3,602	4,157	5,185	5,437	0.86	4.86
LIBYA	24	42	129				
QATAR	4,339	5,774	5,421	6,580	8,697	1.38	32.17
SAUDI ARABIA	12,173	17,260	18,543	21,555	22,163	3.52	2.82
SYRIA	1,694	2,115	3,469	3,345	5,206	0.83	55.64
UNTD ARAB EM	33,862	55,984	65,122	71,697	87,407	13.87	21.91
EGYPT	7,391	9,207	12,759	16,990	16,886	2.68	-0.61
YEMEN			1,034				
OT MIDD EAST	27,400	3,715	6,814	6,256	8,524	1.35	36.25
SOUTH ASIA	**53,887**	**65,555**	**77,033**	**69,818**	**101,971**	**16.19**	**46.05**
SOUTH ASIA	**53,887**	**65,555**	**77,033**	**69,818**	**101,971**	**16.19**	**46.05**
SRI LANKA	2,607	2,756	3,405	3,062	4,032	0.64	31.68

OMAN

3. ARRIVALS OF NON-RESIDENT TOURISTS IN HOTELS AND SIMILAR ESTABLISHMENTS, BY NATIONALITY

	1999	2000	2001	2002	2003	Market share 03	% change 03-02
INDIA	43,339	52,313	61,891	57,212	83,065	13.19	45.19
IRAN	1,115	1,421	1,661	2,092	2,857	0.45	36.57
PAKISTAN	6,826	9,065	10,076	7,452	12,017	1.91	61.26
REG.NOT SPEC			**27,575**	**80,836**	**53,157**	**8.44**	**-34.24**
NOT SPECIFIE			**27,575**	**80,836**	**53,157**	**8.44**	**-34.24**
OTH.WORLD			27,575	80,836	53,157	8.44	-34.24

Source: World Tourism Organization (WTO)

OMAN

5. OVERNIGHT STAYS OF NON-RESIDENT TOURISTS IN HOTELS AND SIMILAR ESTABLISHMENTS, BY NATIONALITY

	1999	2000	2001	2002	2003	Market share 03	% change 03-02
TOTAL				**738,959**	**777,481**	**100.00**	**5.21**
AFRICA				**20,770**	**23,740**	**3.05**	**14.30**
EAST AFRICA				**5,058**	**6,803**	**0.88**	**34.50**
TANZANIA				5,058	6,803	0.88	34.50
NORTH AFRICA				**6,684**	**8,255**	**1.06**	**23.50**
MOROCCO				2,216	2,984	0.38	34.66
SUDAN				3,078	3,399	0.44	10.43
TUNISIA				1,390	1,872	0.24	34.68
SOUTHERN AFR				**4,537**	**4,433**	**0.57**	**-2.29**
SOUTH AFRICA				4,537	4,433	0.57	-2.29
OTHER AFRICA				**4,491**	**4,249**	**0.55**	**-5.39**
OTHER AFRICA				4,491	4,249	0.55	-5.39
AMERICAS				**44,188**	**48,157**	**6.19**	**8.98**
NORTH AMER				**40,795**	**40,485**	**5.21**	**-0.76**
CANADA				9,612	7,560	0.97	-21.35
USA				31,183	32,925	4.23	5.59
SOUTH AMER				**1,041**	**481**	**0.06**	**-53.79**
BRAZIL				1,041	481	0.06	-53.79
OTHER AMERIC				**2,352**	**7,191**	**0.92**	**205.74**
OTH AMERICA				2,352	7,191	0.92	205.74
EAST AS/PACI				**79,123**	**70,623**	**9.08**	**-10.74**
N/EAST ASIA				**13,895**	**15,691**	**2.02**	**12.93**
CHINA				4,644	6,856	0.88	47.63
JAPAN				9,251	8,835	1.14	-4.50
S/EAST ASIA				**8,538**	**8,330**	**1.07**	**-2.44**
PHILIPPINES				8,538	8,330	1.07	-2.44
AUSTRALASIA				**12,066**	**12,527**	**1.61**	**3.82**
AUSTRALIA				9,873	9,822	1.26	-0.52
NEW ZEALAND				2,193	2,705	0.35	23.35
OT.EAST AS/P				**44,624**	**34,075**	**4.38**	**-23.64**
OTHER ASIA				28,292	28,216	3.63	-0.27
OTH OCEANIA				16,332	5,859	0.75	-64.13
EUROPE				**223,052**	**183,806**	**23.64**	**-17.60**
NORTHERN EUR				**93,111**	**72,624**	**9.34**	**-22.00**
DENMARK				3,670	2,101	0.27	-42.75
SWEDEN				2,836	2,279	0.29	-19.64
UK				86,605	68,244	8.78	-21.20
SOUTHERN EUR				**15,278**	**18,256**	**2.35**	**19.49**
ITALY				13,463	16,530	2.13	22.78
SPAIN				1,815	1,726	0.22	-4.90

OMAN

5. OVERNIGHT STAYS OF NON-RESIDENT TOURISTS IN HOTELS AND SIMILAR ESTABLISHMENTS, BY NATIONALITY

	1999	2000	2001	2002	2003	Market share 03	% change 03-02
WESTERN EUR				**85,001**	**68,816**	**8.85**	**-19.04**
AUSTRIA				6,544	2,920	0.38	-55.38
FRANCE				17,541	14,741	1.90	-15.96
GERMANY				38,332	32,626	4.20	-14.89
NETHERLANDS				10,442	10,881	1.40	4.20
SWITZERLAND				12,142	7,648	0.98	-37.01
OTHER EUROPE				**29,662**	**24,110**	**3.10**	**-18.72**
OTHER EUROPE				29,662	24,110	3.10	-18.72
MIDDLE EAST				**210,613**	**242,074**	**31.14**	**14.94**
MIDDLE EAST				**210,613**	**242,074**	**31.14**	**14.94**
BAHRAIN				27,008	31,121	4.00	15.23
JORDAN				10,381	14,350	1.85	38.23
KUWAIT				12,266	14,054	1.81	14.58
LEBANON				8,781	11,206	1.44	27.62
QATAR				8,651	9,562	1.23	10.53
SAUDI ARABIA				24,511	26,262	3.38	7.14
SYRIA				5,999	9,107	1.17	51.81
UNTD ARAB EM				75,910	88,217	11.35	16.21
EGYPT				28,258	24,135	3.10	-14.59
OT MIDD EAST				8,848	14,060	1.81	58.91
SOUTH ASIA				**111,865**	**138,160**	**17.77**	**23.51**
SOUTH ASIA				**111,865**	**138,160**	**17.77**	**23.51**
SRI LANKA				3,886	4,725	0.61	21.59
INDIA				96,330	113,993	14.66	18.34
IRAN				2,817	4,360	0.56	54.77
PAKISTAN				8,832	15,082	1.94	70.77
REG.NOT SPEC				**49,348**	**70,921**	**9.12**	**43.72**
NOT SPECIFIE				**49,348**	**70,921**	**9.12**	**43.72**
OTH.WORLD				49,348	70,921	9.12	43.72

Source: World Tourism Organization (WTO)

PAKISTAN

1. ARRIVALS OF NON-RESIDENT TOURISTS AT NATIONAL BORDERS, BY NATIONALITY

	1999	2000	2001	2002	2003	Market share 03	% change 03-02
TOTAL (*)	**432,217**	**556,805**	**499,719**	**498,059**	**479,052**	**100.00**	**-3.82**
AFRICA	**9,694**	**16,499**	**14,877**	**11,620**	**10,750**	**2.24**	**-7.49**
EAST AFRICA	**2,762**	**4,772**	**3,528**	**2,977**	**2,548**	**0.53**	**-14.41**
ERITREA		8	10	18	7		-61.11
KENYA	2,055	2,388	1,588	1,597	1,134	0.24	-28.99
MAURITIUS		566	517	72	309	0.06	329.17
SOMALIA		316	362	418	420	0.09	0.48
UGANDA		305	249	136	106	0.02	-22.06
TANZANIA	707	1,100	720	709	514	0.11	-27.50
ZAMBIA		89	82	27	58	0.01	114.81
CENTRAL AFR		**47**	**46**	**8**	**23**		**187.50**
CAMEROON		47	46	8	23		187.50
NORTH AFRICA		**4,111**	**2,897**	**1,468**	**1,004**	**0.21**	**-31.61**
ALGERIA		560	435	200	74	0.02	-63.00
MOROCCO		674	281	148	156	0.03	5.41
SUDAN		2,359	1,617	889	632	0.13	-28.91
TUNISIA		518	564	231	142	0.03	-38.53
SOUTHERN AFR	**2,872**	**3,790**	**3,697**	**3,668**	**2,909**	**0.61**	**-20.69**
SOUTH AFRICA	2,872	3,777	3,694	3,667	2,902	0.61	-20.86
SWAZILAND		13	3	1	7		600.00
WEST AFRICA		**2,240**	**2,804**	**2,140**	**2,913**	**0.61**	**36.12**
GHANA		93	58	67	134	0.03	100.00
MALI		64	37	38	37	0.01	-2.63
NIGERIA		2,044	2,684	1,830	2,512	0.52	37.27
SENEGAL		39	25	205	230	0.05	12.20
OTHER AFRICA	**4,060**	**1,539**	**1,905**	**1,359**	**1,353**	**0.28**	**-0.44**
OTHER AFRICA	4,060	1,539	1,905	1,359	1,353	0.28	-0.44
AMERICAS	**60,676**	**89,783**	**82,159**	**87,884**	**78,797**	**16.45**	**-10.34**
CARIBBEAN		**18**	**11**	**13**	**19**		**46.15**
CUBA		18	11	13	19		46.15
NORTH AMER	**60,055**	**84,936**	**81,032**	**87,233**	**78,407**	**16.37**	**-10.12**
CANADA	11,429	12,956	11,813	18,150	12,486	2.61	-31.21
MEXICO	138	462	152	53	76	0.02	43.40
USA	48,488	71,518	69,067	69,030	65,845	13.74	-4.61
SOUTH AMER	**548**	**4,525**	**895**	**544**	**297**	**0.06**	**-45.40**
ARGENTINA	37	489	395	213	123	0.03	-42.25
BRAZIL	511	3,894	378	201	103	0.02	-48.76
CHILE		56	70	52	24	0.01	-53.85
COLOMBIA		42	29	35	22		-37.14
PERU		44	23	43	25	0.01	-41.86
OTHER AMERIC	**73**	**304**	**221**	**94**	**74**	**0.02**	**-21.28**
OTH AMERICA	73	304	221	94	74	0.02	-21.28
EAST AS/PACI	**44,484**	**49,654**	**42,711**	**43,920**	**42,233**	**8.82**	**-3.84**
N/EAST ASIA	**24,546**	**24,898**	**18,835**	**24,392**	**23,466**	**4.90**	**-3.80**

PAKISTAN

1. ARRIVALS OF NON-RESIDENT TOURISTS AT NATIONAL BORDERS, BY NATIONALITY

	1999	2000	2001	2002	2003	Market share 03	% change 03-02
CHINA	7,957	6,191	5,704	8,896	10,055	2.10	13.03
TAIWAN(P.C.)		190	263	183	353	0.07	92.90
HK,CHINA		1,645	801	1,180	233	0.05	-80.25
JAPAN	16,589	12,794	7,580	9,975	9,094	1.90	-8.83
KOREA REP.		4,078	4,487	4,158	3,731	0.78	-10.27
S/EAST ASIA	**7,609**	**15,154**	**14,016**	**12,449**	**11,703**	**2.44**	**-5.99**
MYANMAR		357	436	335	451	0.09	34.63
CAMBODIA		13	21	1	73	0.02	7.200.00
INDONESIA	1,054	2,580	1,756	1,692	1,181	0.25	-30.20
MALAYSIA	3,223	4,317	5,114	4,095	3,637	0.76	-11.18
PHILIPPINES	1,699	2,160	1,679	2,079	1,648	0.34	-20.73
SINGAPORE		2,323	2,639	1,772	2,265	0.47	27.82
VIET NAM		101	43	48	36	0.01	-25.00
THAILAND	1,633	2,001	2,134	2,363	2,335	0.49	-1.18
OTH S/E ASIA		1,302	194	64	77	0.02	20.31
AUSTRALASIA	**6,326**	**9,602**	**9,860**	**7,079**	**7,064**	**1.47**	**-0.21**
AUSTRALIA	4,881	7,697	7,435	5,740	6,065	1.27	5.66
NEW ZEALAND	1,445	1,905	2,425	1,339	999	0.21	-25.39
OT.EAST AS/P	**6,003**						
OEAP	6,003						
EUROPE	**189,979**	**257,504**	**205,140**	**215,280**	**188,291**	**39.30**	**-12.54**
C/E EUROPE	**2,504**	**5,412**	**5,201**	**3,863**	**3,794**	**0.79**	**-1.79**
AZERBAIJAN		184	289	318	363	0.08	14.15
BULGARIA		240	76	69	57	0.01	-17.39
CZECH REP		530	589	199	239	0.05	20.10
HUNGARY		136	107	116	149	0.03	28.45
KAZAKHSTAN		897	699	414	529	0.11	27.78
KYRGYZSTAN		76	107	80	96	0.02	20.00
POLAND	440	411	546	370	386	0.08	4.32
ROMANIA		211	191	174	289	0.06	66.09
RUSSIAN FED		1,828	1,265	1,080	953	0.20	-11.76
TAJIKISTAN				167	271	0.06	62.28
UKRAINE		198	381	595	272	0.06	-54.29
USSR(former)	2,064						
UZBEKISTAN		701	951	281	190	0.04	-32.38
NORTHERN EUR	**139,160**	**198,967**	**158,218**	**167,437**	**144,519**	**30.17**	**-13.69**
DENMARK	2,870	4,887	4,400	4,846	4,172	0.87	-13.91
FINLAND	1,212	819	582	346	319	0.07	-7.80
IRELAND	1,069	1,449	1,417	927	1,270	0.27	37.00
NORWAY	5,368	7,947	4,183	7,075	7,248	1.51	2.45
SWEDEN	2,109	4,107	3,228	2,902	3,082	0.64	6.20
UK	126,532	179,758	144,408	151,341	128,428	26.81	-15.14
SOUTHERN EUR	**5,517**	**8,239**	**6,195**	**5,464**	**5,164**	**1.08**	**-5.49**
ALBANIA		29	15	13	152	0.03	1.069.23
GREECE	757	1,082	546	525	445	0.09	-15.24
ITALY	3,305	3,775	3,046	3,036	2,919	0.61	-3.85
MALTA		311	35	28	46	0.01	64.29
PORTUGAL	163	941	924	444	354	0.07	-20.27
SPAIN	1,292	1,809	1,526	1,344	1,248	0.26	-7.14
SERBIA,MTNEG		292	103	74			
WESTERN EUR	**34,951**	**33,729**	**30,219**	**34,561**	**31,950**	**6.67**	**-7.55**

PAKISTAN

1. ARRIVALS OF NON-RESIDENT TOURISTS AT NATIONAL BORDERS, BY NATIONALITY

	1999	2000	2001	2002	2003	Market share 03	% change 03-02
AUSTRIA	1,324	2,068	1,439	1,667	1,029	0.21	-38.27
BELGIUM	3,050	2,556	2,015	1,694	1,892	0.39	11.69
FRANCE	8,012	517	7,159	6,892	5,500	1.15	-20.20
GERMANY	12,778	14,121	9,047	12,243	13,216	2.76	7.95
NETHERLANDS	6,392	9,794	7,277	9,751	8,972	1.87	-7.99
SWITZERLAND	3,395	4,673	3,282	2,314	1,341	0.28	-42.05
EAST/MED EUR	**3,528**	**4,264**	**3,514**	**3,024**	**2,323**	**0.48**	**-23.18**
CYPRUS		778	478	247	92	0.02	-62.75
TURKEY	3,528	3,486	3,036	2,777	2,231	0.47	-19.66
OTHER EUROPE	**4,319**	**6,893**	**1,793**	**931**	**541**	**0.11**	**-41.89**
OTHER EUROPE	4,319	6,893	1,793	931	541	0.11	-41.89
MIDDLE EAST	**19,792**	**33,107**	**30,466**	**22,329**	**17,701**	**3.70**	**-20.73**
MIDDLE EAST	**19,792**	**33,107**	**30,466**	**22,329**	**17,701**	**3.70**	**-20.73**
BAHRAIN	470	876	618	915	1,233	0.26	34.75
PALESTINE		769	683	254	179	0.04	-29.53
IRAQ	191	463	326	254	96	0.02	-62.20
JORDAN	1,173	1,681	1,899	1,002	1,001	0.21	-0.10
KUWAIT	1,222	1,892	1,131	1,008	491	0.10	-51.29
LEBANON		1,221	1,151	318	443	0.09	39.31
LIBYA	91	195	251	330	162	0.03	-50.91
OMAN	4,795	6,223	5,207	4,702	3,694	0.77	-21.44
QATAR		953	2,012	1,971	934	0.19	-52.61
SAUDI ARABIA	3,900	6,344	5,831	4,220	4,268	0.89	1.14
SYRIA		714	693	482	337	0.07	-30.08
UNTD ARAB EM	4,570	7,548	7,090	4,563	3,471	0.72	-23.93
EGYPT	1,025	2,552	1,915	1,589	1,029	0.21	-35.24
YEMEN		1,674	1,640	719	363	0.08	-49.51
OT MIDD EAST	2,355	2	19	2			
SOUTH ASIA	**107,214**	**108,960**	**123,957**	**116,449**	**140,646**	**29.36**	**20.78**
SOUTH ASIA	**107,214**	**108,960**	**123,957**	**116,449**	**140,646**	**29.36**	**20.78**
AFGHANISTAN	25,586	27,913	46,994	98,498	119,368	24.92	21.19
BANGLADESH	6,287	1,389	6,233	5,581	6,505	1.36	16.56
SRI LANKA	2,551	4,113	3,063	1,960	2,331	0.49	18.93
INDIA	63,225	66,061	58,378	2,618	3,380	0.71	29.11
IRAN	7,124	5,365	6,366	6,394	7,891	1.65	23.41
MALDIVES		487	299	248	176	0.04	-29.03
NEPAL		2,994	2,521	1,139	973	0.20	-14.57
OTH STH ASIA	2,441	638	103	11	22		100.00
REG.NOT SPEC	**378**	**1,298**	**409**	**577**	**634**	**0.13**	**9.88**
NOT SPECIFIE	**378**	**1,298**	**409**	**577**	**634**	**0.13**	**9.88**
OTH.WORLD	378	1,298	409	577	634	0.13	9.88

Source: World Tourism Organization (WTO)

PALAU

1. ARRIVALS OF NON-RESIDENT TOURISTS AT NATIONAL BORDERS, BY COUNTRY OF RESIDENCE

		1999	2000	2001	2002	2003	Market share 03	% change 03-02
TOTAL	(*)	55,493	57,732	54,111	58,560	68,296	100.00	16.63
AMERICAS		**5,587**	**6,704**	**5,375**	**4,774**	**4,511**	**6.61**	**-5.51**
NORTH AMER		**5,587**	**6,704**	**5,375**	**4,774**	**4,511**	**6.61**	**-5.51**
USA		5,587	6,704	5,375	4,774	4,511	6.61	-5.51
EAST AS/PACI		**46,048**	**48,630**	**46,191**	**51,504**	**61,400**	**89.90**	**19.21**
N/EAST ASIA		**34,774**	**37,660**	**36,751**	**41,473**	**51,399**	**75.26**	**23.93**
CHINA		868	889	867	873	724	1.06	-17.07
TAIWAN(P.C.)		10,936	14,122	12,476	15,819	28,088	41.13	77.56
HK,CHINA		344	355	663	536	443	0.65	-17.35
JAPAN		22,087	21,708	22,395	23,748	21,691	31.76	-8.66
KOREA REP.		539	586	350	497	453	0.66	-8.85
S/EAST ASIA		**3,081**	**4,077**	**4,199**	**3,497**	**3,679**	**5.39**	**5.20**
PHILIPPINES		2,952	3,981	4,128	3,410	3,625	5.31	6.30
SINGAPORE		129	96	71	87	54	0.08	-37.93
AUSTRALASIA		**402**	**347**	**430**	**403**	**527**	**0.77**	**30.77**
AUSTRALIA		402	347	430	403	527	0.77	30.77
MICRONESIA		**7,791**	**6,546**	**4,811**	**6,131**	**5,795**	**8.49**	**-5.48**
GUAM		5,594	4,331	2,965	3,729	3,688	5.40	-1.10
N.MARIANA IS		913	1,036	912	1,335	1,010	1.48	-24.34
MICRONESIA		1,284	1,179	934	1,067	1,097	1.61	2.81
EUROPE		**1,418**	**974**	**930**	**834**	**818**	**1.20**	**-1.92**
NORTHERN EUR		**300**	**311**	**288**	**250**	**117**	**0.17**	**-53.20**
UK		300	311	288	250	117	0.17	-53.20
SOUTHERN EUR		**101**	**76**	**106**	**97**	**123**	**0.18**	**26.80**
ITALY		101	76	106	97	123	0.18	26.80
WESTERN EUR		**1,017**	**587**	**536**	**487**	**578**	**0.85**	**18.69**
FRANCE		86	65	68	77	47	0.07	-38.96
GERMANY		796	372	296	256	414	0.61	61.72
SWITZERLAND		135	150	172	154	117	0.17	-24.03
REG.NOT SPEC		**2,440**	**1,424**	**1,615**	**1,448**	**1,567**	**2.29**	**8.22**
NOT SPECIFIE		**2,440**	**1,424**	**1,615**	**1,448**	**1,567**	**2.29**	**8.22**
OTH.WORLD		2,440	1,424	1,615	1,448	1,567	2.29	8.22

Source: World Tourism Organization (WTO)

2. ARRIVALS OF NON-RESIDENT VISITORS AT NATIONAL BORDERS, BY COUNTRY OF RESIDENCE

	1999	2000	2001	2002	2003	Market share 03	% change 03-02
TOTAL (*)	**907,000**	**1,055,000**	**81,472**	**9,453**	**46,356**	**100.00**	**390.38**
AFRICA	**18,000**	**21,000**	**1,682**	**88**	**337**	**0.73**	**282.95**
SOUTHERN AFR	**2,813**	**2,871**	**547**	**24**	**105**	**0.23**	**337.50**
SOUTH AFRICA	2,813	2,871	547	24	105	0.23	337.50
WEST AFRICA			**63**		**75**	**0.16**	
NIGERIA			63		75	0.16	
OTHER AFRICA	**15,187**	**18,129**	**1,072**	**64**	**157**	**0.34**	**145.31**
OTHER AFRICA	15,187	18,129	1,072	64	157	0.34	145.31
AMERICAS	**181,000**	**211,000**	**23,377**	**1,402**	**5,836**	**12.59**	**316.26**
NORTH AMER	**106,951**	**127,522**	**20,742**	**1,262**	**4,791**	**10.34**	**279.64**
CANADA	4,595	4,561	742	100	353	0.76	253.00
MEXICO			1,554	18	528	1.14	2.833.33
USA	102,356	122,961	18,446	1,144	3,910	8.43	241.78
SOUTH AMER	**5,381**	**8,216**	**2,635**	**140**	**1,045**	**2.25**	**646.43**
ARGENTINA			300	11			
BRAZIL	5,381	8,216	1,048		187	0.40	
CHILE			282	53	39	0.08	-26.42
OTH SOUTH AM			1,005	76	819	1.77	977.63
OTHER AMERIC	**68,668**	**75,262**					
OTH AMERICA	68,668	75,262					
EAST AS/PACI	**38,000**	**43,000**	**7,286**	**1,073**	**8,111**	**17.50**	**655.92**
N/EAST ASIA	**5,746**	**10,280**	**2,855**	**509**	**1,596**	**3.44**	**213.56**
CHINA			456	70	126	0.27	80.00
TAIWAN(P.C.)			220	43	36	0.08	-16.28
JAPAN	5,746	10,280	646	131	1,014	2.19	674.05
KOREA REP.			1,533	265	420	0.91	58.49
S/EAST ASIA			**3,645**	**514**	**6,218**	**13.41**	**1,109.73**
INDONESIA			2,431	417	2,090	4.51	401.20
PHILIPPINES			1,142	61	4,128	8.90	6.667.21
THAILAND			72	36			
AUSTRALASIA			**283**	**25**	**154**	**0.33**	**516.00**
AUSTRALIA			283	25	154	0.33	516.00
OT.EAST AS/P	**32,254**	**32,720**	**503**	**25**	**143**	**0.31**	**472.00**
OTHER ASIA			503	25	143	0.31	472.00
OEAP	32,254	32,720					
EUROPE	**608,000**	**717,000**	**24,571**	**4,656**	**18,569**	**40.06**	**298.82**
C/E EUROPE	**74,024**	**85,978**	**7,995**	**1,313**	**3,648**	**7.87**	**177.84**
CZECH REP			519	36	269	0.58	647.22
POLAND	14,475	28,424	4,926	209	709	1.53	239.23
ROMANIA			1,273	716	1,567	3.38	118.85
RUSSIAN FED	59,549	57,554	1,128	335	1,056	2.28	215.22
UKRAINE			149	17	47	0.10	176.47

PALESTINE

2. ARRIVALS OF NON-RESIDENT VISITORS AT NATIONAL BORDERS, BY COUNTRY OF RESIDENCE

	1999	2000	2001	2002	2003	Market share 03	% change 03-02
NORTHERN EUR	**88,873**	**87,662**	**2,728**	**501**	**1,765**	**3.81**	**252.30**
DENMARK			187	22	147	0.32	568.18
FINLAND			38	3	57	0.12	1,800.00
IRELAND			301	23	31	0.07	34.78
NORWAY			426	36	151	0.33	319.44
SWEDEN			398	73	314	0.68	330.14
UK	68,045	69,221	1,378	344	1,065	2.30	209.59
OTH NORT EUR	20,828	18,441					
SOUTHERN EUR	**121,627**	**207,100**	**6,208**	**1,492**	**8,028**	**17.32**	**438.07**
CROATIA			97		61	0.13	
GREECE	24,261	36,905	1,583	419	725	1.56	73.03
ITALY	75,149	132,002	2,516	664	5,081	10.96	665.21
PORTUGAL			131	55	95	0.20	72.73
SPAIN	22,217	38,193	1,881	354	2,066	4.46	483.62
WESTERN EUR	**114,559**	**144,400**	**6,382**	**1,162**	**4,419**	**9.53**	**280.29**
AUSTRIA	4,882	2,119	135	68	185	0.40	172.06
BELGIUM			238	38	143	0.31	276.32
FRANCE	29,767	40,315	2,702	599	2,481	5.35	314.19
GERMANY	59,667	81,301	2,573	404	1,246	2.69	208.42
NETHERLANDS			612	42	246	0.53	485.71
SWITZERLAND			122	11	118	0.25	972.73
OTH WEST EUR	20,243	20,665					
EAST/MED EUR	**16,739**	**7,644**	**147**	**17**	**498**	**1.07**	**2,829.41**
CYPRUS	9,412	2,711	10	17	168	0.36	888.24
ISRAEL	7,327	4,933	137		330	0.71	
OTHER EUROPE	**192,178**	**184,216**	**1,111**	**171**	**211**	**0.46**	**23.39**
OTHER EUROPE	192,178	184,216	1,111	171	211	0.46	23.39
MIDDLE EAST	**45,000**	**42,000**	**58**				
MIDDLE EAST	**45,000**	**42,000**	**58**				
EGYPT			54				
OT MIDD EAST			4				
ALL MID EAST	45,000	42,000					
SOUTH ASIA	**17,000**	**21,000**	**1,742**	**113**	**561**	**1.21**	**396.46**
SOUTH ASIA	**17,000**	**21,000**	**1,742**	**113**	**561**	**1.21**	**396.46**
INDIA	3,609	4,401	1,742	113	561	1.21	396.46
OTH STH ASIA	13,391	16,599					
REG.NOT SPEC			**22,756**	**2,121**	**12,942**	**27.92**	**510.18**
NOT SPECIFIE			**22,756**	**2,121**	**12,942**	**27.92**	**510.18**
OTH.WORLD			22,756	2,121	12,942	27.92	510.18

Source: World Tourism Organization (WTO)

PANAMA

2. ARRIVALS OF NON-RESIDENT VISITORS AT NATIONAL BORDERS, BY COUNTRY OF RESIDENCE

	1999	2000	2001	2002	2003	Market share 03	% change 03-02
TOTAL (*)	**445,957**	**467,228**	**482,040**	**499,643**	**534,208**	**100.00**	**6.92**
AFRICA	**228**	**324**	**425**	**341**	**359**	**0.07**	**5.28**
SOUTHERN AFR	**53**	**100**	**113**	**109**	**131**	**0.02**	**20.18**
SOUTH AFRICA	53	100	113	109	131	0.02	20.18
OTHER AFRICA	**175**	**224**	**312**	**232**	**228**	**0.04**	**-1.72**
OTHER AFRICA	175	224	312	232	228	0.04	-1.72
AMERICAS	**398,852**	**419,348**	**433,103**	**442,890**	**471,033**	**88.17**	**6.35**
CARIBBEAN	**35,475**	**34,718**	**33,303**	**28,816**	**28,108**	**5.26**	**-2.46**
BAHAMAS	366	431	394	408	407	0.08	-0.25
BARBADOS	173	184	229	240	317	0.06	32.08
BERMUDA	49	98	57	70	90	0.02	28.57
CUBA	2,075	3,214	2,841	2,745	2,474	0.46	-9.87
DOMINICAN RP	8,712	9,360	8,843	7,702	6,291	1.18	-18.32
HAITI	6,613	5,331	3,823	3,974	4,120	0.77	3.67
JAMAICA	8,450	8,354	8,491	4,720	4,620	0.86	-2.12
CURACAO	614	475	377	239	494	0.09	106.69
PUERTO RICO	6,669	5,716	6,666	7,254	7,526	1.41	3.75
OTH CARIBBE	1,754	1,555	1,582	1,464	1,769	0.33	20.83
CENTRAL AMER	**103,631**	**104,917**	**100,143**	**101,799**	**101,342**	**18.97**	**-0.45**
BELIZE	655	719	858	1,499	1,330	0.25	-11.27
COSTA RICA	61,327	61,877	56,846	57,550	54,290	10.16	-5.66
EL SALVADOR	8,298	8,162	7,585	7,992	9,837	1.84	23.09
GUATEMALA	11,419	12,428	12,937	14,205	14,284	2.67	0.56
HONDURAS	9,419	8,753	9,012	8,508	9,846	1.84	15.73
NICARAGUA	12,513	12,978	12,905	12,045	11,755	2.20	-2.41
NORTH AMER	**142,776**	**144,080**	**147,691**	**152,799**	**172,464**	**32.28**	**12.87**
CANADA	5,797	6,953	14,652	15,897	15,167	2.84	-4.59
MEXICO	17,805	21,153	20,447	20,784	24,398	4.57	17.39
USA	119,169	115,970	112,585	116,103	132,898	24.88	14.47
OT.NORTH.AME	5	4	7	15	1		-93.33
SOUTH AMER	**116,970**	**135,633**	**151,966**	**159,476**	**169,119**	**31.66**	**6.05**
ARGENTINA	5,889	7,888	9,403	7,196	9,363	1.75	30.11
BOLIVIA	3,182	2,561	2,083	2,204	2,411	0.45	9.39
BRAZIL	3,690	4,889	6,290	6,471	7,877	1.47	21.73
CHILE	4,413	73,611	6,006	6,444	7,116	1.33	10.43
COLOMBIA	64,261	5,547	80,972	88,049	93,821	17.56	6.56
ECUADOR	11,966	14,515	19,171	22,049	20,357	3.81	-7.67
PARAGUAY	597	546	493	423	654	0.12	54.61
PERU	5,412	7,317	8,378	10,643	10,789	2.02	1.37
URUGUAY	1,038	1,247	1,193	1,180	1,399	0.26	18.56
VENEZUELA	16,225	17,129	17,606	14,357	14,827	2.78	3.27
OTH SOUTH AM	297	383	371	460	505	0.09	9.78
EAST AS/PACI	**13,098**	**12,151**	**11,988**	**12,737**	**14,723**	**2.76**	**15.59**
N/EAST ASIA	**6,010**	**5,165**	**4,786**	**4,653**	**5,026**	**0.94**	**8.02**
TAIWAN(P.C.)	2,390	1,880	1,757	1,387	1,669	0.31	20.33
JAPAN	3,620	3,285	3,029	3,266	3,357	0.63	2.79

PANAMA

2. ARRIVALS OF NON-RESIDENT VISITORS AT NATIONAL BORDERS, BY COUNTRY OF RESIDENCE

	1999	2000	2001	2002	2003	Market share 03	% change 03-02
AUSTRALASIA	**786**	**856**	**868**	**855**	**1,258**	**0.24**	**47.13**
AUSTRALIA	590	650	620	683	1,002	0.19	46.71
NEW ZEALAND	196	206	248	172	256	0.05	48.84
OT.EAST AS/P	**6,302**	**6,130**	**6,334**	**7,229**	**8,439**	**1.58**	**16.74**
OTHER ASIA	6,247	6,072	6,276	7,177	8,408	1.57	17.15
OTH OCEANIA	55	58	58	52	31	0.01	-40.38
EUROPE	**33,729**	**35,350**	**36,425**	**43,651**	**48,039**	**8.99**	**10.05**
NORTHERN EUR	**3,815**	**3,760**	**3,778**	**4,583**	**4,789**	**0.90**	**4.49**
UK	3,815	3,760	3,778	4,583	4,789	0.90	4.49
SOUTHERN EUR	**11,749**	**12,679**	**13,001**	**17,064**	**15,531**	**2.91**	**-8.98**
GREECE	595	680	544	553	604	0.11	9.22
ITALY	3,492	3,445	4,510	7,213	5,378	1.01	-25.44
SPAIN	7,662	8,554	7,947	9,298	9,549	1.79	2.70
WESTERN EUR	**10,545**	**10,864**	**10,847**	**12,210**	**16,689**	**3.12**	**36.68**
FRANCE	2,902	2,906	2,788	3,504	7,177	1.34	104.82
GERMANY	4,612	4,320	4,494	4,441	4,941	0.92	11.26
NETHERLANDS	1,574	1,819	1,837	2,365	2,329	0.44	-1.52
SWITZERLAND	1,457	1,819	1,728	1,900	2,242	0.42	18.00
EAST/MED EUR	**1,743**	**2,005**	**2,095**	**2,176**	**2,303**	**0.43**	**5.84**
ISRAEL	1,743	2,005	2,095	2,176	2,303	0.43	5.84
OTHER EUROPE	**5,877**	**6,042**	**6,704**	**7,618**	**8,727**	**1.63**	**14.56**
OTHER EUROPE	5,877	6,042	6,704	7,618	8,727	1.63	14.56
MIDDLE EAST	**50**	**55**	**99**	**24**	**54**	**0.01**	**125.00**
MIDDLE EAST	**50**	**55**	**99**	**24**	**54**	**0.01**	**125.00**
EGYPT	50	55	99	24	54	0.01	125.00

Source: World Tourism Organization (WTO)

PAPUA NEW GUINEA

1. ARRIVALS OF NON-RESIDENT TOURISTS AT NATIONAL BORDERS, BY COUNTRY OF RESIDENCE

	1999	2000	2001	2002	2003	Market share 03	% change 03-02
TOTAL	**67,357**	**58,448**	**54,235**	**53,669**	**56,185**	**100.00**	**4.69**
AFRICA	**320**	**212**	**244**	**271**	**191**	**0.34**	**-29.52**
OTHER AFRICA	**320**	**212**	**244**	**271**	**191**	**0.34**	**-29.52**
ALL AFRICA	320	212	244	271	191	0.34	-29.52
AMERICAS	**6,542**	**7,191**	**6,142**	**6,990**	**4,893**	**8.71**	**-30.00**
NORTH AMER	**6,542**	**6,148**	**6,019**	**6,901**	**4,821**	**8.58**	**-30.14**
CANADA	923	719	705	848	560	1.00	-33.96
USA	5,619	5,429	5,314	6,053	4,261	7.58	-29.61
OTHER AMERIC		**1,043**	**123**	**89**	**72**	**0.13**	**-19.10**
OTH AMERICA		1,043	123	89	72	0.13	-19.10
EAST AS/PACI	**53,055**	**44,828**	**41,675**	**40,912**	**46,266**	**82.35**	**13.09**
N/EAST ASIA	**2,427**	**4,344**	**3,702**	**4,662**	**4,649**	**8.27**	**-0.28**
CHINA		1,100	1,016	858	860	1.53	0.23
JAPAN	2,427	3,244	2,686	3,804	3,789	6.74	-0.39
S/EAST ASIA	**9,063**	**4,722**	**4,371**	**3,986**	**4,577**	**8.15**	**14.83**
MALAYSIA		2,066	1,831	1,538	1,805	3.21	17.36
PHILIPPINES		2,656	2,540	2,448	2,772	4.93	13.24
ALL S/E ASIA	9,063						
AUSTRALASIA	**37,530**	**31,933**	**30,392**	**28,912**	**32,561**	**57.95**	**12.62**
AUSTRALIA	33,818	29,285	27,661	26,562	30,609	54.48	15.24
NEW ZEALAND	3,712	2,648	2,731	2,350	1,952	3.47	-16.94
OT.EAST AS/P	**4,035**	**3,829**	**3,210**	**3,352**	**4,479**	**7.97**	**33.62**
OTHER ASIA	2,361	2,473	1,800	1,926	2,384	4.24	23.78
OTH OCEANIA	1,674	1,356	1,410	1,426	2,095	3.73	46.91
EUROPE	**7,282**	**5,198**	**5,161**	**4,731**	**4,214**	**7.50**	**-10.93**
NORTHERN EUR	**3,067**	**2,279**	**2,133**	**1,803**	**1,459**	**2.60**	**-19.08**
UK	3,067	2,279	2,133	1,803	1,459	2.60	-19.08
WESTERN EUR	**1,701**	**1,265**	**1,478**	**1,048**	**1,102**	**1.96**	**5.15**
FRANCE		289	330	246	206	0.37	-16.26
GERMANY	1,701	976	1,148	802	896	1.59	11.72
OTHER EUROPE	**2,514**	**1,654**	**1,550**	**1,880**	**1,653**	**2.94**	**-12.07**
OTHER EUROPE	2,514	1,654	1,550	1,880	1,653	2.94	-12.07
MIDDLE EAST	**142**						
MIDDLE EAST	**142**						
ALL MID EAST	142						
SOUTH ASIA		**1,019**	**1,013**	**764**	**621**	**1.11**	**-18.72**
SOUTH ASIA		**1,019**	**1,013**	**764**	**621**	**1.11**	**-18.72**
INDIA		1,019	1,013	764	621	1.11	-18.72

PAPUA NEW GUINEA

1. ARRIVALS OF NON-RESIDENT TOURISTS AT NATIONAL BORDERS, BY COUNTRY OF RESIDENCE

	1999	2000	2001	2002	2003	Market share 03	% change 03-02
REG.NOT SPEC	**16**			**1**			
NOT SPECIFIE	**16**			**1**			
OTH.WORLD	16			1			

Source: World Tourism Organization (WTO)

PARAGUAY

1. ARRIVALS OF NON-RESIDENT TOURISTS AT NATIONAL BORDERS, BY NATIONALITY

	1999	2000	2001	2002	2003	Market share 03	% change 03-02
TOTAL (*)	**269,021**	**288,515**	**278,672**	**250,423**	**268,175**	**100.00**	**7.09**
AFRICA	**289**		**139**	**161**	**185**	**0.07**	**14.91**
OTHER AFRICA	**289**		**139**	**161**	**185**	**0.07**	**14.91**
ALL AFRICA	289		139	161	185	0.07	14.91
AMERICAS	**213,662**	**285,977**	**260,112**	**231,727**	**248,364**	**92.61**	**7.18**
CARIBBEAN			**418**	**435**	**419**	**0.16**	**-3.68**
ALL CO CARIB			418	435	419	0.16	-3.68
CENTRAL AMER	**1,198**		**752**	**660**	**636**	**0.24**	**-3.64**
ALL CENT AME	1,198		752	660	636	0.24	-3.64
NORTH AMER	**12,428**	**3,491**	**10,450**	**10,963**	**11,181**	**4.17**	**1.99**
CANADA	924		947	1,062	1,019	0.38	-4.05
MEXICO	1,330		808	889	952	0.35	7.09
USA	10,174	3,491	8,695	9,012	9,210	3.43	2.20
SOUTH AMER	**200,036**	**282,486**	**248,492**	**219,669**	**236,128**	**88.05**	**7.49**
ARGENTINA	98,381	199,220	170,575	160,758	177,741	66.28	10.56
BOLIVIA	6,044	3,001	2,842	3,119	2,177	0.81	-30.20
BRAZIL	62,695	73,283	60,193	43,134	40,651	15.16	-5.76
CHILE	16,146	2,597	5,964	4,694	6,262	2.34	33.40
COLOMBIA	1,536		1,059	815	849	0.32	4.17
ECUADOR	406		334	304	512	0.19	68.42
PERU	5,148		1,588	1,559	1,749	0.65	12.19
URUGUAY	9,424	4,385	5,351	4,939	5,775	2.15	16.93
VENEZUELA	256		585	345	408	0.15	18.26
OTH SOUTH AM			1	2	4		100.00
EAST AS/PACI	**4,260**		**3,010**	**4,620**	**4,251**	**1.59**	**-7.99**
N/EAST ASIA	**2,020**		**2,146**	**2,038**	**1,946**	**0.73**	**-4.51**
JAPAN	2,020		2,146	2,038	1,946	0.73	-4.51
OT.EAST AS/P	**2,240**		**864**	**2,582**	**2,305**	**0.86**	**-10.73**
OTHER ASIA	1,785		585	2,390	2,147	0.80	-10.17
OEAP	455		279	192	158	0.06	-17.71
EUROPE	**32,200**		**15,411**	**13,915**	**15,375**	**5.73**	**10.49**
SOUTHERN EUR	**13,013**		**4,403**	**4,028**	**4,665**	**1.74**	**15.81**
ITALY	5,656		1,588	1,360	1,565	0.58	15.07
SPAIN	7,357		2,815	2,668	3,100	1.16	16.19
WESTERN EUR	**6,110**		**6,075**	**6,015**	**6,436**	**2.40**	**7.00**
FRANCE			1,672	1,510	1,610	0.60	6.62
GERMANY	6,110		4,403	4,505	4,826	1.80	7.13
OTHER EUROPE	**13,077**		**4,933**	**3,872**	**4,274**	**1.59**	**10.38**
OTHER EUROPE	13,077		4,933	3,872	4,274	1.59	10.38
REG.NOT SPEC	**18,610**	**2,538**					

PARAGUAY

1. ARRIVALS OF NON-RESIDENT TOURISTS AT NATIONAL BORDERS, BY NATIONALITY

	1999	2000	2001	2002	2003	Market share 03	% change 03-02
NOT SPECIFIE	**18,610**	**2,538**					
OTH.WORLD	18,610	2,538					

Source: World Tourism Organization (WTO)

PARAGUAY

3. ARRIVALS OF NON-RESIDENT TOURISTS IN HOTELS AND SIMILAR ESTABLISHMENTS, BY NATIONALITY

	1999	2000	2001	2002	2003	Market share 03	% change 03-02
TOTAL	**224,185**	**188,722**	**135,484**	**87,500**			
AFRICA	**241**	**218**	**95**	**109**			
OTHER AFRICA	**241**	**218**	**95**	**109**			
ALL AFRICA	241	218	95	109			
AMERICAS	**178,052**	**154,631**	**110,199**	**71,841**			
CARIBBEAN			**336**	**148**			
ALL CO CARIB			336	148			
CENTRAL AMER	**998**	**517**	**203**	**238**			
ALL CENT AME	998	517	203	238			
NORTH AMER	**10,356**	**8,715**	**7,332**	**4,039**			
CANADA	770	617	461	285			
MEXICO	1,108	835	393	388			
USA	8,478	7,263	6,478	3,366			
SOUTH AMER	**166,698**	**145,399**	**102,328**	**67,416**			
ARGENTINA	81,984	89,858	56,916	41,662			
BOLIVIA	5,037	6,327	4,743	2,933			
BRAZIL	52,246	29,667	26,019	13,756			
CHILE	13,455	7,758	6,505	3,597			
COLOMBIA	1,280	814	515	379			
ECUADOR	338	219	163	102			
PERU	4,290	5,687	3,117	2,636			
URUGUAY	7,854	4,817	4,065	2,234			
VENEZUELA	214	252	285	117			
EAST AS/PACI	**3,550**	**2,641**	**2,534**	**984**			
N/EAST ASIA	**1,683**	**1,295**	**1,043**	**599**			
JAPAN	1,683	1,295	1,043	599			
OT.EAST AS/P	**1,867**	**1,346**	**1,491**	**385**			
OTHER ASIA	1,488	1,112	1,328	275			
OEAP	379	234	163	110			
EUROPE	**26,834**	**21,307**	**15,489**	**10,147**			
SOUTHERN EUR	**10,844**	**6,103**	**5,285**	**2,828**			
ITALY	4,713	2,615	2,534	1,212			
SPAIN	6,131	3,488	2,751	1,616			
WESTERN EUR	**8,068**	**5,887**	**4,364**	**2,729**			
FRANCE	2,976	1,867	1,640	866			
GERMANY	5,092	4,020	2,724	1,863			
OTHER EUROPE	**7,922**	**9,317**	**5,840**	**4,590**			
OTHER EUROPE	7,922	9,317	5,840	4,590			
REG.NOT SPEC	**15,508**	**9,925**	**7,167**	**4,419**			

PARAGUAY

3. ARRIVALS OF NON-RESIDENT TOURISTS IN HOTELS AND SIMILAR ESTABLISHMENTS, BY NATIONALITY

	1999	2000	2001	2002	2003	Market share 03	% change 03-02
NOT SPECIFIE	**15,508**	**9,925**	**7,167**	**4,419**			
OTH.WORLD	15,508	9,925	7,167	4,419			

Source: World Tourism Organization (WTO)

PARAGUAY

5. OVERNIGHT STAYS OF NON-RESIDENT TOURISTS IN HOTELS AND SIMILAR ESTABLISHMENTS, BY NATIONALITY

	1999	2000	2001	2002	2003	Market share 03	% change 03-02
TOTAL	**560,463**	**754,888**	**315,747**	**218,750**			
AFRICA	**603**	**872**	**221**	**273**			
OTHER AFRICA	**603**	**872**	**221**	**273**			
ALL AFRICA	603	872	221	273			
AMERICAS	**445,130**	**618,524**	**256,834**	**179,603**			
CARIBBEAN			**853**	**370**			
ALL CO CARIB			853	370			
CENTRAL AMER	**2,495**	**2,068**	**473**	**595**			
ALL CENT AME	2,495	2,068	473	595			
NORTH AMER	**25,890**	**34,860**	**17,083**	**10,098**			
CANADA	1,925	2,468	1,074	713			
MEXICO	2,770	3,340	915	970			
USA	21,195	29,052	15,094	8,415			
SOUTH AMER	**416,745**	**581,596**	**238,425**	**168,540**			
ARGENTINA	204,960	359,432	132,614	104,155			
BRAZIL	130,615	118,668	11,051	34,390			
CHILE	33,638	31,032	60,624	8,993			
URUGUAY	10,725	19,268	15,157	5,585			
OTH SOUTH AM	36,807	53,196	18,979	15,417			
EAST AS/PACI	**8,875**	**10,564**	**5,904**	**2,460**			
N/EAST ASIA	**4,208**	**5,180**	**2,430**	**1,498**			
JAPAN	4,208	5,180	2,430	1,498			
OT.EAST AS/P	**4,667**	**5,384**	**3,474**	**962**			
OTHER ASIA	3,720	4,448	3,094	687			
OEAP	947	936	380	275			
EUROPE	**67,085**	**85,228**	**36,089**	**23,286**			
SOUTHERN EUR	**27,110**	**24,412**	**12,314**	**7,070**			
ITALY	11,783	10,460	5,905	3,030			
SPAIN	15,327	13,952	6,409	4,040			
WESTERN EUR	**12,730**	**16,080**	**6,347**	**4,658**			
GERMANY	12,730	16,080	6,347	4,658			
OTHER EUROPE	**27,245**	**44,736**	**17,428**	**11,558**			
OTHER EUROPE	27,245	44,736	17,428	11,558			
REG.NOT SPEC	**38,770**	**39,700**	**16,699**	**13,128**			
NOT SPECIFIE	**38,770**	**39,700**	**16,699**	**13,128**			
OTH.WORLD	38,770	39,700	16,699	13,128			

Source: World Tourism Organization (WTO)

PERU

1. ARRIVALS OF NON-RESIDENT TOURISTS AT NATIONAL BORDERS, BY NATIONALITY

	1999	2000	2001	2002	2003	Market share 03	% change 03-02
TOTAL (*)	**694,084**	**800,491**	**801,334**	**865,602**	**933,643**	**100.00**	**7.86**
AFRICA	**1,330**	**1,594**	**1,796**	**1,873**	**1,940**	**0.21**	**3.58**
SOUTHERN AFR	**983**	**1,167**	**1,273**	**1,296**	**1,433**	**0.15**	**10.57**
SOUTH AFRICA	983	1,167	1,273	1,296	1,433	0.15	10.57
OTHER AFRICA	**347**	**427**	**523**	**577**	**507**	**0.05**	**-12.13**
OTHER AFRICA	347	427	523	577	507	0.05	-12.13
AMERICAS	**465,347**	**534,944**	**533,730**	**575,920**	**629,337**	**67.41**	**9.28**
CARIBBEAN	**2,519**	**2,241**	**2,514**	**2,690**	**2,286**	**0.24**	**-15.02**
CUBA	1,014	887	1,059	1,145	1,036	0.11	-9.52
DOMINICAN RP	1,304	1,182	1,264	1,326	1,049	0.11	-20.89
JAMAICA	86	86	96	125	79	0.01	-36.80
TRINIDAD TBG	115	86	95	94	122	0.01	29.79
CENTRAL AMER	**10,080**	**11,463**	**12,331**	**12,978**	**13,452**	**1.44**	**3.65**
COSTA RICA	2,799	3,109	3,183	3,285	3,342	0.36	1.74
EL SALVADOR	985	1,332	1,278	1,531	1,501	0.16	-1.96
GUATEMALA	1,162	1,251	1,641	1,549	1,720	0.18	11.04
HONDURAS	610	700	751	835	901	0.10	7.90
NICARAGUA	476	527	709	652	711	0.08	9.05
PANAMA	2,124	2,532	2,505	2,614	2,836	0.30	8.49
OT CENT AMER	1,924	2,012	2,264	2,512	2,441	0.26	-2.83
NORTH AMER	**195,126**	**218,393**	**220,047**	**234,463**	**242,540**	**25.98**	**3.44**
CANADA	16,472	19,418	19,868	21,572	21,995	2.36	1.96
MEXICO	11,722	12,971	13,720	14,947	17,473	1.87	16.90
USA	166,932	186,004	186,459	197,944	203,072	21.75	2.59
SOUTH AMER	**257,622**	**302,847**	**298,838**	**325,789**	**371,059**	**39.74**	**13.90**
ARGENTINA	31,762	36,097	36,416	34,912	39,242	4.20	12.40
BOLIVIA	27,073	35,984	47,407	58,356	60,849	6.52	4.27
BRAZIL	19,957	20,003	23,744	24,945	29,016	3.11	16.32
CHILE	118,714	134,436	107,994	97,724	138,856	14.87	42.09
COLOMBIA	18,863	24,338	26,220	32,022	30,895	3.31	-3.52
ECUADOR	22,288	31,920	33,632	58,255	54,206	5.81	-6.95
PARAGUAY	1,309	1,355	1,383	1,165	1,631	0.17	40.00
URUGUAY	2,560	3,002	3,541	3,064	3,343	0.36	9.11
VENEZUELA	15,018	15,642	18,408	15,253	12,930	1.38	-15.23
OTH SOUTH AM	78	70	93	93	91	0.01	-2.15
EAST AS/PACI	**38,931**	**48,239**	**38,420**	**45,696**	**50,095**	**5.37**	**9.63**
N/EAST ASIA	**25,489**	**32,085**	**22,257**	**28,193**	**31,885**	**3.42**	**13.10**
CHINA	2,280	3,854	2,786	4,254	4,337	0.46	1.95
TAIWAN(P.C.)	1,146	1,168	967	1,271	1,275	0.14	0.31
JAPAN	19,196	23,071	14,711	17,737	20,823	2.23	17.40
KOREA D P RP	60	112	495	201	98	0.01	-51.24
KOREA REP.	2,807	3,880	3,298	4,730	5,352	0.57	13.15
S/EAST ASIA	**922**	**1,337**	**995**	**2,046**	**1,096**	**0.12**	**-46.43**
MALAYSIA	121	248	160	183	213	0.02	16.39
PHILIPPINES	570	753	655	1,638	725	0.08	-55.74
THAILAND	231	336	180	225	158	0.02	-29.78

PERU

1. ARRIVALS OF NON-RESIDENT TOURISTS AT NATIONAL BORDERS, BY NATIONALITY

	1999	2000	2001	2002	2003	Market share 03	% change 03-02
AUSTRALASIA	**11,213**	**13,161**	**13,436**	**13,527**	**15,604**	**1.67**	**15.35**
AUSTRALIA	9,032	10,845	11,265	11,280	13,251	1.42	17.47
NEW ZEALAND	2,181	2,316	2,171	2,247	2,353	0.25	4.72
OT.EAST AS/P	**1,307**	**1,656**	**1,732**	**1,930**	**1,510**	**0.16**	**-21.76**
OTHER ASIA	1,251	1,604	1,663	1,870	1,424	0.15	-23.85
OTH OCEANIA	56	52	69	60	86	0.01	43.33
EUROPE	**182,756**	**209,289**	**221,151**	**240,652**	**250,659**	**26.85**	**4.16**
C/E EUROPE	**4,896**	**5,252**	**5,196**	**6,046**	**6,607**	**0.71**	**9.28**
CZECH RP/SVK	1,494	1,463	1,610	1,407	1,892	0.20	34.47
HUNGARY	556	670	794	874	1,022	0.11	16.93
POLAND	1,503	1,600	1,598	2,165	1,890	0.20	-12.70
ROMANIA	172	193	180	239	335	0.04	40.17
RUSSIAN FED	1,171	1,326	1,014	1,361	1,468	0.16	7.86
NORTHERN EUR	**38,783**	**47,227**	**55,378**	**57,662**	**63,659**	**6.82**	**10.40**
DENMARK	2,700	2,976	2,499	2,606	2,480	0.27	-4.83
FINLAND	1,176	1,378	1,313	1,320	1,530	0.16	15.91
IRELAND	1,605	2,020	2,945	3,277	3,938	0.42	20.17
NORWAY	2,224	2,823	3,000	3,201	3,487	0.37	8.93
SWEDEN	3,772	4,677	4,878	4,895	5,477	0.59	11.89
UK	27,306	33,353	40,743	42,363	46,747	5.01	10.35
SOUTHERN EUR	**44,911**	**45,612**	**47,564**	**56,275**	**55,505**	**5.94**	**-1.37**
GREECE	925	886	764	1,041	1,376	0.15	32.18
ITALY	17,708	18,679	18,623	22,530	21,922	2.35	-2.70
PORTUGAL	955	1,091	1,073	1,252	1,167	0.12	-6.79
SPAIN	25,140	24,779	26,938	31,224	30,847	3.30	-1.21
YUGOSLAV SFR	183	177	166	228	193	0.02	-15.35
WESTERN EUR	**86,804**	**101,814**	**102,737**	**109,942**	**114,299**	**12.24**	**3.96**
AUSTRIA	3,784	4,233	3,872	3,995	4,072	0.44	1.93
BELGIUM	7,030	7,600	7,236	7,643	7,156	0.77	-6.37
FRANCE	27,823	33,445	33,681	37,571	39,820	4.27	5.99
GERMANY	25,277	30,419	30,174	31,558	33,390	3.58	5.81
LUXEMBOURG	269	303	286	261	265	0.03	1.53
NETHERLANDS	13,263	14,895	15,834	16,882	17,327	1.86	2.64
SWITZERLAND	9,358	10,919	11,654	12,032	12,269	1.31	1.97
EAST/MED EUR	**5,700**	**7,385**	**8,570**	**8,242**	**8,007**	**0.86**	**-2.85**
ISRAEL	5,469	7,069	8,387	8,011	7,725	0.83	-3.57
TURKEY	231	316	183	231	282	0.03	22.08
OTHER EUROPE	**1,662**	**1,999**	**1,706**	**2,485**	**2,582**	**0.28**	**3.90**
OTHER EUROPE	1,662	1,999	1,706	2,485	2,582	0.28	3.90
MIDDLE EAST	**146**	**195**	**146**	**123**	**110**	**0.01**	**-10.57**
MIDDLE EAST	**146**	**195**	**146**	**123**	**110**	**0.01**	**-10.57**
JORDAN	28	32	26	19	23		21.05
LEBANON	46	58	34	31	35		12.90
EGYPT	72	105	86	73	52	0.01	-28.77
SOUTH ASIA	**812**	**1,366**	**1,107**	**1,204**	**1,284**	**0.14**	**6.64**

PERU

1. ARRIVALS OF NON-RESIDENT TOURISTS AT NATIONAL BORDERS, BY NATIONALITY

	1999	2000	2001	2002	2003	Market share 03	% change 03-02
SOUTH ASIA	**812**	**1,366**	**1,107**	**1,204**	**1,284**	**0.14**	**6.64**
INDIA	519	672	714	818	984	0.11	20.29
IRAN	25	42	50	58	39		-32.76
PAKISTAN	268	652	343	328	261	0.03	-20.43
REG.NOT SPEC	**4,762**	**4,864**	**4,984**	**134**	**218**	**0.02**	**62.69**
NOT SPECIFIE	**4,762**	**4,864**	**4,984**	**134**	**218**	**0.02**	**62.69**
OTH.WORLD	4,762	4,864	4,984	134	218	0.02	62.69

Source: World Tourism Organization (WTO)

PERU

3. ARRIVALS OF NON-RESIDENT TOURISTS IN HOTELS AND SIMILAR ESTABLISHMENTS, BY NATIONALITY

	1999	2000	2001	2002	2003	Market share 03	% change 03-02
TOTAL (*)	**1,356,971**	**1,412,686**	**1,446,188**	**1,434,327**	**2,001,810**	**100.00**	**39.56**
AMERICAS	**655,531**	**671,442**	**676,236**	**644,558**	**851,675**	**42.55**	**32.13**
CENTRAL AMER	**15,891**	**17,341**	**15,955**				
PANAMA	15,891	17,341	15,955				
NORTH AMER	**391,637**	**396,940**	**407,780**	**390,120**	**510,598**	**25.51**	**30.88**
CANADA	37,597	40,131	39,040	39,392	56,649	2.83	43.81
MEXICO	24,190	23,425	23,445	25,758	35,929	1.79	39.49
USA	329,850	333,384	345,295	324,970	418,020	20.88	28.63
SOUTH AMER	**248,003**	**257,161**	**252,501**	**254,438**	**341,077**	**17.04**	**34.05**
ARGENTINA	48,454	46,606	45,872	42,865	69,639	3.48	62.46
BOLIVIA	14,946	15,134	18,482	19,015	22,909	1.14	20.48
BRAZIL	32,310	29,260	31,562	35,178	52,541	2.62	49.36
CHILE	82,226	87,822	77,332	63,240	71,805	3.59	13.54
COLOMBIA	31,721	34,212	31,957	38,954	53,123	2.65	36.37
ECUADOR	21,906	24,454	25,809	35,783	53,016	2.65	48.16
VENEZUELA	16,440	19,673	21,487	19,403	18,044	0.90	-7.00
EAST AS/PACI	**59,072**	**67,617**	**41,951**	**48,509**	**76,814**	**3.84**	**58.35**
N/EAST ASIA	**59,072**	**67,617**	**41,951**	**48,509**	**76,814**	**3.84**	**58.35**
JAPAN	59,072	67,617	41,951	48,509	76,814	3.84	58.35
EUROPE	**314,440**	**331,028**	**329,028**	**324,238**	**474,692**	**23.71**	**46.40**
SOUTHERN EUR	**134,918**	**115,903**	**118,070**	**130,159**	**166,548**	**8.32**	**27.96**
ITALY	58,977	53,693	54,257	59,860	75,199	3.76	25.62
SPAIN	75,941	62,210	63,813	70,299	91,349	4.56	29.94
WESTERN EUR	**179,522**	**215,125**	**210,958**	**194,079**	**308,144**	**15.39**	**58.77**
FRANCE	97,627	120,275	114,010	110,666	182,702	9.13	65.09
GERMANY	81,895	94,850	96,948	83,413	125,442	6.27	50.39
REG.NOT SPEC	**327,928**	**342,599**	**398,973**	**417,022**	**598,629**	**29.90**	**43.55**
NOT SPECIFIE	**327,928**	**342,599**	**398,973**	**417,022**	**598,629**	**29.90**	**43.55**
OTH.WORLD	327,928	342,599	398,973	417,022	598,629	29.90	43.55

Source: World Tourism Organization (WTO)

PERU

5. OVERNIGHT STAYS OF NON-RESIDENT TOURISTS IN HOTELS AND SIMILAR ESTABLISHMENTS, BY NATIONALITY

	1999	2000	2001	2002	2003	Market share 03	% change 03-02
TOTAL (*)	**2,703,356**	**2,701,893**	**2,788,297**	**2,801,944**	**3,758,246**	**100.00**	**34.13**
AMERICAS	**1,362,172**	**1,330,582**	**1,351,952**	**1,311,027**	**1,742,771**	**46.37**	**32.93**
CENTRAL AMER	**37,619**	**34,592**	**33,654**				
PANAMA	37,619	34,592	33,654				
NORTH AMER	**794,184**	**777,327**	**788,631**	**765,807**	**998,982**	**26.58**	**30.45**
CANADA	78,991	82,814	79,227	75,384	109,272	2.91	44.95
MEXICO	57,876	51,634	54,728	57,566	84,221	2.24	46.30
USA	657,317	642,879	654,676	632,857	805,489	21.43	27.28
SOUTH AMER	**530,369**	**518,663**	**529,667**	**545,220**	**743,789**	**19.79**	**36.42**
ARGENTINA	104,045	99,957	98,666	95,551	174,053	4.63	82.16
BOLIVIA	29,463	31,865	38,998	35,718	42,758	1.14	19.71
BRAZIL	74,791	64,633	71,741	80,365	113,632	3.02	41.39
CHILE	157,718	162,377	145,900	125,840	143,670	3.82	14.17
COLOMBIA	78,004	78,217	75,250	96,983	128,483	3.42	32.48
ECUADOR	47,728	44,682	53,627	69,994	96,919	2.58	38.47
VENEZUELA	38,620	36,932	45,485	40,769	44,274	1.18	8.60
EAST AS/PACI	**121,159**	**130,829**	**77,707**	**85,793**	**127,552**	**3.39**	**48.67**
N/EAST ASIA	**121,159**	**130,829**	**77,707**	**85,793**	**127,552**	**3.39**	**48.67**
JAPAN	121,159	130,829	77,707	85,793	127,552	3.39	48.67
EUROPE	**600,674**	**609,230**	**614,855**	**603,448**	**808,432**	**21.51**	**33.97**
SOUTHERN EUR	**265,708**	**225,755**	**229,632**	**250,856**	**304,074**	**8.09**	**21.21**
ITALY	106,946	100,020	102,302	110,721	134,005	3.57	21.03
SPAIN	158,762	125,735	127,330	140,135	170,069	4.53	21.36
WESTERN EUR	**334,966**	**383,475**	**385,223**	**352,592**	**504,358**	**13.42**	**43.04**
FRANCE	178,233	207,553	204,657	197,114	285,650	7.60	44.92
GERMANY	156,733	175,922	180,566	155,478	218,708	5.82	40.67
REG.NOT SPEC	**619,351**	**631,252**	**743,783**	**801,676**	**1,079,491**	**28.72**	**34.65**
NOT SPECIFIE	**619,351**	**631,252**	**743,783**	**801,676**	**1,079,491**	**28.72**	**34.65**
OTH.WORLD	619,351	631,252	743,783	801,676	1,079,491	28.72	34.65

Source: World Tourism Organization (WTO)

PHILIPPINES

1. ARRIVALS OF NON-RESIDENT TOURISTS AT NATIONAL BORDERS, BY COUNTRY OF RESIDENCE

	1999	2000	2001	2002	2003	Market share 03	% change 03-02
TOTAL	**2,170,514**	**1,992,169**	**1,796,893**	**1,932,677**	**1,907,226**	**100.00**	**-1.32**
AFRICA	**1,824**	**1,192**	**1,685**	**1,465**	**1,442**	**0.08**	**-1.57**
SOUTHERN AFR	**1,519**	**923**	**1,397**	**1,193**	**1,139**	**0.06**	**-4.53**
SOUTH AFRICA	1,519	923	1,397	1,193	1,139	0.06	-4.53
WEST AFRICA	**305**	**269**	**288**	**272**	**303**	**0.02**	**11.40**
NIGERIA	305	269	288	272	303	0.02	11.40
AMERICAS	**534,480**	**510,862**	**451,008**	**453,667**	**444,264**	**23.29**	**-2.07**
NORTH AMER	**530,120**	**507,222**	**447,921**	**451,201**	**442,390**	**23.20**	**-1.95**
CANADA	64,986	61,004	54,942	54,563	53,601	2.81	-1.76
MEXICO	1,534	1,175	880	1,315	910	0.05	-30.80
USA	463,600	445,043	392,099	395,323	387,879	20.34	-1.88
SOUTH AMER	**4,360**	**3,640**	**3,087**	**2,466**	**1,874**	**0.10**	**-24.01**
ARGENTINA	828	603	512	432	448	0.02	3.70
BRAZIL	2,276	2,029	1,724	1,256	876	0.05	-30.25
COLOMBIA	527	400	364	395	245	0.01	-37.97
PERU	275	311	231	182	171	0.01	-6.04
VENEZUELA	454	297	256	201	134	0.01	-33.33
EAST AS/PACI	**1,076,862**	**1,021,967**	**985,941**	**1,154,439**	**1,128,540**	**59.17**	**-2.24**
N/EAST ASIA	**845,763**	**802,787**	**790,373**	**917,126**	**891,295**	**46.73**	**-2.82**
CHINA	21,220	14,724	18,937	27,803	32,039	1.68	15.24
TAIWAN(P.C.)	143,810	75,722	85,231	103,024	92,740	4.86	-9.98
HK,CHINA	160,152	146,858	134,408	155,964	139,753	7.33	-10.39
JAPAN	387,513	390,517	343,840	341,867	322,896	16.93	-5.55
KOREA REP.	133,068	174,966	207,957	288,468	303,867	15.93	5.34
S/EAST ASIA	**141,329**	**132,742**	**115,566**	**133,790**	**131,136**	**6.88**	**-1.98**
BRUNEI DARSM	2,056	1,827	1,786	2,136	2,070	0.11	-3.09
MYANMAR	2,218	2,314	2,394	1,982	2,149	0.11	8.43
CAMBODIA	400	321	738	1,054	1,040	0.05	-1.33
INDONESIA	16,446	16,272	16,307	15,352	17,051	0.89	11.07
LAO P.DEM.R.	345	199	427	475	502	0.03	5.68
MALAYSIA	49,667	42,067	30,498	31,735	31,161	1.63	-1.81
SINGAPORE	51,244	50,276	44,155	57,662	51,257	2.69	-11.11
VIET NAM	2,856	3,814	4,198	4,577	5,507	0.29	20.32
THAILAND	16,097	15,652	15,063	18,817	20,399	1.07	8.41
AUSTRALASIA	**88,136**	**84,784**	**76,373**	**77,304**	**76,010**	**3.99**	**-1.67**
AUSTRALIA	77,732	75,706	68,541	70,735	69,846	3.66	-1.26
NEW ZEALAND	10,404	9,078	7,832	6,569	6,164	0.32	-6.17
MELANESIA	**1,185**	**784**	**846**	**1,185**	**867**	**0.05**	**-26.84**
PAPUA N.GUIN	1,185	784	846	1,185	867	0.05	-26.84
MICRONESIA	**449**	**870**	**2,783**	**25,034**	**29,232**	**1.53**	**16.77**
GUAM	151	741	2,746	25,013	29,220	1.53	16.82
NAURU	298	129	37	21	12		-42.86
EUROPE	**293,722**	**252,195**	**201,815**	**183,910**	**177,338**	**9.30**	**-3.57**

PHILIPPINES

1. ARRIVALS OF NON-RESIDENT TOURISTS AT NATIONAL BORDERS, BY COUNTRY OF RESIDENCE

	1999	2000	2001	2002	2003	Market share 03	% change 03-02
C/E EUROPE	**3,093**	**2,997**	**3,409**	**4,166**	**3,617**	**0.19**	**-13.18**
POLAND	833	510	636	604	549	0.03	-9.11
CIS	2,260	2,487	2,773	3,562	3,068	0.16	-13.87
NORTHERN EUR	**125,114**	**107,302**	**86,368**	**72,740**	**71,014**	**3.72**	**-2.37**
DENMARK	11,603	10,239	7,902	7,164	6,584	0.35	-8.10
FINLAND	2,980	2,955	2,016	1,597	1,528	0.08	-4.32
IRELAND	3,135	2,678	2,323	1,864	1,977	0.10	6.06
NORWAY	7,872	7,726	6,650	7,025	6,886	0.36	-1.98
SWEDEN	10,604	9,197	7,330	6,612	6,592	0.35	-0.30
UK	88,920	74,507	60,147	48,478	47,447	2.49	-2.13
SOUTHERN EUR	**26,171**	**23,400**	**16,991**	**17,081**	**15,499**	**0.81**	**-9.26**
GREECE	1,368	1,347	940	1,031	944	0.05	-8.44
ITALY	13,880	12,454	8,994	8,483	7,711	0.40	-9.10
PORTUGAL	2,700	1,445	856	636	568	0.03	-10.69
SPAIN	7,478	7,486	5,624	6,349	6,026	0.32	-5.09
YUGOSLAV SFR	745	668	577	582	250	0.01	-57.04
WESTERN EUR	**136,102**	**115,688**	**92,577**	**87,861**	**85,488**	**4.48**	**-2.70**
AUSTRIA	8,563	7,761	6,548	6,281	6,264	0.33	-0.27
BELGIUM	6,995	6,536	5,450	5,512	5,371	0.28	-2.56
FRANCE	24,462	19,179	13,918	12,498	11,549	0.61	-7.59
GERMANY	62,044	51,131	40,605	39,103	38,684	2.03	-1.07
LUXEMBOURG	263	221	248	307	262	0.01	-14.66
NETHERLANDS	17,188	16,150	13,540	12,015	11,441	0.60	-4.78
SWITZERLAND	16,587	14,710	12,268	12,145	11,917	0.62	-1.88
EAST/MED EUR	**3,242**	**2,808**	**2,470**	**2,062**	**1,720**	**0.09**	**-16.59**
ISRAEL	3,242	2,808	2,470	2,062	1,720	0.09	-16.59
MIDDLE EAST	**15,868**	**14,711**	**16,073**	**18,500**	**16,736**	**0.88**	**-9.54**
MIDDLE EAST	**15,868**	**14,711**	**16,073**	**18,500**	**16,736**	**0.88**	**-9.54**
BAHRAIN	1,003	911	1,068	1,358	1,379	0.07	1.55
JORDAN	540	299	404	292	185	0.01	-36.64
KUWAIT	1,058	1,007	1,164	1,469	1,449	0.08	-1.36
SAUDI ARABIA	11,428	10,444	10,409	11,341	9,842	0.52	-13.22
UNTD ARAB EM	1,122	1,568	2,160	3,460	3,305	0.17	-4.48
EGYPT	717	482	868	580	576	0.03	-0.69
SOUTH ASIA	**25,920**	**24,092**	**22,193**	**20,822**	**21,543**	**1.13**	**3.46**
SOUTH ASIA	**25,920**	**24,092**	**22,193**	**20,822**	**21,543**	**1.13**	**3.46**
BANGLADESH	1,509	1,037	1,537	1,457	1,546	0.08	6.11
SRI LANKA	2,004	1,934	1,542	1,341	1,424	0.07	6.19
INDIA	18,637	18,570	15,391	14,826	15,644	0.82	5.52
IRAN	639	388	707	633	604	0.03	-4.58
NEPAL	1,249	996	1,018	974	897	0.05	-7.91
PAKISTAN	1,882	1,167	1,998	1,591	1,428	0.07	-10.25
REG.NOT SPEC	**221,838**	**167,150**	**118,178**	**99,874**	**117,363**	**6.15**	**17.51**
NOT SPECIFIE	**221,838**	**167,150**	**118,178**	**99,874**	**117,363**	**6.15**	**17.51**
OTH.WORLD	22,548	16,764	19,347	16,120	17,039	0.89	5.70
N RESID ABRO (*)	199,290	150,386	98,831	83,754	100,324	5.26	19.78

3. ARRIVALS OF NON-RESIDENT TOURISTS IN HOTELS AND SIMILAR ESTABLISHMENTS, BY COUNTRY OF RESIDENCE

	1999	2000	2001	2002	2003	Market share 03	% change 03-02
TOTAL (*)	**937,623**	**852,569**	**734,720**	**758,474**	**741,886**	**100.00**	**-2.19**
AFRICA	**839**	**477**	**708**	**476**	**472**	**0.06**	**-0.84**
SOUTHERN AFR	**743**	**394**	**630**	**410**	**399**	**0.05**	**-2.68**
SOUTH AFRICA	743	394	630	410	399	0.05	-2.68
WEST AFRICA	**96**	**83**	**78**	**66**	**73**	**0.01**	**10.61**
NIGERIA	96	83	78	66	73	0.01	10.61
AMERICAS	**189,109**	**150,838**	**121,850**	**95,318**	**97,010**	**13.08**	**1.78**
NORTH AMER	**186,965**	**149,020**	**120,456**	**94,358**	**96,246**	**12.97**	**2.00**
CANADA	34,969	33,178	23,954	17,196	16,505	2.22	-4.02
MEXICO	872	645	413	776	376	0.05	-51.55
USA	151,124	115,197	96,089	76,386	79,365	10.70	3.90
SOUTH AMER	**2,144**	**1,818**	**1,394**	**960**	**764**	**0.10**	**-20.42**
ARGENTINA	383	281	183	119	122	0.02	2.52
BRAZIL	1,183	1,046	862	548	439	0.06	-19.89
COLOMBIA	213	177	126	133	62	0.01	-53.38
PERU	150	172	129	110	85	0.01	-22.73
VENEZUELA	215	142	94	50	56	0.01	12.00
EAST AS/PACI	**583,363**	**552,223**	**499,710**	**563,220**	**541,948**	**73.05**	**-3.78**
N/EAST ASIA	**462,769**	**431,840**	**406,240**	**462,113**	**442,129**	**59.60**	**-4.32**
CHINA	3,321	1,727	2,930	4,232	5,249	0.71	24.03
TAIWAN(P.C.)	83,488	39,931	45,527	55,108	39,312	5.30	-28.66
HK,CHINA	100,799	88,332	72,438	77,777	69,395	9.35	-10.78
JAPAN	207,912	205,077	170,860	163,230	151,213	20.38	-7.36
KOREA REP.	67,249	96,773	114,485	161,766	176,960	23.85	9.39
S/EAST ASIA	**68,865**	**67,732**	**54,217**	**64,334**	**63,102**	**8.51**	**-1.92**
BRUNEI DARSM	1,323	1,075	882	1,011	1,062	0.14	5.04
MYANMAR	442	362	245	229	172	0.02	-24.89
CAMBODIA	111	71	177	265	317	0.04	19.62
INDONESIA	7,131	6,663	5,769	5,383	6,619	0.89	22.96
LAO P.DEM.R.	99	61	112	121	174	0.02	43.80
MALAYSIA	20,905	19,083	13,527	13,366	13,037	1.76	-2.46
SINGAPORE	30,209	31,161	25,819	34,072	30,646	4.13	-10.06
VIET NAM	673	833	836	1,066	1,275	0.17	19.61
THAILAND	7,972	8,423	6,850	8,821	9,800	1.32	11.10
AUSTRALASIA	**51,055**	**51,860**	**37,881**	**31,461**	**30,745**	**4.14**	**-2.28**
AUSTRALIA	45,335	46,693	34,077	28,430	27,851	3.75	-2.04
NEW ZEALAND	5,720	5,167	3,804	3,031	2,894	0.39	-4.52
MELANESIA	**358**	**256**	**378**	**643**	**368**	**0.05**	**-42.77**
PAPUA N.GUIN	358	256	378	643	368	0.05	-42.77
MICRONESIA	**316**	**535**	**994**	**4,669**	**5,604**	**0.76**	**20.03**
GUAM	80	445	973	4,653	5,597	0.75	20.29
NAURU	236	90	21	16	7		-56.25

3. ARRIVALS OF NON-RESIDENT TOURISTS IN HOTELS AND SIMILAR ESTABLISHMENTS, BY COUNTRY OF RESIDENCE

	1999	2000	2001	2002	2003	Market share 03	% change 03-02
EUROPE	**135,130**	**115,957**	**82,879**	**68,624**	**66,715**	**8.99**	**-2.78**
C/E EUROPE	**822**	**460**	**807**	**964**	**1,105**	**0.15**	**14.63**
POLAND	285	109	156	124	132	0.02	6.45
CIS	537	351	651	840	973	0.13	15.83
NORTHERN EUR	**60,305**	**51,462**	**36,532**	**24,989**	**24,096**	**3.25**	**-3.57**
DENMARK	3,290	3,148	2,143	1,955	1,886	0.25	-3.53
FINLAND	1,566	1,496	913	659	717	0.10	8.80
IRELAND	1,607	1,330	1,018	712	786	0.11	10.39
NORWAY	3,588	3,665	2,790	2,153	2,250	0.30	4.51
SWEDEN	4,533	3,955	2,693	1,889	1,922	0.26	1.75
UK	45,721	37,868	26,975	17,621	16,535	2.23	-6.16
SOUTHERN EUR	**12,503**	**10,365**	**6,834**	**6,097**	**5,680**	**0.77**	**-6.84**
GREECE	465	461	293	315	314	0.04	-0.32
ITALY	6,560	5,508	3,592	3,190	2,998	0.40	-6.02
PORTUGAL	1,519	735	333	244	208	0.03	-14.75
SPAIN	3,787	3,528	2,511	2,274	2,089	0.28	-8.14
YUGOSLAV SFR	172	133	105	74	71	0.01	-4.05
WESTERN EUR	**59,888**	**52,318**	**37,557**	**35,654**	**35,012**	**4.72**	**-1.80**
AUSTRIA	3,826	3,615	2,503	2,766	2,865	0.39	3.58
BELGIUM	3,549	3,331	2,559	2,877	2,797	0.38	-2.78
FRANCE	10,598	8,233	5,648	4,611	4,339	0.58	-5.90
GERMANY	25,944	22,562	16,187	15,565	14,822	2.00	-4.77
LUXEMBOURG	134	118	118	160	129	0.02	-19.38
NETHERLANDS	8,444	7,914	5,720	4,659	4,620	0.62	-0.84
SWITZERLAND	7,393	6,545	4,822	5,016	5,440	0.73	8.45
EAST/MED EUR	**1,612**	**1,352**	**1,149**	**920**	**822**	**0.11**	**-10.65**
ISRAEL	1,612	1,352	1,149	920	822	0.11	-10.65
MIDDLE EAST	**8,366**	**7,861**	**7,864**	**8,611**	**7,911**	**1.07**	**-8.13**
MIDDLE EAST	**8,366**	**7,861**	**7,864**	**8,611**	**7,911**	**1.07**	**-8.13**
BAHRAIN	573	587	597	670	745	0.10	11.19
JORDAN	253	140	213	114	83	0.01	-27.19
KUWAIT	552	562	594	664	629	0.08	-5.27
SAUDI ARABIA	6,025	5,512	5,079	5,219	4,387	0.59	-15.94
UNTD ARAB EM	619	865	1,046	1,749	1,883	0.25	7.66
EGYPT	344	195	335	195	184	0.02	-5.64
SOUTH ASIA	**9,116**	**7,638**	**6,131**	**4,748**	**4,951**	**0.67**	**4.28**
SOUTH ASIA	**9,116**	**7,638**	**6,131**	**4,748**	**4,951**	**0.67**	**4.28**
BANGLADESH	413	320	362	312	264	0.04	-15.38
SRI LANKA	770	742	501	411	438	0.06	6.57
INDIA	6,523	5,680	4,109	3,128	3,450	0.47	10.29
IRAN	303	169	279	159	161	0.02	1.26
NEPAL	330	264	233	217	220	0.03	1.38
PAKISTAN	777	463	647	521	418	0.06	-19.77
REG.NOT SPEC	**11,700**	**17,575**	**15,578**	**17,477**	**22,879**	**3.08**	**30.91**

3. ARRIVALS OF NON-RESIDENT TOURISTS IN HOTELS AND SIMILAR ESTABLISHMENTS, BY COUNTRY OF RESIDENCE

		1999	2000	2001	2002	2003	Market share 03	% change 03-02
NOT SPECIFIE		**11,700**	**17,575**	**15,578**	**17,477**	**22,879**	**3.08**	**30.91**
OTH.WORLD		7,933	6,117	6,531	5,627	6,010	0.81	6.81
N RESID ABRO	(*)	3,767	11,458	9,047	11,850	16,869	2.27	42.35

Source: World Tourism Organization (WTO)

PHILIPPINES

4. ARRIVALS OF NON-RESIDENT TOURISTS IN ALL TYPES OF ACCOMMODATION ESTABLISHMENTS, BY COUNTRY OF RESIDENCE

	1999	2000	2001	2002	2003	Market share 03	% change 03-02
TOTAL (*)	**2,128,993**	**1,963,659**	**1,770,211**	**1,904,891**	**1,880,067**	**100.00**	**-1.30**
AFRICA	**1,810**	**1,171**	**1,631**	**1,416**	**1,406**	**0.07**	**-0.71**
SOUTHERN AFR	**1,516**	**910**	**1,352**	**1,146**	**1,106**	**0.06**	**-3.49**
SOUTH AFRICA	1,516	910	1,352	1,146	1,106	0.06	-3.49
WEST AFRICA	**294**	**261**	**279**	**270**	**300**	**0.02**	**11.11**
NIGERIA	294	261	279	270	300	0.02	11.11
AMERICAS	**528,903**	**509,081**	**448,621**	**451,614**	**443,636**	**23.60**	**-1.77**
NORTH AMER	**524,557**	**505,459**	**445,538**	**449,249**	**441,775**	**23.50**	**-1.66**
CANADA	64,178	60,890	54,851	54,314	53,546	2.85	-1.41
MEXICO	1,534	1,173	869	1,300	909	0.05	-30.08
USA	458,845	443,396	389,818	393,635	387,320	20.60	-1.60
SOUTH AMER	**4,346**	**3,622**	**3,083**	**2,365**	**1,861**	**0.10**	**-21.31**
ARGENTINA	821	603	512	431	448	0.02	3.94
BRAZIL	2,275	2,027	1,723	1,163	870	0.05	-25.19
COLOMBIA	526	399	364	391	239	0.01	-38.87
PERU	270	300	229	180	170	0.01	-5.56
VENEZUELA	454	293	255	200	134	0.01	-33.00
EAST AS/PACI	**1,057,016**	**1,006,583**	**969,510**	**1,138,437**	**1,110,910**	**59.09**	**-2.42**
N/EAST ASIA	**834,780**	**795,018**	**782,240**	**907,924**	**882,280**	**46.93**	**-2.82**
CHINA	16,887	10,580	14,533	23,247	26,471	1.41	13.87
TAIWAN(P.C.)	141,962	75,400	84,644	102,548	91,931	4.89	-10.35
HK,CHINA	159,825	146,666	134,254	155,583	139,315	7.41	-10.46
JAPAN	385,121	389,039	343,021	340,806	322,644	17.16	-5.33
KOREA REP.	130,985	173,333	205,788	285,740	301,919	16.06	5.66
S/EAST ASIA	**133,593**	**125,439**	**107,627**	**127,987**	**123,392**	**6.56**	**-3.59**
BRUNEI DARSM	2,050	1,821	1,783	2,136	2,053	0.11	-3.89
MYANMAR	1,250	1,108	945	867	854	0.05	-1.50
CAMBODIA	399	321	738	1,054	1,030	0.05	-2.28
INDONESIA	13,909	13,183	12,630	12,513	14,278	0.76	14.11
LAO P.DEM.R.	345	199	427	475	502	0.03	5.68
MALAYSIA	47,882	40,967	29,564	31,287	30,248	1.61	-3.32
SINGAPORE	50,701	50,185	44,010	57,343	51,014	2.71	-11.04
VIET NAM	2,186	2,222	3,058	3,822	4,002	0.21	4.71
THAILAND	14,871	15,433	14,472	18,490	19,411	1.03	4.98
AUSTRALASIA	**87,082**	**84,483**	**76,021**	**76,307**	**75,144**	**4.00**	**-1.52**
AUSTRALIA	76,726	75,429	68,253	69,784	69,019	3.67	-1.10
NEW ZEALAND	10,356	9,054	7,768	6,523	6,125	0.33	-6.10
MELANESIA	**1,112**	**773**	**839**	**1,185**	**862**	**0.05**	**-27.26**
PAPUA N.GUIN	1,112	773	839	1,185	862	0.05	-27.26
MICRONESIA	**449**	**870**	**2,783**	**25,034**	**29,232**	**1.55**	**16.77**
GUAM	151	741	2,746	25,013	29,220	1.55	16.82
NAURU	298	129	37	21	12		-42.86

4. ARRIVALS OF NON-RESIDENT TOURISTS IN ALL TYPES OF ACCOMMODATION ESTABLISHMENTS, BY COUNTRY OF RESIDENCE

	1999	2000	2001	2002	2003	Market share 03	% change 03-02
EUROPE	**285,350**	**244,981**	**198,197**	**178,022**	**172,612**	**9.18**	**-3.04**
C/E EUROPE	**1,986**	**1,263**	**2,189**	**2,654**	**2,601**	**0.14**	**-2.00**
POLAND	655	343	414	388	380	0.02	-2.06
CIS	1,331	920	1,775	2,266	2,221	0.12	-1.99
NORTHERN EUR	**122,536**	**104,985**	**85,041**	**69,965**	**68,434**	**3.64**	**-2.19**
DENMARK	11,325	10,035	7,741	7,103	6,544	0.35	-7.87
FINLAND	2,951	2,942	2,009	1,588	1,523	0.08	-4.09
IRELAND	3,114	2,660	2,306	1,805	1,914	0.10	6.04
NORWAY	7,588	7,482	6,589	6,966	6,845	0.36	-1.74
SWEDEN	10,469	9,106	7,296	6,565	6,571	0.35	0.09
UK	87,089	72,760	59,100	45,938	45,037	2.40	-1.96
SOUTHERN EUR	**25,427**	**22,539**	**16,528**	**16,604**	**15,166**	**0.81**	**-8.66**
GREECE	1,004	950	753	878	762	0.04	-13.21
ITALY	13,740	12,321	8,962	8,465	7,663	0.41	-9.47
PORTUGAL	2,681	1,405	839	619	552	0.03	-10.82
SPAIN	7,382	7,427	5,614	6,301	6,011	0.32	-4.60
YUGOSLAV SFR	620	436	360	341	178	0.01	-47.80
WESTERN EUR	**132,159**	**113,387**	**91,970**	**86,739**	**84,692**	**4.50**	**-2.36**
AUSTRIA	8,507	7,704	6,531	6,236	6,233	0.33	-0.05
BELGIUM	6,937	6,518	5,432	5,461	5,340	0.28	-2.22
FRANCE	23,675	18,700	13,847	12,456	11,491	0.61	-7.75
GERMANY	59,197	49,688	40,286	38,395	38,092	2.03	-0.79
LUXEMBOURG	262	221	248	307	262	0.01	-14.66
NETHERLANDS	17,042	15,929	13,422	11,770	11,374	0.60	-3.36
SWITZERLAND	16,539	14,627	12,204	12,114	11,900	0.63	-1.77
EAST/MED EUR	**3,242**	**2,807**	**2,469**	**2,060**	**1,719**	**0.09**	**-16.55**
ISRAEL	3,242	2,807	2,469	2,060	1,719	0.09	-16.55
MIDDLE EAST	**15,860**	**14,645**	**16,011**	**18,487**	**16,692**	**0.89**	**-9.71**
MIDDLE EAST	**15,860**	**14,645**	**16,011**	**18,487**	**16,692**	**0.89**	**-9.71**
BAHRAIN	1,003	911	1,068	1,358	1,379	0.07	1.55
JORDAN	538	274	404	292	184	0.01	-36.99
KUWAIT	1,055	1,006	1,159	1,469	1,449	0.08	-1.36
SAUDI ARABIA	11,427	10,443	10,409	11,340	9,841	0.52	-13.22
UNTD ARAB EM	1,122	1,568	2,160	3,460	3,305	0.18	-4.48
EGYPT	715	443	811	568	534	0.03	-5.99
SOUTH ASIA	**24,032**	**21,771**	**20,114**	**18,019**	**18,370**	**0.98**	**1.95**
SOUTH ASIA	**24,032**	**21,771**	**20,114**	**18,019**	**18,370**	**0.98**	**1.95**
BANGLADESH	1,435	901	1,334	1,166	1,259	0.07	7.98
SRI LANKA	1,911	1,783	1,448	1,205	1,327	0.07	10.12
INDIA	16,955	16,632	13,768	12,636	13,148	0.70	4.05
IRAN	639	388	688	563	520	0.03	-7.64
NEPAL	1,249	995	1,012	958	883	0.05	-7.83
PAKISTAN	1,843	1,072	1,864	1,491	1,233	0.07	-17.30
REG.NOT SPEC	**216,022**	**165,427**	**116,127**	**98,896**	**116,441**	**6.19**	**17.74**

4. ARRIVALS OF NON-RESIDENT TOURISTS IN ALL TYPES OF ACCOMMODATION ESTABLISHMENTS, BY COUNTRY OF RESIDENCE

		1999	2000	2001	2002	2003	Market share 03	% change 03-02
NOT SPECIFIE		**216,022**	**165,427**	**116,127**	**98,896**	**116,441**	**6.19**	**17.74**
OTH.WORLD		16,732	15,041	17,296	15,142	16,117	0.86	6.44
N RESID ABRO	(*)	199,290	150,386	98,831	83,754	100,324	5.34	19.78

Source: World Tourism Organization (WTO)

2. ARRIVALS OF NON-RESIDENT VISITORS AT NATIONAL BORDERS, BY NATIONALITY

	1999	2000	2001	2002	2003	Market share 03	% change 03-02
TOTAL	**89,117,875**	**84,514,856**	**61,431,266**	**50,734,623**	**52,129,778**	**100.00**	**2.75**
AFRICA	**8,387**	**9,496**	**9,497**	**8,699**	**9,538**	**0.02**	**9.64**
EAST AFRICA	**961**	**886**	**976**	**1,158**	**1,104**		**-4.66**
BR.IND.OC.TR	4	3	1	3	2		-33.33
BURUNDI	8	7	8	14	10		-28.57
COMOROS	2	1	4	2	2		
ETHIOPIA	129	70	80	53	57		7.55
ERITREA	5	9	21	14	24		71.43
DJIBOUTI	2	8	3	3	5		66.67
KENYA	262	212	275	299	366		22.41
MADAGASCAR	31	48	36	59	63		6.78
MALAWI	14	5	1	9	2		-77.78
MAURITIUS	50	94	92	97	102		5.15
MOZAMBIQUE	72	97	94	129	147		13.95
REUNION	4	2	8	8	5		-37.50
RWANDA	22	18	19	22	31		40.91
SEYCHELLES	6	10	19	11	9		-18.18
SOMALIA	17	15	18	8			
ZIMBABWE	123	108	120	118	98		-16.95
UGANDA	46	47	35	155	34		-78.06
TANZANIA	107	89	96	109	117		7.34
ZAMBIA	57	43	46	45	30		-33.33
CENTRAL AFR	**482**	**654**	**711**	**716**	**819**		**14.39**
ANGOLA	126	146	160	172	222		29.07
CAMEROON	178	235	224	227	272		19.82
CENT.AFR.REP	16	11	5	10	12		20.00
CHAD	1	13	17	12	12		
CONGO	97	194	246	240	228		-5.00
DEM.R.CONGO	53	42	19	44	54		22.73
EQ.GUINEA	1		1		2		
GABON	7	9	33	10	15		50.00
SAO TOME PRN	3	4	6	1	2		100.00
NORTH AFRICA	**2,885**	**3,460**	**3,148**	**2,741**	**3,248**	**0.01**	**18.50**
ALGERIA	980	988	1,055	854	1,117		30.80
MOROCCO	745	982	969	837	790		-5.62
WESTN.SAHARA	1		1	2	1		-50.00
SUDAN	136	99	95	79	89		12.66
TUNISIA	1,023	1,391	1,028	969	1,251		29.10
SOUTHERN AFR	**2,611**	**3,098**	**2,975**	**2,499**	**2,733**	**0.01**	**9.36**
BOTSWANA	15	13	7	11	11		
LESOTHO	5	6	5	2	1		-50.00
NAMIBIA	37	55	36	28	33		17.86
SOUTH AFRICA	2,547	3,007	2,918	2,454	2,680	0.01	9.21
SWAZILAND	7	17	9	4	8		100.00
WEST AFRICA	**1,448**	**1,398**	**1,687**	**1,585**	**1,634**		**3.09**
CAPE VERDE	38	18	44	52	22		-57.69
BENIN	36	44	33	45	51		13.33
GAMBIA	31	18	23	20	25		25.00
GHANA	138	133	133	180	230		27.78
GUINEA	53	48	51	30	81		170.00
COTE IVOIRE	61	43	59	75	76		1.33

2. ARRIVALS OF NON-RESIDENT VISITORS AT NATIONAL BORDERS, BY NATIONALITY

	1999	2000	2001	2002	2003	Market share 03	% change 03-02
LIBERIA	32	14	51	26	26		
MALI	57	49	46	53	60		13.21
MAURITANIA	15	14	10	18	17		-5.56
NIGER	9	11	28	24	5		-79.17
NIGERIA	761	755	985	839	790		-5.84
GUINEABISSAU	9	12	9	8	6		-25.00
ST.HELENA	1	1					
SENEGAL	109	115	78	109	119		9.17
SIERRA LEONE	19	39	67	30	32		6.67
TOGO	56	44	37	55	60		9.09
BURKINA FASO	23	40	33	21	34		61.90
AMERICAS	**297,944**	**329,647**	**306,871**	**272,329**	**294,313**	**0.56**	**8.07**
CARIBBEAN	**2,465**	**2,734**	**1,732**	**1,156**	**1,289**		**11.51**
ANTIGUA,BARB	4	2	2	4	7		75.00
BAHAMAS	5	21	13	36	8		-77.78
BARBADOS	10	25	7	23	31		34.78
BERMUDA	1	29	24	21	23		9.52
CAYMAN IS			2	3	6		100.00
CUBA	2,101	2,339	1,235	712	658		-7.58
DOMINICA	160	42	26	16	41		156.25
DOMINICAN RP	38	55	82	76	97		27.63
GRENADA	4	4	3	4	2		-50.00
GUADELOUPE		1		1			
HAITI	7	14	12	12	7		-41.67
JAMAICA	77	70	61	59	95		61.02
MARTINIQUE					1		
MONTSERRAT			1	2			
NETH.ANTILES	5	4	10	2	87		4.250.00
ARUBA					2		
PUERTO RICO	3	2	11	33	1		-96.97
ST.KITTS NEV	1	1	1	3	1		-66.67
ANGUILLA		1	2		1		
ST.LUCIA	9	10	15	27	100		270.37
ST.VINCENT,G	3	4	2	18	2		-88.89
TRINIDAD TBG	37	57	97	72	119		65.28
TURKS,CAICOS		53	125	31			
US.VIRGIN IS			1	1			
CENTRAL AMER	**767**	**1,013**	**747**	**987**	**1,153**		**16.82**
BELIZE	7	5	7	2	8		300.00
COSTA RICA	300	577	254	414	368		-11.11
EL SALVADOR	71	59	81	68	66		-2.94
GUATEMALA	114	89	69	132	145		9.85
HONDURAS	32	55	54	50	147		194.00
NICARAGUA	138	130	175	238	190		-20.17
PANAMA	105	98	107	83	229		175.90
NORTH AMER	**285,231**	**314,042**	**292,138**	**258,485**	**279,012**	**0.54**	**7.94**
CANADA	22,004	21,080	19,273	17,756	20,848	0.04	17.41
GREENLAND	2	1	1	1			
MEXICO	2,554	4,812	5,071	5,286	7,962	0.02	50.62
USA	260,671	288,149	267,793	235,442	250,202	0.48	6.27
SOUTH AMER	**9,481**	**11,858**	**12,254**	**11,701**	**12,859**	**0.02**	**9.90**
ARGENTINA	2,429	3,076	2,907	1,957	2,337		19.42

2. ARRIVALS OF NON-RESIDENT VISITORS AT NATIONAL BORDERS, BY NATIONALITY

	1999	2000	2001	2002	2003	Market share 03	% change 03-02
BOLIVIA	250	255	345	372	475		27.69
BRAZIL	3,279	4,132	4,625	5,021	5,068	0.01	0.94
CHILE	1,279	1,499	1,506	1,501	1,874		24.85
COLOMBIA	507	689	562	681	730		7.20
ECUADOR	290	535	647	680	758		11.47
FALKLAND IS		3	1		1		
FR.GUIANA	6	4	11	8	6		-25.00
GUYANA	21	25	15	16	21		31.25
PARAGUAY	132	56	55	24	48		100.00
PERU	466	668	498	636	629		-1.10
SURINAME	14	16	13	11	42		281.82
URUGUAY	327	237	301	274	356		29.93
VENEZUELA	481	663	768	520	514		-1.15
EAST AS/PACI	**77,679**	**87,693**	**85,061**	**87,430**	**88,693**	**0.17**	**1.44**
N/EAST ASIA	**50,247**	**60,586**	**57,516**	**60,722**	**61,069**	**0.12**	**0.57**
CHINA	5,432	4,953	4,965	6,445	5,077	0.01	-21.23
TAIWAN(P.C.)	4,555	6,476	4,947	3,842	2,250		-41.44
HK,CHINA	241	371	321	552	1,087		96.92
JAPAN	22,738	26,410	24,978	25,900	27,686	0.05	6.90
KOREA D P RP	305	256	339	319	458		43.57
KOREA REP.	12,321	15,572	15,336	19,052	22,033	0.04	15.65
MACAU, CHINA	6	17	9	21	47		123.81
MONGOLIA	4,649	6,531	6,621	4,591	2,431		-47.05
S/EAST ASIA	**8,920**	**9,669**	**9,492**	**10,723**	**11,730**	**0.02**	**9.39**
BRUNEI DARSM	3	2	11	6	13		116.67
MYANMAR	26	26	88	94	68		-27.66
CAMBODIA	16	5	12	9	16		77.78
INDONESIA	616	812	965	867	1,157		33.45
LAO P.DEM.R.	34	31	31	29	42		44.83
MALAYSIA	1,000	1,206	1,359	1,875	2,059		9.81
PHILIPPINES	1,276	1,466	1,442	1,452	1,365		-5.99
SINGAPORE	1,276	1,730	1,516	1,797	1,765		-1.78
VIET NAM	3,952	3,451	3,128	3,528	3,986	0.01	12.98
THAILAND	721	940	940	1,066	1,259		18.11
AUSTRALASIA	**18,462**	**17,315**	**16,423**	**15,864**	**15,451**	**0.03**	**-2.60**
AUSTRALIA	15,550	14,523	13,529	12,917	13,019	0.02	0.79
NEW ZEALAND	2,912	2,792	2,894	2,947	2,432		-17.48
MELANESIA	**21**	**62**	**1,573**	**35**	**411**		**1,074.29**
SOLOMON IS	2	41					
FIJI	5	3	7	13	17		30.77
NEW CALEDNIA	7	12	1,556	17	388		2.182.35
VANUATU	1		3	4	1		-75.00
NORFOLK IS					4		
PAPUA N.GUIN	6	6	7	1	1		
MICRONESIA	**13**	**43**	**26**	**26**	**12**		**-53.85**
CHRISTMAS IS		1	2	1			
COCOS IS	1	13	4	4	3		-25.00
KIRIBATI	6	23	15	15	5		-66.67
GUAM	3	1	1				
NAURU		3	2	6	2		-66.67
MARSHALL IS	2	1					
PALAU	1	1	2		2		

2. ARRIVALS OF NON-RESIDENT VISITORS AT NATIONAL BORDERS, BY NATIONALITY

	1999	2000	2001	2002	2003	Market share 03	% change 03-02
POLYNESIA	**16**	**18**	**31**	**60**	**20**		**-66.67**
AMER SAMOA	1	1	6		1		
FR.POLYNESIA	1	3	11	7	6		-14.29
NIUE		1	8	2			
TOKELAU		1			6		
TONGA	1	2	1	6	6		
TUVALU	9	8	3	5	1		-80.00
SAMOA	4	2	2	40			
EUROPE	**88,677,996**	**84,043,060**	**60,981,868**	**50,315,365**	**51,691,151**	**99.16**	**2.73**
C/E EUROPE	**32,490,687**	**32,812,700**	**27,883,353**	**24,720,972**	**24,300,596**	**46.62**	**-1.70**
AZERBAIJAN	4,085	3,408	2,375	2,281	2,728	0.01	19.60
ARMENIA	2,229	2,163	2,161	2,750	2,692	0.01	-2.11
BULGARIA	41,370	34,758	48,358	57,244	55,235	0.11	-3.51
BELARUS	4,640,343	5,919,553	5,197,070	4,241,711	3,830,074	7.35	-9.70
CZECH REP	13,490,978	11,984,954	9,276,105	8,313,159	8,826,943	16.93	6.18
ESTONIA	351,888	258,527	221,786	186,125	194,442	0.37	4.47
GEORGIA	7,131	7,198	2,470	1,938	2,127		9.75
HUNGARY	163,327	142,963	136,986	138,544	169,931	0.33	22.65
KAZAKHSTAN	77,585	105,055	61,314	50,565	48,578	0.09	-3.93
KYRGYZSTAN	5,325	9,962	4,486	4,033	6,232	0.01	54.53
LATVIA	482,134	421,025	411,682	400,605	421,767	0.81	5.28
LITHUANIA	1,449,455	1,414,338	1,393,171	1,397,746	1,365,823	2.62	-2.28
REP MOLDOVA	69,363	83,928	50,090	43,611	46,537	0.09	6.71
ROMANIA	50,990	48,443	43,461	54,359	64,106	0.12	17.93
RUSSIAN FED	2,114,048	2,275,217	1,969,174	1,843,844	1,534,054	2.94	-16.80
SLOVAKIA	4,234,446	3,913,933	2,642,131	2,126,032	2,896,310	5.56	36.23
TAJIKISTAN	302	376	357	392	474		20.92
TURKMENISTAN	269	332	133	221	162		-26.70
UKRAINE	5,302,828	6,184,395	6,417,693	5,853,478	4,829,789	9.26	-17.49
UZBEKISTAN	2,591	2,172	2,350	2,334	2,592		11.05
NORTHERN EUR	**764,183**	**729,665**	**671,888**	**649,797**	**705,253**	**1.35**	**8.53**
DENMARK	174,354	143,876	122,706	123,060	148,600	0.29	20.75
FAEROE IS	34	12	1	2	6		200.00
FINLAND	70,777	65,856	56,304	50,534	55,935	0.11	10.69
ICELAND	1,553	1,578	2,359	1,937	2,874	0.01	48.37
IRELAND	13,569	15,854	16,993	17,169	20,499	0.04	19.40
NORWAY	60,235	56,959	60,228	64,491	68,696	0.13	6.52
SWEDEN	207,671	205,204	191,572	191,092	197,997	0.38	3.61
UK	235,990	240,326	221,725	201,512	210,646	0.40	4.53
SOUTHERN EUR	**337,776**	**332,565**	**330,298**	**333,766**	**378,443**	**0.73**	**13.39**
ALBANIA	1,387	1,044	985	939	1,014		7.99
ANDORRA	18	317	1,127	226	61		-73.01
BOSNIA HERZG	1,767	2,181	2,411	2,779	2,261		-18.64
CROATIA	19,187	21,155	23,574	29,020	31,494	0.06	8.53
GIBRALTAR	1	1	2				
GREECE	33,947	29,949	29,188	27,746	27,094	0.05	-2.35
HOLY SEE	142	123	136	207	151		-27.05
ITALY	185,465	190,701	188,959	185,126	215,204	0.41	16.25
MALTA	631	666	638	794	933		17.51
PORTUGAL	19,717	14,770	15,918	16,550	19,060	0.04	15.17
SAN MARINO	47	86	72	60	133		121.67
SLOVENIA	15,920	16,621	16,729	17,530	20,117	0.04	14.76
SPAIN	47,971	42,708	38,009	40,503	48,561	0.09	19.89

POLAND

2. ARRIVALS OF NON-RESIDENT VISITORS AT NATIONAL BORDERS, BY NATIONALITY

	1999	2000	2001	2002	2003	Market share 03	% change 03-02
TFYROM	3,677	4,816	4,772	4,041	3,451	0.01	-14.60
SERBIA,MTNEG	7,899	7,427	7,778	8,245	8,909	0.02	8.05
WESTERN EUR	**55,031,062**	**50,108,860**	**32,031,909**	**24,539,779**	**26,233,378**	**50.32**	**6.90**
AUSTRIA	284,955	304,192	297,471	247,761	265,682	0.51	7.23
BELGIUM	176,641	160,418	111,871	92,621	65,230	0.13	-29.57
FRANCE	344,376	291,650	230,469	201,543	179,815	0.34	-10.78
GERMANY	53,787,905	48,902,660	31,010,499	23,654,699	25,456,531	48.83	7.62
LIECHTENSTEN	170	211	158	317	201		-36.59
LUXEMBOURG	3,311	2,998	2,525	2,156	2,612	0.01	21.15
MONACO	52	47	39	50	53		6.00
NETHERLANDS	371,330	401,566	337,243	302,882	224,991	0.43	-25.72
SWITZERLAND	62,322	45,118	41,634	37,750	38,263	0.07	1.36
EAST/MED EUR	**54,288**	**59,270**	**64,420**	**71,051**	**73,481**	**0.14**	**3.42**
CYPRUS	1,611	1,384	1,823	1,602	2,301		43.63
ISRAEL	31,762	39,308	43,476	48,611	48,422	0.09	-0.39
TURKEY	20,915	18,578	19,121	20,838	22,758	0.04	9.21
MIDDLE EAST	**6,430**	**6,763**	**6,414**	**6,277**	**6,065**	**0.01**	**-3.38**
MIDDLE EAST	**6,430**	**6,763**	**6,414**	**6,277**	**6,065**	**0.01**	**-3.38**
BAHRAIN	34	46	31	58	74		27.59
IRAQ	257	233	300	267	192		-28.09
JORDAN	406	486	547	593	510		-14.00
KUWAIT	458	533	454	483	533		10.35
LEBANON	897	1,049	1,069	1,083	1,020		-5.82
LIBYA	1,402	1,253	1,082	1,012	921		-8.99
OMAN	39	49	29	23	21		-8.70
QATAR	33	21	3	100	56		-44.00
SAUDI ARABIA	223	241	328	330	376		13.94
DEM.YEMEN	1		2				
SYRIA	685	754	749	728	634		-12.91
UNTD ARAB EM	210	260	87	98	148		51.02
EGYPT	1,569	1,609	1,514	1,318	1,456		10.47
YEMEN	216	229	219	184	124		-32.61
SOUTH ASIA	**9,198**	**8,990**	**8,554**	**8,875**	**9,483**	**0.02**	**6.85**
SOUTH ASIA	**9,198**	**8,990**	**8,554**	**8,875**	**9,483**	**0.02**	**6.85**
AFGHANISTAN	371	386	285	442	366		-17.19
BANGLADESH	194	203	228	179	132		-26.26
BHUTAN	2	7	4	3	4		33.33
SRI LANKA	188	205	245	236	226		-4.24
INDIA	4,320	4,797	5,015	5,259	6,092	0.01	15.84
IRAN	3,130	1,940	1,535	1,500	1,393		-7.13
MALDIVES	10	1	6	2	1		-50.00
NEPAL	62	78	54	135	97		-28.15
PAKISTAN	921	1,373	1,182	1,119	1,172		4.74
REG.NOT SPEC	**40,241**	**29,207**	**33,001**	**35,648**	**30,535**	**0.06**	**-14.34**
NOT SPECIFIE	**40,241**	**29,207**	**33,001**	**35,648**	**30,535**	**0.06**	**-14.34**
OTH.WORLD	40,241	29,207	33,001	35,648	30,535	0.06	-14.34

Source: World Tourism Organization (WTO)

3. ARRIVALS OF NON-RESIDENT TOURISTS IN HOTELS AND SIMILAR ESTABLISHMENTS, BY COUNTRY OF RESIDENCE

	1999	2000	2001	2002	2003	Market share 03	% change 03-02
TOTAL (*)	**2,494,919**	**2,504,510**	**2,488,198**	**2,535,642**	**2,700,717**	**100.00**	**6.51**
AFRICA		**3,898**	**2,946**	**4,579**	**5,205**	**0.19**	**13.67**
EAST AFRICA		**1,082**	**304**	**215**	**851**	**0.03**	**295.81**
BR.IND.OC.TR				1			
BURUNDI		76	14	4	6		50.00
COMOROS		1	1				
ETHIOPIA		37	27	41	42		2.44
ERITREA			2	4	275	0.01	6.775.00
DJIBOUTI				14	1		-92.86
KENYA		852	36	50	102		104.00
MADAGASCAR		1	13	5	221	0.01	4.320.00
MALAWI			3		50		
MAURITIUS		1	3	13	13		
MOZAMBIQUE		9	6	6	8		33.33
REUNION			8	2			
RWANDA		11	117	7	4		-42.86
SEYCHELLES		4	2		11		
SOMALIA		33	29	12	20		66.67
ZIMBABWE		9	9	10	20		100.00
UGANDA		5	7	8	13		62.50
TANZANIA		19	5	34	50		47.06
ZAMBIA		24	22	4	15		275.00
CENTRAL AFR		**447**	**100**	**1,832**	**370**	**0.01**	**-79.80**
ANGOLA		122	32	1,259	130		-89.67
CAMEROON		191	14	112	82		-26.79
CENT.AFR.REP		10	12	6	40		566.67
CHAD		19		44			
CONGO		88	40	37	102		175.68
DEM.R.CONGO		14	2	369	5		-98.64
EQ.GUINEA		2			9		
GABON		1		3	1		-66.67
SAO TOME PRN				2	1		-50.00
NORTH AFRICA		**830**	**846**	**908**	**2,257**	**0.08**	**148.57**
ALGERIA		368	334	280	1,579	0.06	463.93
MOROCCO		175	190	257	161	0.01	-37.35
WESTN.SAHARA				2	1		-50.00
SUDAN		41	11	19	80		321.05
TUNISIA		246	311	350	436	0.02	24.57
SOUTHERN AFR		**809**	**905**	**557**	**762**	**0.03**	**36.80**
BOTSWANA		1	2	3	6		100.00
LESOTHO			2				
NAMIBIA			1	1	2		100.00
SOUTH AFRICA		765	898	534	746	0.03	39.70
SWAZILAND		43	2	19	8		-57.89
WEST AFRICA		**730**	**791**	**1,067**	**965**	**0.04**	**-9.56**
CAPE VERDE			1		1		
BENIN		123	185	125	140	0.01	12.00
GAMBIA			14		165	0.01	
GHANA		5	9	19	33		73.68
GUINEA		2	4	6	3		-50.00

3. ARRIVALS OF NON-RESIDENT TOURISTS IN HOTELS AND SIMILAR ESTABLISHMENTS, BY COUNTRY OF RESIDENCE

	1999	2000	2001	2002	2003	Market share 03	% change 03-02
COTE IVOIRE		102	76	29	17		-41.38
LIBERIA			2	1	4		300.00
MALI		15	22	27	24		-11.11
MAURITANIA		3	4	9	6		-33.33
NIGER		16	32	17	9		-47.06
NIGERIA		346	336	736	398	0.01	-45.92
GUINEABISSAU			36		13		
ST.HELENA		30	3		2		
SENEGAL		11	10	41	38		-7.32
SIERRA LEONE		73	55	52	100		92.31
TOGO		2	1		8		
BURKINA FASO		2	1	5	4		-20.00
AMERICAS	**169,158**	**197,609**	**181,179**	**174,009**	**164,574**	**6.09**	**-5.42**
CARIBBEAN		**2,115**	**949**	**3,839**	**882**	**0.03**	**-77.03**
ANTIGUA,BARB		117	57	75	133		77.33
BAHAMAS		61	53	29	89		206.90
BARBADOS		17	1	14	26		85.71
BR.VIRGIN IS					2		
CAYMAN IS		6					
CUBA		48	251	102	353	0.01	246.08
DOMINICA		5	4	4			
DOMINICAN RP		14	5	13	10		-23.08
GRENADA		21	3	26	90		246.15
GUADELOUPE		6			1		
HAITI		3	1	5	7		40.00
JAMAICA		22	256	317	14		-95.58
MARTINIQUE		2	2		1		
MONTSERRAT		5		4			
NETH.ANTILES		3	2		17		
ARUBA		2	1				
PUERTO RICO		37	276	53	45		-15.09
ANGUILLA		264		37	43		16.22
TRINIDAD TBG		35		2	28		1,300.00
TURKS,CAICOS		1		5	4		-20.00
US.VIRGIN IS		1,446	37	3,153	19		-99.40
CENTRAL AMER		**103**	**85**	**786**	**268**	**0.01**	**-65.90**
BELIZE				17	1		-94.12
COSTA RICA		39	29	68	99		45.59
EL SALVADOR		25	10	15	27		80.00
GUATEMALA		16	14	17	39		129.41
HONDURAS		7	8	628	61		-90.29
NICARAGUA		10	7	6	22		266.67
PANAMA		6	17	35	19		-45.71
NORTH AMER	**169,158**	**186,316**	**174,447**	**164,681**	**158,654**	**5.87**	**-3.66**
CANADA	13,519	14,752	10,497	14,005	12,238	0.45	-12.62
GREENLAND				1			
MEXICO		1,281	1,301	1,852	2,554	0.09	37.90
ST.PIERRE,MQ		1					
USA	155,639	170,282	162,649	148,823	143,862	5.33	-3.33
SOUTH AMER		**9,075**	**5,698**	**4,703**	**4,770**	**0.18**	**1.42**
ARGENTINA		2,037	1,504	612	909	0.03	48.53
BOLIVIA		21	33	72	81		12.50

3. ARRIVALS OF NON-RESIDENT TOURISTS IN HOTELS AND SIMILAR ESTABLISHMENTS, BY COUNTRY OF RESIDENCE

	1999	2000	2001	2002	2003	Market share 03	% change 03-02
BRAZIL		3,291	3,116	2,990	2,464	0.09	-17.59
CHILE		526	228	625	577	0.02	-7.68
COLOMBIA		89	129	73	168	0.01	130.14
ECUADOR		21	59	39	147	0.01	276.92
FALKLAND IS			21	47			
GUYANA		10	1	1	10		900.00
PARAGUAY		3	7	23	5		-78.26
PERU		166	87	79	96		21.52
SURINAME		42	22	16	34		112.50
URUGUAY		2,649	98	44	127		188.64
VENEZUELA		220	393	82	152	0.01	85.37
EAST AS/PACI	**24,136**	**58,670**	**55,077**	**56,393**	**59,435**	**2.20**	**5.39**
N/EAST ASIA	**24,136**	**49,794**	**47,341**	**47,048**	**48,252**	**1.79**	**2.56**
CHINA		2,548	3,931	4,231	3,598	0.13	-14.96
TAIWAN(P.C.)		3,683	3,205	1,908	1,139	0.04	-40.30
HK,CHINA		986	1,135	990	893	0.03	-9.80
JAPAN	24,136	27,758	25,823	26,825	29,414	1.09	9.65
KOREA D P RP		11,440	3,989	3,684	757	0.03	-79.45
KOREA REP.		2,816	8,960	9,174	12,173	0.45	32.69
MACAU, CHINA		1		1	9		800.00
MONGOLIA		562	298	235	269	0.01	14.47
S/EAST ASIA		**2,023**	**2,124**	**2,825**	**3,580**	**0.13**	**26.73**
BRUNEI DARSM		6	1				
MYANMAR		11	12	13	14		7.69
INDONESIA		183	179	403	733	0.03	81.89
LAO P.DEM.R.			6	7	10		42.86
MALAYSIA		374	364	373	485	0.02	30.03
PHILIPPINES		269	485	585	527	0.02	-9.91
TIMOR-LESTE				5			
SINGAPORE		291	351	749	630	0.02	-15.89
VIET NAM		482	454	359	705	0.03	96.38
THAILAND		407	272	331	476	0.02	43.81
AUSTRALASIA		**6,697**	**5,375**	**6,293**	**7,467**	**0.28**	**18.66**
AUSTRALIA		6,069	4,865	5,697	6,633	0.25	16.43
NEW ZEALAND		628	510	596	834	0.03	39.93
MELANESIA		**37**	**129**	**37**	**24**		**-35.14**
SOLOMON IS		26	109	8	16		100.00
FIJI			2	2	2		
NEW CALEDNIA			17	25	5		-80.00
NORFOLK IS		10					
PAPUA N.GUIN		1	1	2	1		-50.00
MICRONESIA		**14**	**33**	**25**	**16**		**-36.00**
CHRISTMAS IS		3	6	2	14		600.00
COCOS IS		2					
KIRIBATI		3	11	8			
GUAM		2					
NAURU		4	16	15	2		-86.67
POLYNESIA		**105**	**75**	**165**	**96**		**-41.82**
AMER SAMOA		71	11	53	29		-45.28
FR.POLYNESIA		19	2	13	6		-53.85

POLAND

3. ARRIVALS OF NON-RESIDENT TOURISTS IN HOTELS AND SIMILAR ESTABLISHMENTS, BY COUNTRY OF RESIDENCE

	1999	2000	2001	2002	2003	Market share 03	% change 03-02
NIUE		4	52	1	5		400.00
PITCAIRN			1				
TOKELAU		5	1	17	8		-52.94
TONGA				1	3		200.00
TUVALU		1		13	2		-84.62
WALLIS FUT.I		3			1		
SAMOA		2	8	67	42		-37.31
EUROPE	**2,028,421**	**2,166,395**	**2,165,738**	**2,237,073**	**2,418,844**	**89.56**	**8.13**
C/E EUROPE	**366,836**	**364,577**	**366,732**	**406,538**	**451,488**	**16.72**	**11.06**
AZERBAIJAN		655	250	245	381	0.01	55.51
ARMENIA		799	649	512	741	0.03	44.73
BULGARIA		6,743	5,306	4,355	5,658	0.21	29.92
BELARUS	38,522	43,181	55,352	60,872	60,410	2.24	-0.76
CZECH REP	34,763	33,595	30,501	32,176	37,077	1.37	15.23
ESTONIA		6,874	6,877	14,053	16,229	0.60	15.48
GEORGIA		496	485	230	421	0.02	83.04
HUNGARY	21,752	17,054	14,851	16,115	23,477	0.87	45.68
KAZAKHSTAN		1,062	560	822	2,036	0.08	147.69
KYRGYZSTAN		117	27	63	75		19.05
LATVIA		5,493	5,934	7,427	13,036	0.48	75.52
LITHUANIA	78,701	34,705	33,326	36,186	44,562	1.65	23.15
REP MOLDOVA		5,376	3,138	1,688	2,122	0.08	25.71
ROMANIA		7,693	7,263	5,596	7,725	0.29	38.05
RUSSIAN FED	73,243	87,998	108,040	130,172	140,657	5.21	8.05
SLOVAKIA	13,866	12,092	9,905	11,803	14,406	0.53	22.05
TAJIKISTAN		21	27	72	64		-11.11
TURKMENISTAN		27	52	3	16		433.33
UKRAINE	105,989	100,334	84,068	84,013	82,052	3.04	-2.33
UZBEKISTAN		262	121	135	343	0.01	154.07
NORTHERN EUR	**403,333**	**395,220**	**357,109**	**355,640**	**399,671**	**14.80**	**12.38**
DENMARK	85,609	73,942	59,913	65,196	76,306	2.83	17.04
FAEROE IS		1		3	12		300.00
FINLAND	33,351	30,669	26,770	25,465	29,103	1.08	14.29
ICELAND		599	520	582	879	0.03	51.03
IRELAND	7,617	6,116	6,462	6,414	8,956	0.33	39.63
NORWAY	47,474	36,490	38,890	43,779	57,685	2.14	31.76
SVALBARD IS		2		1	1		
SWEDEN	82,349	86,887	76,759	71,315	74,436	2.76	4.38
UK	146,933	160,514	147,795	142,885	152,293	5.64	6.58
SOUTHERN EUR	**143,835**	**146,577**	**166,254**	**190,127**	**219,865**	**8.14**	**15.64**
ALBANIA		262	346	779	868	0.03	11.42
ANDORRA		32	92	15	229	0.01	1,426.67
BOSNIA HERZG		351	202	316	531	0.02	68.04
CROATIA		2,707	3,954	3,472	4,998	0.19	43.95
GIBRALTAR		45	2				
GREECE	5,646	5,443	4,253	6,165	7,357	0.27	19.33
HOLY SEE		6	3	6	10		66.67
ITALY	108,808	95,901	111,205	114,447	136,370	5.05	19.16
MALTA		207	202	340	777	0.03	128.53
PORTUGAL	7,474	7,514	7,985	9,739	8,467	0.31	-13.06
SAN MARINO		104	125	34	139	0.01	308.82
SLOVENIA		3,484	3,892	5,365	4,779	0.18	-10.92

3. ARRIVALS OF NON-RESIDENT TOURISTS IN HOTELS AND SIMILAR ESTABLISHMENTS, BY COUNTRY OF RESIDENCE

	1999	2000	2001	2002	2003	Market share 03	% change 03-02
SPAIN	21,907	28,612	30,965	46,630	52,284	1.94	12.13
TFYROM		258	195	422	453	0.02	7.35
SERBIA,MTNEG		1,651	2,833	2,397	2,603	0.10	8.59
WESTERN EUR	**1,114,417**	**1,168,680**	**1,181,663**	**1,183,876**	**1,246,658**	**46.16**	**5.30**
AUSTRIA	56,251	44,220	46,192	43,685	45,183	1.67	3.43
BELGIUM	32,536	34,281	34,753	36,624	36,783	1.36	0.43
FRANCE	110,663	104,077	113,958	113,197	128,586	4.76	13.59
GERMANY	807,646	879,168	882,244	889,234	928,360	34.37	4.40
LIECHTENSTEN		96	127	82	180	0.01	119.51
LUXEMBOURG	2,513	3,318	5,110	3,973	5,657	0.21	42.39
MONACO		46	37	57	79		38.60
NETHERLANDS	76,258	70,856	68,930	70,512	75,173	2.78	6.61
SWITZERLAND	28,550	32,618	30,312	26,512	26,657	0.99	0.55
EAST/MED EUR		**91,341**	**93,980**	**100,892**	**101,162**	**3.75**	**0.27**
CYPRUS		432	458	457	1,148	0.04	151.20
ISRAEL		87,153	90,406	97,014	93,940	3.48	-3.17
TURKEY		3,756	3,116	3,421	6,074	0.22	77.55
MIDDLE EAST		**2,730**	**2,775**	**2,193**	**3,391**	**0.13**	**54.63**
MIDDLE EAST		**2,730**	**2,775**	**2,193**	**3,391**	**0.13**	**54.63**
BAHRAIN		174	203	118	156	0.01	32.20
IRAQ		177	68	164	86		-47.56
JORDAN		79	99	109	278	0.01	155.05
KUWAIT		186	159	217	250	0.01	15.21
LEBANON		197	161	212	234	0.01	10.38
LIBYA		217	120	151	422	0.02	179.47
OMAN		12	11	53	79		49.06
QATAR		1	16	24	106		341.67
SAUDI ARABIA		881	1,305	193	498	0.02	158.03
SYRIA		56	91	327	170	0.01	-48.01
UNTD ARAB EM		190	107	55	71		29.09
EGYPT		441	404	340	980	0.04	188.24
YEMEN		119	31	230	61		-73.48
SOUTH ASIA		**4,977**	**6,029**	**5,732**	**4,387**	**0.16**	**-23.46**
SOUTH ASIA		**4,977**	**6,029**	**5,732**	**4,387**	**0.16**	**-23.46**
AFGHANISTAN		86	450	250	318	0.01	27.20
BANGLADESH		203	99	695	42		-93.96
BHUTAN		417	3,062	2,383	365	0.01	-84.68
SRI LANKA		671	23	41	51		24.39
INDIA		2,977	1,656	1,657	2,631	0.10	58.78
IRAN		471	583	456	686	0.03	50.44
NEPAL		4	13	76	83		9.21
PAKISTAN		148	143	174	211	0.01	21.26
REG.NOT SPEC	**273,204**	**70,231**	**74,454**	**55,663**	**44,881**	**1.66**	**-19.37**
NOT SPECIFIE	**273,204**	**70,231**	**74,454**	**55,663**	**44,881**	**1.66**	**-19.37**
OTH.WORLD	273,204	70,231	74,454	55,663	44,881	1.66	-19.37

Source: World Tourism Organization (WTO)

POLAND

4. ARRIVALS OF NON-RESIDENT TOURISTS IN ALL TYPES OF ACCOMMODATION ESTABLISHMENTS, BY COUNTRY OF RESIDENCE

	1999	2000	2001	2002	2003	Market share 03	% change 03-02
TOTAL (*)	**3,228,997**	**3,117,146**	**3,151,513**	**3,145,439**	**3,331,870**	**100.00**	**5.93**
AFRICA		**4,758**	**3,788**	**5,051**	**6,009**	**0.18**	**18.97**
EAST AFRICA		**1,173**	**363**	**271**	**992**	**0.03**	**266.05**
BR.IND.OC.TR				1			
BURUNDI		77	25	5	6		20.00
COMOROS		1	1				
ETHIOPIA		40	32	49	53		8.16
ERITREA			11	5	277	0.01	5,440.00
DJIBOUTI				14	1		-92.86
KENYA		864	46	58	127		118.97
MADAGASCAR		2	20	5	227	0.01	4,440.00
MALAWI			3		50		
MAURITIUS		1	3	21	16		-23.81
MOZAMBIQUE		11	10	6	12		100.00
REUNION			12	2			
RWANDA		15	117	7	12		71.43
SEYCHELLES		4	2		12		
SOMALIA		81	33	36	33		-8.33
ZIMBABWE		11	13	11	26		136.36
UGANDA		6	7	8	69		762.50
TANZANIA		34	5	35	56		60.00
ZAMBIA		26	23	8	15		87.50
CENTRAL AFR		**530**	**127**	**1,851**	**450**	**0.01**	**-75.69**
ANGOLA		147	46	1,262	143		-88.67
CAMEROON		223	18	118	100		-15.25
CENT.AFR.REP		10	12	6	41		583.33
CHAD		19	7	44			
CONGO		111	41	45	131		191.11
DEM.R.CONGO		17	2	369	5		-98.64
EQ.GUINEA		2		2	28		1,300.00
GABON		1	1	3	1		-66.67
SAO TOME PRN				2	1		-50.00
NORTH AFRICA		**1,209**	**1,201**	**1,117**	**2,559**	**0.08**	**129.10**
ALGERIA		570	459	346	1,693	0.05	389.31
MOROCCO		202	291	315	179	0.01	-43.17
WESTN.SAHARA				2	1		-50.00
SUDAN		55	19	20	92		360.00
TUNISIA		382	432	434	594	0.02	36.87
SOUTHERN AFR		**968**	**1,051**	**624**	**901**	**0.03**	**44.39**
BOTSWANA		1	2	3	6		100.00
LESOTHO		24	2				
NAMIBIA		1	3	2	2		
SOUTH AFRICA		898	1,042	600	883	0.03	47.17
SWAZILAND		44	2	19	10		-47.37
WEST AFRICA		**878**	**1,046**	**1,188**	**1,107**	**0.03**	**-6.82**
CAPE VERDE			1		1		
BENIN		123	186	125	142		13.60
GAMBIA		30	17	6	179	0.01	2,883.33
GHANA		5	13	20	38		90.00
GUINEA		7	135	7	4		-42.86

POLAND

4. ARRIVALS OF NON-RESIDENT TOURISTS IN ALL TYPES OF ACCOMMODATION ESTABLISHMENTS, BY COUNTRY OF RESIDENCE

	1999	2000	2001	2002	2003	Market share 03	% change 03-02
COTE IVOIRE		102	76	34	19		-44.12
LIBERIA		4	3	1	4		300.00
MALI		21	25	51	26		-49.02
MAURITANIA		3	4	9	9		
NIGER		16	33	19	15		-21.05
NIGERIA		426	407	809	455	0.01	-43.76
GUINEABISSAU		2	62		13		
ST.HELENA		39	3		2		
SENEGAL		20	24	49	48		-2.04
SIERRA LEONE		76	55	53	139		162.26
TOGO		2	1		9		
BURKINA FASO		2	1	5	4		-20.00
AMERICAS	**189,973**	**216,404**	**201,289**	**189,177**	**182,309**	**5.47**	**-3.63**
CARIBBEAN		**2,170**	**1,083**	**3,902**	**915**	**0.03**	**-76.55**
ANTIGUA,BARB		117	57	75	137		82.67
BAHAMAS		63	53	31	89		187.10
BARBADOS		17	1	14	26		85.71
BR.VIRGIN IS		4			2		
CAYMAN IS		7		16			
CUBA		76	323	113	376	0.01	232.74
DOMINICA		7	35	4			
DOMINICAN RP		16	6	15	11		-26.67
GRENADA		25	5	31	90		190.32
GUADELOUPE		6			1		
HAITI		6	3	5	7		40.00
JAMAICA		22	275	331	16		-95.17
MARTINIQUE		2	2		1		
MONTSERRAT		5		5			
NETH.ANTILES		3	2		17		
ARUBA		2	1	5			
PUERTO RICO		37	276	57	46		-19.30
ANGUILLA		266		37	43		16.22
TRINIDAD TBG		35		3	29		866.67
TURKS,CAICOS		5	7	5	4		-20.00
US.VIRGIN IS		1,449	37	3,155	20		-99.37
CENTRAL AMER		**141**	**142**	**840**	**664**	**0.02**	**-20.95**
BELIZE			50	43	360	0.01	737.21
COSTA RICA		44	33	92	112		21.74
EL SALVADOR		27	11	15	28		86.67
GUATEMALA		23	15	21	49		133.33
HONDURAS		26	9	628	70		-88.85
NICARAGUA		14	7	6	25		316.67
PANAMA		7	17	35	20		-42.86
NORTH AMER	**189,973**	**203,649**	**193,458**	**179,150**	**175,129**	**5.26**	**-2.24**
CANADA	16,957	17,666	13,226	16,050	14,674	0.44	-8.57
GREENLAND				1			
MEXICO		1,444	1,660	2,163	2,977	0.09	37.63
ST.PIERRE,MQ		1			47		
USA	173,016	184,538	178,572	160,936	157,431	4.73	-2.18
SOUTH AMER		**10,444**	**6,606**	**5,285**	**5,601**	**0.17**	**5.98**
ARGENTINA		2,216	1,634	727	1,074	0.03	47.73
BOLIVIA		32	44	100	112		12.00

4. ARRIVALS OF NON-RESIDENT TOURISTS IN ALL TYPES OF ACCOMMODATION ESTABLISHMENTS, BY COUNTRY OF RESIDENCE

	1999	2000	2001	2002	2003	Market share 03	% change 03-02
BRAZIL		3,552	3,464	3,159	2,800	0.08	-11.36
CHILE		614	282	669	666	0.02	-0.45
COLOMBIA		322	155	186	228	0.01	22.58
ECUADOR		126	98	82	183	0.01	123.17
FALKLAND IS			21	54			
GUYANA		53	4	1	12		1,100.00
PARAGUAY		4	17	24	5		-79.17
PERU		437	299	117	140		19.66
SURINAME		46	22	16	36		125.00
URUGUAY		2,804	114	54	181	0.01	235.19
VENEZUELA		238	452	96	164		70.83
EAST AS/PACI	**28,941**	**67,584**	**64,127**	**64,206**	**66,951**	**2.01**	**4.28**
N/EAST ASIA	**28,941**	**54,599**	**51,726**	**50,711**	**51,603**	**1.55**	**1.76**
CHINA		3,002	4,375	4,976	4,122	0.12	-17.16
TAIWAN(P.C.)		3,711	3,276	2,005	1,160	0.03	-42.14
HK,CHINA		1,009	1,154	999	927	0.03	-7.21
JAPAN	28,941	30,631	28,631	28,907	31,497	0.95	8.96
KOREA D P RP		12,438	4,261	3,880	908	0.03	-76.60
KOREA REP.		2,907	9,252	9,455	12,563	0.38	32.87
MACAU, CHINA		1		1	9		800.00
MONGOLIA		900	777	488	417	0.01	-14.55
S/EAST ASIA		**2,539**	**2,703**	**3,344**	**4,178**	**0.13**	**24.94**
BRUNEI DARSM		6	6	19			
MYANMAR		11	12	13	14		7.69
CAMBODIA		2					
INDONESIA		194	191	414	754	0.02	82.13
LAO P.DEM.R.		5	7	14	15		7.14
MALAYSIA		417	406	420	567	0.02	35.00
PHILIPPINES		306	669	681	608	0.02	-10.72
TIMOR-LESTE				6	1		-83.33
SINGAPORE		342	403	815	716	0.02	-12.15
VIET NAM		799	698	585	982	0.03	67.86
THAILAND		457	311	377	521	0.02	38.20
AUSTRALASIA		**10,284**	**9,447**	**9,888**	**10,952**	**0.33**	**10.76**
AUSTRALIA		9,091	8,296	8,796	9,356	0.28	6.37
NEW ZEALAND		1,193	1,151	1,092	1,596	0.05	46.15
MELANESIA		**39**	**129**	**37**	**32**		**-13.51**
SOLOMON IS		26	109	8	16		100.00
FIJI			2	2	6		200.00
NEW CALEDNIA		2	17	25	9		-64.00
NORFOLK IS		10					
PAPUA N.GUIN		1	1	2	1		-50.00
MICRONESIA		**14**	**45**	**39**	**16**		**-58.97**
CHRISTMAS IS		3	6	2	14		600.00
COCOS IS		2					
KIRIBATI		3	11	8			
GUAM		2					
NAURU		4	28	29	2		-93.10
POLYNESIA		**109**	**77**	**187**	**170**	**0.01**	**-9.09**
AMER SAMOA		71	12	53	29		-45.28

4. ARRIVALS OF NON-RESIDENT TOURISTS IN ALL TYPES OF ACCOMMODATION ESTABLISHMENTS, BY COUNTRY OF RESIDENCE

	1999	2000	2001	2002	2003	Market share 03	% change 03-02
FR.POLYNESIA		19	3	14	41		192.86
NIUE		4	52	1	5		400.00
PITCAIRN			1				
TOKELAU		5	1	17	8		-52.94
TONGA				1	3		200.00
TUVALU		3		18	2		-88.89
WALLIS FUT.I		5		16	40		150.00
SAMOA		2	8	67	42		-37.31
EUROPE	**2,672,168**	**2,742,901**	**2,791,284**	**2,818,036**	**3,022,645**	**90.72**	**7.26**
C/E EUROPE	**689,299**	**636,462**	**641,457**	**662,382**	**680,373**	**20.42**	**2.72**
AZERBAIJAN		1,096	674	333	611	0.02	83.48
ARMENIA		1,356	1,160	1,104	987	0.03	-10.60
BULGARIA		9,298	7,598	6,658	7,527	0.23	13.05
BELARUS	87,679	93,140	105,325	110,555	102,980	3.09	-6.85
CZECH REP	50,986	45,944	44,451	44,763	50,313	1.51	12.40
ESTONIA		21,082	22,599	22,063	23,248	0.70	5.37
GEORGIA		877	804	326	643	0.02	97.24
HUNGARY	45,602	26,177	24,658	26,206	36,847	1.11	40.61
KAZAKHSTAN		2,133	966	1,527	2,385	0.07	56.19
KYRGYZSTAN		138	44	78	137		75.64
LATVIA		9,549	8,810	11,593	18,790	0.56	62.08
LITHUANIA	104,914	54,249	51,382	54,220	62,718	1.88	15.67
REP MOLDOVA		11,238	6,565	4,473	5,659	0.17	26.51
ROMANIA		13,236	12,985	9,690	11,564	0.35	19.34
RUSSIAN FED	120,064	121,381	140,960	163,391	170,786	5.13	4.53
SLOVAKIA	20,559	17,620	16,302	18,415	21,729	0.65	18.00
TAJIKISTAN		40	52	86	75		-12.79
TURKMENISTAN		61	58	11	16		45.45
UKRAINE	259,495	207,552	195,874	186,709	162,945	4.89	-12.73
UZBEKISTAN		295	190	181	413	0.01	128.18
NORTHERN EUR	**463,058**	**445,132**	**412,042**	**403,289**	**446,363**	**13.40**	**10.68**
DENMARK	102,071	86,772	70,154	74,386	89,030	2.67	19.69
FAEROE IS		14	4	4	14		250.00
FINLAND	38,067	34,595	30,997	29,376	33,265	1.00	13.24
ICELAND		716	626	709	975	0.03	37.52
IRELAND	9,437	7,827	8,268	8,053	10,758	0.32	33.59
NORWAY	53,330	40,087	45,580	48,437	60,680	1.82	25.28
SVALBARD IS		2		1	3		200.00
SWEDEN	92,839	97,938	90,012	84,543	87,088	2.61	3.01
UK	167,314	177,181	166,401	157,780	164,550	4.94	4.29
SOUTHERN EUR	**167,105**	**168,294**	**194,419**	**211,088**	**243,789**	**7.32**	**15.49**
ALBANIA		334	380	794	930	0.03	17.13
ANDORRA		32	99	15	231	0.01	1,440.00
BOSNIA HERZG		429	298	415	654	0.02	57.59
CROATIA		3,446	4,475	4,555	6,274	0.19	37.74
GIBRALTAR		45	2				
GREECE	6,622	6,043	5,259	6,745	7,879	0.24	16.81
HOLY SEE		15	3	170	10		-94.12
ITALY	123,780	109,726	128,986	126,774	150,392	4.51	18.63
MALTA		221	266	398	805	0.02	102.26
PORTUGAL	8,250	8,113	9,787	10,498	9,329	0.28	-11.14
SAN MARINO		104	129	36	140		288.89

4. ARRIVALS OF NON-RESIDENT TOURISTS IN ALL TYPES OF ACCOMMODATION ESTABLISHMENTS, BY COUNTRY OF RESIDENCE

	1999	2000	2001	2002	2003	Market share 03	% change 03-02
SLOVENIA		4,110	4,876	6,407	5,853	0.18	-8.65
SPAIN	28,453	33,016	36,039	50,909	57,746	1.73	13.43
TFYROM		454	422	684	566	0.02	-17.25
SERBIA,MTNEG		2,206	3,398	2,688	2,980	0.09	10.86
WESTERN EUR	**1,352,706**	**1,395,222**	**1,443,653**	**1,436,772**	**1,548,029**	**46.46**	**7.74**
AUSTRIA	63,516	49,711	51,205	47,615	52,119	1.56	9.46
BELGIUM	42,118	40,312	42,218	42,933	43,767	1.31	1.94
FRANCE	132,492	124,816	138,921	132,568	152,873	4.59	15.32
GERMANY	980,445	1,050,520	1,084,264	1,089,917	1,166,907	35.02	7.06
LIECHTENSTEN		107	135	97	195	0.01	101.03
LUXEMBOURG	3,417	3,546	5,418	4,198	5,965	0.18	42.09
MONACO		67	41	59	83		40.68
NETHERLANDS	98,679	90,952	88,920	91,044	96,721	2.90	6.24
SWITZERLAND	32,039	35,191	32,531	28,341	29,399	0.88	3.73
EAST/MED EUR		**97,791**	**99,713**	**104,505**	**104,091**	**3.12**	**-0.40**
CYPRUS		541	509	506	1,225	0.04	142.09
ISRAEL		92,857	95,609	99,995	96,081	2.88	-3.91
TURKEY		4,393	3,595	4,004	6,785	0.20	69.46
MIDDLE EAST		**3,143**	**3,189**	**2,621**	**3,780**	**0.11**	**44.22**
MIDDLE EAST		**3,143**	**3,189**	**2,621**	**3,780**	**0.11**	**44.22**
BAHRAIN		174	230	125	156		24.80
IRAQ		187	89	265	112		-57.74
JORDAN		89	118	113	295	0.01	161.06
KUWAIT		212	165	239	275	0.01	15.06
LEBANON		247	194	259	287	0.01	10.81
LIBYA		255	145	179	466	0.01	160.34
OMAN		24	12	55	79		43.64
QATAR		1	33	24	110		358.33
SAUDI ARABIA		929	1,358	221	550	0.02	148.87
SYRIA		82	140	352	210	0.01	-40.34
UNTD ARAB EM		238	118	75	86		14.67
EGYPT		569	505	416	1,068	0.03	156.73
YEMEN		136	82	298	86		-71.14
SOUTH ASIA		**5,555**	**6,550**	**6,238**	**4,843**	**0.15**	**-22.36**
SOUTH ASIA		**5,555**	**6,550**	**6,238**	**4,843**	**0.15**	**-22.36**
AFGHANISTAN		310	485	303	402	0.01	32.67
BANGLADESH		210	111	720	43		-94.03
BHUTAN		417	3,062	2,383	365	0.01	-84.68
SRI LANKA		742	25	42	65		54.76
INDIA		3,164	1,900	1,939	2,857	0.09	47.34
IRAN		501	633	545	752	0.02	37.98
NEPAL		5	14	87	92		5.75
PAKISTAN		206	320	219	267	0.01	21.92
REG.NOT SPEC	**337,915**	**76,801**	**81,286**	**60,110**	**45,333**	**1.36**	**-24.58**
NOT SPECIFIE	**337,915**	**76,801**	**81,286**	**60,110**	**45,333**	**1.36**	**-24.58**
OTH.WORLD	337,915	76,801	81,286	60,110	45,333	1.36	-24.58

Source: World Tourism Organization (WTO)

5. OVERNIGHT STAYS OF NON-RESIDENT TOURISTS IN HOTELS AND SIMILAR ESTABLISHMENTS, BY COUNTRY OF RESIDENCE

		1999	2000	2001	2002	2003	Market share 03	% change 03-02
TOTAL	(*)	3,051,343	4,944,670	4,918,271	4,999,289	5,450,416	100.00	9.02
AFRICA			8,526	7,441	9,414	15,132	0.28	60.74
EAST AFRICA			1,338	497	568	1,413	0.03	148.77
BR.IND.OC.TR					2			
BURUNDI			149	24	7	15		114.29
COMOROS			2	1				
ETHIOPIA			67	42	62	101		62.90
ERITREA				2	16	276	0.01	1.625.00
DJIBOUTI					42	3		-92.86
KENYA			909	85	121	323	0.01	166.94
MADAGASCAR			2	26	19	237		1.147.37
MALAWI				4		50		
MAURITIUS			6	5	111	26		-76.58
MOZAMBIQUE			17	19	6	38		533.33
REUNION				9	7			
RWANDA			12	155	10	15		50.00
SEYCHELLES			5	3		40		
SOMALIA			43	40	41	32		-21.95
ZIMBABWE			21	21	14	52		271.43
UGANDA			11	11	29	38		31.03
TANZANIA			36	12	75	148		97.33
ZAMBIA			58	38	6	19		216.67
CENTRAL AFR			1,137	200	2,563	883	0.02	-65.55
ANGOLA			206	93	1,620	407	0.01	-74.88
CAMEROON			401	24	200	169		-15.50
CENT.AFR.REP			29	26	8	70		775.00
CHAD			19		57			
CONGO			455	55	75	217		189.33
DEM.R.CONGO			23	2	598	9		-98.49
EQ.GUINEA			2			9		
GABON			2		3	1		-66.67
SAO TOME PRN					2	1		-50.00
NORTH AFRICA			2,507	2,370	2,292	8,531	0.16	272.21
ALGERIA			964	851	1,156	6,417	0.12	455.10
MOROCCO			750	439	473	409	0.01	-13.53
WESTN.SAHARA					4	1		-75.00
SUDAN			113	41	68	216		217.65
TUNISIA			680	1,039	591	1,488	0.03	151.78
SOUTHERN AFR			2,012	2,751	1,777	1,884	0.03	6.02
BOTSWANA			1	9	6	8		33.33
LESOTHO				2				
NAMIBIA				1	1	4		300.00
SOUTH AFRICA			1,768	2,737	1,731	1,844	0.03	6.53
SWAZILAND			243	2	39	28		-28.21
WEST AFRICA			1,532	1,623	2,214	2,421	0.04	9.35
CAPE VERDE				1		1		
BENIN			298	412	319	317	0.01	-0.63
GAMBIA				14		322	0.01	
GHANA			5	29	320	97		-69.69
GUINEA			2	4	13	9		-30.77

POLAND

5. OVERNIGHT STAYS OF NON-RESIDENT TOURISTS IN HOTELS AND SIMILAR ESTABLISHMENTS, BY COUNTRY OF RESIDENCE

	1999	2000	2001	2002	2003	Market share 03	% change 03-02
COTE IVOIRE		118	101	48	55		14.58
LIBERIA			3	3	10		233.33
MALI		36	45	77	42		-45.45
MAURITANIA		5	8	12	26		116.67
NIGER		26	54	20	14		-30.00
NIGERIA		825	689	1,177	1,111	0.02	-5.61
GUINEABISSAU			65		13		
ST.HELENA		39	3		3		
SENEGAL		30	16	113	132		16.81
SIERRA LEONE		136	176	100	207		107.00
TOGO		5	2		48		
BURKINA FASO		7	1	12	14		16.67
AMERICAS	**221,675**	**420,136**	**398,481**	**388,458**	**360,395**	**6.61**	**-7.22**
CARIBBEAN		**6,027**	**2,085**	**8,123**	**2,221**	**0.04**	**-72.66**
ANTIGUA,BARB		248	129	162	250		54.32
BAHAMAS		196	131	86	265		208.14
BARBADOS		31	1	43	42		-2.33
BR.VIRGIN IS					16		
CAYMAN IS		10					
CUBA		93	493	234	920	0.02	293.16
DOMINICA		9	12	5			
DOMINICAN RP		67	5	32	25		-21.88
GRENADA		23	13	33	202		512.12
GUADELOUPE		10			1		
HAITI		14	2	11	8		-27.27
JAMAICA		57	525	670	34		-94.93
MARTINIQUE		9	2		6		
MONTSERRAT		7		4			
NETH.ANTILES		4	6		35		
ARUBA		2	1				
PUERTO RICO		57	684	141	245		73.76
ANGUILLA		295		41	92		124.39
TRINIDAD TBG		72		42	38		-9.52
TURKS,CAICOS		1		9	20		122.22
US.VIRGIN IS		4,822	81	6,610	22		-99.67
CENTRAL AMER		**207**	**185**	**1,704**	**552**	**0.01**	**-67.61**
BELIZE				23	3		-86.96
COSTA RICA		75	78	184	198		7.61
EL SALVADOR		49	20	24	42		75.00
GUATEMALA		36	18	32	75		134.38
HONDURAS		17	10	1,360	148		-89.12
NICARAGUA		19	15	10	47		370.00
PANAMA		11	44	71	39		-45.07
NORTH AMER	**221,675**	**392,544**	**384,117**	**367,700**	**346,450**	**6.36**	**-5.78**
CANADA	19,123	30,375	25,081	32,499	33,053	0.61	1.70
GREENLAND				2			
MEXICO		3,165	2,807	3,934	6,272	0.12	59.43
ST.PIERRE,MQ		1					
USA	202,552	359,003	356,229	331,265	307,125	5.63	-7.29
SOUTH AMER		**21,358**	**12,094**	**10,931**	**11,172**	**0.20**	**2.20**
ARGENTINA		4,198	3,177	1,517	2,304	0.04	51.88
BOLIVIA		41	72	127	128		0.79

5. OVERNIGHT STAYS OF NON-RESIDENT TOURISTS IN HOTELS AND SIMILAR ESTABLISHMENTS, BY COUNTRY OF RESIDENCE

	1999	2000	2001	2002	2003	Market share 03	% change 03-02
BRAZIL		8,990	6,488	6,587	5,650	0.10	-14.22
CHILE		1,012	422	1,643	1,032	0.02	-37.19
COLOMBIA		233	309	154	807	0.01	424.03
ECUADOR		47	91	100	255		155.00
FALKLAND IS			30	115			
GUYANA		21	1	1	21		2,000.00
PARAGUAY		16	13	74	9		-87.84
PERU		673	164	160	179		11.88
SURINAME		56	46	36	62		72.22
URUGUAY		5,140	153	180	262		45.56
VENEZUELA		931	1,128	237	463	0.01	95.36
EAST AS/PACI	**32,913**	**115,617**	**101,164**	**109,834**	**111,681**	**2.05**	**1.68**
N/EAST ASIA	**32,913**	**96,816**	**83,753**	**91,014**	**87,583**	**1.61**	**-3.77**
CHINA		5,679	9,046	9,740	8,297	0.15	-14.82
TAIWAN(P.C.)		4,459	4,231	2,651	2,935	0.05	10.71
HK,CHINA		1,365	1,519	1,616	1,573	0.03	-2.66
JAPAN	32,913	56,929	48,514	55,866	57,085	1.05	2.18
KOREA D P RP		23,349	8,080	8,090	1,545	0.03	-80.90
KOREA REP.		4,047	11,909	12,665	15,638	0.29	23.47
MACAU, CHINA		1		1	9		800.00
MONGOLIA		987	454	385	501	0.01	30.13
S/EAST ASIA		**4,270**	**5,481**	**5,893**	**8,011**	**0.15**	**35.94**
BRUNEI DARSM		6	1				
MYANMAR		25	32	28	30		7.14
INDONESIA		498	307	790	1,324	0.02	67.59
LAO P.DEM.R.			6	9	24		166.67
MALAYSIA		703	1,021	899	1,118	0.02	24.36
PHILIPPINES		554	1,154	1,445	1,400	0.03	-3.11
TIMOR-LESTE				6			
SINGAPORE		582	811	1,460	1,410	0.03	-3.42
VIET NAM		1,209	1,643	568	1,620	0.03	185.21
THAILAND		693	506	688	1,085	0.02	57.70
AUSTRALASIA		**14,116**	**11,418**	**12,503**	**15,674**	**0.29**	**25.36**
AUSTRALIA		12,877	10,428	11,244	13,766	0.25	22.43
NEW ZEALAND		1,239	990	1,259	1,908	0.04	51.55
MELANESIA		**93**	**230**	**71**	**46**		**-35.21**
SOLOMON IS		74	198	17	36		111.76
FIJI			4	8	2		-75.00
NEW CALEDNIA			27	40	5		-87.50
NORFOLK IS		15					
PAPUA N.GUIN		4	1	6	3		-50.00
MICRONESIA		**40**	**72**	**35**	**27**		**-22.86**
CHRISTMAS IS		17	15	4	24		500.00
COCOS IS		4					
KIRIBATI		5	16	11			
GUAM		2					
NAURU		12	41	20	3		-85.00
POLYNESIA		**282**	**210**	**318**	**340**	**0.01**	**6.92**
AMER SAMOA		199	29	94	86		-8.51
FR.POLYNESIA		34	10	14	7		-50.00

5. OVERNIGHT STAYS OF NON-RESIDENT TOURISTS IN HOTELS AND SIMILAR ESTABLISHMENTS, BY COUNTRY OF RESIDENCE

	1999	2000	2001	2002	2003	Market share 03	% change 03-02
NIUE		8	156	3	9		200.00
PITCAIRN			3				
TOKELAU		30	1	23	15		-34.78
TONGA				2	6		200.00
TUVALU		1		13	4		-69.23
WALLIS FUT.I		6			1		
SAMOA		4	11	169	212		25.44
EUROPE	**2,492,688**	**4,249,865**	**4,255,627**	**4,370,601**	**4,858,858**	**89.15**	**11.17**
C/E EUROPE	**355,850**	**624,821**	**619,469**	**665,404**	**748,279**	**13.73**	**12.45**
AZERBAIJAN		1,234	572	844	1,241	0.02	47.04
ARMENIA		6,530	2,288	1,391	1,832	0.03	31.70
BULGARIA		12,127	9,090	8,115	10,726	0.20	32.17
BELARUS	33,067	69,517	84,357	89,589	90,516	1.66	1.03
CZECH REP	40,861	59,033	54,511	56,340	64,746	1.19	14.92
ESTONIA		9,680	9,221	16,317	20,568	0.38	26.05
GEORGIA		942	1,292	695	1,041	0.02	49.78
HUNGARY	27,648	33,173	30,635	32,506	48,120	0.88	48.03
KAZAKHSTAN		2,777	1,516	1,957	4,185	0.08	113.85
KYRGYZSTAN		303	79	210	281	0.01	33.81
LATVIA		8,044	8,941	11,568	20,246	0.37	75.02
LITHUANIA	72,692	52,904	48,589	53,820	64,264	1.18	19.41
REP MOLDOVA		8,875	6,502	4,505	4,288	0.08	-4.82
ROMANIA		13,655	14,727	11,715	14,206	0.26	21.26
RUSSIAN FED	74,184	157,473	184,309	205,638	227,845	4.18	10.80
SLOVAKIA	16,138	20,422	17,599	20,531	23,174	0.43	12.87
TAJIKISTAN		72	45	248	93		-62.50
TURKMENISTAN		55	149	8	50		525.00
UKRAINE	91,260	167,277	144,689	148,960	149,898	2.75	0.63
UZBEKISTAN		728	358	447	959	0.02	114.54
NORTHERN EUR	**524,344**	**828,389**	**748,319**	**754,796**	**831,942**	**15.26**	**10.22**
DENMARK	110,254	167,706	144,185	158,164	171,679	3.15	8.54
FAEROE IS		1		9	20		122.22
FINLAND	42,198	63,517	55,794	52,346	62,766	1.15	19.91
ICELAND		1,391	1,361	1,276	2,270	0.04	77.90
IRELAND	9,778	15,081	14,111	13,987	19,536	0.36	39.67
NORWAY	52,702	70,302	72,427	85,329	116,136	2.13	36.10
SVALBARD IS		8		1	3		200.00
SWEDEN	98,420	160,475	141,696	134,295	140,291	2.57	4.46
UK	210,992	349,908	318,745	309,389	319,241	5.86	3.18
SOUTHERN EUR	**196,494**	**300,879**	**335,423**	**378,552**	**455,162**	**8.35**	**20.24**
ALBANIA		1,048	607	1,289	2,203	0.04	70.91
ANDORRA		50	247	28	793	0.01	2.732.14
BOSNIA HERZG		1,086	593	762	1,083	0.02	42.13
CROATIA		5,353	7,256	6,236	9,464	0.17	51.76
GIBRALTAR		72	2				
GREECE	8,972	12,179	9,154	12,202	16,582	0.30	35.90
HOLY SEE		20	3	10	11		10.00
ITALY	146,913	194,505	220,998	234,989	281,551	5.17	19.81
MALTA		549	501	821	2,248	0.04	173.81
PORTUGAL	11,429	17,255	21,556	19,848	22,214	0.41	11.92
SAN MARINO		352	262	93	241		159.14
SLOVENIA		6,503	7,475	9,600	9,154	0.17	-4.65

5. OVERNIGHT STAYS OF NON-RESIDENT TOURISTS IN HOTELS AND SIMILAR ESTABLISHMENTS, BY COUNTRY OF RESIDENCE

	1999	2000	2001	2002	2003	Market share 03	% change 03-02
SPAIN	29,180	57,509	61,622	87,825	103,769	1.90	18.15
TFYROM		895	413	958	800	0.01	-16.49
SERBIA,MTNEG		3,503	4,734	3,891	5,049	0.09	29.76
WESTERN EUR	**1,416,000**	**2,330,239**	**2,388,068**	**2,398,337**	**2,629,849**	**48.25**	**9.65**
AUSTRIA	66,049	83,239	83,105	75,762	81,461	1.49	7.52
BELGIUM	39,525	65,339	66,321	69,048	71,333	1.31	3.31
FRANCE	146,508	206,212	209,411	211,959	243,327	4.46	14.80
GERMANY	1,030,540	1,777,734	1,841,629	1,856,800	2,037,396	37.38	9.73
LIECHTENSTEN		135	358	159	434	0.01	172.96
LUXEMBOURG	2,840	5,360	6,907	6,585	9,705	0.18	47.38
MONACO		86	75	146	230		57.53
NETHERLANDS	96,379	133,011	126,840	128,642	137,753	2.53	7.08
SWITZERLAND	34,159	59,123	53,422	49,236	48,210	0.88	-2.08
EAST/MED EUR		**165,537**	**164,348**	**173,512**	**193,626**	**3.55**	**11.59**
CYPRUS		1,123	1,271	1,162	2,407	0.04	107.14
ISRAEL		155,459	156,271	164,554	177,857	3.26	8.08
TURKEY		8,955	6,806	7,796	13,362	0.25	71.40
MIDDLE EAST		**8,051**	**6,874**	**5,202**	**7,805**	**0.14**	**50.04**
MIDDLE EAST		**8,051**	**6,874**	**5,202**	**7,805**	**0.14**	**50.04**
BAHRAIN		539	516	355	479	0.01	34.93
IRAQ		235	107	277	141		-49.10
JORDAN		201	200	249	542	0.01	117.67
KUWAIT		419	459	570	575	0.01	0.88
LEBANON		376	392	519	634	0.01	22.16
LIBYA		436	241	337	837	0.02	148.37
OMAN		27	33	152	221		45.39
QATAR		1	16	36	139		286.11
SAUDI ARABIA		2,085	2,290	463	784	0.01	69.33
SYRIA		90	255	445	344	0.01	-22.70
UNTD ARAB EM		1,790	184	156	136		-12.82
EGYPT		1,549	1,784	1,239	2,864	0.05	131.15
YEMEN		303	397	404	109		-73.02
SOUTH ASIA		**10,606**	**12,338**	**12,808**	**12,003**	**0.22**	**-6.29**
SOUTH ASIA		**10,606**	**12,338**	**12,808**	**12,003**	**0.22**	**-6.29**
AFGHANISTAN		201	809	488	954	0.02	95.49
BANGLADESH		275	209	1,077	120		-88.86
BHUTAN		886	4,449	3,525	599	0.01	-83.01
SRI LANKA		1,474	100	129	89		-31.01
INDIA		6,488	5,103	5,333	7,733	0.14	45.00
IRAN		923	1,250	1,366	1,691	0.03	23.79
NEPAL		12	27	395	119		-69.87
PAKISTAN		347	391	495	698	0.01	41.01
REG.NOT SPEC	**304,067**	**131,869**	**136,346**	**102,972**	**84,542**	**1.55**	**-17.90**
NOT SPECIFIE	**304,067**	**131,869**	**136,346**	**102,972**	**84,542**	**1.55**	**-17.90**
OTH.WORLD	304,067	131,869	136,346	102,972	84,542	1.55	-17.90

Source: World Tourism Organization (WTO)

6. OVERNIGHT STAYS OF NON-RESIDENT TOURISTS IN ALL TYPES OF ACCOMMODATION ESTABLISHMENTS, BY COUNTRY OF RESIDENCE

	1999	2000	2001	2002	2003	Market share 03	% change 03-02
TOTAL		**6,891,283**	**6,990,543**	**7,085,019**	**7,828,230**	**100.00**	**10.49**
AFRICA		**13,546**	**9,916**	**11,506**	**18,410**	**0.24**	**60.00**
EAST AFRICA		**2,273**	**636**	**679**	**1,770**	**0.02**	**160.68**
BR.IND.OC.TR				2			
BURUNDI		166	35	8	15		87.50
COMOROS		2	1				
ETHIOPIA		72	59	79	117		48.10
ERITREA			27	17	278		1.535.29
DJIBOUTI				42	3		-92.86
KENYA		936	110	140	364		160.00
MADAGASCAR		6	35	19	243		1.178.95
MALAWI			4		50		
MAURITIUS		6	5	133	30		-77.44
MOZAMBIQUE		19	29	6	43		616.67
REUNION			30	7			
RWANDA		16	155	10	25		150.00
SEYCHELLES		5	3		48		
SOMALIA		864	47	68	215		216.18
ZIMBABWE		38	28	17	64		276.47
UGANDA		16	11	29	97		234.48
TANZANIA		66	12	76	159		109.21
ZAMBIA		61	45	26	19		-26.92
CENTRAL AFR		**1,882**	**243**	**2,698**	**1,513**	**0.02**	**-43.92**
ANGOLA		349	110	1,625	463	0.01	-71.51
CAMEROON		779	31	238	249		4.62
CENT.AFR.REP		29	26	8	71		787.50
CHAD		19	14	57			
CONGO		674	59	165	691	0.01	318.79
DEM.R.CONGO		28	2	598	9		-98.49
EQ.GUINEA		2		2	28		1.300.00
GABON		2	1	3	1		-66.67
SAO TOME PRN				2	1		-50.00
NORTH AFRICA		**4,661**	**3,603**	**3,433**	**9,134**	**0.12**	**166.06**
ALGERIA		2,403	1,124	1,298	6,619	0.08	409.94
MOROCCO		816	1,170	777	437	0.01	-43.76
WESTN.SAHARA				4	1		-75.00
SUDAN		147	55	69	244		253.62
TUNISIA		1,295	1,254	1,285	1,833	0.02	42.65
SOUTHERN AFR		**2,596**	**3,322**	**1,933**	**2,243**	**0.03**	**16.04**
BOTSWANA		1	9	6	8		33.33
LESOTHO		67	2				
NAMIBIA		5	5	4	4		
SOUTH AFRICA		2,270	3,304	1,884	2,200	0.03	16.77
SWAZILAND		253	2	39	31		-20.51
WEST AFRICA		**2,134**	**2,112**	**2,763**	**3,750**	**0.05**	**35.72**
CAPE VERDE			1		1		
BENIN		298	413	319	320		0.31
GAMBIA		51	19	16	369		2.206.25
GHANA		5	33	322	130		-59.63
GUINEA		13	135	17	11		-35.29

6. OVERNIGHT STAYS OF NON-RESIDENT TOURISTS IN ALL TYPES OF ACCOMMODATION ESTABLISHMENTS, BY COUNTRY OF RESIDENCE

	1999	2000	2001	2002	2003	Market share 03	% change 03-02
COTE IVOIRE		118	101	64	57		-10.94
LIBERIA		122	5	3	10		233.33
MALI		42	48	101	44		-56.44
MAURITANIA		5	8	12	31		158.33
NIGER		26	55	22	65		195.45
NIGERIA		1,073	946	1,638	1,924	0.02	17.46
GUINEABISSAU		10	128		13		
ST.HELENA		61	3		3		
SENEGAL		70	38	135	159		17.78
SIERRA LEONE		228	176	102	550	0.01	439.22
TOGO		5	2		49		
BURKINA FASO		7	1	12	14		16.67
AMERICAS		**486,947**	**462,150**	**442,423**	**418,809**	**5.35**	**-5.34**
CARIBBEAN		**6,176**	**2,732**	**8,299**	**2,304**	**0.03**	**-72.24**
ANTIGUA,BARB		248	129	162	266		64.20
BAHAMAS		204	131	93	265		184.95
BARBADOS		31	1	43	42		-2.33
BR.VIRGIN IS		4			16		
CAYMAN IS		11		33			
CUBA		209	1,053	246	971	0.01	294.72
DOMINICA		11	43	5			
DOMINICAN RP		69	6	34	26		-23.53
GRENADA		27	18	55	202		267.27
GUADELOUPE		10			1		
HAITI		17	5	11	8		-27.27
JAMAICA		57	565	708	37		-94.77
MARTINIQUE		9	2		6		
MONTSERRAT		7		6			
NETH.ANTILES		4	6		35		
ARUBA		2	1	40			
PUERTO RICO		57	684	145	249		71.72
ANGUILLA		297		41	92		124.39
TRINIDAD TBG		72		56	40		-28.57
TURKS,CAICOS		5	7	9	20		122.22
US.VIRGIN IS		4,825	81	6,612	28		-99.58
CENTRAL AMER		**342**	**284**	**1,772**	**2,773**	**0.04**	**56.49**
BELIZE			82	51	2,160	0.03	4.135.29
COSTA RICA		80	88	218	222		1.83
EL SALVADOR		53	21	24	43		79.17
GUATEMALA		44	22	38	90		136.84
HONDURAS		118	12	1,360	165		-87.87
NICARAGUA		35	15	10	53		430.00
PANAMA		12	44	71	40		-43.66
NORTH AMER		**455,682**	**444,971**	**419,576**	**400,408**	**5.11**	**-4.57**
CANADA		38,349	32,941	37,999	39,931	0.51	5.08
GREENLAND				2			
MEXICO		3,414	3,403	4,613	7,186	0.09	55.78
ST.PIERRE,MQ		1			141		
USA		413,918	408,627	376,962	353,150	4.51	-6.32
SOUTH AMER		**24,747**	**14,163**	**12,776**	**13,324**	**0.17**	**4.29**
ARGENTINA		4,582	3,471	1,868	2,707	0.03	44.91
BOLIVIA		82	96	175	193		10.29

6. OVERNIGHT STAYS OF NON-RESIDENT TOURISTS IN ALL TYPES OF ACCOMMODATION ESTABLISHMENTS, BY COUNTRY OF RESIDENCE

	1999	2000	2001	2002	2003	Market share 03	% change 03-02
BRAZIL		9,710	7,321	7,383	6,555	0.08	-11.21
CHILE		1,262	512	1,720	1,201	0.02	-30.17
COLOMBIA		800	363	532	1,122	0.01	110.90
ECUADOR		250	176	150	319		112.67
FALKLAND IS			30	124			
GUYANA		437	9	1	33		3.200.00
PARAGUAY		19	43	75	9		-88.00
PERU		1,177	508	235	270		14.89
SURINAME		60	46	36	72		100.00
URUGUAY		5,385	182	205	344		67.80
VENEZUELA		983	1,406	272	499	0.01	83.46
EAST AS/PACI		**148,617**	**122,186**	**129,087**	**127,470**	**1.63**	**-1.25**
N/EAST ASIA		**119,504**	**95,083**	**100,065**	**94,525**	**1.21**	**-5.54**
CHINA		7,182	10,602	11,650	9,440	0.12	-18.97
TAIWAN(P.C.)		4,500	4,342	2,756	2,988	0.04	8.42
HK,CHINA		1,403	1,574	1,636	1,628	0.02	-0.49
JAPAN		64,524	55,707	61,290	61,198	0.78	-0.15
KOREA D P RP		35,200	8,808	8,647	1,942	0.02	-77.54
KOREA REP.		4,192	12,484	13,179	16,389	0.21	24.36
MACAU, CHINA		1		1	9		800.00
MONGOLIA		2,502	1,566	906	931	0.01	2.76
S/EAST ASIA		**5,513**	**7,044**	**8,219**	**9,698**	**0.12**	**17.99**
BRUNEI DARSM		6	6	19			
MYANMAR		25	32	28	30		7.14
CAMBODIA		2					
INDONESIA		540	350	876	1,389	0.02	58.56
LAO P.DEM.R.		12	7	180	147		-18.33
MALAYSIA		798	1,203	1,137	1,261	0.02	10.91
PHILIPPINES		626	1,715	1,807	1,522	0.02	-15.77
TIMOR-LESTE				8	6		-25.00
SINGAPORE		670	902	1,569	1,600	0.02	1.98
VIET NAM		1,921	2,262	1,598	2,546	0.03	59.32
THAILAND		913	567	997	1,197	0.02	20.06
AUSTRALASIA		**23,169**	**19,520**	**20,288**	**22,601**	**0.29**	**11.40**
AUSTRALIA		20,065	17,193	17,850	19,332	0.25	8.30
NEW ZEALAND		3,104	2,327	2,438	3,269	0.04	34.09
MELANESIA		**95**	**230**	**71**	**185**		**160.56**
SOLOMON IS		74	198	17	36		111.76
FIJI			4	8	137		1.612.50
NEW CALEDNIA		2	27	40	9		-77.50
NORFOLK IS		15					
PAPUA N.GUIN		4	1	6	3		-50.00
MICRONESIA		**40**	**93**	**49**	**27**		**-44.90**
CHRISTMAS IS		17	15	4	24		500.00
COCOS IS		4					
KIRIBATI		5	16	11			
GUAM		2					
NAURU		12	62	34	3		-91.18
POLYNESIA		**296**	**216**	**395**	**434**	**0.01**	**9.87**
AMER SAMOA		199	34	94	86		-8.51

6. OVERNIGHT STAYS OF NON-RESIDENT TOURISTS IN ALL TYPES OF ACCOMMODATION ESTABLISHMENTS, BY COUNTRY OF RESIDENCE

	1999	2000	2001	2002	2003	Market share 03	% change 03-02
FR.POLYNESIA		34	11	15	42		180.00
NIUE		8	156	3	9		200.00
PITCAIRN			3				
TOKELAU		30	1	23	15		-34.78
TONGA				2	6		200.00
TUVALU		5		18	4		-77.78
WALLIS FUT.I		16		71	60		-15.49
SAMOA		4	11	169	212		25.44
EUROPE		**6,070,106**	**6,221,381**	**6,368,093**	**7,154,760**	**91.40**	**12.35**
C/E EUROPE		**1,202,266**	**1,204,024**	**1,166,151**	**1,258,839**	**16.08**	**7.95**
AZERBAIJAN		1,874	1,189	1,130	2,052	0.03	81.59
ARMENIA		11,817	7,916	4,078	2,489	0.03	-38.97
BULGARIA		23,712	21,176	14,401	14,767	0.19	2.54
BELARUS		156,516	176,146	178,761	186,181	2.38	4.15
CZECH REP		92,210	88,942	85,424	95,988	1.23	12.37
ESTONIA		25,180	26,908	25,306	28,957	0.37	14.43
GEORGIA		3,263	2,022	905	2,095	0.03	131.49
HUNGARY		56,850	54,009	54,816	80,258	1.03	46.41
KAZAKHSTAN		7,840	3,595	3,243	5,063	0.06	56.12
KYRGYZSTAN		347	122	257	425	0.01	65.37
LATVIA		15,737	13,869	17,795	30,357	0.39	70.59
LITHUANIA		86,514	82,497	86,836	94,933	1.21	9.32
REP MOLDOVA		21,631	17,961	13,486	11,240	0.14	-16.65
ROMANIA		34,165	32,274	22,252	23,172	0.30	4.13
RUSSIAN FED		228,915	253,105	266,867	290,297	3.71	8.78
SLOVAKIA		35,770	35,000	34,451	38,432	0.49	11.56
TAJIKISTAN		368	125	288	132		-54.17
TURKMENISTAN		386	169	30	50		66.67
UKRAINE		398,246	386,550	355,301	350,801	4.48	-1.27
UZBEKISTAN		925	449	524	1,150	0.01	119.47
NORTHERN EUR		**968,602**	**892,805**	**893,725**	**962,272**	**12.29**	**7.67**
DENMARK		208,233	174,547	188,265	208,023	2.66	10.49
FAEROE IS		34	10	14	26		85.71
FINLAND		70,473	63,963	59,992	70,273	0.90	17.14
ICELAND		1,847	1,609	1,655	2,455	0.03	48.34
IRELAND		18,496	17,893	17,395	23,646	0.30	35.94
NORWAY		78,316	88,828	96,818	124,470	1.59	28.56
SVALBARD IS		8		1	11		1,000.00
SWEDEN		193,537	181,359	179,298	181,872	2.32	1.44
UK		397,658	364,596	350,287	351,496	4.49	0.35
SOUTHERN EUR		**355,559**	**399,975**	**432,580**	**514,641**	**6.57**	**18.97**
ALBANIA		1,212	703	1,350	2,352	0.03	74.22
ANDORRA		50	258	28	799	0.01	2,753.57
BOSNIA HERZG		1,252	1,208	1,023	1,724	0.02	68.52
CROATIA		7,562	8,959	8,623	13,384	0.17	55.21
GIBRALTAR		72	2				
GREECE		14,547	11,594	14,573	18,512	0.24	27.03
HOLY SEE		31	3	269	11		-95.91
ITALY		228,157	260,313	266,083	315,567	4.03	18.60
MALTA		578	664	1,006	2,318	0.03	130.42
PORTUGAL		18,365	25,113	22,252	24,572	0.31	10.43
SAN MARINO		352	274	95	253		166.32

6. OVERNIGHT STAYS OF NON-RESIDENT TOURISTS IN ALL TYPES OF ACCOMMODATION ESTABLISHMENTS, BY COUNTRY OF RESIDENCE

	1999	2000	2001	2002	2003	Market share 03	% change 03-02
SLOVENIA		7,832	9,768	12,049	11,645	0.15	-3.35
SPAIN		67,058	73,609	97,959	115,759	1.48	18.17
TFYROM		2,039	1,160	2,390	1,234	0.02	-48.37
SERBIA,MTNEG		6,452	6,347	4,880	6,511	0.08	33.42
WESTERN EUR		**3,359,649**	**3,544,423**	**3,689,163**	**4,212,369**	**53.81**	**14.18**
AUSTRIA		96,869	95,290	85,462	98,593	1.26	15.36
BELGIUM		81,007	84,309	85,412	88,619	1.13	3.75
FRANCE		263,968	271,842	261,958	307,437	3.93	17.36
GERMANY		2,661,451	2,851,919	3,016,245	3,460,318	44.20	14.72
LIECHTENSTEN		152	389	187	515	0.01	175.40
LUXEMBOURG		6,037	7,555	7,292	10,330	0.13	41.66
MONACO		151	90	149	245		64.43
NETHERLANDS		184,907	174,495	179,055	192,233	2.46	7.36
SWITZERLAND		65,107	58,534	53,403	54,079	0.69	1.27
EAST/MED EUR		**184,030**	**180,154**	**186,474**	**206,639**	**2.64**	**10.81**
CYPRUS		1,454	1,419	1,289	2,743	0.04	112.80
ISRAEL		171,774	170,695	175,641	188,686	2.41	7.43
TURKEY		10,802	8,040	9,544	15,210	0.19	59.37
MIDDLE EAST		**10,185**	**8,775**	**8,159**	**9,571**	**0.12**	**17.31**
MIDDLE EAST		**10,185**	**8,775**	**8,159**	**9,571**	**0.12**	**17.31**
BAHRAIN		539	567	376	479	0.01	27.39
IRAQ		267	145	453	304		-32.89
JORDAN		235	249	267	618	0.01	131.46
KUWAIT		539	516	714	800	0.01	12.04
LEBANON		502	568	810	1,017	0.01	25.56
LIBYA		575	311	426	954	0.01	123.94
OMAN		315	34	154	221		43.51
QATAR		1	43	36	153		325.00
SAUDI ARABIA		2,211	2,426	542	1,015	0.01	87.27
SYRIA		161	352	497	488	0.01	-1.81
UNTD ARAB EM		2,527	327	495	175		-64.65
EGYPT		1,890	2,074	1,713	3,192	0.04	86.34
YEMEN		423	1,163	1,676	155		-90.75
SOUTH ASIA		**16,143**	**13,861**	**14,307**	**13,477**	**0.17**	**-5.80**
SOUTH ASIA		**16,143**	**13,861**	**14,307**	**13,477**	**0.17**	**-5.80**
AFGHANISTAN		2,683	900	576	1,131	0.01	96.35
BANGLADESH		284	232	1,133	122		-89.23
BHUTAN		886	4,449	3,525	599	0.01	-83.01
SRI LANKA		2,824	107	130	115		-11.54
INDIA		7,295	5,992	5,995	8,315	0.11	38.70
IRAN		1,040	1,566	1,896	2,043	0.03	7.75
NEPAL		13	31	413	151		-63.44
PAKISTAN		1,118	584	639	1,001	0.01	56.65
REG.NOT SPEC		**145,739**	**152,274**	**111,444**	**85,733**	**1.10**	**-23.07**
NOT SPECIFIE		**145,739**	**152,274**	**111,444**	**85,733**	**1.10**	**-23.07**
OTH.WORLD		145,739	152,274	111,444	85,733	1.10	-23.07

Source: World Tourism Organization (WTO)

PORTUGAL

1. ARRIVALS OF NON-RESIDENT TOURISTS AT NATIONAL BORDERS, BY NATIONALITY

	1999	2000	2001	2002	2003	Market share 03	% change 03-02
TOTAL (*)	11,631,996	12,096,680	12,167,200	11,644,231			
AMERICAS	417,122	479,501	454,425	434,694			
NORTH AMER	321,780	365,183	346,970	329,080			
CANADA	93,915	106,296	109,005	99,155			
USA	227,865	258,887	237,965	229,925			
SOUTH AMER	95,342	114,318	107,455	105,614			
BRAZIL	95,342	114,318	107,455	105,614			
EAST AS/PACI	40,570	46,135	43,570	46,292			
N/EAST ASIA	40,570	46,135	43,570	46,292			
JAPAN	40,570	46,135	43,570	46,292			
EUROPE	10,869,577	11,191,804	11,365,683	10,901,171			
NORTHERN EUR	2,361,817	2,403,598	2,496,336	2,362,125			
DENMARK	138,653	140,391	133,867	127,958			
FINLAND	77,779	75,308	73,059	73,246			
IRELAND	128,273	126,842	130,087	137,273			
NORWAY	43,671	48,172	48,737	45,193			
SWEDEN	125,748	135,064	143,993	136,685			
UK	1,847,693	1,877,821	1,966,593	1,841,770			
SOUTHERN EUR	6,006,500	6,155,757	6,239,306	5,991,771			
ITALY	269,638	290,902	312,355	290,766			
SPAIN	5,736,862	5,864,855	5,926,951	5,701,005			
WESTERN EUR	2,501,260	2,632,449	2,630,041	2,547,275			
AUSTRIA	55,156	57,619	57,682	56,642			
BELGIUM	232,517	242,532	252,387	243,690			
FRANCE	727,210	763,293	802,332	823,761			
GERMANY	889,906	931,255	883,306	814,286			
LUXEMBOURG	30,358	33,636	33,393	33,455			
NETHERLANDS	463,959	500,352	495,363	476,609			
SWITZERLAND	102,154	103,762	105,578	98,832			
REG.NOT SPEC	304,727	379,240	303,522	262,074			
NOT SPECIFIE	304,727	379,240	303,522	262,074			
OTH.WORLD	304,727	379,240	303,522	262,074			

Source: World Tourism Organization (WTO)

PORTUGAL

1. ARRIVALS OF NON-RESIDENT TOURISTS AT NATIONAL BORDERS, BY COUNTRY OF RESIDENCE

	1999	2000	2001	2002	2003	Market share 03	% change 03-02
TOTAL (*)	**11,631,996**	**12,096,680**	**12,167,200**	**11,644,231**	**11,707,228**	**100.00**	**0.54**
AMERICAS	**453,642**	**563,992**	**536,248**	**463,847**	**480,544**	**4.10**	**3.60**
NORTH AMER	**358,705**	**418,329**	**396,119**	**351,751**	**362,298**	**3.09**	**3.00**
CANADA	97,367	120,655	121,707	105,552	109,717	0.94	3.95
USA	261,338	297,674	274,412	246,199	252,581	2.16	2.59
SOUTH AMER	**94,937**	**145,663**	**140,129**	**112,096**	**118,246**	**1.01**	**5.49**
BRAZIL	94,937	145,663	140,129	112,096	118,246	1.01	5.49
EAST AS/PACI	**42,536**	**42,595**	**40,053**	**43,964**	**40,055**	**0.34**	**-8.89**
N/EAST ASIA	**42,536**	**42,595**	**40,053**	**43,964**	**40,055**	**0.34**	**-8.89**
JAPAN	42,536	42,595	40,053	43,964	40,055	0.34	-8.89
EUROPE	**10,790,574**	**11,125,806**	**11,281,780**	**10,849,103**	**10,887,861**	**93.00**	**0.36**
NORTHERN EUR	**2,384,150**	**2,404,891**	**2,492,659**	**2,370,314**	**2,398,240**	**20.49**	**1.18**
DENMARK	129,852	133,475	127,365	121,574	126,287	1.08	3.88
FINLAND	81,250	74,670	72,474	74,671	78,686	0.67	5.38
IRELAND	136,784	124,374	127,483	138,397	142,964	1.22	3.30
NORWAY	43,177	49,115	49,415	45,619	46,571	0.40	2.09
SWEDEN	125,030	131,177	139,052	131,876	129,733	1.11	-1.63
UK	1,868,057	1,892,080	1,976,870	1,858,177	1,873,999	16.01	0.85
SOUTHERN EUR	**5,660,420**	**5,916,724**	**5,989,483**	**5,802,760**	**5,809,030**	**49.62**	**0.11**
GREECE	26,431	24,558	23,301	39,265	43,933	0.38	11.89
ITALY	312,671	277,197	297,279	367,185	333,809	2.85	-9.09
SPAIN	5,321,318	5,614,969	5,668,903	5,396,310	5,431,288	46.39	0.65
WESTERN EUR	**2,746,004**	**2,804,191**	**2,799,638**	**2,676,029**	**2,680,591**	**22.90**	**0.17**
AUSTRIA	55,217	63,570	63,448	58,073	61,539	0.53	5.97
BELGIUM	240,594	262,153	270,998	262,253	271,078	2.32	3.37
FRANCE	778,571	842,716	875,855	844,905	843,762	7.21	-0.14
GERMANY	1,010,223	951,887	908,625	851,596	848,339	7.25	-0.38
LUXEMBOURG	35,939	34,572	34,333	37,497	39,219	0.33	4.59
NETHERLANDS	487,165	499,470	494,603	482,613	479,271	4.09	-0.69
SWITZERLAND	138,295	149,823	151,776	139,092	137,383	1.17	-1.23
REG.NOT SPEC	**345,244**	**364,287**	**309,119**	**287,317**	**298,768**	**2.55**	**3.99**
NOT SPECIFIE	**345,244**	**364,287**	**309,119**	**287,317**	**298,768**	**2.55**	**3.99**
OTH.WORLD	345,244	364,287	309,119	287,317	298,768	2.55	3.99

Source: World Tourism Organization (WTO)

PORTUGAL

2. ARRIVALS OF NON-RESIDENT VISITORS AT NATIONAL BORDERS, BY NATIONALITY

	1999	2000	2001	2002	2003	Market share 03	% change 03-02
TOTAL	**27,016,307**	**28,013,963**	**28,149,911**	**27,193,920**	**27,532,354**	**100.00**	**1.24**
AMERICAS	**488,428**	**553,551**	**506,810**	**485,292**	**508,010**	**1.85**	**4.68**
NORTH AMER	**381,718**	**426,647**	**386,963**	**367,066**	**387,527**	**1.41**	**5.57**
CANADA	99,635	111,638	113,307	103,205	108,458	0.39	5.09
USA	282,083	315,009	273,656	263,861	279,069	1.01	5.76
SOUTH AMER	**106,710**	**126,904**	**119,847**	**118,226**	**120,483**	**0.44**	**1.91**
BRAZIL	106,710	126,904	119,847	118,226	120,483	0.44	1.91
EAST AS/PACI	**44,471**	**47,998**	**45,274**	**48,176**	**45,460**	**0.17**	**-5.64**
N/EAST ASIA	**44,471**	**47,998**	**45,274**	**48,176**	**45,460**	**0.17**	**-5.64**
JAPAN	44,471	47,998	45,274	48,176	45,460	0.17	-5.64
EUROPE	**26,000,206**	**26,911,495**	**27,190,110**	**26,285,125**	**26,580,675**	**96.54**	**1.12**
NORTHERN EUR	**2,496,517**	**2,555,252**	**2,636,997**	**2,501,179**	**2,639,861**	**9.59**	**5.54**
DENMARK	141,577	141,538	135,190	129,296	132,163	0.48	2.22
FINLAND	79,286	78,030	75,428	75,888	81,285	0.30	7.11
IRELAND	130,211	127,861	130,886	138,042	146,897	0.53	6.41
NORWAY	44,935	49,144	49,533	46,042	48,179	0.17	4.64
SWEDEN	131,001	138,143	146,272	138,924	137,024	0.50	-1.37
UK	1,969,507	2,020,536	2,099,688	1,972,987	2,094,313	7.61	6.15
SOUTHERN EUR	**20,837,938**	**21,518,053**	**21,727,888**	**21,047,471**	**21,167,866**	**76.88**	**0.57**
GREECE	23,415	21,108	19,880	20,351	22,061	0.08	8.40
ITALY	307,103	322,437	344,967	321,259	320,497	1.16	-0.24
SPAIN	20,507,420	21,174,508	21,363,041	20,705,861	20,825,308	75.64	0.58
WESTERN EUR	**2,665,751**	**2,838,190**	**2,825,225**	**2,736,475**	**2,772,948**	**10.07**	**1.33**
AUSTRIA	61,623	60,950	60,158	59,287	61,050	0.22	2.97
BELGIUM	238,980	255,558	265,535	251,021	264,595	0.96	5.41
FRANCE	763,404	809,416	849,233	866,747	866,921	3.15	0.02
GERMANY	979,817	1,035,823	978,264	905,970	917,095	3.33	1.23
LUXEMBOURG	31,023	34,417	34,057	34,253	38,051	0.14	11.09
NETHERLANDS	483,348	526,175	520,334	507,553	512,121	1.86	0.90
SWITZERLAND	107,556	115,851	117,644	111,644	113,115	0.41	1.32
REG.NOT SPEC	**483,202**	**500,919**	**407,717**	**375,327**	**398,209**	**1.45**	**6.10**
NOT SPECIFIE	**483,202**	**500,919**	**407,717**	**375,327**	**398,209**	**1.45**	**6.10**
OTH.WORLD	483,202	500,919	407,717	375,327	398,209	1.45	6.10

Source: World Tourism Organization (WTO)

PORTUGAL

2. ARRIVALS OF NON-RESIDENT VISITORS AT NATIONAL BORDERS, BY COUNTRY OF RESIDENCE

	1999	2000	2001	2002	2003	Market share 03	% change 03-02
TOTAL	**27,016,307**	**28,013,963**	**28,149,911**	**27,193,920**	**27,532,354**	**100.00**	**1.24**
AMERICAS	**518,361**	**638,059**	**588,005**	**511,029**	**546,289**	**1.98**	**6.90**
NORTH AMER	**413,789**	**480,600**	**436,812**	**389,213**	**417,355**	**1.52**	**7.23**
CANADA	103,502	126,373	126,257	109,403	116,475	0.42	6.46
USA	310,287	354,227	310,555	279,810	300,880	1.09	7.53
SOUTH AMER	**104,572**	**157,459**	**151,193**	**121,816**	**128,934**	**0.47**	**5.84**
BRAZIL	104,572	157,459	151,193	121,816	128,934	0.47	5.84
EAST AS/PACI	**43,656**	**43,705**	**40,975**	**44,877**	**41,430**	**0.15**	**-7.68**
N/EAST ASIA	**43,656**	**43,705**	**40,975**	**44,877**	**41,430**	**0.15**	**-7.68**
JAPAN	43,656	43,705	40,975	44,877	41,430	0.15	-7.68
EUROPE	**26,029,004**	**26,890,971**	**27,151,610**	**26,288,255**	**26,571,956**	**96.51**	**1.08**
NORTHERN EUR	**2,504,532**	**2,546,131**	**2,622,576**	**2,502,803**	**2,635,031**	**9.57**	**5.28**
DENMARK	131,449	134,478	128,534	122,742	127,676	0.46	4.02
FINLAND	82,738	77,312	74,779	77,375	81,301	0.30	5.07
IRELAND	138,069	125,222	128,116	139,024	144,395	0.52	3.86
NORWAY	44,456	49,979	50,083	46,577	48,494	0.18	4.12
SWEDEN	126,714	133,980	141,049	133,632	131,891	0.48	-1.30
UK	1,981,106	2,025,160	2,100,015	1,983,453	2,101,274	7.63	5.94
SOUTHERN EUR	**20,686,854**	**21,380,317**	**21,580,959**	**20,965,713**	**21,074,571**	**76.54**	**0.52**
GREECE	28,705	25,025	23,756	39,927	44,790	0.16	12.18
ITALY	341,267	306,892	327,778	396,377	364,220	1.32	-8.11
SPAIN	20,316,882	21,048,400	21,229,425	20,529,409	20,665,561	75.06	0.66
WESTERN EUR	**2,837,618**	**2,964,523**	**2,948,075**	**2,819,739**	**2,862,354**	**10.40**	**1.51**
AUSTRIA	57,467	66,893	65,921	60,322	64,486	0.23	6.90
BELGIUM	244,282	270,188	279,175	269,918	279,403	1.01	3.51
FRANCE	797,960	887,917	921,248	886,355	886,310	3.22	-0.01
GERMANY	1,060,111	1,023,230	969,941	908,067	929,334	3.38	2.34
LUXEMBOURG	36,626	35,364	35,002	38,344	41,289	0.15	7.68
NETHERLANDS	498,203	524,039	518,169	511,974	514,434	1.87	0.48
SWITZERLAND	142,969	156,892	158,619	144,759	147,098	0.53	1.62
REG.NOT SPEC	**425,286**	**441,228**	**369,321**	**349,759**	**372,679**	**1.35**	**6.55**
NOT SPECIFIE	**425,286**	**441,228**	**369,321**	**349,759**	**372,679**	**1.35**	**6.55**
OTH.WORLD	425,286	441,228	369,321	349,759	372,679	1.35	6.55

Source: World Tourism Organization (WTO)

3. ARRIVALS OF NON-RESIDENT TOURISTS IN HOTELS AND SIMILAR ESTABLISHMENTS, BY COUNTRY OF RESIDENCE

	1999	2000	2001	2002	2003	Market share 03	% change 03-02
TOTAL	**4,910,562**	**5,118,550**	**4,933,855**	**4,944,621**	**4,824,463**	**100.00**	**-2.43**
AFRICA	**33,700**	**42,794**	**40,334**	**40,458**	**40,931**	**0.85**	**1.17**
EAST AFRICA	**257**	**692**	**357**	**241**	**372**	**0.01**	**54.36**
KENYA	155	563	266	157	278	0.01	77.07
ZIMBABWE	102	129	91	84	94		11.90
NORTH AFRICA	**2,994**	**4,439**	**4,375**	**4,522**	**4,900**	**0.10**	**8.36**
ALGERIA	670	765	682	1,357	1,590	0.03	17.17
MOROCCO	2,324	3,674	3,693	3,165	3,310	0.07	4.58
SOUTHERN AFR	**9,394**	**11,459**	**10,152**	**9,048**	**7,707**	**0.16**	**-14.82**
SOUTH AFRICA	9,394	11,459	10,152	9,048	7,707	0.16	-14.82
WEST AFRICA	**441**	**522**	**466**	**571**	**520**	**0.01**	**-8.93**
NIGERIA	441	522	466	571	520	0.01	-8.93
OTHER AFRICA	**20,614**	**25,682**	**24,984**	**26,076**	**27,432**	**0.57**	**5.20**
OTHER AFRICA	20,614	25,682	24,984	26,076	27,432	0.57	5.20
AMERICAS	**532,535**	**626,180**	**519,800**	**479,394**	**432,534**	**8.97**	**-9.77**
CARIBBEAN	**1,158**	**1,229**	**1,196**	**1,044**	**931**	**0.02**	**-10.82**
CUBA	1,158	1,229	1,196	1,044	931	0.02	-10.82
NORTH AMER	**356,660**	**402,390**	**347,179**	**320,833**	**282,447**	**5.85**	**-11.96**
CANADA	54,516	68,477	77,982	69,097	59,092	1.22	-14.48
MEXICO	7,595	9,058	9,724	12,217	11,359	0.24	-7.02
USA	294,549	324,855	259,473	239,519	211,996	4.39	-11.49
SOUTH AMER	**167,885**	**216,306**	**166,157**	**151,708**	**142,584**	**2.96**	**-6.01**
ARGENTINA	11,951	14,495	13,968	6,968	7,907	0.16	13.48
BRAZIL	146,296	189,584	140,845	132,783	126,038	2.61	-5.08
CHILE	2,568	2,981	2,924	3,316	2,603	0.05	-21.50
COLOMBIA	1,670	2,157	2,294	2,517	2,165	0.04	-13.98
VENEZUELA	5,400	7,089	6,126	6,124	3,871	0.08	-36.79
OTHER AMERIC	**6,832**	**6,255**	**5,268**	**5,809**	**6,572**	**0.14**	**13.13**
OTH AMERICA	6,832	6,255	5,268	5,809	6,572	0.14	13.13
EAST AS/PACI	**139,837**	**123,132**	**113,856**	**142,165**	**125,471**	**2.60**	**-11.74**
N/EAST ASIA	**112,174**	**93,708**	**85,219**	**109,755**	**93,256**	**1.93**	**-15.03**
CHINA	7,477	8,200	9,831	10,416	9,567	0.20	-8.15
TAIWAN(P.C.)	984	317	351	215	172		-20.00
JAPAN	101,562	80,977	69,647	94,066	78,025	1.62	-17.05
KOREA REP.	1,569	3,774	4,786	4,351	4,776	0.10	9.77
OT NORTH AS	582	440	604	707	716	0.01	1.27
S/EAST ASIA	**5,867**	**6,418**	**4,994**	**5,582**	**5,845**	**0.12**	**4.71**
MALAYSIA	790	933	779	850	875	0.02	2.94
PHILIPPINES	2,085	3,484	1,971	2,700	2,584	0.05	-4.30
SINGAPORE	1,050	869	944	881	1,260	0.03	43.02
THAILAND	1,942	1,132	1,300	1,151	1,126	0.02	-2.17
AUSTRALASIA	**17,507**	**19,238**	**20,683**	**23,564**	**21,230**	**0.44**	**-9.90**

3. ARRIVALS OF NON-RESIDENT TOURISTS IN HOTELS AND SIMILAR ESTABLISHMENTS, BY COUNTRY OF RESIDENCE

	1999	2000	2001	2002	2003	Market share 03	% change 03-02
AUSTRALIA	14,723	16,205	17,235	19,802	17,989	0.37	-9.16
NEW ZEALAND	2,784	3,033	3,448	3,762	3,241	0.07	-13.85
OT.EAST AS/P	**4,289**	**3,768**	**2,960**	**3,264**	**5,140**	**0.11**	**57.48**
OTHER ASIA	4,136	3,615	2,764	3,218	5,058	0.10	57.18
OTH OCEANIA	153	153	196	46	82		78.26
EUROPE	**4,196,757**	**4,317,524**	**4,249,761**	**4,272,078**	**4,214,728**	**87.36**	**-1.34**
C/E EUROPE	**49,082**	**55,158**	**60,141**	**67,022**	**66,775**	**1.38**	**-0.37**
BULGARIA	1,446	1,871	2,252	3,154	2,909	0.06	-7.77
HUNGARY	9,399	10,066	10,020	9,159	11,717	0.24	27.93
POLAND	17,596	19,942	18,482	23,550	21,455	0.44	-8.90
ROMANIA	2,281	2,740	2,977	4,443	5,674	0.12	27.71
USSR(former)	18,360	20,539	26,410	26,716	25,020	0.52	-6.35
NORTHERN EUR	**1,297,161**	**1,408,209**	**1,413,321**	**1,416,831**	**1,411,513**	**29.26**	**-0.38**
DENMARK	78,709	78,654	67,978	59,021	63,244	1.31	7.16
FINLAND	50,590	49,088	47,744	52,811	54,627	1.13	3.44
ICELAND	9,649	12,188	9,636	5,346	5,917	0.12	10.68
IRELAND	71,779	89,923	88,977	105,734	127,071	2.63	20.18
NORWAY	58,631	63,267	71,462	64,871	67,387	1.40	3.88
SWEDEN	102,075	107,087	120,212	115,939	96,440	2.00	-16.82
UK	925,728	1,008,002	1,007,312	1,013,109	996,827	20.66	-1.61
SOUTHERN EUR	**1,074,009**	**1,094,965**	**1,099,090**	**1,134,156**	**1,148,508**	**23.81**	**1.27**
ALBANIA	766	2,523	1,046	1,230	1,383	0.03	12.44
GREECE	12,897	16,013	12,927	15,356	15,395	0.32	0.25
ITALY	339,529	325,078	329,281	314,463	290,862	6.03	-7.51
SPAIN	720,817	751,351	755,836	803,107	840,868	17.43	4.70
WESTERN EUR	**1,735,286**	**1,716,647**	**1,634,314**	**1,611,063**	**1,543,698**	**32.00**	**-4.18**
AUSTRIA	72,975	59,696	51,914	50,569	48,726	1.01	-3.64
BELGIUM	111,917	116,086	114,247	108,874	106,364	2.20	-2.31
FRANCE	370,914	369,312	375,043	419,280	431,440	8.94	2.90
GERMANY	810,340	803,557	730,069	670,566	617,162	12.79	-7.96
LIECHTENSTEN	210	442	573	885	1,958	0.04	121.24
LUXEMBOURG	8,810	8,457	7,455	7,589	7,782	0.16	2.54
NETHERLANDS	258,101	264,943	263,064	267,160	247,584	5.13	-7.33
SWITZERLAND	102,019	94,154	91,949	86,140	82,682	1.71	-4.01
EAST/MED EUR	**18,881**	**19,570**	**18,179**	**15,386**	**16,478**	**0.34**	**7.10**
ISRAEL	15,482	14,884	14,425	11,038	10,537	0.22	-4.54
TURKEY	3,399	4,686	3,754	4,348	5,941	0.12	36.64
OTHER EUROPE	**22,338**	**22,975**	**24,716**	**27,620**	**27,756**	**0.58**	**0.49**
OTHER EUROPE	22,338	22,975	24,716	27,620	27,756	0.58	0.49
MIDDLE EAST	**3,272**	**3,410**	**4,203**	**3,776**	**3,681**	**0.08**	**-2.52**
MIDDLE EAST	**3,272**	**3,410**	**4,203**	**3,776**	**3,681**	**0.08**	**-2.52**
IRAQ	88	122	105	97	174		79.38
JORDAN	132	190	191	253	239		-5.53
KUWAIT	156	168	134	262	215		-17.94
LEBANON	629	563	879	667	602	0.01	-9.75
LIBYA	456	64	57	79	60		-24.05
OMAN	23	10	14	25	18		-28.00

3. ARRIVALS OF NON-RESIDENT TOURISTS IN HOTELS AND SIMILAR ESTABLISHMENTS, BY COUNTRY OF RESIDENCE

	1999	2000	2001	2002	2003	Market share 03	% change 03-02
SAUDI ARABIA	881	768	1,124	820	732	0.02	-10.73
SYRIA	76	97	68	190	47		-75.26
UNTD ARAB EM	77	280	240	217	203		-6.45
EGYPT	754	1,148	1,391	1,166	1,391	0.03	19.30
SOUTH ASIA	**4,461**	**5,510**	**5,901**	**6,750**	**7,118**	**0.15**	**5.45**
SOUTH ASIA	**4,461**	**5,510**	**5,901**	**6,750**	**7,118**	**0.15**	**5.45**
INDIA	2,968	3,865	4,114	4,970	5,066	0.11	1.93
IRAN	958	1,235	1,066	1,027	1,221	0.03	18.89
PAKISTAN	535	410	721	753	831	0.02	10.36

Source: World Tourism Organization (WTO)

PORTUGAL

4. ARRIVALS OF NON-RESIDENT TOURISTS IN ALL TYPES OF ACCOMMODATION ESTABLISHMENTS, BY COUNTRY OF RESIDENCE

	1999	2000	2001	2002	2003	Market share 03	% change 03-02
TOTAL (*)	**5,378,526**	**5,599,127**	**5,391,886**	**5,444,072**	**5,301,778**	**100.00**	**-2.61**
AFRICA	**35,250**	**44,974**	**42,641**	**42,960**	**42,758**	**0.81**	**-0.47**
EAST AFRICA	**264**	**708**	**369**	**272**	**421**	**0.01**	**54.78**
KENYA	162	568	273	181	322	0.01	77.90
ZIMBABWE	102	140	96	91	99		8.79
NORTH AFRICA	**3,410**	**4,966**	**4,891**	**4,988**	**5,255**	**0.10**	**5.35**
ALGERIA	707	798	709	1,383	1,633	0.03	18.08
MOROCCO	2,703	4,168	4,182	3,605	3,622	0.07	0.47
SOUTHERN AFR	**10,115**	**12,317**	**10,981**	**9,841**	**8,330**	**0.16**	**-15.35**
SOUTH AFRICA	10,115	12,317	10,981	9,841	8,330	0.16	-15.35
WEST AFRICA	**443**	**527**	**466**	**573**	**521**	**0.01**	**-9.08**
NIGERIA	443	527	466	573	521	0.01	-9.08
OTHER AFRICA	**21,018**	**26,456**	**25,934**	**27,286**	**28,231**	**0.53**	**3.46**
OTHER AFRICA	21,018	26,456	25,934	27,286	28,231	0.53	3.46
AMERICAS	**545,935**	**643,042**	**536,373**	**496,163**	**448,955**	**8.47**	**-9.51**
CARIBBEAN	**1,178**	**1,253**	**1,205**	**1,052**	**957**	**0.02**	**-9.03**
CUBA	1,178	1,253	1,205	1,052	957	0.02	-9.03
NORTH AMER	**365,786**	**412,719**	**358,217**	**331,441**	**291,851**	**5.50**	**-11.94**
CANADA	58,410	73,012	82,911	74,191	63,728	1.20	-14.10
MEXICO	7,841	9,429	10,123	12,628	11,952	0.23	-5.35
USA	299,535	330,278	265,183	244,622	216,171	4.08	-11.63
SOUTH AMER	**171,753**	**222,437**	**171,297**	**157,536**	**148,567**	**2.80**	**-5.69**
ARGENTINA	12,405	15,047	14,674	7,675	8,365	0.16	8.99
BRAZIL	149,313	194,594	144,692	137,268	130,835	2.47	-4.69
CHILE	2,728	3,202	3,187	3,589	3,060	0.06	-14.74
COLOMBIA	1,755	2,311	2,428	2,685	2,293	0.04	-14.60
VENEZUELA	5,552	7,283	6,316	6,319	4,014	0.08	-36.48
OTHER AMERIC	**7,218**	**6,633**	**5,654**	**6,134**	**7,580**	**0.14**	**23.57**
OTH AMERICA	7,218	6,633	5,654	6,134	7,580	0.14	23.57
EAST AS/PACI	**153,471**	**135,782**	**127,461**	**155,682**	**138,217**	**2.61**	**-11.22**
N/EAST ASIA	**113,890**	**95,315**	**86,875**	**111,773**	**95,531**	**1.80**	**-14.53**
CHINA	7,609	8,330	9,963	10,662	9,844	0.19	-7.67
TAIWAN(P.C.)	997	327	356	253	226		-10.67
JAPAN	102,964	82,232	70,881	95,561	79,726	1.50	-16.57
KOREA REP.	1,729	3,980	5,065	4,589	5,007	0.09	9.11
OT NORTH AS	591	446	610	708	728	0.01	2.82
S/EAST ASIA	**5,940**	**6,500**	**5,150**	**5,775**	**5,947**	**0.11**	**2.98**
MALAYSIA	796	944	803	868	893	0.02	2.88
PHILIPPINES	2,093	3,515	1,992	2,724	2,601	0.05	-4.52
SINGAPORE	1,057	889	1,005	910	1,284	0.02	41.10
THAILAND	1,994	1,152	1,350	1,273	1,169	0.02	-8.17
AUSTRALASIA	**28,933**	**29,932**	**32,278**	**34,748**	**31,460**	**0.59**	**-9.46**

PORTUGAL

4. ARRIVALS OF NON-RESIDENT TOURISTS IN ALL TYPES OF ACCOMMODATION ESTABLISHMENTS, BY COUNTRY OF RESIDENCE

	1999	2000	2001	2002	2003	Market share 03	% change 03-02
AUSTRALIA	21,928	22,854	24,792	27,763	25,272	0.48	-8.97
NEW ZEALAND	7,005	7,078	7,486	6,985	6,188	0.12	-11.41
OT.EAST AS/P	**4,708**	**4,035**	**3,158**	**3,386**	**5,279**	**0.10**	**55.91**
OTHER ASIA	4,279	3,761	2,840	3,331	5,191	0.10	55.84
OTH OCEANIA	429	274	318	55	88		60.00
EUROPE	**4,635,983**	**4,766,163**	**4,675,170**	**4,738,548**	**4,660,911**	**87.91**	**-1.64**
C/E EUROPE	**56,227**	**62,297**	**67,137**	**74,120**	**73,081**	**1.38**	**-1.40**
BULGARIA	1,482	1,927	2,373	3,348	3,049	0.06	-8.93
HUNGARY	10,634	11,392	11,171	10,486	12,919	0.24	23.20
POLAND	23,032	24,806	23,087	27,691	25,077	0.47	-9.44
ROMANIA	2,435	2,889	3,188	5,226	6,274	0.12	20.05
USSR(former)	18,644	21,283	27,318	27,369	25,762	0.49	-5.87
NORTHERN EUR	**1,334,837**	**1,449,354**	**1,454,689**	**1,458,695**	**1,457,247**	**27.49**	**-0.10**
DENMARK	84,962	84,608	73,619	63,862	68,518	1.29	7.29
FINLAND	51,737	50,374	49,895	54,298	56,200	1.06	3.50
ICELAND	9,677	12,235	9,672	5,373	5,960	0.11	10.92
IRELAND	73,569	92,013	91,357	107,899	129,905	2.45	20.39
NORWAY	59,751	64,332	72,616	66,405	69,181	1.30	4.18
SWEDEN	103,881	108,912	122,348	117,642	98,257	1.85	-16.48
UK	951,260	1,036,880	1,035,182	1,043,216	1,029,226	19.41	-1.34
SOUTHERN EUR	**1,173,466**	**1,197,191**	**1,197,006**	**1,247,449**	**1,264,449**	**23.85**	**1.36**
ALBANIA	768	2,526	1,062	1,245	1,387	0.03	11.41
GREECE	13,264	16,480	13,627	16,433	15,884	0.30	-3.34
ITALY	366,592	353,065	354,329	341,686	315,603	5.95	-7.63
SPAIN	792,842	825,120	827,988	888,085	931,575	17.57	4.90
WESTERN EUR	**2,024,440**	**2,008,845**	**1,906,152**	**1,907,138**	**1,812,897**	**34.19**	**-4.94**
AUSTRIA	78,293	64,095	56,787	55,938	53,461	1.01	-4.43
BELGIUM	132,973	136,579	134,206	129,530	125,952	2.38	-2.76
FRANCE	479,385	487,196	485,281	554,276	549,716	10.37	-0.82
GERMANY	898,195	888,950	805,993	743,342	681,507	12.85	-8.32
LIECHTENSTEN	223	456	590	899	1,975	0.04	119.69
LUXEMBOURG	9,295	9,339	8,125	8,489	8,798	0.17	3.64
NETHERLANDS	317,664	321,856	316,989	322,635	302,194	5.70	-6.34
SWITZERLAND	108,412	100,374	98,181	92,029	89,294	1.68	-2.97
EAST/MED EUR	**19,160**	**20,154**	**18,541**	**15,831**	**17,133**	**0.32**	**8.22**
ISRAEL	15,686	15,375	14,697	11,421	11,113	0.21	-2.70
TURKEY	3,474	4,779	3,844	4,410	6,020	0.11	36.51
OTHER EUROPE	**27,853**	**28,322**	**31,645**	**35,315**	**36,104**	**0.68**	**2.23**
OTHER EUROPE	27,853	28,322	31,645	35,315	36,104	0.68	2.23
MIDDLE EAST	**3,302**	**3,495**	**4,238**	**3,824**	**3,700**	**0.07**	**-3.24**
MIDDLE EAST	**3,302**	**3,495**	**4,238**	**3,824**	**3,700**	**0.07**	**-3.24**
IRAQ	89	130	107	97	174		79.38
JORDAN	132	200	194	253	241		-4.74
KUWAIT	156	172	134	262	215		-17.94
LEBANON	642	600	891	672	611	0.01	-9.08
LIBYA	456	68	59	81	60		-25.93
OMAN	23	11	16	25	18		-28.00

4. ARRIVALS OF NON-RESIDENT TOURISTS IN ALL TYPES OF ACCOMMODATION ESTABLISHMENTS, BY COUNTRY OF RESIDENCE

	1999	2000	2001	2002	2003	Market share 03	% change 03-02
SAUDI ARABIA	881	769	1,126	831	736	0.01	-11.43
SYRIA	76	97	70	190	47		-75.26
UNTD ARAB EM	77	280	240	217	203		-6.45
EGYPT	770	1,168	1,401	1,196	1,395	0.03	16.64
SOUTH ASIA	**4,585**	**5,671**	**6,003**	**6,895**	**7,237**	**0.14**	**4.96**
SOUTH ASIA	**4,585**	**5,671**	**6,003**	**6,895**	**7,237**	**0.14**	**4.96**
INDIA	3,045	3,970	4,166	5,071	5,145	0.10	1.46
IRAN	1,000	1,283	1,103	1,038	1,236	0.02	19.08
PAKISTAN	540	418	734	786	856	0.02	8.91

Source: World Tourism Organization (WTO)

5. OVERNIGHT STAYS OF NON-RESIDENT TOURISTS IN HOTELS AND SIMILAR ESTABLISHMENTS, BY COUNTRY OF RESIDENCE

		1999	2000	2001	2002	2003	Market share 03	% change 03-02
TOTAL	(*)	**23,330,836**	**24,101,963**	**23,577,571**	**23,018,014**	**22,714,016**	**100.00**	**-1.32**
AFRICA		**152,084**	**171,066**	**172,112**	**169,342**	**149,089**	**0.66**	**-11.96**
EAST AFRICA		**940**	**2,071**	**1,663**	**1,104**	**1,463**	**0.01**	**32.52**
KENYA		583	1,645	1,301	780	1,180	0.01	51.28
ZIMBABWE		357	426	362	324	283		-12.65
NORTH AFRICA		**8,195**	**12,728**	**14,898**	**13,991**	**14,442**	**0.06**	**3.22**
ALGERIA		1,931	2,490	2,427	3,548	4,265	0.02	20.21
MOROCCO		6,264	10,238	12,471	10,443	10,177	0.04	-2.55
SOUTHERN AFR		**32,345**	**41,363**	**38,233**	**38,717**	**27,876**	**0.12**	**-28.00**
SOUTH AFRICA		32,345	41,363	38,233	38,717	27,876	0.12	-28.00
WEST AFRICA		**1,497**	**1,672**	**1,420**	**2,937**	**2,080**	**0.01**	**-29.18**
NIGERIA		1,497	1,672	1,420	2,937	2,080	0.01	-29.18
OTHER AFRICA		**109,107**	**113,232**	**115,898**	**112,593**	**103,228**	**0.45**	**-8.32**
OTHER AFRICA		109,107	113,232	115,898	112,593	103,228	0.45	-8.32
AMERICAS		**1,407,579**	**1,684,303**	**1,504,019**	**1,332,631**	**1,236,931**	**5.45**	**-7.18**
CARIBBEAN		**4,809**	**6,595**	**7,781**	**8,648**	**4,451**	**0.02**	**-48.53**
CUBA		4,809	6,595	7,781	8,648	4,451	0.02	-48.53
NORTH AMER		**1,015,122**	**1,168,313**	**1,071,512**	**936,736**	**870,340**	**3.83**	**-7.09**
CANADA		260,709	318,689	371,372	295,867	290,618	1.28	-1.77
MEXICO		21,899	22,571	23,840	28,135	26,736	0.12	-4.97
USA		732,514	827,053	676,300	612,734	552,986	2.43	-9.75
SOUTH AMER		**369,051**	**493,635**	**410,072**	**371,430**	**338,622**	**1.49**	**-8.83**
ARGENTINA		30,165	35,504	34,088	18,793	21,788	0.10	15.94
BRAZIL		313,833	426,297	345,943	317,951	295,218	1.30	-7.15
CHILE		6,481	7,313	7,438	8,898	6,801	0.03	-23.57
COLOMBIA		4,352	5,126	5,492	6,353	5,290	0.02	-16.73
VENEZUELA		14,220	19,395	17,111	19,435	9,525	0.04	-50.99
OTHER AMERIC		**18,597**	**15,760**	**14,654**	**15,817**	**23,518**	**0.10**	**48.69**
OTH AMERICA		18,597	15,760	14,654	15,817	23,518	0.10	48.69
EAST AS/PACI		**272,697**	**258,162**	**246,169**	**286,481**	**260,096**	**1.15**	**-9.21**
N/EAST ASIA		**202,996**	**184,212**	**172,231**	**201,649**	**176,427**	**0.78**	**-12.51**
CHINA		16,605	17,913	23,057	23,762	23,194	0.10	-2.39
TAIWAN(P.C.)		1,723	470	819	392	287		-26.79
JAPAN		177,204	156,240	134,213	166,117	141,331	0.62	-14.92
KOREA REP.		5,352	8,347	12,596	9,550	9,799	0.04	2.61
OT NORTH AS		2,112	1,242	1,546	1,828	1,816	0.01	-0.66
S/EAST ASIA		**13,547**	**13,627**	**13,306**	**13,496**	**13,698**	**0.06**	**1.50**
MALAYSIA		2,481	2,232	1,941	1,981	2,899	0.01	46.34
PHILIPPINES		4,489	6,826	5,411	5,734	4,429	0.02	-22.76
SINGAPORE		2,521	2,090	3,034	2,944	3,801	0.02	29.11
THAILAND		4,056	2,479	2,920	2,837	2,569	0.01	-9.45
AUSTRALASIA		**44,788**	**49,591**	**52,703**	**61,486**	**56,656**	**0.25**	**-7.86**

5. OVERNIGHT STAYS OF NON-RESIDENT TOURISTS IN HOTELS AND SIMILAR ESTABLISHMENTS, BY COUNTRY OF RESIDENCE

	1999	2000	2001	2002	2003	Market share 03	% change 03-02
AUSTRALIA	38,137	42,031	44,261	51,752	48,214	0.21	-6.84
NEW ZEALAND	6,651	7,560	8,442	9,734	8,442	0.04	-13.27
OT.EAST AS/P	**11,366**	**10,732**	**7,929**	**9,850**	**13,315**	**0.06**	**35.18**
OTHER ASIA	11,085	10,422	7,402	9,707	12,945	0.06	33.36
OTH OCEANIA	281	310	527	143	370		158.74
EUROPE	**21,474,415**	**21,960,314**	**21,620,830**	**21,194,648**	**21,033,576**	**92.60**	**-0.76**
C/E EUROPE	**216,765**	**236,588**	**269,872**	**293,747**	**290,825**	**1.28**	**-0.99**
BULGARIA	5,090	6,736	8,426	11,787	10,795	0.05	-8.42
HUNGARY	30,484	34,960	34,425	34,692	41,006	0.18	18.20
POLAND	75,473	83,735	79,684	99,284	94,305	0.42	-5.01
ROMANIA	9,592	10,665	12,137	16,039	17,783	0.08	10.87
USSR(former)	96,126	100,492	135,200	131,945	126,936	0.56	-3.80
NORTHERN EUR	**9,351,175**	**9,839,870**	**9,948,039**	**9,894,311**	**9,988,194**	**43.97**	**0.95**
DENMARK	470,260	473,835	375,284	307,089	309,121	1.36	0.66
FINLAND	334,045	337,505	307,089	342,260	361,604	1.59	5.65
ICELAND	110,691	139,781	95,262	51,785	56,990	0.25	10.05
IRELAND	620,203	745,625	766,520	930,930	1,064,675	4.69	14.37
NORWAY	350,740	378,684	425,394	376,333	422,383	1.86	12.24
SWEDEN	572,899	612,015	711,652	668,867	574,750	2.53	-14.07
UK	6,892,337	7,152,425	7,266,838	7,217,047	7,198,671	31.69	-0.25
SOUTHERN EUR	**2,575,322**	**2,694,170**	**2,756,140**	**2,832,625**	**2,886,492**	**12.71**	**1.90**
ALBANIA	1,596	6,839	4,934	5,899	7,366	0.03	24.87
GREECE	36,070	47,918	39,461	44,028	48,622	0.21	10.43
ITALY	815,435	796,561	799,229	761,517	711,423	3.13	-6.58
SPAIN	1,722,221	1,842,852	1,912,516	2,021,181	2,119,081	9.33	4.84
WESTERN EUR	**9,195,421**	**9,041,123**	**8,497,775**	**8,026,419**	**7,710,086**	**33.94**	**-3.94**
AUSTRIA	344,528	274,730	248,316	224,863	221,729	0.98	-1.39
BELGIUM	553,685	545,979	546,545	518,710	530,781	2.34	2.33
FRANCE	983,114	1,001,519	1,046,164	1,133,117	1,183,177	5.21	4.42
GERMANY	5,127,075	5,010,959	4,532,232	4,030,261	3,820,169	16.82	-5.21
LIECHTENSTEN	964	2,599	3,046	4,103	6,993	0.03	70.44
LUXEMBOURG	50,534	45,061	39,895	36,954	36,725	0.16	-0.62
NETHERLANDS	1,753,986	1,814,267	1,755,514	1,773,924	1,618,878	7.13	-8.74
SWITZERLAND	381,535	346,009	326,063	304,487	291,634	1.28	-4.22
EAST/MED EUR	**44,646**	**48,724**	**49,529**	**40,148**	**46,674**	**0.21**	**16.25**
ISRAEL	35,198	34,083	36,804	26,761	28,758	0.13	7.46
TURKEY	9,448	14,641	12,725	13,387	17,916	0.08	33.83
OTHER EUROPE	**91,086**	**99,839**	**99,475**	**107,398**	**111,305**	**0.49**	**3.64**
OTHER EUROPE	91,086	99,839	99,475	107,398	111,305	0.49	3.64
MIDDLE EAST	**10,561**	**12,288**	**16,426**	**14,582**	**13,839**	**0.06**	**-5.10**
MIDDLE EAST	**10,561**	**12,288**	**16,426**	**14,582**	**13,839**	**0.06**	**-5.10**
IRAQ	258	455	445	438	1,081		146.80
JORDAN	463	597	751	702	682		-2.85
KUWAIT	565	679	532	1,146	892		-22.16
LEBANON	2,515	1,934	2,240	2,276	1,869	0.01	-17.88
LIBYA	713	183	193	203	214		5.42
OMAN	63	51	30	55	54		-1.82

5. OVERNIGHT STAYS OF NON-RESIDENT TOURISTS IN HOTELS AND SIMILAR ESTABLISHMENTS, BY COUNTRY OF RESIDENCE

	1999	2000	2001	2002	2003	Market share 03	% change 03-02
SAUDI ARABIA	3,444	3,063	4,480	3,398	2,847	0.01	-16.22
SYRIA	199	393	425	867	172		-80.16
UNTD ARAB EM	347	901	684	624	665		6.57
EGYPT	1,994	4,032	6,646	4,873	5,363	0.02	10.06
SOUTH ASIA	**13,500**	**15,830**	**18,015**	**20,330**	**20,485**	**0.09**	**0.76**
SOUTH ASIA	**13,500**	**15,830**	**18,015**	**20,330**	**20,485**	**0.09**	**0.76**
INDIA	8,627	10,560	12,333	14,844	14,729	0.06	-0.77
IRAN	2,775	4,031	2,886	3,201	3,337	0.01	4.25
PAKISTAN	2,098	1,239	2,796	2,285	2,419	0.01	5.86

Source: World Tourism Organization (WTO)

PORTUGAL

6. OVERNIGHT STAYS OF NON-RESIDENT TOURISTS IN ALL TYPES OF ACCOMMODATION ESTABLISHMENTS, BY COUNTRY OF RESIDENCE

	1999	2000	2001	2002	2003	Market share 03	% change 03-02
TOTAL (*)	**25,080,002**	**25,785,146**	**25,228,612**	**24,574,060**	**24,369,264**	**100.00**	**-0.83**
AFRICA	**158,318**	**178,556**	**182,308**	**177,966**	**156,765**	**0.64**	**-11.91**
EAST AFRICA	**948**	**2,122**	**1,700**	**1,194**	**1,607**	**0.01**	**34.59**
KENYA	591	1,675	1,330	851	1,314	0.01	54.41
ZIMBABWE	357	447	370	343	293		-14.58
NORTH AFRICA	**9,765**	**14,778**	**18,137**	**16,001**	**16,192**	**0.07**	**1.19**
ALGERIA	2,095	2,562	2,515	3,630	4,366	0.02	20.28
MOROCCO	7,670	12,216	15,622	12,371	11,826	0.05	-4.41
SOUTHERN AFR	**34,125**	**43,163**	**40,456**	**41,092**	**30,412**	**0.12**	**-25.99**
SOUTH AFRICA	34,125	43,163	40,456	41,092	30,412	0.12	-25.99
WEST AFRICA	**1,500**	**1,702**	**1,420**	**2,943**	**2,081**	**0.01**	**-29.29**
NIGERIA	1,500	1,702	1,420	2,943	2,081	0.01	-29.29
OTHER AFRICA	**111,980**	**116,791**	**120,595**	**116,736**	**106,473**	**0.44**	**-8.79**
OTHER AFRICA	111,980	116,791	120,595	116,736	106,473	0.44	-8.79
AMERICAS	**1,442,438**	**1,728,820**	**1,548,989**	**1,375,609**	**1,280,784**	**5.26**	**-6.89**
CARIBBEAN	**4,915**	**6,643**	**7,805**	**8,659**	**4,506**	**0.02**	**-47.96**
CUBA	4,915	6,643	7,805	8,659	4,506	0.02	-47.96
NORTH AMER	**1,039,230**	**1,196,591**	**1,100,051**	**962,390**	**893,655**	**3.67**	**-7.14**
CANADA	271,164	330,930	383,949	308,516	301,694	1.24	-2.21
MEXICO	22,351	23,312	24,613	28,996	28,216	0.12	-2.69
USA	745,715	842,349	691,489	624,878	563,745	2.31	-9.78
SOUTH AMER	**378,604**	**509,127**	**425,363**	**388,076**	**356,049**	**1.46**	**-8.25**
ARGENTINA	31,108	36,772	35,701	20,879	23,304	0.10	11.61
BRAZIL	321,655	439,147	358,068	330,700	309,316	1.27	-6.47
CHILE	6,782	7,788	8,095	9,506	7,970	0.03	-16.16
COLOMBIA	4,495	5,516	5,822	6,841	5,556	0.02	-18.78
VENEZUELA	14,564	19,904	17,677	20,150	9,903	0.04	-50.85
OTHER AMERIC	**19,689**	**16,459**	**15,770**	**16,484**	**26,574**	**0.11**	**61.21**
OTH AMERICA	19,689	16,459	15,770	16,484	26,574	0.11	61.21
EAST AS/PACI	**308,369**	**305,206**	**286,931**	**323,626**	**293,826**	**1.21**	**-9.21**
N/EAST ASIA	**206,369**	**187,707**	**175,727**	**205,787**	**181,218**	**0.74**	**-11.94**
CHINA	16,873	18,225	23,346	24,355	23,841	0.10	-2.11
TAIWAN(P.C.)	1,737	491	825	461	410		-11.06
JAPAN	180,013	159,019	136,898	169,112	144,894	0.59	-14.32
KOREA REP.	5,621	8,724	13,099	10,030	10,245	0.04	2.14
OT NORTH AS	2,125	1,248	1,559	1,829	1,828	0.01	-0.05
S/EAST ASIA	**13,674**	**13,835**	**13,706**	**13,792**	**13,914**	**0.06**	**0.88**
MALAYSIA	2,488	2,279	1,991	2,016	2,946	0.01	46.13
PHILIPPINES	4,501	6,879	5,487	5,769	4,486	0.02	-22.24
TIMOR-LESTE	2,531	2,131	3,127	2,989	3,831	0.02	28.17
THAILAND	4,154	2,546	3,101	3,018	2,651	0.01	-12.16
AUSTRALASIA	**74,654**	**79,041**	**84,313**	**92,123**	**83,361**	**0.34**	**-9.51**

6. OVERNIGHT STAYS OF NON-RESIDENT TOURISTS IN ALL TYPES OF ACCOMMODATION ESTABLISHMENTS, BY COUNTRY OF RESIDENCE

	1999	2000	2001	2002	2003	Market share 03	% change 03-02
AUSTRALIA	57,365	60,191	63,785	71,895	65,988	0.27	-8.22
NEW ZEALAND	17,289	18,850	20,528	20,228	17,373	0.07	-14.11
OT.EAST AS/P	**13,672**	**24,623**	**13,185**	**11,924**	**15,333**	**0.06**	**28.59**
OTHER ASIA	12,949	24,117	12,471	11,755	14,934	0.06	27.04
OTH OCEANIA	723	506	714	169	399		136.09
EUROPE	**23,146,379**	**23,543,791**	**23,175,331**	**22,661,365**	**22,603,236**	**92.75**	**-0.26**
C/E EUROPE	**233,976**	**254,794**	**292,191**	**314,248**	**306,791**	**1.26**	**-2.37**
BULGARIA	5,195	6,812	9,122	12,498	11,165	0.05	-10.67
HUNGARY	33,351	38,316	37,599	37,847	43,708	0.18	15.49
POLAND	88,378	96,148	90,992	109,173	102,332	0.42	-6.27
ROMANIA	10,047	11,040	12,972	19,302	19,675	0.08	1.93
USSR(former)	97,005	102,478	141,506	135,428	129,911	0.53	-4.07
NORTHERN EUR	**9,558,424**	**10,049,782**	**10,172,670**	**10,105,849**	**10,238,660**	**42.01**	**1.31**
DENMARK	493,507	494,953	396,759	323,861	327,398	1.34	1.09
FINLAND	341,392	346,788	317,931	349,226	370,852	1.52	6.19
ICELAND	110,752	139,883	95,365	51,822	57,083	0.23	10.15
IRELAND	625,935	752,109	774,942	937,511	1,073,222	4.40	14.48
NORWAY	356,834	386,170	433,641	386,826	433,967	1.78	12.19
SWEDEN	579,086	619,733	721,992	676,421	584,093	2.40	-13.65
UK	7,050,918	7,310,146	7,432,040	7,380,182	7,392,045	30.33	0.16
SOUTHERN EUR	**2,924,268**	**2,985,204**	**3,041,341**	**3,125,239**	**3,207,954**	**13.16**	**2.65**
ALBANIA	1,598	6,844	4,978	5,922	7,372	0.03	24.48
GREECE	36,881	48,977	40,875	46,519	50,052	0.21	7.59
ITALY	893,917	861,611	856,572	820,044	768,616	3.15	-6.27
SPAIN	1,991,872	2,067,772	2,138,916	2,252,754	2,381,914	9.77	5.73
WESTERN EUR	**10,281,673**	**10,092,697**	**9,503,263**	**8,951,630**	**8,674,384**	**35.60**	**-3.10**
AUSTRIA	358,923	287,665	261,964	237,715	233,149	0.96	-1.92
BELGIUM	628,210	615,266	621,435	588,350	601,347	2.47	2.21
FRANCE	1,329,360	1,347,771	1,388,654	1,499,497	1,533,858	6.29	2.29
GERMANY	5,481,584	5,342,607	4,826,735	4,268,694	4,068,108	16.69	-4.70
LIECHTENSTEN	995	2,621	3,096	4,139	7,031	0.03	69.87
LUXEMBOURG	52,257	47,603	41,939	39,469	39,644	0.16	0.44
NETHERLANDS	2,031,108	2,083,700	2,016,353	1,993,389	1,881,745	7.72	-5.60
SWITZERLAND	399,236	365,464	343,087	320,377	309,502	1.27	-3.39
EAST/MED EUR	**45,188**	**50,013**	**50,305**	**41,156**	**47,849**	**0.20**	**16.26**
ISRAEL	35,562	35,124	37,331	27,634	29,749	0.12	7.65
TURKEY	9,626	14,889	12,974	13,522	18,100	0.07	33.86
OTHER EUROPE	**102,850**	**111,301**	**115,561**	**123,243**	**127,598**	**0.52**	**3.53**
OTHER EUROPE	102,850	111,301	115,561	123,243	127,598	0.52	3.53
MIDDLE EAST	**10,632**	**12,538**	**16,701**	**14,754**	**13,877**	**0.06**	**-5.94**
MIDDLE EAST	**10,632**	**12,538**	**16,701**	**14,754**	**13,877**	**0.06**	**-5.94**
IRAQ	259	494	590	438	1,081		146.80
JORDAN	463	633	764	702	684		-2.56
KUWAIT	565	683	532	1,146	892		-22.16
LEBANON	2,534	2,014	2,290	2,287	1,885	0.01	-17.58
LIBYA	713	187	197	207	214		3.38
OMAN	63	54	36	55	54		-1.82

6. OVERNIGHT STAYS OF NON-RESIDENT TOURISTS IN ALL TYPES OF ACCOMMODATION ESTABLISHMENTS, BY COUNTRY OF RESIDENCE

	1999	2000	2001	2002	2003	Market share 03	% change 03-02
SAUDI ARABIA	3,444	3,064	4,486	3,426	2,858	0.01	-16.58
SYRIA	199	393	429	867	172		-80.16
UNTD ARAB EM	347	901	684	624	665		6.57
EGYPT	2,045	4,115	6,693	5,002	5,372	0.02	7.40
SOUTH ASIA	**13,866**	**16,235**	**18,352**	**20,740**	**20,776**	**0.09**	**0.17**
SOUTH ASIA	**13,866**	**16,235**	**18,352**	**20,740**	**20,776**	**0.09**	**0.17**
INDIA	8,827	10,762	12,462	15,078	14,939	0.06	-0.92
IRAN	2,911	4,217	2,999	3,231	3,365	0.01	4.15
PAKISTAN	2,128	1,256	2,891	2,431	2,472	0.01	1.69

Source: World Tourism Organization (WTO)

PUERTO RICO

1. ARRIVALS OF NON-RESIDENT TOURISTS AT NATIONAL BORDERS, BY COUNTRY OF RESIDENCE

	1999	2000	2001	2002	2003	Market share 03	% change 03-02
TOTAL (*)	**3,024,088**	**3,341,400**	**3,551,200**	**3,087,100**	**3,238,300**	**100.00**	**4.90**
AMERICAS	**2,284,058**	**2,500,800**	**2,635,000**	**2,230,400**	**2,470,500**	**76.29**	**10.76**
CARIBBEAN	**19,069**	**21,400**	**18,800**	**17,500**	**16,200**	**0.50**	**-7.43**
US.VIRGIN IS	19,069	21,400	18,800	17,500	16,200	0.50	-7.43
NORTH AMER	**2,264,989**	**2,479,400**	**2,616,200**	**2,212,900**	**2,454,300**	**75.79**	**10.91**
USA	2,264,989	2,479,400	2,616,200	2,212,900	2,454,300	75.79	10.91
REG.NOT SPEC	**740,030**	**840,600**	**916,200**	**856,700**	**767,800**	**23.71**	**-10.38**
NOT SPECIFIE	**740,030**	**840,600**	**916,200**	**856,700**	**767,800**	**23.71**	**-10.38**
OTH.WORLD	740,030	840,600	916,200	856,700	767,800	23.71	-10.38

Source: World Tourism Organization (WTO)

PUERTO RICO

3. ARRIVALS OF NON-RESIDENT TOURISTS IN HOTELS AND SIMILAR ESTABLISHMENTS, BY COUNTRY OF RESIDENCE

		1999	2000	2001	2002	2003	Market share 03	% change 03-02
TOTAL	(*)	**1,095,107**	**1,102,912**	**1,250,460**	**1,203,832**	**1,304,610**	**100.00**	**8.37**
AFRICA		**479**	**158**	**2,345**	**1,393**	**669**	**0.05**	**-51.97**
OTHER AFRICA		**479**	**158**	**2,345**	**1,393**	**669**	**0.05**	**-51.97**
ALL AFRICA		479	158	2,345	1,393	669	0.05	-51.97
AMERICAS		**947,749**	**989,137**	**1,167,991**	**1,123,499**	**1,219,366**	**93.47**	**8.53**
CARIBBEAN		**41,789**	**44,426**	**44,263**	**42,232**	**40,769**	**3.12**	**-3.46**
CUBA		47	27	195	124	231	0.02	86.29
DOMINICAN RP		6,081	5,698	6,459	6,490	7,631	0.58	17.58
US.VIRGIN IS	(*)	16,513	18,187	3,609	5,601	5,580	0.43	-0.37
OTH CARIBBE	(*)	19,148	20,514	34,000	30,017	27,327	2.09	-8.96
CENTRAL AMER		**7,482**	**9,286**	**7,938**	**4,552**	**4,350**	**0.33**	**-4.44**
BELIZE		106	23	90	70	146	0.01	108.57
COSTA RICA		3,809	4,653	4,323	1,079	1,326	0.10	22.89
EL SALVADOR		114	90	103	214	183	0.01	-14.49
GUATEMALA		258	213	300	323	361	0.03	11.76
HONDURAS		100	141	178	121	99	0.01	-18.18
NICARAGUA		101	87	86	89	113	0.01	26.97
PANAMA		1,010	752	683	774	755	0.06	-2.45
OT CENT AMER		1,984	3,327	2,175	1,882	1,367	0.10	-27.36
NORTH AMER		**879,135**	**921,781**	**1,095,535**	**1,057,743**	**1,156,300**	**88.63**	**9.32**
CANADA		10,234	10,413	15,063	12,530	12,238	0.94	-2.33
MEXICO		10,564	11,352	13,740	12,049	12,113	0.93	0.53
USA		858,337	900,016	1,066,732	1,033,164	1,131,949	86.77	9.56
SOUTH AMER		**19,343**	**13,644**	**20,255**	**18,972**	**17,947**	**1.38**	**-5.40**
ARGENTINA		2,812	2,766	4,013	2,470	2,444	0.19	-1.05
BOLIVIA		113	85	112	183	271	0.02	48.09
BRAZIL		1,156	1,120	1,851	1,671	1,662	0.13	-0.54
CHILE		1,735	551	701	920	1,525	0.12	65.76
COLOMBIA		2,222	2,280	2,658	2,645	3,230	0.25	22.12
ECUADOR		134	172	161	276	341	0.03	23.55
FR.GUIANA		6	4	5	16	5		-68.75
GUYANA		46	9	26	28	11		-60.71
PARAGUAY		44	78	34	54	33		-38.89
PERU		524	599	635	760	594	0.05	-21.84
SURINAME		9		23	19	12		-36.84
URUGUAY		232	267	237	115	243	0.02	111.30
VENEZUELA		3,545	3,024	6,088	5,785	4,568	0.35	-21.04
OTH SOUTH AM		6,765	2,689	3,711	4,030	3,008	0.23	-25.36
EAST AS/PACI		**4,574**	**2,591**	**3,882**	**2,936**	**3,735**	**0.29**	**27.21**
N/EAST ASIA		**1,013**	**960**	**1,337**	**1,155**	**1,091**	**0.08**	**-5.54**
CHINA		115	116	252	193	278	0.02	44.04
TAIWAN(P.C.)		37	71	35	44	36		-18.18
HK,CHINA		86	64	89	43	80	0.01	86.05
JAPAN		775	709	961	875	697	0.05	-20.34
S/EAST ASIA		**218**	**184**	**293**	**298**	**302**	**0.02**	**1.34**

PUERTO RICO

3. ARRIVALS OF NON-RESIDENT TOURISTS IN HOTELS AND SIMILAR ESTABLISHMENTS, BY COUNTRY OF RESIDENCE

	1999	2000	2001	2002	2003	Market share 03	% change 03-02
PHILIPPINES	186	176	260	269	232	0.02	-13.75
THAILAND	32	8	33	29	70	0.01	141.38
AUSTRALASIA	**775**	**908**	**862**	**947**	**1,551**	**0.12**	**63.78**
AUSTRALIA	727	877	834	894	1,493	0.11	67.00
NEW ZEALAND	48	31	28	53	58		9.43
OT.EAST AS/P	**2,568**	**539**	**1,390**	**536**	**791**	**0.06**	**47.57**
OTHER ASIA	2,568	539	1,390	536	791	0.06	47.57
EUROPE	**37,225**	**26,327**	**35,852**	**32,202**	**27,345**	**2.10**	**-15.08**
C/E EUROPE	**201**	**298**	**332**	**352**	**411**	**0.03**	**16.76**
BULGARIA	11	22	21	33	23		-30.30
CZECH RP/SVK	9	51	17	34	66	0.01	94.12
HUNGARY	28	43	39	65	46		-29.23
POLAND	47	42	54	43	65		51.16
ROMANIA	31	28	55	36	43		19.44
USSR(former)	75	112	146	141	168	0.01	19.15
NORTHERN EUR	**13,421**	**6,022**	**7,624**	**7,458**	**7,272**	**0.56**	**-2.49**
DENMARK	282	255	272	840	211	0.02	-74.88
FINLAND	125	104	117	112	291	0.02	159.82
ICELAND	116	41	9	30	31		3.33
IRELAND	1,235	209	180	205	171	0.01	-16.59
NORWAY	317	306	400	272	225	0.02	-17.28
SWEDEN	415	434	523	478	640	0.05	33.89
UK	10,931	4,673	6,123	5,521	5,703	0.44	3.30
SOUTHERN EUR	**8,254**	**7,101**	**7,468**	**8,938**	**9,961**	**0.76**	**11.45**
GIBRALTAR	20	28	1		12		
GREECE	299	64	95	173	120	0.01	-30.64
ITALY	1,876	1,387	1,713	1,679	1,827	0.14	8.81
MALTA	11	14	25	18	12		-33.33
PORTUGAL	139	191	277	233	268	0.02	15.02
SAN MARINO	4	4	6	2	18		800.00
SPAIN	5,903	5,412	5,335	6,816	7,696	0.59	12.91
YUGOSLAV SFR	2	1	16	17	8		-52.94
WESTERN EUR	**9,554**	**8,951**	**7,663**	**8,162**	**7,317**	**0.56**	**-10.35**
AUSTRIA	224	241	418	515	546	0.04	6.02
BELGIUM	453	421	484	453	486	0.04	7.28
FRANCE	2,001	1,498	1,551	1,957	1,775	0.14	-9.30
GERMANY	4,014	4,256	2,946	3,371	2,858	0.22	-15.22
LUXEMBOURG	32	49	40	21	19		-9.52
NETHERLANDS	1,705	1,541	1,429	1,152	916	0.07	-20.49
SWITZERLAND	1,125	945	795	693	717	0.05	3.46
EAST/MED EUR	**921**	**357**	**423**	**359**	**310**	**0.02**	**-13.65**
ISRAEL	259	232	337	241	242	0.02	0.41
TURKEY	662	125	86	118	68	0.01	-42.37
OTHER EUROPE	**4,874**	**3,598**	**12,342**	**6,933**	**2,074**	**0.16**	**-70.09**
OTHER EUROPE	4,874	3,598	12,342	6,933	2,074	0.16	-70.09
MIDDLE EAST	**77**	**54**	**85**	**72**	**197**	**0.02**	**173.61**
MIDDLE EAST	**77**	**54**	**85**	**72**	**197**	**0.02**	**173.61**

PUERTO RICO

3. ARRIVALS OF NON-RESIDENT TOURISTS IN HOTELS AND SIMILAR ESTABLISHMENTS, BY COUNTRY OF RESIDENCE

	1999	2000	2001	2002	2003	Market share 03	% change 03-02
IRAQ	4		2	2			
SAUDI ARABIA	59	40	25	22	154	0.01	600.00
EGYPT	14	14	58	48	43		-10.42
REG.NOT SPEC	**105,003**	**84,645**	**40,305**	**43,730**	**53,298**	**4.09**	**21.88**
NOT SPECIFIE	**105,003**	**84,645**	**40,305**	**43,730**	**53,298**	**4.09**	**21.88**
OTH.WORLD (*)	41,145	48,985	17,790	23,243	32,880	2.52	41.46
N RESID ABRO	63,858	35,660	22,515	20,487	20,418	1.57	-0.34

Source: World Tourism Organization (WTO)

QATAR

3. ARRIVALS OF NON-RESIDENT TOURISTS IN HOTELS AND SIMILAR ESTABLISHMENTS, BY COUNTRY OF RESIDENCE

		1999	2000	2001	2002	2003	Market share 03	% change 03-02
TOTAL	(*)		**377,979**	**375,954**	**586,645**	**556,965**	**100.00**	**-5.06**
EAST AS/PACI			**62,031**	**59,755**	**107,832**	**127,348**	**22.86**	**18.10**
OT.EAST AS/P			**62,031**	**59,755**	**107,832**	**127,348**	**22.86**	**18.10**
ALL ASIA			62,031	59,755	107,832	127,348	22.86	18.10
EUROPE			**105,758**	**56,426**	**102,983**	**88,620**	**15.91**	**-13.95**
OTHER EUROPE			**105,758**	**56,426**	**102,983**	**88,620**	**15.91**	**-13.95**
ALL EUROPE			105,758	56,426	102,983	88,620	15.91	-13.95
MIDDLE EAST			**166,375**	**231,456**	**312,063**	**282,538**	**50.73**	**-9.46**
MIDDLE EAST			**166,375**	**231,456**	**312,063**	**282,538**	**50.73**	**-9.46**
ALL MID EAST			166,375	231,456	312,063	282,538	50.73	-9.46
REG.NOT SPEC			**43,815**	**28,317**	**63,767**	**58,459**	**10.50**	**-8.32**
NOT SPECIFIE			**43,815**	**28,317**	**63,767**	**58,459**	**10.50**	**-8.32**
OTH.WORLD			43,815	28,317	63,767	58,459	10.50	-8.32

Source: World Tourism Organization (WTO)

QATAR

5. OVERNIGHT STAYS OF NON-RESIDENT TOURISTS IN HOTELS AND SIMILAR ESTABLISHMENTS, BY COUNTRY OF RESIDENCE

	1999	2000	2001	2002	2003	Market share 03	% change 03-02
TOTAL (*)		**434,901**	**506,505**	**697,616**	**848,395**	**100.00**	**21.61**
EAST AS/PACI		**85,354**	**75,887**	**129,372**	**165,060**	**19.46**	**27.59**
OT.EAST AS/P		**85,354**	**75,887**	**129,372**	**165,060**	**19.46**	**27.59**
ALL ASIA		85,354	75,887	129,372	165,060	19.46	27.59
EUROPE		**110,671**	**83,945**	**155,321**	**165,335**	**19.49**	**6.45**
OTHER EUROPE		**110,671**	**83,945**	**155,321**	**165,335**	**19.49**	**6.45**
ALL EUROPE		110,671	83,945	155,321	165,335	19.49	6.45
MIDDLE EAST		**179,989**	**298,476**	**327,458**	**405,781**	**47.83**	**23.92**
MIDDLE EAST		**179,989**	**298,476**	**327,458**	**405,781**	**47.83**	**23.92**
ALL MID EAST		179,989	298,476	327,458	405,781	47.83	23.92
REG.NOT SPEC		**58,887**	**48,197**	**85,465**	**112,219**	**13.23**	**31.30**
NOT SPECIFIE		**58,887**	**48,197**	**85,465**	**112,219**	**13.23**	**31.30**
OTH.WORLD		58,887	48,197	85,465	112,219	13.23	31.30

Source: World Tourism Organization (WTO)

REPUBLIC OF MOLDOVA

2. ARRIVALS OF NON-RESIDENT VISITORS AT NATIONAL BORDERS, BY NATIONALITY

	1999	2000	2001	2002	2003	Market share 03	% change 03-02
TOTAL (*)	**14,088**	**18,964**	**15,690**	**20,161**	**23,598**	**100.00**	**17.05**
AFRICA	**10**	**20**	**27**	**40**	**45**	**0.19**	**12.50**
EAST AFRICA	**1**	**2**	**19**	**4**	**8**	**0.03**	**100.00**
KENYA	1	1	15		4	0.02	
MADAGASCAR			1				
RWANDA					1		
ZIMBABWE			2		1		
UGANDA				2	2	0.01	
TANZANIA			1	1			
ZAMBIA		1		1			
CENTRAL AFR	**7**			**1**	**2**	**0.01**	**100.00**
CAMEROON	2				1		
CONGO	5			1	1		
NORTH AFRICA	**1**	**8**		**5**	**21**	**0.09**	**320.00**
ALGERIA		3			1		
MOROCCO		1			5	0.02	
SUDAN	1	4		3	14	0.06	366.67
TUNISIA				2	1		-50.00
SOUTHERN AFR		**1**	**2**	**1**	**6**	**0.03**	**500.00**
SOUTH AFRICA		1	2	1	6	0.03	500.00
WEST AFRICA	**1**	**9**	**6**	**29**	**8**	**0.03**	**-72.41**
GAMBIA		1					
LIBERIA		2					
MAURITANIA	1		2	1			
NIGER				1			
NIGERIA		2	4	1	5	0.02	400.00
SENEGAL					3	0.01	
SIERRA LEONE				26			
BURKINA FASO		4					
AMERICAS	**910**	**1,109**	**1,148**	**1,788**	**2,556**	**10.83**	**42.95**
CARIBBEAN			**5**		**2**	**0.01**	
CUBA			5		1		
DOMINICAN RP					1		
CENTRAL AMER	**2**	**1**		**11**			
COSTA RICA				11			
EL SALVADOR	2						
PANAMA		1					
NORTH AMER	**905**	**1,102**	**1,122**	**1,762**	**2,543**	**10.78**	**44.32**
CANADA	15	46	42	52	49	0.21	-5.77
GREENLAND		1	2				
MEXICO	1	25	6	3			
USA	889	1,030	1,072	1,707	2,494	10.57	46.10
SOUTH AMER	**3**	**6**	**21**	**15**	**11**	**0.05**	**-26.67**
ARGENTINA			4	5	2	0.01	-60.00
BOLIVIA				1			
BRAZIL	1	3	15		4	0.02	
CHILE		2	2	1			

REPUBLIC OF MOLDOVA

2. ARRIVALS OF NON-RESIDENT VISITORS AT NATIONAL BORDERS, BY NATIONALITY

	1999	2000	2001	2002	2003	Market share 03	% change 03-02
COLOMBIA	2			3			
PERU				2	2	0.01	
SURINAME					1		
VENEZUELA		1		3	2	0.01	-33.33
EAST AS/PACI	**224**	**398**	**377**	**411**	**295**	**1.25**	**-28.22**
N/EAST ASIA	**203**	**374**	**359**	**394**	**259**	**1.10**	**-34.26**
CHINA	100	197	201	247	85	0.36	-65.59
TAIWAN(P.C.)	5	63		13	14	0.06	7.69
JAPAN	78	79	87	118	139	0.59	17.80
KOREA D P RP	20	31	18	1	2	0.01	100.00
KOREA REP.			1	14	19	0.08	35.71
MONGOLIA		4	52	1			
S/EAST ASIA	**10**	**4**	**8**	**3**	**12**	**0.05**	**300.00**
CAMBODIA			1				
INDONESIA		2	2	1	7	0.03	600.00
MALAYSIA			1	1	1		
PHILIPPINES			3				
SINGAPORE	2				2	0.01	
VIET NAM	3	2	1	1	1		
THAILAND	5				1		
AUSTRALASIA	**11**	**20**	**10**	**11**	**24**	**0.10**	**118.18**
AUSTRALIA	9	5	10	6	19	0.08	216.67
NEW ZEALAND	2	15		5	5	0.02	
MELANESIA				**3**			
NEW CALEDNIA				3			
EUROPE	**12,832**	**17,230**	**14,028**	**17,631**	**20,152**	**85.40**	**14.30**
C/E EUROPE	**8,517**	**11,402**	**8,416**	**11,283**	**11,336**	**48.04**	**0.47**
AZERBAIJAN	23	15	24	97	23	0.10	-76.29
ARMENIA	39	16	25	36	26	0.11	-27.78
BULGARIA	458	528	295	326	625	2.65	91.72
BELARUS	550	546	509	720	750	3.18	4.17
CZECH REP	183	158	88	224	100	0.42	-55.36
ESTONIA	20	34	53	27	75	0.32	177.78
GEORGIA	51	23	67	88	35	0.15	-60.23
HUNGARY	147	65	128	160	171	0.72	6.88
KAZAKHSTAN	25	49	92	85	45	0.19	-47.06
KYRGYZSTAN	19	10	18	29	19	0.08	-34.48
LATVIA	23	26	17	223	39	0.17	-82.51
LITHUANIA	34	29	126	83	115	0.49	38.55
POLAND	278	358	237	486	320	1.36	-34.16
ROMANIA	2,087	2,341	2,076	1,929	2,381	10.09	23.43
RUSSIAN FED	2,595	5,146	2,361	3,758	3,270	13.86	-12.99
SLOVAKIA	16	11	16	5	23	0.10	360.00
TAJIKISTAN	5	15	4	16	4	0.02	-75.00
TURKMENISTAN	8	4		3	4	0.02	33.33
UKRAINE	1,944	1,969	2,261	2,947	3,283	13.91	11.40
UZBEKISTAN	12	59	19	41	28	0.12	-31.71
NORTHERN EUR	**887**	**585**	**447**	**518**	**664**	**2.81**	**28.19**
DENMARK	74	28	58	23	44	0.19	91.30

REPUBLIC OF MOLDOVA

2. ARRIVALS OF NON-RESIDENT VISITORS AT NATIONAL BORDERS, BY NATIONALITY

	1999	2000	2001	2002	2003	Market share 03	% change 03-02
FINLAND	39	39	31	32	17	0.07	-46.88
ICELAND	2	7		3	25	0.11	733.33
IRELAND	44	42	35	70	39	0.17	-44.29
NORWAY	53	36	40	44	69	0.29	56.82
SWEDEN	60	106	120	156	251	1.06	60.90
UK	615	327	163	190	219	0.93	15.26
SOUTHERN EUR	**816**	**1,262**	**979**	**998**	**1,117**	**4.73**	**11.92**
ALBANIA	27	104	28	10	30	0.13	200.00
ANDORRA				1			
BOSNIA HERZG	3	8	11	9	13	0.06	44.44
CROATIA	23	58	18	17	9	0.04	-47.06
GREECE	239	277	99	120	103	0.44	-14.17
ITALY	409	594	572	491	702	2.97	42.97
MALTA		21	8	1			
PORTUGAL	3	4	20	62	12	0.05	-80.65
SAN MARINO		2	1	2			
SLOVENIA	32	48	68	96	56	0.24	-41.67
SPAIN	29	62	57	118	58	0.25	-50.85
TFYROM	21	35	24	16	18	0.08	12.50
SERBIA,MTNEG	30	49	73	55	116	0.49	110.91
WESTERN EUR	**725**	**1,078**	**1,171**	**1,033**	**2,400**	**10.17**	**132.33**
AUSTRIA	46	95	105	63	451	1.91	615.87
BELGIUM	49	40	38	43	39	0.17	-9.30
FRANCE	217	203	304	179	305	1.29	70.39
GERMANY	277	537	558	560	717	3.04	28.04
LUXEMBOURG		5	5	2	2	0.01	
NETHERLANDS	121	153	125	161	529	2.24	228.57
SWITZERLAND	15	45	36	25	357	1.51	1,328.00
EAST/MED EUR	**1,887**	**2,903**	**3,015**	**3,799**	**4,635**	**19.64**	**22.01**
CYPRUS	64	127	319	514	266	1.13	-48.25
ISRAEL	211	228	291	416	404	1.71	-2.88
TURKEY	1,612	2,548	2,405	2,869	3,965	16.80	38.20
MIDDLE EAST	**89**	**159**	**80**	**281**	**525**	**2.22**	**86.83**
MIDDLE EAST	**89**	**159**	**80**	**281**	**525**	**2.22**	**86.83**
IRAQ	4	12		5			
JORDAN	13	17	10	10	47	0.20	370.00
KUWAIT	2		1	3	10	0.04	233.33
LEBANON	29	74	39	220	333	1.41	51.36
LIBYA		10	1		1		
OMAN					2	0.01	
SAUDI ARABIA			1	8	15	0.06	87.50
SYRIA	17	8	5	19	86	0.36	352.63
UNTD ARAB EM	1	13	13	4	5	0.02	25.00
EGYPT	23	20	7	5	26	0.11	420.00
YEMEN		5	3	7			
SOUTH ASIA	**23**	**48**	**30**	**10**	**25**	**0.11**	**150.00**
SOUTH ASIA	**23**	**48**	**30**	**10**	**25**	**0.11**	**150.00**
AFGHANISTAN	4	1					
BANGLADESH	2	3	1	2			
SRI LANKA			1				

REPUBLIC OF MOLDOVA

2. ARRIVALS OF NON-RESIDENT VISITORS AT NATIONAL BORDERS, BY NATIONALITY

	1999	2000	2001	2002	2003	Market share 03	% change 03-02
INDIA	12	24	25	6	12	0.05	100.00
IRAN	5	11	1	1	8	0.03	700.00
NEPAL		3					
PAKISTAN		6	2	1	5	0.02	400.00

Source: World Tourism Organization (WTO)

REUNION

1. ARRIVALS OF NON-RESIDENT TOURISTS AT NATIONAL BORDERS, BY COUNTRY OF RESIDENCE

	1999	2000	2001	2002	2003	Market share 03	% change 03-02
TOTAL	**394,000**	**429,999**	**424,000**	**426,000**	**432,000**	**100.00**	**1.41**
AFRICA	**52,769**	**44,240**	**45,805**	**30,600**	**27,400**	**6.34**	**-10.46**
EAST AFRICA	**52,769**	**44,240**	**45,805**	**30,600**	**27,400**	**6.34**	**-10.46**
MADAGASCAR	12,345	7,252	8,515				
MAURITIUS	40,424	36,988	37,290	30,600	27,400	6.34	-10.46
EUROPE	**316,642**	**359,689**	**342,663**	**351,500**	**363,600**	**84.17**	**3.44**
OTHER EUROPE	**316,642**	**359,689**	**342,663**	**351,500**	**363,600**	**84.17**	**3.44**
ALL EUROPE	316,642	359,689	342,663	351,500	363,600	84.17	3.44
REG.NOT SPEC	**24,589**	**26,070**	**35,532**	**43,900**	**41,000**	**9.49**	**-6.61**
NOT SPECIFIE	**24,589**	**26,070**	**35,532**	**43,900**	**41,000**	**9.49**	**-6.61**
OTH.WORLD	24,589	26,070	35,532	43,900	41,000	9.49	-6.61

Source: World Tourism Organization (WTO)

2. ARRIVALS OF NON-RESIDENT VISITORS AT NATIONAL BORDERS, BY COUNTRY OF RESIDENCE

	1999	2000	2001	2002	2003	Market share 03	% change 03-02
TOTAL	**5,223,896**	**5,263,715**	**4,938,375**	**4,793,722**	**5,594,828**	**100.00**	**16.71**
AFRICA	**4,667**	**5,131**	**4,735**	**4,984**	**5,461**	**0.10**	**9.57**
EAST AFRICA	**392**	**595**	**409**	**366**	**404**	**0.01**	**10.38**
BURUNDI	4	3	13	1	6		500.00
COMOROS	1	3	2	3	1		-66.67
ETHIOPIA	80	69	33	28	28		
ERITREA	5	25		8	2		-75.00
DJIBOUTI	3	2	2	3	6		100.00
KENYA	37	51	29	31	66		112.90
MADAGASCAR	10	18	13	4	19		375.00
MAURITIUS	55	75	91	82	103		25.61
MOZAMBIQUE	1	5	9	5	2		-60.00
RWANDA	10	10	3	9	9		
SOMALIA	14	175	100	80	62		-22.50
ZIMBABWE	30	27	19	25	31		24.00
UGANDA	31	36	33	34	19		-44.12
TANZANIA	98	85	52	45	29		-35.56
ZAMBIA	13	11	10	8	21		162.50
CENTRAL AFR	**399**	**307**	**238**	**257**	**310**	**0.01**	**20.62**
ANGOLA	80	32	28	46	67		45.65
CAMEROON	69	43	35	41	56		36.59
CENT.AFR.REP	94	71	53	50	26		-48.00
CHAD			2		1		
CONGO	125	123	92	96	111		15.63
DEM.R.CONGO	11	3	1		2		
EQ.GUINEA	1	3	15	2	21		950.00
GABON	17	21	10	22	26		18.18
SAO TOME PRN	2	11	2				
NORTH AFRICA	**2,400**	**2,438**	**2,410**	**2,555**	**2,781**	**0.05**	**8.85**
ALGERIA	315	251	300	314	355	0.01	13.06
MOROCCO	1,032	958	785	730	721	0.01	-1.23
SUDAN	453	439	331	302	292	0.01	-3.31
TUNISIA	600	790	994	1,209	1,413	0.03	16.87
SOUTHERN AFR	**859**	**1,076**	**993**	**983**	**1,170**	**0.02**	**19.02**
BOTSWANA	4	3	3	1	9		800.00
LESOTHO	3	3	2	1	2		100.00
NAMIBIA	5	16	26	12	34		183.33
SOUTH AFRICA	847	1,054	962	969	1,125	0.02	16.10
WEST AFRICA	**617**	**715**	**685**	**823**	**796**	**0.01**	**-3.28**
CAPE VERDE	15	12	23	23	26		13.04
BENIN	38	32	30	17	8		-52.94
GAMBIA	6	7	4	16	2		-87.50
GHANA	99	130	90	115	92		-20.00
GUINEA	66	41	61	68	61		-10.29
COTE IVOIRE	3	8	17	26	35		34.62
LIBERIA	13	13	48	11	7		-36.36
MALI	3	3	8	18	9		-50.00
MAURITANIA	12	14	17	13	7		-46.15
NIGER	1	2	4	3	1		-66.67
NIGERIA	308	345	283	403	415	0.01	2.98
GUINEABISSAU	3	3	2	2	9		350.00

2. ARRIVALS OF NON-RESIDENT VISITORS AT NATIONAL BORDERS, BY COUNTRY OF RESIDENCE

	1999	2000	2001	2002	2003	Market share 03	% change 03-02
SENEGAL	20	77	63	81	92		13.58
SIERRA LEONE	9	5	4	2	5		150.00
TOGO	9	16	22	12	8		-33.33
BURKINA FASO	12	7	9	13	19		46.15
AMERICAS	**84,184**	**94,642**	**96,012**	**102,481**	**115,373**	**2.06**	**12.58**
CARIBBEAN	**293**	**232**	**321**	**148**	**244**		**64.86**
CUBA	249	178	271	100	184		84.00
DOMINICAN RP	14	15	23	13	36		176.92
HAITI	10	13	5		3		
JAMAICA	20	26	22	35	21		-40.00
CENTRAL AMER	**314**	**309**	**606**	**308**	**301**	**0.01**	**-2.27**
COSTA RICA	100	108	165	126	123		-2.38
EL SALVADOR	10	15	51	14	11		-21.43
GUATEMALA	39	58	90	24	17		-29.17
HONDURAS	75	72	191	58	88		51.72
NICARAGUA	19	10	30	14	15		7.14
PANAMA	71	46	79	68	42		-38.24
OT CENT AMER				4	5		25.00
NORTH AMER	**80,636**	**91,051**	**91,777**	**98,813**	**111,851**	**2.00**	**13.19**
CANADA	10,991	11,643	12,420	16,347	19,091	0.34	16.79
MEXICO	519	591	1,527	729	830	0.01	13.85
USA	69,126	78,817	77,830	81,737	91,930	1.64	12.47
SOUTH AMER	**2,941**	**3,050**	**3,308**	**3,212**	**2,977**	**0.05**	**-7.32**
ARGENTINA	517	571	580	493	551	0.01	11.76
BOLIVIA	59	76	76	56	57		1.79
BRAZIL	707	815	979	954	901	0.02	-5.56
CHILE	365	333	285	306	356	0.01	16.34
COLOMBIA	340	324	449	527	305	0.01	-42.13
ECUADOR	421	305	285	219	188		-14.16
GUYANA	3	3	11	1	2		100.00
PARAGUAY	3	6	28	27	10		-62.96
PERU	184	222	210	225	247		9.78
SURINAME	2	9	2	1	1		
URUGUAY	49	79	59	91	40		-56.04
VENEZUELA	291	307	344	312	319	0.01	2.24
EAST AS/PACI	**36,020**	**37,260**	**36,393**	**41,703**	**41,610**	**0.74**	**-0.22**
N/EAST ASIA	**20,409**	**21,636**	**21,071**	**23,118**	**22,333**	**0.40**	**-3.40**
CHINA	8,420	9,457	8,055	7,854	6,807	0.12	-13.33
TAIWAN(P.C.)	52	123	42	334	463	0.01	38.62
HK,CHINA	56	12	10	95	133		40.00
JAPAN	7,822	8,024	9,046	10,391	10,615	0.19	2.16
KOREA D P RP	275	226	137	293	153		-47.78
KOREA REP.	3,379	3,356	3,527	3,944	3,977	0.07	0.84
MONGOLIA	405	438	254	207	185		-10.63
S/EAST ASIA	**9,873**	**8,822**	**9,144**	**12,006**	**13,478**	**0.24**	**12.26**
MYANMAR	37	162	70	210	313	0.01	49.05
CAMBODIA	1	6	1	3	1		-66.67
INDONESIA	1,041	529	545	517	867	0.02	67.70
LAO P.DEM.R.	1	2		1	7		600.00

2. ARRIVALS OF NON-RESIDENT VISITORS AT NATIONAL BORDERS, BY COUNTRY OF RESIDENCE

	1999	2000	2001	2002	2003	Market share 03	% change 03-02
MALAYSIA	288	397	398	315	428	0.01	35.87
PHILIPPINES	7,735	6,843	7,133	9,778	10,518	0.19	7.57
SINGAPORE	150	156	194	176	221		25.57
VIET NAM	431	331	349	463	543	0.01	17.28
THAILAND	189	396	454	543	580	0.01	6.81
AUSTRALASIA	**5,738**	**6,800**	**6,136**	**6,081**	**5,700**	**0.10**	**-6.27**
AUSTRALIA	4,625	5,526	5,105	5,010	4,725	0.08	-5.69
NEW ZEALAND	1,113	1,274	1,031	1,071	975	0.02	-8.96
MELANESIA		**2**	**1**	**1**	**6**		**500.00**
FIJI		2	1	1	6		500.00
OT.EAST AS/P			**41**	**497**	**93**		**-81.29**
OEAP			41	497	93		-81.29
EUROPE	**5,048,614**	**5,074,204**	**4,757,141**	**4,603,867**	**5,391,609**	**96.37**	**17.11**
C/E EUROPE	**3,692,401**	**3,706,112**	**3,273,047**	**3,071,413**	**3,663,122**	**65.47**	**19.27**
AZERBAIJAN	2,903	1,309	1,009	910	1,380	0.02	51.65
ARMENIA	3,144	1,415	569	542	506	0.01	-6.64
BULGARIA	488,779	362,540	392,312	362,660	340,291	6.08	-6.17
BELARUS	39,765	28,233	26,056	25,480	23,228	0.42	-8.84
CZECH REP	68,940	70,918	78,345	77,890	64,881	1.16	-16.70
ESTONIA	1,518	1,228	1,344	1,110	1,288	0.02	16.04
GEORGIA	1,924	1,139	919	1,074	803	0.01	-25.23
HUNGARY	1,030,676	1,202,713	1,131,475	1,152,599	1,537,114	27.47	33.36
KAZAKHSTAN	1,099	836	363	409	485	0.01	18.58
KYRGYZSTAN	46	69	40	50	97		94.00
LATVIA	621	661	905	1,664	2,495	0.04	49.94
LITHUANIA	5,277	4,961	5,367	5,143	3,994	0.07	-22.34
REP MOLDOVA	1,454,734	1,435,912	1,033,116	856,723	1,058,636	18.92	23.57
POLAND	103,348	101,610	106,089	112,888	108,729	1.94	-3.68
RUSSIAN FED	77,645	82,689	86,493	79,868	85,251	1.52	6.74
SLOVAKIA	91,573	79,645	84,173	102,747	84,450	1.51	-17.81
TAJIKISTAN	24	17	17	42	12		-71.43
TURKMENISTAN	282	113	65	33	27		-18.18
UKRAINE	319,059	329,695	324,158	289,383	349,268	6.24	20.69
USSR(former)	877	226	119	40	27		-32.50
UZBEKISTAN	167	183	113	158	160		1.27
NORTHERN EUR	**91,401**	**96,794**	**104,732**	**111,705**	**124,977**	**2.23**	**11.88**
DENMARK	9,314	10,440	12,092	12,178	12,958	0.23	6.40
FINLAND	3,516	3,774	4,056	4,008	4,360	0.08	8.78
ICELAND	103	333	214	238	279		17.23
IRELAND	3,372	3,865	4,731	5,565	6,344	0.11	14.00
NORWAY	6,231	8,073	8,791	9,448	10,419	0.19	10.28
SWEDEN	16,408	17,049	18,452	20,641	21,956	0.39	6.37
UK	52,457	53,260	56,396	59,627	68,661	1.23	15.15
SOUTHERN EUR	**474,177**	**465,117**	**476,306**	**528,389**	**655,126**	**11.71**	**23.99**
ALBANIA	2,504	2,821	2,449	2,411	2,514	0.04	4.27
BOSNIA HERZG	15,019	8,489	6,964	2,393	2,160	0.04	-9.74
CROATIA	13,892	15,168	17,582	19,810	20,277	0.36	2.36
GREECE	71,377	69,669	66,973	59,338	59,942	1.07	1.02
HOLY SEE		13	17	11	17		54.55
ITALY	158,255	189,208	218,592	230,454	258,830	4.63	12.31
MALTA	280	351	301	305	516	0.01	69.18

ROMANIA

2. ARRIVALS OF NON-RESIDENT VISITORS AT NATIONAL BORDERS, BY COUNTRY OF RESIDENCE

	1999	2000	2001	2002	2003	Market share 03	% change 03-02
PORTUGAL	2,414	2,519	3,141	3,658	4,291	0.08	17.30
SAN MARINO		166	143	170	208		22.35
SLOVENIA	9,233	7,739	8,392	7,572	8,212	0.15	8.45
SPAIN	9,512	11,778	14,320	17,356	21,328	0.38	22.89
TFYROM	39,313	14,612	10,673	10,268	5,541	0.10	-46.04
SERBIA,MTNEG	152,195	142,584	126,759	174,643	271,290	4.85	55.34
OT SOUTH EUR	183						
WESTERN EUR	**461,814**	**496,718**	**606,075**	**641,784**	**688,499**	**12.31**	**7.28**
AUSTRIA	62,811	66,150	85,075	87,995	101,182	1.81	14.99
BELGIUM	17,514	19,264	23,040	24,098	26,798	0.48	11.20
FRANCE	61,584	76,076	87,585	91,788	101,080	1.81	10.12
GERMANY	248,992	255,145	327,885	358,738	380,478	6.80	6.06
LIECHTENSTEN	56	79	96	135	129		-4.44
LUXEMBOURG	834	837	917	1,007	1,256	0.02	24.73
MONACO	9	10	11	11	9		-18.18
NETHERLANDS	47,081	54,711	57,752	56,490	58,277	1.04	3.16
SWITZERLAND	22,933	24,446	23,714	21,522	19,290	0.34	-10.37
EAST/MED EUR	**328,821**	**309,423**	**296,981**	**250,576**	**259,885**	**4.65**	**3.72**
CYPRUS	5,292	5,947	6,088	6,318	6,840	0.12	8.26
ISRAEL	42,739	50,508	229,762	52,811	47,850	0.86	-9.39
TURKEY	280,790	252,968	61,131	191,447	205,195	3.67	7.18
OTHER EUROPE		**40**					
OTHER EUROPE		40					
MIDDLE EAST	**32,140**	**33,647**	**28,181**	**27,105**	**26,867**	**0.48**	**-0.88**
MIDDLE EAST	**32,140**	**33,647**	**28,181**	**27,105**	**26,867**	**0.48**	**-0.88**
BAHRAIN	59	79	57	40	77		92.50
PALESTINE	540	583	287	227	282	0.01	24.23
IRAQ	1,651	2,154	1,249	1,279	801	0.01	-37.37
JORDAN	2,560	2,257	1,940	2,048	1,792	0.03	-12.50
KUWAIT	699	1,284	1,620	1,251	1,144	0.02	-8.55
LEBANON	5,144	4,790	3,883	4,122	4,060	0.07	-1.50
LIBYA	429	457	366	383	288	0.01	-24.80
OMAN	58	55	57	59	36		-38.98
QATAR	49	84	60	142	125		-11.97
SAUDI ARABIA	1,092	2,014	1,688	1,314	873	0.02	-33.56
SYRIA	13,798	14,345	12,612	11,570	12,328	0.22	6.55
UNTD ARAB EM	473	585	739	792	714	0.01	-9.85
EGYPT	5,368	4,782	3,473	3,720	4,214	0.08	13.28
YEMEN	220	178	150	158	133		-15.82
SOUTH ASIA	**16,174**	**16,909**	**13,971**	**12,423**	**12,856**	**0.23**	**3.49**
SOUTH ASIA	**16,174**	**16,909**	**13,971**	**12,423**	**12,856**	**0.23**	**3.49**
AFGHANISTAN	41	25	14	23	39		69.57
BANGLADESH	171	192	133	110	101		-8.18
SRI LANKA	418	393	328	507	420	0.01	-17.16
INDIA	3,160	3,337	3,529	4,773	4,024	0.07	-15.69
IRAN	10,060	10,790	8,290	5,709	7,149	0.13	25.22
MALDIVES	51	110	99	99	36		-63.64
NEPAL	20	26	10	22	16		-27.27
PAKISTAN	2,253	2,036	1,568	1,180	1,071	0.02	-9.24

ROMANIA

2. ARRIVALS OF NON-RESIDENT VISITORS AT NATIONAL BORDERS, BY COUNTRY OF RESIDENCE

	1999	2000	2001	2002	2003	Market share 03	% change 03-02
REG.NOT SPEC	**2,097**	**1,922**	**1,942**	**1,159**	**1,052**	**0.02**	**-9.23**
NOT SPECIFIE	**2,097**	**1,922**	**1,942**	**1,159**	**1,052**	**0.02**	**-9.23**
OTH.WORLD	2,097	1,922	1,942	1,159	1,052	0.02	-9.23

Source: World Tourism Organization (WTO)

3. ARRIVALS OF NON-RESIDENT TOURISTS IN HOTELS AND SIMILAR ESTABLISHMENTS, BY COUNTRY OF RESIDENCE

		1999	2000	2001	2002	2003	Market share 03	% change 03-02
TOTAL		**786,616**	**851,897**	**894,712**	**981,797**	**1,085,569**	**100.00**	**10.57**
AFRICA		**5,741**	**4,721**	**4,044**	**4,683**	**5,239**	**0.48**	**11.87**
OTHER AFRICA		**5,741**	**4,721**	**4,044**	**4,683**	**5,239**	**0.48**	**11.87**
ALL AFRICA	(*)	5,741	4,721	4,044	4,683	5,239	0.48	11.87
AMERICAS		**65,750**	**65,449**	**65,856**	**70,540**	**78,853**	**7.26**	**11.78**
CENTRAL AMER		**1,509**	**1,240**	**2,117**	**2,015**	**1,790**	**0.16**	**-11.17**
ALL CENT AME	(*)	1,509	1,240	2,117	2,015	1,790	0.16	-11.17
NORTH AMER		**62,411**	**61,457**	**60,524**	**66,149**	**74,842**	**6.89**	**13.14**
CANADA		6,782	6,484	5,898	7,943	8,023	0.74	1.01
USA		55,629	54,973	54,626	58,206	66,819	6.16	14.80
SOUTH AMER		**1,830**	**2,752**	**3,215**	**2,376**	**2,221**	**0.20**	**-6.52**
ALL SOUTH AM		1,830	2,752	3,215	2,376	2,221	0.20	-6.52
EAST AS/PACI		**33,981**	**34,898**	**37,243**	**42,180**	**40,113**	**3.70**	**-4.90**
N/EAST ASIA		**16,412**	**16,864**	**18,333**	**22,698**	**22,002**	**2.03**	**-3.07**
CHINA		4,197	3,637	3,211	4,250	3,605	0.33	-15.18
JAPAN		12,215	13,227	15,122	18,448	18,397	1.69	-0.28
OT.EAST AS/P		**17,569**	**18,034**	**18,910**	**19,482**	**18,111**	**1.67**	**-7.04**
OTHER ASIA		13,410	13,828	15,102	15,760	14,641	1.35	-7.10
ALL OCEANIA		4,159	4,206	3,808	3,722	3,470	0.32	-6.77
EUROPE		**676,219**	**746,829**	**787,569**	**864,394**	**961,364**	**88.56**	**11.22**
C/E EUROPE		**115,431**	**120,833**	**122,995**	**141,095**	**165,898**	**15.28**	**17.58**
BULGARIA		7,451	7,476	8,605	8,677	10,550	0.97	21.59
CZECH REP		6,382	6,661	6,769	8,379	10,071	0.93	20.19
HUNGARY		48,328	50,872	48,652	61,313	77,638	7.15	26.63
REP MOLDOVA		29,582	31,734	29,252	28,934	28,765	2.65	-0.58
POLAND		4,778	5,378	8,845	9,802	13,095	1.21	33.60
RUSSIAN FED		8,097	9,652	9,897	10,960	13,070	1.20	19.25
SLOVAKIA		2,920	2,647	3,727	4,182	4,103	0.38	-1.89
UKRAINE		7,893	6,413	7,248	8,848	8,606	0.79	-2.74
NORTHERN EUR		**70,176**	**71,943**	**80,742**	**92,858**	**108,171**	**9.96**	**16.49**
DENMARK		7,583	8,849	10,687	11,516	12,690	1.17	10.19
FINLAND		2,595	2,485	2,703	4,141	3,670	0.34	-11.37
IRELAND		2,837	3,395	3,527	4,099	4,909	0.45	19.76
NORWAY		4,731	4,702	7,864	7,423	8,939	0.82	20.42
SWEDEN		8,697	8,707	9,689	11,831	12,021	1.11	1.61
UK		43,733	43,805	46,272	53,848	65,942	6.07	22.46
SOUTHERN EUR		**158,711**	**190,540**	**186,318**	**204,269**	**232,281**	**21.40**	**13.71**
GREECE		22,997	21,269	19,847	20,899	24,273	2.24	16.14
ITALY		97,340	109,963	122,704	138,747	159,319	14.68	14.83
PORTUGAL		2,135	1,502	2,009	3,377	3,537	0.33	4.74
SLOVENIA		1,878	1,767	2,331	3,104	3,176	0.29	2.32
SPAIN		13,861	18,642	23,588	28,709	31,223	2.88	8.76

3. ARRIVALS OF NON-RESIDENT TOURISTS IN HOTELS AND SIMILAR ESTABLISHMENTS, BY COUNTRY OF RESIDENCE

	1999	2000	2001	2002	2003	Market share 03	% change 03-02
SERBIA,MTNEG	20,500	37,397	15,839	9,433	10,753	0.99	13.99
WESTERN EUR	**235,665**	**255,753**	**277,602**	**313,263**	**344,335**	**31.72**	**9.92**
AUSTRIA	29,115	31,403	33,428	34,842	40,278	3.71	15.60
BELGIUM	13,004	12,286	14,099	16,105	15,273	1.41	-5.17
FRANCE	54,104	62,429	69,565	83,252	91,719	8.45	10.17
GERMANY	96,747	97,483	115,830	128,628	147,900	13.62	14.98
LUXEMBOURG	610	595	720	1,111	1,171	0.11	5.40
NETHERLANDS	26,169	35,773	28,249	31,616	30,687	2.83	-2.94
SWITZERLAND	15,916	15,784	15,711	17,709	17,307	1.59	-2.27
EAST/MED EUR	**82,453**	**89,434**	**101,943**	**95,484**	**90,209**	**8.31**	**-5.52**
ISRAEL	50,094	58,874	74,818	68,307	63,120	5.81	-7.59
TURKEY	32,359	30,560	27,125	27,177	27,089	2.50	-0.32
OTHER EUROPE	**13,783**	**18,326**	**17,969**	**17,425**	**20,470**	**1.89**	**17.47**
OTHER EUROPE	13,783	18,326	17,969	17,425	20,470	1.89	17.47
REG.NOT SPEC	**4,925**						
NOT SPECIFIE	**4,925**						
N RESID ABRO	4,925						

Source: World Tourism Organization (WTO)

ROMANIA

4. ARRIVALS OF NON-RESIDENT TOURISTS IN ALL TYPES OF ACCOMMODATION ESTABLISHMENTS, BY COUNTRY OF RESIDENCE

		1999	2000	2001	2002	2003	Market share 03	% change 03-02
TOTAL		**795,112**	**867,024**	**914,509**	**999,208**	**1,104,975**	**100.00**	**10.59**
AFRICA		**5,749**	**4,734**	**4,052**	**4,685**	**5,244**	**0.47**	**11.93**
OTHER AFRICA		**5,749**	**4,734**	**4,052**	**4,685**	**5,244**	**0.47**	**11.93**
ALL AFRICA	(*)	5,749	4,734	4,052	4,685	5,244	0.47	11.93
AMERICAS		**66,019**	**65,775**	**66,434**	**70,861**	**79,110**	**7.16**	**11.64**
CENTRAL AMER		**1,536**	**1,240**	**2,115**	**2,028**	**1,791**	**0.16**	**-11.69**
ALL CENT AME	(*)	1,536	1,240	2,115	2,028	1,791	0.16	-11.69
NORTH AMER		**62,653**	**61,775**	**61,079**	**66,457**	**75,096**	**6.80**	**13.00**
CANADA		6,818	6,530	5,972	7,993	8,059	0.73	0.83
USA		55,835	55,245	55,107	58,464	67,037	6.07	14.66
SOUTH AMER		**1,830**	**2,760**	**3,240**	**2,376**	**2,223**	**0.20**	**-6.44**
ALL SOUTH AM		1,830	2,760	3,240	2,376	2,223	0.20	-6.44
EAST AS/PACI		**34,083**	**35,178**	**37,927**	**42,861**	**40,291**	**3.65**	**-6.00**
N/EAST ASIA		**16,455**	**16,956**	**18,374**	**22,714**	**22,028**	**1.99**	**-3.02**
CHINA		4,209	3,714	3,245	4,262	3,627	0.33	-14.90
JAPAN		12,246	13,242	15,129	18,452	18,401	1.67	-0.28
OT.EAST AS/P		**17,628**	**18,222**	**19,553**	**20,147**	**18,263**	**1.65**	**-9.35**
OTHER ASIA		12,914	13,996	15,708	16,329	14,745	1.33	-9.70
ALL OCEANIA		4,714	4,226	3,845	3,818	3,518	0.32	-7.86
EUROPE		**689,261**	**761,337**	**806,096**	**880,801**	**980,330**	**88.72**	**11.30**
C/E EUROPE		**121,355**	**124,074**	**127,295**	**144,767**	**171,223**	**15.50**	**18.27**
BULGARIA		7,467	7,481	8,691	8,722	10,692	0.97	22.59
CZECH REP		6,415	6,714	7,162	8,666	10,425	0.94	20.30
HUNGARY		52,402	52,937	50,709	63,147	80,710	7.30	27.81
REP MOLDOVA		30,872	32,549	30,213	29,554	29,404	2.66	-0.51
POLAND		4,975	5,539	9,236	10,411	13,799	1.25	32.54
RUSSIAN FED		8,173	9,772	9,991	10,993	13,218	1.20	20.24
SLOVAKIA		2,955	2,649	3,735	4,247	4,171	0.38	-1.79
UKRAINE		8,096	6,433	7,558	9,027	8,804	0.80	-2.47
NORTHERN EUR		**70,894**	**73,343**	**82,896**	**94,473**	**109,573**	**9.92**	**15.98**
DENMARK		7,660	9,546	11,423	12,429	13,200	1.19	6.20
FINLAND		2,649	2,519	2,714	4,234	3,932	0.36	-7.13
IRELAND		2,949	3,436	3,564	4,120	4,959	0.45	20.36
NORWAY		4,737	4,711	7,864	7,432	9,048	0.82	21.74
SWEDEN		8,765	8,749	9,756	12,053	12,091	1.09	0.32
UK		44,134	44,382	47,575	54,205	66,343	6.00	22.39
SOUTHERN EUR		**159,770**	**191,394**	**187,743**	**205,679**	**234,272**	**21.20**	**13.90**
GREECE		23,158	21,281	19,938	20,920	24,341	2.20	16.35
ITALY		97,962	110,627	123,803	139,860	160,774	14.55	14.95
PORTUGAL		2,137	1,514	2,013	3,395	3,612	0.33	6.39
SLOVENIA		1,900	1,786	2,361	3,158	3,212	0.29	1.71
SPAIN		13,948	18,710	23,746	28,814	31,400	2.84	8.97

4. ARRIVALS OF NON-RESIDENT TOURISTS IN ALL TYPES OF ACCOMMODATION ESTABLISHMENTS, BY COUNTRY OF RESIDENCE

	1999	2000	2001	2002	2003	Market share 03	% change 03-02
SERBIA,MTNEG	20,665	37,476	15,882	9,532	10,933	0.99	14.70
WESTERN EUR	**240,694**	**264,039**	**287,742**	**322,181**	**354,297**	**32.06**	**9.97**
AUSTRIA	29,298	31,647	33,671	35,179	40,664	3.68	15.59
BELGIUM	13,440	12,710	14,631	16,331	15,702	1.42	-3.85
FRANCE	55,352	63,092	70,551	84,153	92,760	8.39	10.23
GERMANY	98,239	102,844	122,105	134,963	154,242	13.96	14.28
LUXEMBOURG	621	640	795	1,156	1,172	0.11	1.38
NETHERLANDS	27,587	37,135	30,173	32,614	32,103	2.91	-1.57
SWITZERLAND	16,157	15,971	15,816	17,785	17,654	1.60	-0.74
EAST/MED EUR	**82,692**	**89,828**	**102,269**	**96,061**	**90,454**	**8.19**	**-5.84**
ISRAEL	50,188	59,104	74,982	68,535	63,222	5.72	-7.75
TURKEY	32,504	30,724	27,287	27,526	27,232	2.46	-1.07
OTHER EUROPE	**13,856**	**18,659**	**18,151**	**17,640**	**20,511**	**1.86**	**16.28**
OTHER EUROPE	13,856	18,659	18,151	17,640	20,511	1.86	16.28

Source: World Tourism Organization (WTO)

5. OVERNIGHT STAYS OF NON-RESIDENT TOURISTS IN HOTELS AND SIMILAR ESTABLISHMENTS, BY COUNTRY OF RESIDENCE

		1999	2000	2001	2002	2003	Market share 03	% change 03-02
TOTAL		**1,960,367**	**2,084,927**	**2,300,661**	**2,470,622**	**2,687,832**	**100.00**	**8.79**
AFRICA		**16,663**	**17,625**	**16,253**	**12,075**	**14,691**	**0.55**	**21.66**
OTHER AFRICA		**16,663**	**17,625**	**16,253**	**12,075**	**14,691**	**0.55**	**21.66**
ALL AFRICA	(*)	16,663	17,625	16,253	12,075	14,691	0.55	21.66
AMERICAS		**136,495**	**141,280**	**154,800**	**169,773**	**185,941**	**6.92**	**9.52**
CENTRAL AMER		**3,061**	**2,801**	**4,255**	**4,041**	**3,933**	**0.15**	**-2.67**
ALL CENT AME	(*)	3,061	2,801	4,255	4,041	3,933	0.15	-2.67
NORTH AMER		**129,485**	**132,945**	**141,941**	**160,536**	**176,526**	**6.57**	**9.96**
CANADA		14,375	12,494	13,795	18,214	19,113	0.71	4.94
USA		115,110	120,451	128,146	142,322	157,413	5.86	10.60
SOUTH AMER		**3,949**	**5,534**	**8,604**	**5,196**	**5,482**	**0.20**	**5.50**
ALL SOUTH AM		3,949	5,534	8,604	5,196	5,482	0.20	5.50
EAST AS/PACI		**87,688**	**75,612**	**86,735**	**92,858**	**84,465**	**3.14**	**-9.04**
N/EAST ASIA		**33,441**	**33,841**	**34,450**	**43,313**	**38,779**	**1.44**	**-10.47**
CHINA		9,922	9,035	7,401	8,323	7,101	0.26	-14.68
JAPAN		23,519	24,806	27,049	34,990	31,678	1.18	-9.47
OT.EAST AS/P		**54,247**	**41,771**	**52,285**	**49,545**	**45,686**	**1.70**	**-7.79**
OTHER ASIA		45,592	34,247	44,588	42,617	38,969	1.45	-8.56
ALL OCEANIA		8,655	7,524	7,697	6,928	6,717	0.25	-3.05
EUROPE		**1,708,751**	**1,850,410**	**2,042,873**	**2,195,916**	**2,402,735**	**89.39**	**9.42**
C/E EUROPE		**242,942**	**258,696**	**277,253**	**313,858**	**397,603**	**14.79**	**26.68**
BULGARIA		13,428	13,644	17,021	16,575	21,537	0.80	29.94
CZECH REP		11,835	13,435	12,030	16,283	21,282	0.79	30.70
HUNGARY		94,864	102,053	111,619	123,159	159,453	5.93	29.47
REP MOLDOVA		69,410	71,108	67,884	74,029	75,005	2.79	1.32
POLAND		9,897	11,922	17,221	18,749	34,403	1.28	83.49
RUSSIAN FED		20,689	26,462	29,760	33,914	54,442	2.03	60.53
SLOVAKIA		7,753	6,573	7,275	9,542	10,233	0.38	7.24
UKRAINE		15,066	13,499	14,443	21,607	21,248	0.79	-1.66
NORTHERN EUR		**190,736**	**180,821**	**220,403**	**261,954**	**298,271**	**11.10**	**13.86**
DENMARK		14,877	18,539	30,143	31,602	37,750	1.40	19.45
FINLAND		8,443	6,790	8,079	10,878	8,437	0.31	-22.44
IRELAND		6,649	9,741	8,050	8,809	11,289	0.42	28.15
NORWAY		24,955	22,498	51,308	38,019	46,633	1.73	22.66
SWEDEN		23,668	21,314	25,581	36,949	37,540	1.40	1.60
UK		112,144	101,939	97,242	135,697	156,622	5.83	15.42
SOUTHERN EUR		**341,099**	**401,557**	**404,326**	**449,167**	**495,014**	**18.42**	**10.21**
GREECE		48,455	46,492	46,550	47,935	52,612	1.96	9.76
ITALY		215,572	250,433	277,473	314,352	347,775	12.94	10.63
PORTUGAL		4,986	3,469	5,714	8,824	9,338	0.35	5.83
SLOVENIA		3,728	3,956	4,918	6,593	6,574	0.24	-0.29
SPAIN		26,050	34,655	40,063	51,573	56,283	2.09	9.13

5. OVERNIGHT STAYS OF NON-RESIDENT TOURISTS IN HOTELS AND SIMILAR ESTABLISHMENTS, BY COUNTRY OF RESIDENCE

	1999	2000	2001	2002	2003	Market share 03	% change 03-02
SERBIA,MTNEG	42,308	62,552	29,608	19,890	22,432	0.83	12.78
WESTERN EUR	**633,116**	**685,969**	**800,089**	**880,626**	**929,885**	**34.60**	**5.59**
AUSTRIA	62,941	60,891	63,567	65,730	78,297	2.91	19.12
BELGIUM	33,908	35,221	40,973	40,538	38,376	1.43	-5.33
FRANCE	133,302	156,425	179,966	196,066	215,466	8.02	9.89
GERMANY	306,820	326,394	412,641	463,660	493,827	18.37	6.51
LUXEMBOURG	1,610	1,289	1,532	3,935	3,793	0.14	-3.61
NETHERLANDS	69,988	80,563	76,439	82,423	68,843	2.56	-16.48
SWITZERLAND	24,547	25,186	24,971	28,274	31,283	1.16	10.64
EAST/MED EUR	**267,601**	**279,052**	**301,708**	**244,866**	**236,317**	**8.79**	**-3.49**
ISRAEL	198,096	205,670	238,320	186,711	175,220	6.52	-6.15
TURKEY	69,505	73,382	63,388	58,155	61,097	2.27	5.06
OTHER EUROPE	**33,257**	**44,315**	**39,094**	**45,445**	**45,645**	**1.70**	**0.44**
OTHER EUROPE	33,257	44,315	39,094	45,445	45,645	1.70	0.44
REG.NOT SPEC	**10,770**						
NOT SPECIFIE	**10,770**						
N RESID ABRO	10,770						

Source: World Tourism Organization (WTO)

6. OVERNIGHT STAYS OF NON-RESIDENT TOURISTS IN ALL TYPES OF ACCOMMODATION ESTABLISHMENTS, BY COUNTRY OF RESIDENCE

		1999	2000	2001	2002	2003	Market share 03	% change 03-02
TOTAL		**1,980,516**	**2,149,358**	**2,390,531**	**2,534,219**	**2,765,500**	**100.00**	**9.13**
AFRICA		**16,671**	**17,652**	**16,275**	**12,077**	**14,696**	**0.53**	**21.69**
OTHER AFRICA		**16,671**	**17,652**	**16,275**	**12,077**	**14,696**	**0.53**	**21.69**
ALL AFRICA	(*)	16,671	17,652	16,275	12,077	14,696	0.53	21.69
AMERICAS		**137,041**	**143,263**	**159,053**	**171,286**	**187,131**	**6.77**	**9.25**
CENTRAL AMER		**3,102**	**2,801**	**4,269**	**4,056**	**3,934**	**0.14**	**-3.01**
ALL CENT AME	(*)	3,102	2,801	4,269	4,056	3,934	0.14	-3.01
NORTH AMER		**129,990**	**134,875**	**146,005**	**162,034**	**177,713**	**6.43**	**9.68**
CANADA		14,442	12,735	14,224	18,464	19,221	0.70	4.10
USA		115,548	122,140	131,781	143,570	158,492	5.73	10.39
SOUTH AMER		**3,949**	**5,587**	**8,779**	**5,196**	**5,484**	**0.20**	**5.54**
ALL SOUTH AM		3,949	5,587	8,779	5,196	5,484	0.20	5.54
EAST AS/PACI		**87,855**	**76,512**	**89,147**	**94,728**	**85,288**	**3.08**	**-9.97**
N/EAST ASIA		**33,541**	**34,111**	**34,549**	**43,340**	**38,823**	**1.40**	**-10.42**
CHINA		9,966	9,254	7,489	8,350	7,139	0.26	-14.50
JAPAN		23,575	24,857	27,060	34,990	31,684	1.15	-9.45
OT.EAST AS/P		**54,314**	**42,401**	**54,598**	**51,388**	**46,465**	**1.68**	**-9.58**
OTHER ASIA		45,641	34,852	46,864	44,236	39,700	1.44	-10.25
ALL OCEANIA		8,673	7,549	7,734	7,152	6,765	0.24	-5.41
EUROPE		**1,738,949**	**1,911,931**	**2,126,056**	**2,256,128**	**2,478,385**	**89.62**	**9.85**
C/E EUROPE		**257,840**	**266,150**	**293,453**	**320,953**	**413,870**	**14.97**	**28.95**
BULGARIA		13,444	13,649	17,407	16,665	22,223	0.80	33.35
CZECH REP		11,966	13,562	14,112	17,916	22,432	0.81	25.21
HUNGARY		104,075	107,057	117,767	125,849	169,046	6.11	34.32
REP MOLDOVA		73,334	72,380	69,900	75,264	76,523	2.77	1.67
POLAND		10,348	12,093	17,754	19,594	35,794	1.29	82.68
RUSSIAN FED		20,814	27,297	30,173	34,006	55,291	2.00	62.59
SLOVAKIA		7,849	6,575	7,286	9,676	10,407	0.38	7.55
UKRAINE		16,010	13,537	19,054	21,983	22,154	0.80	0.78
NORTHERN EUR		**194,836**	**189,550**	**234,126**	**269,803**	**304,113**	**11.00**	**12.72**
DENMARK		15,017	22,027	35,306	37,660	40,936	1.48	8.70
FINLAND		8,514	6,824	8,102	10,980	8,713	0.32	-20.65
IRELAND		6,779	10,006	8,190	8,854	11,410	0.41	28.87
NORWAY		24,964	22,507	51,309	38,048	47,101	1.70	23.79
SWEDEN		23,801	21,507	25,675	38,012	37,890	1.37	-0.32
UK		115,761	106,679	105,544	136,249	158,063	5.72	16.01
SOUTHERN EUR		**343,443**	**404,015**	**407,606**	**452,095**	**499,029**	**18.04**	**10.38**
GREECE		49,054	46,625	47,038	47,962	53,090	1.92	10.69
ITALY		216,452	252,310	279,700	316,736	350,530	12.68	10.67
PORTUGAL		4,988	3,483	5,730	8,854	9,429	0.34	6.49
SLOVENIA		3,773	3,979	4,995	6,663	6,671	0.24	0.12
SPAIN		26,165	34,859	40,410	51,729	56,548	2.04	9.32

6. OVERNIGHT STAYS OF NON-RESIDENT TOURISTS IN ALL TYPES OF ACCOMMODATION ESTABLISHMENTS, BY COUNTRY OF RESIDENCE

	1999	2000	2001	2002	2003	Market share 03	% change 03-02
SERBIA,MTNEG	43,011	62,759	29,733	20,151	22,761	0.82	12.95
WESTERN EUR	**641,048**	**726,290**	**848,777**	**921,685**	**978,744**	**35.39**	**6.19**
AUSTRIA	63,129	61,699	64,319	67,191	79,237	2.87	17.93
BELGIUM	34,470	36,129	43,523	41,245	39,171	1.42	-5.03
FRANCE	135,520	159,265	181,832	197,683	218,771	7.91	10.67
GERMANY	309,643	358,826	451,106	497,817	533,942	19.31	7.26
LUXEMBOURG	1,628	1,583	2,150	4,202	3,797	0.14	-9.64
NETHERLANDS	71,822	82,564	80,599	84,863	71,790	2.60	-15.40
SWITZERLAND	24,836	26,224	25,248	28,684	32,036	1.16	11.69
EAST/MED EUR	**268,095**	**280,479**	**302,529**	**245,762**	**236,909**	**8.57**	**-3.60**
ISRAEL	198,352	206,873	238,871	187,103	175,399	6.34	-6.26
TURKEY	69,743	73,606	63,658	58,659	61,510	2.22	4.86
OTHER EUROPE	**33,687**	**45,447**	**39,565**	**45,830**	**45,720**	**1.65**	**-0.24**
OTHER EUROPE	33,687	45,447	39,565	45,830	45,720	1.65	-0.24

Source: World Tourism Organization (WTO)

RUSSIAN FEDERATION

2. ARRIVALS OF NON-RESIDENT VISITORS AT NATIONAL BORDERS, BY NATIONALITY

	1999	2000	2001	2002	2003	Market share 03	% change 03-02
TOTAL	**18,819,558**	**21,169,100**	**21,570,000**	**23,296,000**	**22,521,059**	**100.00**	**-3.33**
AFRICA	**28,616**	**38,438**	**33,377**	**31,502**	**28,985**	**0.13**	**-7.99**
EAST AFRICA	**1,790**	**4,478**	**2,247**	**3,529**	**3,145**	**0.01**	**-10.88**
BURUNDI	26	36	37	50	126		152.00
COMOROS		35	7	1	7		600.00
ETHIOPIA	346	342	260	542	457		-15.68
ERITREA	49	18	49	953	69		-92.76
DJIBOUTI	6	795	4	5	8		60.00
KENYA	258	246	295	399	368		-7.77
MADAGASCAR	98	77	333	54	124		129.63
MALAWI	2	3	10	6	36		500.00
MAURITIUS	234	209	279	493	389		-21.10
MOZAMBIQUE	50	170	50	179	137		-23.46
RWANDA	37	68	62	43	51		18.60
SEYCHELLES	39	75	12	33	76		130.30
SOMALIA	62	222	255	154	370		140.26
ZIMBABWE	119	120	106	137	166		21.17
UGANDA	64	1,724	72	79	299		278.48
TANZANIA	231	210	223	196	241		22.96
ZAMBIA	169	128	193	205	221		7.80
CENTRAL AFR	**1,239**	**1,605**	**1,492**	**1,663**	**1,802**	**0.01**	**8.36**
ANGOLA	426	522	450	722	925		28.12
CAMEROON	318	453	378	365	381		4.38
CENT.AFR.REP	34	34	4	10	16		60.00
CHAD	75	78	50	78	80		2.56
CONGO	180	175	309	288	309		7.29
EQ.GUINEA	148	268	111	126	37		-70.63
GABON	54	31	107	73	51		-30.14
SAO TOME PRN	4	44	83	1	3		200.00
NORTH AFRICA	**6,339**	**5,165**	**4,783**	**12,582**	**6,287**	**0.03**	**-50.03**
ALGERIA	1,696	1,741	1,853	7,862	1,713	0.01	-78.21
MOROCCO	2,882	2,621	2,253	2,670	2,345	0.01	-12.17
SUDAN	491	593	454	538	656		21.93
TUNISIA	1,270	210	223	1,512	1,573	0.01	4.03
SOUTHERN AFR	**2,698**	**2,791**	**3,498**	**3,671**	**4,241**	**0.02**	**15.53**
BOTSWANA	13	18	12	8	24		200.00
LESOTHO	1	15	9	13	24		84.62
NAMIBIA	71	264	151	129	162		25.58
SOUTH AFRICA	2,611	2,492	3,324	3,514	4,025	0.02	14.54
SWAZILAND	2	2	2	7	6		-14.29
WEST AFRICA	**16,550**	**24,399**	**21,357**	**10,057**	**13,510**	**0.06**	**34.33**
CAPE VERDE	73	68	104	176	135		-23.30
BENIN	78	98	111	145	154		6.21
GAMBIA	4	8	13	52	59		13.46
GHANA	322	253	271	225	313		39.11
GUINEA	233	210	208	190	265		39.47
COTE IVOIRE	93	79	99	131	193		47.33
LIBERIA	14,506	22,530	18,998	7,680	10,919	0.05	42.17
MALI	100	97	97	147	185		25.85
MAURITANIA	163	81	51	109	77		-29.36
NIGER	23	6	5	14	36		157.14

RUSSIAN FEDERATION

2. ARRIVALS OF NON-RESIDENT VISITORS AT NATIONAL BORDERS, BY NATIONALITY

	1999	2000	2001	2002	2003	Market share 03	% change 03-02
NIGERIA	764	676	1,003	848	843		-0.59
GUINEABISSAU	30	17	156	76	76		
SENEGAL	44	123	91	127	144		13.39
SIERRA LEONE	48	84	50	55	64		16.36
TOGO	55	60	94	68	40		-41.18
BURKINA FASO	14	9	6	14	7		-50.00
AMERICAS	**255,017**	**292,865**	**305,604**	**342,625**	**420,867**	**1.87**	**22.84**
CARIBBEAN	**24,324**	**33,642**	**44,213**	**42,632**	**76,111**	**0.34**	**78.53**
ANTIGUA,BARB	1,325	1,157	1,090	1,066	1,720	0.01	61.35
BAHAMAS	19,059	24,646	31,210	32,297	61,762	0.27	91.23
BARBADOS	78	86	133	142	138		-2.82
BERMUDA	70	3,836	7,429	41	1,374	0.01	3,251.22
CAYMAN IS	522	1,071	893	1,456	1,642	0.01	12.77
CUBA	1,613	1,324	1,360	2,453	3,518	0.02	43.42
DOMINICA	11	15	43	36	275		663.89
DOMINICAN RP	78	72	103	238	106		-55.46
GRENADA	5	15	143	60	389		548.33
HAITI	44	67	47	58	82		41.38
JAMAICA	163	209	711	1,804	851		-52.83
MARTINIQUE			2				
NETH.ANTILES	49	14	60	112	140		25.00
PUERTO RICO					2		
ST.KITTS NEV	7	3	4	4	3		-25.00
ANGUILLA		7	15	56	6		-89.29
ST.LUCIA	1		1	4	6		50.00
ST.VINCENT,G	1,265	1,086	933	2,750	4,035	0.02	46.73
TRINIDAD TBG	34	34	36	55	62		12.73
CENTRAL AMER	**10,792**	**11,765**	**10,719**	**14,534**	**13,278**	**0.06**	**-8.64**
BELIZE	2,353	2,668	571	1,137	617		-45.73
COSTA RICA	219	280	342	236	384		62.71
EL SALVADOR	124	631	111	122	136		11.48
GUATEMALA	159	420	136	169	251		48.52
HONDURAS	521	189	396	174	1,406	0.01	708.05
NICARAGUA	128	329	190	187	134		-28.34
PANAMA	7,288	7,248	8,973	12,509	10,350	0.05	-17.26
NORTH AMER	**207,615**	**226,387**	**237,421**	**272,337**	**316,510**	**1.41**	**16.22**
CANADA	19,893	23,536	21,952	30,314	29,778	0.13	-1.77
MEXICO	3,679	3,530	5,384	6,327	5,884	0.03	-7.00
USA	184,043	199,321	210,085	235,696	280,848	1.25	19.16
SOUTH AMER	**12,286**	**21,071**	**13,251**	**13,122**	**14,968**	**0.07**	**14.07**
ARGENTINA	4,613	4,132	3,303	2,060	3,424	0.02	66.21
BOLIVIA	305	383	243	313	288		-7.99
BRAZIL	3,049	4,038	3,622	4,068	4,685	0.02	15.17
CHILE	1,147	940	1,475	1,447	1,400	0.01	-3.25
COLOMBIA	846	932	1,484	1,298	1,685	0.01	29.82
ECUADOR	353	486	676	1,035	752		-27.34
FALKLAND IS	1	15	12	1	64		6,300.00
GUYANA	16	17	5	29	14		-51.72
PARAGUAY	24	49	116	29	36		24.14
PERU	1,040	963	958	1,192	1,132	0.01	-5.03
SURINAME	4	66	8	5	4		-20.00
URUGUAY	402	744	446	455	615		35.16

2. ARRIVALS OF NON-RESIDENT VISITORS AT NATIONAL BORDERS, BY NATIONALITY

	1999	2000	2001	2002	2003	Market share 03	% change 03-02
VENEZUELA	486	8,306	903	1,190	869		-26.97
EAST AS/PACI	**747,677**	**838,803**	**868,590**	**1,150,399**	**1,106,605**	**4.91**	**-3.81**
N/EAST ASIA	**685,878**	**772,754**	**791,022**	**1,056,682**	**1,006,310**	**4.47**	**-4.77**
CHINA	445,924	493,800	461,175	725,825	679,608	3.02	-6.37
TAIWAN(P.C.)	5,002	4,031	5,887	6,090	6,660	0.03	9.36
HK,CHINA	1,712				3,585	0.02	
JAPAN	60,658	62,619	70,751	73,734	86,764	0.39	17.67
KOREA D P RP	10,017	16,088	10,319	20,536	18,412	0.08	-10.34
KOREA REP.	33,862	60,789	116,967	96,010	94,563	0.42	-1.51
MACAU, CHINA				3	34		1.033.33
MONGOLIA	128,703	135,427	125,923	134,484	116,684	0.52	-13.24
S/EAST ASIA	**48,481**	**50,578**	**59,460**	**72,065**	**73,327**	**0.33**	**1.75**
BRUNEI DARSM	25	21	29	14	18		28.57
MYANMAR	926	4,335	1,947	1,672	1,470	0.01	-12.08
CAMBODIA	8,864	3,479	4,222	5,535	5,002	0.02	-9.63
INDONESIA	1,653	2,041	2,586	4,413	4,931	0.02	11.74
LAO P.DEM.R.	46	31	25	61	128		109.84
MALAYSIA	1,784	1,843	2,216	3,612	3,560	0.02	-1.44
PHILIPPINES	16,170	15,401	21,377	23,327	26,082	0.12	11.81
SINGAPORE	4,085	5,265	3,446	3,246	3,665	0.02	12.91
VIET NAM	12,314	14,903	19,542	26,614	23,911	0.11	-10.16
THAILAND	2,614	3,259	4,070	3,571	4,560	0.02	27.70
AUSTRALASIA	**12,535**	**14,201**	**17,432**	**20,529**	**21,474**	**0.10**	**4.60**
AUSTRALIA	9,960	11,744	14,608	16,672	16,961	0.08	1.73
NEW ZEALAND	2,575	2,457	2,824	3,857	4,513	0.02	17.01
MELANESIA	**69**	**310**	**125**	**124**	**323**		**160.48**
SOLOMON IS	1	240	2		14		
FIJI	14	19	25	46	51		10.87
NEW CALEDNIA	10	7	38	1			
VANUATU	44	43	58	74	250		237.84
NORFOLK IS		1	2				
PAPUA N.GUIN				3	8		166.67
MICRONESIA	**614**	**778**	**408**	**900**	**5,021**	**0.02**	**457.89**
KIRIBATI	21	24	87	46	14		-69.57
GUAM		83	22	6			
NAURU	2		1	1			
MICRONESIA				2	7		250.00
MARSHALL IS	591	671	298	844	4,998	0.02	492.18
PALAU				1	2		100.00
POLYNESIA	**100**	**182**	**143**	**99**	**150**		**51.52**
TONGA	5	4	2	1	21		2.000.00
TUVALU	95	178	141	98	129		31.63
EUROPE	**16,780,247**	**19,269,425**	**19,703,592**	**21,097,264**	**20,239,128**	**89.87**	**-4.07**
C/E EUROPE	**14,208,436**	**16,596,210**	**17,140,365**	**18,366,351**	**17,336,497**	**76.98**	**-5.61**
AZERBAIJAN	930,518	1,074,100	842,439	844,318	825,974	3.67	-2.17
ARMENIA	185,778	234,900	316,504	309,049	331,922	1.47	7.40
BULGARIA	32,632	40,100	24,017	28,997	31,718	0.14	9.38
BELARUS	190,012	243,700	188,856	197,492	148,979	0.66	-24.56
CZECH REP	19,365	25,119	26,149	28,140	30,212	0.13	7.36

RUSSIAN FEDERATION

2. ARRIVALS OF NON-RESIDENT VISITORS AT NATIONAL BORDERS, BY NATIONALITY

	1999	2000	2001	2002	2003	Market share 03	% change 03-02
ESTONIA	463,925	418,400	358,680	386,537	406,004	1.80	5.04
GEORGIA	1,044,447	948,000	974,569	988,203	737,936	3.28	-25.33
HUNGARY	12,884	12,294	11,836	15,602	17,059	0.08	9.34
KAZAKHSTAN	358,826	2,189,400	2,539,454	2,955,993	2,674,895	11.88	-9.51
KYRGYZSTAN	64,959	164,000	222,678	307,700	271,956	1.21	-11.62
LATVIA	259,838	329,900	245,277	292,629	344,971	1.53	17.89
LITHUANIA	980,382	1,048,800	1,058,692	950,567	873,814	3.88	-8.07
REP MOLDOVA	493,720	599,900	657,716	694,985	751,598	3.34	8.15
POLAND	958,740	947,900	884,580	1,209,790	1,232,942	5.47	1.91
ROMANIA	7,782	7,731	7,612	14,097	12,474	0.06	-11.51
SLOVAKIA	5,848	6,966	8,417	13,032	14,687	0.07	12.70
TAJIKISTAN	156,134	314,100	332,237	358,452	366,927	1.63	2.36
TURKMENISTAN	61,633	109,900	18,719	33,973	22,249	0.10	-34.51
UKRAINE	7,757,131	7,391,700	7,924,812	8,229,840	7,686,224	34.13	-6.61
UZBEKISTAN	223,882	489,300	497,121	506,955	553,956	2.46	9.27
NORTHERN EUR	**1,655,478**	**1,694,972**	**1,546,523**	**1,454,068**	**1,486,943**	**6.60**	**2.26**
DENMARK	30,387	24,679	26,183	30,105	33,388	0.15	10.91
FAEROE IS	5	136	70	41	59		43.90
FINLAND	1,406,659	1,453,500	1,290,660	1,161,233	1,154,129	5.12	-0.61
ICELAND	894	1,328	1,423	2,072	1,906	0.01	-8.01
IRELAND	5,748	5,147	6,073	11,960	12,093	0.05	1.11
NORWAY	37,503	44,600	39,946	43,621	45,254	0.20	3.74
SWEDEN	53,075	47,482	43,434	55,652	63,347	0.28	13.83
UK	121,207	118,100	138,734	149,384	176,767	0.78	18.33
SOUTHERN EUR	**178,528**	**202,711**	**200,109**	**287,889**	**309,771**	**1.38**	**7.60**
ALBANIA	611	958	868	1,210	914		-24.46
ANDORRA	54	208	86	88	134		52.27
BOSNIA HERZG	1,304	1,873	1,395	3,900	5,007	0.02	28.38
CROATIA	3,702	4,695	2,986	7,510	8,798	0.04	17.15
GREECE	21,422	26,948	20,708	25,829	29,262	0.13	13.29
HOLY SEE	18	20	30	15	11		-26.67
ITALY	83,688	105,300	110,817	154,319	169,730	0.75	9.99
MALTA	21,424	25,390	16,652	21,254	21,395	0.09	0.66
PORTUGAL	4,621	5,677	6,681	7,107	10,523	0.05	48.07
SAN MARINO	47	36	127	82	256		212.20
SLOVENIA	4,567	4,865	6,894	8,018	8,109	0.04	1.13
SPAIN	20,021	26,741	32,865	58,557	52,205	0.23	-10.85
TFYROM	847				2,307	0.01	
SERBIA,MTNEG	16,202				1,120		
WESTERN EUR	**576,970**	**606,869**	**651,600**	**792,573**	**887,910**	**3.94**	**12.03**
AUSTRIA	30,623	29,939	30,769	37,869	46,968	0.21	24.03
BELGIUM	17,763	15,904	19,127	22,468	26,102	0.12	16.17
FRANCE	94,700	95,400	107,461	146,604	189,145	0.84	29.02
GERMANY	361,392	363,200	414,979	493,267	516,217	2.29	4.65
LIECHTENSTEN	83	84	121	103	142		37.86
LUXEMBOURG	648	2,390	1,654	2,712	3,258	0.01	20.13
MONACO	57	52	129	80	244		205.00
NETHERLANDS	44,692	52,400	50,997	63,975	68,264	0.30	6.70
SWITZERLAND	27,012	47,500	26,363	25,495	37,570	0.17	47.36
EAST/MED EUR	**160,835**	**168,663**	**164,995**	**196,383**	**218,007**	**0.97**	**11.01**
CYPRUS	20,515	28,763	18,138	19,325	18,151	0.08	-6.08
ISRAEL	37,742	36,500	47,447	58,358	60,111	0.27	3.00
TURKEY	102,578	103,400	99,410	118,700	139,745	0.62	17.73

2. ARRIVALS OF NON-RESIDENT VISITORS AT NATIONAL BORDERS, BY NATIONALITY

	1999	2000	2001	2002	2003	Market share 03	% change 03-02
MIDDLE EAST	**28,290**	**32,983**	**24,341**	**28,312**	**31,792**	**0.14**	**12.29**
MIDDLE EAST	**28,290**	**32,983**	**24,341**	**28,312**	**31,792**	**0.14**	**12.29**
BAHRAIN	66	72	108	136	99		-27.21
PALESTINE	549	682	387	388	384		-1.03
IRAQ	1,090	1,099	1,500	2,258	857		-62.05
JORDAN	2,077	2,465	1,863	2,675	3,147	0.01	17.64
KUWAIT	330	587	268	413	400		-3.15
LEBANON	4,361	4,587	3,392	3,532	4,138	0.02	17.16
LIBYA	790	543	591	705	697		-1.13
OMAN	111	152	225	278	318		14.39
QATAR	80	46	141	98	621		533.67
SAUDI ARABIA	516	383	416	844	1,220	0.01	44.55
SYRIA	11,034	9,663	9,080	8,773	9,950	0.04	13.42
UNTD ARAB EM	817	4,635	763	1,771	2,396	0.01	35.29
EGYPT	5,737	7,566	4,652	5,317	6,848	0.03	28.79
YEMEN	732	503	955	1,124	717		-36.21
SOUTH ASIA	**43,137**	**44,970**	**48,236**	**57,708**	**58,804**	**0.26**	**1.90**
SOUTH ASIA	**43,137**	**44,970**	**48,236**	**57,708**	**58,804**	**0.26**	**1.90**
AFGHANISTAN	2,644	4,038	2,377	3,101	4,548	0.02	46.66
BANGLADESH	3,277	2,232	2,193	2,104	1,154	0.01	-45.15
BHUTAN	15	1	3	1			
SRI LANKA	3,128	2,896	1,466	1,664	1,541	0.01	-7.39
INDIA	23,372	23,476	27,576	33,546	32,954	0.15	-1.76
IRAN	7,125	8,274	11,244	13,481	13,983	0.06	3.72
MALDIVES	91	142	143	119	165		38.66
NEPAL	589	645	743	662	773		16.77
PAKISTAN	2,896	3,266	2,491	3,030	3,686	0.02	21.65
REG.NOT SPEC	**936,574**	**651,616**	**586,260**	**588,190**	**634,878**	**2.82**	**7.94**
NOT SPECIFIE	**936,574**	**651,616**	**586,260**	**588,190**	**634,878**	**2.82**	**7.94**
OTH.WORLD	936,574	651,616	586,260	588,190	634,878	2.82	7.94

Source: World Tourism Organization (WTO)

RWANDA

1. ARRIVALS OF NON-RESIDENT TOURISTS AT NATIONAL BORDERS, BY COUNTRY OF RESIDENCE

	1999	2000	2001	2002	2003	Market share 03	% change 03-02
TOTAL (*)		**104,216**	**113,185**				
AFRICA		**93,058**	**99,928**				
EAST AFRICA		**80,710**	**69,242**				
BURUNDI		20,972	9,455				
COMOROS		3	6				
ETHIOPIA		224					
ERITREA		30	55				
DJIBOUTI		2	8				
KENYA		2,050	2,243				
MADAGASCAR		37	43				
MALAWI		14	64				
MAURITIUS		33	52				
MOZAMBIQUE		2	8				
SEYCHELLES		5	26				
SOMALIA		20	29				
ZIMBABWE		24	38				
UGANDA		38,897	38,472				
TANZANIA		18,320	18,697				
ZAMBIA		77	46				
CENTRAL AFR		**10,739**	**28,846**				
ANGOLA		14	7				
CAMEROON		223	228				
CENT.AFR.REP		16	12				
CHAD		13	27				
CONGO		3	11				
DEM.R.CONGO		10,450	28,514				
EQ.GUINEA			36				
GABON		20	11				
NORTH AFRICA		**117**	**121**				
ALGERIA		14	15				
MOROCCO		21	17				
SUDAN		51	53				
TUNISIA		31	36				
SOUTHERN AFR		**452**	**661**				
BOTSWANA		5	5				
LESOTHO		5	1				
NAMIBIA		10	3				
SOUTH AFRICA		431	645				
SWAZILAND		1	7				
WEST AFRICA		**1,040**	**1,058**				
BENIN		40	60				
GAMBIA		33	16				
GHANA		89	117				
GUINEA		41	38				
COTE IVOIRE		87	88				
LIBERIA		21	41				
MALI		122	166				
MAURITANIA		45	55				
NIGER		27	37				
NIGERIA		71	126				
ST.HELENA			30				

RWANDA

1. ARRIVALS OF NON-RESIDENT TOURISTS AT NATIONAL BORDERS, BY COUNTRY OF RESIDENCE

	1999	2000	2001	2002	2003	Market share 03	% change 03-02
SENEGAL		164	157				
SIERRA LEONE		12	24				
TOGO		43	35				
BURKINA FASO		245	68				
AMERICAS		**2,250**	**2,785**				
CARIBBEAN		**13**	**29**				
BARBADOS		3					
HAITI		7					
JAMAICA		3	29				
CENTRAL AMER		**9**	**9**				
COSTA RICA		1	3				
GUATEMALA		1					
NICARAGUA		5	3				
PANAMA		2	3				
NORTH AMER		**2,192**	**2,732**				
CANADA		601	827				
GREENLAND		1					
MEXICO		4	1				
USA		1,586	1,904				
SOUTH AMER		**36**	**15**				
ARGENTINA		7	5				
BRAZIL		10	6				
CHILE		2					
COLOMBIA		9					
GUYANA		1					
PERU		1					
URUGUAY		1					
VENEZUELA		4	4				
OTH SOUTH AM		1					
EAST AS/PACI		**751**	**699**				
N/EAST ASIA		**508**	**459**				
CHINA		354	310				
TAIWAN(P.C.)		10					
JAPAN		105	101				
KOREA REP.		39	48				
S/EAST ASIA		**34**	**18**				
INDONESIA		3	6				
MALAYSIA		5					
PHILIPPINES		21	12				
VIET NAM		1					
THAILAND		4					
AUSTRALASIA		**208**	**220**				
AUSTRALIA		142	170				
NEW ZEALAND		66	50				
MELANESIA		**1**	**2**				
FIJI		1	2				

RWANDA

1. ARRIVALS OF NON-RESIDENT TOURISTS AT NATIONAL BORDERS, BY COUNTRY OF RESIDENCE

	1999	2000	2001	2002	2003	Market share 03	% change 03-02
EUROPE		**6,412**	**8,395**				
C/E EUROPE		**257**	**400**				
ARMENIA			1				
BULGARIA		18	35				
BELARUS		1					
CZECH REP		1					
ESTONIA		1					
HUNGARY		5					
KAZAKHSTAN		4	9				
REP MOLDOVA		14					
POLAND		73	88				
ROMANIA		7	6				
RUSSIAN FED		111	217				
UKRAINE		22	44				
NORTHERN EUR		**1,215**	**2,178**				
DENMARK		64	121				
FINLAND		11	10				
NORWAY		119	135				
SWEDEN		169	157				
UK		150	1,536				
OTH NORT EUR		702	219				
SOUTHERN EUR		**727**	**768**				
BOSNIA HERZG		3					
CROATIA		27	33				
HOLY SEE		2	1				
ITALY		485	521				
PORTUGAL		25	38				
SLOVENIA		4					
SPAIN		168	172				
SERBIA,MTNEG		13	3				
WESTERN EUR		**4,147**	**4,974**				
AUSTRIA		61	47				
BELGIUM		1,866	2,057				
FRANCE		848	1,064				
GERMANY		853	895				
LUXEMBOURG		15	11				
NETHERLANDS		218	533				
SWITZERLAND		286	367				
EAST/MED EUR		**66**	**75**				
ISRAEL		65	74				
TURKEY		1	1				
MIDDLE EAST		**504**	**333**				
MIDDLE EAST		**504**	**333**				
JORDAN			14				
KUWAIT			5				
LEBANON		58	41				
LIBYA		49	32				
OMAN		307	166				
SAUDI ARABIA			5				
SYRIA		4					

RWANDA

1. ARRIVALS OF NON-RESIDENT TOURISTS AT NATIONAL BORDERS, BY COUNTRY OF RESIDENCE

	1999	2000	2001	2002	2003	Market share 03	% change 03-02
UNTD ARAB EM			1				
EGYPT		86	69				
SOUTH ASIA		**1,241**	**1,045**				
SOUTH ASIA		**1,241**	**1,045**				
BANGLADESH		22					
SRI LANKA		29	14				
INDIA		1,021	948				
IRAN		13	4				
NEPAL		18					
PAKISTAN		138	79				

Source: World Tourism Organization (WTO)

SABA

1. ARRIVALS OF NON-RESIDENT TOURISTS AT NATIONAL BORDERS, BY COUNTRY OF RESIDENCE

	1999	2000	2001	2002	2003	Market share 03	% change 03-02
TOTAL	**9,252**	**9,120**	**9,005**				
AMERICAS	**7,022**	**6,695**	**7,036**				
CARIBBEAN	**2,898**	**2,618**	**3,183**				
DOMINICAN RP	100		88				
NETH.ANTILES	2,798	2,618	2,658				
OTH CARIBBE			437				
NORTH AMER	**4,124**	**4,077**	**3,853**				
CANADA	243	337	401				
USA	3,881	3,740	3,452				
EUROPE	**850**	**848**	**1,354**				
NORTHERN EUR	**366**	**414**	**431**				
UK	366	414	353				
SCANDINAVIA			78				
SOUTHERN EUR			**35**				
ITALY			35				
WESTERN EUR	**484**	**434**	**888**				
FRANCE	484	434	453				
GERMANY			435				
REG.NOT SPEC	**1,380**	**1,577**	**615**				
NOT SPECIFIE	**1,380**	**1,577**	**615**				
OTH.WORLD	1,380	1,577	615				

Source: World Tourism Organization (WTO)

2. ARRIVALS OF NON-RESIDENT VISITORS AT NATIONAL BORDERS, BY COUNTRY OF RESIDENCE

	1999	2000	2001	2002	2003	Market share 03	% change 03-02
TOTAL	**24,276**	**24,407**					
AMERICAS	**12,170**	**10,378**					
CARIBBEAN	**2,916**	**1,337**					
DOMINICAN RP	118						
NETH.ANTILES	2,798						
ALL CO CARIB		1,337					
NORTH AMER	**9,254**	**9,041**					
CANADA	699	845					
USA	8,555	8,196					
EUROPE	**6,938**	**7,837**					
NORTHERN EUR	**1,045**	**1,136**					
UK	1,045	1,059					
OTH NORT EUR		77					
WESTERN EUR	**5,893**	**6,701**					
FRANCE	2,353	2,505					
OTH WEST EUR	3,540	4,196					
REG.NOT SPEC	**5,168**	**6,192**					
NOT SPECIFIE	**5,168**	**6,192**					
OTH.WORLD	5,168	6,192					

Source: World Tourism Organization (WTO)

SAINT EUSTATIUS

1. ARRIVALS OF NON-RESIDENT TOURISTS AT NATIONAL BORDERS, BY COUNTRY OF RESIDENCE

	1999	2000	2001	2002	2003	Market share 03	% change 03-02
TOTAL (*)	**9,176**	**9,072**	**9,690**	**9,781**	**10,466**	**100.00**	**7.00**
AMERICAS	**2,888**	**3,393**	**3,532**	**3,403**	**3,483**	**33.28**	**2.35**
CARIBBEAN	**537**	**577**	**459**	**417**	**391**	**3.74**	**-6.24**
DOMINICAN RP	537	577	459	417	391	3.74	-6.24
NORTH AMER	**1,951**	**2,256**	**2,530**	**2,563**	**2,562**	**24.48**	**-0.04**
CANADA	171	155	198	192	184	1.76	-4.17
USA	1,780	2,101	2,332	2,371	2,378	22.72	0.30
SOUTH AMER	**131**	**193**	**216**	**145**	**198**	**1.89**	**36.55**
GUYANA	131	193	216	145	198	1.89	36.55
OTHER AMERIC	**269**	**367**	**327**	**278**	**332**	**3.17**	**19.42**
OTH AMERICA	269	367	327	278	332	3.17	19.42
EUROPE	**4,293**	**3,988**	**4,529**	**4,600**	**5,287**	**50.52**	**14.93**
WESTERN EUR	**3,061**	**2,903**	**3,269**	**3,394**	**4,015**	**38.36**	**18.30**
GERMANY	122	225	132	89	85	0.81	-4.49
NETHERLANDS	2,939	2,678	3,137	3,305	3,930	37.55	18.91
OTHER EUROPE	**1,232**	**1,085**	**1,260**	**1,206**	**1,272**	**12.15**	**5.47**
OTHER EUROPE	1,232	1,085	1,260	1,206	1,272	12.15	5.47
REG.NOT SPEC	**1,995**	**1,691**	**1,629**	**1,778**	**1,696**	**16.20**	**-4.61**
NOT SPECIFIE	**1,995**	**1,691**	**1,629**	**1,778**	**1,696**	**16.20**	**-4.61**
OTH.WORLD	1,995	1,691	1,629	1,778	1,696	16.20	-4.61

Source: World Tourism Organization (WTO)

SAINT EUSTATIUS

2. ARRIVALS OF NON-RESIDENT VISITORS AT NATIONAL BORDERS, BY COUNTRY OF RESIDENCE

		1999	2000	2001	2002	2003	Market share 03	% change 03-02
TOTAL	(*)	**19,065**	**19,066**	**19,595**				
AMERICAS		**13,835**	**13,941**	**14,081**				
CARIBBEAN		**9,889**	**10,136**	**9,998**				
NETH.ANTILES	(*)	9,889	10,136	9,998				
NORTH AMER		**1,951**	**2,256**	**2,432**				
CANADA		171	155	195				
USA		1,780	2,101	2,237				
OTHER AMERIC		**1,995**	**1,549**	**1,651**				
OTH AMERICA		1,995	1,549	1,651				
EUROPE		**4,293**	**3,988**	**4,499**				
WESTERN EUR		**3,061**	**2,903**	**3,252**				
GERMANY		122	225	140				
NETHERLANDS		2,939	2,678	3,112				
OTHER EUROPE		**1,232**	**1,085**	**1,247**				
OTHER EUROPE		1,232	1,085	1,247				
REG.NOT SPEC		**937**	**1,137**	**1,015**				
NOT SPECIFIE		**937**	**1,137**	**1,015**				
OTH.WORLD		937	1,137	1,015				

Source: World Tourism Organization (WTO)

SAINT KITTS AND NEVIS

1. ARRIVALS OF NON-RESIDENT TOURISTS AT NATIONAL BORDERS, BY COUNTRY OF RESIDENCE

	1999	2000	2001	2002	2003	Market share 03	% change 03-02
TOTAL (*)	**84,002**	**73,149**	**70,565**	**67,531**			
AMERICAS	**67,684**	**45,407**	**59,285**	**60,023**			
CARIBBEAN	**26,296**	**28,513**	**28,490**	**28,146**			
ANTIGUA,BARB	3,616						
BAHAMAS	54						
BARBADOS	1,468						
BERMUDA	443						
BR.VIRGIN IS	2,009						
CAYMAN IS	100						
DOMINICA	375						
DOMINICAN RP	215						
GRENADA	156						
GUADELOUPE	49						
HAITI	7						
JAMAICA	769						
MARTINIQUE	13						
MONTSERRAT	533						
ARUBA	10						
CURACAO	45						
PUERTO RICO	1,499						
ANGUILLA	2,094						
ST.LUCIA	263						
SAINT MAARTE	2,882						
ST.VINCENT,G	815						
TRINIDAD TBG	1,322						
TURKS,CAICOS	28						
US.VIRGIN IS	6,199						
OTH CARIBBE	1,332						
ALL CO CARIB		28,513	28,490	28,146			
CENTRAL AMER	**16**						
BELIZE	16						
NORTH AMER	**40,652**		**30,795**	**31,877**			
CANADA	5,880		5,237	4,352			
MEXICO	56						
USA	34,716		25,558	27,525			
SOUTH AMER	**720**						
ARGENTINA	17						
BRAZIL	17						
COLOMBIA	37						
GUYANA	614						
SURINAME	10						
VENEZUELA	25						
OTHER AMERIC		**16,894**					
OTH AMERICA		16,894					
EAST AS/PACI	**114**						
N/EAST ASIA	**114**						
JAPAN	114						

SAINT KITTS AND NEVIS

1. ARRIVALS OF NON-RESIDENT TOURISTS AT NATIONAL BORDERS, BY COUNTRY OF RESIDENCE

	1999	2000	2001	2002	2003	Market share 03	% change 03-02
EUROPE	**15,759**	**15,155**	**8,726**	**5,464**			
NORTHERN EUR	**13,314**		**8,726**	**5,464**			
DENMARK	15						
IRELAND	42						
NORWAY	46						
SWEDEN	48						
UK	13,163		8,726	5,464			
SOUTHERN EUR	**196**						
GREECE	4						
ITALY	138						
PORTUGAL	8						
SPAIN	46						
WESTERN EUR	**1,661**						
AUSTRIA	38						
BELGIUM	65						
FRANCE	511						
GERMANY	854						
NETHERLANDS	73						
SWITZERLAND	120						
OTHER EUROPE	**588**	**15,155**					
OTHER EUROPE	588						
ALL EUROPE		15,155					
REG.NOT SPEC	**445**	**12,587**	**2,554**	**2,044**			
NOT SPECIFIE	**445**	**12,587**	**2,554**	**2,044**			
OTH.WORLD	445	12,587	2,554	2,044			

Source: World Tourism Organization (WTO)

SAINT LUCIA

1. ARRIVALS OF NON-RESIDENT TOURISTS AT NATIONAL BORDERS, BY COUNTRY OF RESIDENCE

	1999	2000	2001	2002	2003	Market share 03	% change 03-02
TOTAL (*)	**263,793**	**269,850**	**250,132**	**253,463**	**276,948**	**100.00**	**9.27**
AMERICAS	**162,010**	**168,150**	**165,239**	**175,390**	**183,349**	**66.20**	**4.54**
CARIBBEAN	**61,148**	**52,271**	**58,549**	**66,409**	**67,540**	**24.39**	**1.70**
ANTIGUA,BARB	1,510	1,194	1,531	3,217	3,783	1.37	17.59
BARBADOS	9,483	9,995	10,681	16,973	16,156	5.83	-4.81
DOMINICA	2,972	2,811	2,734	3,685	4,048	1.46	9.85
DOMINICAN RP	58	50	184	134	135	0.05	0.75
GRENADA	1,658	1,882	1,527	2,401	3,421	1.24	42.48
HAITI	109	95	128	134	188	0.07	40.30
JAMAICA	2,229	2,729	2,028	3,563	4,049	1.46	13.64
NETH.ANTILES	579	659	638	775	661	0.24	-14.71
PUERTO RICO	780	579	981	807	952	0.34	17.97
ST.KITTS NEV	451	471	638	1,158	1,066	0.38	-7.94
ST.VINCENT,G	2,593	2,444	2,668	4,289	4,932	1.78	14.99
TRINIDAD TBG	7,786	8,550	8,307	11,040	11,410	4.12	3.35
US.VIRGIN IS	2,408	801	1,083	1,618	1,490	0.54	-7.91
OTH CARIBBE	28,532	20,011	25,421	16,615	15,249	5.51	-8.22
NORTH AMER	**96,734**	**112,500**	**103,502**	**106,971**	**111,572**	**40.29**	**4.30**
CANADA	13,159	14,968	12,254	12,927	13,494	4.87	4.39
USA	83,575	97,532	91,248	94,044	98,078	35.41	4.29
SOUTH AMER	**3,210**	**2,324**	**1,974**	**900**	**3,003**	**1.08**	**233.67**
GUYANA	3,210	2,324	1,974	900	3,003	1.08	233.67
OTHER AMERIC	**918**	**1,055**	**1,214**	**1,110**	**1,234**	**0.45**	**11.17**
OTH AMERICA	918	1,055	1,214	1,110	1,234	0.45	11.17
EAST AS/PACI	**237**	**503**	**205**	**278**	**373**	**0.13**	**34.17**
N/EAST ASIA	**237**	**503**	**205**	**278**	**373**	**0.13**	**34.17**
JAPAN	237	503	205	278	373	0.13	34.17
EUROPE	**98,555**	**98,869**	**82,672**	**76,199**	**90,193**	**32.57**	**18.37**
NORTHERN EUR	**71,340**	**73,433**	**67,046**	**63,702**	**75,820**	**27.38**	**19.02**
SWEDEN	232			425	394	0.14	-7.29
UK	71,108	73,433	67,046	63,277	75,426	27.23	19.20
SOUTHERN EUR	**1,119**	**818**	**760**	**910**	**884**	**0.32**	**-2.86**
ITALY	1,068	818	760	698	697	0.25	-0.14
SPAIN	51			212	187	0.07	-11.79
WESTERN EUR	**22,667**	**20,680**	**11,511**	**9,042**	**11,188**	**4.04**	**23.73**
AUSTRIA	1,018	1,121	539	402	431	0.16	7.21
BELGIUM				225	194	0.07	-13.78
FRANCE	12,390	10,992	5,091	3,405	6,017	2.17	76.71
GERMANY	7,968	7,292	4,818	3,929	3,582	1.29	-8.83
NETHERLANDS	322	412	348	337	398	0.14	18.10
SWITZERLAND	969	863	715	744	566	0.20	-23.92
OTHER EUROPE	**3,429**	**3,938**	**3,355**	**2,545**	**2,301**	**0.83**	**-9.59**
OTHER EUROPE	3,429	3,938	3,355	2,545	2,301	0.83	-9.59

SAINT LUCIA

1. ARRIVALS OF NON-RESIDENT TOURISTS AT NATIONAL BORDERS, BY COUNTRY OF RESIDENCE

	1999	2000	2001	2002	2003	Market share 03	% change 03-02
REG.NOT SPEC	**2,991**	**2,328**	**2,016**	**1,596**	**3,033**	**1.10**	**90.04**
NOT SPECIFIE	**2,991**	**2,328**	**2,016**	**1,596**	**3,033**	**1.10**	**90.04**
OTH.WORLD	2,991	2,328	2,016	1,596	3,033	1.10	90.04

Source: World Tourism Organization (WTO)

SAINT MAARTEN

1. ARRIVALS OF NON-RESIDENT TOURISTS AT NATIONAL BORDERS, BY NATIONALITY

	1999	2000	2001	2002	2003	Market share 03	% change 03-02
TOTAL (*)	**444,812**	**432,292**	**402,649**	**380,801**	**427,587**	**100.00**	**12.29**
AMERICAS	**281,213**	**271,753**	**269,613**	**259,506**	**301,018**	**70.40**	**16.00**
CARIBBEAN	**28,380**	**31,260**	**31,652**	**33,371**	**39,913**	**9.33**	**19.60**
ANTIGUA,BARB	2,976	3,065	3,512	6,072			
DOMINICAN RP	4,558	4,366	4,733	3,504			
HAITI	3,136	3,765	4,063	2,946			
ST.KITTS NEV	6,798	7,839	7,330	8,325			
TRINIDAD TBG	1,807	1,956	1,898	2,061			
OTH CARIBBE	9,105	10,269	10,116	10,463			
ALL CO CARIB					39,913	9.33	
NORTH AMER	**228,313**	**216,256**	**217,991**	**215,368**	**251,792**	**58.89**	**16.91**
CANADA	29,694	28,470	25,093	23,460	29,545	6.91	25.94
USA	198,619	187,786	192,898	191,908	222,247	51.98	15.81
SOUTH AMER	**24,520**	**24,237**	**19,970**	**10,767**	**2,485**	**0.58**	**-76.92**
ARGENTINA	11,654	10,413	6,848	931			
BRAZIL	1,776	1,082	1,048	697			
CHILE	271	349	156	152			
VENEZUELA	5,886	6,891	5,148	3,447	2,485	0.58	-27.91
OTH SOUTH AM	4,933	5,502	6,770	5,540			
OTHER AMERIC					**6,828**	**1.60**	
OTH AMERICA					6,828	1.60	
EUROPE	**125,828**	**121,819**	**97,449**	**87,147**	**88,259**	**20.64**	**1.28**
C/E EUROPE	**271**	**247**	**284**	**215**			
RUSSIAN FED	271	247	284	215			
SOUTHERN EUR	**7,661**	**6,828**	**5,355**	**4,178**	**4,842**	**1.13**	**15.89**
ITALY	7,661	6,828	5,355	4,178	4,842	1.13	15.89
WESTERN EUR	**99,827**	**96,631**	**75,161**	**71,644**	**71,719**	**16.77**	**0.10**
FRANCE (*)	86,193	89,803	69,806	62,457	58,801	13.75	-5.85
NETHERLANDS	13,634	6,828	5,355	9,187	12,918	3.02	40.61
OTHER EUROPE	**18,069**	**18,113**	**16,649**	**11,110**	**11,698**	**2.74**	**5.29**
OTHER EUROPE	18,069	18,113	16,649	11,110	11,698	2.74	5.29
REG.NOT SPEC	**37,771**	**38,720**	**35,587**	**34,148**	**38,310**	**8.96**	**12.19**
NOT SPECIFIE	**37,771**	**38,720**	**35,587**	**34,148**	**38,310**	**8.96**	**12.19**
OTH.WORLD	22,281	23,485	21,001	20,673	38,310	8.96	85.31
N RESID ABRO	15,490	15,235	14,586	13,475			

Source: World Tourism Organization (WTO)

SAINT VINCENT AND THE GRENADINES

1. ARRIVALS OF NON-RESIDENT TOURISTS AT NATIONAL BORDERS, BY COUNTRY OF RESIDENCE

	1999	2000	2001	2002	2003	Market share 03	% change 03-02
TOTAL (*)	**68,293**	**72,895**	**70,686**	**77,631**	**78,535**	**100.00**	**1.16**
AMERICAS	**46,980**		**50,572**	**58,465**	**61,314**	**78.07**	**4.87**
CARIBBEAN	**22,543**		**26,428**	**30,229**	**33,775**	**43.01**	**11.73**
ANTIGUA,BARB	725		878	988	1,109	1.41	12.25
BARBADOS	6,815		8,326	10,217	9,906	12.61	-3.04
GRENADA	1,484		2,553	2,001	2,667	3.40	33.28
NETH.ANTILES	294		196	312	518	0.66	66.03
ST.LUCIA	2,325		2,213	2,127	3,862	4.92	81.57
TRINIDAD TBG	5,215		7,520	8,975	9,654	12.29	7.57
OTH CARIBBE	5,685		4,742	5,609	6,059	7.72	8.02
NORTH AMER	**23,665**		**23,290**	**27,680**	**27,112**	**34.52**	**-2.05**
CANADA	4,509		3,929	5,268	4,918	6.26	-6.64
USA	19,156		19,361	22,412	22,194	28.26	-0.97
OTHER AMERIC	**772**		**854**	**556**	**427**	**0.54**	**-23.20**
OTH AMERICA	772		854	556	427	0.54	-23.20
EUROPE	**20,264**		**18,850**	**17,997**	**17,202**	**21.90**	**-4.42**
NORTHERN EUR	**12,380**		**11,833**	**12,432**	**12,193**	**15.53**	**-1.92**
IRELAND			278	299	216	0.28	-27.76
NORWAY			210	170	96	0.12	-43.53
SWEDEN	479		501	332	334	0.43	0.60
UK	11,901		10,844	11,631	11,547	14.70	-0.72
SOUTHERN EUR	**1,777**		**1,457**	**1,204**	**1,192**	**1.52**	**-1.00**
ITALY	1,640		1,227	985	1,030	1.31	4.57
SPAIN	137		230	219	162	0.21	-26.03
WESTERN EUR	**5,350**		**5,025**	**3,917**	**3,311**	**4.22**	**-15.47**
BELGIUM			188	217	151	0.19	-30.41
FRANCE	2,568		2,432	2,142	1,750	2.23	-18.30
GERMANY	1,912		1,426	894	815	1.04	-8.84
NETHERLANDS	344		423	243	127	0.16	-47.74
SWITZERLAND	526		556	421	468	0.60	11.16
OTHER EUROPE	**757**		**535**	**444**	**506**	**0.64**	**13.96**
OTHER EUROPE	757		535	444	506	0.64	13.96
REG.NOT SPEC	**1,049**	**72,895**	**1,264**	**1,169**	**19**	**0.02**	**-98.37**
NOT SPECIFIE	**1,049**	**72,895**	**1,264**	**1,169**	**19**	**0.02**	**-98.37**
OTH.WORLD	1,049	72,895	1,264	1,169	19	0.02	-98.37

Source: World Tourism Organization (WTO)

2. ARRIVALS OF NON-RESIDENT VISITORS AT NATIONAL BORDERS, BY COUNTRY OF RESIDENCE

	1999	2000	2001	2002	2003	Market share 03	% change 03-02
TOTAL (*)	**85,761**	**94,030**	**85,735**	**90,693**	**92,231**	**100.00**	**1.70**
AMERICAS	**51,412**		**55,447**	**64,125**	**64,863**	**70.33**	**1.15**
CARIBBEAN	**25,486**		**29,042**	**33,989**	**35,747**	**38.76**	**5.17**
ANTIGUA,BARB			933	1,101	1,180	1.28	7.18
BARBADOS			9,107	11,595	10,228	11.09	-11.79
GRENADA			2,983	2,610	3,226	3.50	23.60
NETH.ANTILES			202	321	590	0.64	83.80
ST.LUCIA			2,657	2,558	3,583	3.88	40.07
TRINIDAD TBG			8,107	9,785	10,440	11.32	6.69
OTH CARIBBE			5,053	6,019	6,500	7.05	7.99
ALL CO CARIB	25,486						
NORTH AMER	**25,122**		**25,497**	**29,545**	**28,648**	**31.06**	**-3.04**
CANADA	4,789		4,367	5,642	5,189	5.63	-8.03
USA	20,333		21,130	23,903	23,459	25.44	-1.86
OTHER AMERIC	**804**		**908**	**591**	**468**	**0.51**	**-20.81**
OTH AMERICA	804		908	591	468	0.51	-20.81
EUROPE	**33,121**		**28,929**	**25,271**	**25,241**	**27.37**	**-0.12**
NORTHERN EUR	**20,936**		**18,750**	**17,466**	**18,401**	**19.95**	**5.35**
IRELAND			440	424	319	0.35	-24.76
NORWAY			255	213	111	0.12	-47.89
SWEDEN	582		584	389	379	0.41	-2.57
UK	20,354		17,471	16,440	17,592	19.07	7.01
SOUTHERN EUR	**2,207**		**1,827**	**1,473**	**1,383**	**1.50**	**-6.11**
ITALY	2,207		1,578	1,220	1,211	1.31	-0.74
SPAIN			249	253	172	0.19	-32.02
WESTERN EUR	**8,390**		**7,622**	**5,726**	**4,781**	**5.18**	**-16.50**
BELGIUM			245	284	166	0.18	-41.55
FRANCE	4,520		4,193	3,371	2,654	2.88	-21.27
GERMANY	3,105		1,992	1,251	1,236	1.34	-1.20
NETHERLANDS			476	297	167	0.18	-43.77
SWITZERLAND	765		716	523	558	0.61	6.69
OTHER EUROPE	**1,588**		**730**	**606**	**676**	**0.73**	**11.55**
OTHER EUROPE	1,588		730	606	676	0.73	11.55
REG.NOT SPEC	**1,228**	**94,030**	**1,359**	**1,297**	**2,127**	**2.31**	**63.99**
NOT SPECIFIE	**1,228**	**94,030**	**1,359**	**1,297**	**2,127**	**2.31**	**63.99**
OTH.WORLD	1,228	94,030	1,359	1,297	2,127	2.31	63.99

Source: World Tourism Organization (WTO)

SAMOA

1. ARRIVALS OF NON-RESIDENT TOURISTS AT NATIONAL BORDERS, BY COUNTRY OF RESIDENCE

	1999	2000	2001	2002	2003	Market share 03	% change 03-02
TOTAL	85,124	87,688	88,263	88,960	92,313	100.00	3.77
AMERICAS	**8,252**	**9,422**	**8,837**	**9,095**	**8,951**	**9.70**	**-1.58**
NORTH AMER	**8,252**	**9,422**	**8,837**	**9,095**	**8,951**	**9.70**	**-1.58**
CANADA	320	390	370	375	406	0.44	8.27
USA	7,932	9,032	8,467	8,720	8,545	9.26	-2.01
EAST AS/PACI	**70,603**	**71,314**	**73,403**	**74,822**	**77,990**	**84.48**	**4.23**
N/EAST ASIA	**812**	**713**	**718**	**577**	**683**	**0.74**	**18.37**
JAPAN	812	713	718	577	683	0.74	18.37
AUSTRALASIA	**32,559**	**33,772**	**34,561**	**35,228**	**39,075**	**42.33**	**10.92**
AUSTRALIA	9,311	10,954	11,224	11,438	12,101	13.11	5.80
NEW ZEALAND	23,248	22,818	23,337	23,790	26,974	29.22	13.38
MELANESIA	**1,685**	**2,032**	**2,104**	**1,928**	**2,184**	**2.37**	**13.28**
FIJI	1,685	2,032	2,104	1,928	2,184	2.37	13.28
POLYNESIA	**31,205**	**30,139**	**31,103**	**31,914**	**30,321**	**32.85**	**-4.99**
AMER SAMOA	31,099	30,063	31,016	31,803	30,166	32.68	-5.15
COOK IS	106	76	87	111	155	0.17	39.64
OT.EAST AS/P	**4,342**	**4,658**	**4,917**	**5,175**	**5,727**	**6.20**	**10.67**
OTHER ASIA	1,352	1,263	1,753	1,310	1,780	1.93	35.88
OTH OCEANIA	2,990	3,395	3,164	3,865	3,947	4.28	2.12
EUROPE	**5,460**	**6,396**	**5,797**	**4,762**	**5,136**	**5.56**	**7.85**
NORTHERN EUR	**2,275**	**2,805**	**2,602**	**2,283**	**2,759**	**2.99**	**20.85**
UK	1,588	2,092	1,722	1,480	2,092	2.27	41.35
SCANDINAVIA	687	713	880	803	667	0.72	-16.94
WESTERN EUR	**1,713**	**2,046**	**2,129**	**1,381**	**1,436**	**1.56**	**3.98**
GERMANY	1,541	1,784	1,928	1,196	1,207	1.31	0.92
BENELUX	172	262	201	185	229	0.25	23.78
OTHER EUROPE	**1,472**	**1,545**	**1,066**	**1,098**	**941**	**1.02**	**-14.30**
OTHER EUROPE	1,472	1,545	1,066	1,098	941	1.02	-14.30
REG.NOT SPEC	**809**	**556**	**226**	**281**	**236**	**0.26**	**-16.01**
NOT SPECIFIE	**809**	**556**	**226**	**281**	**236**	**0.26**	**-16.01**
OTH.WORLD	809	556	226	281	236	0.26	-16.01

Source: World Tourism Organization (WTO)

SAO TOME AND PRINCIPE

1. ARRIVALS OF NON-RESIDENT TOURISTS AT NATIONAL BORDERS, BY COUNTRY OF RESIDENCE

	1999	2000	2001	2002	2003	Market share 03	% change 03-02
TOTAL	**5,800**	**7,137**	**7,569**				
AFRICA	**1,159**	**1,141**	**2,615**				
CENTRAL AFR			**1,032**				
ANGOLA			660				
GABON			372				
WEST AFRICA			**651**				
CAPE VERDE			179				
NIGERIA			472				
OTHER AFRICA	**1,159**	**1,141**	**932**				
OTHER AFRICA			932				
ALL AFRICA	1,159	1,141					
AMERICAS			**456**				
NORTH AMER			**330**				
USA			330				
OTHER AMERIC			**126**				
OTH AMERICA			126				
EAST AS/PACI			**62**				
OT.EAST AS/P			**62**				
AEAP			62				
EUROPE	**4,333**	**3,818**	**4,380**				
NORTHERN EUR			**122**				
UK			122				
SOUTHERN EUR			**2,166**				
PORTUGAL			1,886				
SPAIN			280				
WESTERN EUR			**1,567**				
BELGIUM			115				
FRANCE			1,233				
GERMANY			147				
NETHERLANDS			72				
OTHER EUROPE	**4,333**	**3,818**	**525**				
OTHER EUROPE			525				
ALL EUROPE	4,333	3,818					
MIDDLE EAST			**33**				
MIDDLE EAST			**33**				
ALL MID EAST			33				
SOUTH ASIA			**23**				
SOUTH ASIA			**23**				

SAO TOME AND PRINCIPE

1. ARRIVALS OF NON-RESIDENT TOURISTS AT NATIONAL BORDERS, BY COUNTRY OF RESIDENCE

	1999	2000	2001	2002	2003	Market share 03	% change 03-02
ALL STH ASIA			23				
REG.NOT SPEC	**308**	**2,178**					
NOT SPECIFIE	**308**	**2,178**					
OTH.WORLD	308	2,178					

Source: World Tourism Organization (WTO)

SAUDI ARABIA

1. ARRIVALS OF NON-RESIDENT TOURISTS AT NATIONAL BORDERS, BY NATIONALITY

	1999	2000	2001	2002	2003	Market share 03	% change 03-02
TOTAL		**6,585,326**	**6,726,620**	**7,511,299**	**7,332,233**	**100.00**	**-2.38**
AFRICA		**566,204**	**535,099**	**606,791**	**525,045**	**7.16**	**-13.47**
EAST AFRICA		**46,968**	**40,407**	**57,116**	**56,185**	**0.77**	**-1.63**
BURUNDI		38	40	39	33		-15.38
COMOROS		1,469	1,310	1,316	1,941	0.03	47.49
ETHIOPIA		18,496	15,646	27,248	26,332	0.36	-3.36
ERITREA		4,365	3,487	3,699	3,555	0.05	-3.89
DJIBOUTI		1,639	1,321	1,381	1,284	0.02	-7.02
KENYA		3,730	2,565	2,663	2,847	0.04	6.91
MADAGASCAR		138	111	111	122		9.91
MALAWI		193	199	135	134		-0.74
MAURITIUS		2,393	2,082	2,536	2,420	0.03	-4.57
MOZAMBIQUE		374	330	419	364		-13.13
RWANDA		29	30	28	27		-3.57
SEYCHELLES		63	53	65	47		-27.69
SOMALIA		10,719	10,522	14,854	14,546	0.20	-2.07
ZIMBABWE		186	212	179	95		-46.93
UGANDA		862	788	650	773	0.01	18.92
TANZANIA		2,117	1,518	1,639	1,524	0.02	-7.02
ZAMBIA		157	193	154	141		-8.44
CENTRAL AFR		**15,285**	**12,361**	**14,345**	**11,981**	**0.16**	**-16.48**
ANGOLA		22	17	7	14		100.00
CAMEROON		2,674	2,434	2,625	2,723	0.04	3.73
CENT.AFR.REP		737	760	763	459	0.01	-39.84
CHAD		11,732	9,069	10,856	8,662	0.12	-20.21
CONGO		50	33	42	22		-47.62
DEM.R.CONGO		18	9	6	1		-83.33
EQ.GUINEA		5	6	2	3		50.00
GABON		47	33	44	97		120.45
NORTH AFRICA		**332,288**	**322,474**	**366,095**	**296,905**	**4.05**	**-18.90**
ALGERIA		90,632	85,335	92,788	85,352	1.16	-8.01
MOROCCO		78,971	64,335	78,095	70,238	0.96	-10.06
SUDAN		121,779	139,760	156,342	108,742	1.48	-30.45
TUNISIA		40,906	33,044	38,870	32,573	0.44	-16.20
SOUTHERN AFR		**20,102**	**17,096**	**17,104**	**17,483**	**0.24**	**2.22**
BOTSWANA		36	23	20	24		20.00
LESOTHO		18	30	38	22		-42.11
NAMIBIA		9	6	7	11		57.14
SOUTH AFRICA		20,036	17,031	17,012	17,388	0.24	2.21
SWAZILAND		3	6	27	38		40.74
WEST AFRICA		**151,561**	**142,761**	**152,131**	**142,491**	**1.94**	**-6.34**
BENIN		1,799	1,799	1,799	2,367	0.03	31.57
GAMBIA		2,478	2,353	2,403	2,476	0.03	3.04
GHANA		2,568	2,401	2,546	2,495	0.03	-2.00
GUINEA		4,829	4,580	4,693	6,243	0.09	33.03
COTE IVOIRE		2,819	2,766	2,765	1,616	0.02	-41.56
LIBERIA		250	248	261	337		29.12
MALI		6,286	5,095	5,468	5,291	0.07	-3.24
MAURITANIA		4,180	3,636	4,501	3,960	0.05	-12.02
NIGER		11,214	7,141	7,230	6,549	0.09	-9.42
NIGERIA		102,263	101,680	109,316	99,028	1.35	-9.41

1. ARRIVALS OF NON-RESIDENT TOURISTS AT NATIONAL BORDERS, BY NATIONALITY

	1999	2000	2001	2002	2003	Market share 03	% change 03-02
GUINEABISSAU		168	179	175	561	0.01	220.57
SENEGAL		9,374	7,765	7,806	8,179	0.11	4.78
SIERRA LEONE		514	475	489	602	0.01	23.11
TOGO		869	853	856	1,071	0.01	25.12
BURKINA FASO		1,950	1,790	1,823	1,716	0.02	-5.87
AMERICAS		**53,725**	**47,109**	**51,981**	**46,496**	**0.63**	**-10.55**
CARIBBEAN		**422**	**400**	**454**	**408**	**0.01**	**-10.13**
BAHAMAS		20	20	23	13		-43.48
BARBADOS		118	128	119	81		-31.93
BR.VIRGIN IS			6				
CUBA		7	2	6	9		50.00
DOMINICA		76	43	51	43		-15.69
DOMINICAN RP		9	2	20	8		-60.00
HAITI		6	4	1			
JAMAICA		7	6	9	16		77.78
PUERTO RICO		1	1	2			
ST.LUCIA		1	2				
TRINIDAD TBG		177	186	223	238		6.73
CENTRAL AMER		**119**	**125**	**146**	**111**		**-23.97**
BELIZE		27	23	13	24		84.62
COSTA RICA		13	13	8	11		37.50
EL SALVADOR		6	10	5			
GUATEMALA		7	12	13	12		-7.69
HONDURAS		10	22	57	22		-61.40
NICARAGUA		1	2		4		
PANAMA		55	43	50	38		-24.00
NORTH AMER		**51,719**	**45,164**	**49,920**	**44,668**	**0.61**	**-10.52**
CANADA		10,067	8,739	9,972	9,081	0.12	-8.94
MEXICO		188	148	179	178		-0.56
USA		41,461	36,274	39,756	35,405	0.48	-10.94
OT.NORTH.AME		3	3	13	4		-69.23
SOUTH AMER		**1,465**	**1,420**	**1,461**	**1,309**	**0.02**	**-10.40**
ARGENTINA		393	277	235	193		-17.87
BOLIVIA		21	14	25	19		-24.00
BRAZIL		486	627	623	637	0.01	2.25
CHILE		27	51	48	88		83.33
COLOMBIA		128	106	74	83		12.16
ECUADOR		15	16	60	19		-68.33
FR.GUIANA			4				
GUYANA		35	41	30			
PARAGUAY		4	12	8	5		-37.50
PERU		15	26	14	17		21.43
SURINAME		43	47	48	53		10.42
URUGUAY		19	16	112	21		-81.25
VENEZUELA		279	183	184	174		-5.43
EAST AS/PACI		**630,023**	**595,847**	**660,329**	**612,340**	**8.35**	**-7.27**
N/EAST ASIA		**18,751**	**17,702**	**20,774**	**23,131**	**0.32**	**11.35**
CHINA		9,842	9,522	11,552	15,136	0.21	31.02
TAIWAN(P.C.)		230	230	230			
HK,CHINA		12	17		20		

SAUDI ARABIA

1. ARRIVALS OF NON-RESIDENT TOURISTS AT NATIONAL BORDERS, BY NATIONALITY

	1999	2000	2001	2002	2003	Market share 03	% change 03-02
JAPAN		5,744	5,140	6,291	5,466	0.07	-13.11
KOREA D P RP		357	314	193	201		4.15
KOREA REP.		2,519	2,460	2,488	2,284	0.03	-8.20
MONGOLIA		47	19	20	24		20.00
S/EAST ASIA		**604,931**	**571,245**	**632,345**	**582,503**	**7.94**	**-7.88**
BRUNEI DARSM		6,136	5,507	5,655	2,617	0.04	-53.72
MYANMAR		609	458	577	224		-61.18
CAMBODIA		68	70	71	153		115.49
INDONESIA		390,953	371,962	418,704	396,709	5.41	-5.25
LAO P.DEM.R.			2		2		
MALAYSIA		108,768	96,844	105,000	84,473	1.15	-19.55
PHILIPPINES		71,016	72,508	78,863	79,490	1.08	0.80
SINGAPORE		17,387	14,594	12,618	7,149	0.10	-43.34
VIET NAM		53	9	2			
THAILAND		9,941	9,291	10,855	11,686	0.16	7.66
AUSTRALASIA		**6,274**	**6,840**	**7,152**	**6,609**	**0.09**	**-7.59**
AUSTRALIA		5,336	5,583	5,649	5,273	0.07	-6.66
NEW ZEALAND		938	1,257	1,503	1,336	0.02	-11.11
MELANESIA		**57**	**54**	**57**	**96**		**68.42**
FIJI		57	54	57	96		68.42
MICRONESIA		**5**	**5**	**1**			
KIRIBATI			1				
GUAM			2				
N.MARIANA IS		1	1				
MICRONESIA		1	1	1			
MARSHALL IS		3					
POLYNESIA		**5**	**1**		**1**		
AMER SAMOA		1					
FR.POLYNESIA			1		1		
TONGA		4					
EUROPE		**338,449**	**304,894**	**338,580**	**334,159**	**4.56**	**-1.31**
C/E EUROPE		**21,449**	**20,276**	**21,686**	**20,307**	**0.28**	**-6.36**
AZERBAIJAN		1,020	985	1,206	1,358	0.02	12.60
ARMENIA		6	13	23	32		39.13
BULGARIA		321	284	379	492	0.01	29.82
BELARUS		77	71	327	168		-48.62
CZECH REP		228	263	450	377	0.01	-16.22
ESTONIA		9	9	13	49		276.92
GEORGIA		25	41	35	53		51.43
HUNGARY		209	187	219	159		-27.40
KAZAKHSTAN		568	547	650	906	0.01	39.38
KYRGYZSTAN			4	46	683	0.01	1,384.78
LATVIA		32	66	37	46		24.32
LITHUANIA		24	13	29	13		-55.17
REP MOLDOVA		73	87	36	84		133.33
POLAND		302	292	432	460	0.01	6.48
ROMANIA		280	433	577	479	0.01	-16.98
RUSSIAN FED		1,929	1,589	1,942	5,679	0.08	192.43
SLOVAKIA		114	95	136	113		-16.91
TAJIKISTAN		5,548	5,595	5,525	3,292	0.04	-40.42
TURKMENISTAN		211	216	236	234		-0.85

SAUDI ARABIA

1. ARRIVALS OF NON-RESIDENT TOURISTS AT NATIONAL BORDERS, BY NATIONALITY

	1999	2000	2001	2002	2003	Market share 03	% change 03-02
UKRAINE		249	276	500	621	0.01	24.20
UZBEKISTAN		6,253	5,976	5,733	5,009	0.07	-12.63
OTH C/E EUR		3,971	3,234	3,155			
NORTHERN EUR		**88,573**	**75,108**	**85,035**	**78,669**	**1.07**	**-7.49**
DENMARK		2,309	1,852	2,236	1,990	0.03	-11.00
FINLAND		592	616	704	616	0.01	-12.50
ICELAND		345	355	82	150		82.93
IRELAND		2,015	1,858	1,886	1,971	0.03	4.51
NORWAY		1,789	1,538	1,721	1,481	0.02	-13.95
SWEDEN		3,851	3,283	3,556	2,909	0.04	-18.19
UK		77,672	65,606	74,850	69,552	0.95	-7.08
SOUTHERN EUR		**15,100**	**14,284**	**15,332**	**18,177**	**0.25**	**18.56**
ALBANIA		261	228	269	568	0.01	111.15
ANDORRA		2	1				
BOSNIA HERZG		1,471	1,337	1,405	1,521	0.02	8.26
CROATIA		158	270	320	397	0.01	24.06
GREECE		1,422	1,392	1,435	1,367	0.02	-4.74
ITALY		5,985	5,720	6,194	5,615	0.08	-9.35
MALTA		53	41	51	56		9.80
PORTUGAL		581	461	567	469	0.01	-17.28
SAN MARINO		2	3	3			
SLOVENIA		33	46	69	58		-15.94
SPAIN		1,930	1,671	1,925	1,712	0.02	-11.06
SERBIA,MTNEG		2	1	1			
OT SOUTH EUR		3,200	3,113	3,093	6,414	0.09	107.37
WESTERN EUR		**37,999**	**35,260**	**40,195**	**39,273**	**0.54**	**-2.29**
AUSTRIA		1,472	1,541	1,569	1,824	0.02	16.25
BELGIUM		1,887	1,735	2,094	1,970	0.03	-5.92
FRANCE		15,028	13,928	15,851	15,237	0.21	-3.87
GERMANY		11,574	10,837	12,185	12,007	0.16	-1.46
LIECHTENSTEN		1					
LUXEMBOURG		25	22	15	18		20.00
MONACO		6	1				
NETHERLANDS		6,028	5,221	6,127	5,832	0.08	-4.81
SWITZERLAND		1,978	1,975	2,354	2,385	0.03	1.32
EAST/MED EUR		**175,328**	**159,966**	**176,332**	**177,733**	**2.42**	**0.79**
CYPRUS		419	373	344	266		-22.67
TURKEY		174,909	159,593	175,988	177,467	2.42	0.84
MIDDLE EAST		**3,598,746**	**3,853,143**	**4,212,598**	**3,923,873**	**53.52**	**-6.85**
MIDDLE EAST		**3,598,746**	**3,853,143**	**4,212,598**	**3,923,873**	**53.52**	**-6.85**
BAHRAIN		214,463	235,415	252,697	281,875	3.84	11.55
PALESTINE		40,370	47,965	52,034	46,301	0.63	-11.02
IRAQ		22,027	24,933	23,987	25,099	0.34	4.64
JORDAN		250,495	247,719	263,592	240,356	3.28	-8.82
KUWAIT		907,521	903,017	1,010,943	971,341	13.25	-3.92
LEBANON		51,646	55,737	61,977	63,793	0.87	2.93
LIBYA		44,229	39,829	44,558	39,546	0.54	-11.25
OMAN		94,247	109,272	126,976	136,389	1.86	7.41
QATAR		322,185	342,155	363,345	388,239	5.29	6.85
SYRIA		479,251	533,105	564,776	541,894	7.39	-4.05
UNTD ARAB EM		158,679	172,196	177,581	189,471	2.58	6.70
EGYPT		888,585	957,764	1,015,078	787,277	10.74	-22.44

SAUDI ARABIA

1. ARRIVALS OF NON-RESIDENT TOURISTS AT NATIONAL BORDERS, BY NATIONALITY

	1999	2000	2001	2002	2003	Market share 03	% change 03-02
YEMEN		125,048	184,036	255,054	212,292	2.90	-16.77
SOUTH ASIA		**1,380,304**	**1,371,162**	**1,618,928**	**1,868,897**	**25.49**	**15.44**
SOUTH ASIA		**1,380,304**	**1,371,162**	**1,618,928**	**1,868,897**	**25.49**	**15.44**
AFGHANISTAN		13,140	12,074	14,249	31,481	0.43	120.93
BANGLADESH		199,270	195,400	221,447	209,560	2.86	-5.37
BHUTAN		1	4				
SRI LANKA		67,231	71,876	75,847	81,695	1.11	7.71
INDIA		293,944	313,131	373,636	362,609	4.95	-2.95
IRAN		321,370	309,687	376,774	618,897	8.44	64.26
MALDIVES		2,069	1,947	2,042	1,341	0.02	-34.33
NEPAL		21,215	20,295	25,091	23,843	0.33	-4.97
PAKISTAN		462,064	446,748	529,842	539,471	7.36	1.82
REG.NOT SPEC		**17,875**	**19,366**	**22,092**	**21,423**	**0.29**	**-3.03**
NOT SPECIFIE		**17,875**	**19,366**	**22,092**	**21,423**	**0.29**	**-3.03**
OTH.WORLD		17,875	19,366	22,092	21,423	0.29	-3.03

Source: World Tourism Organization (WTO)

SENEGAL

3. ARRIVALS OF NON-RESIDENT TOURISTS IN HOTELS AND SIMILAR ESTABLISHMENTS, BY NATIONALITY

	1999	2000	2001	2002	2003	Market share 03	% change 03-02
TOTAL	**369,116**	**389,433**	**396,254**	**426,825**	**353,539**	**100.00**	**-17.17**
AFRICA	**81,101**	**96,834**	**77,623**	**86,037**	**85,664**	**24.23**	**-0.43**
OTHER AFRICA	**81,101**	**96,834**	**77,623**	**86,037**	**85,664**	**24.23**	**-0.43**
ALL AFRICA	81,101	96,834	77,623	86,037	85,664	24.23	-0.43
AMERICAS	**10,057**	**13,192**	**10,683**	**9,536**	**10,025**	**2.84**	**5.13**
NORTH AMER	**9,608**	**12,917**	**9,999**	**9,164**	**9,676**	**2.74**	**5.59**
CANADA	1,199	900	819	923	1,158	0.33	25.46
USA	8,409	12,017	9,180	8,241	8,518	2.41	3.36
OTHER AMERIC	**449**	**275**	**684**	**372**	**349**	**0.10**	**-6.18**
OTH AMERICA	449	275	684	372	349	0.10	-6.18
EAST AS/PACI	**2,680**	**2,669**	**2,208**	**1,864**	**2,273**	**0.64**	**21.94**
OT.EAST AS/P	**2,680**	**2,669**	**2,208**	**1,864**	**2,273**	**0.64**	**21.94**
AEAP	2,680	2,669	2,208	1,864	2,273	0.64	21.94
EUROPE	**269,692**	**274,035**	**301,087**	**322,631**	**252,568**	**71.44**	**-21.72**
C/E EUROPE	**486**	**507**	**433**	**410**	**532**	**0.15**	**29.76**
USSR(former)	486	507	433	410	532	0.15	29.76
NORTHERN EUR	**3,100**	**5,319**	**4,795**	**5,745**	**4,512**	**1.28**	**-21.46**
DENMARK	232	199	330	167	639	0.18	282.63
FINLAND	228	160	165	159	119	0.03	-25.16
NORWAY	151	163	144	152	415	0.12	173.03
SWEDEN	435	264	364	195	276	0.08	41.54
UK	2,054	4,533	3,792	5,072	3,063	0.87	-39.61
SOUTHERN EUR	**35,972**	**35,429**	**40,410**	**44,122**	**23,470**	**6.64**	**-46.81**
ITALY	13,063	13,923	15,616	19,496	9,279	2.62	-52.41
PORTUGAL	1,432	892	1,295	1,402	1,511	0.43	7.77
SPAIN	21,477	20,614	23,499	23,224	12,680	3.59	-45.40
WESTERN EUR	**216,876**	**218,635**	**241,479**	**255,057**	**207,955**	**58.82**	**-18.47**
FRANCE	186,477	193,135	209,641	230,088	181,470	51.33	-21.13
GERMANY	17,261	8,199	10,847	8,458	7,985	2.26	-5.59
SWITZERLAND	1,480	2,068	2,205	883	1,475	0.42	67.04
BENELUX	11,658	15,233	18,786	15,628	17,025	4.82	8.94
OTHER EUROPE	**13,258**	**14,145**	**13,970**	**17,297**	**16,099**	**4.55**	**-6.93**
OTHER EUROPE	13,258	14,145	13,970	17,297	16,099	4.55	-6.93
MIDDLE EAST	**955**	**988**	**915**	**994**	**1,253**	**0.35**	**26.06**
MIDDLE EAST	**955**	**988**	**915**	**994**	**1,253**	**0.35**	**26.06**
ALL MID EAST	955	988	915	994	1,253	0.35	26.06
REG.NOT SPEC	**4,631**	**1,715**	**3,738**	**5,763**	**1,756**	**0.50**	**-69.53**

SENEGAL

3. ARRIVALS OF NON-RESIDENT TOURISTS IN HOTELS AND SIMILAR ESTABLISHMENTS, BY NATIONALITY

	1999	2000	2001	2002	2003	Market share 03	% change 03-02
NOT SPECIFIE	**4,631**	**1,715**	**3,738**	**5,763**	**1,756**	**0.50**	**-69.53**
OTH.WORLD	4,631	1,715	3,738	5,763	1,756	0.50	-69.53

Source: World Tourism Organization (WTO)

SENEGAL

5. OVERNIGHT STAYS OF NON-RESIDENT TOURISTS IN HOTELS AND SIMILAR ESTABLISHMENTS, BY NATIONALITY

	1999	2000	2001	2002	2003	Market share 03	% change 03-02
TOTAL	**1,468,713**	**1,401,470**	**1,499,248**	**1,569,123**	**1,451,213**	**100.00**	**-7.51**
AFRICA	**209,035**	**208,408**	**192,353**	**226,702**	**223,917**	**15.43**	**-1.23**
OTHER AFRICA	**209,035**	**208,408**	**192,353**	**226,702**	**223,917**	**15.43**	**-1.23**
ALL AFRICA	209,035	208,408	192,353	226,702	223,917	15.43	-1.23
AMERICAS	**29,261**	**27,145**	**24,027**	**20,150**	**58,624**	**4.04**	**190.94**
NORTH AMER	**27,881**	**26,528**	**22,486**	**19,313**	**57,771**	**3.98**	**199.13**
CANADA	4,277	2,704	2,611	2,499	3,781	0.26	51.30
USA	23,604	23,824	19,875	16,814	53,990	3.72	221.10
OTHER AMERIC	**1,380**	**617**	**1,541**	**837**	**853**	**0.06**	**1.91**
OTH AMERICA	1,380	617	1,541	837	853	0.06	1.91
EAST AS/PACI	**6,751**	**6,284**	**6,520**	**4,278**	**7,146**	**0.49**	**67.04**
OT.EAST AS/P	**6,751**	**6,284**	**6,520**	**4,278**	**7,146**	**0.49**	**67.04**
AEAP	6,751	6,284	6,520	4,278	7,146	0.49	67.04
EUROPE	**1,201,474**	**1,152,185**	**1,254,814**	**1,290,136**	**1,132,104**	**78.01**	**-12.25**
C/E EUROPE	**898**	**1,351**	**857**	**1,626**	**1,531**	**0.11**	**-5.84**
RUSSIAN FED	898	1,351	857	1,626	1,531	0.11	-5.84
NORTHERN EUR	**7,785**	**14,848**	**11,789**	**14,230**	**13,771**	**0.95**	**-3.23**
DENMARK	564	417	1,021	516	1,205	0.08	133.53
FINLAND	402	371	624	309	331	0.02	7.12
NORWAY	347	415	495	529	1,015	0.07	91.87
SWEDEN	949	831	876	493	655	0.05	32.86
UK	5,523	12,814	8,773	12,383	10,565	0.73	-14.68
SOUTHERN EUR	**93,297**	**89,765**	**108,195**	**107,866**	**79,683**	**5.49**	**-26.13**
ITALY	48,982	45,858	37,923	65,281	41,608	2.87	-36.26
PORTUGAL	2,643	3,492	4,925		5,372	0.37	
SPAIN	41,672	40,415	65,347	42,585	32,703	2.25	-23.21
WESTERN EUR	**1,074,568**	**1,020,280**	**1,102,471**	**1,114,890**	**988,345**	**68.10**	**-11.35**
FRANCE	885,742	849,103	911,333	964,507	852,973	58.78	-11.56
GERMANY	126,624	73,786	79,404	68,610	41,608	2.87	-39.36
SWITZERLAND	8,072	14,267	9,567	5,559	6,487	0.45	16.69
BENELUX	54,130	83,124	102,167	76,214	87,277	6.01	14.52
OTHER EUROPE	**24,926**	**25,941**	**31,502**	**51,524**	**48,774**	**3.36**	**-5.34**
OTHER EUROPE	24,926	25,941	31,502	51,524	48,774	3.36	-5.34
MIDDLE EAST	**2,631**	**3,351**	**2,423**		**2,928**	**0.20**	
MIDDLE EAST	**2,631**	**3,351**	**2,423**		**2,928**	**0.20**	
ALL MID EAST	2,631	3,351	2,423		2,928	0.20	
REG.NOT SPEC	**19,561**	**4,097**	**19,111**	**27,857**	**26,494**	**1.83**	**-4.89**

SENEGAL

5. OVERNIGHT STAYS OF NON-RESIDENT TOURISTS IN HOTELS AND SIMILAR ESTABLISHMENTS, BY NATIONALITY

	1999	2000	2001	2002	2003	Market share 03	% change 03-02
NOT SPECIFIE	**19,561**	**4,097**	**19,111**	**27,857**	**26,494**	**1.83**	**-4.89**
OTH.WORLD	19,561	4,097	19,111	27,857	26,494	1.83	-4.89

Source: World Tourism Organization (WTO)

SERBIA AND MONTENEGRO

3. ARRIVALS OF NON-RESIDENT TOURISTS IN HOTELS AND SIMILAR ESTABLISHMENTS, BY NATIONALITY

	1999	2000	2001	2002	2003	Market share 03	% change 03-02
TOTAL	**139,476**	**212,889**	**313,476**	**408,072**	**434,669**	**100.00**	**6.52**
AMERICAS	**2,467**	**3,503**	**9,963**	**14,122**	**16,293**	**3.75**	**15.37**
NORTH AMER	**2,467**	**3,503**	**9,963**	**14,122**	**16,293**	**3.75**	**15.37**
CANADA	433	839	1,556	2,348	2,755	0.63	17.33
USA	2,034	2,664	8,407	11,774	13,538	3.11	14.98
EAST AS/PACI	**1,498**	**2,314**	**3,027**	**3,337**	**4,073**	**0.94**	**22.06**
N/EAST ASIA	**1,105**	**1,526**	**1,692**	**1,693**	**1,790**	**0.41**	**5.73**
JAPAN	1,105	1,526	1,692	1,693	1,790	0.41	5.73
AUSTRALASIA	**393**	**788**	**1,335**	**1,644**	**2,283**	**0.53**	**38.87**
AUSTRALIA	335	706	1,204	1,378	1,966	0.45	42.67
NEW ZEALAND	58	82	131	266	317	0.07	19.17
EUROPE	**128,943**	**196,462**	**290,227**	**379,403**	**404,426**	**93.04**	**6.60**
C/E EUROPE	**21,290**	**39,108**	**70,035**	**106,465**	**103,016**	**23.70**	**-3.24**
BULGARIA	4,921	7,065	10,039	13,373	16,983	3.91	26.99
CZECH RP/SVK	2,945	7,245	18,942	38,555	31,713	7.30	-17.75
HUNGARY	2,371	4,446	9,055	13,086	12,729	2.93	-2.73
POLAND	624	1,879	7,446	14,040	15,498	3.57	10.38
ROMANIA	3,670	5,757	8,759	9,659	8,912	2.05	-7.73
RUSSIAN FED	6,759	12,716	15,794	17,752	17,181	3.95	-3.22
NORTHERN EUR	**5,141**	**7,645**	**16,072**	**21,453**	**27,565**	**6.34**	**28.49**
DENMARK	476	955	1,949	2,256	2,682	0.62	18.88
FINLAND	362	422	773	1,010	1,155	0.27	14.36
ICELAND	88	59	80	277	329	0.08	18.77
IRELAND	255	548	1,095	1,305	1,811	0.42	38.77
NORWAY	723	919	1,807	2,529	3,079	0.71	21.75
SWEDEN	1,093	1,593	2,953	3,939	4,775	1.10	21.22
UK	2,144	3,149	7,415	10,137	13,734	3.16	35.48
SOUTHERN EUR	**86,430**	**118,542**	**142,106**	**163,616**	**174,922**	**40.24**	**6.91**
BOSNIA HERZG	52,593	66,495	60,332	53,283	49,428	11.37	-7.23
CROATIA	3,251	7,222	13,149	18,320	22,452	5.17	22.55
GREECE	7,691	6,711	7,427	10,890	13,967	3.21	28.26
ITALY	7,950	12,035	16,075	22,330	23,766	5.47	6.43
PORTUGAL	125	391	619	613	813	0.19	32.63
SLOVENIA	3,001	7,056	19,518	26,989	33,138	7.62	22.78
SPAIN	599	1,018	1,946	2,312	2,922	0.67	26.38
TFYROM	11,220	17,614	23,040	28,879	28,436	6.54	-1.53
WESTERN EUR	**10,382**	**19,902**	**42,135**	**65,261**	**75,434**	**17.35**	**15.59**
AUSTRIA	1,874	3,744	7,883	11,430	12,733	2.93	11.40
BELGIUM	481	1,365	2,091	3,837	3,737	0.86	-2.61
FRANCE	2,166	2,996	6,580	8,410	9,730	2.24	15.70
GERMANY	3,841	8,035	18,341	32,280	37,696	8.67	16.78
LUXEMBOURG	74	171	184	244	339	0.08	38.93
NETHERLANDS	951	1,741	3,729	5,035	6,650	1.53	32.08
SWITZERLAND	995	1,850	3,327	4,025	4,549	1.05	13.02
EAST/MED EUR	**1,220**	**2,467**	**6,030**	**8,094**	**9,784**	**2.25**	**20.88**

SERBIA AND MONTENEGRO

3. ARRIVALS OF NON-RESIDENT TOURISTS IN HOTELS AND SIMILAR ESTABLISHMENTS, BY NATIONALITY

	1999	2000	2001	2002	2003	Market share 03	% change 03-02
ISRAEL	518	838	1,758	2,804	3,924	0.90	39.94
TURKEY	702	1,629	4,272	5,290	5,860	1.35	10.78
OTHER EUROPE	**4,480**	**8,798**	**13,849**	**14,514**	**13,705**	**3.15**	**-5.57**
OTHER EUROPE	4,480	8,798	13,849	14,514	13,705	3.15	-5.57
REG.NOT SPEC	**6,568**	**10,610**	**10,259**	**11,210**	**9,877**	**2.27**	**-11.89**
NOT SPECIFIE	**6,568**	**10,610**	**10,259**	**11,210**	**9,877**	**2.27**	**-11.89**
OTH.WORLD	6,568	10,610	10,259	11,210	9,877	2.27	-11.89

Source: World Tourism Organization (WTO)

SERBIA AND MONTENEGRO

4. ARRIVALS OF NON-RESIDENT TOURISTS IN ALL TYPES OF ACCOMMODATION ESTABLISHMENTS, BY NATIONALITY

	1999	2000	2001	2002	2003	Market share 03	% change 03-02
TOTAL	**151,650**	**238,957**	**351,333**	**448,223**	**481,070**	**100.00**	**7.33**
AMERICAS	**2,595**	**3,631**	**10,555**	**14,593**	**16,812**	**3.49**	**15.21**
NORTH AMER	**2,595**	**3,631**	**10,555**	**14,593**	**16,812**	**3.49**	**15.21**
CANADA	447	891	1,647	2,494	2,874	0.60	15.24
USA	2,148	2,740	8,908	12,099	13,938	2.90	15.20
EAST AS/PACI	**1,525**	**2,360**	**3,089**	**3,442**	**4,156**	**0.86**	**20.74**
N/EAST ASIA	**1,128**	**1,539**	**1,715**	**1,704**	**1,797**	**0.37**	**5.46**
JAPAN	1,128	1,539	1,715	1,704	1,797	0.37	5.46
AUSTRALASIA	**397**	**821**	**1,374**	**1,738**	**2,359**	**0.49**	**35.73**
AUSTRALIA	339	734	1,241	1,458	2,042	0.42	40.05
NEW ZEALAND	58	87	133	280	317	0.07	13.21
EUROPE	**140,806**	**222,074**	**327,263**	**418,676**	**449,932**	**93.53**	**7.47**
C/E EUROPE	**23,397**	**45,638**	**78,633**	**116,919**	**112,655**	**23.42**	**-3.65**
BULGARIA	5,946	8,605	10,562	14,334	18,149	3.77	26.62
CZECH RP/SVK	3,057	8,668	21,186	40,712	34,326	7.14	-15.69
HUNGARY	2,477	4,808	9,743	14,205	14,343	2.98	0.97
POLAND	662	1,921	7,818	14,448	15,871	3.30	9.85
ROMANIA	4,309	7,611	10,931	12,322	11,360	2.36	-7.81
RUSSIAN FED	6,946	14,025	18,393	20,898	18,606	3.87	-10.97
NORTHERN EUR	**5,256**	**7,884**	**17,364**	**23,395**	**29,616**	**6.16**	**26.59**
DENMARK	482	967	2,010	2,347	2,794	0.58	19.05
FINLAND	366	434	791	1,038	1,185	0.25	14.16
ICELAND	88	63	87	281	333	0.07	18.51
IRELAND	261	560	1,136	1,338	1,833	0.38	37.00
NORWAY	733	975	2,582	3,745	4,475	0.93	19.49
SWEDEN	1,155	1,660	3,172	4,205	5,042	1.05	19.90
UK	2,171	3,225	7,586	10,441	13,954	2.90	33.65
SOUTHERN EUR	**94,146**	**133,410**	**161,727**	**182,802**	**199,464**	**41.46**	**9.11**
BOSNIA HERZG	58,447	75,902	73,533	62,646	63,403	13.18	1.21
CROATIA	3,585	7,920	13,775	19,341	23,191	4.82	19.91
GREECE	8,317	8,725	8,299	12,453	15,582	3.24	25.13
ITALY	8,133	12,605	16,813	23,410	24,795	5.15	5.92
PORTUGAL	143	403	639	638	935	0.19	46.55
SLOVENIA	3,131	7,336	20,851	29,829	36,382	7.56	21.97
SPAIN	603	1,035	1,971	2,335	3,014	0.63	29.08
TFYROM	11,787	19,484	25,846	32,150	32,162	6.69	0.04
WESTERN EUR	**12,114**	**23,264**	**47,008**	**71,422**	**82,605**	**17.17**	**15.66**
AUSTRIA	2,933	5,189	10,059	13,999	15,507	3.22	10.77
BELGIUM	494	1,630	2,501	3,955	4,108	0.85	3.87
FRANCE	2,194	3,147	6,770	8,593	10,101	2.10	17.55
GERMANY	3,907	8,327	18,850	33,454	38,644	8.03	15.51
LUXEMBOURG	76	187	185	250	356	0.07	42.40
NETHERLANDS	988	1,850	3,926	5,648	7,624	1.58	34.99
SWITZERLAND	1,522	2,934	4,717	5,523	6,265	1.30	13.43
EAST/MED EUR	**1,333**	**2,542**	**6,281**	**8,587**	**10,234**	**2.13**	**19.18**

4. ARRIVALS OF NON-RESIDENT TOURISTS IN ALL TYPES OF ACCOMMODATION ESTABLISHMENTS, BY NATIONALITY

	1999	2000	2001	2002	2003	Market share 03	% change 03-02
ISRAEL	529	859	1,801	2,850	4,207	0.87	47.61
TURKEY	804	1,683	4,480	5,737	6,027	1.25	5.05
OTHER EUROPE	**4,560**	**9,336**	**16,250**	**15,551**	**15,358**	**3.19**	**-1.24**
OTHER EUROPE	4,560	9,336	16,250	15,551	15,358	3.19	-1.24
REG.NOT SPEC	**6,724**	**10,892**	**10,426**	**11,512**	**10,170**	**2.11**	**-11.66**
NOT SPECIFIE	**6,724**	**10,892**	**10,426**	**11,512**	**10,170**	**2.11**	**-11.66**
OTH.WORLD	6,724	10,892	10,426	11,512	10,170	2.11	-11.66

Source: World Tourism Organization (WTO)

SERBIA AND MONTENEGRO

5. OVERNIGHT STAYS OF NON-RESIDENT TOURISTS IN HOTELS AND SIMILAR ESTABLISHMENTS, BY NATIONALITY

	1999	2000	2001	2002	2003	Market share 03	% change 03-02
TOTAL	**410,175**	**715,865**	**1,047,307**	**1,404,115**	**1,424,535**	**100.00**	**1.45**
AMERICAS	**9,249**	**13,026**	**44,987**	**52,856**	**50,306**	**3.53**	**-4.82**
NORTH AMER	**9,249**	**13,026**	**44,987**	**52,856**	**50,306**	**3.53**	**-4.82**
CANADA	1,888	3,050	4,552	7,212	8,127	0.57	12.69
USA	7,361	9,976	40,435	45,644	42,179	2.96	-7.59
EAST AS/PACI	**5,337**	**6,524**	**7,733**	**9,241**	**10,399**	**0.73**	**12.53**
N/EAST ASIA	**3,932**	**4,368**	**4,204**	**4,704**	**4,225**	**0.30**	**-10.18**
JAPAN	3,932	4,368	4,204	4,704	4,225	0.30	-10.18
AUSTRALASIA	**1,405**	**2,156**	**3,529**	**4,537**	**6,174**	**0.43**	**36.08**
AUSTRALIA	1,228	1,950	3,144	3,855	5,354	0.38	38.88
NEW ZEALAND	177	206	385	682	820	0.06	20.23
EUROPE	**373,334**	**657,009**	**956,868**	**1,303,662**	**1,334,954**	**93.71**	**2.40**
C/E EUROPE	**65,503**	**158,344**	**286,007**	**493,877**	**454,186**	**31.88**	**-8.04**
BULGARIA	10,775	14,236	21,274	26,221	36,919	2.59	40.80
CZECH RP/SVK	7,043	39,057	114,654	260,733	212,745	14.93	-18.41
HUNGARY	4,434	11,035	21,981	27,947	32,785	2.30	17.31
POLAND	1,729	6,817	19,154	53,688	44,959	3.16	-16.26
ROMANIA	10,252	14,310	22,451	21,030	23,454	1.65	11.53
RUSSIAN FED	31,270	72,889	86,493	104,258	103,324	7.25	-0.90
NORTHERN EUR	**16,545**	**23,514**	**47,278**	**62,617**	**82,531**	**5.79**	**31.80**
DENMARK	1,145	2,699	4,632	6,348	6,635	0.47	4.52
FINLAND	870	1,032	1,951	2,621	3,024	0.21	15.38
ICELAND	104	180	192	840	1,117	0.08	32.98
IRELAND	760	1,682	3,622	3,297	6,464	0.45	96.06
NORWAY	2,024	2,478	4,423	7,076	8,209	0.58	16.01
SWEDEN	3,376	4,542	8,676	10,650	12,401	0.87	16.44
UK	8,266	10,901	23,782	31,785	44,681	3.14	40.57
SOUTHERN EUR	**249,716**	**381,306**	**454,286**	**444,382**	**448,187**	**31.46**	**0.86**
BOSNIA HERZG	166,780	235,906	224,204	165,322	155,359	10.91	-6.03
CROATIA	14,336	32,824	52,545	55,887	49,765	3.49	-10.95
GREECE	16,880	15,769	18,101	26,405	29,972	2.10	13.51
ITALY	21,076	33,740	41,278	56,511	57,114	4.01	1.07
PORTUGAL	791	1,100	1,606	1,731	2,855	0.20	64.93
SLOVENIA	6,440	21,199	60,119	73,171	79,205	5.56	8.25
SPAIN	1,877	3,378	6,012	6,121	7,224	0.51	18.02
TFYROM	21,536	37,390	50,421	59,234	66,693	4.68	12.59
WESTERN EUR	**28,886**	**57,248**	**106,184**	**235,116**	**285,212**	**20.02**	**21.31**
AUSTRIA	4,832	8,893	17,231	24,800	27,118	1.90	9.35
BELGIUM	1,730	4,282	6,363	15,691	14,076	0.99	-10.29
FRANCE	6,507	8,772	17,903	22,409	24,182	1.70	7.91
GERMANY	10,488	23,767	45,453	145,550	188,372	13.22	29.42
LUXEMBOURG	139	699	403	715	1,177	0.08	64.62
NETHERLANDS	2,441	5,298	9,225	12,459	16,621	1.17	33.41
SWITZERLAND	2,749	5,537	9,606	13,492	13,666	0.96	1.29
EAST/MED EUR	**3,093**	**7,425**	**13,843**	**21,249**	**22,479**	**1.58**	**5.79**

SERBIA AND MONTENEGRO

5. OVERNIGHT STAYS OF NON-RESIDENT TOURISTS IN HOTELS AND SIMILAR ESTABLISHMENTS, BY NATIONALITY

	1999	2000	2001	2002	2003	Market share 03	% change 03-02
ISRAEL	1,644	2,484	4,738	11,519	9,487	0.67	-17.64
TURKEY	1,449	4,941	9,105	9,730	12,992	0.91	33.53
OTHER EUROPE	**9,591**	**29,172**	**49,270**	**46,421**	**42,359**	**2.97**	**-8.75**
OTHER EUROPE	9,591	29,172	49,270	46,421	42,359	2.97	-8.75
REG.NOT SPEC	**22,255**	**39,306**	**37,719**	**38,356**	**28,876**	**2.03**	**-24.72**
NOT SPECIFIE	**22,255**	**39,306**	**37,719**	**38,356**	**28,876**	**2.03**	**-24.72**
OTH.WORLD	22,255	39,306	37,719	38,356	28,876	2.03	-24.72

Source: World Tourism Organization (WTO)

6. OVERNIGHT STAYS OF NON-RESIDENT TOURISTS IN ALL TYPES OF ACCOMMODATION ESTABLISHMENTS, BY NATIONALITY

	1999	2000	2001	2002	2003	Market share 03	% change 03-02
TOTAL	497,967	865,014	1,281,029	1,650,170	1,707,440	100.00	3.47
AMERICAS	9,827	13,733	47,420	55,524	53,174	3.11	-4.23
NORTH AMER	9,827	13,733	47,420	55,524	53,174	3.11	-4.23
CANADA	1,945	3,414	5,059	8,243	8,825	0.52	7.06
USA	7,882	10,319	42,361	47,281	44,349	2.60	-6.20
EAST AS/PACI	5,469	6,818	8,040	9,544	10,722	0.63	12.34
N/EAST ASIA	4,039	4,400	4,254	4,747	4,241	0.25	-10.66
JAPAN	4,039	4,400	4,254	4,747	4,241	0.25	-10.66
AUSTRALASIA	1,430	2,418	3,786	4,797	6,481	0.38	35.11
AUSTRALIA	1,253	2,168	3,396	4,074	5,661	0.33	38.95
NEW ZEALAND	177	250	390	723	820	0.05	13.42
EUROPE	459,383	803,344	1,187,218	1,544,442	1,613,037	94.47	4.44
C/E EUROPE	70,767	189,745	336,403	555,640	501,883	29.39	-9.67
BULGARIA	11,876	16,297	22,401	28,605	38,345	2.25	34.05
CZECH RP/SVK	7,757	52,173	131,312	277,380	230,909	13.52	-16.75
HUNGARY	4,941	12,996	26,075	34,587	42,388	2.48	22.55
POLAND	1,907	7,049	20,337	56,435	47,193	2.76	-16.38
ROMANIA	11,552	17,096	25,653	25,966	27,320	1.60	5.21
RUSSIAN FED	32,734	84,134	110,625	132,667	115,728	6.78	-12.77
NORTHERN EUR	16,828	24,911	63,204	91,836	114,579	6.71	24.76
DENMARK	1,161	2,755	4,886	6,753	7,514	0.44	11.27
FINLAND	878	1,094	2,020	2,876	3,109	0.18	8.10
ICELAND	104	192	219	845	1,143	0.07	35.27
IRELAND	788	1,744	3,737	3,367	6,517	0.38	93.56
NORWAY	2,069	2,940	17,780	32,744	36,871	2.16	12.60
SWEDEN	3,466	4,944	9,999	12,408	13,806	0.81	11.27
UK	8,362	11,242	24,563	32,843	45,619	2.67	38.90
SOUTHERN EUR	327,391	483,517	589,945	563,576	606,816	35.54	7.67
BOSNIA HERZG	236,041	315,841	331,633	244,234	270,137	15.82	10.61
CROATIA	17,681	38,155	55,813	60,135	53,133	3.11	-11.64
GREECE	18,113	18,199	19,092	28,319	32,727	1.92	15.57
ITALY	21,778	35,561	43,447	60,137	60,308	3.53	0.28
PORTUGAL	869	1,188	1,682	1,889	3,520	0.21	86.34
SLOVENIA	6,889	22,744	64,293	79,213	85,649	5.02	8.12
SPAIN	1,898	3,497	6,080	6,187	7,400	0.43	19.61
TFYROM	24,122	48,332	67,905	83,462	93,942	5.50	12.56
WESTERN EUR	31,254	65,997	122,670	259,846	313,684	18.37	20.72
AUSTRIA	5,994	11,689	20,510	29,106	30,964	1.81	6.38
BELGIUM	1,743	5,422	9,913	16,594	16,166	0.95	-2.58
FRANCE	6,593	9,476	18,970	23,492	25,922	1.52	10.34
GERMANY	10,863	25,957	48,745	154,228	193,191	11.31	25.26
LUXEMBOURG	141	774	412	737	1,210	0.07	64.18
NETHERLANDS	2,601	5,887	11,327	19,817	29,833	1.75	50.54
SWITZERLAND	3,319	6,792	12,793	15,872	16,398	0.96	3.31
EAST/MED EUR	3,218	7,636	14,567	21,907	23,388	1.37	6.76

SERBIA AND MONTENEGRO

6. OVERNIGHT STAYS OF NON-RESIDENT TOURISTS IN ALL TYPES OF ACCOMMODATION ESTABLISHMENTS, BY NATIONALITY

	1999	2000	2001	2002	2003	Market share 03	% change 03-02
ISRAEL	1,660	2,548	5,072	11,606	10,102	0.59	-12.96
TURKEY	1,558	5,088	9,495	10,301	13,286	0.78	28.98
OTHER EUROPE	**9,925**	**31,538**	**60,429**	**51,637**	**52,687**	**3.09**	**2.03**
OTHER EUROPE	9,925	31,538	60,429	51,637	52,687	3.09	2.03
REG.NOT SPEC	**23,288**	**41,119**	**38,351**	**40,660**	**30,507**	**1.79**	**-24.97**
NOT SPECIFIE	**23,288**	**41,119**	**38,351**	**40,660**	**30,507**	**1.79**	**-24.97**
OTH.WORLD	23,288	41,119	38,351	40,660	30,507	1.79	-24.97

Source: World Tourism Organization (WTO)

SEYCHELLES

1. ARRIVALS OF NON-RESIDENT TOURISTS AT NATIONAL BORDERS, BY COUNTRY OF RESIDENCE

	1999	2000	2001	2002	2003	Market share 03	% change 03-02
TOTAL	**124,865**	**130,046**	**129,762**	**132,246**	**122,038**	**100.00**	**-7.72**
AFRICA	**14,188**	**13,746**	**13,821**	**13,819**	**13,578**	**11.13**	**-1.74**
EAST AFRICA	**9,256**	**8,471**	**8,216**	**8,233**	**7,221**	**5.92**	**-12.29**
ETHIOPIA	160	77	83	72	104	0.09	44.44
DJIBOUTI	19	5	88	12	21	0.02	75.00
KENYA	1,179	1,333	1,068	1,163	1,038	0.85	-10.75
MADAGASCAR	637	342	478	300	329	0.27	9.67
MALAWI	41	27	48	41	29	0.02	-29.27
MAURITIUS	3,536	3,068	2,744	3,100	2,351	1.93	-24.16
MOZAMBIQUE	53	57	100	45	56	0.05	24.44
REUNION	3,047	2,842	3,049	2,909	2,816	2.31	-3.20
RWANDA	23	33	25	30	32	0.03	6.67
SOMALIA		10		1			
ZIMBABWE	173	264	171	178	143	0.12	-19.66
UGANDA	155	154	108	153	103	0.08	-32.68
TANZANIA	134	150	131	155	97	0.08	-37.42
ZAMBIA	99	109	123	74	102	0.08	37.84
CENTRAL AFR					**15**	**0.01**	
DEM.R.CONGO					15	0.01	
NORTH AFRICA	**44**	**35**	**26**	**32**	**51**	**0.04**	**59.38**
ALGERIA	35	17	10	9	7	0.01	-22.22
SUDAN	9	18	16	23	44	0.04	91.30
SOUTHERN AFR	**4,047**	**4,384**	**4,546**	**4,265**	**5,087**	**4.17**	**19.27**
BOTSWANA	91	82	110	66	67	0.05	1.52
LESOTHO	19	24	17	11	6		-45.45
SOUTH AFRICA	3,902	4,260	4,396	4,173	5,003	4.10	19.89
SWAZILAND	35	18	23	15	11	0.01	-26.67
WEST AFRICA	**97**	**160**	**187**	**129**	**138**	**0.11**	**6.98**
GHANA	38	61	48	36	34	0.03	-5.56
NIGERIA	59	99	139	93	104	0.09	11.83
OTHER AFRICA	**744**	**696**	**846**	**1,160**	**1,066**	**0.87**	**-8.10**
OTHER AFRICA	744	696	846	1,160	1,066	0.87	-8.10
AMERICAS	**4,144**	**6,239**	**6,854**	**3,670**	**3,477**	**2.85**	**-5.26**
NORTH AMER	**2,994**	**5,111**	**6,200**	**3,331**	**3,169**	**2.60**	**-4.86**
CANADA	335	334	368	342	331	0.27	-3.22
MEXICO	40	31	27	35	45	0.04	28.57
USA	2,619	4,746	5,805	2,954	2,793	2.29	-5.45
SOUTH AMER	**960**	**902**	**564**	**212**	**200**	**0.16**	**-5.66**
ARGENTINA	850	810	509	99	120	0.10	21.21
BRAZIL	110	92	55	113	80	0.07	-29.20
OTHER AMERIC	**190**	**226**	**90**	**127**	**108**	**0.09**	**-14.96**
OTH AMERICA	190	226	90	127	108	0.09	-14.96
EAST AS/PACI	**2,543**	**2,716**	**2,624**	**2,678**	**1,977**	**1.62**	**-26.18**
N/EAST ASIA	**873**	**1,150**	**965**	**1,108**	**871**	**0.71**	**-21.39**
CHINA	324	472	413	551	407	0.33	-26.13

SEYCHELLES

1. ARRIVALS OF NON-RESIDENT TOURISTS AT NATIONAL BORDERS, BY COUNTRY OF RESIDENCE

	1999	2000	2001	2002	2003	Market share 03	% change 03-02
TAIWAN(P.C.)	41	73	49	55	54	0.04	-1.82
HK,CHINA	80	129	96	119	79	0.06	-33.61
JAPAN	405	414	376	362	306	0.25	-15.47
KOREA REP.	23	62	31	21	25	0.02	19.05
S/EAST ASIA	**1,114**	**1,043**	**1,086**	**1,077**	**598**	**0.49**	**-44.48**
INDONESIA	63	230	254	88	65	0.05	-26.14
MALAYSIA	131	146	171	140	77	0.06	-45.00
PHILIPPINES	174	116	112	143	115	0.09	-19.58
SINGAPORE	637	468	355	442	254	0.21	-42.53
THAILAND	109	83	194	264	87	0.07	-67.05
AUSTRALASIA	**529**	**494**	**538**	**441**	**488**	**0.40**	**10.66**
AUSTRALIA	449	430	469	396	432	0.35	9.09
NEW ZEALAND	80	64	69	45	56	0.05	24.44
OT.EAST AS/P	**27**	**29**	**35**	**52**	**20**	**0.02**	**-61.54**
OEAP	15	20	9	33	6		-81.82
OTH OCEANIA	12	9	26	19	14	0.01	-26.32
EUROPE	**101,320**	**104,545**	**103,270**	**108,246**	**99,961**	**81.91**	**-7.65**
C/E EUROPE	**2,935**	**2,419**	**2,405**	**3,248**	**3,644**	**2.99**	**12.19**
POLAND	300	287	324	390	260	0.21	-33.33
CIS	2,635	2,132	2,081	2,858	3,384	2.77	18.40
NORTHERN EUR	**19,733**	**20,787**	**21,006**	**22,978**	**22,189**	**18.18**	**-3.43**
DENMARK	1,730	1,454	1,056	1,307	882	0.72	-32.52
FINLAND	560	521	381	368	420	0.34	14.13
IRELAND	325	341	424	446	374	0.31	-16.14
NORWAY	818	683	744	744	717	0.59	-3.63
SWEDEN	994	1,671	1,325	1,223	1,031	0.84	-15.70
UK	15,306	16,117	17,076	18,890	18,765	15.38	-0.66
SOUTHERN EUR	**23,251**	**23,379**	**25,875**	**23,799**	**20,740**	**16.99**	**-12.85**
GREECE	198	137	130	171	144	0.12	-15.79
ITALY	19,520	19,951	21,151	20,000	17,778	14.57	-11.11
PORTUGAL	1,127	1,047	2,388	846	522	0.43	-38.30
SPAIN	2,009	1,989	1,962	2,550	2,062	1.69	-19.14
YUGOSLAV SFR	397	255	244	232	234	0.19	0.86
WESTERN EUR	**53,467**	**55,939**	**51,934**	**53,594**	**51,076**	**41.85**	**-4.70**
AUSTRIA	2,096	1,929	1,804	2,275	1,889	1.55	-16.97
BELGIUM	1,447	1,529	1,382	1,426	1,392	1.14	-2.38
FRANCE	24,283	28,282	25,459	28,326	25,990	21.30	-8.25
GERMANY	18,835	17,720	16,822	15,145	15,903	13.03	5.00
LUXEMBOURG	153	211	184	195	187	0.15	-4.10
NETHERLANDS	1,400	1,267	1,040	1,067	978	0.80	-8.34
SWITZERLAND	5,253	5,001	5,243	5,160	4,737	3.88	-8.20
EAST/MED EUR	**359**	**390**	**364**	**2,625**	**309**	**0.25**	**-88.23**
ISRAEL	210	322	261	2,495	149	0.12	-94.03
TURKEY	149	68	103	130	160	0.13	23.08
OTHER EUROPE	**1,575**	**1,631**	**1,686**	**2,002**	**2,003**	**1.64**	**0.05**
OTHER EUROPE	1,575	1,631	1,686	2,002	2,003	1.64	0.05
MIDDLE EAST	**1,419**	**1,512**	**1,503**	**2,023**	**1,770**	**1.45**	**-12.51**

SEYCHELLES

1. ARRIVALS OF NON-RESIDENT TOURISTS AT NATIONAL BORDERS, BY COUNTRY OF RESIDENCE

	1999	2000	2001	2002	2003	Market share 03	% change 03-02
MIDDLE EAST	**1,419**	**1,512**	**1,503**	**2,023**	**1,770**	**1.45**	**-12.51**
BAHRAIN	126	122	69	193	182	0.15	-5.70
KUWAIT	68	87	96	111	77	0.06	-30.63
LIBYA	1	12	14	2	5		150.00
OMAN	23	14	40	37	76	0.06	105.41
QATAR	25	31	37	19	24	0.02	26.32
SAUDI ARABIA	361	344	295	363	247	0.20	-31.96
UNTD ARAB EM	623	679	671	1,040	888	0.73	-14.62
EGYPT	48	30	91	49	51	0.04	4.08
YEMEN	22	8	2	3	33	0.03	1.000.00
OT MIDD EAST	122	185	188	206	187	0.15	-9.22
SOUTH ASIA	**1,251**	**1,288**	**1,690**	**1,810**	**1,275**	**1.04**	**-29.56**
SOUTH ASIA	**1,251**	**1,288**	**1,690**	**1,810**	**1,275**	**1.04**	**-29.56**
BANGLADESH	6	21	26	94	5		-94.68
SRI LANKA	104	177	149	205	212	0.17	3.41
INDIA	952	941	1,352	1,271	893	0.73	-29.74
IRAN	14	22	29	34	34	0.03	
PAKISTAN	152	110	93	114	64	0.05	-43.86
OTH STH ASIA	23	17	41	92	67	0.05	-27.17

Source: World Tourism Organization (WTO)

SIERRA LEONE

1. ARRIVALS OF NON-RESIDENT TOURISTS AT NATIONAL BORDERS, BY COUNTRY OF RESIDENCE

	1999	2000	2001	2002	2003	Market share 03	% change 03-02
TOTAL (*)	**10,615**	**15,713**	**24,067**	**28,463**	**37,201**	**100.00**	**30.70**
AFRICA	**4,265**	**4,810**	**11,427**	**13,519**	**22,435**	**60.31**	**65.95**
OTHER AFRICA	**4,265**	**4,810**	**11,427**	**13,519**	**22,435**	**60.31**	**65.95**
ALL AFRICA	4,265	4,810	11,427	13,519	22,435	60.31	65.95
AMERICAS	**139**	**2,454**	**3,211**	**3,785**	**4,699**	**12.63**	**24.15**
OTHER AMERIC	**139**	**2,454**	**3,211**	**3,785**	**4,699**	**12.63**	**24.15**
ALL AMERICAS	139	2,454	3,211	3,785	4,699	12.63	24.15
EAST AS/PACI	**600**	**1,923**	**1,812**	**2,134**	**1,995**	**5.36**	**-6.51**
OT.EAST AS/P	**600**	**1,923**	**1,812**	**2,134**	**1,995**	**5.36**	**-6.51**
ALL ASIA	600	1,923	1,812	2,134	1,995	5.36	-6.51
EUROPE	**4,205**	**5,658**	**6,250**	**7,403**	**6,460**	**17.37**	**-12.74**
OTHER EUROPE	**4,205**	**5,658**	**6,250**	**7,403**	**6,460**	**17.37**	**-12.74**
ALL EUROPE	4,205	5,658	6,250	7,403	6,460	17.37	-12.74
MIDDLE EAST	**1,406**	**868**	**1,367**	**1,622**	**1,612**	**4.33**	**-0.62**
MIDDLE EAST	**1,406**	**868**	**1,367**	**1,622**	**1,612**	**4.33**	**-0.62**
ALL MID EAST	1,406	868	1,367	1,622	1,612	4.33	-0.62

Source: World Tourism Organization (WTO)

SIERRA LEONE

5. OVERNIGHT STAYS OF NON-RESIDENT TOURISTS IN HOTELS AND SIMILAR ESTABLISHMENTS, BY COUNTRY OF RESIDENCE

	1999	2000	2001	2002	2003	Market share 03	% change 03-02
TOTAL	**33,355**	**205,375**	**258,989**	**284,885**			
AFRICA	**7,387**	**41,585**	**76,917**	**84,611**			
OTHER AFRICA	**7,387**	**41,585**	**76,917**	**84,611**			
ALL AFRICA	7,387	41,585	76,917	84,611			
AMERICAS	**274**	**31,224**	**33,589**	**37,035**			
OTHER AMERIC	**274**	**31,224**	**33,589**	**37,035**			
ALL AMERICAS	274	31,224	33,589	37,035			
EAST AS/PACI	**4,726**	**21,831**	**21,386**	**23,645**			
OT.EAST AS/P	**4,726**	**21,831**	**21,386**	**23,645**			
ALL ASIA	4,726	21,831	21,386	23,645			
EUROPE	**18,954**	**102,587**	**120,525**	**132,472**			
OTHER EUROPE	**18,954**	**102,587**	**120,525**	**132,472**			
ALL EUROPE	18,954	102,587	120,525	132,472			
MIDDLE EAST	**2,014**	**8,148**	**6,572**	**7,122**			
MIDDLE EAST	**2,014**	**8,148**	**6,572**	**7,122**			
ALL MID EAST	2,014	8,148	6,572	7,122			

Source: World Tourism Organization (WTO)

SINGAPORE

2. ARRIVALS OF NON-RESIDENT VISITORS AT NATIONAL BORDERS, BY NATIONALITY

	1999	2000	2001	2002	2003	Market share 03	% change 03-02
TOTAL (*)	**6,958,201**	**7,691,399**	**7,522,163**	**7,567,110**	**6,127,029**	**100.00**	**-19.03**
AFRICA	**78,518**	**85,560**	**74,724**	**65,672**	**53,975**	**0.88**	**-17.81**
EAST AFRICA	**19,429**	**19,746**	**14,844**	**11,854**	**8,282**	**0.14**	**-30.13**
MAURITIUS	19,429	19,746	14,844	11,854	8,282	0.14	-30.13
SOUTHERN AFR	**37,485**	**41,170**	**34,279**	**30,543**	**27,650**	**0.45**	**-9.47**
SOUTH AFRICA	37,485	41,170	34,279	30,543	27,650	0.45	-9.47
OTHER AFRICA	**21,604**	**24,644**	**25,601**	**23,275**	**18,043**	**0.29**	**-22.48**
OTHER AFRICA	21,604	24,644	25,601	23,275	18,043	0.29	-22.48
AMERICAS	**491,248**	**532,965**	**481,589**	**460,247**	**355,257**	**5.80**	**-22.81**
CARIBBEAN	**1,774**	**2,856**	**3,859**	**3,241**	**2,141**	**0.03**	**-33.94**
ALL CO CARIB	1,774	2,856	3,859	3,241	2,141	0.03	-33.94
CENTRAL AMER	**2,069**	**2,038**	**2,168**	**2,004**	**1,214**	**0.02**	**-39.42**
ALL CENT AME	2,069	2,038	2,168	2,004	1,214	0.02	-39.42
NORTH AMER	**473,511**	**513,127**	**462,660**	**442,567**	**342,527**	**5.59**	**-22.60**
CANADA	93,090	96,015	92,294	90,901	71,386	1.17	-21.47
MEXICO	6,253	11,009	7,542	8,655	4,453	0.07	-48.55
USA	374,168	406,103	362,824	343,011	266,688	4.35	-22.25
SOUTH AMER	**13,894**	**14,944**	**12,902**	**12,435**	**9,375**	**0.15**	**-24.61**
ARGENTINA	3,524	3,805	3,285	1,599	1,319	0.02	-17.51
BRAZIL	4,514	4,909	4,026	4,611	3,695	0.06	-19.87
CHILE	1,222	1,425	1,290	1,294	979	0.02	-24.34
COLOMBIA	1,544	1,810	1,706	2,191	1,556	0.03	-28.98
URUGUAY	384	216	100	177	111		-37.29
VENEZUELA	972	896	899	931	686	0.01	-26.32
OTH SOUTH AM	1,734	1,883	1,596	1,632	1,029	0.02	-36.95
EAST AS/PACI	**4,598,524**	**5,090,984**	**5,021,605**	**5,176,210**	**4,207,058**	**68.66**	**-18.72**
N/EAST ASIA	**2,013,125**	**2,240,464**	**2,050,448**	**2,193,906**	**1,591,897**	**25.98**	**-27.44**
CHINA	372,685	439,957	500,545	666,315	559,724	9.14	-16.00
TAIWAN(P.C.)	317,695	292,827	223,740	212,943	147,281	2.40	-30.84
HK,CHINA	158,357	160,502	147,698	154,643	133,976	2.19	-13.36
JAPAN	905,393	978,761	804,342	774,330	475,726	7.76	-38.56
KOREA D P RP	470	319	217	301	377	0.01	25.25
KOREA REP.	255,979	365,034	369,490	380,170	269,818	4.40	-29.03
MACAU, CHINA	1,162	1,879	2,656	3,308	2,987	0.05	-9.70
MONGOLIA	1,384	1,185	1,760	1,896	2,008	0.03	5.91
S/EAST ASIA	**2,046,928**	**2,258,388**	**2,347,290**	**2,368,145**	**2,160,516**	**35.26**	**-8.77**
BRUNEI DARSM	35,990	39,438	44,537	43,816	29,541	0.48	-32.58
MYANMAR	20,648	22,971	22,943	23,170	20,069	0.33	-13.38
CAMBODIA	7,033	6,708	7,132	6,412	6,495	0.11	1.29
INDONESIA	1,179,156	1,293,175	1,349,536	1,384,409	1,335,083	21.79	-3.56
LAO P.DEM.R.	613	736	960	833	750	0.01	-9.96
MALAYSIA	411,714	459,558	462,257	434,136	333,444	5.44	-23.19
PHILIPPINES	164,647	185,182	195,334	202,283	181,940	2.97	-10.06
VIET NAM	21,632	27,935	30,139	35,651	40,041	0.65	12.31
THAILAND	205,495	222,685	234,452	237,435	213,153	3.48	-10.23

2. ARRIVALS OF NON-RESIDENT VISITORS AT NATIONAL BORDERS, BY NATIONALITY

	1999	2000	2001	2002	2003	Market share 03	% change 03-02
AUSTRALASIA	**531,851**	**585,494**	**617,957**	**607,974**	**449,402**	**7.33**	**-26.08**
AUSTRALIA	441,522	484,561	515,421	505,621	370,029	6.04	-26.82
NEW ZEALAND	90,329	100,933	102,536	102,353	79,373	1.30	-22.45
MELANESIA	**4,590**	**4,534**	**4,199**	**4,398**	**3,979**	**0.06**	**-9.53**
FIJI	2,161	2,263	2,003	2,230	2,486	0.04	11.48
NEW CALEDNIA	25	13	5	9	9		
PAPUA N.GUIN	2,404	2,258	2,191	2,159	1,484	0.02	-31.26
MICRONESIA	**698**	**429**	**221**	**245**	**182**		**-25.71**
GUAM	105	70	37	20	4		-80.00
NAURU	593	359	184	225	178		-20.89
OT.EAST AS/P	**1,332**	**1,675**	**1,490**	**1,542**	**1,082**	**0.02**	**-29.83**
OTH OCEANIA	1,332	1,675	1,490	1,542	1,082	0.02	-29.83
EUROPE	**1,231,829**	**1,339,125**	**1,316,111**	**1,285,220**	**1,025,979**	**16.75**	**-20.17**
C/E EUROPE	**31,939**	**35,193**	**37,150**	**38,132**	**33,224**	**0.54**	**-12.87**
CZECH REP	3,337	3,193	3,678	4,062	3,112	0.05	-23.39
HUNGARY	2,281	2,636	2,929	2,880	2,472	0.04	-14.17
POLAND	6,427	7,253	7,490	6,930	6,314	0.10	-8.89
CIS	19,894	22,111	23,053	24,260	21,326	0.35	-12.09
NORTHERN EUR	**638,398**	**715,265**	**721,622**	**700,744**	**584,843**	**9.55**	**-16.54**
DENMARK	30,530	31,302	32,028	31,046	25,392	0.41	-18.21
FINLAND	19,187	20,921	16,714	13,969	11,853	0.19	-15.15
IRELAND	24,233	29,148	30,233	31,252	24,639	0.40	-21.16
NORWAY	22,871	25,885	25,117	24,739	19,620	0.32	-20.69
SWEDEN	42,980	48,081	43,060	40,020	32,525	0.53	-18.73
UK	498,597	559,928	574,470	559,718	470,814	7.68	-15.88
SOUTHERN EUR	**86,479**	**84,862**	**74,910**	**78,913**	**49,703**	**0.81**	**-37.02**
GREECE	13,896	13,600	11,669	13,080	8,232	0.13	-37.06
ITALY	47,723	47,038	40,491	41,271	23,639	0.39	-42.72
PORTUGAL	9,479	7,845	6,543	6,466	4,491	0.07	-30.54
SPAIN	13,996	14,802	14,577	16,677	12,099	0.20	-27.45
SERBIA,MTNEG	1,385	1,577	1,630	1,419	1,242	0.02	-12.47
WESTERN EUR	**436,521**	**460,593**	**443,491**	**425,674**	**324,472**	**5.30**	**-23.77**
AUSTRIA	19,096	18,763	16,359	16,379	10,911	0.18	-33.38
BELGIUM	19,430	23,220	23,076	21,548	14,756	0.24	-31.52
FRANCE	91,743	96,350	91,097	90,579	69,695	1.14	-23.06
GERMANY	181,594	184,619	180,332	170,956	132,877	2.17	-22.27
LUXEMBOURG	1,097	928	964	845	484	0.01	-42.72
NETHERLANDS	77,525	90,807	87,995	83,921	65,529	1.07	-21.92
SWITZERLAND	46,036	45,906	43,668	41,446	30,220	0.49	-27.09
EAST/MED EUR	**23,567**	**26,220**	**21,238**	**23,550**	**19,765**	**0.32**	**-16.07**
ISRAEL	8,660	10,794	10,003	10,548	8,050	0.13	-23.68
TURKEY	14,907	15,426	11,235	13,002	11,715	0.19	-9.90
OTHER EUROPE	**14,925**	**16,992**	**17,700**	**18,207**	**13,972**	**0.23**	**-23.26**
OTHER EUROPE	14,925	16,992	17,700	18,207	13,972	0.23	-23.26
MIDDLE EAST	**41,650**	**45,896**	**44,996**	**20,906**	**12,597**	**0.21**	**-39.74**
MIDDLE EAST	**41,650**	**45,896**	**44,996**	**20,906**	**12,597**	**0.21**	**-39.74**
BAHRAIN	1,697	1,698	1,604	1,480	861	0.01	-41.82

2. ARRIVALS OF NON-RESIDENT VISITORS AT NATIONAL BORDERS, BY NATIONALITY

	1999	2000	2001	2002	2003	Market share 03	% change 03-02
JORDAN	599	663	569	751	338	0.01	-54.99
KUWAIT	5,941	6,949	7,369	5,925	2,667	0.04	-54.99
LEBANON	763	576	533	500	336	0.01	-32.80
LIBYA	99	157	128	106	75		-29.25
SAUDI ARABIA	17,725	20,259	20,452	2,282	1,610	0.03	-29.45
UNTD ARAB EM	4,670	4,501	4,515	4,672	3,280	0.05	-29.79
EGYPT	7,006	7,690	6,509	1,949	1,772	0.03	-9.08
OT MIDD EAST	3,150	3,403	3,317	3,241	1,658	0.03	-48.84
SOUTH ASIA	**510,495**	**594,038**	**581,328**	**556,742**	**470,688**	**7.68**	**-15.46**
SOUTH ASIA	**510,495**	**594,038**	**581,328**	**556,742**	**470,688**	**7.68**	**-15.46**
AFGHANISTAN	220	177	86	64	65		1.56
BANGLADESH	33,718	39,073	42,918	27,049	26,330	0.43	-2.66
SRI LANKA	62,733	68,639	63,274	61,650	55,944	0.91	-9.26
INDIA	344,713	409,999	397,902	434,199	359,476	5.87	-17.21
IRAN	7,922	8,657	9,166	2,901	3,301	0.05	13.79
NEPAL	14,683	13,831	16,342	14,589	10,885	0.18	-25.39
PAKISTAN	40,938	47,874	45,243	10,524	9,575	0.16	-9.02
OTH STH ASIA	5,568	5,788	6,397	5,766	5,112	0.08	-11.34
REG.NOT SPEC	**5,937**	**2,831**	**1,810**	**2,113**	**1,475**	**0.02**	**-30.19**
NOT SPECIFIE	**5,937**	**2,831**	**1,810**	**2,113**	**1,475**	**0.02**	**-30.19**
OTH.WORLD	5,937	2,831	1,810	2,113	1,475	0.02	-30.19

Source: World Tourism Organization (WTO)

SINGAPORE

2. ARRIVALS OF NON-RESIDENT VISITORS AT NATIONAL BORDERS, BY COUNTRY OF RESIDENCE

		1999	2000	2001	2002	2003	Market share 03	% change 03-02
TOTAL	(*)	**6,958,201**	**7,691,399**	**7,522,163**	**7,567,110**	**6,127,029**	**100.00**	**-19.03**
AFRICA		**83,808**	**92,003**	**81,150**	**70,117**	**55,992**	**0.91**	**-20.14**
EAST AFRICA		**20,111**	**21,141**	**17,292**	**13,927**	**9,363**	**0.15**	**-32.77**
MAURITIUS		20,111	21,141	17,292	13,927	9,363	0.15	-32.77
SOUTHERN AFR		**39,627**	**43,119**	**35,558**	**30,524**	**27,486**	**0.45**	**-9.95**
SOUTH AFRICA		39,627	43,119	35,558	30,524	27,486	0.45	-9.95
OTHER AFRICA		**24,070**	**27,743**	**28,300**	**25,666**	**19,143**	**0.31**	**-25.41**
OTHER AFRICA		24,070	27,743	28,300	25,666	19,143	0.31	-25.41
AMERICAS		**444,252**	**482,984**	**433,552**	**416,375**	**314,704**	**5.14**	**-24.42**
CARIBBEAN		**1,713**	**2,119**	**2,000**	**2,019**	**1,464**	**0.02**	**-27.49**
ALL CO CARIB		1,713	2,119	2,000	2,019	1,464	0.02	-27.49
CENTRAL AMER		**1,436**	**1,263**	**1,336**	**1,370**	**750**	**0.01**	**-45.26**
ALL CENT AME		1,436	1,263	1,336	1,370	750	0.01	-45.26
NORTH AMER		**429,420**	**466,859**	**419,616**	**403,220**	**305,727**	**4.99**	**-24.18**
CANADA		72,529	71,393	69,273	67,970	51,256	0.84	-24.59
MEXICO		5,432	9,881	6,538	7,602	3,815	0.06	-49.82
USA		351,459	385,585	343,805	327,648	250,656	4.09	-23.50
SOUTH AMER		**10,937**	**12,189**	**10,034**	**9,434**	**6,568**	**0.11**	**-30.38**
ARGENTINA		2,964	3,074	2,650	1,162	876	0.01	-24.61
BRAZIL		3,904	4,465	3,497	4,191	3,004	0.05	-28.32
CHILE		1,009	1,224	1,012	1,015	809	0.01	-20.30
COLOMBIA		1,057	1,398	1,136	1,325	858	0.01	-35.25
URUGUAY		324	218	83	169	87		-48.52
VENEZUELA		734	699	690	621	393	0.01	-36.71
OTH SOUTH AM		945	1,111	966	951	541	0.01	-43.11
OTHER AMERIC		**746**	**554**	**566**	**332**	**195**		**-41.27**
OTH AMERICA		746	554	566	332	195		-41.27
EAST AS/PACI		**4,849,620**	**5,347,318**	**5,297,821**	**5,426,216**	**4,426,061**	**72.24**	**-18.43**
N/EAST ASIA		**2,061,151**	**2,303,086**	**2,118,417**	**2,249,216**	**1,643,356**	**26.82**	**-26.94**
CHINA		372,881	434,335	497,398	670,098	568,497	9.28	-15.16
TAIWAN(P.C.)		317,502	290,904	222,087	209,321	144,932	2.37	-30.76
HK,CHINA		260,033	285,975	276,157	265,970	226,255	3.69	-14.93
JAPAN		860,662	929,895	755,766	723,431	434,064	7.08	-40.00
KOREA D P RP		699	789	884	1,076	1,068	0.02	-0.74
KOREA REP.		242,226	354,353	359,083	371,050	261,396	4.27	-29.55
MACAU, CHINA		5,752	5,604	5,196	6,315	5,149	0.08	-18.46
MONGOLIA		1,396	1,231	1,846	1,955	1,995	0.03	2.05
S/EAST ASIA		**2,223,971**	**2,427,668**	**2,522,922**	**2,532,887**	**2,307,124**	**37.65**	**-8.91**
BRUNEI DARSM		57,300	57,913	62,264	60,052	41,152	0.67	-31.47
MYANMAR		20,146	22,091	21,675	22,340	19,531	0.32	-12.57
CAMBODIA		8,294	9,030	8,572	7,710	7,640	0.12	-0.91
INDONESIA		1,210,024	1,313,316	1,364,380	1,393,020	1,341,708	21.90	-3.68
LAO P.DEM.R.		820	949	1,091	1,024	887	0.01	-13.38
MALAYSIA		509,199	564,750	578,719	548,659	439,413	7.17	-19.91
PHILIPPINES		161,932	181,032	190,630	195,564	176,574	2.88	-9.71

2. ARRIVALS OF NON-RESIDENT VISITORS AT NATIONAL BORDERS, BY COUNTRY OF RESIDENCE

	1999	2000	2001	2002	2003	Market share 03	% change 03-02
VIET NAM	26,781	31,837	34,633	40,652	44,419	0.72	9.27
THAILAND	229,475	246,750	260,958	263,866	235,800	3.85	-10.64
AUSTRALASIA	**552,724**	**604,621**	**644,964**	**632,523**	**466,390**	**7.61**	**-26.27**
AUSTRALIA	466,067	510,347	550,681	538,408	392,898	6.41	-27.03
NEW ZEALAND	86,657	94,274	94,283	94,115	73,492	1.20	-21.91
MELANESIA	**7,993**	**8,186**	**8,119**	**8,007**	**6,672**	**0.11**	**-16.67**
FIJI	1,882	2,072	2,012	2,195	2,351	0.04	7.11
NEW CALEDNIA	882	1,194	1,179	1,080	913	0.01	-15.46
PAPUA N.GUIN	5,229	4,920	4,928	4,732	3,408	0.06	-27.98
MICRONESIA	**1,621**	**1,242**	**1,096**	**1,041**	**830**	**0.01**	**-20.27**
GUAM	896	852	943	889	723	0.01	-18.67
NAURU	725	390	153	152	107		-29.61
OT.EAST AS/P	**2,160**	**2,515**	**2,303**	**2,542**	**1,689**	**0.03**	**-33.56**
OTH OCEANIA	2,160	2,515	2,303	2,542	1,689	0.03	-33.56
EUROPE	**1,058,433**	**1,138,518**	**1,124,435**	**1,112,156**	**885,118**	**14.45**	**-20.41**
C/E EUROPE	**32,401**	**34,731**	**37,317**	**37,455**	**32,681**	**0.53**	**-12.75**
CZECH REP	3,044	2,748	3,492	3,775	3,057	0.05	-19.02
HUNGARY	2,340	2,610	2,818	2,823	2,408	0.04	-14.70
POLAND	6,975	7,990	8,780	7,686	6,557	0.11	-14.69
CIS	20,042	21,383	22,227	23,171	20,659	0.34	-10.84
NORTHERN EUR	**519,650**	**575,049**	**582,912**	**577,985**	**484,000**	**7.90**	**-16.26**
DENMARK	25,229	25,243	25,431	25,706	21,176	0.35	-17.62
FINLAND	16,770	18,171	14,123	11,317	9,543	0.16	-15.68
IRELAND	17,012	20,330	21,763	23,202	17,828	0.29	-23.16
NORWAY	21,079	23,914	23,138	22,820	18,003	0.29	-21.11
SWEDEN	38,086	42,415	38,439	36,412	29,480	0.48	-19.04
UK	401,474	444,976	460,018	458,528	387,970	6.33	-15.39
SOUTHERN EUR	**76,059**	**75,185**	**66,642**	**71,087**	**43,777**	**0.71**	**-38.42**
GREECE	13,344	13,170	11,319	12,801	7,894	0.13	-38.33
ITALY	43,814	42,230	35,739	36,737	20,342	0.33	-44.63
PORTUGAL	3,738	3,152	3,019	3,008	1,917	0.03	-36.27
SPAIN	13,909	15,117	15,268	17,324	12,527	0.20	-27.69
SERBIA,MTNEG	1,254	1,516	1,297	1,217	1,097	0.02	-9.86
WESTERN EUR	**391,097**	**409,707**	**397,416**	**382,934**	**290,280**	**4.74**	**-24.20**
AUSTRIA	16,725	15,979	14,051	14,645	9,373	0.15	-36.00
BELGIUM	18,415	22,436	21,895	20,357	14,059	0.23	-30.94
FRANCE	74,049	74,773	71,456	72,153	55,760	0.91	-22.72
GERMANY	167,856	169,408	166,981	157,510	121,370	1.98	-22.94
LUXEMBOURG	1,542	1,462	1,525	1,384	918	0.01	-33.67
NETHERLANDS	64,665	77,326	74,989	71,651	55,355	0.90	-22.74
SWITZERLAND	47,845	48,323	46,519	45,234	33,445	0.55	-26.06
EAST/MED EUR	**22,318**	**25,068**	**20,221**	**22,471**	**18,872**	**0.31**	**-16.02**
ISRAEL	8,440	10,646	9,803	10,288	7,779	0.13	-24.39
TURKEY	13,878	14,422	10,418	12,183	11,093	0.18	-8.95
OTHER EUROPE	**16,908**	**18,778**	**19,927**	**20,224**	**15,508**	**0.25**	**-23.32**
OTHER EUROPE	16,908	18,778	19,927	20,224	15,508	0.25	-23.32
MIDDLE EAST	**66,045**	**70,628**	**71,516**	**46,770**	**29,842**	**0.49**	**-36.19**

SINGAPORE

2. ARRIVALS OF NON-RESIDENT VISITORS AT NATIONAL BORDERS, BY COUNTRY OF RESIDENCE

	1999	2000	2001	2002	2003	Market share 03	% change 03-02
MIDDLE EAST	**66,045**	**70,628**	**71,516**	**46,770**	**29,842**	**0.49**	**-36.19**
BAHRAIN	2,928	3,058	2,970	2,676	1,654	0.03	-38.19
JORDAN	545	596	614	741	288		-61.13
KUWAIT	7,137	8,221	8,690	7,113	3,174	0.05	-55.38
LEBANON	564	463	494	645	265		-58.91
LIBYA	74	94	102	96	43		-55.21
SAUDI ARABIA	23,109	24,751	25,113	6,753	3,477	0.06	-48.51
UNTD ARAB EM	20,244	21,017	21,619	20,784	15,684	0.26	-24.54
EGYPT	6,275	7,411	6,737	2,621	2,318	0.04	-11.56
OT MIDD EAST	5,169	5,017	5,177	5,341	2,939	0.05	-44.97
SOUTH ASIA	**444,088**	**516,293**	**508,302**	**490,262**	**415,124**	**6.78**	**-15.33**
SOUTH ASIA	**444,088**	**516,293**	**508,302**	**490,262**	**415,124**	**6.78**	**-15.33**
AFGHANISTAN	146	105	76	63	58		-7.94
BANGLADESH	33,278	38,646	42,415	27,552	26,380	0.43	-4.25
SRI LANKA	60,101	63,170	56,248	54,690	51,405	0.84	-6.01
INDIA	288,383	346,356	339,813	375,659	309,446	5.05	-17.63
IRAN	6,166	6,809	7,551	2,530	3,089	0.05	22.09
NEPAL	13,464	12,674	14,780	13,202	10,013	0.16	-24.16
PAKISTAN	36,264	42,495	40,842	10,569	9,398	0.15	-11.08
OTH STH ASIA	6,286	6,038	6,577	5,997	5,335	0.09	-11.04
REG.NOT SPEC	**11,955**	**43,655**	**5,387**	**5,214**	**188**		**-96.39**
NOT SPECIFIE	**11,955**	**43,655**	**5,387**	**5,214**	**188**		**-96.39**
OTH.WORLD	11,955	43,655	5,387	5,214	188		-96.39

Source: World Tourism Organization (WTO)

SLOVAKIA

4. ARRIVALS OF NON-RESIDENT TOURISTS IN ALL TYPES OF ACCOMMODATION ESTABLISHMENTS, BY NATIONALITY

	1999	2000	2001	2002	2003	Market share 03	% change 03-02
TOTAL (*)	**975,105**	**1,045,614**	**1,219,099**	**1,398,740**	**1,386,791**	**100.00**	**-0.85**
AFRICA	**2,664**	**2,670**	**3,131**	**2,960**	**2,581**	**0.19**	**-12.80**
EAST AFRICA	**14**	**14**	**9**	**5**	**7**		**40.00**
KENYA	14	14	9	5	7		40.00
NORTH AFRICA	**195**	**79**	**163**	**143**	**45**		**-68.53**
TUNISIA	195	79	163	143	45		-68.53
SOUTHERN AFR	**232**	**292**	**518**	**404**	**330**	**0.02**	**-18.32**
SOUTH AFRICA	232	292	518	404	330	0.02	-18.32
OTHER AFRICA	**2,223**	**2,285**	**2,441**	**2,408**	**2,199**	**0.16**	**-8.68**
OTHER AFRICA	2,223	2,285	2,441	2,408	2,199	0.16	-8.68
AMERICAS	**30,683**	**35,821**	**35,922**	**33,352**	**33,981**	**2.45**	**1.89**
CARIBBEAN	**45**	**47**	**49**	**14**	**23**		**64.29**
DOMINICAN RP	45	47	49	14	23		64.29
NORTH AMER	**26,860**	**32,529**	**33,096**	**30,595**	**31,133**	**2.24**	**1.76**
CANADA	3,505	3,623	4,738	4,958	5,542	0.40	11.78
MEXICO	45	55	175	255	208	0.01	-18.43
USA	23,310	28,851	28,183	25,382	25,383	1.83	
SOUTH AMER	**185**	**382**	**673**	**773**	**614**	**0.04**	**-20.57**
ARGENTINA	99	214	457	394	295	0.02	-25.13
BRAZIL	86	168	216	379	319	0.02	-15.83
OTHER AMERIC	**3,593**	**2,863**	**2,104**	**1,970**	**2,211**	**0.16**	**12.23**
OTH AMERICA	3,593	2,863	2,104	1,970	2,211	0.16	12.23
EAST AS/PACI	**23,204**	**25,417**	**30,089**	**34,130**	**32,258**	**2.33**	**-5.48**
N/EAST ASIA	**9,922**	**10,747**	**9,991**	**10,469**	**9,133**	**0.66**	**-12.76**
CHINA	606	537	550	780	684	0.05	-12.31
JAPAN	9,169	9,775	8,878	9,153	7,278	0.52	-20.49
KOREA REP.	147	435	563	536	1,171	0.08	118.47
S/EAST ASIA	**26**	**28**	**305**	**132**	**331**	**0.02**	**150.76**
THAILAND	26	28	305	132	331	0.02	150.76
AUSTRALASIA	**2,730**	**2,436**	**4,130**	**5,277**	**7,590**	**0.55**	**43.83**
AUSTRALIA			3,795	4,799	6,965	0.50	45.13
NEW ZEALAND			335	478	625	0.05	30.75
AUST/N.ZLND	2,730	2,436					
OT.EAST AS/P	**10,526**	**12,206**	**15,663**	**18,252**	**15,204**	**1.10**	**-16.70**
OTHER ASIA	10,526	12,206	15,663	18,252	15,204	1.10	-16.70
EUROPE	**917,862**	**980,250**	**1,147,970**	**1,326,492**	**1,316,120**	**94.90**	**-0.78**
C/E EUROPE	**578,888**	**616,174**	**734,344**	**869,216**	**857,005**	**61.80**	**-1.40**
BULGARIA	5,306	3,147	3,718	3,464	3,235	0.23	-6.61
BELARUS	2,318	3,800	1,437	1,578	1,985	0.14	25.79
CZECH REP	275,031	277,401	327,607	447,962	469,991	33.89	4.92

4. ARRIVALS OF NON-RESIDENT TOURISTS IN ALL TYPES OF ACCOMMODATION ESTABLISHMENTS, BY NATIONALITY

	1999	2000	2001	2002	2003	Market share 03	% change 03-02
ESTONIA	1,027	1,308	2,978	3,034	2,979	0.21	-1.81
HUNGARY	53,057	59,322	73,937	88,268	100,546	7.25	13.91
LATVIA	1,173	912	1,906	2,913	3,528	0.25	21.11
LITHUANIA	6,399	7,392	10,224	9,452	9,789	0.71	3.57
REP MOLDOVA	111	189	224	657	1,427	0.10	117.20
POLAND	173,135	201,082	264,631	266,911	215,383	15.53	-19.31
ROMANIA	7,238	6,548	8,943	5,123	5,776	0.42	12.75
RUSSIAN FED	22,361	30,861	19,876	20,313	22,681	1.64	11.66
UKRAINE	31,732	24,212	18,863	19,541	19,685	1.42	0.74
NORTHERN EUR	**34,021**	**36,068**	**43,053**	**57,129**	**54,129**	**3.90**	**-5.25**
DENMARK	5,570	5,260	6,475	9,390	7,946	0.57	-15.38
FINLAND	2,797	2,795	4,329	7,467	8,017	0.58	7.37
ICELAND			95	143	98	0.01	-31.47
IRELAND	365	788	1,085	1,847	2,059	0.15	11.48
NORWAY	2,618	2,530	2,713	3,213	3,301	0.24	2.74
SWEDEN	4,622	5,603	6,722	6,977	6,646	0.48	-4.74
UK	18,049	19,092	21,634	28,092	26,062	1.88	-7.23
SOUTHERN EUR	**51,166**	**53,004**	**62,745**	**67,625**	**74,756**	**5.39**	**10.54**
ALBANIA	488	896	518	447	831	0.06	85.91
BOSNIA HERZG	211	611	611	486	852	0.06	75.31
CROATIA	7,989	8,311	8,981	9,489	11,499	0.83	21.18
GREECE	1,732	1,691	2,200	1,906	2,163	0.16	13.48
ITALY	27,076	28,097	32,737	34,998	37,996	2.74	8.57
MALTA	70	29	49	187	107	0.01	-42.78
PORTUGAL			622	981	894	0.06	-8.87
SLOVENIA	5,542	5,650	7,286	9,351	10,404	0.75	11.26
SPAIN	2,976	3,568	4,985	5,463	5,464	0.39	0.02
TFYROM	219	175	214	227	203	0.01	-10.57
SERBIA,MTNEG	4,863	3,976	4,542	4,090	4,343	0.31	6.19
WESTERN EUR	**220,616**	**242,564**	**278,572**	**305,437**	**301,617**	**21.75**	**-1.25**
AUSTRIA	32,643	36,779	44,046	47,072	51,365	3.70	9.12
BELGIUM	8,735	8,443	11,123	11,338	10,626	0.77	-6.28
FRANCE	14,833	16,015	19,523	21,890	28,629	2.06	30.79
GERMANY	137,964	155,129	172,446	188,733	175,746	12.67	-6.88
LUXEMBOURG	112	106	114	254	217	0.02	-14.57
NETHERLANDS	16,540	18,772	22,068	23,945	24,487	1.77	2.26
SWITZERLAND	9,789	7,320	9,252	12,205	10,547	0.76	-13.58
EAST/MED EUR	**14,087**	**12,682**	**11,055**	**8,188**	**9,831**	**0.71**	**20.07**
CYPRUS	238	247	627	506	452	0.03	-10.67
ISRAEL	12,841	10,879	9,123	6,563	7,988	0.58	21.71
TURKEY	1,008	1,556	1,305	1,119	1,391	0.10	24.31
OTHER EUROPE	**19,084**	**19,758**	**18,201**	**18,897**	**18,782**	**1.35**	**-0.61**
OTHER EUROPE	19,084	19,758	18,201	18,897	18,782	1.35	-0.61
MIDDLE EAST	**180**	**238**	**334**	**224**	**241**	**0.02**	**7.59**
MIDDLE EAST	**180**	**238**	**334**	**224**	**241**	**0.02**	**7.59**
EGYPT	180	238	334	224	241	0.02	7.59
SOUTH ASIA	**425**	**1,117**	**1,515**	**1,437**	**1,305**	**0.09**	**-9.19**
SOUTH ASIA	**425**	**1,117**	**1,515**	**1,437**	**1,305**	**0.09**	**-9.19**

SLOVAKIA

4. ARRIVALS OF NON-RESIDENT TOURISTS IN ALL TYPES OF ACCOMMODATION ESTABLISHMENTS, BY NATIONALITY

	1999	2000	2001	2002	2003	Market share 03	% change 03-02
INDIA	425	1,117	1,515	1,437	1,305	0.09	-9.19
REG.NOT SPEC	**87**	**101**	**138**	**145**	**305**	**0.02**	**110.34**
NOT SPECIFIE	**87**	**101**	**138**	**145**	**305**	**0.02**	**110.34**
OTH.WORLD	87	101	138	145	305	0.02	110.34

Source: World Tourism Organization (WTO)

6. OVERNIGHT STAYS OF NON-RESIDENT TOURISTS IN ALL TYPES OF ACCOMMODATION ESTABLISHMENTS, BY NATIONALITY

		1999	2000	2001	2002	2003	Market share 03	% change 03-02
TOTAL	(*)	**3,523,874**	**3,703,866**	**4,377,556**	**5,043,135**	**4,964,392**	**100.00**	**-1.56**
AFRICA		**9,289**	**10,538**	**10,737**	**10,068**	**8,936**	**0.18**	**-11.24**
EAST AFRICA		**26**	**22**	**18**	**17**	**14**		**-17.65**
KENYA		26	22	18	17	14		-17.65
NORTH AFRICA		**831**	**530**	**663**	**521**	**147**		**-71.79**
TUNISIA		831	530	663	521	147		-71.79
SOUTHERN AFR		**596**	**804**	**1,954**	**1,069**	**1,092**	**0.02**	**2.15**
SOUTH AFRICA		596	804	1,954	1,069	1,092	0.02	2.15
OTHER AFRICA		**7,836**	**9,182**	**8,102**	**8,461**	**7,683**	**0.15**	**-9.20**
OTHER AFRICA		7,836	9,182	8,102	8,461	7,683	0.15	-9.20
AMERICAS		**85,775**	**108,420**	**106,053**	**102,281**	**95,994**	**1.93**	**-6.15**
CARIBBEAN		**129**	**140**	**196**	**38**	**67**		**76.32**
DOMINICAN RP		129	140	196	38	67		76.32
NORTH AMER		**74,590**	**96,163**	**94,814**	**91,440**	**85,262**	**1.72**	**-6.76**
CANADA		10,099	10,016	12,441	15,368	15,551	0.31	1.19
MEXICO		95	169	519	1,456	630	0.01	-56.73
USA		64,396	85,978	81,854	74,616	69,081	1.39	-7.42
SOUTH AMER		**419**	**1,143**	**2,211**	**2,797**	**2,228**	**0.04**	**-20.34**
ARGENTINA		242	460	1,318	776	710	0.01	-8.51
BRAZIL		177	683	893	2,021	1,518	0.03	-24.89
OTHER AMERIC		**10,637**	**10,974**	**8,832**	**8,006**	**8,437**	**0.17**	**5.38**
OTH AMERICA		10,637	10,974	8,832	8,006	8,437	0.17	5.38
EAST AS/PACI		**74,027**	**74,789**	**93,410**	**98,758**	**90,426**	**1.82**	**-8.44**
N/EAST ASIA		**16,302**	**16,708**	**19,302**	**18,878**	**19,618**	**0.40**	**3.92**
CHINA		967	1,817	2,211	1,559	1,346	0.03	-13.66
JAPAN		15,044	13,933	15,677	15,651	14,102	0.28	-9.90
KOREA REP.		291	958	1,414	1,668	4,170	0.08	150.00
S/EAST ASIA		**50**	**54**	**1,125**	**538**	**1,050**	**0.02**	**95.17**
THAILAND		50	54	1,125	538	1,050	0.02	95.17
AUSTRALASIA		**6,721**	**6,559**	**9,580**	**12,676**	**16,519**	**0.33**	**30.32**
AUSTRALIA				8,998	11,768	15,469	0.31	31.45
NEW ZEALAND				582	908	1,050	0.02	15.64
AUST/N.ZLND		6,721	6,559					
OT.EAST AS/P		**50,954**	**51,468**	**63,403**	**66,666**	**53,239**	**1.07**	**-20.14**
OTHER ASIA		50,954	51,468	63,403	66,666	53,239	1.07	-20.14
EUROPE		**3,352,154**	**3,506,433**	**4,162,425**	**4,823,625**	**4,764,280**	**95.97**	**-1.23**
C/E EUROPE		**1,936,755**	**2,018,033**	**2,477,680**	**2,936,097**	**2,937,754**	**59.18**	**0.06**
BULGARIA		10,095	7,204	7,215	7,609	7,264	0.15	-4.53
BELARUS		9,337	11,617	6,481	9,127	12,171	0.25	33.35
CZECH REP		899,541	887,999	1,069,202	1,478,155	1,674,918	33.74	13.31

6. OVERNIGHT STAYS OF NON-RESIDENT TOURISTS IN ALL TYPES OF ACCOMMODATION ESTABLISHMENTS, BY NATIONALITY

	1999	2000	2001	2002	2003	Market share 03	% change 03-02
ESTONIA	3,018	2,152	8,050	8,226	7,373	0.15	-10.37
HUNGARY	171,064	191,466	233,235	268,066	295,686	5.96	10.30
LATVIA	3,110	2,331	6,659	7,730	8,662	0.17	12.06
LITHUANIA	19,778	18,433	24,046	24,988	25,038	0.50	0.20
REP MOLDOVA	248	478	591	1,421	3,244	0.07	128.29
POLAND	611,171	690,950	939,399	940,805	703,067	14.16	-25.27
ROMANIA	15,036	13,733	22,051	15,344	15,454	0.31	0.72
RUSSIAN FED	93,419	98,937	86,596	87,250	96,873	1.95	11.03
UKRAINE	100,938	92,733	74,155	87,376	88,004	1.77	0.72
NORTHERN EUR	**86,627**	**87,769**	**107,945**	**148,910**	**135,873**	**2.74**	**-8.75**
DENMARK	16,677	14,783	18,245	32,075	22,461	0.45	-29.97
FINLAND	6,006	5,885	10,987	19,023	22,005	0.44	15.68
ICELAND			153	277	425	0.01	53.43
IRELAND	1,003	2,584	3,090	4,701	4,696	0.09	-0.11
NORWAY	6,260	5,757	6,663	8,397	8,564	0.17	1.99
SWEDEN	10,632	12,130	15,573	15,971	14,684	0.30	-8.06
UK	46,049	46,630	53,234	68,466	63,038	1.27	-7.93
SOUTHERN EUR	**151,973**	**135,163**	**156,597**	**164,881**	**173,144**	**3.49**	**5.01**
ALBANIA	1,211	2,526	1,852	2,026	2,217	0.04	9.43
BOSNIA HERZG	420	1,347	2,173	1,490	2,288	0.05	53.56
CROATIA	26,722	26,203	30,332	28,084	30,370	0.61	8.14
GREECE	5,760	5,804	6,911	5,638	5,729	0.12	1.61
ITALY	60,778	61,188	70,931	75,371	79,203	1.60	5.08
MALTA	202	86	96	402	332	0.01	-17.41
PORTUGAL			1,353	2,744	2,972	0.06	8.31
SLOVENIA	26,863	14,022	15,730	22,257	24,100	0.49	8.28
SPAIN	7,869	9,343	12,661	13,909	11,755	0.24	-15.49
TFYROM	449	389	434	502	625	0.01	24.50
SERBIA,MTNEG	21,699	14,255	14,124	12,458	13,553	0.27	8.79
WESTERN EUR	**1,046,341**	**1,140,000**	**1,301,294**	**1,463,075**	**1,407,062**	**28.34**	**-3.83**
AUSTRIA	113,441	121,209	146,079	160,328	176,115	3.55	9.85
BELGIUM	29,879	26,948	30,544	32,465	28,638	0.58	-11.79
FRANCE	33,808	35,235	43,060	49,129	59,226	1.19	20.55
GERMANY	797,892	884,616	990,765	1,111,066	1,037,062	20.89	-6.66
LUXEMBOURG	247	214	320	627	490	0.01	-21.85
NETHERLANDS	49,884	55,118	69,608	79,273	80,114	1.61	1.06
SWITZERLAND	21,190	16,660	20,918	30,187	25,417	0.51	-15.80
EAST/MED EUR	**65,617**	**70,952**	**64,250**	**54,377**	**53,706**	**1.08**	**-1.23**
CYPRUS	1,178	1,345	3,379	3,553	2,616	0.05	-26.37
ISRAEL	61,866	65,679	58,129	48,442	48,156	0.97	-0.59
TURKEY	2,573	3,928	2,742	2,382	2,934	0.06	23.17
OTHER EUROPE	**64,841**	**54,516**	**54,659**	**56,285**	**56,741**	**1.14**	**0.81**
OTHER EUROPE	64,841	54,516	54,659	56,285	56,741	1.14	0.81
MIDDLE EAST	**1,206**	**1,470**	**1,970**	**1,857**	**1,749**	**0.04**	**-5.82**
MIDDLE EAST	**1,206**	**1,470**	**1,970**	**1,857**	**1,749**	**0.04**	**-5.82**
EGYPT	1,206	1,470	1,970	1,857	1,749	0.04	-5.82
SOUTH ASIA	**1,311**	**2,090**	**2,508**	**5,993**	**1,957**	**0.04**	**-67.35**
SOUTH ASIA	**1,311**	**2,090**	**2,508**	**5,993**	**1,957**	**0.04**	**-67.35**

6. OVERNIGHT STAYS OF NON-RESIDENT TOURISTS IN ALL TYPES OF ACCOMMODATION ESTABLISHMENTS, BY NATIONALITY

	1999	2000	2001	2002	2003	Market share 03	% change 03-02
INDIA	1,311	2,090	2,508	5,993	1,957	0.04	-67.35
REG.NOT SPEC	**112**	**126**	**453**	**553**	**1,050**	**0.02**	**89.87**
NOT SPECIFIE	**112**	**126**	**453**	**553**	**1,050**	**0.02**	**89.87**
OTH.WORLD	112	126	453	553	1,050	0.02	89.87

Source: World Tourism Organization (WTO)

SLOVENIA

3. ARRIVALS OF NON-RESIDENT TOURISTS IN HOTELS AND SIMILAR ESTABLISHMENTS, BY NATIONALITY

	1999	2000	2001	2002	2003	Market share 03	% change 03-02
TOTAL	**739,756**	**884,362**	**933,275**	**1,005,567**	**1,052,847**	**100.00**	**4.70**
AMERICAS	**20,217**	**27,413**	**28,458**	**31,520**	**30,815**	**2.93**	**-2.24**
NORTH AMER	**20,217**	**27,413**	**28,458**	**31,520**	**30,815**	**2.93**	**-2.24**
CANADA	2,864	4,303	4,144	5,046	5,237	0.50	3.79
USA	17,353	23,110	24,314	26,474	25,578	2.43	-3.38
EAST AS/PACI	**6,661**	**9,550**	**10,712**	**12,263**	**11,925**	**1.13**	**-2.76**
N/EAST ASIA	**3,657**	**5,640**	**5,953**	**6,260**	**5,809**	**0.55**	**-7.20**
JAPAN	3,657	5,640	5,953	6,260	5,809	0.55	-7.20
AUSTRALASIA	**3,004**	**3,910**	**4,759**	**6,003**	**6,116**	**0.58**	**1.88**
AUSTRALIA	2,582	3,364	4,075	5,062	5,065	0.48	0.06
NEW ZEALAND	422	546	684	941	1,051	0.10	11.69
EUROPE	**704,859**	**838,598**	**885,291**	**951,052**	**999,215**	**94.91**	**5.06**
C/E EUROPE	**61,586**	**76,208**	**87,579**	**89,750**	**93,643**	**8.89**	**4.34**
BULGARIA	2,944	4,892	6,571	7,159	7,197	0.68	0.53
BELARUS	374	402	393	504	512	0.05	1.59
CZECH REP	11,465	12,477	13,372	13,335	14,615	1.39	9.60
HUNGARY	15,661	20,495	20,897	20,585	22,451	2.13	9.06
POLAND	7,305	11,848	14,922	14,202	12,630	1.20	-11.07
ROMANIA	4,544	3,854	5,612	6,768	7,080	0.67	4.61
RUSSIAN FED	9,741	11,482	14,200	14,277	14,603	1.39	2.28
SLOVAKIA	4,930	5,412	5,893	5,738	7,000	0.66	21.99
UKRAINE	3,284	3,637	3,337	3,751	4,522	0.43	20.55
BALTIC COUNT	1,338	1,709	2,382	3,431	3,033	0.29	-11.60
NORTHERN EUR	**40,004**	**48,391**	**55,574**	**61,576**	**69,528**	**6.60**	**12.91**
DENMARK	3,555	4,125	5,452	4,866	5,892	0.56	21.09
FINLAND	2,209	2,198	2,217	3,028	4,220	0.40	39.37
ICELAND	448	350	535	757	791	0.08	4.49
IRELAND	1,998	2,649	3,563	4,717	6,442	0.61	36.57
NORWAY	3,073	2,334	3,266	4,181	4,584	0.44	9.64
SWEDEN	7,466	9,159	8,164	7,638	8,360	0.79	9.45
UK	21,255	27,576	32,377	36,389	39,239	3.73	7.83
SOUTHERN EUR	**311,536**	**361,217**	**363,629**	**376,134**	**392,923**	**37.32**	**4.46**
BOSNIA HERZG	24,516	27,069	24,856	24,590	24,803	2.36	0.87
CROATIA	69,980	76,068	76,677	75,812	75,685	7.19	-0.17
GREECE	1,754	1,582	1,971	1,996	3,036	0.29	52.10
ITALY	190,884	230,868	232,956	238,534	247,668	23.52	3.83
PORTUGAL	1,176	1,097	1,205	1,512	2,445	0.23	61.71
SPAIN	3,208	4,917	4,469	6,489	8,553	0.81	31.81
TFYROM	11,440	9,001	8,099	9,354	8,493	0.81	-9.20
SERBIA,MTNEG	8,578	10,615	13,396	17,847	22,240	2.11	24.61
WESTERN EUR	**276,696**	**334,128**	**358,562**	**384,321**	**399,464**	**37.94**	**3.94**
AUSTRIA	106,467	125,366	138,127	152,134	161,138	15.30	5.92
BELGIUM	9,510	11,746	13,275	15,726	16,573	1.57	5.39
FRANCE	15,825	18,338	17,804	21,246	25,307	2.40	19.11
GERMANY	122,640	151,309	160,442	161,418	159,077	15.11	-1.45

SLOVENIA

3. ARRIVALS OF NON-RESIDENT TOURISTS IN HOTELS AND SIMILAR ESTABLISHMENTS, BY NATIONALITY

	1999	2000	2001	2002	2003	Market share 03	% change 03-02
LUXEMBOURG	478	449	558	701	756	0.07	7.85
NETHERLANDS	11,482	14,277	14,477	16,417	18,463	1.75	12.46
SWITZERLAND	10,294	12,643	13,879	16,679	18,150	1.72	8.82
EAST/MED EUR	**10,296**	**14,325**	**15,634**	**35,100**	**39,469**	**3.75**	**12.45**
ISRAEL	5,546	10,352	12,828	29,342	35,140	3.34	19.76
TURKEY	4,750	3,973	2,806	5,758	4,329	0.41	-24.82
OTHER EUROPE	**4,741**	**4,329**	**4,313**	**4,171**	**4,188**	**0.40**	**0.41**
OTHER EUROPE	4,741	4,329	4,313	4,171	4,188	0.40	0.41
REG.NOT SPEC	**8,019**	**8,801**	**8,814**	**10,732**	**10,892**	**1.03**	**1.49**
NOT SPECIFIE	**8,019**	**8,801**	**8,814**	**10,732**	**10,892**	**1.03**	**1.49**
OTH.WORLD	8,019	8,801	8,814	10,732	10,892	1.03	1.49

Source: World Tourism Organization (WTO)

4. ARRIVALS OF NON-RESIDENT TOURISTS IN ALL TYPES OF ACCOMMODATION ESTABLISHMENTS, BY NATIONALITY

	1999	2000	2001	2002	2003	Market share 03	% change 03-02
TOTAL	**884,048**	**1,089,549**	**1,218,721**	**1,302,019**	**1,373,137**	**100.00**	**5.46**
AMERICAS	**22,290**	**30,221**	**33,344**	**36,232**	**35,945**	**2.62**	**-0.79**
NORTH AMER	**22,290**	**30,221**	**33,344**	**36,232**	**35,945**	**2.62**	**-0.79**
CANADA	3,387	4,859	5,090	6,129	6,298	0.46	2.76
USA	18,903	25,362	28,254	30,103	29,647	2.16	-1.51
EAST AS/PACI	**8,286**	**11,725**	**15,065**	**17,430**	**17,141**	**1.25**	**-1.66**
N/EAST ASIA	**4,008**	**6,015**	**6,770**	**6,921**	**6,539**	**0.48**	**-5.52**
JAPAN	4,008	6,015	6,770	6,921	6,539	0.48	-5.52
AUSTRALASIA	**4,278**	**5,710**	**8,295**	**10,509**	**10,602**	**0.77**	**0.88**
AUSTRALIA	3,405	4,482	6,755	8,499	8,360	0.61	-1.64
NEW ZEALAND	873	1,228	1,540	2,010	2,242	0.16	11.54
EUROPE	**844,728**	**1,037,797**	**1,159,864**	**1,235,856**	**1,307,775**	**95.24**	**5.82**
C/E EUROPE	**91,353**	**113,694**	**132,892**	**136,590**	**141,165**	**10.28**	**3.35**
BULGARIA	3,059	5,097	7,213	7,831	7,915	0.58	1.07
BELARUS	434	419	913	1,036	572	0.04	-44.79
CZECH REP	22,550	26,652	28,960	30,030	31,314	2.28	4.28
HUNGARY	25,120	30,374	32,607	32,774	37,111	2.70	13.23
POLAND	13,384	21,248	26,037	24,805	20,360	1.48	-17.92
ROMANIA	4,783	4,321	6,443	7,596	8,080	0.59	6.37
RUSSIAN FED	10,418	12,071	15,514	15,370	16,030	1.17	4.29
SLOVAKIA	6,414	6,902	7,900	7,832	10,370	0.76	32.41
UKRAINE	3,489	3,941	3,755	4,249	5,008	0.36	17.86
BALTIC COUNT	1,702	2,669	3,550	5,067	4,405	0.32	-13.06
NORTHERN EUR	**45,792**	**56,884**	**72,899**	**81,281**	**91,556**	**6.67**	**12.64**
DENMARK	4,728	6,002	8,588	8,712	9,740	0.71	11.80
FINLAND	2,506	2,757	3,088	3,844	5,568	0.41	44.85
ICELAND	506	387	605	814	922	0.07	13.27
IRELAND	2,231	3,120	4,908	6,496	8,624	0.63	32.76
NORWAY	3,449	2,799	4,103	5,131	5,542	0.40	8.01
SWEDEN	8,669	10,606	11,184	10,167	10,940	0.80	7.60
UK	23,703	31,213	40,423	46,117	50,220	3.66	8.90
SOUTHERN EUR	**344,615**	**407,513**	**427,495**	**441,014**	**463,687**	**33.77**	**5.14**
BOSNIA HERZG	26,304	28,910	27,885	27,770	27,644	2.01	-0.45
CROATIA	81,988	91,286	95,540	94,176	93,639	6.82	-0.57
GREECE	1,852	1,683	2,188	2,273	3,372	0.25	48.35
ITALY	207,230	256,212	269,338	274,792	288,507	21.01	4.99
PORTUGAL	1,411	1,696	1,653	2,264	3,222	0.23	42.31
SPAIN	4,123	6,837	6,828	9,860	12,951	0.94	31.35
TFYROM	12,098	9,454	8,907	10,292	9,233	0.67	-10.29
SERBIA,MTNEG	9,609	11,435	15,156	19,587	25,119	1.83	28.24
WESTERN EUR	**346,602**	**439,649**	**504,184**	**534,313**	**560,873**	**40.85**	**4.97**
AUSTRIA	126,370	150,309	174,403	193,422	201,367	14.66	4.11
BELGIUM	11,553	16,114	19,094	23,637	25,000	1.82	5.77
FRANCE	17,874	22,169	23,452	27,863	34,745	2.53	24.70
GERMANY	157,502	204,003	234,209	229,211	229,372	16.70	0.07

SLOVENIA

4. ARRIVALS OF NON-RESIDENT TOURISTS IN ALL TYPES OF ACCOMMODATION ESTABLISHMENTS, BY NATIONALITY

	1999	2000	2001	2002	2003	Market share 03	% change 03-02
LUXEMBOURG	529	511	658	872	1,113	0.08	27.64
NETHERLANDS	20,982	31,494	34,813	38,682	46,762	3.41	20.89
SWITZERLAND	11,792	15,049	17,555	20,626	22,514	1.64	9.15
EAST/MED EUR	**10,818**	**15,017**	**17,319**	**37,917**	**44,361**	**3.23**	**17.00**
ISRAEL	5,958	10,896	14,372	31,972	39,852	2.90	24.65
TURKEY	4,860	4,121	2,947	5,945	4,509	0.33	-24.15
OTHER EUROPE	**5,548**	**5,040**	**5,075**	**4,741**	**6,133**	**0.45**	**29.36**
OTHER EUROPE	5,548	5,040	5,075	4,741	6,133	0.45	29.36
REG.NOT SPEC	**8,744**	**9,806**	**10,448**	**12,501**	**12,276**	**0.89**	**-1.80**
NOT SPECIFIE	**8,744**	**9,806**	**10,448**	**12,501**	**12,276**	**0.89**	**-1.80**
OTH.WORLD	8,744	9,806	10,448	12,501	12,276	0.89	-1.80

Source: World Tourism Organization (WTO)

SLOVENIA

5. OVERNIGHT STAYS OF NON-RESIDENT TOURISTS IN HOTELS AND SIMILAR ESTABLISHMENTS, BY NATIONALITY

	1999	2000	2001	2002	2003	Market share 03	% change 03-02
TOTAL	2,267,183	2,757,751	2,878,885	3,049,389	3,165,602	100.00	3.81
AMERICAS	54,602	71,607	68,806	74,670	72,064	2.28	-3.49
NORTH AMER	54,602	71,607	68,806	74,670	72,064	2.28	-3.49
CANADA	7,936	10,776	10,803	13,248	14,190	0.45	7.11
USA	46,666	60,831	58,003	61,422	57,874	1.83	-5.78
EAST AS/PACI	14,859	19,419	22,263	28,885	26,906	0.85	-6.85
N/EAST ASIA	8,259	10,991	12,093	12,502	11,156	0.35	-10.77
JAPAN	8,259	10,991	12,093	12,502	11,156	0.35	-10.77
AUSTRALASIA	6,600	8,428	10,170	16,383	15,750	0.50	-3.86
AUSTRALIA	5,712	7,167	8,797	14,240	13,593	0.43	-4.54
NEW ZEALAND	888	1,261	1,373	2,143	2,157	0.07	0.65
EUROPE	2,173,630	2,638,905	2,757,558	2,905,824	3,037,532	95.95	4.53
C/E EUROPE	205,411	235,692	264,377	276,466	306,131	9.67	10.73
BULGARIA	15,545	9,482	11,264	12,658	13,069	0.41	3.25
BELARUS	1,823	1,668	2,250	2,073	2,030	0.06	-2.07
CZECH REP	25,776	28,246	30,308	29,712	33,734	1.07	13.54
HUNGARY	44,172	55,933	54,252	52,913	59,880	1.89	13.17
POLAND	19,028	24,307	30,570	29,991	30,100	0.95	0.36
ROMANIA	12,684	10,387	11,812	14,935	16,196	0.51	8.44
RUSSIAN FED	47,922	65,233	85,791	86,786	93,439	2.95	7.67
SLOVAKIA	13,141	13,753	12,243	17,210	24,584	0.78	42.85
UKRAINE	20,978	21,890	20,321	21,741	25,055	0.79	15.24
BALTIC COUNT	4,342	4,793	5,566	8,447	8,044	0.25	-4.77
NORTHERN EUR	170,692	202,350	224,380	233,046	255,722	8.08	9.73
DENMARK	10,652	12,705	14,899	13,037	16,589	0.52	27.25
FINLAND	5,766	5,046	6,396	7,540	11,956	0.38	58.57
ICELAND	2,134	1,116	946	3,540	3,371	0.11	-4.77
IRELAND	8,458	10,766	14,131	18,635	25,307	0.80	35.80
NORWAY	7,926	6,121	9,223	10,899	10,510	0.33	-3.57
SWEDEN	24,899	25,234	20,764	18,282	20,982	0.66	14.77
UK	110,857	141,362	158,021	161,113	167,007	5.28	3.66
SOUTHERN EUR	753,811	938,899	926,370	972,717	1,028,702	32.50	5.76
BOSNIA HERZG	60,318	76,781	62,836	65,439	87,381	2.76	33.53
CROATIA	175,971	198,440	198,915	195,848	204,996	6.48	4.67
GREECE	4,016	4,023	5,741	4,955	7,995	0.25	61.35
ITALY	447,162	584,928	590,368	618,314	626,530	19.79	1.33
PORTUGAL	8,554	3,434	3,259	3,508	6,606	0.21	88.31
SPAIN	8,114	12,243	10,145	14,032	20,185	0.64	43.85
TFYROM	24,526	26,345	18,466	19,677	18,051	0.57	-8.26
SERBIA,MTNEG	25,150	32,705	36,640	50,944	56,958	1.80	11.81
WESTERN EUR	995,279	1,207,316	1,291,579	1,344,816	1,354,524	42.79	0.72
AUSTRIA	377,294	440,407	494,829	531,586	553,728	17.49	4.17
BELGIUM	35,643	46,680	54,662	67,503	66,167	2.09	-1.98
FRANCE	37,275	43,543	40,772	46,836	54,237	1.71	15.80
GERMANY	477,312	592,396	616,859	599,993	572,161	18.07	-4.64

SLOVENIA

5. OVERNIGHT STAYS OF NON-RESIDENT TOURISTS IN HOTELS AND SIMILAR ESTABLISHMENTS, BY NATIONALITY

	1999	2000	2001	2002	2003	Market share 03	% change 03-02
LUXEMBOURG	1,373	1,613	1,745	2,711	2,262	0.07	-16.56
NETHERLANDS	38,243	48,204	45,245	49,566	55,148	1.74	11.26
SWITZERLAND	28,139	34,473	37,467	46,621	50,821	1.61	9.01
EAST/MED EUR	**35,174**	**41,845**	**39,089**	**67,566**	**82,188**	**2.60**	**21.64**
ISRAEL	17,749	29,094	33,045	58,975	73,708	2.33	24.98
TURKEY	17,425	12,751	6,044	8,591	8,480	0.27	-1.29
OTHER EUROPE	**13,263**	**12,803**	**11,763**	**11,213**	**10,265**	**0.32**	**-8.45**
OTHER EUROPE	13,263	12,803	11,763	11,213	10,265	0.32	-8.45
REG.NOT SPEC	**24,092**	**27,820**	**30,258**	**40,010**	**29,100**	**0.92**	**-27.27**
NOT SPECIFIE	**24,092**	**27,820**	**30,258**	**40,010**	**29,100**	**0.92**	**-27.27**
OTH.WORLD	24,092	27,820	30,258	40,010	29,100	0.92	-27.27

Source: World Tourism Organization (WTO)

SLOVENIA

6. OVERNIGHT STAYS OF NON-RESIDENT TOURISTS IN ALL TYPES OF ACCOMMODATION ESTABLISHMENTS, BY NATIONALITY

	1999	2000	2001	2002	2003	Market share 03	% change 03-02
TOTAL	**2,741,218**	**3,404,097**	**3,813,477**	**4,020,799**	**4,175,385**	**100.00**	**3.84**
AMERICAS	**59,272**	**79,157**	**80,742**	**85,816**	**84,407**	**2.02**	**-1.64**
NORTH AMER	**59,272**	**79,157**	**80,742**	**85,816**	**84,407**	**2.02**	**-1.64**
CANADA	9,176	12,238	13,018	15,978	16,678	0.40	4.38
USA	50,096	66,919	67,724	69,838	67,729	1.62	-3.02
EAST AS/PACI	**18,440**	**23,806**	**31,544**	**39,784**	**37,013**	**0.89**	**-6.97**
N/EAST ASIA	**9,240**	**11,992**	**13,949**	**13,834**	**12,554**	**0.30**	**-9.25**
JAPAN	9,240	11,992	13,949	13,834	12,554	0.30	-9.25
AUSTRALASIA	**9,200**	**11,814**	**17,595**	**25,950**	**24,459**	**0.59**	**-5.75**
AUSTRALIA	7,453	9,404	14,596	21,766	20,116	0.48	-7.58
NEW ZEALAND	1,747	2,410	2,999	4,184	4,343	0.10	3.80
EUROPE	**2,636,179**	**3,270,425**	**3,666,417**	**3,847,883**	**4,019,677**	**96.27**	**4.46**
C/E EUROPE	**284,861**	**325,950**	**388,612**	**403,325**	**429,108**	**10.28**	**6.39**
BULGARIA	15,943	10,001	13,841	14,144	14,695	0.35	3.90
BELARUS	2,189	1,740	11,781	11,680	2,394	0.06	-79.50
CZECH REP	46,623	55,957	60,857	62,401	64,834	1.55	3.90
HUNGARY	75,204	86,175	89,822	91,048	102,671	2.46	12.77
POLAND	32,826	43,439	57,752	56,018	50,378	1.21	-10.07
ROMANIA	13,552	12,535	14,753	17,283	18,980	0.45	9.82
RUSSIAN FED	51,771	68,567	92,675	92,553	100,656	2.41	8.75
SLOVAKIA	19,028	17,794	17,138	22,461	36,787	0.88	63.78
UKRAINE	22,648	23,164	22,375	24,013	27,303	0.65	13.70
BALTIC COUNT	5,077	6,578	7,618	11,724	10,410	0.25	-11.21
NORTHERN EUR	**188,514**	**226,734**	**285,658**	**294,567**	**321,136**	**7.69**	**9.02**
DENMARK	14,638	18,004	24,512	25,104	28,960	0.69	15.36
FINLAND	6,507	6,153	8,266	9,149	14,908	0.36	62.95
ICELAND	2,256	1,290	1,077	3,650	3,700	0.09	1.37
IRELAND	9,059	12,178	17,996	23,064	30,633	0.73	32.82
NORWAY	8,910	7,173	11,647	13,414	12,723	0.30	-5.15
SWEDEN	29,058	29,439	31,479	26,165	28,031	0.67	7.13
UK	118,086	152,497	190,681	194,021	202,181	4.84	4.21
SOUTHERN EUR	**858,340**	**1,076,708**	**1,117,529**	**1,168,095**	**1,226,894**	**29.38**	**5.03**
BOSNIA HERZG	69,574	85,992	76,161	80,475	98,970	2.37	22.98
CROATIA	217,239	251,073	260,312	256,145	264,827	6.34	3.39
GREECE	4,241	4,393	6,626	5,879	8,945	0.21	52.15
ITALY	489,696	650,566	688,227	718,384	729,181	17.46	1.50
PORTUGAL	9,168	4,418	4,167	5,107	8,295	0.20	62.42
SPAIN	10,154	15,969	15,858	21,158	29,458	0.71	39.23
TFYROM	28,360	28,331	21,819	22,505	20,151	0.48	-10.46
SERBIA,MTNEG	29,908	35,966	44,359	58,442	67,067	1.61	14.76
WESTERN EUR	**1,252,196**	**1,582,593**	**1,816,978**	**1,895,618**	**1,934,730**	**46.34**	**2.06**
AUSTRIA	443,408	526,996	619,822	677,043	690,827	16.55	2.04
BELGIUM	43,578	61,484	73,985	95,241	94,117	2.25	-1.18
FRANCE	42,489	53,300	55,737	63,494	75,891	1.82	19.52
GERMANY	607,316	772,833	877,795	848,418	813,241	19.48	-4.15

6. OVERNIGHT STAYS OF NON-RESIDENT TOURISTS IN ALL TYPES OF ACCOMMODATION ESTABLISHMENTS, BY NATIONALITY

	1999	2000	2001	2002	2003	Market share 03	% change 03-02
LUXEMBOURG	1,568	1,801	1,984	3,157	3,133	0.08	-0.76
NETHERLANDS	81,320	125,210	139,385	150,345	195,356	4.68	29.94
SWITZERLAND	32,517	40,969	48,270	57,920	62,165	1.49	7.33
EAST/MED EUR	**36,794**	**43,647**	**43,323**	**73,363**	**92,312**	**2.21**	**25.83**
ISRAEL	18,831	30,624	36,933	64,142	83,339	2.00	29.93
TURKEY	17,963	13,023	6,390	9,221	8,973	0.21	-2.69
OTHER EUROPE	**15,474**	**14,793**	**14,317**	**12,915**	**15,497**	**0.37**	**19.99**
OTHER EUROPE	15,474	14,793	14,317	12,915	15,497	0.37	19.99
REG.NOT SPEC	**27,327**	**30,709**	**34,774**	**47,316**	**34,288**	**0.82**	**-27.53**
NOT SPECIFIE	**27,327**	**30,709**	**34,774**	**47,316**	**34,288**	**0.82**	**-27.53**
OTH.WORLD	27,327	30,709	34,774	47,316	34,288	0.82	-27.53

Source: World Tourism Organization (WTO)

SOUTH AFRICA

1. ARRIVALS OF NON-RESIDENT TOURISTS AT NATIONAL BORDERS, BY COUNTRY OF RESIDENCE

	1999	2000	2001	2002	2003	Market share 03	% change 03-02
TOTAL (*)			**5,787,368**	**6,429,583**	**6,504,890**	**100.00**	**1.17**
AFRICA			**4,130,975**	**4,452,762**	**4,450,212**	**68.41**	**-0.06**
EAST AFRICA			**1,173,725**	**1,410,188**	**1,247,051**	**19.17**	**-11.57**
KENYA			14,804	17,031	17,743	0.27	4.18
MALAWI			77,325	95,117	88,942	1.37	-6.49
MAURITIUS			12,167	15,738	15,235	0.23	-3.20
MOZAMBIQUE			456,860	527,028	421,201	6.48	-20.08
REUNION			906	845	1,095	0.02	29.59
SEYCHELLES			1,646	4,170	3,913	0.06	-6.16
ZIMBABWE			498,572	608,986	563,877	8.67	-7.41
UGANDA			6,418	8,361	9,484	0.15	13.43
TANZANIA			8,976	10,546	10,855	0.17	2.93
ZAMBIA			96,051	122,366	114,706	1.76	-6.26
CENTRAL AFR			**29,472**	**35,585**	**34,765**	**0.53**	**-2.30**
ANGOLA			26,672	30,769	28,872	0.44	-6.17
DEM.R.CONGO			2,800	4,816	5,893	0.09	22.36
SOUTHERN AFR			**2,871,701**	**2,935,224**	**3,093,737**	**47.56**	**5.40**
BOTSWANA			641,194	779,794	791,785	12.17	1.54
LESOTHO			1,282,785	1,157,930	1,284,953	19.75	10.97
NAMIBIA			203,105	216,566	216,313	3.33	-0.12
SWAZILAND			744,617	780,934	800,686	12.31	2.53
WEST AFRICA			**24,198**	**30,074**	**30,866**	**0.47**	**2.63**
GHANA			6,127	7,983	8,221	0.13	2.98
NIGERIA			18,071	22,091	22,645	0.35	2.51
OTHER AFRICA			**31,879**	**41,691**	**43,793**	**0.67**	**5.04**
OTHER AFRICA			31,879	41,691	43,793	0.67	5.04
AMERICAS			**241,991**	**254,586**	**262,496**	**4.04**	**3.11**
NORTH AMER			**199,957**	**218,884**	**224,882**	**3.46**	**2.74**
CANADA			27,401	33,684	34,692	0.53	2.99
MEXICO			1,945	2,609	2,743	0.04	5.14
USA			170,611	182,591	187,447	2.88	2.66
SOUTH AMER			**34,505**	**26,851**	**28,816**	**0.44**	**7.32**
ARGENTINA			14,212	5,131	7,744	0.12	50.93
BRAZIL			17,066	18,187	17,452	0.27	-4.04
CHILE			2,485	2,628	2,982	0.05	13.47
VENEZUELA			742	905	638	0.01	-29.50
OTHER AMERIC			**7,529**	**8,851**	**8,798**	**0.14**	**-0.60**
OTH AMERICA			7,529	8,851	8,798	0.14	-0.60
EAST AS/PACI			**193,955**	**229,128**	**224,610**	**3.45**	**-1.97**
N/EAST ASIA			**75,626**	**90,785**	**88,689**	**1.36**	**-2.31**
CHINA (*)			29,681	36,957	42,822	0.66	15.87
TAIWAN(P.C.)			13,032	16,012	13,401	0.21	-16.31
JAPAN			24,598	26,239	21,311	0.33	-18.78
KOREA REP.			8,315	11,577	11,155	0.17	-3.65
S/EAST ASIA			**31,444**	**39,854**	**33,210**	**0.51**	**-16.67**

SOUTH AFRICA

1. ARRIVALS OF NON-RESIDENT TOURISTS AT NATIONAL BORDERS, BY COUNTRY OF RESIDENCE

	1999	2000	2001	2002	2003	Market share 03	% change 03-02
INDONESIA			4,040	4,662	3,980	0.06	-14.63
MALAYSIA			9,830	12,771	12,049	0.19	-5.65
PHILIPPINES			6,894	8,421	5,781	0.09	-31.35
SINGAPORE			6,103	6,456	5,337	0.08	-17.33
THAILAND			4,577	7,544	6,063	0.09	-19.63
AUSTRALASIA			**74,075**	**84,739**	**88,074**	**1.35**	**3.94**
AUSTRALIA			60,684	69,832	71,687	1.10	2.66
NEW ZEALAND			13,391	14,907	16,387	0.25	9.93
OT.EAST AS/P			**12,810**	**13,750**	**14,637**	**0.23**	**6.45**
OTHER ASIA			11,943	12,714	13,649	0.21	7.35
OTH OCEANIA			867	1,036	988	0.02	-4.63
EUROPE			**1,028,236**	**1,274,365**	**1,338,976**	**20.58**	**5.07**
C/E EUROPE			**17,841**	**23,766**	**21,313**	**0.33**	**-10.32**
CZECH REP			3,383	3,596	4,383	0.07	21.89
HUNGARY			3,382	5,094	2,864	0.04	-43.78
POLAND			4,599	6,527	6,368	0.10	-2.44
RUSSIAN FED			6,477	8,549	7,698	0.12	-9.95
NORTHERN EUR			**426,108**	**534,202**	**564,252**	**8.67**	**5.63**
DENMARK			13,852	16,726	19,292	0.30	15.34
FINLAND			5,163	6,135	7,099	0.11	15.71
IRELAND			20,630	29,506	34,379	0.53	16.52
NORWAY			11,128	14,998	17,633	0.27	17.57
SWEDEN			18,576	23,927	29,381	0.45	22.79
UK			356,759	442,910	456,468	7.02	3.06
SOUTHERN EUR			**82,850**	**108,626**	**112,204**	**1.72**	**3.29**
GREECE			6,518	7,527	7,869	0.12	4.54
ITALY			36,899	47,756	49,818	0.77	4.32
PORTUGAL			21,729	29,088	28,920	0.44	-0.58
SPAIN			17,704	24,255	25,597	0.39	5.53
WESTERN EUR			**468,319**	**569,309**	**605,797**	**9.31**	**6.41**
AUSTRIA			18,639	21,633	21,711	0.33	0.36
BELGIUM			34,453	39,242	42,735	0.66	8.90
FRANCE			82,745	112,078	127,760	1.96	13.99
GERMANY			203,911	248,990	257,018	3.95	3.22
NETHERLANDS			96,090	110,389	120,933	1.86	9.55
SWITZERLAND			32,481	36,977	35,640	0.55	-3.62
EAST/MED EUR			**19,937**	**21,655**	**19,804**	**0.30**	**-8.55**
ISRAEL			15,116	16,445	15,025	0.23	-8.63
TURKEY			4,821	5,210	4,779	0.07	-8.27
OTHER EUROPE			**13,181**	**16,807**	**15,606**	**0.24**	**-7.15**
OTHER EUROPE			13,181	16,807	15,606	0.24	-7.15
MIDDLE EAST			**13,062**	**14,955**	**15,048**	**0.23**	**0.62**
MIDDLE EAST			**13,062**	**14,955**	**15,048**	**0.23**	**0.62**
SAUDI ARABIA			2,128	2,865	3,523	0.05	22.97
UNTD ARAB EM			1,687	1,439	1,788	0.03	24.25
EGYPT			3,166	3,209	3,038	0.05	-5.33
OT MIDD EAST			6,081	7,442	6,699	0.10	-9.98

SOUTH AFRICA

1. ARRIVALS OF NON-RESIDENT TOURISTS AT NATIONAL BORDERS, BY COUNTRY OF RESIDENCE

	1999	2000	2001	2002	2003	Market share 03	% change 03-02
SOUTH ASIA			**28,012**	**34,062**	**41,018**	**0.63**	**20.42**
SOUTH ASIA			**28,012**	**34,062**	**41,018**	**0.63**	**20.42**
INDIA			28,012	34,062	41,018	0.63	20.42
REG.NOT SPEC			**151,137**	**169,725**	**172,530**	**2.65**	**1.65**
NOT SPECIFIE			**151,137**	**169,725**	**172,530**	**2.65**	**1.65**
OTH.WORLD			151,137	169,725	172,530	2.65	1.65

Source: World Tourism Organization (WTO)

SOUTH AFRICA

2. ARRIVALS OF NON-RESIDENT VISITORS AT NATIONAL BORDERS, BY COUNTRY OF RESIDENCE

		1999	2000	2001	2002	2003	Market share 03	% change 03-02
TOTAL	(*)	**6,026,086**	**6,000,538**	**5,908,024**	**6,549,916**	**6,640,095**	**100.00**	**1.38**
AFRICA		**4,362,677**	**4,309,893**	**4,204,904**	**4,530,022**	**4,536,397**	**68.32**	**0.14**
EAST AFRICA		**1,158,132**	**1,165,884**	**1,236,936**	**1,480,109**	**1,321,128**	**19.90**	**-10.74**
BURUNDI		1,595	837	967	996	1,190	0.02	19.48
COMOROS		622	291	180	178	199		11.80
ETHIOPIA		2,580	2,448	2,476	3,395	4,873	0.07	43.53
ERITREA		361	215	561	691	565	0.01	-18.23
DJIBOUTI		27	49	58	74	66		-10.81
KENYA		15,481	14,646	15,573	17,853	18,780	0.28	5.19
MADAGASCAR		1,678	1,326	1,319	1,601	1,864	0.03	16.43
MALAWI		69,686	70,732	77,680	95,518	89,469	1.35	-6.33
MAURITIUS		11,156	12,042	12,447	15,962	15,468	0.23	-3.09
MOZAMBIQUE		473,939	491,526	506,077	579,768	474,790	7.15	-18.11
REUNION		952	808	911	850	1,095	0.02	28.82
RWANDA		1,713	1,523	2,230	2,928	2,855	0.04	-2.49
SEYCHELLES		1,191	1,473	1,667	4,192	3,923	0.06	-6.42
SOMALIA		1,260	883	439	746	653	0.01	-12.47
ZIMBABWE		494,530	477,380	501,698	612,543	568,626	8.56	-7.17
UGANDA		6,419	6,294	6,768	8,824	9,889	0.15	12.07
TANZANIA		7,260	7,529	9,219	10,909	11,173	0.17	2.42
ZAMBIA		67,682	75,882	96,666	123,081	115,650	1.74	-6.04
CENTRAL AFR		**44,940**	**42,133**	**42,870**	**52,224**	**53,551**	**0.81**	**2.54**
ANGOLA		29,927	28,281	27,206	31,230	29,511	0.44	-5.50
CAMEROON		2,548	2,126	1,938	2,375	3,118	0.05	31.28
CENT.AFR.REP		133	87	103	102	117		14.71
CHAD		111	94	78	112	108		-3.57
CONGO		5,098	6,897	8,475	10,469	10,515	0.16	0.44
DEM.R.CONGO		4,980	2,437	2,864	4,938	6,042	0.09	22.36
EQ.GUINEA		152	298	304	404	490	0.01	21.29
GABON		1,881	1,757	1,747	2,463	3,535	0.05	43.52
SAO TOME PRN		110	156	155	131	115		-12.21
NORTH AFRICA		**2,984**	**2,370**	**2,902**	**4,036**	**3,177**	**0.05**	**-21.28**
ALGERIA		951	551	962	1,697	1,129	0.02	-33.47
MOROCCO		694	645	660	1,011	613	0.01	-39.37
WESTN.SAHARA		2	6	1	2	2		
SUDAN		755	691	784	760	845	0.01	11.18
TUNISIA		582	477	495	566	588	0.01	3.89
SOUTHERN AFR		**3,130,035**	**3,071,430**	**2,887,618**	**2,950,894**	**3,114,584**	**46.91**	**5.55**
BOTSWANA		554,923	563,365	644,253	782,189	797,315	12.01	1.93
LESOTHO		1,588,365	1,559,422	1,288,160	1,162,786	1,291,242	19.45	11.05
NAMIBIA		201,685	206,022	203,667	217,077	216,978	3.27	-0.05
SWAZILAND		785,062	742,621	751,538	788,842	809,049	12.18	2.56
WEST AFRICA		**26,033**	**27,764**	**34,233**	**42,669**	**43,182**	**0.65**	**1.20**
CAPE VERDE		786	701	792	1,040	911	0.01	-12.40
BENIN		869	901	861	1,303	1,212	0.02	-6.98
GAMBIA		307	265	336	475	664	0.01	39.79
GHANA		6,022	6,193	6,481	8,392	8,700	0.13	3.67
GUINEA		449	364	525	659	817	0.01	23.98
COTE IVOIRE		2,385	1,920	2,030	2,723	2,100	0.03	-22.88
LIBERIA		376	387	294	344	323		-6.10
MALI		630	446	567	605	745	0.01	23.14

SOUTH AFRICA

2. ARRIVALS OF NON-RESIDENT VISITORS AT NATIONAL BORDERS, BY COUNTRY OF RESIDENCE

	1999	2000	2001	2002	2003	Market share 03	% change 03-02
MAURITANIA	74	79	91	149	153		2.68
NIGER	147	157	152	226	149		-34.07
NIGERIA	10,114	13,451	18,931	22,981	23,477	0.35	2.16
GUINEABISSAU	189	143	154	139	170		22.30
ST.HELENA	236	355	325	341	196		-42.52
SENEGAL	2,095	1,257	1,624	1,915	2,300	0.03	20.10
SIERRA LEONE	642	515	482	609	620	0.01	1.81
TOGO	347	285	277	361	319		-11.63
BURKINA FASO	365	345	311	407	326		-19.90
OTHER AFRICA	**553**	**312**	**345**	**90**	**775**	**0.01**	**761.11**
OTHER AFRICA	553	312	345	90	775	0.01	761.11
AMERICAS	**245,297**	**257,697**	**250,042**	**261,831**	**270,022**	**4.07**	**3.13**
CARIBBEAN	**2,466**	**2,441**	**2,984**	**2,784**	**2,330**	**0.04**	**-16.31**
ANTIGUA,BARB	36	36	45	33	39		18.18
BAHAMAS	119	107	86	68	79		16.18
BARBADOS	212	171	153	202	256		26.73
BERMUDA	149	99	116	91	105		15.38
BR.VIRGIN IS	31	12	24	40	38		-5.00
CAYMAN IS	1,045						
CUBA		1,205	1,494	1,327	1,232	0.02	-7.16
DOMINICA	51						
DOMINICAN RP	29	63	45	72	38		-47.22
GRENADA		32	32	32	30		-6.25
JAMAICA	429	363	419	498			
ST.LUCIA	24	23	33	42	37		-11.90
ST.VINCENT,G	38	24	22	27	33		22.22
TRINIDAD TBG	299	304	512	333	438	0.01	31.53
TURKS,CAICOS	4	2	3	15	4		-73.33
US.VIRGIN IS				4	1		-75.00
CENTRAL AMER	**661**	**970**	**771**	**1,028**	**984**	**0.01**	**-4.28**
BELIZE	36	88	61	75	99		32.00
COSTA RICA	199	232	228	280	271		-3.21
EL SALVADOR	68	113	76	89	99		11.24
GUATEMALA	114	154	110	168	164		-2.38
HONDURAS	58	103	93	129	85		-34.11
NICARAGUA	36	138	108	119	107		-10.08
PANAMA	150	142	95	168	159		-5.36
NORTH AMER	**203,697**	**212,523**	**206,774**	**225,030**	**231,073**	**3.48**	**2.69**
CANADA	28,562	28,717	28,361	34,664	35,683	0.54	2.94
GREENLAND	16	20	33	44	42		-4.55
MEXICO	1,586	2,154	1,968	2,641	2,787	0.04	5.53
USA	173,533	181,632	176,412	187,681	192,561	2.90	2.60
SOUTH AMER	**38,020**	**41,138**	**39,053**	**32,320**	**34,411**	**0.52**	**6.47**
ARGENTINA	15,771	15,487	14,310	5,256	7,904	0.12	50.38
BOLIVIA	172	172	202	302	439	0.01	45.36
BRAZIL	14,820	17,659	17,396	18,460	17,883	0.27	-3.13
CHILE	2,779	3,370	2,555	2,697	3,085	0.05	14.39
COLOMBIA	447	586	563	876	699	0.01	-20.21
ECUADOR	147	173	212	257	257		
FALKLAND IS	12	15	9	4	6		50.00
FR.GUIANA	81	79	91	113	91		-19.47
GUYANA	364	274	342	378	329		-12.96

SOUTH AFRICA

2. ARRIVALS OF NON-RESIDENT VISITORS AT NATIONAL BORDERS, BY COUNTRY OF RESIDENCE

	1999	2000	2001	2002	2003	Market share 03	% change 03-02
PARAGUAY	393	220	381	392	366	0.01	-6.63
PERU	691	763	872	1,294	1,161	0.02	-10.28
SURINAME	91	50	63	56	46		-17.86
URUGUAY	1,618	1,505	1,294	1,285	1,489	0.02	15.88
VENEZUELA	634	785	763	950	656	0.01	-30.95
OTHER AMERIC	**453**	**625**	**460**	**669**	**1,224**	**0.02**	**82.96**
OTH AMERICA	453	625	460	669	1,224	0.02	82.96
EAST AS/PACI	**187,576**	**189,717**	**189,909**	**223,980**	**220,415**	**3.32**	**-1.59**
N/EAST ASIA	**83,954**	**81,217**	**79,945**	**95,088**	**94,021**	**1.42**	**-1.12**
CHINA	19,337	19,722	20,577	25,849	33,128	0.50	28.16
TAIWAN(P.C.)	19,454	15,825	13,510	16,420	13,959	0.21	-14.99
HK,CHINA	12,086	12,251	10,874	12,776	12,132	0.18	-5.04
JAPAN	24,711	24,104	25,975	27,581	22,741	0.34	-17.55
KOREA D P RP	182	48	41	43	40		-6.98
KOREA REP.	7,901	9,081	8,767	12,096	11,737	0.18	-2.97
MACAU, CHINA	251	113	125	172	169		-1.74
MONGOLIA	32	73	76	151	115		-23.84
S/EAST ASIA	**33,397**	**37,208**	**33,373**	**41,601**	**36,003**	**0.54**	**-13.46**
BRUNEI DARSM	112	97	101	120	156		30.00
MYANMAR	797	618	551	370	535	0.01	44.59
CAMBODIA	105	87	60	75	59		-21.33
INDONESIA	3,550	5,444	4,188	4,837	4,347	0.07	-10.13
LAO P.DEM.R.	8	66	80	132	72		-45.45
MALAYSIA	8,017	9,944	10,172	13,078	12,289	0.19	-6.03
PHILIPPINES	7,548	7,333	7,249	8,707	6,723	0.10	-22.79
SINGAPORE	7,758	6,920	6,273	6,583	5,497	0.08	-16.50
THAILAND	5,502	6,699	4,699	7,699	6,325	0.10	-17.85
AUSTRALASIA	**69,193**	**70,226**	**75,546**	**86,084**	**89,362**	**1.35**	**3.81**
AUSTRALIA	56,606	57,191	61,779	70,871	72,728	1.10	2.62
NEW ZEALAND	12,587	13,035	13,767	15,213	16,634	0.25	9.34
MELANESIA	**264**	**214**	**227**	**317**	**273**		**-13.88**
SOLOMON IS	15	4	13	15	18		20.00
FIJI	185	143	155	241	188		-21.99
NEW CALEDNIA	24	13	10	11	1		-90.91
NORFOLK IS	5	5	5	1	5		400.00
PAPUA N.GUIN	35	49	44	49	61		24.49
MICRONESIA	**308**	**322**	**292**	**250**	**268**		**7.20**
CHRISTMAS IS		29	28	56	19		-66.07
COCOS IS	48	34	17	14	50		257.14
KIRIBATI	42	68	47	40	29		-27.50
GUAM	47	14	16	11	25		127.27
NAURU	42	29	17	14	10		-28.57
N.MARIANA IS	118	94	103	48	66		37.50
MICRONESIA		48	49	56	52		-7.14
MARSHALL IS	11	6	15	11	17		54.55
POLYNESIA	**460**	**370**	**348**	**473**	**457**	**0.01**	**-3.38**
COOK IS	1	1	1	1			
FR.POLYNESIA	311	258	176	268	319		19.03
PITCAIRN	1	9	2	2	2		
TOKELAU	5	5	3	4	7		75.00
TONGA	60	21	57	28	17		-39.29

SOUTH AFRICA

2. ARRIVALS OF NON-RESIDENT VISITORS AT NATIONAL BORDERS, BY COUNTRY OF RESIDENCE

	1999	2000	2001	2002	2003	Market share 03	% change 03-02
TUVALU	8	10	13	22	37		68.18
SAMOA	74	66	96	148	75		-49.32
OT.EAST AS/P		**160**	**178**	**167**	**31**		**-81.44**
OTHER ASIA		131	149	155			
OTH OCEANIA		29	29	12	31		158.33
EUROPE	**1,048,633**	**1,070,284**	**1,052,916**	**1,297,647**	**1,365,004**	**20.56**	**5.19**
C/E EUROPE	**24,618**	**24,742**	**26,688**	**35,098**	**33,754**	**0.51**	**-3.83**
AZERBAIJAN	35	48	43	64	55		-14.06
ARMENIA	45	36	36	61	53		-13.11
BULGARIA	2,036	1,702	1,722	1,923	2,366	0.04	23.04
BELARUS	10	4	6	10	14		40.00
CZECH REP	3,230	3,338	3,475	3,700	4,482	0.07	21.14
ESTONIA	281	243	292	359	371	0.01	3.34
HUNGARY	2,591	2,518	3,462	5,157	2,940	0.04	-42.99
KAZAKHSTAN	75	53	107	210	264		25.71
KYRGYZSTAN	70	94	94	94	62		-34.04
LATVIA	344	341	306	708	408	0.01	-42.37
LITHUANIA	585	584	494	612	564	0.01	-7.84
REP MOLDOVA	79	50	70	88	80		-9.09
POLAND	5,830	5,282	4,785	6,648	6,694	0.10	0.69
ROMANIA	1,030	1,008	899	1,136	1,295	0.02	14.00
RUSSIAN FED	5,265	6,207	7,492	8,907	8,604	0.13	-3.40
SLOVAKIA	912	1,068	901	1,067	1,078	0.02	1.03
TURKMENISTAN	13	21	15	14	16		14.29
UKRAINE	2,160	2,101	2,449	4,297	4,307	0.06	0.23
UZBEKISTAN	27	44	40	43	101		134.88
NORTHERN EUR	**417,569**	**431,178**	**436,497**	**543,172**	**573,905**	**8.64**	**5.66**
DENMARK	16,361	15,189	14,320	17,217	19,888	0.30	15.51
FAEROE IS	26	36	40	43	48		11.63
FINLAND	5,259	5,245	5,335	6,311	7,265	0.11	15.12
ICELAND	452	855	957	633	765	0.01	20.85
IRELAND	19,152	19,753	21,137	29,885	34,806	0.52	16.47
NORWAY	10,533	10,839	11,474	15,270	17,982	0.27	17.76
SWEDEN	21,707	21,072	19,331	24,590	30,053	0.45	22.22
UK	343,934	358,072	363,825	449,166	463,021	6.97	3.08
CHANNEL IS	36	41	17	21	44		109.52
ISLE OF MAN	109	76	61	36	33		-8.33
SOUTHERN EUR	**99,477**	**93,130**	**88,628**	**114,739**	**118,220**	**1.78**	**3.03**
ALBANIA	182	175	177	212	233		9.91
ANDORRA	54	35	40	29	68		134.48
CROATIA	1,471	1,334	1,276	1,704	1,293	0.02	-24.12
GIBRALTAR	27	18	17	19	28		47.37
GREECE	7,019	6,637	6,806	7,734	8,159	0.12	5.50
HOLY SEE				11			
ITALY	39,725	38,979	37,565	48,342	50,403	0.76	4.26
MALTA	426	241	351	388	304		-21.65
PORTUGAL	28,337	25,013	22,021	29,492	29,347	0.44	-0.49
SAN MARINO	31	39	21	35	81		131.43
SLOVENIA	568	807	1,035	968	837	0.01	-13.53
SPAIN	20,377	18,234	17,985	24,446	26,167	0.39	7.04
SERBIA,MTNEG	1,260	1,618	1,334	1,359	1,300	0.02	-4.34
WESTERN EUR	**484,915**	**499,669**	**479,280**	**580,938**	**617,338**	**9.30**	**6.27**

SOUTH AFRICA

2. ARRIVALS OF NON-RESIDENT VISITORS AT NATIONAL BORDERS, BY COUNTRY OF RESIDENCE

	1999	2000	2001	2002	2003	Market share 03	% change 03-02
AUSTRIA	24,188	22,137	18,932	21,910	21,960	0.33	0.23
BELGIUM	36,950	41,550	35,265	40,023	43,537	0.66	8.78
FRANCE	87,887	92,750	85,663	114,797	130,365	1.96	13.56
GERMANY	211,052	215,011	207,511	253,411	261,194	3.93	3.07
LIECHTENSTEN	195	171	153	183	186		1.64
LUXEMBOURG	947	958	801	1,138	1,292	0.02	13.53
MONACO	117	63	56	72	36		-50.00
NETHERLANDS	87,606	93,091	97,780	111,873	122,565	1.85	9.56
SWITZERLAND	35,973	33,938	33,119	37,531	36,203	0.55	-3.54
EAST/MED EUR	**21,885**	**21,501**	**21,687**	**23,700**	**21,787**	**0.33**	**-8.07**
CYPRUS	1,495	1,384	1,272	1,497	1,343	0.02	-10.29
ISRAEL	15,670	14,161	15,468	16,837	15,427	0.23	-8.37
TURKEY	4,720	5,956	4,947	5,366	5,017	0.08	-6.50
OTHER EUROPE	**169**	**64**	**136**				
OTHER EUROPE	169	64	136				
MIDDLE EAST	**10,582**	**10,210**	**11,865**	**13,897**	**13,915**	**0.21**	**0.13**
MIDDLE EAST	**10,582**	**10,210**	**11,865**	**13,897**	**13,915**	**0.21**	**0.13**
BAHRAIN	121	132	182	184	136		-26.09
PALESTINE		163	173		209		
IRAQ	67	123	145	154	139		-9.74
JORDAN	772	933	1,006	1,249	1,087	0.02	-12.97
KUWAIT	394	556	477	841	693	0.01	-17.60
LEBANON	965	1,012	1,409	1,491	1,396	0.02	-6.37
LIBYA	764	605	469	1,116	617	0.01	-44.71
OMAN	151	167	179	237	202		-14.77
QATAR	61	67	129	233	142		-39.06
SAUDI ARABIA	2,304	2,032	2,188	2,946	3,595	0.05	22.03
SYRIA	313	260	292	374	329		-12.03
UNTD ARAB EM	1,432	1,553	1,728	1,469	1,820	0.03	23.89
EGYPT	3,117	2,438	3,384	3,435	3,428	0.05	-0.20
YEMEN	121	169	104	168	122		-27.38
SOUTH ASIA	**38,656**	**38,839**	**42,594**	**48,777**	**57,275**	**0.86**	**17.42**
SOUTH ASIA	**38,656**	**38,839**	**42,594**	**48,777**	**57,275**	**0.86**	**17.42**
AFGHANISTAN	361	273	282	416	432	0.01	3.85
BANGLADESH	1,608	1,797	2,374	2,240	1,983	0.03	-11.47
BHUTAN	12	7	15	25	11		-56.00
SRI LANKA	1,500	1,663	1,499	1,580	1,834	0.03	16.08
INDIA	27,252	27,810	29,538	35,402	42,954	0.65	21.33
IRAN	752	787	961	1,066	1,181	0.02	10.79
MALDIVES	55	54	76	101	57		-43.56
NEPAL	133	183	333	355	292		-17.75
PAKISTAN	6,983	6,265	7,516	7,592	8,531	0.13	12.37
REG.NOT SPEC	**132,665**	**123,898**	**155,794**	**173,762**	**177,067**	**2.67**	**1.90**
NOT SPECIFIE	**132,665**	**123,898**	**155,794**	**173,762**	**177,067**	**2.67**	**1.90**
OTH.WORLD	132,665	123,898	155,794	173,762	177,067	2.67	1.90

Source: World Tourism Organization (WTO)

SPAIN

1. ARRIVALS OF NON-RESIDENT TOURISTS AT NATIONAL BORDERS, BY COUNTRY OF RESIDENCE

	1999	2000	2001	2002	2003	Market share 03	% change 03-02
TOTAL	**46,775,870**	**47,897,915**	**50,093,557**	**52,326,766**	**51,829,596**	**100.00**	**-0.95**
AMERICAS	**2,238,148**	**2,518,590**	**2,174,344**	**2,079,643**	**1,940,705**	**3.74**	**-6.68**
NORTH AMER	**1,317,958**	**1,491,853**	**1,453,626**	**1,308,309**	**1,247,056**	**2.41**	**-4.68**
CANADA	104,709	118,417	144,412	154,989	128,560	0.25	-17.05
MEXICO	179,149	227,807	172,947	213,266	189,580	0.37	-11.11
USA	1,034,100	1,145,629	1,136,267	940,054	928,916	1.79	-1.18
SOUTH AMER	**648,166**	**629,320**	**546,851**	**507,308**	**440,653**	**0.85**	**-13.14**
ARGENTINA	266,169	242,367	178,803	166,496	185,310	0.36	11.30
BRAZIL	219,173	203,015	164,592	145,582	100,162	0.19	-31.20
CHILE	74,206	91,877	66,117	61,750	59,073	0.11	-4.34
VENEZUELA	88,618	92,061	137,339	133,480	96,108	0.19	-28.00
OTHER AMERIC	**272,024**	**397,417**	**173,867**	**264,026**	**252,996**	**0.49**	**-4.18**
OTH AMERICA	272,024	397,417	173,867	264,026	252,996	0.49	-4.18
EAST AS/PACI	**359,113**	**300,828**	**265,047**	**240,637**	**247,991**	**0.48**	**3.06**
N/EAST ASIA	**359,113**	**300,828**	**265,047**	**240,637**	**247,991**	**0.48**	**3.06**
JAPAN	359,113	300,828	265,047	240,637	247,991	0.48	3.06
EUROPE	**43,587,461**	**44,499,469**	**46,827,387**	**49,303,582**	**49,004,902**	**94.55**	**-0.61**
C/E EUROPE	**212,544**	**237,459**	**298,863**	**270,039**	**216,124**	**0.42**	**-19.97**
RUSSIAN FED	212,544	237,459	298,863	270,039	216,124	0.42	-19.97
NORTHERN EUR	**14,886,199**	**16,130,400**	**17,840,693**	**18,806,836**	**20,133,825**	**38.85**	**7.06**
DENMARK	629,105	613,984	670,401	639,071	659,581	1.27	3.21
FINLAND	423,873	431,271	436,569	431,491	399,285	0.77	-7.46
IRELAND			791,493	1,129,239	1,360,598	2.63	20.49
NORWAY	568,035	636,497	747,264	771,160	788,068	1.52	2.19
SWEDEN	1,083,731	1,209,675	1,183,741	1,138,488	1,000,921	1.93	-12.08
UK	12,181,455	13,238,973	14,011,225	14,697,387	15,925,372	30.73	8.36
SOUTHERN EUR	**3,374,221**	**3,587,522**	**4,111,685**	**4,448,259**	**4,150,924**	**8.01**	**-6.68**
GREECE			67,071	154,654	103,436	0.20	-33.12
ITALY	2,087,697	2,097,666	2,412,126	2,532,055	2,367,091	4.57	-6.52
PORTUGAL	1,286,524	1,489,856	1,632,488	1,761,550	1,680,397	3.24	-4.61
WESTERN EUR	**22,934,497**	**22,160,019**	**23,121,555**	**24,414,631**	**23,158,925**	**44.68**	**-5.14**
AUSTRIA	558,514	462,028	421,013	461,000	434,522	0.84	-5.74
BELGIUM	1,809,811	1,679,874	1,716,924	1,774,970	1,766,437	3.41	-0.48
FRANCE	5,732,640	5,680,578	6,712,905	8,143,463	7,653,835	14.77	-6.01
GERMANY	11,586,318	11,171,050	10,783,029	10,211,494	9,754,352	18.82	-4.48
LUXEMBOURG			105,695	185,308	143,949	0.28	-22.32
NETHERLANDS	2,043,774	1,968,010	2,148,486	2,415,193	2,362,298	4.56	-2.19
SWITZERLAND	1,203,440	1,198,479	1,233,503	1,223,203	1,043,532	2.01	-14.69
OTHER EUROPE	**2,180,000**	**2,384,069**	**1,454,591**	**1,363,817**	**1,345,104**	**2.60**	**-1.37**
OTHER EUROPE	2,180,000	2,384,069	1,454,591	1,363,817	1,345,104	2.60	-1.37
REG.NOT SPEC	**591,148**	**579,028**	**826,779**	**702,904**	**635,998**	**1.23**	**-9.52**
NOT SPECIFIE	**591,148**	**579,028**	**826,779**	**702,904**	**635,998**	**1.23**	**-9.52**
OTH.WORLD	591,148	579,028	826,779	702,904	635,998	1.23	-9.52

3. ARRIVALS OF NON-RESIDENT TOURISTS IN HOTELS AND SIMILAR ESTABLISHMENTS, BY COUNTRY OF RESIDENCE

	1999	2000	2001	2002	2003	Market share 03	% change 03-02
TOTAL (*)	**26,799,259**	**27,149,526**	**27,012,002**	**26,610,690**	**27,248,610**	**100.00**	**2.40**
AFRICA	**196,058**	**228,978**	**269,438**	**265,328**	**285,307**	**1.05**	**7.53**
OTHER AFRICA	**196,058**	**228,978**	**269,438**	**265,328**	**285,307**	**1.05**	**7.53**
ALL AFRICA	196,058	228,978	269,438	265,328	285,307	1.05	7.53
AMERICAS	**2,623,327**	**3,139,763**	**3,037,713**	**2,754,604**	**2,627,163**	**9.64**	**-4.63**
NORTH AMER	**1,844,708**	**2,056,450**	**1,989,262**	**1,885,772**	**1,841,878**	**6.76**	**-2.33**
CANADA	133,497	151,627	161,748	186,325	184,701	0.68	-0.87
MEXICO	167,225	206,669	229,096	267,913	248,716	0.91	-7.17
USA	1,543,986	1,698,154	1,598,418	1,431,534	1,408,461	5.17	-1.61
SOUTH AMER	**413,180**	**648,273**	**604,795**	**428,534**	**412,215**	**1.51**	**-3.81**
ARGENTINA	365,302	402,517	377,989	212,708	210,852	0.77	-0.87
BRAZIL		192,358	161,548	148,933	142,331	0.52	-4.43
VENEZUELA	47,878	53,398	65,258	66,893	59,032	0.22	-11.75
OTHER AMERIC	**365,439**	**435,040**	**443,656**	**440,298**	**373,070**	**1.37**	**-15.27**
OTH AMERICA	365,439	435,040	443,656	440,298	373,070	1.37	-15.27
EAST AS/PACI	**1,688,561**	**1,118,081**	**913,448**	**961,481**	**919,579**	**3.37**	**-4.36**
N/EAST ASIA	**763,357**	**780,378**	**576,771**	**596,382**	**545,653**	**2.00**	**-8.51**
JAPAN	763,357	780,378	576,771	596,382	545,653	2.00	-8.51
AUSTRALASIA		**141,895**	**132,102**	**143,019**	**154,490**	**0.57**	**8.02**
AUSTRALIA		119,540	109,600	117,996	126,677	0.46	7.36
NEW ZEALAND		22,355	22,502	25,023	27,813	0.10	11.15
OT.EAST AS/P	**925,204**	**195,808**	**204,575**	**222,080**	**219,436**	**0.81**	**-1.19**
OTHER ASIA	925,204	195,808	204,575	222,080	219,436	0.81	-1.19
EUROPE	**22,266,523**	**22,094,332**	**22,267,525**	**22,080,020**	**22,856,178**	**83.88**	**3.52**
C/E EUROPE		**634,072**	**642,745**	**558,280**	**553,028**	**2.03**	**-0.94**
CZECH REP		169,136	140,527	138,408	147,887	0.54	6.85
HUNGARY		45,900	45,483	45,174	48,363	0.18	7.06
POLAND		180,291	161,918	128,964	110,216	0.40	-14.54
RUSSIAN FED		195,198	263,497	218,423	210,766	0.77	-3.51
SLOVAKIA		43,547	31,320	27,311	35,796	0.13	31.07
NORTHERN EUR	**6,656,082**	**6,844,277**	**7,289,188**	**7,537,941**	**8,080,075**	**29.65**	**7.19**
DENMARK	220,531	209,613	189,972	203,191	210,770	0.77	3.73
FINLAND	125,901	137,211	137,969	128,466	131,196	0.48	2.13
ICELAND		18,385	16,499	17,077	22,108	0.08	29.46
IRELAND	170,871	198,033	222,994	271,201	322,977	1.19	19.09
NORWAY	175,629	213,572	231,263	239,472	217,264	0.80	-9.27
SWEDEN	393,466	442,104	457,037	399,355	367,267	1.35	-8.03
UK	5,569,684	5,625,359	6,033,454	6,279,179	6,808,493	24.99	8.43
SOUTHERN EUR	**2,643,927**	**2,708,479**	**2,666,636**	**2,848,857**	**2,817,563**	**10.34**	**-1.10**
GREECE	84,602	78,825	78,296	92,757	82,751	0.30	-10.79
ITALY	1,702,111	1,690,482	1,689,339	1,788,290	1,741,685	6.39	-2.61
PORTUGAL	857,214	939,172	899,001	967,810	993,127	3.64	2.62

SPAIN

3. ARRIVALS OF NON-RESIDENT TOURISTS IN HOTELS AND SIMILAR ESTABLISHMENTS, BY COUNTRY OF RESIDENCE

	1999	2000	2001	2002	2003	Market share 03	% change 03-02
WESTERN EUR	**11,953,428**	**11,580,528**	**11,321,794**	**10,736,760**	**11,004,489**	**40.39**	**2.49**
AUSTRIA	213,964	210,910	185,284	185,271	205,225	0.75	10.77
BELGIUM	1,030,827	953,409	911,658	906,991	931,155	3.42	2.66
FRANCE	2,487,025	2,486,487	2,642,484	2,856,615	2,970,755	10.90	4.00
GERMANY	6,629,013	6,352,796	6,037,823	5,215,352	5,390,488	19.78	3.36
LUXEMBOURG	72,098	65,586	64,727	63,104	70,021	0.26	10.96
NETHERLANDS	1,032,881	1,032,814	996,178	1,056,563	1,011,883	3.71	-4.23
SWITZERLAND	487,620	478,526	483,640	452,864	424,962	1.56	-6.16
EAST/MED EUR		**36,677**	**31,482**	**30,184**	**36,023**	**0.13**	**19.34**
TURKEY		36,677	31,482	30,184	36,023	0.13	19.34
OTHER EUROPE	**1,013,086**	**290,299**	**315,680**	**367,998**	**365,000**	**1.34**	**-0.81**
OTHER EUROPE	1,013,086	290,299	315,680	367,998	365,000	1.34	-0.81
REG.NOT SPEC	**24,790**	**568,372**	**523,878**	**549,257**	**560,383**	**2.06**	**2.03**
NOT SPECIFIE	**24,790**	**568,372**	**523,878**	**549,257**	**560,383**	**2.06**	**2.03**
OTH.WORLD	24,790	568,372	523,878	549,257	560,383	2.06	2.03

Source: World Tourism Organization (WTO)

SPAIN

4. ARRIVALS OF NON-RESIDENT TOURISTS IN ALL TYPES OF ACCOMMODATION ESTABLISHMENTS, BY COUNTRY OF RESIDENCE

	1999	2000	2001	2002	2003	Market share 03	% change 03-02
TOTAL (*)		**36,838,614**	**36,377,482**	**36,038,355**	**36,643,764**	**100.00**	**1.68**
AFRICA		**246,660**	**289,419**	**280,001**	**298,098**	**0.81**	**6.46**
OTHER AFRICA		**246,660**	**289,419**	**280,001**	**298,098**	**0.81**	**6.46**
ALL AFRICA		246,660	289,419	280,001	298,098	0.81	6.46
AMERICAS		**3,224,348**	**3,142,283**	**2,853,427**	**2,739,029**	**7.47**	**-4.01**
NORTH AMER		**1,735,042**	**1,645,897**	**1,472,392**	**1,458,359**	**3.98**	**-0.95**
USA		1,735,042	1,645,897	1,472,392	1,458,359	3.98	-0.95
OTHER AMERIC		**1,489,306**	**1,496,386**	**1,381,035**	**1,280,670**	**3.49**	**-7.27**
OTH AMERICA		1,489,306	1,496,386	1,381,035	1,280,670	3.49	-7.27
EAST AS/PACI		**983,249**	**790,796**	**828,136**	**930,783**	**2.54**	**12.39**
OT.EAST AS/P		**983,249**	**790,796**	**828,136**	**930,783**	**2.54**	**12.39**
ALL ASIA		983,249	790,796	828,136	930,783	2.54	12.39
EUROPE		**31,631,369**	**31,454,839**	**31,338,684**	**32,053,355**	**87.47**	**2.28**
NORTHERN EUR		**11,374,150**	**11,690,144**	**12,362,334**	**12,784,757**	**34.89**	**3.42**
DENMARK		454,637	422,737	422,220	395,636	1.08	-6.30
FINLAND		338,270	312,282	282,113	283,271	0.77	0.41
IRELAND		544,226	523,840	589,789	681,277	1.86	15.51
NORWAY				475,358	415,496	1.13	-12.59
SWEDEN		927,734	931,074	803,142	712,684	1.94	-11.26
UK		9,109,283	9,500,211	9,789,712	10,296,393	28.10	5.18
SOUTHERN EUR		**3,058,614**	**2,997,833**	**3,213,096**	**3,201,372**	**8.74**	**-0.36**
GREECE		92,016	92,406	100,977	89,253	0.24	-11.61
ITALY		1,908,315	1,897,946	2,037,616	2,007,080	5.48	-1.50
PORTUGAL		1,058,283	1,007,481	1,074,503	1,105,039	3.02	2.84
WESTERN EUR		**14,964,230**	**14,479,443**	**14,007,146**	**14,340,037**	**39.13**	**2.38**
AUSTRIA		260,524	231,762	239,208	256,830	0.70	7.37
BELGIUM		1,154,235	1,125,051	1,119,254	1,146,309	3.13	2.42
FRANCE		3,064,148	3,280,074	3,605,718	3,804,008	10.38	5.50
GERMANY		8,496,703	7,875,583	6,962,131	7,048,022	19.23	1.23
LUXEMBOURG		75,198	74,997	70,089	77,310	0.21	10.30
NETHERLANDS		1,913,422	1,891,976	2,010,746	2,007,558	5.48	-0.16
OTHER EUROPE		**2,234,375**	**2,287,419**	**1,756,108**	**1,727,189**	**4.71**	**-1.65**
OTHER EUROPE		2,234,375	2,287,419	1,756,108	1,727,189	4.71	-1.65
REG.NOT SPEC		**752,988**	**700,145**	**738,107**	**622,499**	**1.70**	**-15.66**
NOT SPECIFIE		**752,988**	**700,145**	**738,107**	**622,499**	**1.70**	**-15.66**
OTH.WORLD		752,988	700,145	738,107	622,499	1.70	-15.66

Source: World Tourism Organization (WTO)

SPAIN

5. OVERNIGHT STAYS OF NON-RESIDENT TOURISTS IN HOTELS AND SIMILAR ESTABLISHMENTS, BY COUNTRY OF RESIDENCE

	1999	2000	2001	2002	2003	Market share 03	% change 03-02
TOTAL (*)	**149,035,992**	**143,761,604**	**143,420,602**	**135,836,394**	**136,865,483**	**100.00**	**0.76**
AFRICA	**492,141**	**586,803**	**761,158**	**722,685**	**694,328**	**0.51**	**-3.92**
OTHER AFRICA	**492,141**	**586,803**	**761,158**	**722,685**	**694,328**	**0.51**	**-3.92**
ALL AFRICA	492,141	586,803	761,158	722,685	694,328	0.51	-3.92
AMERICAS	**5,906,670**	**7,315,819**	**7,221,695**	**6,525,878**	**6,147,464**	**4.49**	**-5.80**
NORTH AMER	**4,105,227**	**4,736,731**	**4,571,990**	**4,362,589**	**4,232,145**	**3.09**	**-2.99**
CANADA	369,274	424,751	423,406	452,671	500,792	0.37	10.63
MEXICO	391,432	485,915	543,680	631,645	581,607	0.42	-7.92
USA	3,344,521	3,826,065	3,604,904	3,278,273	3,149,746	2.30	-3.92
SOUTH AMER	**978,872**	**1,524,955**	**1,484,462**	**1,102,165**	**993,724**	**0.73**	**-9.84**
ARGENTINA	862,021	956,462	932,555	571,147	524,673	0.38	-8.14
BRAZIL		424,826	378,438	358,451	317,803	0.23	-11.34
VENEZUELA	116,851	143,667	173,469	172,567	151,248	0.11	-12.35
OTHER AMERIC	**822,571**	**1,054,133**	**1,165,243**	**1,061,124**	**921,595**	**0.67**	**-13.15**
OTH AMERICA	822,571	1,054,133	1,165,243	1,061,124	921,595	0.67	-13.15
EAST AS/PACI	**2,798,244**	**1,912,387**	**1,752,369**	**1,795,394**	**1,778,783**	**1.30**	**-0.93**
N/EAST ASIA	**1,214,834**	**1,228,190**	**954,934**	**985,750**	**963,535**	**0.70**	**-2.25**
JAPAN	1,214,834	1,228,190	954,934	985,750	963,535	0.70	-2.25
AUSTRALASIA		**297,672**	**287,532**	**303,389**	**323,408**	**0.24**	**6.60**
AUSTRALIA		253,328	242,082	254,775	267,747	0.20	5.09
NEW ZEALAND		44,344	45,450	48,614	55,661	0.04	14.50
OT.EAST AS/P	**1,583,410**	**386,525**	**509,903**	**506,255**	**491,840**	**0.36**	**-2.85**
OTHER ASIA	1,583,410	386,525	509,903	506,255	491,840	0.36	-2.85
EUROPE	**139,057,566**	**132,417,575**	**132,247,091**	**125,351,926**	**126,840,401**	**92.68**	**1.19**
C/E EUROPE		**4,006,843**	**3,960,151**	**3,406,388**	**3,061,855**	**2.24**	**-10.11**
CZECH REP		1,059,500	925,280	919,974	872,895	0.64	-5.12
HUNGARY		261,736	217,148	202,494	200,403	0.15	-1.03
POLAND		996,635	759,832	637,889	482,487	0.35	-24.36
RUSSIAN FED		1,420,872	1,885,276	1,506,677	1,336,879	0.98	-11.27
SLOVAKIA		268,100	172,615	139,354	169,191	0.12	21.41
NORTHERN EUR	**46,913,340**	**46,167,218**	**49,876,493**	**50,368,499**	**51,087,614**	**37.33**	**1.43**
DENMARK	1,206,568	1,077,985	949,406	966,702	987,754	0.72	2.18
FINLAND	713,391	708,212	695,004	646,350	623,288	0.46	-3.57
ICELAND		91,901	104,722	90,123	151,668	0.11	68.29
IRELAND	903,133	1,023,678	1,247,710	1,483,135	1,735,687	1.27	17.03
NORWAY	1,072,769	1,281,853	1,242,122	1,204,940	1,124,578	0.82	-6.67
SWEDEN	2,428,131	2,704,019	2,685,335	2,315,221	2,060,669	1.51	-10.99
UK	40,589,348	39,279,570	42,952,194	43,662,028	44,403,970	32.44	1.70
SOUTHERN EUR	**9,031,756**	**8,949,119**	**8,868,750**	**9,573,579**	**9,432,002**	**6.89**	**-1.48**
GREECE	203,834	199,357	189,140	224,258	217,447	0.16	-3.04
ITALY	6,562,983	6,357,998	6,397,612	6,790,623	6,608,280	4.83	-2.69
PORTUGAL	2,264,939	2,391,764	2,281,998	2,558,698	2,606,275	1.90	1.86

SPAIN

5. OVERNIGHT STAYS OF NON-RESIDENT TOURISTS IN HOTELS AND SIMILAR ESTABLISHMENTS, BY COUNTRY OF RESIDENCE

	1999	2000	2001	2002	2003	Market share 03	% change 03-02
WESTERN EUR	**77,787,396**	**72,165,517**	**68,363,002**	**60,692,637**	**61,882,352**	**45.21**	**1.96**
AUSTRIA	1,192,681	1,067,930	937,656	849,079	1,038,943	0.76	22.36
BELGIUM	6,767,174	6,272,116	5,729,692	5,533,379	5,615,284	4.10	1.48
FRANCE	8,357,369	8,193,305	8,750,295	9,003,762	9,174,828	6.70	1.90
GERMANY	52,366,748	47,794,260	44,562,378	37,206,735	38,160,674	27.88	2.56
LUXEMBOURG	481,048	430,165	409,072	381,405	418,851	0.31	9.82
NETHERLANDS	6,051,905	5,910,974	5,407,277	5,538,314	5,378,812	3.93	-2.88
SWITZERLAND	2,570,471	2,496,767	2,566,632	2,179,963	2,094,960	1.53	-3.90
EAST/MED EUR		**100,946**	**86,291**	**83,290**	**92,116**	**0.07**	**10.60**
TURKEY		100,946	86,291	83,290	92,116	0.07	10.60
OTHER EUROPE	**5,325,074**	**1,027,932**	**1,092,404**	**1,227,533**	**1,284,462**	**0.94**	**4.64**
OTHER EUROPE	5,325,074	1,027,932	1,092,404	1,227,533	1,284,462	0.94	4.64
REG.NOT SPEC	**781,371**	**1,529,020**	**1,438,289**	**1,440,511**	**1,404,507**	**1.03**	**-2.50**
NOT SPECIFIE	**781,371**	**1,529,020**	**1,438,289**	**1,440,511**	**1,404,507**	**1.03**	**-2.50**
OTH.WORLD	781,371	1,529,020	1,438,289	1,440,511	1,404,507	1.03	-2.50

Source: World Tourism Organization (WTO)

SPAIN

6. OVERNIGHT STAYS OF NON-RESIDENT TOURISTS IN ALL TYPES OF ACCOMMODATION ESTABLISHMENTS, BY COUNTRY OF RESIDENCE

	1999	2000	2001	2002	2003	Market share 03	% change 03-02
TOTAL (*)		**233,896,548**	**232,035,196**	**220,707,302**	**217,851,793**	**100.00**	**-1.29**
AFRICA		**687,551**	**881,969**	**818,264**	**794,014**	**0.36**	**-2.96**
OTHER AFRICA		**687,551**	**881,969**	**818,264**	**794,014**	**0.36**	**-2.96**
ALL AFRICA		687,551	881,969	818,264	794,014	0.36	-2.96
AMERICAS		**7,881,001**	**7,845,695**	**7,122,349**	**6,787,707**	**3.12**	**-4.70**
NORTH AMER		**4,046,482**	**3,843,115**	**3,481,056**	**3,410,561**	**1.57**	**-2.03**
USA		4,046,482	3,843,115	3,481,056	3,410,561	1.57	-2.03
OTHER AMERIC		**3,834,519**	**4,002,580**	**3,641,293**	**3,377,146**	**1.55**	**-7.25**
OTH AMERICA		3,834,519	4,002,580	3,641,293	3,377,146	1.55	-7.25
EAST AS/PACI		**1,666,830**	**1,523,713**	**1,549,601**	**1,518,628**	**0.70**	**-2.00**
OT.EAST AS/P		**1,666,830**	**1,523,713**	**1,549,601**	**1,518,628**	**0.70**	**-2.00**
ALL ASIA		1,666,830	1,523,713	1,549,601	1,518,628	0.70	-2.00
EUROPE		**221,626,888**	**219,807,196**	**209,256,759**	**206,759,181**	**94.91**	**-1.19**
NORTHERN EUR		**90,336,101**	**93,936,719**	**96,026,773**	**94,672,916**	**43.46**	**-1.41**
DENMARK		3,095,353	2,982,146	2,815,478	2,543,140	1.17	-9.67
FINLAND		2,623,424	2,275,764	2,034,045	1,979,945	0.91	-2.66
IRELAND		4,310,313	4,261,183	4,584,868	4,797,124	2.20	4.63
NORWAY				3,542,615	2,997,812	1.38	-15.38
SWEDEN		7,127,138	6,935,373	5,901,146	5,098,783	2.34	-13.60
UK		73,179,873	77,482,253	77,148,621	77,256,112	35.46	0.14
SOUTHERN EUR		**10,846,546**	**10,784,604**	**11,438,548**	**11,282,846**	**5.18**	**-1.36**
GREECE		327,377	403,992	263,384	262,852	0.12	-0.20
ITALY		7,507,427	7,418,290	8,082,632	7,911,067	3.63	-2.12
PORTUGAL		3,011,742	2,962,322	3,092,532	3,108,927	1.43	0.53
WESTERN EUR		**106,361,160**	**101,009,624**	**92,139,870**	**91,628,417**	**42.06**	**-0.56**
AUSTRIA		1,482,644	1,297,334	1,225,980	1,392,331	0.64	13.57
BELGIUM		8,014,149	7,615,704	7,363,098	7,298,323	3.35	-0.88
FRANCE		11,842,696	12,695,502	13,566,205	13,671,925	6.28	0.78
GERMANY		70,031,611	64,739,350	54,867,175	54,651,503	25.09	-0.39
LUXEMBOURG		509,151	482,663	439,596	477,918	0.22	8.72
NETHERLANDS		14,480,909	14,179,071	14,677,816	14,136,417	6.49	-3.69
OTHER EUROPE		**14,083,081**	**14,076,249**	**9,651,568**	**9,175,002**	**4.21**	**-4.94**
OTHER EUROPE		14,083,081	14,076,249	9,651,568	9,175,002	4.21	-4.94
REG.NOT SPEC		**2,034,278**	**1,976,623**	**1,960,329**	**1,992,263**	**0.91**	**1.63**
NOT SPECIFIE		**2,034,278**	**1,976,623**	**1,960,329**	**1,992,263**	**0.91**	**1.63**
OTH.WORLD		2,034,278	1,976,623	1,960,329	1,992,263	0.91	1.63

Source: World Tourism Organization (WTO)

SRI LANKA

1. ARRIVALS OF NON-RESIDENT TOURISTS AT NATIONAL BORDERS, BY NATIONALITY

		1999	2000	2001	2002	2003	Market share 03	% change 03-02
TOTAL	(*)	**436,440**	**400,414**	**336,794**	**393,171**	**500,642**	**100.00**	**27.33**
AFRICA		**1,236**	**891**	**902**	**1,545**	**1,925**	**0.38**	**24.60**
SOUTHERN AFR		**282**						
SOUTH AFRICA		282						
OTHER AFRICA		**954**	**891**	**902**	**1,545**	**1,925**	**0.38**	**24.60**
OTHER AFRICA		954						
ALL AFRICA			891	902	1,545	1,925	0.38	24.60
AMERICAS		**18,870**	**17,694**	**16,704**	**20,553**	**25,735**	**5.14**	**25.21**
NORTH AMER		**18,534**	**17,352**	**16,304**	**20,004**	**25,099**	**5.01**	**25.47**
CANADA		7,935	7,521	7,804	8,337	11,109	2.22	33.25
USA		10,599	9,831	8,500	11,667	13,990	2.79	19.91
OTHER AMERIC		**336**	**342**	**400**	**549**	**636**	**0.13**	**15.85**
OTH AMERICA		336	342	400	549	636	0.13	15.85
EAST AS/PACI		**66,405**	**58,076**	**48,590**	**67,008**	**85,726**	**17.12**	**27.93**
N/EAST ASIA		**27,672**	**21,911**	**20,761**	**27,522**	**32,940**	**6.58**	**19.69**
CHINA		1,707	2,220	3,789	4,350	7,380	1.47	69.66
TAIWAN(P.C.)		3,957	3,546	2,821	3,417	2,532	0.51	-25.90
HK,CHINA		3,168	3,243	2,115	3,582	3,150	0.63	-12.06
JAPAN		16,353	10,287	9,241	13,566	17,178	3.43	26.63
KOREA REP.		2,487	2,615	2,795	2,607	2,700	0.54	3.57
S/EAST ASIA		**22,851**	**17,304**	**13,850**	**24,234**	**27,524**	**5.50**	**13.58**
INDONESIA		4,260	2,607	1,075	1,473	1,392	0.28	-5.50
MALAYSIA		6,003	4,830	3,917	9,603	9,283	1.85	-3.33
PHILIPPINES		1,431	1,428	1,422	1,626	2,418	0.48	48.71
SINGAPORE		6,864	5,010	4,505	7,578	8,423	1.68	11.15
THAILAND		4,293	3,429	2,931	3,954	6,008	1.20	51.95
AUSTRALASIA		**15,066**	**18,198**	**12,863**	**13,254**	**22,933**	**4.58**	**73.03**
AUSTRALIA		13,284	16,476	11,330	11,334	20,075	4.01	77.12
NEW ZEALAND		1,782	1,722	1,533	1,920	2,858	0.57	48.85
OT.EAST AS/P		**816**	**663**	**1,116**	**1,998**	**2,329**	**0.47**	**16.57**
OTHER ASIA		750	639	1,053	1,941	2,195	0.44	13.09
OTH OCEANIA		66	24	63	57	134	0.03	135.09
EUROPE		**282,126**	**267,851**	**211,555**	**208,722**	**265,779**	**53.09**	**27.34**
C/E EUROPE		**6,255**	**6,840**	**7,045**	**8,046**	**10,600**	**2.12**	**31.74**
RUSSIAN FED		3,174	3,552	2,534	2,943	3,683	0.74	25.14
OTH C/E EUR		3,081	3,288	4,511	5,103	6,917	1.38	35.55
NORTHERN EUR		**89,040**	**95,136**	**77,325**	**76,053**	**104,734**	**20.92**	**37.71**
DENMARK		2,010	1,662	1,630	1,980	2,732	0.55	37.98
FINLAND		1,278	2,319	538	726	1,103	0.22	51.93
NORWAY		2,046	2,010	2,285	2,892	3,677	0.73	27.14
SWEDEN		2,673	4,338	4,318	2,523	3,916	0.78	55.21
UK		81,033	84,807	68,554	67,932	93,306	18.64	37.35

SRI LANKA

1. ARRIVALS OF NON-RESIDENT TOURISTS AT NATIONAL BORDERS, BY NATIONALITY

	1999	2000	2001	2002	2003	Market share 03	% change 03-02
SOUTHERN EUR	**22,224**	**18,585**	**14,830**	**14,520**	**18,449**	**3.69**	**27.06**
ITALY	19,818	16,719	13,283	12,171	15,648	3.13	28.57
SPAIN	2,406	1,866	1,547	2,349	2,801	0.56	19.24
WESTERN EUR	**161,667**	**144,422**	**109,857**	**107,067**	**128,445**	**25.66**	**19.97**
AUSTRIA	6,123	6,312	5,788	6,144	7,337	1.47	19.42
BELGIUM	5,667	10,230	5,226	4,731	4,268	0.85	-9.79
FRANCE	34,491	26,120	20,989	19,980	28,576	5.71	43.02
GERMANY	77,340	70,635	60,370	55,137	58,875	11.76	6.78
NETHERLANDS	29,682	22,632	11,257	11,763	18,212	3.64	54.82
SWITZERLAND	8,364	8,493	6,227	9,312	11,177	2.23	20.03
OTHER EUROPE	**2,940**	**2,868**	**2,498**	**3,036**	**3,551**	**0.71**	**16.96**
OTHER EUROPE	2,940	2,868	2,498	3,036	3,551	0.71	16.96
MIDDLE EAST	**4,815**	**4,347**	**5,364**	**6,462**	**6,759**	**1.35**	**4.60**
MIDDLE EAST	**4,815**	**4,347**	**5,364**	**6,462**	**6,759**	**1.35**	**4.60**
ALL MID EAST	4,815	4,347	5,364	6,462	6,759	1.35	4.60
SOUTH ASIA	**62,988**	**51,555**	**53,679**	**88,881**	**114,718**	**22.91**	**29.07**
SOUTH ASIA	**62,988**	**51,555**	**53,679**	**88,881**	**114,718**	**22.91**	**29.07**
BANGLADESH	1,140	1,218	1,738	1,518	1,851	0.37	21.94
INDIA	42,267	31,851	33,932	69,996	90,639	18.10	29.49
MALDIVES	7,587	7,941	8,975	9,855	11,577	2.31	17.47
NEPAL	570	528	512	786	977	0.20	24.30
PAKISTAN	11,424	10,017	8,522	6,726	9,674	1.93	43.83

Source: World Tourism Organization (WTO)

SRI LANKA

1. ARRIVALS OF NON-RESIDENT TOURISTS AT NATIONAL BORDERS, BY COUNTRY OF RESIDENCE

	1999	2000	2001	2002	2003	Market share 03	% change 03-02
TOTAL (*)	**436,440**	**400,414**	**336,794**	**393,171**	**500,642**	**100.00**	**27.33**
AFRICA	**1,236**	**894**	**952**	**1,611**	**1,991**	**0.40**	**23.59**
SOUTHERN AFR	**282**	**372**	**341**	**660**	**980**	**0.20**	**48.48**
SOUTH AFRICA	282	372	341	660	980	0.20	48.48
OTHER AFRICA	**954**	**522**	**611**	**951**	**1,011**	**0.20**	**6.31**
OTHER AFRICA	954	522	611	951	1,011	0.20	6.31
AMERICAS	**18,849**	**17,766**	**16,412**	**20,421**	**25,744**	**5.14**	**26.07**
NORTH AMER	**18,477**	**17,319**	**15,983**	**19,869**	**25,110**	**5.02**	**26.38**
CANADA	7,905	7,503	7,609	8,304	11,164	2.23	34.44
USA	10,572	9,816	8,374	11,565	13,946	2.79	20.59
OTHER AMERIC	**372**	**447**	**429**	**552**	**634**	**0.13**	**14.86**
OTH AMERICA	372	447	429	552	634	0.13	14.86
EAST AS/PACI	**66,528**	**58,197**	**49,079**	**66,084**	**84,145**	**16.81**	**27.33**
N/EAST ASIA	**27,723**	**21,978**	**20,889**	**27,747**	**32,697**	**6.53**	**17.84**
CHINA	1,704	2,208	3,721	4,338	7,251	1.45	67.15
TAIWAN(P.C.)	3,948	3,543	2,834	3,432	2,547	0.51	-25.79
HK,CHINA	3,255	3,348	2,319	3,759	3,075	0.61	-18.20
JAPAN	16,332	10,266	9,237	13,602	17,115	3.42	25.83
KOREA REP.	2,484	2,613	2,778	2,616	2,709	0.54	3.56
S/EAST ASIA	**22,833**	**17,292**	**14,015**	**24,312**	**27,602**	**5.51**	**13.53**
INDONESIA	4,254	2,604	1,081	1,476	1,395	0.28	-5.49
MALAYSIA	6,012	4,833	3,910	9,651	9,331	1.86	-3.32
PHILIPPINES	1,431	1,428	1,427	1,641	2,433	0.49	48.26
SINGAPORE	6,858	5,019	4,641	7,599	8,444	1.69	11.12
THAILAND	4,278	3,408	2,956	3,945	5,999	1.20	52.07
AUSTRALASIA	**15,003**	**18,180**	**12,985**	**13,137**	**22,816**	**4.56**	**73.68**
AUSTRALIA	13,218	16,443	11,457	11,217	19,958	3.99	77.93
NEW ZEALAND	1,785	1,737	1,528	1,920	2,858	0.57	48.85
OT.EAST AS/P	**969**	**747**	**1,190**	**888**	**1,030**	**0.21**	**15.99**
OTHER ASIA	813	699	1,070	816	881	0.18	7.97
OTH OCEANIA	156	48	120	72	149	0.03	106.94
EUROPE	**282,000**	**267,664**	**211,049**	**208,374**	**265,802**	**53.09**	**27.56**
C/E EUROPE	**6,204**	**6,840**	**7,065**	**8,079**	**10,633**	**2.12**	**31.61**
RUSSIAN FED	3,183	3,552	2,542	2,946	3,686	0.74	25.12
OTH C/E EUR	3,021	3,288	4,523	5,133	6,947	1.39	35.34
NORTHERN EUR	**89,220**	**95,016**	**76,519**	**75,606**	**104,658**	**20.90**	**38.43**
DENMARK	2,016	1,653	1,628	1,968	2,720	0.54	38.21
FINLAND	1,569	2,316	535	729	1,106	0.22	51.71
NORWAY	2,025	2,010	2,261	2,889	3,674	0.73	27.17
SWEDEN	2,691	4,344	4,265	2,487	3,880	0.78	56.01
UK	80,919	84,693	67,830	67,533	93,278	18.63	38.12
SOUTHERN EUR	**22,215**	**18,731**	**13,603**	**14,505**	**18,434**	**3.68**	**27.09**

SRI LANKA

1. ARRIVALS OF NON-RESIDENT TOURISTS AT NATIONAL BORDERS, BY COUNTRY OF RESIDENCE

	1999	2000	2001	2002	2003	Market share 03	% change 03-02
ITALY	19,815	16,883	12,074	12,177	15,654	3.13	28.55
SPAIN	2,400	1,848	1,529	2,328	2,780	0.56	19.42
WESTERN EUR	**161,448**	**144,202**	**111,369**	**107,166**	**128,544**	**25.68**	**19.95**
AUSTRIA	6,108	6,294	5,968	6,117	7,310	1.46	19.50
BELGIUM	5,643	10,224	5,250	4,767	4,304	0.86	-9.71
FRANCE	34,458	25,992	20,949	19,989	28,585	5.71	43.00
GERMANY	77,259	70,584	60,405	55,170	58,908	11.77	6.78
NETHERLANDS	29,670	22,618	12,569	11,748	18,197	3.63	54.89
SWITZERLAND	8,310	8,490	6,228	9,375	11,240	2.25	19.89
OTHER EUROPE	**2,913**	**2,875**	**2,493**	**3,018**	**3,533**	**0.71**	**17.06**
OTHER EUROPE	2,913	2,875	2,493	3,018	3,533	0.71	17.06
MIDDLE EAST	**4,821**	**4,341**	**5,544**	**6,492**	**6,789**	**1.36**	**4.57**
MIDDLE EAST	**4,821**	**4,341**	**5,544**	**6,492**	**6,789**	**1.36**	**4.57**
ALL MID EAST	4,821	4,341	5,544	6,492	6,789	1.36	4.57
SOUTH ASIA	**63,006**	**51,552**	**53,758**	**90,189**	**116,171**	**23.20**	**28.81**
SOUTH ASIA	**63,006**	**51,552**	**53,758**	**90,189**	**116,171**	**23.20**	**28.81**
BANGLADESH	1,137	1,218	1,745	1,521	1,830	0.37	20.32
INDIA	42,315	31,860	33,924	69,960	90,603	18.10	29.51
MALDIVES	7,557	7,935	9,019	9,861	11,583	2.31	17.46
NEPAL	576	534	508	789	980	0.20	24.21
PAKISTAN	11,421	10,005	8,562	6,756	9,704	1.94	43.64
OTH STH ASIA				1,302	1,471	0.29	12.98

Source: World Tourism Organization (WTO)

SRI LANKA

6. OVERNIGHT STAYS OF NON-RESIDENT TOURISTS IN ALL TYPES OF ACCOMMODATION ESTABLISHMENTS, BY NATIONALITY

	1999	2000	2001	2002	2003	Market share 03	% change 03-02
TOTAL	**4,478,762**	**4,056,306**	**3,342,233**	**3,989,058**	**5,092,782**	**100.00**	**27.67**
AFRICA	**12,484**	**8,999**	**8,648**	**14,987**	**18,288**	**0.36**	**22.03**
OTHER AFRICA	**12,484**	**8,999**	**8,648**	**14,987**	**18,288**	**0.36**	**22.03**
ALL AFRICA	12,484	8,999	8,648	14,987	18,288	0.36	22.03
AMERICAS	**185,102**	**168,773**	**178,004**	**214,312**	**275,267**	**5.41**	**28.44**
NORTH AMER	**182,676**	**165,213**	**173,980**	**206,954**	**267,566**	**5.25**	**29.29**
CANADA	87,265	69,553	79,627	82,700	123,380	2.42	49.19
USA	95,411	95,660	94,353	124,254	144,186	2.83	16.04
OTHER AMERIC	**2,426**	**3,560**	**4,024**	**7,358**	**7,701**	**0.15**	**4.66**
OTH AMERICA	2,426	3,560	4,024	7,358	7,701	0.15	4.66
EAST AS/PACI	**447,728**	**467,826**	**422,697**	**577,039**	**793,694**	**15.58**	**37.55**
N/EAST ASIA	**169,838**	**181,404**	**171,297**	**222,707**	**278,022**	**5.46**	**24.84**
CHINA	11,198	19,159	31,183	30,015	59,040	1.16	96.70
TAIWAN(P.C.)	20,907	28,368	23,753	23,724	15,952	0.31	-32.76
HK,CHINA	16,410	18,453	14,086	23,856	22,680	0.45	-4.93
JAPAN	105,804	90,320	80,027	120,737	156,320	3.07	29.47
KOREA REP.	15,519	25,104	22,248	24,375	24,030	0.47	-1.42
S/EAST ASIA	**117,382**	**103,403**	**103,002**	**166,627**	**216,402**	**4.25**	**29.87**
INDONESIA	12,354	7,482	4,343	8,617	8,491	0.17	-1.46
MALAYSIA	28,994	4,830	24,599	58,962	75,192	1.48	27.53
PHILIPPINES	9,960	14,537	14,647	9,984	14,508	0.28	45.31
SINGAPORE	41,184	47,545	34,148	59,336	66,542	1.31	12.14
THAILAND	24,890	29,009	25,265	29,728	51,669	1.01	73.81
AUSTRALASIA	**150,410**	**174,332**	**135,750**	**164,926**	**271,017**	**5.32**	**64.33**
AUSTRALIA	133,641	157,009	120,108	140,542	235,006	4.61	67.21
NEW ZEALAND	16,769	17,323	15,642	24,384	36,011	0.71	47.68
OT.EAST AS/P	**10,098**	**8,687**	**12,648**	**22,779**	**28,253**	**0.55**	**24.03**
OTHER ASIA	9,636	8,519	12,207	22,089	26,645	0.52	20.63
OTH OCEANIA	462	168	441	690	1,608	0.03	133.04
EUROPE	**3,345,428**	**2,987,776**	**2,296,658**	**2,461,444**	**3,066,972**	**60.22**	**24.60**
C/E EUROPE	**59,878**	**37,577**	**53,677**	**81,827**	**108,710**	**2.13**	**32.85**
RUSSIAN FED	30,670	24,884	20,938	32,648	40,832	0.80	25.07
OTH C/E EUR	29,208	12,693	32,739	49,179	67,878	1.33	38.02
NORTHERN EUR	**1,012,145**	**1,019,179**	**788,462**	**833,012**	**1,078,464**	**21.18**	**29.47**
DENMARK	20,809	17,868	20,290	24,923	31,051	0.61	24.59
FINLAND	14,015	31,111	5,391	8,579	12,175	0.24	41.92
NORWAY	19,333	19,650	24,568	31,260	40,479	0.79	29.49
SWEDEN	27,603	45,604	47,734	28,225	41,379	0.81	46.60
UK	930,385	904,946	690,479	740,025	953,380	18.72	28.83
SOUTHERN EUR	**212,884**	**174,272**	**136,028**	**145,991**	**199,855**	**3.92**	**36.90**
ITALY	190,209	154,730	122,933	123,206	174,605	3.43	41.72
SPAIN	22,675	19,542	13,095	22,785	25,250	0.50	10.82

6. OVERNIGHT STAYS OF NON-RESIDENT TOURISTS IN ALL TYPES OF ACCOMMODATION ESTABLISHMENTS, BY NATIONALITY

	1999	2000	2001	2002	2003	Market share 03	% change 03-02
WESTERN EUR	**2,021,874**	**1,723,487**	**1,291,833**	**1,367,778**	**1,647,588**	**32.35**	**20.46**
AUSTRIA	78,022	94,728	72,101	81,233	91,864	1.80	13.09
BELGIUM	58,207	137,417	60,087	52,484	49,140	0.96	-6.37
FRANCE	328,747	271,452	222,988	213,898	292,084	5.74	36.55
GERMANY	1,077,834	845,294	724,387	750,130	830,322	16.30	10.69
NETHERLANDS	400,083	278,871	142,562	152,116	242,924	4.77	59.70
SWITZERLAND	78,981	95,725	69,708	117,917	141,254	2.77	19.79
OTHER EUROPE	**38,647**	**33,261**	**26,658**	**32,836**	**32,355**	**0.64**	**-1.46**
OTHER EUROPE	38,647	33,261	26,658	32,836	32,355	0.64	-1.46
MIDDLE EAST	**38,414**	**41,383**	**42,966**	**51,050**	**54,836**	**1.08**	**7.42**
MIDDLE EAST	**38,414**	**41,383**	**42,966**	**51,050**	**54,836**	**1.08**	**7.42**
ALL MID EAST	38,414	41,383	42,966	51,050	54,836	1.08	7.42
SOUTH ASIA	**449,606**	**381,549**	**393,260**	**670,226**	**883,725**	**17.35**	**31.85**
SOUTH ASIA	**449,606**	**381,549**	**393,260**	**670,226**	**883,725**	**17.35**	**31.85**
BANGLADESH	6,156	6,577	11,297	10,778	13,512	0.27	25.37
INDIA	314,466	239,201	251,097	531,970	716,048	14.06	34.60
MALDIVES	47,874	56,937	61,838	69,971	84,512	1.66	20.78
PAKISTAN	81,110	78,834	69,028	57,507	69,653	1.37	21.12

Source: World Tourism Organization (WTO)

SUDAN

1. ARRIVALS OF NON-RESIDENT TOURISTS AT NATIONAL BORDERS, BY NATIONALITY

	1999	2000	2001	2002	2003	Market share 03	% change 03-02
TOTAL	**39,000**	**38,000**	**50,000**				
AFRICA	**7,000**	**5,000**	**7,000**				
OTHER AFRICA	**7,000**	**5,000**	**7,000**				
ALL AFRICA	7,000	5,000	7,000				
AMERICAS	**6,000**	**4,000**	**4,000**				
OTHER AMERIC	**6,000**	**4,000**	**4,000**				
ALL AMERICAS	6,000	4,000	4,000				
EAST AS/PACI	**4,000**	**7,000**	**10,000**				
OT.EAST AS/P	**4,000**	**7,000**	**10,000**				
ALL ASIA	4,000	7,000	10,000				
EUROPE	**7,000**	**9,000**	**11,000**				
OTHER EUROPE	**7,000**	**9,000**	**11,000**				
ALL EUROPE	7,000	9,000	11,000				
MIDDLE EAST	**12,000**	**9,000**	**13,000**				
MIDDLE EAST	**12,000**	**9,000**	**13,000**				
ALL MID EAST	12,000	9,000	13,000				
SOUTH ASIA	**3,000**	**4,000**	**5,000**				
SOUTH ASIA	**3,000**	**4,000**	**5,000**				
ALL STH ASIA	3,000	4,000	5,000				

Source: World Tourism Organization (WTO)

SWAZILAND

3. ARRIVALS OF NON-RESIDENT TOURISTS IN HOTELS AND SIMILAR ESTABLISHMENTS, BY COUNTRY OF RESIDENCE

	1999	2000	2001	2002	2003	Market share 03	% change 03-02
TOTAL (*)	**289,383**	**280,870**	**283,177**	**255,927**	**218,813**	**100.00**	**-14.50**
AFRICA	**198,921**	**177,216**	**145,169**	**173,420**	**110,054**	**50.30**	**-36.54**
EAST AFRICA	**27,457**	**23,650**	**19,455**	**17,304**	**11,642**	**5.32**	**-32.72**
MOZAMBIQUE	27,457	23,650	19,455	17,304	11,642	5.32	-32.72
SOUTHERN AFR	**146,417**	**126,296**	**112,157**	**146,286**	**85,899**	**39.26**	**-41.28**
SOUTH AFRICA	146,417	126,296	112,157	146,286	85,899	39.26	-41.28
OTHER AFRICA	**25,047**	**27,270**	**13,557**	**9,830**	**12,513**	**5.72**	**27.29**
OTHER AFRICA	25,047	27,270	13,557	9,830	12,513	5.72	27.29
AMERICAS	**9,733**	**10,823**	**20,217**	**10,380**	**11,092**	**5.07**	**6.86**
OTHER AMERIC	**9,733**	**10,823**	**20,217**	**10,380**	**11,092**	**5.07**	**6.86**
ALL AMERICAS	9,733	10,823	20,217	10,380	11,092	5.07	6.86
EAST AS/PACI	**6,313**	**7,053**	**5,676**	**5,244**	**2,343**	**1.07**	**-55.32**
AUSTRALASIA	**5,515**	**6,304**	**3,784**	**1,496**	**701**	**0.32**	**-53.14**
AUSTRALIA	5,515	6,304	3,784	1,496	701	0.32	-53.14
OT.EAST AS/P	**798**	**749**	**1,892**	**3,748**	**1,642**	**0.75**	**-56.19**
OTHER ASIA	798	749	1,892	3,748	1,642	0.75	-56.19
EUROPE	**72,916**	**84,514**	**84,988**	**40,483**	**87,999**	**40.22**	**117.37**
NORTHERN EUR	**24,546**	**26,562**	**13,684**	**5,818**	**13,702**	**6.26**	**135.51**
UK	24,546	26,562	13,684	5,818	13,702	6.26	135.51
SOUTHERN EUR	**836**	**818**	**2,014**	**2,006**	**8,666**	**3.96**	**332.00**
PORTUGAL	836	818	2,014	2,006	8,666	3.96	332.00
OTHER EUROPE	**47,534**	**57,134**	**69,290**	**32,659**	**65,631**	**29.99**	**100.96**
OTHER EUROPE	47,534	57,134	69,290	32,659	65,631	29.99	100.96
REG.NOT SPEC	**1,500**	**1,264**	**27,127**	**26,400**	**7,325**	**3.35**	**-72.25**
NOT SPECIFIE	**1,500**	**1,264**	**27,127**	**26,400**	**7,325**	**3.35**	**-72.25**
OTH.WORLD	1,500	1,264	27,127	26,400	7,325	3.35	-72.25

Source: World Tourism Organization (WTO)

SWEDEN

1. ARRIVALS OF NON-RESIDENT TOURISTS AT NATIONAL BORDERS, BY COUNTRY OF RESIDENCE

	1999	2000	2001	2002	2003	Market share 03	% change 03-02
TOTAL (*)			**7,431,000**	**7,459,000**	**7,627,000**	**100.00**	**2.25**
AFRICA			**37,000**	**42,000**	**46,000**	**0.60**	**9.52**
OTHER AFRICA			**37,000**	**42,000**	**46,000**	**0.60**	**9.52**
ALL AFRICA			37,000	42,000	46,000	0.60	9.52
AMERICAS			**546,000**	**413,000**	**467,000**	**6.12**	**13.08**
NORTH AMER			**475,000**	**369,000**	**399,000**	**5.23**	**8.13**
CANADA			73,000	41,000	50,000	0.66	21.95
USA			402,000	328,000	349,000	4.58	6.40
OTHER AMERIC			**71,000**	**44,000**	**68,000**	**0.89**	**54.55**
OTH AMERICA			71,000	44,000	68,000	0.89	54.55
EAST AS/PACI			**411,000**	**348,000**	**380,000**	**4.98**	**9.20**
OT.EAST AS/P			**411,000**	**348,000**	**380,000**	**4.98**	**9.20**
ALL ASIA			357,000	282,000	309,000	4.05	9.57
ALL OCEANIA			54,000	66,000	71,000	0.93	7.58
EUROPE			**6,437,000**	**6,656,000**	**6,696,000**	**87.79**	**0.60**
C/E EUROPE			**304,000**	**326,000**	**375,000**	**4.92**	**15.03**
ALL C/E EUR			304,000	326,000	375,000	4.92	15.03
NORTHERN EUR			**3,222,000**	**3,242,000**	**3,241,000**	**42.49**	**-0.03**
DENMARK			1,351,000	1,361,000	1,556,000	20.40	14.33
FINLAND			817,000	795,000	639,000	8.38	-19.62
NORWAY			477,000	587,000	519,000	6.80	-11.58
UK			577,000	499,000	527,000	6.91	5.61
WESTERN EUR			**2,099,000**	**2,284,000**	**2,293,000**	**30.06**	**0.39**
FRANCE			284,000	279,000	239,000	3.13	-14.34
GERMANY			1,493,000	1,696,000	1,736,000	22.76	2.36
NETHERLANDS			322,000	309,000	318,000	4.17	2.91
OTHER EUROPE			**812,000**	**804,000**	**787,000**	**10.32**	**-2.11**
OTHER EUROPE			812,000	804,000	787,000	10.32	-2.11
REG.NOT SPEC					**38,000**	**0.50**	
NOT SPECIFIE					**38,000**	**0.50**	
OTH.WORLD					38,000	0.50	

Source: World Tourism Organization (WTO)

SWEDEN

5. OVERNIGHT STAYS OF NON-RESIDENT TOURISTS IN HOTELS AND SIMILAR ESTABLISHMENTS, BY COUNTRY OF RESIDENCE

	1999	2000	2001	2002	2003	Market share 03	% change 03-02
TOTAL (*)	**4,515,500**	**4,678,806**	**4,926,857**	**4,867,679**	**4,833,186**	**100.00**	**-0.71**
AMERICAS	**421,943**	**430,763**	**474,333**	**445,191**	**394,864**	**8.17**	**-11.30**
NORTH AMER	**411,157**	**415,635**	**463,691**	**435,879**	**379,674**	**7.86**	**-12.89**
CANADA	43,224	34,322	53,392	59,048	30,576	0.63	-48.22
USA	367,933	381,313	410,299	376,831	349,098	7.22	-7.36
OTHER AMERIC	**10,786**	**15,128**	**10,642**	**9,312**	**15,190**	**0.31**	**63.12**
OTH AMERICA	10,786	15,128	10,642	9,312	15,190	0.31	63.12
EAST AS/PACI	**212,504**	**225,455**	**197,165**	**213,441**	**183,273**	**3.79**	**-14.13**
N/EAST ASIA	**138,539**	**143,728**	**127,080**	**138,561**	**110,179**	**2.28**	**-20.48**
JAPAN	127,788	132,722	117,153	123,302	99,237	2.05	-19.52
KOREA REP.	10,751	11,006	9,927	15,259	10,942	0.23	-28.29
AUSTRALASIA	**21,036**	**22,119**	**22,151**	**25,242**	**22,821**	**0.47**	**-9.59**
AUSTRALIA	19,146	20,397	21,135	24,259	21,326	0.44	-12.09
NEW ZEALAND	1,890	1,722	1,016	983	1,495	0.03	52.09
OT.EAST AS/P	**52,929**	**59,608**	**47,934**	**49,638**	**50,273**	**1.04**	**1.28**
OTHER ASIA	52,929	59,608	47,934	49,638	50,273	1.04	1.28
EUROPE	**3,367,281**	**3,405,892**	**3,601,666**	**3,677,557**	**3,697,125**	**76.49**	**0.53**
C/E EUROPE	**164,066**	**150,300**	**182,334**	**192,300**	**193,439**	**4.00**	**0.59**
CZECH REP	6,148	5,622	6,639	5,765	9,381	0.19	62.72
ESTONIA	23,259	25,559	18,731	17,143	14,620	0.30	-14.72
HUNGARY	5,181	5,376	6,428	4,036	6,170	0.13	52.87
LATVIA	9,876	8,395	11,178	8,311	9,701	0.20	16.72
LITHUANIA	9,283	7,702	9,097	6,896	10,349	0.21	50.07
POLAND	40,244	34,947	46,796	44,918	38,716	0.80	-13.81
RUSSIAN FED	67,275	60,732	80,884	103,696	102,871	2.13	-0.80
SLOVAKIA	2,800	1,967	2,581	1,535	1,631	0.03	6.25
NORTHERN EUR	**1,657,631**	**1,713,953**	**1,838,396**	**1,956,075**	**2,011,374**	**41.62**	**2.83**
DENMARK	298,613	315,584	343,649	331,597	368,657	7.63	11.18
FINLAND	282,234	261,402	264,756	265,453	262,487	5.43	-1.12
ICELAND	4,855	6,350	3,653	3,840	7,401	0.15	92.73
IRELAND	10,006	8,956	10,339	10,928	15,586	0.32	42.62
NORWAY	621,956	653,435	680,736	837,232	868,342	17.97	3.72
UK	439,967	468,226	535,263	507,025	488,901	10.12	-3.57
SOUTHERN EUR	**239,478**	**247,803**	**262,809**	**253,996**	**241,480**	**5.00**	**-4.93**
GREECE	9,053	6,463	5,335	4,354	6,215	0.13	42.74
ITALY	145,629	138,281	153,140	150,910	141,726	2.93	-6.09
PORTUGAL	7,179	6,259	5,231	5,565	7,360	0.15	32.26
SPAIN	77,617	96,800	99,103	93,167	86,179	1.78	-7.50
WESTERN EUR	**1,045,219**	**1,047,815**	**1,062,442**	**1,054,764**	**1,038,842**	**21.49**	**-1.51**
AUSTRIA	35,926	26,866	32,292	31,963	34,072	0.70	6.60
BELGIUM	56,489	55,578	62,155	50,247	56,098	1.16	11.64
FRANCE	137,360	146,117	153,647	153,231	141,441	2.93	-7.69
GERMANY	589,674	611,009	602,734	601,608	601,609	12.45	
LUXEMBOURG	1,696	1,846	1,550	1,245	3,323	0.07	166.91

5. OVERNIGHT STAYS OF NON-RESIDENT TOURISTS IN HOTELS AND SIMILAR ESTABLISHMENTS, BY COUNTRY OF RESIDENCE

	1999	2000	2001	2002	2003	Market share 03	% change 03-02
NETHERLANDS	132,570	135,030	130,360	126,101	124,824	2.58	-1.01
SWITZERLAND	91,504	71,369	79,704	90,369	77,475	1.60	-14.27
EAST/MED EUR	**4,295**	**2,451**	**2,777**	**3,232**	**6,984**	**0.14**	**116.09**
TURKEY	4,295	2,451	2,777	3,232	6,984	0.14	116.09
OTHER EUROPE	**256,592**	**243,570**	**252,908**	**217,190**	**205,006**	**4.24**	**-5.61**
OTHER EUROPE	256,592	243,570	252,908	217,190	205,006	4.24	-5.61
REG.NOT SPEC	**513,772**	**616,696**	**653,693**	**531,490**	**557,924**	**11.54**	**4.97**
NOT SPECIFIE	**513,772**	**616,696**	**653,693**	**531,490**	**557,924**	**11.54**	**4.97**
OTH.WORLD	513,772	616,696	653,693	531,490	557,924	11.54	4.97

Source: World Tourism Organization (WTO)

SWEDEN

6. OVERNIGHT STAYS OF NON-RESIDENT TOURISTS IN ALL TYPES OF ACCOMMODATION ESTABLISHMENTS, BY COUNTRY OF RESIDENCE

	1999	2000	2001	2002	2003	Market share 03	% change 03-02
TOTAL	**8,600,785**	**8,654,086**	**9,133,450**	**9,767,708**	**9,714,883**	**100.00**	**-0.54**
AMERICAS	**439,999**	**449,137**	**493,077**	**467,468**	**418,587**	**4.31**	**-10.46**
NORTH AMER	**426,242**	**431,538**	**479,663**	**454,271**	**398,710**	**4.10**	**-12.23**
CANADA	45,911	36,817	55,947	62,476	33,931	0.35	-45.69
USA	380,331	394,721	423,716	391,795	364,779	3.75	-6.90
OTHER AMERIC	**13,757**	**17,599**	**13,414**	**13,197**	**19,877**	**0.20**	**50.62**
OTH AMERICA	13,757	17,599	13,414	13,197	19,877	0.20	50.62
EAST AS/PACI	**231,566**	**247,026**	**219,596**	**243,763**	**209,612**	**2.16**	**-14.01**
N/EAST ASIA	**148,341**	**157,012**	**141,384**	**154,443**	**122,791**	**1.26**	**-20.49**
JAPAN	136,647	144,973	130,350	137,598	109,557	1.13	-20.38
KOREA REP.	11,694	12,039	11,034	16,845	13,234	0.14	-21.44
AUSTRALASIA	**27,905**	**27,226**	**27,517**	**33,571**	**31,635**	**0.33**	**-5.77**
AUSTRALIA	24,997	24,575	25,506	31,347	28,845	0.30	-7.98
NEW ZEALAND	2,908	2,651	2,011	2,224	2,790	0.03	25.45
OT.EAST AS/P	**55,320**	**62,788**	**50,695**	**55,749**	**55,186**	**0.57**	**-1.01**
OTHER ASIA	55,320	62,788	50,695	55,749	55,186	0.57	-1.01
EUROPE	**7,344,071**	**7,280,481**	**7,684,392**	**8,452,417**	**8,439,628**	**86.87**	**-0.15**
C/E EUROPE	**240,075**	**231,279**	**267,673**	**297,354**	**279,049**	**2.87**	**-6.16**
CZECH REP	10,005	9,793	12,950	14,238	18,159	0.19	27.54
ESTONIA	26,309	29,066	23,915	30,183	23,318	0.24	-22.74
HUNGARY	6,281	6,502	7,185	5,137	7,387	0.08	43.80
LATVIA	11,578	10,031	13,276	16,017	14,559	0.15	-9.10
LITHUANIA	10,849	10,687	12,818	9,826	12,572	0.13	27.95
POLAND	94,432	98,993	110,208	105,624	87,909	0.90	-16.77
RUSSIAN FED	77,134	64,069	84,444	114,054	113,137	1.16	-0.80
SLOVAKIA	3,487	2,138	2,877	2,275	2,008	0.02	-11.74
NORTHERN EUR	**3,813,324**	**3,735,409**	**3,997,315**	**4,625,562**	**4,527,873**	**46.61**	**-2.11**
DENMARK	839,127	832,138	909,617	999,674	1,024,094	10.54	2.44
FINLAND	502,288	463,750	407,010	448,890	417,770	4.30	-6.93
ICELAND	5,724	7,929	4,378	5,250	9,081	0.09	72.97
IRELAND	11,643	10,181	11,772	13,106	18,579	0.19	41.76
NORWAY	1,951,556	1,867,966	2,052,696	2,541,303	2,465,835	25.38	-2.97
UK	502,986	553,445	611,842	617,339	592,514	6.10	-4.02
SOUTHERN EUR	**289,433**	**295,736**	**306,727**	**304,549**	**288,827**	**2.97**	**-5.16**
GREECE	9,695	6,910	5,587	4,851	6,915	0.07	42.55
ITALY	188,790	180,123	190,237	192,511	178,995	1.84	-7.02
PORTUGAL	8,213	7,082	6,192	6,511	8,258	0.09	26.83
SPAIN	82,735	101,621	104,711	100,676	94,659	0.97	-5.98
WESTERN EUR	**2,689,460**	**2,714,374**	**2,783,128**	**2,935,356**	**3,035,188**	**31.24**	**3.40**
AUSTRIA	43,953	33,537	37,407	39,603	40,549	0.42	2.39
BELGIUM	59,651	58,708	66,806	56,074	61,283	0.63	9.29
FRANCE	199,697	210,451	212,229	215,766	200,845	2.07	-6.92
GERMANY	1,757,033	1,797,113	1,831,844	1,913,612	2,012,896	20.72	5.19
LUXEMBOURG	2,342	2,908	1,928	1,696	4,150	0.04	144.69

SWEDEN

6. OVERNIGHT STAYS OF NON-RESIDENT TOURISTS IN ALL TYPES OF ACCOMMODATION ESTABLISHMENTS, BY COUNTRY OF RESIDENCE

	1999	2000	2001	2002	2003	Market share 03	% change 03-02
NETHERLANDS	472,158	477,761	491,267	541,383	576,531	5.93	6.49
SWITZERLAND	154,626	133,896	141,647	167,222	138,934	1.43	-16.92
EAST/MED EUR	**4,418**	**2,591**	**2,869**	**3,457**	**7,476**	**0.08**	**116.26**
TURKEY	4,418	2,591	2,869	3,457	7,476	0.08	116.26
OTHER EUROPE	**307,361**	**301,092**	**326,680**	**286,139**	**301,215**	**3.10**	**5.27**
OTHER EUROPE	307,361	301,092	326,680	286,139	301,215	3.10	5.27
REG.NOT SPEC	**585,149**	**677,442**	**736,385**	**604,060**	**647,056**	**6.66**	**7.12**
NOT SPECIFIE	**585,149**	**677,442**	**736,385**	**604,060**	**647,056**	**6.66**	**7.12**
OTH.WORLD	585,149	677,442	736,385	604,060	647,056	6.66	7.12

Source: World Tourism Organization (WTO)

SWITZERLAND

3. ARRIVALS OF NON-RESIDENT TOURISTS IN HOTELS AND SIMILAR ESTABLISHMENTS, BY COUNTRY OF RESIDENCE

	1999	2000	2001	2002	2003	Market share 03	% change 03-02
TOTAL	**7,153,967**	**7,821,158**	**7,454,855**	**6,867,696**	**6,530,108**	**100.00**	**-4.92**
AFRICA	**73,139**	**77,345**	**79,164**	**74,195**	**72,786**	**1.11**	**-1.90**
NORTH AFRICA	**20,005**	**19,597**	**19,985**	**18,747**	**16,921**	**0.26**	**-9.74**
ALL NORT AFR (*)	20,005	19,597	19,985	18,747	16,921	0.26	-9.74
SOUTHERN AFR	**23,447**	**28,059**	**25,865**	**21,836**	**21,517**	**0.33**	**-1.46**
SOUTH AFRICA	23,447	28,059	25,865	21,836	21,517	0.33	-1.46
OTHER AFRICA	**29,687**	**29,689**	**33,314**	**33,612**	**34,348**	**0.53**	**2.19**
OTHER AFRICA	29,687	29,689	33,314	33,612	34,348	0.53	2.19
AMERICAS	**1,019,743**	**1,198,553**	**1,026,667**	**871,279**	**757,015**	**11.59**	**-13.11**
NORTH AMER	**898,257**	**1,064,882**	**903,191**	**758,404**	**663,819**	**10.17**	**-12.47**
CANADA	65,393	73,921	76,036	69,584	65,773	1.01	-5.48
USA	832,864	990,961	827,155	688,820	598,046	9.16	-13.18
SOUTH AMER	**84,435**	**92,124**	**84,968**	**72,455**	**59,442**	**0.91**	**-17.96**
ARGENTINA	14,874	18,649	17,948	10,321	9,214	0.14	-10.73
BRAZIL	39,466	40,816	35,593	34,447	27,961	0.43	-18.83
CHILE	3,615	4,438	3,957	3,526	3,280	0.05	-6.98
OTH SOUTH AM	26,480	28,221	27,470	24,161	18,987	0.29	-21.41
OTHER AMERIC	**37,051**	**41,547**	**38,508**	**40,420**	**33,754**	**0.52**	**-16.49**
OTH AMERICA	37,051	41,547	38,508	40,420	33,754	0.52	-16.49
EAST AS/PACI	**923,645**	**1,079,068**	**937,554**	**865,244**	**727,005**	**11.13**	**-15.98**
N/EAST ASIA	**681,457**	**820,579**	**706,513**	**632,078**	**516,919**	**7.92**	**-18.22**
CHINA	38,600	44,752	49,379	69,268	62,542	0.96	-9.71
TAIWAN(P.C.)	44,647	50,205	39,218	41,518	34,396	0.53	-17.15
HK,CHINA	35,586	43,438	38,548	35,991	28,142	0.43	-21.81
JAPAN	528,416	623,291	522,674	416,306	320,593	4.91	-22.99
KOREA REP.	34,208	58,893	56,694	68,995	71,246	1.09	3.26
S/EAST ASIA	**131,742**	**137,650**	**127,918**	**136,717**	**126,800**	**1.94**	**-7.25**
INDONESIA	10,526	12,515	9,754	11,430	10,096	0.15	-11.67
MALAYSIA	11,668	19,873	15,211	18,108	15,661	0.24	-13.51
PHILIPPINES	3,378	3,891	3,146	3,895	3,685	0.06	-5.39
SINGAPORE	18,056	22,758	21,030	20,215	18,879	0.29	-6.61
THAILAND	23,616	26,122	30,348	32,918	30,323	0.46	-7.88
OTH S/E ASIA	64,498	52,491	48,429	50,151	48,156	0.74	-3.98
OT.EAST AS/P	**110,446**	**120,839**	**103,123**	**96,449**	**83,286**	**1.28**	**-13.65**
OTHER ASIA	17,747	16,935	16,954	16,444	14,792	0.23	-10.05
ALL OCEANIA	92,699	103,904	86,169	80,005	68,494	1.05	-14.39
EUROPE	**5,029,798**	**5,343,044**	**5,277,161**	**4,906,368**	**4,821,157**	**73.83**	**-1.74**
C/E EUROPE	**143,437**	**164,941**	**179,072**	**177,217**	**183,853**	**2.82**	**3.74**
BULGARIA	6,152	7,026	7,567	6,875	8,456	0.13	23.00
BELARUS	1,611	2,379	2,831	2,896	2,832	0.04	-2.21
CZECH REP	18,211	20,750	22,103	19,983	20,222	0.31	1.20
HUNGARY	18,848	20,721	20,950	22,213	21,071	0.32	-5.14

SWITZERLAND

3. ARRIVALS OF NON-RESIDENT TOURISTS IN HOTELS AND SIMILAR ESTABLISHMENTS, BY COUNTRY OF RESIDENCE

	1999	2000	2001	2002	2003	Market share 03	% change 03-02
POLAND	29,041	27,759	30,512	27,371	26,451	0.41	-3.36
ROMANIA	7,001	7,837	7,913	8,396	9,696	0.15	15.48
RUSSIAN FED	40,811	53,385	61,266	64,145	68,759	1.05	7.19
SLOVAKIA	8,834	9,677	9,134	8,997	8,727	0.13	-3.00
UKRAINE	5,705	8,000	8,452	8,394	9,498	0.15	13.15
BALTIC COUNT	7,223	7,407	8,344	7,947	8,141	0.12	2.44
NORTHERN EUR	**778,328**	**861,669**	**859,598**	**802,023**	**800,374**	**12.26**	**-0.21**
DENMARK	41,519	41,297	41,047	40,755	39,602	0.61	-2.83
FINLAND	27,395	27,981	26,900	23,977	23,767	0.36	-0.88
ICELAND	5,304	7,858	7,253	6,275	5,363	0.08	-14.53
IRELAND	17,741	18,948	18,467	18,731	23,255	0.36	24.15
NORWAY	28,216	31,495	30,960	27,687	30,798	0.47	11.24
SWEDEN	72,516	81,535	73,474	65,285	65,154	1.00	-0.20
UK	585,637	652,555	661,497	619,313	612,435	9.38	-1.11
SOUTHERN EUR	**683,382**	**711,994**	**689,261**	**671,827**	**663,715**	**10.16**	**-1.21**
CROATIA	6,446	7,317	7,929	8,381	8,349	0.13	-0.38
GREECE	37,808	41,469	34,088	38,387	36,460	0.56	-5.02
ITALY	437,926	448,718	438,736	429,436	434,515	6.65	1.18
PORTUGAL	26,713	29,167	28,698	27,269	25,375	0.39	-6.95
SLOVENIA	8,207	8,489	7,472	8,363	7,583	0.12	-9.33
SPAIN	138,804	156,349	156,045	145,149	137,904	2.11	-4.99
SERBIA,MTNEG	27,478	20,485	16,293	14,842	13,529	0.21	-8.85
WESTERN EUR	**3,255,831**	**3,447,674**	**3,394,435**	**3,117,191**	**3,032,366**	**46.44**	**-2.72**
AUSTRIA	139,744	150,585	146,553	144,890	144,189	2.21	-0.48
BELGIUM	201,620	216,916	208,505	197,957	191,463	2.93	-3.28
FRANCE	448,477	499,301	502,797	488,817	488,468	7.48	-0.07
GERMANY	2,143,498	2,221,557	2,179,224	1,952,214	1,881,932	28.82	-3.60
LIECHTENSTEN	7,214	8,425	8,852	8,961	9,019	0.14	0.65
LUXEMBOURG	30,708	35,611	36,424	35,234	32,313	0.49	-8.29
NETHERLANDS	284,570	315,279	312,080	289,118	284,982	4.36	-1.43
EAST/MED EUR	**107,025**	**107,471**	**102,954**	**89,438**	**85,174**	**1.30**	**-4.77**
ISRAEL	79,839	76,931	78,869	66,015	60,539	0.93	-8.30
TURKEY	27,186	30,540	24,085	23,423	24,635	0.38	5.17
OTHER EUROPE	**61,795**	**49,295**	**51,841**	**48,672**	**55,675**	**0.85**	**14.39**
OTHER EUROPE	61,795	49,295	51,841	48,672	55,675	0.85	14.39
MIDDLE EAST	**43,099**	**51,236**	**62,018**	**70,180**	**67,460**	**1.03**	**-3.88**
MIDDLE EAST	**43,099**	**51,236**	**62,018**	**70,180**	**67,460**	**1.03**	**-3.88**
EGYPT	9,973	9,796	10,843	11,325	11,624	0.18	2.64
OT MIDD EAST	33,126	41,440	51,175	58,855	55,836	0.86	-5.13
SOUTH ASIA	**64,543**	**71,912**	**72,291**	**80,430**	**84,685**	**1.30**	**5.29**
SOUTH ASIA	**64,543**	**71,912**	**72,291**	**80,430**	**84,685**	**1.30**	**5.29**
INDIA	64,543	71,912	72,291	80,430	84,685	1.30	5.29

Source: World Tourism Organization (WTO)

SWITZERLAND

5. OVERNIGHT STAYS OF NON-RESIDENT TOURISTS IN HOTELS AND SIMILAR ESTABLISHMENTS, BY COUNTRY OF RESIDENCE

	1999	2000	2001	2002	2003	Market share 03	% change 03-02
TOTAL	**18,544,486**	**19,914,293**	**19,273,175**	**17,767,537**	**16,964,160**	**100.00**	**-4.52**
AFRICA	**236,253**	**238,241**	**249,682**	**242,468**	**242,269**	**1.43**	**-0.08**
NORTH AFRICA	**78,078**	**73,747**	**71,795**	**75,222**	**71,947**	**0.42**	**-4.35**
ALL NORT AFR (*)	78,078	73,747	71,795	75,222	71,947	0.42	-4.35
SOUTHERN AFR	**66,417**	**72,242**	**70,135**	**56,814**	**58,373**	**0.34**	**2.74**
SOUTH AFRICA	66,417	72,242	70,135	56,814	58,373	0.34	2.74
OTHER AFRICA	**91,758**	**92,252**	**107,752**	**110,432**	**111,949**	**0.66**	**1.37**
OTHER AFRICA	91,758	92,252	107,752	110,432	111,949	0.66	1.37
AMERICAS	**2,339,795**	**2,662,801**	**2,380,650**	**2,057,695**	**1,827,312**	**10.77**	**-11.20**
NORTH AMER	**2,028,390**	**2,345,872**	**2,064,419**	**1,752,300**	**1,561,515**	**9.20**	**-10.89**
CANADA	156,274	173,590	187,114	165,356	163,533	0.96	-1.10
USA	1,872,116	2,172,282	1,877,305	1,586,944	1,397,982	8.24	-11.91
SOUTH AMER	**213,640**	**226,398**	**224,125**	**209,061**	**179,647**	**1.06**	**-14.07**
ARGENTINA	35,575	42,949	43,439	31,637	27,022	0.16	-14.59
BRAZIL	100,395	108,664	106,551	105,524	93,833	0.55	-11.08
CHILE	8,832	11,745	11,653	10,778	9,197	0.05	-14.67
OTH SOUTH AM	68,838	63,040	62,482	61,122	49,595	0.29	-18.86
OTHER AMERIC	**97,765**	**90,531**	**92,106**	**96,334**	**86,150**	**0.51**	**-10.57**
OTH AMERICA	97,765	90,531	92,106	96,334	86,150	0.51	-10.57
EAST AS/PACI	**1,652,729**	**1,862,595**	**1,661,949**	**1,552,555**	**1,364,776**	**8.05**	**-12.09**
N/EAST ASIA	**1,115,122**	**1,293,229**	**1,133,482**	**1,030,819**	**870,174**	**5.13**	**-15.58**
CHINA	75,131	83,239	95,257	119,261	106,037	0.63	-11.09
TAIWAN(P.C.)	69,276	74,335	60,173	63,336	51,526	0.30	-18.65
HK,CHINA	67,001	76,875	67,570	59,217	49,069	0.29	-17.14
JAPAN	850,060	970,416	829,089	690,452	558,222	3.29	-19.15
KOREA REP.	53,654	88,364	81,393	98,553	105,320	0.62	6.87
S/EAST ASIA	**283,268**	**300,229**	**284,879**	**288,889**	**280,615**	**1.65**	**-2.86**
INDONESIA	22,979	26,157	22,705	25,079	22,046	0.13	-12.09
MALAYSIA	29,712	48,362	40,987	41,876	39,619	0.23	-5.39
PHILIPPINES	9,801	11,606	10,623	12,525	12,823	0.08	2.38
SINGAPORE	41,285	51,696	49,347	45,634	43,716	0.26	-4.20
THAILAND	39,746	50,565	56,626	57,103	57,086	0.34	-0.03
OTH S/E ASIA	139,745	111,843	104,591	106,672	105,325	0.62	-1.26
OT.EAST AS/P	**254,339**	**269,137**	**243,588**	**232,847**	**213,987**	**1.26**	**-8.10**
OTHER ASIA	54,039	52,204	52,636	54,674	51,786	0.31	-5.28
ALL OCEANIA	200,300	216,933	190,952	178,173	162,201	0.96	-8.96
EUROPE	**13,969,293**	**14,746,521**	**14,543,403**	**13,390,553**	**13,048,429**	**76.92**	**-2.55**
C/E EUROPE	**406,684**	**501,977**	**538,644**	**546,967**	**557,861**	**3.29**	**1.99**
BULGARIA	16,004	23,531	23,368	19,508	21,600	0.13	10.72
BELARUS	4,607	7,921	9,381	7,292	7,860	0.05	7.79
CZECH REP	43,134	50,439	56,098	53,085	53,446	0.32	0.68
HUNGARY	57,622	63,378	61,480	62,994	59,062	0.35	-6.24

SWITZERLAND

5. OVERNIGHT STAYS OF NON-RESIDENT TOURISTS IN HOTELS AND SIMILAR ESTABLISHMENTS, BY COUNTRY OF RESIDENCE

	1999	2000	2001	2002	2003	Market share 03	% change 03-02
POLAND	68,152	72,739	76,008	70,046	66,098	0.39	-5.64
ROMANIA	22,468	25,465	26,071	28,292	28,113	0.17	-0.63
RUSSIAN FED	128,253	181,315	209,155	231,816	239,511	1.41	3.32
SLOVAKIA	22,030	23,558	24,513	23,025	23,352	0.14	1.42
UKRAINE	18,802	26,585	30,145	28,584	34,577	0.20	20.97
BALTIC COUNT	25,612	27,046	22,425	22,325	24,242	0.14	8.59
NORTHERN EUR	**2,209,130**	**2,415,845**	**2,456,350**	**2,292,835**	**2,256,617**	**13.30**	**-1.58**
DENMARK	95,333	97,872	94,712	91,470	89,542	0.53	-2.11
FINLAND	66,338	65,233	63,860	57,474	58,321	0.34	1.47
ICELAND	11,954	19,215	19,611	17,397	12,988	0.08	-25.34
IRELAND	51,878	50,875	49,040	48,284	59,455	0.35	23.14
NORWAY	64,058	69,471	70,422	61,936	72,473	0.43	17.01
SWEDEN	166,226	183,885	175,854	149,816	150,762	0.89	0.63
UK	1,753,343	1,929,294	1,982,851	1,866,458	1,813,076	10.69	-2.86
SOUTHERN EUR	**1,479,046**	**1,530,847**	**1,492,184**	**1,477,964**	**1,475,697**	**8.70**	**-0.15**
CROATIA	18,775	21,122	20,722	23,963	21,748	0.13	-9.24
GREECE	96,997	106,975	86,755	95,598	93,228	0.55	-2.48
ITALY	940,929	956,744	947,915	932,663	958,484	5.65	2.77
PORTUGAL	64,437	72,092	73,679	69,489	64,036	0.38	-7.85
SLOVENIA	16,115	17,830	16,506	18,757	16,632	0.10	-11.33
SPAIN	285,397	313,613	312,934	304,108	292,185	1.72	-3.92
SERBIA,MTNEG	56,396	42,471	33,673	33,386	29,384	0.17	-11.99
WESTERN EUR	**9,419,488**	**9,882,340**	**9,649,300**	**8,705,200**	**8,393,686**	**49.48**	**-3.58**
AUSTRIA	314,825	346,297	331,698	326,794	326,341	1.92	-0.14
BELGIUM	755,720	795,962	748,942	714,817	699,452	4.12	-2.15
FRANCE	1,104,687	1,235,539	1,244,150	1,166,228	1,149,441	6.78	-1.44
GERMANY	6,283,095	6,443,857	6,277,677	5,543,920	5,301,798	31.25	-4.37
LIECHTENSTEN	16,109	18,766	19,474	20,182	20,011	0.12	-0.85
LUXEMBOURG	107,725	119,223	123,658	115,638	109,404	0.64	-5.39
NETHERLANDS	837,327	922,696	903,701	817,621	787,239	4.64	-3.72
EAST/MED EUR	**277,950**	**287,751**	**271,753**	**240,145**	**228,071**	**1.34**	**-5.03**
ISRAEL	204,627	198,920	202,925	175,833	163,770	0.97	-6.86
TURKEY	73,323	88,831	68,828	64,312	64,301	0.38	-0.02
OTHER EUROPE	**176,995**	**127,761**	**135,172**	**127,442**	**136,497**	**0.80**	**7.11**
OTHER EUROPE	176,995	127,761	135,172	127,442	136,497	0.80	7.11
MIDDLE EAST	**180,530**	**224,506**	**253,868**	**324,114**	**284,505**	**1.68**	**-12.22**
MIDDLE EAST	**180,530**	**224,506**	**253,868**	**324,114**	**284,505**	**1.68**	**-12.22**
EGYPT	33,070	35,329	37,299	35,348	37,565	0.22	6.27
OT MIDD EAST	147,460	189,177	216,569	288,766	246,940	1.46	-14.48
SOUTH ASIA	**165,886**	**179,629**	**183,623**	**200,152**	**196,869**	**1.16**	**-1.64**
SOUTH ASIA	**165,886**	**179,629**	**183,623**	**200,152**	**196,869**	**1.16**	**-1.64**
INDIA	165,886	179,629	183,623	200,152	196,869	1.16	-1.64

Source: World Tourism Organization (WTO)

SWITZERLAND

6. OVERNIGHT STAYS OF NON-RESIDENT TOURISTS IN ALL TYPES OF ACCOMMODATION ESTABLISHMENTS, BY COUNTRY OF RESIDENCE

	1999	2000	2001	2002	2003	Market share 03	% change 03-02
TOTAL	**31,863,421**	**32,844,102**	**32,110,820**	**29,641,451**	**28,568,994**	**100.00**	**-3.62**
AFRICA	**271,081**	**277,755**	**289,907**	**284,956**	**290,245**	**1.02**	**1.86**
NORTH AFRICA	**82,251**	**79,399**	**77,105**	**80,289**	**80,015**	**0.28**	**-0.34**
ALL NORT AFR	82,251	79,399	77,105	80,289	80,015	0.28	-0.34
SOUTHERN AFR	**84,513**	**93,605**	**92,137**	**74,412**	**77,890**	**0.27**	**4.67**
SOUTH AFRICA	84,513	93,605	92,137	74,412	77,890	0.27	4.67
OTHER AFRICA	**104,317**	**104,751**	**120,665**	**130,255**	**132,340**	**0.46**	**1.60**
OTHER AFRICA	104,317	104,751	120,665	130,255	132,340	0.46	1.60
AMERICAS	**2,637,028**	**2,969,695**	**2,707,924**	**2,347,189**	**2,126,040**	**7.44**	**-9.42**
NORTH AMER	**2,290,140**	**2,620,100**	**2,358,609**	**2,008,075**	**1,820,824**	**6.37**	**-9.32**
CANADA	192,940	209,773	227,541	202,066	197,173	0.69	-2.42
USA	2,097,200	2,410,327	2,131,068	1,806,009	1,623,651	5.68	-10.10
SOUTH AMER	**238,360**	**247,743**	**246,927**	**231,864**	**204,909**	**0.72**	**-11.63**
ARGENTINA	39,902	47,266	48,301	35,326	29,090	0.10	-17.65
BRAZIL	110,787	117,303	115,037	112,463	107,524	0.38	-4.39
CHILE	10,066	13,135	12,898	12,168	10,843	0.04	-10.89
OTH SOUTH AM	77,605	70,039	70,691	71,907	57,452	0.20	-20.10
OTHER AMERIC	**108,528**	**101,852**	**102,388**	**107,250**	**100,307**	**0.35**	**-6.47**
OTH AMERICA	108,528	101,852	102,388	107,250	100,307	0.35	-6.47
EAST AS/PACI	**1,850,307**	**2,060,917**	**1,859,331**	**1,737,986**	**1,564,112**	**5.47**	**-10.00**
N/EAST ASIA	**1,207,187**	**1,385,753**	**1,230,319**	**1,121,642**	**961,625**	**3.37**	**-14.27**
CHINA	81,502	89,190	105,007	129,430	117,725	0.41	-9.04
TAIWAN(P.C.)	73,250	80,279	64,589	68,677	55,899	0.20	-18.61
HK,CHINA	76,585	87,433	75,583	65,383	55,063	0.19	-15.78
JAPAN	899,975	1,014,683	874,610	726,348	590,005	2.07	-18.77
KOREA REP.	75,875	114,168	110,530	131,804	142,933	0.50	8.44
S/EAST ASIA	**311,818**	**326,408**	**310,582**	**316,108**	**310,449**	**1.09**	**-1.79**
INDONESIA	23,781	27,776	24,208	26,986	23,528	0.08	-12.81
MALAYSIA	31,781	49,967	43,111	43,397	42,054	0.15	-3.09
PHILIPPINES	10,657	12,564	11,680	13,388	13,833	0.05	3.32
SINGAPORE	44,672	55,548	53,480	49,266	47,342	0.17	-3.91
THAILAND	42,234	53,775	59,496	60,221	60,624	0.21	0.67
OTH S/E ASIA	158,693	126,778	118,607	122,850	123,068	0.43	0.18
OT.EAST AS/P	**331,302**	**348,756**	**318,430**	**300,236**	**292,038**	**1.02**	**-2.73**
OTHER ASIA	58,799	57,493	59,219	59,733	56,202	0.20	-5.91
ALL OCEANIA	272,503	291,263	259,211	240,503	235,836	0.83	-1.94
EUROPE	**26,727,607**	**27,090,551**	**26,787,388**	**24,712,235**	**24,070,937**	**84.26**	**-2.60**
C/E EUROPE	**599,575**	**682,446**	**748,114**	**724,845**	**763,861**	**2.67**	**5.38**
BULGARIA	18,930	26,410	26,352	21,480	28,261	0.10	31.57
BELARUS	6,285	9,689	14,380	9,776	10,105	0.04	3.37
CZECH REP	109,293	115,142	145,133	116,305	126,810	0.44	9.03
HUNGARY	78,287	82,536	79,733	81,231	83,091	0.29	2.29

SWITZERLAND

6. OVERNIGHT STAYS OF NON-RESIDENT TOURISTS IN ALL TYPES OF ACCOMMODATION ESTABLISHMENTS, BY COUNTRY OF RESIDENCE

	1999	2000	2001	2002	2003	Market share 03	% change 03-02
POLAND	122,972	117,293	123,322	109,426	106,573	0.37	-2.61
ROMANIA	27,338	32,072	31,938	33,521	31,933	0.11	-4.74
RUSSIAN FED	145,840	199,175	227,850	258,568	268,210	0.94	3.73
SLOVAKIA	29,517	30,633	30,566	30,152	31,029	0.11	2.91
UKRAINE	24,147	33,522	36,446	33,444	42,705	0.15	27.69
BALTIC COUNT	36,966	35,974	32,394	30,942	35,144	0.12	13.58
NORTHERN EUR	**2,928,461**	**3,199,121**	**3,227,730**	**3,037,670**	**3,032,404**	**10.61**	**-0.17**
DENMARK	182,424	200,718	166,347	154,345	157,640	0.55	2.13
FINLAND	95,582	92,991	84,625	78,382	80,682	0.28	2.93
ICELAND	15,174	20,504	20,687	19,352	15,977	0.06	-17.44
IRELAND	63,593	63,370	61,488	59,794	74,631	0.26	24.81
NORWAY	81,992	90,295	87,695	83,078	91,846	0.32	10.55
SWEDEN	214,141	238,194	230,865	199,612	198,332	0.69	-0.64
UK	2,275,555	2,493,049	2,576,023	2,443,107	2,413,296	8.45	-1.22
SOUTHERN EUR	**2,064,038**	**2,104,588**	**2,061,011**	**2,042,186**	**2,027,661**	**7.10**	**-0.71**
CROATIA	22,615	23,795	23,928	26,589	26,769	0.09	0.68
GREECE	104,563	114,099	92,330	99,982	99,614	0.35	-0.37
ITALY	1,380,344	1,392,984	1,377,754	1,361,641	1,380,328	4.83	1.37
PORTUGAL	79,678	87,244	86,353	81,800	77,267	0.27	-5.54
SLOVENIA	25,591	25,520	24,739	28,868	25,769	0.09	-10.74
SPAIN	389,945	414,042	418,719	405,664	384,259	1.35	-5.28
SERBIA,MTNEG	61,302	46,904	37,188	37,642	33,655	0.12	-10.59
WESTERN EUR	**20,552,867**	**20,522,342**	**20,175,329**	**18,429,734**	**17,783,592**	**62.25**	**-3.51**
AUSTRIA	425,609	449,683	436,680	419,546	430,729	1.51	2.67
BELGIUM	1,620,163	1,603,547	1,558,808	1,470,718	1,443,809	5.05	-1.83
FRANCE	1,755,328	1,888,372	1,865,249	1,774,477	1,793,396	6.28	1.07
GERMANY	13,770,004	13,521,299	13,303,539	12,031,555	11,467,317	40.14	-4.69
LIECHTENSTEN	36,195	40,692	37,731	38,001	40,144	0.14	5.64
LUXEMBOURG	167,926	181,772	182,639	170,900	164,802	0.58	-3.57
NETHERLANDS	2,777,642	2,836,977	2,790,683	2,524,537	2,443,395	8.55	-3.21
EAST/MED EUR	**331,397**	**347,387**	**330,378**	**295,097**	**279,542**	**0.98**	**-5.27**
ISRAEL	251,840	253,775	255,543	226,122	210,470	0.74	-6.92
TURKEY	79,557	93,612	74,835	68,975	69,072	0.24	0.14
OTHER EUROPE	**251,269**	**234,667**	**244,826**	**182,703**	**183,877**	**0.64**	**0.64**
OTHER EUROPE	251,269	234,667	244,826	182,703	183,877	0.64	0.64
MIDDLE EAST	**199,519**	**251,956**	**268,441**	**342,362**	**299,054**	**1.05**	**-12.65**
MIDDLE EAST	**199,519**	**251,956**	**268,441**	**342,362**	**299,054**	**1.05**	**-12.65**
EGYPT	34,642	37,361	39,723	37,628	40,106	0.14	6.59
OT MIDD EAST	164,877	214,595	228,718	304,734	258,948	0.91	-15.02
SOUTH ASIA	**177,879**	**193,228**	**197,829**	**216,723**	**218,606**	**0.77**	**0.87**
SOUTH ASIA	**177,879**	**193,228**	**197,829**	**216,723**	**218,606**	**0.77**	**0.87**
INDIA	177,879	193,228	197,829	216,723	218,606	0.77	0.87

Source: World Tourism Organization (WTO)

SYRIAN ARAB REPUBLIC

2. ARRIVALS OF NON-RESIDENT VISITORS AT NATIONAL BORDERS, BY NATIONALITY

	1999	2000	2001	2002	2003	Market share 03	% change 03-02
TOTAL (*)	**2,681,534**	**3,014,758**	**3,389,091**	**4,272,911**	**4,388,119**	**100.00**	**2.70**
AFRICA	**64,920**	**66,131**	**71,383**	**71,089**	**73,487**	**1.67**	**3.37**
NORTH AFRICA	**64,920**	**66,131**	**71,383**	**71,089**	**73,487**	**1.67**	**3.37**
ALGERIA	18,582	18,340	19,712	21,170	25,382	0.58	19.90
MOROCCO	6,393	7,874	9,337	9,182	9,754	0.22	6.23
SUDAN	23,518	21,778	21,724	19,280	17,303	0.39	-10.25
TUNISIA	16,427	18,139	20,610	21,457	21,048	0.48	-1.91
AMERICAS	**30,591**	**38,209**	**43,415**	**44,588**	**43,901**	**1.00**	**-1.54**
NORTH AMER	**26,791**	**33,217**	**38,019**	**39,895**	**38,887**	**0.89**	**-2.53**
CANADA	6,663	8,123	9,984	11,417	9,864	0.22	-13.60
USA	20,128	25,094	28,035	28,478	29,023	0.66	1.91
SOUTH AMER	**3,800**	**4,992**	**5,396**	**4,693**	**5,014**	**0.11**	**6.84**
ARGENTINA	1,144	1,386	1,216	564	778	0.02	37.94
BRAZIL	1,264	1,695	1,629	1,665	1,753	0.04	5.29
VENEZUELA	1,392	1,911	2,551	2,464	2,483	0.06	0.77
EAST AS/PACI	**22,287**	**24,088**	**23,178**	**27,767**	**25,897**	**0.59**	**-6.73**
N/EAST ASIA	**7,280**	**8,166**	**5,984**	**6,491**	**4,787**	**0.11**	**-26.25**
JAPAN	7,280	8,166	5,984	6,491	4,787	0.11	-26.25
S/EAST ASIA	**5,445**	**6,949**	**8,614**	**12,239**	**13,513**	**0.31**	**10.41**
INDONESIA	5,445	6,949	8,614	12,239	13,513	0.31	10.41
AUSTRALASIA	**9,562**	**8,973**	**8,580**	**9,037**	**7,597**	**0.17**	**-15.93**
AUSTRALIA	9,562	8,973	8,580	9,037	7,597	0.17	-15.93
EUROPE	**369,479**	**397,871**	**471,541**	**645,942**	**651,800**	**14.85**	**0.91**
C/E EUROPE	**31,984**	**34,804**	**35,636**	**36,539**	**42,157**	**0.96**	**15.38**
BULGARIA	4,049	5,035	4,131	3,939	4,232	0.10	7.44
CZECH RP/SVK	2,311	2,800	2,971	2,605	1,951	0.04	-25.11
HUNGARY	2,429	3,047	2,970	2,825	2,526	0.06	-10.58
POLAND	2,053	2,000	3,392	1,880	1,399	0.03	-25.59
ROMANIA	2,998	3,051	3,239	3,684	3,353	0.08	-8.98
USSR(former)	18,144	18,871	18,933	21,606	28,696	0.65	32.81
NORTHERN EUR	**26,909**	**38,863**	**43,924**	**38,104**	**37,802**	**0.86**	**-0.79**
DENMARK	2,878	4,402	4,778	5,041	5,616	0.13	11.41
NORWAY	1,871	3,219	2,957	2,285	2,328	0.05	1.88
SWEDEN	7,392	11,141	12,405	11,567	12,950	0.30	11.96
UK	14,768	20,101	23,784	19,211	16,908	0.39	-11.99
SOUTHERN EUR	**30,976**	**34,734**	**25,665**	**24,091**	**24,300**	**0.55**	**0.87**
GREECE	3,068	2,728	3,892	2,773	3,207	0.07	15.65
ITALY	18,695	20,441	12,135	9,607	8,859	0.20	-7.79
SPAIN	7,659	9,168	6,794	6,263	6,890	0.16	10.01
YUGOSLAV SFR	1,554	2,397	2,844	5,448	5,344	0.12	-1.91
WESTERN EUR	**88,098**	**100,539**	**80,741**	**73,806**	**70,014**	**1.60**	**-5.14**
AUSTRIA	4,807	5,166	4,046	3,809	3,730	0.09	-2.07
BELGIUM	5,502	5,930	3,874	3,591	3,376	0.08	-5.99

SYRIAN ARAB REPUBLIC

2. ARRIVALS OF NON-RESIDENT VISITORS AT NATIONAL BORDERS, BY NATIONALITY

	1999	2000	2001	2002	2003	Market share 03	% change 03-02
FRANCE	35,168	36,059	31,084	28,586	26,910	0.61	-5.86
GERMANY	31,272	38,297	29,843	26,425	25,036	0.57	-5.26
NETHERLANDS	7,741	10,015	8,347	7,426	7,862	0.18	5.87
SWITZERLAND	3,608	5,072	3,547	3,969	3,100	0.07	-21.89
EAST/MED EUR	**191,512**	**188,931**	**285,575**	**473,402**	**477,527**	**10.88**	**0.87**
CYPRUS	4,742	6,130	4,116	5,754	6,627	0.15	15.17
TURKEY	186,770	182,801	281,459	467,648	470,900	10.73	0.70
MIDDLE EAST	**1,928,846**	**2,196,287**	**2,425,119**	**3,093,856**	**3,325,490**	**75.78**	**7.49**
MIDDLE EAST	**1,928,846**	**2,196,287**	**2,425,119**	**3,093,856**	**3,325,490**	**75.78**	**7.49**
BAHRAIN	27,522	32,263	43,922	76,402	60,648	1.38	-20.62
PALESTINE	36,338	37,082	43,321	50,166	52,087	1.19	3.83
IRAQ	58,136	85,439	187,954	278,934	253,120	5.77	-9.25
JORDAN	513,783	538,493	609,225	692,211	752,935	17.16	8.77
KUWAIT	65,868	69,075	80,344	99,906	72,693	1.66	-27.24
LEBANON	868,051	995,235	1,025,101	1,410,511	1,654,001	37.69	17.26
LIBYA	13,994	24,358	21,260	19,101	18,230	0.42	-4.56
QATAR	5,904	5,160	5,910	8,362	9,883	0.23	18.19
SAUDI ARABIA	273,161	283,653	330,639	371,601	361,758	8.24	-2.65
UNTD ARAB EM	11,819	14,698	14,603	18,984	24,274	0.55	27.87
EGYPT	25,040	32,320	29,075	31,010	31,423	0.72	1.33
YEMEN	18,478	19,656	21,389	23,387	22,046	0.50	-5.73
OT MIDD EAST	10,752	58,855	12,376	13,281	12,392	0.28	-6.69
SOUTH ASIA	**220,741**	**242,529**	**237,188**	**340,457**	**228,357**	**5.20**	**-32.93**
SOUTH ASIA	**220,741**	**242,529**	**237,188**	**340,457**	**228,357**	**5.20**	**-32.93**
AFGHANISTAN	507	543	647	636	649	0.01	2.04
INDIA	11,772	10,685	10,688	16,689	9,560	0.22	-42.72
IRAN	199,307	221,380	216,542	310,839	213,931	4.88	-31.18
PAKISTAN	9,155	9,921	9,311	12,293	4,217	0.10	-65.70
REG.NOT SPEC	**44,670**	**49,643**	**117,267**	**49,212**	**39,187**	**0.89**	**-20.37**
NOT SPECIFIE	**44,670**	**49,643**	**117,267**	**49,212**	**39,187**	**0.89**	**-20.37**
OTH.WORLD	44,670	49,643	117,267	49,212	39,187	0.89	-20.37

Source: World Tourism Organization (WTO)

SYRIAN ARAB REPUBLIC

3. ARRIVALS OF NON-RESIDENT TOURISTS IN HOTELS AND SIMILAR ESTABLISHMENTS, BY NATIONALITY

	1999	2000	2001	2002	2003	Market share 03	% change 03-02
TOTAL	**916,208**	**909,321**	**878,421**	**847,308**			
AFRICA	**52,334**	**48,011**	**52,605**	**57,652**			
NORTH AFRICA	**52,334**	**48,011**	**52,605**	**57,652**			
ALGERIA	16,896	15,237	18,042	16,981			
MOROCCO	3,774	4,208	5,518	15,177			
SUDAN	17,132	13,864	13,345	11,585			
TUNISIA	14,532	14,702	15,700	13,909			
AMERICAS	**20,359**	**24,821**	**18,813**	**12,405**			
NORTH AMER	**18,298**	**21,826**	**17,398**	**11,485**			
CANADA	4,767	5,211	5,483	3,691			
USA	13,531	16,615	11,915	7,794			
SOUTH AMER	**2,061**	**2,995**	**1,415**	**920**			
ARGENTINA	1,160	1,634	840	273			
BRAZIL	901	1,361	575	647			
EAST AS/PACI	**23,124**	**26,056**	**20,357**	**12,999**			
N/EAST ASIA	**16,551**	**18,767**	**14,884**	**9,244**			
JAPAN	16,551	18,767	14,884	9,244			
AUSTRALASIA	**6,573**	**7,289**	**5,473**	**3,755**			
AUSTRALIA	6,573	7,289	5,473	3,755			
EUROPE	**368,036**	**377,541**	**260,563**	**181,458**			
C/E EUROPE	**25,291**	**24,156**	**23,948**	**19,005**			
BULGARIA	1,245	1,297	1,131	1,312			
CZECH RP/SVK	1,688	2,672	2,217	1,850			
HUNGARY	1,557	1,736	2,194	1,828			
POLAND	1,972	2,545	4,203	2,199			
USSR(former)	18,829	15,906	14,203	11,816			
NORTHERN EUR	**26,194**	**31,290**	**26,458**	**29,856**			
DENMARK	3,121	3,400	3,104	3,078			
NORWAY	1,726	2,999	2,686	3,564			
SWEDEN	2,929	3,702	3,287	5,074			
UK	18,418	21,189	17,381	18,140			
SOUTHERN EUR	**78,513**	**84,891**	**50,572**	**29,823**			
GREECE	4,690	3,908	3,028	2,085			
ITALY	55,297	61,293	33,838	19,457			
SPAIN	17,948	19,086	13,093	7,748			
YUGOSLAV SFR	578	604	613	533			
WESTERN EUR	**213,529**	**215,680**	**140,689**	**83,570**			
AUSTRIA	9,084	10,145	8,194	4,990			
BELGIUM	13,152	13,084	6,829	4,635			
FRANCE	94,539	89,920	57,813	37,862			
GERMANY	70,910	72,751	46,831	29,589			
NETHERLANDS	15,486	16,822	12,497				

SYRIAN ARAB REPUBLIC

3. ARRIVALS OF NON-RESIDENT TOURISTS IN HOTELS AND SIMILAR ESTABLISHMENTS, BY NATIONALITY

	1999	2000	2001	2002	2003	Market share 03	% change 03-02
SWITZERLAND	10,358	12,958	8,525	6,494			
EAST/MED EUR	**24,509**	**21,524**	**18,896**	**19,204**			
CYPRUS	8,620	11,972	7,298	6,904			
TURKEY	15,889	9,552	11,598	12,300			
MIDDLE EAST	**360,379**	**341,205**	**399,910**	**425,181**			
MIDDLE EAST	**360,379**	**341,205**	**399,910**	**425,181**			
BAHRAIN	2,020	2,831	2,801	3,063			
PALESTINE	8,426	7,880	9,489	9,108			
IRAQ	18,506	20,711	38,726	44,968			
JORDAN	91,415	84,117	104,675	118,606			
KUWAIT	8,612	8,316	10,203	9,984			
LEBANON	137,370	119,960	125,519	124,785			
LIBYA	6,915	12,512	13,040	12,672			
QATAR	1,407	1,526	1,738	1,960			
SAUDI ARABIA	51,848	48,825	56,487	55,637			
UNTD ARAB EM	2,991	3,151	3,656	4,309			
EGYPT	18,174	17,916	18,248	16,889			
YEMEN	10,167	11,426	12,134	12,958			
OT MIDD EAST	2,528	2,034	3,194	10,242			
SOUTH ASIA	**68,781**	**65,883**	**102,414**	**127,326**			
SOUTH ASIA	**68,781**	**65,883**	**102,414**	**127,326**			
INDIA	2,491	2,971	3,277	3,570			
IRAN	64,897	61,515	97,255	121,777			
PAKISTAN	1,393	1,397	1,882	1,979			
REG.NOT SPEC	**23,195**	**25,804**	**23,759**	**30,287**			
NOT SPECIFIE	**23,195**	**25,804**	**23,759**	**30,287**			
OTH.WORLD	23,195	25,804	23,759	30,287			

Source: World Tourism Organization (WTO)

SYRIAN ARAB REPUBLIC

5. OVERNIGHT STAYS OF NON-RESIDENT TOURISTS IN HOTELS AND SIMILAR ESTABLISHMENTS, BY NATIONALITY

	1999	2000	2001	2002	2003	Market share 03	% change 03-02
TOTAL	**1,845,146**	**1,836,879**	**1,888,384**	**1,940,939**			
AFRICA	**161,399**	**156,543**	**168,666**	**177,741**			
NORTH AFRICA	**161,399**	**156,543**	**168,666**	**177,741**			
ALGERIA	48,097	41,997	47,894	49,672			
MOROCCO	20,512	25,377	38,567	55,690			
SUDAN	47,645	40,476	36,088	30,853			
TUNISIA	45,145	48,693	46,117	41,526			
AMERICAS	**39,349**	**45,786**	**35,676**	**25,305**			
NORTH AMER	**35,218**	**40,647**	**33,044**	**23,355**			
CANADA	10,076	10,416	10,469	7,648			
USA	25,142	30,231	22,575	15,707			
SOUTH AMER	**4,131**	**5,139**	**2,632**	**1,950**			
ARGENTINA	2,310	2,604	1,542	645			
BRAZIL	1,821	2,535	1,090	1,305			
EAST AS/PACI	**40,660**	**46,542**	**42,359**	**34,525**			
N/EAST ASIA	**28,819**	**33,640**	**31,868**	**27,235**			
JAPAN	28,819	33,640	31,868	27,235			
AUSTRALASIA	**11,841**	**12,902**	**10,491**	**7,290**			
AUSTRALIA	11,841	12,902	10,491	7,290			
EUROPE	**686,866**	**689,428**	**514,253**	**381,728**			
C/E EUROPE	**127,832**	**117,005**	**109,750**	**91,156**			
BULGARIA	4,528	4,061	2,978	3,845			
CZECH RP/SVK	3,157	5,087	3,713	3,320			
HUNGARY	2,825	3,714	3,166	2,775			
POLAND	3,669	4,031	6,869	3,587			
USSR(former)	113,653	100,112	93,024	77,629			
NORTHERN EUR	**50,829**	**56,909**	**51,654**	**54,394**			
DENMARK	6,338	7,159	6,649	6,349			
NORWAY	4,665	5,945	4,594	4,513			
SWEDEN	6,814	6,975	6,727	9,526			
UK	33,012	36,830	33,684	34,006			
SOUTHERN EUR	**127,285**	**132,415**	**85,765**	**53,082**			
GREECE	8,733	8,194	5,456	4,120			
ITALY	86,481	91,730	56,123	34,138			
SPAIN	30,513	31,118	22,283	13,614			
YUGOSLAV SFR	1,558	1,373	1,903	1,210			
WESTERN EUR	**335,513**	**341,607**	**231,277**	**147,032**			
AUSTRIA	15,566	16,304	12,959	9,782			
BELGIUM	21,323	20,341	11,361	7,706			
FRANCE	142,073	140,348	91,533	64,383			
GERMANY	113,570	115,935	79,302	53,299			
NETHERLANDS	26,031	28,996	22,278				

5. OVERNIGHT STAYS OF NON-RESIDENT TOURISTS IN HOTELS AND SIMILAR ESTABLISHMENTS, BY NATIONALITY

	1999	2000	2001	2002	2003	Market share 03	% change 03-02
SWITZERLAND	16,950	19,683	13,844	11,862			
EAST/MED EUR	**45,407**	**41,492**	**35,807**	**36,064**			
CYPRUS	30,341	23,547	14,360	13,643			
TURKEY	15,066	17,945	21,447	22,421			
MIDDLE EAST	**643,117**	**624,740**	**719,538**	**744,326**			
MIDDLE EAST	**643,117**	**624,740**	**719,538**	**744,326**			
BAHRAIN	4,088	6,168	6,240	6,374			
PALESTINE	15,481	15,185	18,229	17,437			
IRAQ	36,506	36,904	66,156	83,384			
JORDAN	153,112	145,448	177,230	189,110			
KUWAIT	17,183	16,761	21,364	21,989			
LEBANON	221,425	193,784	200,123	199,126			
LIBYA	16,211	30,107	33,653	30,815			
QATAR	3,639	4,541	4,921	5,295			
SAUDI ARABIA	90,588	90,599	103,038	101,645			
UNTD ARAB EM	7,077	8,294	9,205	11,009			
EGYPT	48,954	44,367	43,365	39,011			
YEMEN	22,843	27,549	29,300	31,876			
OT MIDD EAST	6,010	5,033	6,714	7,255			
SOUTH ASIA	**217,282**	**210,078**	**348,199**	**491,250**			
SOUTH ASIA	**217,282**	**210,078**	**348,199**	**491,250**			
INDIA	6,570	7,033	6,710	7,867			
IRAN	207,743	199,592	337,553	478,843			
PAKISTAN	2,969	3,453	3,936	4,540			
REG.NOT SPEC	**56,473**	**63,762**	**59,693**	**86,064**			
NOT SPECIFIE	**56,473**	**63,762**	**59,693**	**86,064**			
OTH.WORLD	56,473	63,762	59,693	86,064			

Source: World Tourism Organization (WTO)

TAIWAN (PROVINCE OF CHINA)

2. ARRIVALS OF NON-RESIDENT VISITORS AT NATIONAL BORDERS, BY COUNTRY OF RESIDENCE

	1999	2000	2001	2002	2003	Market share 03	% change 03-02
TOTAL	2,411,248	2,624,037	2,831,035	2,977,692	2,248,117	100.00	-24.50
AFRICA	7,716	8,667	8,663	9,120	7,375	0.33	-19.13
EAST AFRICA	399	376	295	353	152	0.01	-56.94
MADAGASCAR	28	28	14	17	9		-47.06
MAURITIUS	371	348	281	336	143	0.01	-57.44
SOUTHERN AFR	3,852	4,849	5,151	5,724	5,182	0.23	-9.47
SOUTH AFRICA	3,852	4,849	5,151	5,724	5,182	0.23	-9.47
WEST AFRICA	827	930	1,020	835	585	0.03	-29.94
NIGERIA	827	930	1,020	835	585	0.03	-29.94
OTHER AFRICA	2,638	2,512	2,197	2,208	1,456	0.06	-34.06
OTHER AFRICA	2,638	2,512	2,197	2,208	1,456	0.06	-34.06
AMERICAS	357,455	405,749	388,507	406,227	311,594	13.86	-23.30
NORTH AMER	348,257	396,427	380,329	398,421	305,609	13.59	-23.29
CANADA	34,568	38,016	40,176	42,815	33,873	1.51	-20.89
MEXICO	1,694	1,876	1,605	2,195	1,213	0.05	-44.74
USA	311,995	356,535	338,548	353,411	270,523	12.03	-23.45
SOUTH AMER	3,793	3,819	3,043	2,758	2,261	0.10	-18.02
ARGENTINA	1,326	1,052	888	552	438	0.02	-20.65
BRAZIL	2,467	2,767	2,155	2,206	1,823	0.08	-17.36
OTHER AMERIC	5,405	5,503	5,135	5,048	3,724	0.17	-26.23
OTH AMERICA	5,405	5,503	5,135	5,048	3,724	0.17	-26.23
EAST AS/PACI	1,560,358	1,703,884	1,718,334	1,761,660	1,348,597	59.99	-23.45
N/EAST ASIA	961,533	1,071,072	1,133,574	1,142,128	801,381	35.65	-29.83
HK,CHINA	63,323	73,708	80,752	76,690	56,076	2.49	-26.88
JAPAN	823,799	914,884	970,741	985,564	655,131	29.14	-33.53
KOREA REP.	74,411	82,480	82,081	79,874	90,174	4.01	12.90
S/EAST ASIA	498,601	523,221	474,965	508,742	447,395	19.90	-12.06
INDONESIA	76,424	106,787	89,027	86,098	37,116	1.65	-56.89
MALAYSIA	52,358	57,728	56,615	64,483	66,487	2.96	3.11
PHILIPPINES	120,319	83,137	68,955	74,022	75,851	3.37	2.47
SINGAPORE	85,569	94,691	96,645	107,069	78,300	3.48	-26.87
THAILAND	137,664	132,998	116,296	105,688	97,478	4.34	-7.77
OTH S/E ASIA	26,267	47,880	47,427	71,382	92,163	4.10	29.11
AUSTRALASIA	35,088	37,684	35,746	37,601	31,559	1.40	-16.07
AUSTRALIA	29,731	31,711	29,978	31,477	26,287	1.17	-16.49
NEW ZEALAND	5,357	5,973	5,768	6,124	5,272	0.23	-13.91
OT.EAST AS/P	65,136	71,907	74,049	73,189	68,262	3.04	-6.73
OTHER ASIA	64,683	71,542	73,654	72,941	67,972	3.02	-6.81
OTH OCEANIA	453	365	395	248	290	0.01	16.94
EUROPE	161,377	160,728	147,610	146,730	118,273	5.26	-19.39
NORTHERN EUR	38,536	41,056	38,414	39,009	32,188	1.43	-17.49

TAIWAN (PROVINCE OF CHINA)

2. ARRIVALS OF NON-RESIDENT VISITORS AT NATIONAL BORDERS, BY COUNTRY OF RESIDENCE

	1999	2000	2001	2002	2003	Market share 03	% change 03-02
SWEDEN	5,400	5,585	4,845	4,927	3,872	0.17	-21.41
UK	33,136	35,471	33,569	34,082	28,316	1.26	-16.92
SOUTHERN EUR	**16,522**	**17,311**	**15,469**	**15,664**	**11,297**	**0.50**	**-27.88**
GREECE	1,318	1,193	1,094	1,174	856	0.04	-27.09
ITALY	11,329	12,055	10,639	10,664	7,678	0.34	-28.00
SPAIN	3,875	4,063	3,736	3,826	2,763	0.12	-27.78
WESTERN EUR	**86,588**	**85,746**	**79,435**	**77,455**	**62,305**	**2.77**	**-19.56**
AUSTRIA	4,199	4,238	4,313	4,098	3,119	0.14	-23.89
BELGIUM	4,098	4,147	3,506	3,833	3,014	0.13	-21.37
FRANCE	23,508	23,675	20,988	20,179	15,188	0.68	-24.73
GERMANY	34,096	34,769	33,687	33,469	28,476	1.27	-14.92
NETHERLANDS	14,235	12,592	11,032	10,237	8,022	0.36	-21.64
SWITZERLAND	6,452	6,325	5,909	5,639	4,486	0.20	-20.45
OTHER EUROPE	**19,731**	**16,615**	**14,292**	**14,602**	**12,483**	**0.56**	**-14.51**
OTHER EUROPE	19,731	16,615	14,292	14,602	12,483	0.56	-14.51
MIDDLE EAST	**10,578**	**11,202**	**9,194**	**9,929**	**7,696**	**0.34**	**-22.49**
MIDDLE EAST	**10,578**	**11,202**	**9,194**	**9,929**	**7,696**	**0.34**	**-22.49**
ALL MID EAST	10,578	11,202	9,194	9,929	7,696	0.34	-22.49
SOUTH ASIA	**11,498**	**13,195**	**13,062**	**13,945**	**12,405**	**0.55**	**-11.04**
SOUTH ASIA	**11,498**	**13,195**	**13,062**	**13,945**	**12,405**	**0.55**	**-11.04**
INDIA	11,498	13,195	13,062	13,945	12,405	0.55	-11.04
REG.NOT SPEC	**302,266**	**320,612**	**545,665**	**630,081**	**442,177**	**19.67**	**-29.82**
NOT SPECIFIE	**302,266**	**320,612**	**545,665**	**630,081**	**442,177**	**19.67**	**-29.82**
OTH.WORLD	6,671	7,245	6,501	6,406	6,094	0.27	-4.87
N RESID ABRO	295,595	313,367	539,164	623,675	436,083	19.40	-30.08

Source: World Tourism Organization (WTO)

TAIWAN (PROVINCE OF CHINA)

4. ARRIVALS OF NON-RESIDENT TOURISTS IN ALL TYPES OF ACCOMMODATION ESTABLISHMENTS, BY COUNTRY OF RESIDENCE

	1999	2000	2001	2002	2003	Market share 03	% change 03-02
TOTAL	**2,061,691**	**2,228,701**	**2,305,905**	**2,236,936**	**1,813,814**	**100.00**	**-18.92**
AFRICA	**7,139**	**7,233**	**6,777**	**6,549**	**4,940**	**0.27**	**-24.57**
EAST AFRICA	**351**	**340**	**245**	**315**	**8**		**-97.46**
MADAGASCAR	27	26	12	18	7		-61.11
MAURITIUS	324	314	233	297	1		-99.66
SOUTHERN AFR	**3,654**	**3,854**	**3,690**	**3,689**	**3,054**	**0.17**	**-17.21**
SOUTH AFRICA	3,654	3,854	3,690	3,689	3,054	0.17	-17.21
WEST AFRICA	**665**	**771**	**813**	**646**	**503**	**0.03**	**-22.14**
NIGERIA	665	771	813	646	503	0.03	-22.14
OTHER AFRICA	**2,469**	**2,268**	**2,029**	**1,899**	**1,375**	**0.08**	**-27.59**
OTHER AFRICA	2,469	2,268	2,029	1,899	1,375	0.08	-27.59
AMERICAS	**343,004**	**375,899**	**356,922**	**371,449**	**283,085**	**15.61**	**-23.79**
NORTH AMER	**333,817**	**367,138**	**349,533**	**364,514**	**277,857**	**15.32**	**-23.77**
CANADA	32,345	33,674	34,532	35,872	27,298	1.51	-23.90
MEXICO	1,579	1,768	1,537	1,946	1,082	0.06	-44.40
USA	299,893	331,696	313,464	326,696	249,477	13.75	-23.64
SOUTH AMER	**4,002**	**3,781**	**2,870**	**2,487**	**1,999**	**0.11**	**-19.62**
ARGENTINA	1,423	1,039	811	479	353	0.02	-26.30
BRAZIL	2,579	2,742	2,059	2,008	1,646	0.09	-18.03
OTHER AMERIC	**5,185**	**4,980**	**4,519**	**4,448**	**3,229**	**0.18**	**-27.41**
OTH AMERICA	5,185	4,980	4,519	4,448	3,229	0.18	-27.41
EAST AS/PACI	**1,516,825**	**1,656,830**	**1,775,679**	**1,694,291**	**1,370,891**	**75.58**	**-19.09**
N/EAST ASIA	**1,172,644**	**1,290,387**	**1,392,049**	**1,273,802**	**1,004,488**	**55.38**	**-21.14**
HK,CHINA	293,483	332,980	370,720	244,103	287,312	15.84	17.70
JAPAN	809,947	880,551	944,621	955,439	631,219	34.80	-33.93
KOREA REP.	69,214	76,856	76,708	74,260	85,957	4.74	15.75
S/EAST ASIA	**229,678**	**245,385**	**242,733**	**263,726**	**224,277**	**12.36**	**-14.96**
INDONESIA	31,773	36,636	32,817	32,527	23,699	1.31	-27.14
MALAYSIA	44,327	49,632	48,087	56,420	58,225	3.21	3.20
PHILIPPINES	32,802	25,038	25,398	23,155	22,257	1.23	-3.88
SINGAPORE	84,326	91,537	94,120	105,056	76,118	4.20	-27.55
THAILAND	27,176	30,043	28,391	29,103	24,881	1.37	-14.51
OTH S/E ASIA	9,274	12,499	13,920	17,465	19,097	1.05	9.34
AUSTRALASIA	**33,562**	**34,860**	**32,918**	**34,093**	**28,367**	**1.56**	**-16.80**
AUSTRALIA	28,480	29,542	27,926	28,833	23,814	1.31	-17.41
NEW ZEALAND	5,082	5,318	4,992	5,260	4,553	0.25	-13.44
OT.EAST AS/P	**80,941**	**86,198**	**107,979**	**122,670**	**113,759**	**6.27**	**-7.26**
OTHER ASIA	80,557	85,872	107,645	122,471	113,503	6.26	-7.32
OTH OCEANIA	384	326	334	199	256	0.01	28.64
EUROPE	**150,368**	**148,384**	**135,442**	**133,050**	**106,125**	**5.85**	**-20.24**
NORTHERN EUR	**35,827**	**37,560**	**34,651**	**34,832**	**28,873**	**1.59**	**-17.11**

4. ARRIVALS OF NON-RESIDENT TOURISTS IN ALL TYPES OF ACCOMMODATION ESTABLISHMENTS, BY COUNTRY OF RESIDENCE

	1999	2000	2001	2002	2003	Market share 03	% change 03-02
SWEDEN	5,011	5,172	4,519	4,633	3,615	0.20	-21.97
UK	30,816	32,388	30,132	30,199	25,258	1.39	-16.36
SOUTHERN EUR	**15,545**	**16,225**	**14,359**	**14,280**	**10,099**	**0.56**	**-29.28**
GREECE	1,076	1,009	927	989	625	0.03	-36.80
ITALY	10,767	11,349	9,961	9,782	6,952	0.38	-28.93
SPAIN	3,702	3,867	3,471	3,509	2,522	0.14	-28.13
WESTERN EUR	**80,442**	**79,644**	**73,521**	**70,993**	**56,391**	**3.11**	**-20.57**
AUSTRIA	3,853	3,863	4,008	3,783	2,819	0.16	-25.48
BELGIUM	3,731	3,823	3,332	3,484	2,771	0.15	-20.46
FRANCE	21,809	21,762	19,166	18,492	13,766	0.76	-25.56
GERMANY	31,823	32,527	31,364	30,692	25,644	1.41	-16.45
NETHERLANDS	13,132	11,685	10,020	9,219	7,139	0.39	-22.56
SWITZERLAND	6,094	5,984	5,631	5,323	4,252	0.23	-20.12
OTHER EUROPE	**18,554**	**14,955**	**12,911**	**12,945**	**10,762**	**0.59**	**-16.86**
OTHER EUROPE	18,554	14,955	12,911	12,945	10,762	0.59	-16.86
MIDDLE EAST	**9,958**	**10,652**	**8,710**	**9,320**	**7,186**	**0.40**	**-22.90**
MIDDLE EAST	**9,958**	**10,652**	**8,710**	**9,320**	**7,186**	**0.40**	**-22.90**
ALL MID EAST	9,958	10,652	8,710	9,320	7,186	0.40	-22.90
SOUTH ASIA	**9,766**	**11,205**	**11,001**	**11,793**	**9,996**	**0.55**	**-15.24**
SOUTH ASIA	**9,766**	**11,205**	**11,001**	**11,793**	**9,996**	**0.55**	**-15.24**
INDIA	9,766	11,205	11,001	11,793	9,996	0.55	-15.24
REG.NOT SPEC	**24,631**	**18,498**	**11,374**	**10,484**	**31,591**	**1.74**	**201.33**
NOT SPECIFIE	**24,631**	**18,498**	**11,374**	**10,484**	**31,591**	**1.74**	**201.33**
OTH.WORLD	24,631	18,498	11,374	10,484	31,591	1.74	201.33

Source: World Tourism Organization (WTO)

TAIWAN (PROVINCE OF CHINA)

6. OVERNIGHT STAYS OF NON-RESIDENT TOURISTS IN ALL TYPES OF ACCOMMODATION ESTABLISHMENTS, BY COUNTRY OF RESIDENCE

	1999	2000	2001	2002	2003	Market share 03	% change 03-02
TOTAL	**15,966,101**	**16,487,081**	**16,986,990**	**16,856,168**	**14,460,852**	**100.00**	**-14.21**
AFRICA	**70,960**	**79,786**	**81,637**	**81,135**	**71,214**	**0.49**	**-12.23**
EAST AFRICA	**3,108**	**3,317**	**1,949**	**3,308**	**38**		**-98.85**
MADAGASCAR	630	397	83	258	31		-87.98
MAURITIUS	2,478	2,920	1,866	3,050	7		-99.77
SOUTHERN AFR	**36,999**	**44,628**	**46,439**	**49,841**	**45,151**	**0.31**	**-9.41**
SOUTH AFRICA	36,999	44,628	46,439	49,841	45,151	0.31	-9.41
WEST AFRICA	**11,513**	**14,109**	**15,405**	**12,333**	**12,844**	**0.09**	**4.14**
NIGERIA	11,513	14,109	15,405	12,333	12,844	0.09	4.14
OTHER AFRICA	**19,340**	**17,732**	**17,844**	**15,653**	**13,181**	**0.09**	**-15.79**
OTHER AFRICA	19,340	17,732	17,844	15,653	13,181	0.09	-15.79
AMERICAS	**3,521,623**	**3,710,258**	**3,668,405**	**3,790,449**	**2,929,600**	**20.26**	**-22.71**
NORTH AMER	**3,413,443**	**3,612,374**	**3,583,956**	**3,714,087**	**2,867,900**	**19.83**	**-22.78**
CANADA	366,529	361,683	365,659	377,030	317,346	2.19	-15.83
MEXICO	12,012	12,566	13,187	14,477	8,531	0.06	-41.07
USA	3,034,902	3,238,125	3,205,110	3,322,580	2,542,023	17.58	-23.49
SOUTH AMER	**48,913**	**43,224**	**34,265**	**29,585**	**25,803**	**0.18**	**-12.78**
ARGENTINA	17,873	12,438	10,808	7,873	5,573	0.04	-29.21
BRAZIL	31,040	30,786	23,457	21,712	20,230	0.14	-6.83
OTHER AMERIC	**59,267**	**54,660**	**50,184**	**46,777**	**35,897**	**0.25**	**-23.26**
OTH AMERICA	59,267	54,660	50,184	46,777	35,897	0.25	-23.26
EAST AS/PACI	**10,674,211**	**11,108,493**	**11,837,944**	**11,639,663**	**10,218,702**	**70.66**	**-12.21**
N/EAST ASIA	**6,211,544**	**6,476,587**	**6,741,642**	**6,236,387**	**5,432,610**	**37.57**	**-12.89**
HK,CHINA	1,773,195	1,774,908	1,818,696	1,321,527	1,400,068	9.68	5.94
JAPAN	4,020,124	4,294,752	4,489,876	4,506,849	3,591,033	24.83	-20.32
KOREA REP.	418,225	406,927	433,070	408,011	441,509	3.05	8.21
S/EAST ASIA	**2,454,101**	**2,598,287**	**2,598,556**	**2,734,813**	**2,403,631**	**16.62**	**-12.11**
INDONESIA	474,727	540,439	503,754	499,814	345,119	2.39	-30.95
MALAYSIA	413,887	475,689	445,369	499,243	483,919	3.35	-3.07
PHILIPPINES	461,058	332,749	319,005	285,725	321,357	2.22	12.47
SINGAPORE	636,805	683,370	719,359	762,479	528,789	3.66	-30.65
THAILAND	322,929	340,192	338,499	346,215	318,284	2.20	-8.07
OTH S/E ASIA	144,695	225,848	272,570	341,337	406,163	2.81	18.99
AUSTRALASIA	**268,152**	**272,637**	**264,742**	**267,598**	**241,444**	**1.67**	**-9.77**
AUSTRALIA	218,165	223,116	217,945	219,083	194,369	1.34	-11.28
NEW ZEALAND	49,987	49,521	46,797	48,515	47,075	0.33	-2.97
OT.EAST AS/P	**1,740,414**	**1,760,982**	**2,233,004**	**2,400,865**	**2,141,017**	**14.81**	**-10.82**
OTHER ASIA	1,736,861	1,757,224	2,229,906	2,398,400	2,138,423	14.79	-10.84
OTH OCEANIA	3,553	3,758	3,098	2,465	2,594	0.02	5.23
EUROPE	**1,151,999**	**1,137,256**	**1,076,182**	**1,027,500**	**832,011**	**5.75**	**-19.03**
NORTHERN EUR	**252,719**	**272,796**	**264,149**	**268,485**	**229,981**	**1.59**	**-14.34**

TAIWAN (PROVINCE OF CHINA)

6. OVERNIGHT STAYS OF NON-RESIDENT TOURISTS IN ALL TYPES OF ACCOMMODATION ESTABLISHMENTS, BY COUNTRY OF RESIDENCE

	1999	2000	2001	2002	2003	Market share 03	% change 03-02
SWEDEN	36,249	34,354	30,706	32,621	25,196	0.17	-22.76
UK	216,470	238,442	233,443	235,864	204,785	1.42	-13.18
SOUTHERN EUR	**108,614**	**104,279**	**96,339**	**90,339**	**63,998**	**0.44**	**-29.16**
GREECE	6,089	5,825	6,601	6,060	3,273	0.02	-45.99
ITALY	76,883	73,010	67,054	61,625	42,544	0.29	-30.96
SPAIN	25,642	25,444	22,684	22,654	18,181	0.13	-19.74
WESTERN EUR	**663,003**	**639,981**	**605,310**	**567,880**	**460,298**	**3.18**	**-18.94**
AUSTRIA	36,301	38,198	42,114	37,844	27,112	0.19	-28.36
BELGIUM	25,328	24,361	21,769	19,617	18,665	0.13	-4.85
FRANCE	188,134	175,901	161,003	154,739	119,653	0.83	-22.67
GERMANY	277,134	276,393	268,977	254,570	212,808	1.47	-16.40
NETHERLANDS	80,315	74,881	64,017	61,209	48,061	0.33	-21.48
SWITZERLAND	55,791	50,247	47,430	39,901	33,999	0.24	-14.79
OTHER EUROPE	**127,663**	**120,200**	**110,384**	**100,796**	**77,734**	**0.54**	**-22.88**
OTHER EUROPE	127,663	120,200	110,384	100,796	77,734	0.54	-22.88
MIDDLE EAST	**66,197**	**71,262**	**59,583**	**63,202**	**50,807**	**0.35**	**-19.61**
MIDDLE EAST	**66,197**	**71,262**	**59,583**	**63,202**	**50,807**	**0.35**	**-19.61**
ALL MID EAST	66,197	71,262	59,583	63,202	50,807	0.35	-19.61
SOUTH ASIA	**87,836**	**99,328**	**105,650**	**111,513**	**98,841**	**0.68**	**-11.36**
SOUTH ASIA	**87,836**	**99,328**	**105,650**	**111,513**	**98,841**	**0.68**	**-11.36**
INDIA	87,836	99,328	105,650	111,513	98,841	0.68	-11.36
REG.NOT SPEC	**393,275**	**280,698**	**157,589**	**142,706**	**259,677**	**1.80**	**81.97**
NOT SPECIFIE	**393,275**	**280,698**	**157,589**	**142,706**	**259,677**	**1.80**	**81.97**
OTH.WORLD	393,275	280,698	157,589	142,706	259,677	1.80	81.97

Source: World Tourism Organization (WTO)

TAJIKISTAN

2. ARRIVALS OF NON-RESIDENT VISITORS AT NATIONAL BORDERS, BY COUNTRY OF RESIDENCE

	1999	2000	2001	2002	2003	Market share 03	% change 03-02
TOTAL	4,500	7,673	5,200				
AFRICA	15	72					
EAST AFRICA	1						
ETHIOPIA	1						
SOUTHERN AFR	14	72					
SOUTH AFRICA	14	72					
AMERICAS	401	796	887				
NORTH AMER	401	796	887				
CANADA	50	231	254				
USA	351	565	633				
EAST AS/PACI	416	1,093	467				
N/EAST ASIA	368	1,016	455				
CHINA	75	181	78				
JAPAN	49	72	85				
KOREA D P RP	244	763	292				
S/EAST ASIA		20	5				
PHILIPPINES		7	5				
SINGAPORE		5					
THAILAND		8					
AUSTRALASIA	48	57	7				
AUSTRALIA	42	51	7				
NEW ZEALAND	6	6					
EUROPE	3,069	4,921	3,300				
C/E EUROPE	1,681	2,243	1,940				
BULGARIA	15	30	17				
HUNGARY	16	15	14				
KAZAKHSTAN	14	92	8				
KYRGYZSTAN	11	65	15				
POLAND	36	40	15				
ROMANIA	2	6					
RUSSIAN FED	1,529	1,823	1,871				
SLOVAKIA	3	5					
UKRAINE	7	99					
UZBEKISTAN	48	68					
NORTHERN EUR	167	437	147				
DENMARK	12	15	5				
FINLAND	3	10	3				
NORWAY	4	12	3				
SWEDEN	13	15	4				
UK	135	385	132				
SOUTHERN EUR	157	241	67				
GREECE	62	75	11				
ITALY	85	135	51				

TAJIKISTAN

2. ARRIVALS OF NON-RESIDENT VISITORS AT NATIONAL BORDERS, BY COUNTRY OF RESIDENCE

	1999	2000	2001	2002	2003	Market share 03	% change 03-02
SPAIN	10	31	5				
WESTERN EUR	**933**	**1,882**	**1,051**				
AUSTRIA	46	58	13				
BELGIUM	48	161	65				
FRANCE	515	953	570				
GERMANY	249	546	283				
NETHERLANDS	25	63	31				
SWITZERLAND	50	101	89				
EAST/MED EUR	**131**	**118**	**95**				
ISRAEL	12	8	7				
TURKEY	119	110	88				
MIDDLE EAST	**105**	**123**	**34**				
MIDDLE EAST	**105**	**123**	**34**				
IRAQ	27	20	12				
JORDAN	15	26					
LIBYA	17	15	13				
OMAN	38	40					
SYRIA	4	10					
UNTD ARAB EM	4	12	9				
SOUTH ASIA	**494**	**668**	**512**				
SOUTH ASIA	**494**	**668**	**512**				
AFGHANISTAN	157	225	243				
BANGLADESH	6	4	8				
INDIA	48	57	45				
IRAN	239	290	183				
PAKISTAN	44	92	33				

Source: World Tourism Organization (WTO)

THAILAND

1. ARRIVALS OF NON-RESIDENT TOURISTS AT NATIONAL BORDERS, BY NATIONALITY

	1999	2000	2001	2002	2003	Market share 03	% change 03-02
TOTAL (*)	**8,651,260**	**9,578,826**	**10,132,509**	**10,872,976**	**10,082,109**	**100.00**	**-7.27**
AFRICA	**76,008**	**84,487**	**97,413**	**98,290**	**74,285**	**0.74**	**-24.42**
SOUTHERN AFR	**31,833**	**35,381**	**40,133**	**39,262**	**35,560**	**0.35**	**-9.43**
SOUTH AFRICA	31,833	35,381	40,133	39,262	35,560	0.35	-9.43
OTHER AFRICA	**44,175**	**49,106**	**57,280**	**59,028**	**38,725**	**0.38**	**-34.40**
OTHER AFRICA	44,175	49,106	57,280	59,028	38,725	0.38	-34.40
AMERICAS	**595,381**	**663,276**	**682,995**	**730,402**	**679,210**	**6.74**	**-7.01**
NORTH AMER	**567,528**	**630,593**	**648,799**	**691,021**	**652,826**	**6.48**	**-5.53**
CANADA	105,857	112,540	121,020	135,668	137,963	1.37	1.69
USA	461,671	518,053	527,779	555,353	514,863	5.11	-7.29
SOUTH AMER	**10,618**	**11,357**	**12,312**	**12,358**	**9,132**	**0.09**	**-26.10**
ARGENTINA	5,319	5,535	6,295	3,398	2,348	0.02	-30.90
BRAZIL	5,299	5,822	6,017	8,960	6,784	0.07	-24.29
OTHER AMERIC	**17,235**	**21,326**	**21,884**	**27,023**	**17,252**	**0.17**	**-36.16**
OTH AMERICA	17,235	21,326	21,884	27,023	17,252	0.17	-36.16
EAST AS/PACI	**5,345,580**	**5,924,638**	**6,206,954**	**6,663,355**	**6,139,091**	**60.89**	**-7.87**
N/EAST ASIA	**2,989,100**	**3,357,726**	**3,511,499**	**3,752,228**	**3,257,112**	**32.31**	**-13.20**
CHINA	813,596	753,781	801,362	797,976	606,635	6.02	-23.98
TAIWAN(P.C.)	528,291	706,482	738,642	674,366	501,573	4.97	-25.62
HK,CHINA	244,474	243,952	245,170	335,816	411,242	4.08	22.46
JAPAN	1,059,872	1,202,164	1,177,599	1,239,421	1,042,349	10.34	-15.90
KOREA REP.	342,867	451,347	548,726	704,649	695,313	6.90	-1.32
S/EAST ASIA	**1,864,278**	**2,135,206**	**2,241,562**	**2,474,523**	**2,504,231**	**24.84**	**1.20**
BRUNEI DARSM	2,405	4,776	10,177	10,129	8,863	0.09	-12.50
MYANMAR		43,573	36,843	36,111	32,702	0.32	-9.44
CAMBODIA		35,244	45,479	70,187	65,502	0.65	-6.68
INDONESIA	133,252	156,764	156,411	164,645	168,568	1.67	2.38
LAO P.DEM.R.	68,809	70,985	82,307	90,717	100,747	1.00	11.06
MALAYSIA	1,009,821	1,111,687	1,185,891	1,332,355	1,354,295	13.43	1.65
PHILIPPINES	86,835	103,013	124,841	139,364	140,371	1.39	0.72
SINGAPORE	528,889	563,679	531,818	546,796	515,630	5.11	-5.70
VIET NAM	34,267	45,485	67,795	84,219	117,553	1.17	39.58
AUSTRALASIA	**342,656**	**377,116**	**418,836**	**425,218**	**361,259**	**3.58**	**-15.04**
AUSTRALIA	283,498	314,531	350,322	351,508	291,872	2.89	-16.97
NEW ZEALAND	59,158	62,585	68,514	73,710	69,387	0.69	-5.86
OT.EAST AS/P	**149,546**	**54,590**	**35,057**	**11,386**	**16,489**	**0.16**	**44.82**
OTHER ASIA	147,323	52,924	33,342	9,495	15,015	0.15	58.14
OTH OCEANIA	2,223	1,666	1,715	1,891	1,474	0.01	-22.05
EUROPE	**2,182,600**	**2,377,605**	**2,600,109**	**2,749,683**	**2,587,034**	**25.66**	**-5.92**
C/E EUROPE	**82,856**	**100,749**	**116,769**	**143,585**	**152,312**	**1.51**	**6.08**
RUSSIAN FED	36,622	46,417	54,488	70,692	89,329	0.89	26.36
OTH C/E EUR	46,234	54,332	62,281	72,893	62,983	0.62	-13.60

THAILAND

1. ARRIVALS OF NON-RESIDENT TOURISTS AT NATIONAL BORDERS, BY NATIONALITY

	1999	2000	2001	2002	2003	Market share 03	% change 03-02
NORTHERN EUR	**808,754**	**954,225**	**1,120,024**	**1,152,169**	**1,161,748**	**11.52**	**0.83**
DENMARK	79,094	79,040	83,216	90,480	82,828	0.82	-8.46
FINLAND	45,933	51,109	64,370	66,772	66,513	0.66	-0.39
NORWAY	48,630	53,902	73,620	74,607	71,885	0.71	-3.65
SWEDEN	119,935	150,515	238,369	215,894	204,002	2.02	-5.51
UK	515,162	619,659	660,449	704,416	736,520	7.31	4.56
SOUTHERN EUR	**155,512**	**166,805**	**160,475**	**176,724**	**129,052**	**1.28**	**-26.98**
ITALY	126,572	133,247	122,263	129,293	97,526	0.97	-24.57
SPAIN	28,940	33,558	38,212	47,431	31,526	0.31	-33.53
WESTERN EUR	**983,321**	**983,913**	**1,013,430**	**1,062,294**	**976,655**	**9.69**	**-8.06**
AUSTRIA	59,098	52,240	50,376	54,020	53,646	0.53	-0.69
BELGIUM	52,231	52,256	53,813	56,865	52,052	0.52	-8.46
FRANCE	255,247	256,948	251,717	271,395	237,690	2.36	-12.42
GERMANY	389,466	390,030	402,992	411,049	386,532	3.83	-5.96
NETHERLANDS	118,780	126,848	142,560	150,138	138,839	1.38	-7.53
SWITZERLAND	108,499	105,591	111,972	118,827	107,896	1.07	-9.20
EAST/MED EUR	**65,794**	**75,798**	**91,543**	**98,691**	**69,837**	**0.69**	**-29.24**
ISRAEL	65,794	75,798	91,543	98,691	69,837	0.69	-29.24
OTHER EUROPE	**86,363**	**96,115**	**97,868**	**116,220**	**97,430**	**0.97**	**-16.17**
OTHER EUROPE	86,363	96,115	97,868	116,220	97,430	0.97	-16.17
MIDDLE EAST	**88,966**	**106,610**	**123,605**	**147,131**	**117,792**	**1.17**	**-19.94**
MIDDLE EAST	**88,966**	**106,610**	**123,605**	**147,131**	**117,792**	**1.17**	**-19.94**
KUWAIT	14,924	18,599	20,597	25,251	19,977	0.20	-20.89
SAUDI ARABIÀ	5,048	6,150	7,093	6,886	4,849	0.05	-29.58
UNTD ARAB EM	17,455	20,798	21,369	26,565	22,914	0.23	-13.74
EGYPT	5,139	6,281	6,371	7,719	5,264	0.05	-31.80
OT MIDD EAST	46,400	54,782	68,175	80,710	64,788	0.64	-19.73
SOUTH ASIA	**291,797**	**352,007**	**350,874**	**410,206**	**407,041**	**4.04**	**-0.77**
SOUTH ASIA	**291,797**	**352,007**	**350,874**	**410,206**	**407,041**	**4.04**	**-0.77**
BANGLADESH	22,243	25,681	28,397	35,928	53,421	0.53	48.69
SRI LANKA	26,263	28,668	28,657	31,649	38,483	0.38	21.59
INDIA	181,033	224,104	229,751	280,641	253,752	2.52	-9.58
NEPAL	14,957	16,389	17,284	19,933	19,909	0.20	-0.12
PAKISTAN	39,466	49,407	36,946	31,246	31,315	0.31	0.22
OTH STH ASIA	7,835	7,758	9,839	10,809	10,161	0.10	-6.00
REG.NOT SPEC	**70,928**	**70,203**	**70,559**	**73,909**	**77,656**	**0.77**	**5.07**
NOT SPECIFIE	**70,928**	**70,203**	**70,559**	**73,909**	**77,656**	**0.77**	**5.07**
N RESID ABRO	70,928	70,203	70,559	73,909	77,656	0.77	5.07

Source: World Tourism Organization (WTO)

THAILAND

1. ARRIVALS OF NON-RESIDENT TOURISTS AT NATIONAL BORDERS, BY COUNTRY OF RESIDENCE

	1999	2000	2001	2002	2003	Market share 03	% change 03-02
TOTAL (*)	**8,651,260**	**9,578,826**	**10,132,509**	**10,872,976**	**10,082,109**	**100.00**	**-7.27**
AFRICA	**73,233**	**80,389**	**90,963**	**89,449**	**67,117**	**0.67**	**-24.97**
SOUTHERN AFR	**33,821**	**37,521**	**42,026**	**37,721**	**34,522**	**0.34**	**-8.48**
SOUTH AFRICA	33,821	37,521	42,026	37,721	34,522	0.34	-8.48
OTHER AFRICA	**39,412**	**42,868**	**48,937**	**51,728**	**32,595**	**0.32**	**-36.99**
OTHER AFRICA	39,412	42,868	48,937	51,728	32,595	0.32	-36.99
AMERICAS	**514,595**	**584,967**	**604,041**	**640,143**	**576,589**	**5.72**	**-9.93**
NORTH AMER	**494,361**	**559,564**	**578,079**	**611,210**	**557,478**	**5.53**	**-8.79**
CANADA	76,501	86,279	92,803	101,369	97,616	0.97	-3.70
USA	417,860	473,285	485,276	509,841	459,862	4.56	-9.80
SOUTH AMER	**8,750**	**9,242**	**9,929**	**7,915**	**6,241**	**0.06**	**-21.15**
ARGENTINA	4,989	5,256	5,674	2,380	1,585	0.02	-33.40
BRAZIL	3,761	3,986	4,255	5,535	4,656	0.05	-15.88
OTHER AMERIC	**11,484**	**16,161**	**16,033**	**21,018**	**12,870**	**0.13**	**-38.77**
OTH AMERICA	11,484	16,161	16,033	21,018	12,870	0.13	-38.77
EAST AS/PACI	**5,546,527**	**6,134,335**	**6,491,790**	**6,955,047**	**6,510,374**	**64.57**	**-6.39**
N/EAST ASIA	**3,165,777**	**3,544,265**	**3,664,645**	**3,901,977**	**3,504,928**	**34.76**	**-10.18**
CHINA	775,626	704,080	694,886	763,139	624,214	6.19	-18.20
TAIWAN(P.C.)	557,629	707,305	724,769	673,652	521,941	5.18	-22.52
HK,CHINA	429,944	487,151	523,465	526,138	649,920	6.45	23.53
JAPAN	1,064,539	1,197,931	1,168,548	1,222,270	1,014,513	10.06	-17.00
KOREA REP.	338,039	447,798	552,977	716,778	694,340	6.89	-3.13
S/EAST ASIA	**2,017,372**	**2,196,847**	**2,385,528**	**2,614,627**	**2,646,003**	**26.24**	**1.20**
BRUNEI DARSM	9,277	12,762	13,912	13,755	17,244	0.17	25.37
MYANMAR	43,815	47,164	42,903	42,266	37,180	0.37	-12.03
CAMBODIA	32,142	43,104	54,399	79,219	73,868	0.73	-6.75
INDONESIA	132,216	145,066	153,458	164,994	167,414	1.66	1.47
LAO P.DEM.R.	71,722	74,832	86,357	94,052	104,468	1.04	11.07
MALAYSIA	991,060	1,054,469	1,159,630	1,296,109	1,338,624	13.28	3.28
PHILIPPINES	87,326	106,724	129,818	142,940	143,015	1.42	0.05
SINGAPORE	604,867	655,767	664,980	683,296	629,103	6.24	-7.93
VIET NAM	44,947	56,959	80,071	97,996	135,087	1.34	37.85
AUSTRALASIA	**348,027**	**379,050**	**424,886**	**420,300**	**341,366**	**3.39**	**-18.78**
AUSTRALIA	303,844	323,275	363,696	355,529	281,361	2.79	-20.86
NEW ZEALAND	44,183	55,775	61,190	64,771	60,005	0.60	-7.36
OT.EAST AS/P	**15,351**	**14,173**	**16,731**	**18,143**	**18,077**	**0.18**	**-0.36**
OTHER ASIA	12,823	11,759	13,944	14,942	15,529	0.15	3.93
OTH OCEANIA	2,528	2,414	2,787	3,201	2,548	0.03	-20.40
EUROPE	**2,055,430**	**2,242,466**	**2,395,806**	**2,549,507**	**2,320,810**	**23.02**	**-8.97**
C/E EUROPE	**87,547**	**104,906**	**117,701**	**134,339**	**148,650**	**1.47**	**10.65**
RUSSIAN FED	36,574	49,586	58,927	68,978	90,665	0.90	31.44
OTH C/E EUR	50,973	55,320	58,774	65,361	57,985	0.58	-11.29

THAILAND

1. ARRIVALS OF NON-RESIDENT TOURISTS AT NATIONAL BORDERS, BY COUNTRY OF RESIDENCE

	1999	2000	2001	2002	2003	Market share 03	% change 03-02
NORTHERN EUR	**771,126**	**885,088**	**951,057**	**1,014,357**	**966,234**	**9.58**	**-4.74**
DENMARK	78,446	79,915	78,728	84,617	78,587	0.78	-7.13
FINLAND	49,465	55,144	58,530	64,115	62,509	0.62	-2.50
NORWAY	55,062	64,550	72,785	74,947	70,694	0.70	-5.67
SWEDEN	162,465	209,092	223,040	220,866	209,444	2.08	-5.17
UK	425,688	476,387	517,974	569,812	545,000	5.41	-4.35
SOUTHERN EUR	**143,823**	**153,631**	**158,765**	**174,713**	**124,506**	**1.23**	**-28.74**
ITALY	113,884	119,677	119,953	126,222	92,656	0.92	-26.59
SPAIN	29,939	33,954	38,812	48,491	31,850	0.32	-34.32
WESTERN EUR	**906,247**	**944,829**	**993,792**	**1,028,132**	**938,150**	**9.31**	**-8.75**
AUSTRIA	42,874	44,793	46,461	48,067	46,717	0.46	-2.81
BELGIUM	46,352	50,374	54,350	56,179	50,772	0.50	-9.62
FRANCE	227,219	239,532	237,511	253,463	219,227	2.17	-13.51
GERMANY	375,345	378,562	398,034	403,240	378,642	3.76	-6.10
NETHERLANDS	105,825	119,533	136,929	140,966	129,211	1.28	-8.34
SWITZERLAND	108,632	112,035	120,507	126,217	113,581	1.13	-10.01
EAST/MED EUR	**64,981**	**73,470**	**91,166**	**98,629**	**64,650**	**0.64**	**-34.45**
ISRAEL	64,981	73,470	91,166	98,629	64,650	0.64	-34.45
OTHER EUROPE	**81,706**	**80,542**	**83,325**	**99,337**	**78,620**	**0.78**	**-20.86**
OTHER EUROPE	81,706	80,542	83,325	99,337	78,620	0.78	-20.86
MIDDLE EAST	**110,125**	**127,053**	**146,102**	**174,176**	**139,228**	**1.38**	**-20.06**
MIDDLE EAST	**110,125**	**127,053**	**146,102**	**174,176**	**139,228**	**1.38**	**-20.06**
KUWAIT	17,203	19,699	22,167	28,448	21,264	0.21	-25.25
SAUDI ARABIA	12,362	13,719	13,593	14,254	9,886	0.10	-30.64
UNTD ARAB EM	29,599	34,124	36,692	43,549	39,317	0.39	-9.72
EGYPT	4,920	6,322	6,077	7,489	5,209	0.05	-30.44
OT MIDD EAST	46,041	53,189	67,573	80,436	63,552	0.63	-20.99
SOUTH ASIA	**280,422**	**339,413**	**333,248**	**390,745**	**390,335**	**3.87**	**-0.10**
SOUTH ASIA	**280,422**	**339,413**	**333,248**	**390,745**	**390,335**	**3.87**	**-0.10**
BANGLADESH	25,300	29,708	32,941	41,145	57,651	0.57	40.12
SRI LANKA	26,612	29,586	29,147	32,441	38,309	0.38	18.09
INDIA	163,980	202,868	206,132	253,110	230,316	2.28	-9.01
NEPAL	16,681	19,603	19,009	23,001	22,397	0.22	-2.63
PAKISTAN	39,054	49,148	35,737	29,902	30,894	0.31	3.32
OTH STH ASIA	8,795	8,500	10,282	11,146	10,768	0.11	-3.39
REG.NOT SPEC	**70,928**	**70,203**	**70,559**	**73,909**	**77,656**	**0.77**	**5.07**
NOT SPECIFIE	**70,928**	**70,203**	**70,559**	**73,909**	**77,656**	**0.77**	**5.07**
N RESID ABRO	70,928	70,203	70,559	73,909	77,656	0.77	5.07

Source: World Tourism Organization (WTO)

THAILAND

3. ARRIVALS OF NON-RESIDENT TOURISTS IN HOTELS AND SIMILAR ESTABLISHMENTS, BY COUNTRY OF RESIDENCE

	1999	2000	2001	2002	2003	Market share 03	% change 03-02
TOTAL	**8,324,758**	**9,271,023**	**9,814,892**				
AFRICA	**71,105**	**77,725**	**88,734**				
SOUTHERN AFR	**33,057**	**37,025**	**41,165**				
SOUTH AFRICA	33,057	37,025	41,165				
OTHER AFRICA	**38,048**	**40,700**	**47,569**				
OTHER AFRICA	38,048	40,700	47,569				
AMERICAS	**485,583**	**559,787**	**573,681**				
NORTH AMER	**466,338**	**535,174**	**548,898**				
CANADA	72,295	82,468	88,520				
USA	394,043	452,706	460,378				
SOUTH AMER	**8,288**	**8,820**	**9,479**				
ARGENTINA	4,804	5,049	5,430				
BRAZIL	3,484	3,771	4,049				
OTHER AMERIC	**10,957**	**15,793**	**15,304**				
OTH AMERICA	10,957	15,793	15,304				
EAST AS/PACI	**5,426,869**	**6,009,964**	**6,379,302**				
N/EAST ASIA	**3,103,482**	**3,498,163**	**3,607,245**				
CHINA	761,819	694,980	681,811				
TAIWAN(P.C.)	551,182	702,500	718,296				
HK,CHINA	422,930	482,765	516,877				
JAPAN	1,036,606	1,175,989	1,145,712				
KOREA REP.	330,945	441,929	544,549				
S/EAST ASIA	**1,903,124**	**2,130,372**	**2,344,890**				
BRUNEI DARSM	9,036	12,628	13,606				
MYANMAR		44,103	39,267				
CAMBODIA		41,770	51,494				
INDONESIA	130,111	141,821	151,070				
LAO P.DEM.R.	65,067	69,756	83,274				
MALAYSIA	983,083	1,020,475	1,150,976				
PHILIPPINES	83,301	102,902	125,084				
SINGAPORE	589,016	641,613	653,254				
VIET NAM	43,510	55,304	76,865				
AUSTRALASIA	**335,056**	**367,964**	**410,588**				
AUSTRALIA	293,197	314,415	352,382				
NEW ZEALAND	41,859	53,549	58,206				
OT.EAST AS/P	**85,207**	**13,465**	**16,579**				
OTHER ASIA	82,824	11,073	13,835				
OTH OCEANIA	2,383	2,392	2,744				
EUROPE	**1,970,900**	**2,175,651**	**2,314,363**				
C/E EUROPE	**83,671**	**102,209**	**114,602**				
RUSSIAN FED	35,281	48,421	57,688				
OTH C/E EUR	48,390	53,788	56,914				

3. ARRIVALS OF NON-RESIDENT TOURISTS IN HOTELS AND SIMILAR ESTABLISHMENTS, BY COUNTRY OF RESIDENCE

	1999	2000	2001	2002	2003	Market share 03	% change 03-02
NORTHERN EUR	**740,507**	**858,356**	**920,785**				
DENMARK	75,382	77,037	76,042				
FINLAND	47,779	54,395	57,385				
NORWAY	51,837	62,189	70,482				
SWEDEN	157,849	204,375	218,086				
UK	407,660	460,360	498,790				
SOUTHERN EUR	**138,552**	**150,104**	**155,034**				
ITALY	109,827	117,109	117,263				
SPAIN	28,725	32,995	37,771				
WESTERN EUR	**867,887**	**915,695**	**956,657**				
AUSTRIA	41,465	43,757	45,092				
BELGIUM	44,084	48,708	51,720				
FRANCE	215,201	231,198	227,007				
GERMANY	362,502	368,396	385,161				
NETHERLANDS	100,078	114,495	131,289				
SWITZERLAND	104,557	109,141	116,388				
EAST/MED EUR	**61,732**	**70,942**	**87,194**				
ISRAEL	61,732	70,942	87,194				
OTHER EUROPE	**78,551**	**78,345**	**80,091**				
OTHER EUROPE	78,551	78,345	80,091				
MIDDLE EAST	**106,391**	**124,843**	**141,728**				
MIDDLE EAST	**106,391**	**124,843**	**141,728**				
KUWAIT	16,490	19,412	21,553				
SAUDI ARABIA	11,907	13,338	13,297				
UNTD ARAB EM	28,796	33,593	35,755				
EGYPT	4,700	6,154	5,885				
OT MIDD EAST	44,498	52,346	65,238				
SOUTH ASIA	**263,910**	**323,053**	**317,084**				
SOUTH ASIA	**263,910**	**323,053**	**317,084**				
BANGLADESH	24,298	28,714	31,918				
SRI LANKA	25,489	28,947	28,545				
INDIA	152,323	190,388	193,757				
NEPAL	15,911	18,815	18,105				
PAKISTAN	37,663	48,042	34,848				
OTH STH ASIA	8,226	8,147	9,911				

Source: World Tourism Organization (WTO)

5. OVERNIGHT STAYS OF NON-RESIDENT TOURISTS IN HOTELS AND SIMILAR ESTABLISHMENTS, BY NATIONALITY

	1999	2000	2001	2002	2003	Market share 03	% change 03-02
TOTAL	**68,293,242**	**73,855,073**	**79,795,758**				
AFRICA	**726,332**	**805,783**	**903,655**				
SOUTHERN AFR	**212,906**	**257,845**	**295,686**				
SOUTH AFRICA	212,906	257,845	295,686				
OTHER AFRICA	**513,426**	**547,938**	**607,969**				
OTHER AFRICA	513,426	547,938	607,969				
AMERICAS	**5,217,176**	**5,893,068**	**6,522,145**				
NORTH AMER	**5,008,710**	**5,650,228**	**6,261,854**				
CANADA	1,019,421	1,088,178	1,257,896				
USA	3,989,289	4,562,050	5,003,958				
SOUTH AMER	**87,686**	**93,149**	**106,556**				
ARGENTINA	46,246	48,385	57,126				
BRAZIL	41,440	44,764	49,430				
OTHER AMERIC	**120,780**	**149,691**	**153,735**				
OTH AMERICA	120,780	149,691	153,735				
EAST AS/PACI	**30,562,563**	**32,698,762**	**34,346,256**				
N/EAST ASIA	**18,054,306**	**19,320,876**	**20,097,860**				
CHINA	5,194,214	4,801,086	4,694,111				
TAIWAN(P.C.)	3,424,797	4,140,658	4,340,866				
HK,CHINA	1,134,924	1,097,338	1,081,634				
JAPAN	6,533,321	7,107,340	7,353,189				
KOREA REP.	1,767,050	2,174,454	2,628,060				
S/EAST ASIA	**8,127,159**	**9,505,227**	**10,074,695**				
BRUNEI DARSM	9,666	19,474	44,200				
MYANMAR		404,997	334,011				
CAMBODIA		242,566	313,177				
INDONESIA	534,715	610,134	648,086				
LAO P.DEM.R.	935,443	1,000,092	1,033,101				
MALAYSIA	3,497,136	3,835,991	4,071,954				
PHILIPPINES	625,492	744,925	882,680				
SINGAPORE	2,294,331	2,355,680	2,328,384				
VIET NAM	230,376	291,368	419,102				
AUSTRALASIA	**3,246,617**	**3,435,137**	**3,853,322**				
AUSTRALIA	2,647,164	2,858,305	3,245,643				
NEW ZEALAND	599,453	576,832	607,679				
OT.EAST AS/P	**1,134,481**	**437,522**	**320,379**				
OTHER ASIA	1,116,803	424,365	307,953				
OTH OCEANIA	17,678	13,157	12,426				
EUROPE	**28,353,074**	**30,573,970**	**34,116,207**				
C/E EUROPE	**936,324**	**1,167,752**	**1,355,378**				
RUSSIAN FED	408,035	530,382	634,610				
OTH C/E EUR	528,289	637,370	720,768				

THAILAND

5. OVERNIGHT STAYS OF NON-RESIDENT TOURISTS IN HOTELS AND SIMILAR ESTABLISHMENTS, BY NATIONALITY

	1999	2000	2001	2002	2003	Market share 03	% change 03-02
NORTHERN EUR	**10,192,424**	**11,807,307**	**14,367,069**				
DENMARK	1,112,267	1,097,920	1,165,930				
FINLAND	601,096	686,268	881,514				
NORWAY	677,819	762,326	1,068,461				
SWEDEN	1,725,257	2,144,666	3,457,701				
UK	6,075,985	7,116,127	7,793,463				
SOUTHERN EUR	**1,717,288**	**1,829,600**	**1,777,616**				
ITALY	1,461,392	1,539,099	1,444,855				
SPAIN	255,896	290,501	332,761				
WESTERN EUR	**14,018,821**	**13,969,978**	**14,479,166**				
AUSTRIA	890,392	768,684	730,556				
BELGIUM	701,379	705,391	731,590				
FRANCE	2,884,819	2,921,237	2,886,627				
GERMANY	6,168,600	6,107,472	6,274,350				
NETHERLANDS	1,746,053	1,886,107	2,182,765				
SWITZERLAND	1,627,578	1,581,087	1,673,278				
EAST/MED EUR	**737,479**	**902,637**	**1,156,087**				
ISRAEL	737,479	902,637	1,156,087				
OTHER EUROPE	**750,738**	**896,696**	**980,891**				
OTHER EUROPE	750,738	896,696	980,891				
MIDDLE EAST	**907,940**	**1,032,423**	**1,204,483**				
MIDDLE EAST	**907,940**	**1,032,423**	**1,204,483**				
KUWAIT	162,601	196,402	217,866				
SAUDI ARABIA	48,900	56,447	71,857				
UNTD ARAB EM	193,729	226,778	231,849				
EGYPT	39,986	40,867	44,755				
OT MIDD EAST	462,724	511,929	638,156				
SOUTH ASIA	**2,526,157**	**2,851,067**	**2,703,012**				
SOUTH ASIA	**2,526,157**	**2,851,067**	**2,703,012**				
BANGLADESH	127,066	151,064	171,767				
SRI LANKA	156,641	154,770	168,279				
INDIA	1,687,813	1,867,591	1,817,514				
NEPAL	146,504	144,735	148,522				
PAKISTAN	350,769	479,135	330,860				
OTH STH ASIA	57,364	53,772	66,070				

Source: World Tourism Organization (WTO)

3. ARRIVALS OF NON-RESIDENT TOURISTS IN HOTELS AND SIMILAR ESTABLISHMENTS, BY NATIONALITY

	1999	2000	2001	2002	2003	Market share 03	% change 03-02
TOTAL	**168,686**	**202,933**	**92,491**	**115,391**	**148,508**	**100.00**	**28.70**
AMERICAS	**15,325**	**16,703**	**7,742**	**7,704**	**8,209**	**5.53**	**6.56**
NORTH AMER	**15,325**	**16,703**	**7,742**	**7,704**	**8,209**	**5.53**	**6.56**
CANADA	1,587	1,654	733	765	923	0.62	20.65
USA	13,738	15,049	7,009	6,939	7,286	4.91	5.00
EAST AS/PACI	**2,372**	**2,663**	**1,035**	**1,540**	**2,289**	**1.54**	**48.64**
N/EAST ASIA	**1,283**	**981**	**404**	**584**	**1,050**	**0.71**	**79.79**
JAPAN	1,283	981	404	584	1,050	0.71	79.79
AUSTRALASIA	**1,089**	**1,682**	**631**	**956**	**1,239**	**0.83**	**29.60**
AUSTRALIA	921	1,504	563	832	1,146	0.77	37.74
NEW ZEALAND	168	178	68	124	93	0.06	-25.00
EUROPE	**147,162**	**178,478**	**81,200**	**103,525**	**134,549**	**90.60**	**29.97**
C/E EUROPE	**24,595**	**40,110**	**16,808**	**18,325**	**20,705**	**13.94**	**12.99**
BULGARIA	16,934	25,269	7,115	10,510	12,375	8.33	17.75
BELARUS	561	421	160	153	156	0.11	1.96
CZECH REP	675	948	537	921	1,129	0.76	22.58
HUNGARY	636	2,168	2,098	1,973	2,171	1.46	10.04
POLAND	654	1,017	670	1,043	1,007	0.68	-3.45
ROMANIA	846	1,559	980	1,198	1,304	0.88	8.85
RUSSIAN FED	3,209	2,889	1,599	1,227	1,310	0.88	6.76
SLOVAKIA	493	399	300	481	558	0.38	16.01
UKRAINE	587	5,440	3,349	819	695	0.47	-15.14
NORTHERN EUR	**16,216**	**14,846**	**7,970**	**8,142**	**9,420**	**6.34**	**15.70**
DENMARK	2,175	2,213	692	780	1,002	0.67	28.46
FINLAND	757	1,198	692	679	760	0.51	11.93
ICELAND	128	113	112	152	157	0.11	3.29
IRELAND	839	617	375	522	471	0.32	-9.77
NORWAY	1,876	2,208	861	1,049	1,104	0.74	5.24
SWEDEN	1,441	1,938	945	1,059	1,464	0.99	38.24
UK	9,000	6,559	4,293	3,901	4,462	3.00	14.38
SOUTHERN EUR	**70,541**	**88,271**	**40,193**	**56,107**	**78,664**	**52.97**	**40.20**
ALBANIA	19,245	22,465	6,003	8,314	11,338	7.63	36.37
BOSNIA HERZG	1,071	1,490	1,261	1,737	2,450	1.65	41.05
CROATIA	3,054	3,890	2,364	3,647	4,754	3.20	30.35
GREECE	9,767	20,478	10,294	14,200	26,514	17.85	86.72
ITALY	6,135	4,252	2,469	3,025	3,558	2.40	17.62
PORTUGAL	417	451	215	308	412	0.28	33.77
SLOVENIA	4,330	4,696	2,454	3,576	4,094	2.76	14.49
SPAIN	1,126	1,245	867	833	1,354	0.91	62.55
SERBIA,MTNEG	25,396	29,304	14,266	20,467	24,190	16.29	18.19
WESTERN EUR	**28,947**	**26,612**	**11,461**	**14,200**	**17,128**	**11.53**	**20.62**
AUSTRIA	1,928	2,291	1,232	1,836	2,511	1.69	36.76
BELGIUM	2,924	1,671	795	947	1,196	0.81	26.29
FRANCE	4,676	4,597	2,271	2,508	3,429	2.31	36.72
GERMANY	11,992	9,740	4,735	5,986	6,159	4.15	2.89

THE FORMER YUGOSLAV REP. OF MACEDONIA

3. ARRIVALS OF NON-RESIDENT TOURISTS IN HOTELS AND SIMILAR ESTABLISHMENTS, BY NATIONALITY

	1999	2000	2001	2002	2003	Market share 03	% change 03-02
NETHERLANDS	5,852	6,645	1,529	1,973	2,380	1.60	20.63
SWITZERLAND	1,575	1,668	899	950	1,453	0.98	52.95
EAST/MED EUR	**4,939**	**6,472**	**3,275**	**5,249**	**6,024**	**4.06**	**14.76**
ISRAEL	340	540	360	429	526	0.35	22.61
TURKEY	4,599	5,932	2,915	4,820	5,498	3.70	14.07
OTHER EUROPE	**1,924**	**2,167**	**1,493**	**1,502**	**2,608**	**1.76**	**73.64**
OTHER EUROPE	1,924	2,167	1,493	1,502	2,608	1.76	73.64
REG.NOT SPEC	**3,827**	**5,089**	**2,514**	**2,622**	**3,461**	**2.33**	**32.00**
NOT SPECIFIE	**3,827**	**5,089**	**2,514**	**2,622**	**3,461**	**2.33**	**32.00**
OTH.WORLD	3,827	5,089	2,514	2,622	3,461	2.33	32.00

Source: World Tourism Organization (WTO)

4. ARRIVALS OF NON-RESIDENT TOURISTS IN ALL TYPES OF ACCOMMODATION ESTABLISHMENTS, BY NATIONALITY

	1999	2000	2001	2002	2003	Market share 03	% change 03-02
TOTAL	**180,788**	**224,016**	**98,946**	**122,861**	**157,692**	**100.00**	**28.35**
AMERICAS	**15,526**	**17,023**	**7,846**	**7,773**	**8,373**	**5.31**	**7.72**
NORTH AMER	**15,526**	**17,023**	**7,846**	**7,773**	**8,373**	**5.31**	**7.72**
CANADA	1,626	1,711	747	776	970	0.62	25.00
USA	13,900	15,312	7,099	6,997	7,403	4.69	5.80
EAST AS/PACI	**2,440**	**2,803**	**1,082**	**1,566**	**2,362**	**1.50**	**50.83**
N/EAST ASIA	**1,301**	**1,025**	**419**	**594**	**1,076**	**0.68**	**81.14**
JAPAN	1,301	1,025	419	594	1,076	0.68	81.14
AUSTRALASIA	**1,139**	**1,778**	**663**	**972**	**1,286**	**0.82**	**32.30**
AUSTRALIA	967	1,578	586	844	1,187	0.75	40.64
NEW ZEALAND	172	200	77	128	99	0.06	-22.66
EUROPE	**158,754**	**198,298**	**87,396**	**110,878**	**143,387**	**90.93**	**29.32**
C/E EUROPE	**27,041**	**44,242**	**18,529**	**19,754**	**22,608**	**14.34**	**14.45**
BULGARIA	18,770	27,623	8,484	11,703	14,147	8.97	20.88
BELARUS	562	452	166	154	157	0.10	1.95
CZECH REP	715	1,032	560	927	1,155	0.73	24.60
HUNGARY	803	2,372	2,130	1,985	2,173	1.38	9.47
POLAND	779	1,134	725	1,095	1,029	0.65	-6.03
ROMANIA	910	1,759	1,101	1,255	1,330	0.84	5.98
RUSSIAN FED	3,366	3,078	1,647	1,246	1,352	0.86	8.51
SLOVAKIA	514	445	311	481	559	0.35	16.22
UKRAINE	622	6,347	3,405	908	706	0.45	-22.25
NORTHERN EUR	**16,625**	**15,582**	**8,127**	**8,204**	**9,585**	**6.08**	**16.83**
DENMARK	2,207	2,468	704	786	1,048	0.66	33.33
FINLAND	859	1,278	711	683	768	0.49	12.45
ICELAND	128	134	119	153	159	0.10	3.92
IRELAND	879	672	389	525	482	0.31	-8.19
NORWAY	1,921	2,304	885	1,059	1,108	0.70	4.63
SWEDEN	1,505	2,033	962	1,082	1,503	0.95	38.91
UK	9,126	6,693	4,357	3,916	4,517	2.86	15.35
SOUTHERN EUR	**77,767**	**99,536**	**43,745**	**61,047**	**84,632**	**53.67**	**38.63**
ALBANIA	21,248	24,747	6,419	9,086	12,088	7.67	33.04
BOSNIA HERZG	1,258	1,841	1,377	1,885	2,687	1.70	42.55
CROATIA	3,260	4,651	2,609	4,097	5,467	3.47	33.44
GREECE	10,152	21,304	10,637	14,677	27,042	17.15	84.25
ITALY	6,259	4,410	2,511	3,076	3,626	2.30	17.88
PORTUGAL	423	487	226	308	432	0.27	40.26
SLOVENIA	4,606	5,288	2,658	3,837	4,579	2.90	19.34
SPAIN	1,215	1,286	879	842	1,386	0.88	64.61
SERBIA,MTNEG	29,346	35,522	16,429	23,239	27,325	17.33	17.58
WESTERN EUR	**29,840**	**28,112**	**11,785**	**14,496**	**17,592**	**11.16**	**21.36**
AUSTRIA	2,098	2,559	1,300	1,919	2,564	1.63	33.61
BELGIUM	2,961	1,759	814	970	1,243	0.79	28.14
FRANCE	4,735	4,768	2,313	2,542	3,513	2.23	38.20
GERMANY	12,370	10,349	4,860	6,084	6,317	4.01	3.83

4. ARRIVALS OF NON-RESIDENT TOURISTS IN ALL TYPES OF ACCOMMODATION ESTABLISHMENTS, BY NATIONALITY

	1999	2000	2001	2002	2003	Market share 03	% change 03-02
NETHERLANDS	5,953	6,809	1,564	2,016	2,470	1.57	22.52
SWITZERLAND	1,723	1,868	934	965	1,485	0.94	53.89
EAST/MED EUR	**5,380**	**7,295**	**3,476**	**5,610**	**6,281**	**3.98**	**11.96**
ISRAEL	342	595	375	430	526	0.33	22.33
TURKEY	5,038	6,700	3,101	5,180	5,755	3.65	11.10
OTHER EUROPE	**2,101**	**3,531**	**1,734**	**1,767**	**2,689**	**1.71**	**52.18**
OTHER EUROPE	2,101	3,531	1,734	1,767	2,689	1.71	52.18
REG.NOT SPEC	**4,068**	**5,892**	**2,622**	**2,644**	**3,570**	**2.26**	**35.02**
NOT SPECIFIE	**4,068**	**5,892**	**2,622**	**2,644**	**3,570**	**2.26**	**35.02**
OTH.WORLD	4,068	5,892	2,622	2,644	3,570	2.26	35.02

Source: World Tourism Organization (WTO)

5. OVERNIGHT STAYS OF NON-RESIDENT TOURISTS IN HOTELS AND SIMILAR ESTABLISHMENTS, BY NATIONALITY

	1999	2000	2001	2002	2003	Market share 03	% change 03-02
TOTAL	**438,531**	**438,959**	**197,163**	**249,463**	**320,932**	**100.00**	**28.65**
AMERICAS	**58,518**	**42,003**	**19,446**	**20,866**	**21,957**	**6.84**	**5.23**
NORTH AMER	**58,518**	**42,003**	**19,446**	**20,866**	**21,957**	**6.84**	**5.23**
CANADA	4,891	3,186	1,546	1,752	2,142	0.67	22.26
USA	53,627	38,817	17,900	19,114	19,815	6.17	3.67
EAST AS/PACI	**6,228**	**5,861**	**2,608**	**3,481**	**5,014**	**1.56**	**44.04**
N/EAST ASIA	**3,337**	**2,044**	**959**	**1,209**	**2,187**	**0.68**	**80.89**
JAPAN	3,337	2,044	959	1,209	2,187	0.68	80.89
AUSTRALASIA	**2,891**	**3,817**	**1,649**	**2,272**	**2,827**	**0.88**	**24.43**
AUSTRALIA	2,526	3,404	1,452	1,993	2,663	0.83	33.62
NEW ZEALAND	365	413	197	279	164	0.05	-41.22
EUROPE	**363,152**	**379,050**	**169,781**	**218,368**	**284,192**	**88.55**	**30.14**
C/E EUROPE	**62,556**	**87,619**	**39,400**	**42,067**	**45,606**	**14.21**	**8.41**
BULGARIA	38,885	53,152	13,515	21,398	24,631	7.67	15.11
BELARUS	2,685	1,166	322	381	492	0.15	29.13
CZECH REP	1,906	3,004	1,587	2,673	3,157	0.98	18.11
HUNGARY	1,799	3,605	4,122	3,805	4,010	1.25	5.39
POLAND	1,882	2,629	2,284	3,336	3,407	1.06	2.13
ROMANIA	1,777	3,756	2,296	2,661	3,108	0.97	16.80
RUSSIAN FED	10,624	8,871	4,853	3,449	3,801	1.18	10.21
SLOVAKIA	931	687	566	1,783	1,267	0.39	-28.94
UKRAINE	2,067	10,749	9,855	2,581	1,733	0.54	-32.86
NORTHERN EUR	**44,023**	**30,315**	**19,760**	**18,346**	**21,775**	**6.78**	**18.69**
DENMARK	4,618	4,530	1,396	1,473	2,312	0.72	56.96
FINLAND	1,626	1,928	1,040	1,122	1,352	0.42	20.50
ICELAND	265	202	211	288	287	0.09	-0.35
IRELAND	2,447	1,055	954	1,618	1,105	0.34	-31.71
NORWAY	4,607	4,882	1,755	2,200	2,820	0.88	28.18
SWEDEN	3,403	3,854	2,095	2,404	3,294	1.03	37.02
UK	27,057	13,864	12,309	9,241	10,605	3.30	14.76
SOUTHERN EUR	**169,283**	**186,664**	**75,626**	**113,072**	**157,419**	**49.05**	**39.22**
ALBANIA	47,400	55,695	9,879	17,476	22,232	6.93	27.21
BOSNIA HERZG	2,382	3,215	2,226	3,752	5,050	1.57	34.59
CROATIA	6,964	9,114	4,871	8,005	10,278	3.20	28.39
GREECE	18,973	37,454	19,167	29,694	51,995	16.20	75.10
ITALY	34,623	9,030	5,595	6,620	7,928	2.47	19.76
PORTUGAL	906	772	411	620	888	0.28	43.23
SLOVENIA	8,130	10,192	4,450	6,883	8,431	2.63	22.49
SPAIN	3,198	2,302	1,567	1,506	2,536	0.79	68.39
SERBIA,MTNEG	46,707	58,890	27,460	38,516	48,081	14.98	24.83
WESTERN EUR	**70,558**	**53,467**	**25,798**	**31,848**	**43,039**	**13.41**	**35.14**
AUSTRIA	5,740	4,599	2,259	2,875	4,606	1.44	60.21
BELGIUM	4,250	3,108	1,571	1,795	2,613	0.81	45.57
FRANCE	12,248	7,688	4,984	5,906	9,848	3.07	66.75
GERMANY	34,869	23,927	11,371	14,509	15,829	4.93	9.10

5. OVERNIGHT STAYS OF NON-RESIDENT TOURISTS IN HOTELS AND SIMILAR ESTABLISHMENTS, BY NATIONALITY

	1999	2000	2001	2002	2003	Market share 03	% change 03-02
NETHERLANDS	9,590	10,890	3,796	4,791	6,590	2.05	37.55
SWITZERLAND	3,861	3,255	1,817	1,972	3,553	1.11	80.17
EAST/MED EUR	**9,995**	**15,423**	**6,136**	**10,176**	**11,742**	**3.66**	**15.39**
ISRAEL	843	1,365	676	829	1,176	0.37	41.86
TURKEY	9,152	14,058	5,460	9,347	10,566	3.29	13.04
OTHER EUROPE	**6,737**	**5,562**	**3,061**	**2,859**	**4,611**	**1.44**	**61.28**
OTHER EUROPE	6,737	5,562	3,061	2,859	4,611	1.44	61.28
REG.NOT SPEC	**10,633**	**12,045**	**5,328**	**6,748**	**9,769**	**3.04**	**44.77**
NOT SPECIFIE	**10,633**	**12,045**	**5,328**	**6,748**	**9,769**	**3.04**	**44.77**
OTH.WORLD	10,633	12,045	5,328	6,748	9,769	3.04	44.77

Source: World Tourism Organization (WTO)

THE FORMER YUGOSLAV REP. OF MACEDONIA

6. OVERNIGHT STAYS OF NON-RESIDENT TOURISTS IN ALL TYPES OF ACCOMMODATION ESTABLISHMENTS, BY NATIONALITY

	1999	2000	2001	2002	2003	Market share 03	% change 03-02
TOTAL	**474,394**	**493,867**	**212,751**	**274,720**	**346,200**	**100.00**	**26.02**
AMERICAS	**58,847**	**42,604**	**19,601**	**21,154**	**22,251**	**6.43**	**5.19**
NORTH AMER	**58,847**	**42,604**	**19,601**	**21,154**	**22,251**	**6.43**	**5.19**
CANADA	4,950	3,267	1,562	1,791	2,238	0.65	24.96
USA	53,897	39,337	18,039	19,363	20,013	5.78	3.36
EAST AS/PACI	**6,373**	**6,118**	**2,667**	**3,546**	**5,278**	**1.52**	**48.84**
N/EAST ASIA	**3,387**	**2,090**	**975**	**1,219**	**2,345**	**0.68**	**92.37**
JAPAN	3,387	2,090	975	1,219	2,345	0.68	92.37
AUSTRALASIA	**2,986**	**4,028**	**1,692**	**2,327**	**2,933**	**0.85**	**26.04**
AUSTRALIA	2,612	3,592	1,486	2,044	2,763	0.80	35.18
NEW ZEALAND	374	436	206	283	170	0.05	-39.93
EUROPE	**397,974**	**432,183**	**185,014**	**243,206**	**308,453**	**89.10**	**26.83**
C/E EUROPE	**69,179**	**96,409**	**44,185**	**45,901**	**50,136**	**14.48**	**9.23**
BULGARIA	43,849	59,027	17,177	24,413	28,772	8.31	17.86
BELARUS	2,686	1,208	328	382	493	0.14	29.06
CZECH REP	1,971	3,252	1,616	2,687	3,202	0.92	19.17
HUNGARY	1,972	3,835	4,154	3,825	4,014	1.16	4.94
POLAND	2,200	2,813	2,402	3,600	3,543	1.02	-1.58
ROMANIA	1,946	4,560	2,576	2,852	3,144	0.91	10.24
RUSSIAN FED	11,393	9,275	5,140	3,488	3,936	1.14	12.84
SLOVAKIA	959	754	577	1,783	1,272	0.37	-28.66
UKRAINE	2,203	11,685	10,215	2,871	1,760	0.51	-38.70
NORTHERN EUR	**44,713**	**31,489**	**20,008**	**18,469**	**22,295**	**6.44**	**20.72**
DENMARK	4,664	4,948	1,418	1,483	2,497	0.72	68.37
FINLAND	1,750	2,020	1,070	1,132	1,376	0.40	21.55
ICELAND	265	227	218	289	291	0.08	0.69
IRELAND	2,495	1,124	973	1,629	1,119	0.32	-31.31
NORWAY	4,792	5,104	1,790	2,220	2,832	0.82	27.57
SWEDEN	3,496	4,015	2,120	2,442	3,472	1.00	42.18
UK	27,251	14,051	12,419	9,274	10,708	3.09	15.46
SOUTHERN EUR	**191,887**	**221,121**	**83,369**	**130,894**	**174,262**	**50.34**	**33.13**
ALBANIA	54,907	65,141	11,510	20,665	24,095	6.96	16.60
BOSNIA HERZG	2,796	3,781	2,415	4,091	5,494	1.59	34.29
CROATIA	7,309	10,218	5,178	8,537	11,313	3.27	32.52
GREECE	20,441	39,229	19,867	30,730	53,447	15.44	73.92
ITALY	34,874	9,476	5,646	6,694	8,120	2.35	21.30
PORTUGAL	912	808	422	620	1,028	0.30	65.81
SLOVENIA	9,088	10,993	4,804	7,546	9,262	2.68	22.74
SPAIN	3,291	2,388	1,581	1,515	2,704	0.78	78.48
SERBIA,MTNEG	58,269	79,087	31,946	50,496	58,799	16.98	16.44
WESTERN EUR	**72,797**	**56,275**	**26,899**	**33,272**	**44,424**	**12.83**	**33.52**
AUSTRIA	6,019	5,169	2,883	3,715	4,704	1.36	26.62
BELGIUM	4,304	3,202	1,606	1,850	2,746	0.79	48.43
FRANCE	12,393	7,887	5,051	5,986	10,115	2.92	68.98
GERMANY	36,243	25,222	11,598	14,849	16,390	4.73	10.38

6. OVERNIGHT STAYS OF NON-RESIDENT TOURISTS IN ALL TYPES OF ACCOMMODATION ESTABLISHMENTS, BY NATIONALITY

	1999	2000	2001	2002	2003	Market share 03	% change 03-02
NETHERLANDS	9,800	11,159	3,864	4,876	6,874	1.99	40.98
SWITZERLAND	4,038	3,636	1,897	1,996	3,595	1.04	80.11
EAST/MED EUR	**12,272**	**18,481**	**6,794**	**11,445**	**12,426**	**3.59**	**8.57**
ISRAEL	851	1,444	691	830	1,176	0.34	41.69
TURKEY	11,421	17,037	6,103	10,615	11,250	3.25	5.98
OTHER EUROPE	**7,126**	**8,408**	**3,759**	**3,225**	**4,910**	**1.42**	**52.25**
OTHER EUROPE	7,126	8,408	3,759	3,225	4,910	1.42	52.25
REG.NOT SPEC	**11,200**	**12,962**	**5,469**	**6,814**	**10,218**	**2.95**	**49.96**
NOT SPECIFIE	**11,200**	**12,962**	**5,469**	**6,814**	**10,218**	**2.95**	**49.96**
OTH.WORLD	11,200	12,962	5,469	6,814	10,218	2.95	49.96

Source: World Tourism Organization (WTO)

TOGO

3. ARRIVALS OF NON-RESIDENT TOURISTS IN HOTELS AND SIMILAR ESTABLISHMENTS, BY COUNTRY OF RESIDENCE

	1999	2000	2001	2002	2003	Market share 03	% change 03-02
TOTAL	**69,818**	**59,541**	**56,629**	**57,539**	**60,592**	**100.00**	**5.31**
AFRICA	**41,268**	**29,546**	**33,554**	**28,636**	**31,334**	**51.71**	**9.42**
WEST AFRICA	**30,479**	**18,167**	**24,998**	**20,104**	**19,935**	**32.90**	**-0.84**
BENIN	7,743	4,964	6,521	5,371	5,111	8.44	-4.84
GHANA	2,927	1,530	2,167	1,755	1,585	2.62	-9.69
COTE IVOIRE	4,795	2,415	3,438	3,071	4,134	6.82	34.61
NIGERIA	5,201	3,179	4,976	3,919	3,152	5.20	-19.57
BURKINA FASO (*)	9,813	6,079	7,896	5,988	5,953	9.82	-0.58
OTHER AFRICA	**10,789**	**11,379**	**8,556**	**8,532**	**11,399**	**18.81**	**33.60**
OTHER AFRICA	10,789	11,379	8,556	8,532	11,399	18.81	33.60
AMERICAS	**3,339**	**2,050**	**2,343**	**1,975**	**1,785**	**2.95**	**-9.62**
NORTH AMER	**3,073**	**1,937**	**2,016**	**1,895**	**1,699**	**2.80**	**-10.34**
CANADA	718	249	424	269	315	0.52	17.10
USA	2,355	1,688	1,592	1,626	1,384	2.28	-14.88
OTHER AMERIC	**266**	**113**	**327**	**80**	**86**	**0.14**	**7.50**
OTH AMERICA	266	113	327	80	86	0.14	7.50
EAST AS/PACI	**1,453**	**1,271**	**1,311**	**1,125**	**1,452**	**2.40**	**29.07**
N/EAST ASIA	**177**	**104**	**119**	**47**	**60**	**0.10**	**27.66**
JAPAN	177	104	119	47	60	0.10	27.66
OT.EAST AS/P	**1,276**	**1,167**	**1,192**	**1,078**	**1,392**	**2.30**	**29.13**
OTHER ASIA	1,276	1,167	1,192	1,078	1,392	2.30	29.13
EUROPE	**21,336**	**25,376**	**17,680**	**24,097**	**24,484**	**40.41**	**1.61**
C/E EUROPE	**225**	**87**	**154**	**147**	**79**	**0.13**	**-46.26**
USSR(former)	225	87	154	147	79	0.13	-46.26
NORTHERN EUR	**4,140**	**477**	**391**	**554**	**679**	**1.12**	**22.56**
UK	3,970	414	352	526	655	1.08	24.52
SCANDINAVIA	170	63	39	28	24	0.04	-14.29
SOUTHERN EUR	**1,064**	**524**	**351**	**527**	**570**	**0.94**	**8.16**
ITALY	1,064	524	351	527	570	0.94	8.16
WESTERN EUR	**13,756**	**12,626**	**10,598**	**15,048**	**15,767**	**26.02**	**4.78**
FRANCE	9,834	9,690	8,480	12,764	14,154	23.36	10.89
GERMANY	2,088	1,391	1,107	991	830	1.37	-16.25
SWITZERLAND	582	418	351	393	274	0.45	-30.28
BENELUX	1,252	1,127	660	900	509	0.84	-43.44
OTHER EUROPE	**2,151**	**11,662**	**6,186**	**7,821**	**7,389**	**12.19**	**-5.52**
OTHER EUROPE	2,151	11,662	6,186	7,821	7,389	12.19	-5.52
MIDDLE EAST	**2,344**	**1,203**	**1,619**	**1,680**	**1,495**	**2.47**	**-11.01**
MIDDLE EAST	**2,344**	**1,203**	**1,619**	**1,680**	**1,495**	**2.47**	**-11.01**
ALL MID EAST	2,344	1,203	1,619	1,680	1,495	2.47	-11.01

TOGO

3. ARRIVALS OF NON-RESIDENT TOURISTS IN HOTELS AND SIMILAR ESTABLISHMENTS, BY COUNTRY OF RESIDENCE

	1999	2000	2001	2002	2003	Market share 03	% change 03-02
REG.NOT SPEC	**78**	**95**	**122**	**26**	**42**	**0.07**	**61.54**
NOT SPECIFIE	**78**	**95**	**122**	**26**	**42**	**0.07**	**61.54**
OTH.WORLD	78	95	122	26	42	0.07	61.54

Source: World Tourism Organization (WTO)

TOGO

5. OVERNIGHT STAYS OF NON-RESIDENT TOURISTS IN HOTELS AND SIMILAR ESTABLISHMENTS, BY COUNTRY OF RESIDENCE

	1999	2000	2001	2002	2003	Market share 03	% change 03-02
TOTAL	**162,233**	**132,211**	**120,744**	**117,079**	**136,422**	**100.00**	**16.52**
AFRICA	**91,057**	**69,262**	**71,986**	**70,154**	**70,552**	**51.72**	**0.57**
WEST AFRICA	**64,087**	**38,715**	**49,973**	**47,357**	**42,551**	**31.19**	**-10.15**
BENIN	12,626	8,475	9,490	9,122	8,293	6.08	-9.09
GHANA	6,692	3,055	2,934	4,026	3,181	2.33	-20.99
COTE IVOIRE	11,497	6,249	7,390	9,561	11,373	8.34	18.95
NIGERIA	10,017	6,302	8,668	7,983	5,961	4.37	-25.33
BURKINA FASO (*)	23,255	14,634	21,491	16,665	13,743	10.07	-17.53
OTHER AFRICA	**26,970**	**30,547**	**22,013**	**22,797**	**28,001**	**20.53**	**22.83**
OTHER AFRICA	26,970	30,547	22,013	22,797	28,001	20.53	22.83
AMERICAS	**8,893**	**6,172**	**6,326**	**4,689**	**6,024**	**4.42**	**28.47**
NORTH AMER	**8,086**	**5,865**	**5,337**	**4,359**	**4,755**	**3.49**	**9.08**
CANADA	2,541	777	1,612	724	1,015	0.74	40.19
USA	5,545	5,088	3,725	3,635	3,740	2.74	2.89
OTHER AMERIC	**807**	**307**	**989**	**330**	**1,269**	**0.93**	**284.55**
OTH AMERICA	807	307	989	330	1,269	0.93	284.55
EAST AS/PACI	**3,774**	**2,507**	**2,935**	**2,363**	**3,072**	**2.25**	**30.00**
N/EAST ASIA	**1,402**	**231**	**589**	**230**	**263**	**0.19**	**14.35**
JAPAN	1,402	231	589	230	263	0.19	14.35
OT.EAST AS/P	**2,372**	**2,276**	**2,346**	**2,133**	**2,809**	**2.06**	**31.69**
OTHER ASIA	2,372	2,276	2,346	2,133	2,809	2.06	31.69
EUROPE	**54,121**	**52,372**	**36,677**	**37,600**	**54,700**	**40.10**	**45.48**
C/E EUROPE	**729**	**168**	**442**	**236**	**373**	**0.27**	**58.05**
USSR(former)	729	168	442	236	373	0.27	58.05
NORTHERN EUR	**9,564**	**1,168**	**715**	**1,072**	**2,122**	**1.56**	**97.95**
UK	9,042	996	661	1,009	2,114	1.55	109.51
SCANDINAVIA	522	172	54	63	8	0.01	-87.30
SOUTHERN EUR	**4,015**	**1,259**	**1,037**	**1,386**	**1,538**	**1.13**	**10.97**
ITALY	4,015	1,259	1,037	1,386	1,538	1.13	10.97
WESTERN EUR	**34,536**	**26,441**	**24,019**	**21,691**	**33,141**	**24.29**	**52.79**
FRANCE	22,594	18,754	18,116	16,268	27,765	20.35	70.67
GERMANY	5,736	3,281	2,680	2,155	2,199	1.61	2.04
SWITZERLAND	2,215	1,422	1,031	962	1,350	0.99	40.33
BENELUX	3,991	2,984	2,192	2,306	1,827	1.34	-20.77
OTHER EUROPE	**5,277**	**23,336**	**10,464**	**13,215**	**17,526**	**12.85**	**32.62**
OTHER EUROPE	5,277	23,336	10,464	13,215	17,526	12.85	32.62
MIDDLE EAST	**4,176**	**1,672**	**2,664**	**2,177**	**1,779**	**1.30**	**-18.28**
MIDDLE EAST	**4,176**	**1,672**	**2,664**	**2,177**	**1,779**	**1.30**	**-18.28**
ALL MID EAST	4,176	1,672	2,664	2,177	1,779	1.30	-18.28

5. OVERNIGHT STAYS OF NON-RESIDENT TOURISTS IN HOTELS AND SIMILAR ESTABLISHMENTS, BY COUNTRY OF RESIDENCE

	1999	2000	2001	2002	2003	Market share 03	% change 03-02
REG.NOT SPEC	**212**	**226**	**156**	**96**	**295**	**0.22**	**207.29**
NOT SPECIFIE	**212**	**226**	**156**	**96**	**295**	**0.22**	**207.29**
OTH.WORLD	212	226	156	96	295	0.22	207.29

Source: World Tourism Organization (WTO)

TONGA

1. ARRIVALS OF NON-RESIDENT TOURISTS AT NATIONAL BORDERS, BY COUNTRY OF RESIDENCE

	1999	2000	2001	2002	2003	Market share 03	% change 03-02
TOTAL (*)	**30,949**	**34,694**	**32,386**	**36,588**	**40,110**	**100.00**	**9.63**
AFRICA	**67**	**53**	**55**	**92**			
SOUTHERN AFR	**46**	**43**	**30**	**59**			
SOUTH AFRICA	46	43	30	59			
OTHER AFRICA	**21**	**10**	**25**	**33**			
OTHER AFRICA	21	10	25	33			
AMERICAS	**6,153**	**8,005**	**6,706**	**7,860**	**7,930**	**19.77**	**0.89**
NORTH AMER	**6,113**	**7,980**	**6,672**	**7,801**	**7,930**	**19.77**	**1.65**
CANADA	326	359	370	328	365	0.91	11.28
USA	5,787	7,621	6,302	7,473	7,565	18.86	1.23
OTHER AMERIC	**40**	**25**	**34**	**59**			
OTH AMERICA	40	25	34	59			
EAST AS/PACI	**19,790**	**20,557**	**20,920**	**24,477**	**27,932**	**69.64**	**14.12**
N/EAST ASIA	**1,141**	**1,263**	**1,283**	**1,254**	**790**	**1.97**	**-37.00**
TAIWAN(P.C.)	319	468	269	414			
HK,CHINA	26	11	182	44			
JAPAN	796	784	832	796	790	1.97	-0.75
AUSTRALASIA	**15,520**	**16,126**	**16,480**	**19,199**	**22,954**	**57.23**	**19.56**
AUSTRALIA	5,746	5,662	5,416	6,261	8,272	20.62	32.12
NEW ZEALAND	9,774	10,464	11,064	12,938	14,682	36.60	13.48
MELANESIA	**1,642**	**1,782**	**1,696**	**2,112**	**2,012**	**5.02**	**-4.73**
FIJI	1,642	1,782	1,696	2,112	2,012	5.02	-4.73
POLYNESIA	**676**	**573**	**681**	**898**			
AMER SAMOA	80	46	24	114			
SAMOA	596	527	657	784			
OT.EAST AS/P	**811**	**813**	**780**	**1,014**	**2,176**	**5.43**	**114.60**
OTHER ASIA	345	323	311	352	765	1.91	117.33
OTH OCEANIA	466	490	469	662	1,411	3.52	113.14
EUROPE	**4,855**	**5,977**	**4,601**	**4,082**	**4,131**	**10.30**	**1.20**
NORTHERN EUR	**1,766**	**2,356**	**1,712**	**1,303**	**1,385**	**3.45**	**6.29**
SWEDEN	376	387	328	212			
UK	1,390	1,969	1,384	1,091	1,385	3.45	26.95
SOUTHERN EUR	**479**	**540**	**350**	**322**			
ITALY	479	540	350	322			
WESTERN EUR	**1,845**	**2,041**	**1,758**	**1,723**	**979**	**2.44**	**-43.18**
AUSTRIA	122	176	126	137			
FRANCE	359	254	217	271			
GERMANY	1,189	1,349	1,273	1,188	979	2.44	-17.59
SWITZERLAND	175	262	142	127			
OTHER EUROPE	**765**	**1,040**	**781**	**734**	**1,767**	**4.41**	**140.74**
OTHER EUROPE	765	1,040	781	734	1,767	4.41	140.74

TONGA

1. ARRIVALS OF NON-RESIDENT TOURISTS AT NATIONAL BORDERS, BY COUNTRY OF RESIDENCE

	1999	2000	2001	2002	2003	Market share 03	% change 03-02
SOUTH ASIA	**84**	**102**	**104**	**77**			
SOUTH ASIA	**84**	**102**	**104**	**77**			
INDIA	84	102	104	77			
REG.NOT SPEC					**117**	**0.29**	
NOT SPECIFIE					**117**	**0.29**	
OTH.WORLD					117	0.29	

Source: World Tourism Organization (WTO)

TRINIDAD AND TOBAGO

1. ARRIVALS OF NON-RESIDENT TOURISTS AT NATIONAL BORDERS, BY COUNTRY OF RESIDENCE

	1999	2000	2001	2002	2003	Market share 03	% change 03-02
TOTAL (*)	**358,220**	**398,559**	**383,101**	**384,212**	**409,069**	**100.00**	**6.47**
AFRICA	**904**	**996**	**935**	**997**	**935**	**0.23**	**-6.22**
EAST AFRICA	**83**	**91**	**105**	**178**	**141**	**0.03**	**-20.79**
BR.IND.OC.TR				4			
BURUNDI	1	1			3		
COMOROS					2		
ETHIOPIA	1	1		4	4		
ERITREA				1			
DJIBOUTI				3			
KENYA	20	10	12	49	41	0.01	-16.33
MADAGASCAR				3			
MALAWI		15	17	3	3		
MAURITIUS	6	15	20	11	9		-18.18
MOZAMBIQUE				2	2		
REUNION				1			
RWANDA				3	4		33.33
SEYCHELLES	10	6	7	7	2		-71.43
SOMALIA	10	4	5				
ZIMBABWE	9	25	29	38	15		-60.53
UGANDA		1		15	9		-40.00
TANZANIA		2	2	16	22	0.01	37.50
ZAMBIA	26	11	13	18	25	0.01	38.89
CENTRAL AFR	**12**	**15**	**17**	**27**	**37**	**0.01**	**37.04**
ANGOLA	10			2	3		50.00
CAMEROON		1	3	13	3		-76.92
CENT.AFR.REP					3		
CHAD				1			
CONGO		2		4	7		75.00
DEM.R.CONGO				2			
EQ.GUINEA				2	18		800.00
GABON	2			1	3		200.00
SAO TOME PRN		12	14	2			
NORTH AFRICA	**22**	**24**	**36**	**26**	**17**		**-34.62**
ALGERIA	1	1	1	7	2		-71.43
MOROCCO	20	22	33	6	4		-33.33
SUDAN	1	1	1	7	3		-57.14
TUNISIA			1	6	8		33.33
SOUTHERN AFR	**400**	**440**	**396**	**386**	**373**	**0.09**	**-3.37**
BOTSWANA	63	69	62	67	112	0.03	67.16
LESOTHO		1		1	1		
NAMIBIA	21	23	21	3	3		
SOUTH AFRICA	293	322	291	303	249	0.06	-17.82
SWAZILAND	23	25	22	12	8		-33.33
WEST AFRICA	**387**	**426**	**381**	**380**	**367**	**0.09**	**-3.42**
CAPE VERDE	20	22	20		3		
BENIN				1			
GAMBIA	12	13	12	8	4		-50.00
GHANA	90	99	89	37	44	0.01	18.92
GUINEA				5	13		160.00
COTE IVOIRE	3	3		1	2		100.00
LIBERIA		2		4			

TRINIDAD AND TOBAGO

1. ARRIVALS OF NON-RESIDENT TOURISTS AT NATIONAL BORDERS, BY COUNTRY OF RESIDENCE

	1999	2000	2001	2002	2003	Market share 03	% change 03-02
MALI				1			
MAURITANIA		20	18	2	8		300.00
NIGER	3	3		4	1		-75.00
NIGERIA	218	220	204	300	258	0.06	-14.00
GUINEABISSAU				2			
ST.HELENA				2	1		-50.00
SENEGAL	41	43	38	2	24	0.01	1,100.00
SIERRA LEONE		1		9	7		-22.22
TOGO				2	1		-50.00
BURKINA FASO					1		
AMERICAS	**277,819**	**309,122**	**285,882**	**308,018**	**324,175**	**79.25**	**5.25**
CARIBBEAN	**78,669**	**87,543**	**84,058**	**91,792**	**100,690**	**24.61**	**9.69**
ANTIGUA,BARB	2,728	3,249	3,110	4,233	4,334	1.06	2.39
BAHAMAS	782	927	840	1,179	1,343	0.33	13.91
BARBADOS	28,694	31,126	27,878	33,989	37,320	9.12	9.80
BERMUDA	479	620	783	522	575	0.14	10.15
BR.VIRGIN IS	438	561	882	981	960	0.23	-2.14
CAYMAN IS	488	622	786	464	556	0.14	19.83
CUBA	133	173	219	231	227	0.06	-1.73
DOMINICA	1,035	1,096	1,344	1,277	1,535	0.38	20.20
DOMINICAN RP	397	376	546	525	574	0.14	9.33
GRENADA	14,050	15,492	15,130	16,539	19,220	4.70	16.21
GUADELOUPE	734	879	756	668	712	0.17	6.59
HAITI	326	279	353	174	184	0.04	5.75
JAMAICA	4,828	6,255	5,968	6,044	6,186	1.51	2.35
MARTINIQUE	1,350	1,452	1,428	1,005	1,076	0.26	7.06
MONTSERRAT	166	245	310	209	220	0.05	5.26
NETH.ANTILES	1,737	2,062	2,101	563	466	0.11	-17.23
ARUBA	370	428	541	403	437	0.11	8.44
CURACAO				1,003	1,060	0.26	5.68
PUERTO RICO	1,342	1,797	1,428	1,479	1,616	0.40	9.26
ST.KITTS NEV	1,007	1,199	1,092	1,280	1,438	0.35	12.34
ANGUILLA	293	321	406	330	254	0.06	-23.03
ST.LUCIA	6,740	7,374	7,228	6,892	7,423	1.81	7.70
ST.VINCENT,G	8,000	8,265	8,405	9,636	11,041	2.70	14.58
TURKS,CAICOS	94	135	171	127	143	0.03	12.60
US.VIRGIN IS	2,458	2,610	2,353	2,039	1,790	0.44	-12.21
CENTRAL AMER	**1,088**	**1,206**	**1,267**	**1,433**	**1,592**	**0.39**	**11.10**
BELIZE	246	248	260	280	360	0.09	28.57
COSTA RICA	232	330	347	403	516	0.13	28.04
EL SALVADOR	62	45	47	64	37	0.01	-42.19
GUATEMALA	110	133	140	113	115	0.03	1.77
HONDURAS	28	29	30	104	98	0.02	-5.77
NICARAGUA	23	14	15	18	21	0.01	16.67
PANAMA	387	407	428	451	445	0.11	-1.33
NORTH AMER	**162,317**	**180,589**	**162,827**	**175,873**	**182,677**	**44.66**	**3.87**
CANADA	43,459	47,382	43,291	41,506	43,036	10.52	3.69
GREENLAND				1			
MEXICO	468	629	574	801	703	0.17	-12.23
ST.PIERRE,MQ					3		
USA	118,390	132,578	118,962	133,565	138,935	33.96	4.02
SOUTH AMER	**35,745**	**39,784**	**37,730**	**38,920**	**39,216**	**9.59**	**0.76**

TRINIDAD AND TOBAGO

1. ARRIVALS OF NON-RESIDENT TOURISTS AT NATIONAL BORDERS, BY COUNTRY OF RESIDENCE

	1999	2000	2001	2002	2003	Market share 03	% change 03-02
ARGENTINA	308	352	769	437	429	0.10	-1.83
BOLIVIA	21	19	34	42	70	0.02	66.67
BRAZIL	604	749	1,198	974	836	0.20	-14.17
CHILE	122	119	203	103	188	0.05	82.52
COLOMBIA	808	777	1,278	923	1,353	0.33	46.59
ECUADOR	45	56	145	109	116	0.03	6.42
FALKLAND IS				1	3		200.00
FR.GUIANA	86	183	311	433	536	0.13	23.79
GUYANA	21,607	23,686	20,062	22,299	22,783	5.57	2.17
PARAGUAY	10	6	45	7	8		14.29
PERU	34	127	182	88	187	0.05	112.50
SURINAME	1,906	2,212	3,181	2,344	2,354	0.58	0.43
URUGUAY	12	48	115	53	80	0.02	50.94
VENEZUELA	10,182	11,450	10,207	11,107	10,273	2.51	-7.51
EAST AS/PACI	**3,141**	**3,507**	**3,874**	**2,670**	**3,313**	**0.81**	**24.08**
N/EAST ASIA	**1,184**	**1,322**	**1,675**	**1,123**	**1,170**	**0.29**	**4.19**
CHINA	289	303	384	278	377	0.09	35.61
TAIWAN(P.C.)	75	116	147	109	66	0.02	-39.45
HK,CHINA	65	140	177	70	81	0.02	15.71
JAPAN	669	712	902	578	599	0.15	3.63
KOREA D P RP	10	18	23	31	13		-58.06
KOREA REP.	76	33	42	56	29	0.01	-48.21
MACAU, CHINA				1	1		
MONGOLIA					4		
S/EAST ASIA	**313**	**349**	**351**	**496**	**418**	**0.10**	**-15.73**
MYANMAR				15	23	0.01	53.33
CAMBODIA				1	3		200.00
INDONESIA	22	15	13	43	67	0.02	55.81
MALAYSIA	85	116	119	111	95	0.02	-14.41
PHILIPPINES	23	39	41	163	110	0.03	-32.52
SINGAPORE	117	114	116	102	93	0.02	-8.82
VIET NAM	3	3	2	5	3		-40.00
THAILAND	63	62	60	56	24	0.01	-57.14
AUSTRALASIA	**1,580**	**1,764**	**1,813**	**1,005**	**1,679**	**0.41**	**67.06**
AUSTRALIA	1,313	1,469	1,510	799	1,516	0.37	89.74
NEW ZEALAND	267	295	303	206	163	0.04	-20.87
MELANESIA	**42**	**47**	**35**	**16**	**14**		**-12.50**
SOLOMON IS	10	9	7	2	7		250.00
FIJI	21	28	21	8	5		-37.50
NEW CALEDNIA	11	10	7	1			
VANUATU				1	2		100.00
NORFOLK IS				2			
PAPUA N.GUIN				2			
MICRONESIA	**2**	**3**		**25**	**19**		**-24.00**
GUAM	2	3		1			
NAURU				20	12		-40.00
N.MARIANA IS				1	6		500.00
MARSHALL IS				1			
WAKE IS				2	1		-50.00
POLYNESIA	**20**	**22**		**5**	**13**		**160.00**
AMER SAMOA				1			

TRINIDAD AND TOBAGO

1. ARRIVALS OF NON-RESIDENT TOURISTS AT NATIONAL BORDERS, BY COUNTRY OF RESIDENCE

	1999	2000	2001	2002	2003	Market share 03	% change 03-02
COOK IS	10	11					
FR.POLYNESIA				3	2		-33.33
NIUE					1		
PITCAIRN					1		
TONGA	10	11					
TUVALU					1		
WALLIS FUT.I				1	4		300.00
SAMOA					4		
EUROPE	**74,260**	**82,661**	**89,002**	**71,133**	**79,236**	**19.37**	**11.39**
C/E EUROPE	**176**	**198**	**244**	**326**	**432**	**0.11**	**32.52**
AZERBAIJAN				6	9		50.00
ARMENIA				3	1		-66.67
BULGARIA	5	22	27	5	6		20.00
BELARUS				6	4		-33.33
CZECH RP/SVK	32	35	43	11	2		-81.82
CZECH REP				19	60	0.01	215.79
ESTONIA		11	14	9	4		-55.56
GEORGIA	10	1			3		
HUNGARY	45	8	10	30	38	0.01	26.67
KAZAKHSTAN				12	5		-58.33
KYRGYZSTAN					2		
LATVIA	16	3	4	19	49	0.01	157.89
LITHUANIA	14	18	22	16	12		-25.00
REP MOLDOVA				1			
POLAND	28	50	63	75	79	0.02	5.33
ROMANIA	14	4	5	20	16		-20.00
RUSSIAN FED	11	36	44	43	79	0.02	83.72
SLOVAKIA				8	11		37.50
TAJIKISTAN				3	6		100.00
TURKMENISTAN					2		
UKRAINE	1	10	12	21	10		-52.38
UZBEKISTAN				19	34	0.01	78.95
NORTHERN EUR	**54,685**	**60,872**	**59,984**	**56,115**	**61,840**	**15.12**	**10.20**
DENMARK	787	978	1,713	803	811	0.20	1.00
FAEROE IS				2	1		-50.00
FINLAND	202	198	373	194	141	0.03	-27.32
ICELAND	5	6	8	7	14		100.00
IRELAND	916	1,049	1,517	1,059	1,103	0.27	4.15
NORWAY	1,113	1,464	2,563	1,155	1,019	0.25	-11.77
SWEDEN	2,169	2,107	5,015	1,187	1,167	0.29	-1.68
UK	49,480	55,048	48,570	51,688	57,566	14.07	11.37
ISLE OF MAN	13	22	225	20	18		-10.00
SOUTHERN EUR	**2,107**	**2,348**	**4,221**	**1,977**	**1,812**	**0.44**	**-8.35**
ALBANIA	24	13	23	6	6		
ANDORRA		2		2	4		100.00
BOSNIA HERZG				2			
CROATIA				34	19		-44.12
GIBRALTAR		1	8	1	2		100.00
GREECE	28	66	119	51	45	0.01	-11.76
HOLY SEE					1		
ITALY	1,489	1,654	2,973	1,099	1,028	0.25	-6.46
MALTA	56	49	88	36	12		-66.67
PORTUGAL	101	103	185	82	129	0.03	57.32

TRINIDAD AND TOBAGO

1. ARRIVALS OF NON-RESIDENT TOURISTS AT NATIONAL BORDERS, BY COUNTRY OF RESIDENCE

	1999	2000	2001	2002	2003	Market share 03	% change 03-02
SAN MARINO		1		1			
SLOVENIA				9	12		33.33
SPAIN	391	441	793	640	543	0.13	-15.16
SERBIA,MTNEG	18	18	32	14	11		-21.43
WESTERN EUR	**17,098**	**19,028**	**24,324**	**12,504**	**14,966**	**3.66**	**19.69**
AUSTRIA	868	1,009	1,610	546	850	0.21	55.68
BELGIUM	416	414	720	441	401	0.10	-9.07
FRANCE	1,983	2,132	3,392	2,194	2,203	0.54	0.41
GERMANY	10,306	11,266	11,371	5,659	7,491	1.83	32.37
LIECHTENSTEN				2	4		100.00
LUXEMBOURG	20	32	48	22	11		-50.00
MONACO	16	11	17	19	9		-52.63
NETHERLANDS	2,283	2,618	3,990	2,591	2,817	0.69	8.72
SWITZERLAND	1,206	1,546	3,176	1,030	1,180	0.29	14.56
EAST/MED EUR	**194**	**215**	**229**	**211**	**186**	**0.05**	**-11.85**
CYPRUS	22	19	18	15	33	0.01	120.00
ISRAEL	143	171	184	165	135	0.03	-18.18
TURKEY	29	25	27	31	18		-41.94
MIDDLE EAST	**267**	**279**	**262**	**219**	**239**	**0.06**	**9.13**
MIDDLE EAST	**267**	**279**	**262**	**219**	**239**	**0.06**	**9.13**
BAHRAIN		20	19	1	4		300.00
IRAQ				2	3		50.00
JORDAN				4	16		300.00
KUWAIT	8	9	8	9	13		44.44
LEBANON	45	21	20	8	9		12.50
LIBYA	10	7	6	2	4		100.00
OMAN	1	1		13	11		-15.38
QATAR		10	9	11	16		45.45
SAUDI ARABIA	73	57	55	56	46	0.01	-17.86
SYRIA	19	51	48	41	38	0.01	-7.32
UNTD ARAB EM	57	48	45	25	29	0.01	16.00
EGYPT	54	55	52	47	49	0.01	4.26
YEMEN					1		
SOUTH ASIA	**1,093**	**1,196**	**1,492**	**1,164**	**1,136**	**0.28**	**-2.41**
SOUTH ASIA	**1,093**	**1,196**	**1,492**	**1,164**	**1,136**	**0.28**	**-2.41**
AFGHANISTAN				14	13		-7.14
BANGLADESH	3	171	213	30	49	0.01	63.33
SRI LANKA	54	26	32	27	40	0.01	48.15
INDIA	908	818	1,022	962	931	0.23	-3.22
IRAN	40	22	27	24	30	0.01	25.00
NEPAL				8	2		-75.00
PAKISTAN	88	159	198	99	71	0.02	-28.28
REG.NOT SPEC	**736**	**798**	**1,654**	**11**	**35**	**0.01**	**218.18**
NOT SPECIFIE	**736**	**798**	**1,654**	**11**	**35**	**0.01**	**218.18**
OTH.WORLD	736	798	1,654	11	35	0.01	218.18

Source: World Tourism Organization (WTO)

TUNISIA

1. ARRIVALS OF NON-RESIDENT TOURISTS AT NATIONAL BORDERS, BY NATIONALITY

	1999	2000	2001	2002	2003	Market share 03	% change 03-02
TOTAL (*)	**4,831,658**	**5,057,513**	**5,387,300**	**5,063,538**	**5,114,303**	**100.00**	**1.00**
AFRICA	**671,501**	**666,199**	**676,236**	**786,053**	**871,560**	**17.04**	**10.88**
NORTH AFRICA	**654,746**	**649,696**	**659,260**	**767,784**	**846,466**	**16.55**	**10.25**
ALGERIA	616,447	611,620	623,337	728,309	811,463	15.87	11.42
MOROCCO	37,785	37,689	35,525	38,865	35,003	0.68	-9.94
SUDAN	514	387	398	610			
WEST AFRICA	**5,382**	**5,558**	**5,394**	**5,788**	**6,962**	**0.14**	**20.28**
MAURITANIA	5,382	5,558	5,394	5,788	6,962	0.14	20.28
OTHER AFRICA	**11,373**	**10,945**	**11,582**	**12,481**	**18,132**	**0.35**	**45.28**
OTHER AFRICA	11,373	10,945	11,582	12,481	18,132	0.35	45.28
AMERICAS	**27,050**	**31,275**	**28,486**	**21,920**	**22,192**	**0.43**	**1.24**
NORTH AMER	**27,050**	**31,275**	**28,486**	**21,920**	**22,192**	**0.43**	**1.24**
CANADA	13,423	14,902	14,378	10,339	11,913	0.23	15.22
USA	13,627	16,373	14,108	11,581	10,279	0.20	-11.24
EAST AS/PACI	**9,314**	**8,343**	**7,804**	**7,167**	**6,833**	**0.13**	**-4.66**
N/EAST ASIA	**9,314**	**8,343**	**7,804**	**7,167**	**6,833**	**0.13**	**-4.66**
JAPAN	9,314	8,343	7,804	7,167	6,833	0.13	-4.66
EUROPE	**3,460,857**	**3,615,793**	**3,609,526**	**2,918,526**	**2,840,307**	**55.54**	**-2.68**
C/E EUROPE	**211,336**	**186,004**	**196,710**	**195,113**	**305,734**	**5.98**	**56.70**
BULGARIA	3,180	2,141	1,532	1,728	1,791	0.04	3.65
CZECH REP	59,733	54,762	57,186	58,813	90,038	1.76	53.09
HUNGARY	23,281	33,445	30,782	30,468	55,532	1.09	82.26
POLAND	77,135	49,837	53,901	36,720	54,443	1.06	48.27
ROMANIA	7,247	6,428	6,411	4,133	8,656	0.17	109.44
RUSSIAN FED	22,067	20,979	27,198	47,207	73,376	1.43	55.43
SLOVAKIA	18,693	18,412	19,700	16,044	21,898	0.43	36.49
NORTHERN EUR	**349,673**	**408,115**	**421,262**	**354,648**	**316,283**	**6.18**	**-10.82**
DENMARK	20,623	19,574	16,503	9,392			
FINLAND	17,509	18,257	12,859	12,759			
IRELAND	23,097	32,945	29,631	30,320	22,713	0.44	-25.09
NORWAY	10,368	13,312	19,112	23,703			
SWEDEN	16,199	24,651	28,416	20,675			
UK	261,877	299,376	314,741	257,799	223,189	4.36	-13.43
SCANDINAVIA					70,381	1.38	
SOUTHERN EUR	**483,217**	**540,537**	**531,632**	**498,169**	**523,304**	**10.23**	**5.05**
GREECE	12,042	11,332	9,410	8,086	8,381	0.16	3.65
ITALY	354,616	393,891	398,349	375,160	379,773	7.43	1.23
MALTA	7,868	7,832	6,189	8,288	14,311	0.28	72.67
PORTUGAL	12,993	17,668	22,591	24,912	28,197	0.55	13.19
SPAIN	86,857	102,828	87,441	74,325	78,223	1.53	5.24
YUGOSLAV SFR	8,841	6,986	7,652	7,398	14,419	0.28	94.90
WESTERN EUR	**2,385,839**	**2,452,085**	**2,431,549**	**1,846,492**	**1,660,193**	**32.46**	**-10.09**
AUSTRIA	138,261	110,160	114,818	77,168	70,065	1.37	-9.20

TUNISIA

1. ARRIVALS OF NON-RESIDENT TOURISTS AT NATIONAL BORDERS, BY NATIONALITY

	1999	2000	2001	2002	2003	Market share 03	% change 03-02
BELGIUM	132,361	139,846	150,674	122,111	132,596	2.59	8.59
FRANCE	893,664	997,882	1,047,426	885,167	833,989	16.31	-5.78
GERMANY	1,036,262	1,011,298	934,747	613,666	488,481	9.55	-20.40
LUXEMBOURG	5,942	6,863	7,224	5,558	4,807	0.09	-13.51
NETHERLANDS	69,147	67,587	62,432	48,885	44,490	0.87	-8.99
SWITZERLAND	110,202	118,449	114,228	93,937	85,765	1.68	-8.70
EAST/MED EUR	**12,201**	**12,477**	**8,490**	**8,509**	**11,520**	**0.23**	**35.39**
TURKEY	12,201	12,477	8,490	8,509	11,520	0.23	35.39
OTHER EUROPE	**18,591**	**16,575**	**19,883**	**15,595**	**23,273**	**0.46**	**49.23**
OTHER EUROPE	18,591	16,575	19,883	15,595	23,273	0.46	49.23
MIDDLE EAST	**634,898**	**712,545**	**1,046,184**	**1,310,607**	**1,356,569**	**26.53**	**3.51**
MIDDLE EAST	**634,898**	**712,545**	**1,046,184**	**1,310,607**	**1,356,569**	**26.53**	**3.51**
BAHRAIN	333	223	496	869			
PALESTINE	2,261	1,800	2,000	1,778			
IRAQ	3,864	1,905	1,875	1,434			
JORDAN	2,665	1,812	2,001	1,846			
KUWAIT	914	1,039	1,071	1,093			
LEBANON	3,205	2,520	2,805	2,589			
LIBYA	603,074	685,208	1,016,569	1,280,733	1,325,660	25.92	3.51
OMAN	382	540	443	448			
QATAR	569	431	434	768			
SAUDI ARABIA	5,965	5,745	6,333	6,506			
SYRIA	3,128	2,912	2,765	2,729			
UNTD ARAB EM	664	506	621	543			
EGYPT	7,388	7,140	8,166	8,575			
YEMEN	486	764	605	696			
OT MIDD EAST					30,909	0.60	
REG.NOT SPEC	**28,038**	**23,358**	**19,064**	**19,265**	**16,842**	**0.33**	**-12.58**
NOT SPECIFIE	**28,038**	**23,358**	**19,064**	**19,265**	**16,842**	**0.33**	**-12.58**
OTH.WORLD	28,038	23,358	19,064	19,265	16,842	0.33	-12.58

Source: World Tourism Organization (WTO)

3. ARRIVALS OF NON-RESIDENT TOURISTS IN HOTELS AND SIMILAR ESTABLISHMENTS, BY NATIONALITY

	1999	2000	2001	2002	2003	Market share 03	% change 03-02
TOTAL	**5,141,805**	**5,314,534**	**5,232,708**	**4,244,985**	**4,064,176**	**100.00**	**-4.26**
AFRICA	**229,442**	**233,069**	**236,514**	**232,139**	**245,376**	**6.04**	**5.70**
NORTH AFRICA	**216,748**	**218,485**	**217,932**	**215,876**	**220,638**	**5.43**	**2.21**
ALGERIA	194,474	195,578	199,765	197,100	202,759	4.99	2.87
MOROCCO	22,274	22,907	18,167	18,776	17,879	0.44	-4.78
OTHER AFRICA	**12,694**	**14,584**	**18,582**	**16,263**	**24,738**	**0.61**	**52.11**
OTHER AFRICA	12,694	14,584	18,582	16,263	24,738	0.61	52.11
AMERICAS	**60,553**	**69,802**	**66,265**	**38,015**	**41,102**	**1.01**	**8.12**
NORTH AMER	**60,553**	**69,802**	**66,265**	**38,015**	**41,102**	**1.01**	**8.12**
CANADA	37,823	43,174	47,039	24,253	29,509	0.73	21.67
USA	22,730	26,628	19,226	13,762	11,593	0.29	-15.76
EAST AS/PACI	**32,468**	**27,006**	**23,027**	**22,272**	**20,899**	**0.51**	**-6.16**
N/EAST ASIA	**32,468**	**27,006**	**23,027**	**22,272**	**20,899**	**0.51**	**-6.16**
JAPAN	32,468	27,006	23,027	22,272	20,899	0.51	-6.16
EUROPE	**4,605,402**	**4,748,507**	**4,643,028**	**3,704,079**	**3,512,217**	**86.42**	**-5.18**
C/E EUROPE	**266,436**	**226,550**	**245,587**	**245,663**	**381,813**	**9.39**	**55.42**
BULGARIA	2,020	2,101	922	1,274	1,421	0.03	11.54
CZECH REP	78,957	65,258	71,716	71,835	114,233	2.81	59.02
HUNGARY	20,807	31,163	31,062	34,810	57,010	1.40	63.77
POLAND	110,695	74,088	76,185	49,748	66,050	1.63	32.77
ROMANIA	3,594	4,080	3,649	2,168	3,718	0.09	71.49
RUSSIAN FED	34,507	33,852	43,508	70,438	119,448	2.94	69.58
SLOVAKIA	15,856	16,008	18,545	15,390	19,933	0.49	29.52
NORTHERN EUR	**405,250**	**468,552**	**493,601**	**410,699**	**373,469**	**9.19**	**-9.07**
IRELAND	6,467	11,779	8,140	6,673	6,615	0.16	-0.87
UK	321,523	369,298	398,050	331,987	287,872	7.08	-13.29
SCANDINAVIA	77,260	87,475	87,411	72,039	78,982	1.94	9.64
SOUTHERN EUR	**792,839**	**916,152**	**858,364**	**771,233**	**776,938**	**19.12**	**0.74**
GREECE	34,751	32,569	24,656	22,292	17,913	0.44	-19.64
ITALY	453,411	520,126	514,992	469,164	467,888	11.51	-0.27
MALTA	5,590	7,290	4,480	7,086	10,122	0.25	42.85
PORTUGAL	23,751	23,216	24,323	26,201	20,503	0.50	-21.75
SPAIN	267,059	324,712	282,748	237,087	245,757	6.05	3.66
YUGOSLAV SFR	8,277	8,239	7,165	9,403	14,755	0.36	56.92
WESTERN EUR	**3,104,269**	**3,092,282**	**3,015,160**	**2,235,831**	**1,934,552**	**47.60**	**-13.48**
AUSTRIA	127,059	95,497	105,536	67,339	55,400	1.36	-17.73
BELGIUM	149,407	167,042	174,159	134,011	149,898	3.69	11.85
FRANCE	1,341,375	1,399,342	1,412,048	1,144,750	1,010,428	24.86	-11.73
GERMANY	1,258,394	1,203,133	1,117,419	716,393	560,033	13.78	-21.83
LUXEMBOURG	11,351	11,586	13,649	12,839	16,328	0.40	27.18
NETHERLANDS	87,749	75,484	67,218	57,881	51,814	1.27	-10.48
SWITZERLAND	128,934	140,198	125,131	102,618	90,651	2.23	-11.66

TUNISIA

3. ARRIVALS OF NON-RESIDENT TOURISTS IN HOTELS AND SIMILAR ESTABLISHMENTS, BY NATIONALITY

	1999	2000	2001	2002	2003	Market share 03	% change 03-02
EAST/MED EUR	**9,789**	**9,985**	**5,901**	**7,010**	**11,742**	**0.29**	**67.50**
TURKEY	9,789	9,985	5,901	7,010	11,742	0.29	67.50
OTHER EUROPE	**26,819**	**34,986**	**24,415**	**33,643**	**33,703**	**0.83**	**0.18**
OTHER EUROPE	26,819	34,986	24,415	33,643	33,703	0.83	0.18
MIDDLE EAST	**137,438**	**156,712**	**168,302**	**171,200**	**161,260**	**3.97**	**-5.81**
MIDDLE EAST	**137,438**	**156,712**	**168,302**	**171,200**	**161,260**	**3.97**	**-5.81**
LIBYA	106,689	128,716	140,983	144,597	131,770	3.24	-8.87
OT MIDD EAST	30,749	27,996	27,319	26,603	29,490	0.73	10.85
REG.NOT SPEC	**76,502**	**79,438**	**95,572**	**77,280**	**83,322**	**2.05**	**7.82**
NOT SPECIFIE	**76,502**	**79,438**	**95,572**	**77,280**	**83,322**	**2.05**	**7.82**
OTH.WORLD	76,502	79,438	95,572	77,280	83,322	2.05	7.82

Source: World Tourism Organization (WTO)

TUNISIA

5. OVERNIGHT STAYS OF NON-RESIDENT TOURISTS IN HOTELS AND SIMILAR ESTABLISHMENTS, BY NATIONALITY

	1999	2000	2001	2002	2003	Market share 03	% change 03-02
TOTAL	**33,150,730**	**33,168,301**	**33,005,617**	**25,897,226**	**25,301,322**	**100.00**	**-2.30**
AFRICA	**552,546**	**563,431**	**581,145**	**606,880**	**726,309**	**2.87**	**19.68**
NORTH AFRICA	**504,148**	**496,892**	**518,552**	**547,921**	**633,256**	**2.50**	**15.57**
ALGERIA	445,761	437,757	467,373	497,832	581,137	2.30	16.73
MOROCCO	58,387	59,135	51,179	50,089	52,119	0.21	4.05
OTHER AFRICA	**48,398**	**66,539**	**62,593**	**58,959**	**93,053**	**0.37**	**57.83**
OTHER AFRICA	48,398	66,539	62,593	58,959	93,053	0.37	57.83
AMERICAS	**179,501**	**225,515**	**232,449**	**140,131**	**184,757**	**0.73**	**31.85**
NORTH AMER	**179,501**	**225,515**	**232,449**	**140,131**	**184,757**	**0.73**	**31.85**
CANADA	130,420	157,126	167,000	91,973	132,463	0.52	44.02
USA	49,081	68,389	65,449	48,158	52,294	0.21	8.59
EAST AS/PACI	**53,941**	**48,229**	**43,646**	**40,397**	**40,275**	**0.16**	**-0.30**
N/EAST ASIA	**53,941**	**48,229**	**43,646**	**40,397**	**40,275**	**0.16**	**-0.30**
JAPAN	53,941	48,229	43,646	40,397	40,275	0.16	-0.30
EUROPE	**31,719,249**	**31,679,054**	**31,412,977**	**24,417,881**	**23,669,982**	**93.55**	**-3.06**
C/E EUROPE	**1,826,464**	**1,491,856**	**1,722,529**	**1,748,381**	**2,886,959**	**11.41**	**65.12**
BULGARIA	8,988	13,937	9,118	3,853	8,470	0.03	119.83
CZECH REP	636,609	503,709	577,998	583,142	984,417	3.89	68.81
HUNGARY	111,352	194,788	167,644	187,747	357,055	1.41	90.18
POLAND	752,349	481,044	545,394	353,216	524,725	2.07	48.56
ROMANIA	14,263	18,704	12,648	9,702	19,203	0.08	97.93
RUSSIAN FED	202,601	190,827	296,943	502,600	859,273	3.40	70.97
SLOVAKIA	100,302	88,847	112,784	108,121	133,816	0.53	23.77
NORTHERN EUR	**3,260,607**	**3,761,656**	**3,985,587**	**3,308,966**	**2,970,758**	**11.74**	**-10.22**
IRELAND	81,715	107,556	77,842	60,929	56,737	0.22	-6.88
UK	2,637,481	3,036,300	3,227,460	2,678,069	2,289,934	9.05	-14.49
SCANDINAVIA	541,411	617,800	680,285	569,968	624,087	2.47	9.50
SOUTHERN EUR	**3,476,561**	**3,896,122**	**3,844,257**	**3,491,269**	**3,607,281**	**14.26**	**3.32**
GREECE	64,413	63,419	49,032	42,832	37,824	0.15	-11.69
ITALY	2,620,586	2,922,107	2,967,663	2,678,635	2,711,719	10.72	1.24
MALTA	25,878	24,838	21,382	32,933	51,515	0.20	56.42
PORTUGAL	71,818	85,200	98,393	102,833	88,140	0.35	-14.29
SPAIN	640,671	753,359	663,477	581,673	626,072	2.47	7.63
YUGOSLAV SFR	53,195	47,199	44,310	52,363	92,011	0.36	75.72
WESTERN EUR	**23,008,648**	**22,322,885**	**21,711,087**	**15,750,501**	**13,995,618**	**55.32**	**-11.14**
AUSTRIA	1,186,971	819,600	895,746	553,312	465,220	1.84	-15.92
BELGIUM	1,253,099	1,306,600	1,432,152	1,102,259	1,267,594	5.01	15.00
FRANCE	6,767,897	7,205,700	7,294,392	6,066,662	5,671,187	22.41	-6.52
GERMANY	12,092,699	11,284,300	10,465,927	6,805,286	5,498,718	21.73	-19.20
LUXEMBOURG	103,494	103,785	126,679	113,484	113,472	0.45	-0.01
NETHERLANDS	579,418	540,700	479,330	351,656	329,628	1.30	-6.26
SWITZERLAND	1,025,070	1,062,200	1,016,861	757,842	649,799	2.57	-14.26

5. OVERNIGHT STAYS OF NON-RESIDENT TOURISTS IN HOTELS AND SIMILAR ESTABLISHMENTS, BY NATIONALITY

	1999	2000	2001	2002	2003	Market share 03	% change 03-02
EAST/MED EUR	**31,881**	**36,078**	**23,526**	**27,225**	**41,976**	**0.17**	**54.18**
TURKEY	31,881	36,078	23,526	27,225	41,976	0.17	54.18
OTHER EUROPE	**115,088**	**170,457**	**125,991**	**91,539**	**167,390**	**0.66**	**82.86**
OTHER EUROPE	115,088	170,457	125,991	91,539	167,390	0.66	82.86
MIDDLE EAST	**316,250**	**335,700**	**384,008**	**384,706**	**370,980**	**1.47**	**-3.57**
MIDDLE EAST	**316,250**	**335,700**	**384,008**	**384,706**	**370,980**	**1.47**	**-3.57**
LIBYA	198,843	234,700	271,280	283,701	256,658	1.01	-9.53
OT MIDD EAST	117,407	101,000	112,728	101,005	114,322	0.45	13.18
REG.NOT SPEC	**329,243**	**316,372**	**351,392**	**307,231**	**309,019**	**1.22**	**0.58**
NOT SPECIFIE	**329,243**	**316,372**	**351,392**	**307,231**	**309,019**	**1.22**	**0.58**
OTH.WORLD	329,243	316,372	351,392	307,231	309,019	1.22	0.58

Source: World Tourism Organization (WTO)

TURKEY

1. ARRIVALS OF NON-RESIDENT TOURISTS AT NATIONAL BORDERS, BY NATIONALITY

	1999	2000	2001	2002	2003	Market share 03	% change 03-02
TOTAL	**6,892,636**	**9,585,695**	**10,782,673**	**12,789,827**	**13,340,956**	**100.00**	**4.31**
AFRICA	**82,332**	**106,289**	**118,870**	**130,758**	**119,122**	**0.89**	**-8.90**
NORTH AFRICA	**60,762**	**83,937**	**95,233**	**105,436**	**102,174**	**0.77**	**-3.09**
ALGERIA	19,997	31,458	37,725	39,490	39,945	0.30	1.15
MOROCCO	9,759	10,976	10,761	12,548	13,704	0.10	9.21
SUDAN	1,443	1,879	1,936	2,209	1,911	0.01	-13.49
TUNISIA	29,563	39,624	44,811	51,189	46,614	0.35	-8.94
SOUTHERN AFR			**14,428**	**15,193**	**7,270**	**0.05**	**-52.15**
SOUTH AFRICA			14,428	15,193	7,270	0.05	-52.15
OTHER AFRICA	**21,570**	**22,352**	**9,209**	**10,129**	**9,678**	**0.07**	**-4.45**
OTHER AFRICA	21,570	22,352	9,209	10,129	9,678	0.07	-4.45
AMERICAS	**282,616**	**360,920**	**326,732**	**253,804**	**213,136**	**1.60**	**-16.02**
CENTRAL AMER	**3,761**	**3,460**	**3,671**	**1,614**	**918**	**0.01**	**-43.12**
ALL CENT AME	3,761	3,460	3,671	1,614	918	0.01	-43.12
NORTH AMER	**264,939**	**337,758**	**302,791**	**235,723**	**197,491**	**1.48**	**-16.22**
CANADA	26,859	32,741	35,265	28,686	27,732	0.21	-3.33
MEXICO	4,613	8,334	10,719	8,171	6,395	0.05	-21.74
USA	230,795	295,921	255,405	197,402	162,198	1.22	-17.83
OT.NORTH.AME	2,672	762	1,402	1,464	1,166	0.01	-20.36
SOUTH AMER	**13,916**	**19,702**	**20,270**	**16,467**	**14,727**	**0.11**	**-10.57**
ARGENTINA	4,810	7,456	6,020	2,371	2,769	0.02	16.79
BRAZIL	4,178	7,033	6,281	6,040	5,072	0.04	-16.03
CHILE	1,682	2,763	2,428	2,480	2,171	0.02	-12.46
COLOMBIA	805	271	1,122	1,396	983	0.01	-29.58
VENEZUELA	490	349	1,238	1,321	865	0.01	-34.52
OTH SOUTH AM	1,951	1,830	3,181	2,859	2,867	0.02	0.28
EAST AS/PACI	**167,166**	**233,669**	**247,202**	**280,607**	**241,996**	**1.81**	**-13.76**
N/EAST ASIA	**88,211**	**125,041**	**136,534**	**164,917**	**137,127**	**1.03**	**-16.85**
CHINA	10,288	21,084	24,391	31,637	26,506	0.20	-16.22
JAPAN	63,568	82,374	83,543	91,153	64,664	0.48	-29.06
KOREA REP.	14,355	21,583	28,600	42,127	45,957	0.34	9.09
S/EAST ASIA	**13,738**	**21,756**	**31,182**	**33,534**	**31,317**	**0.23**	**-6.61**
INDONESIA			5,783	8,080	5,324	0.04	-34.11
MALAYSIA	3,603	8,571	8,967	8,070	6,828	0.05	-15.39
PHILIPPINES	4,964	7,157	7,826	9,253	11,044	0.08	19.36
SINGAPORE	5,171	6,028	5,686	4,959	5,802	0.04	17.00
THAILAND			2,920	3,172	2,319	0.02	-26.89
AUSTRALASIA	**46,738**	**58,963**	**60,529**	**64,272**	**54,020**	**0.40**	**-15.95**
AUSTRALIA	38,315	47,220	48,595	52,551	45,289	0.34	-13.82
NEW ZEALAND	8,423	11,743	11,934	11,721	8,731	0.07	-25.51
OT.EAST AS/P	**18,479**	**27,909**	**18,957**	**17,884**	**19,532**	**0.15**	**9.21**
OTHER ASIA	18,160	27,103	18,741	17,432	19,252	0.14	10.44
OTH OCEANIA	319	806	216	452	280		-38.05

TURKEY

1. ARRIVALS OF NON-RESIDENT TOURISTS AT NATIONAL BORDERS, BY NATIONALITY

	1999	2000	2001	2002	2003	Market share 03	% change 03-02
EUROPE	**5,786,258**	**8,234,233**	**9,473,313**	**11,359,447**	**11,871,694**	**88.99**	**4.51**
C/E EUROPE	**1,887,434**	**2,189,684**	**2,387,126**	**2,935,932**	**3,501,961**	**26.25**	**19.28**
AZERBAIJAN			177,258	162,503	192,698	1.44	18.58
ARMENIA			7,057	17,519	23,104	0.17	31.88
BULGARIA	258,441	379,837	539,425	832,220	1,005,684	7.54	20.84
BELARUS			17,133	36,271	43,607	0.33	20.23
CZECH RP/SVK	39,762	47,922					
CZECH REP			49,800	61,446	46,341	0.35	-24.58
GEORGIA			163,215	161,095	167,551	1.26	4.01
HUNGARY	23,707	35,254	36,936	49,920	46,767	0.35	-6.32
KAZAKHSTAN			37,843	43,749	64,968	0.49	48.50
KYRGYZSTAN			7,886	10,379	13,793	0.10	32.89
REP MOLDOVA			45,432	45,772	54,828	0.41	19.79
POLAND	63,506	115,511	148,599	148,836	100,538	0.75	-32.45
ROMANIA	482,371	263,907	179,322	177,397	184,366	1.38	3.93
RUSSIAN FED			750,173	937,298	1,272,140	9.54	35.72
SLOVAKIA			26,837	33,064	23,597	0.18	-28.63
TAJIKISTAN			1,252	1,526	3,557	0.03	133.09
TURKMENISTAN			14,999	21,317	15,784	0.12	-25.96
UKRAINE			162,600	175,247	223,619	1.68	27.60
UZBEKISTAN			21,359	20,373	19,019	0.14	-6.65
CIS	1,019,647	1,347,253					
NORTHERN EUR	**1,005,160**	**1,148,024**	**1,175,395**	**1,487,981**	**1,470,435**	**11.02**	**-1.18**
DENMARK	76,737	93,341	117,868	159,795	147,730	1.11	-7.55
FINLAND	35,660	49,059	57,653	76,728	55,354	0.41	-27.86
ICELAND	5,836	3,166	2,802	1,168	1,137	0.01	-2.65
IRELAND	35,158	38,211	44,480	49,412	54,055	0.41	9.40
NORWAY	48,870	58,632	78,695	85,827	81,670	0.61	-4.84
SWEDEN	98,445	137,514	189,795	197,179	194,724	1.46	-1.25
UK	704,454	768,101	684,102	917,872	935,765	7.01	1.95
SOUTHERN EUR	**463,841**	**742,005**	**795,496**	**930,210**	**988,234**	**7.41**	**6.24**
ALBANIA	27,136	29,561	26,009	29,075	32,206	0.24	10.77
BOSNIA HERZG			28,208	32,482	34,618	0.26	6.58
CROATIA			12,320	14,045	14,861	0.11	5.81
GREECE	129,397	192,665	173,264	255,867	364,571	2.73	42.48
ITALY	63,845	155,844	215,645	193,669	144,095	1.08	-25.60
PORTUGAL	5,173	9,475	13,819	12,233	9,179	0.07	-24.97
SLOVENIA			7,262	10,488	15,078	0.11	43.76
SPAIN	25,327	69,836	80,093	73,379	68,415	0.51	-6.76
TFYROM			113,544	120,945	119,299	0.89	-1.36
YUGOSLAV SFR	212,963	284,624					
SERBIA,MTNEG			125,332	188,027	185,912	1.39	-1.12
WESTERN EUR	**2,108,429**	**3,701,481**	**4,697,079**	**5,600,689**	**5,448,832**	**40.84**	**-2.71**
AUSTRIA	125,453	314,983	351,111	369,866	370,306	2.78	0.12
BELGIUM	143,973	247,629	302,079	306,911	299,583	2.25	-2.39
FRANCE	256,542	419,184	489,488	510,381	444,142	3.33	-12.98
GERMANY	1,342,139	2,218,550	2,818,888	3,421,112	3,231,115	24.22	-5.55
LUXEMBOURG	955	1,692	2,965	3,983	3,111	0.02	-21.89
NETHERLANDS	203,672	425,567	616,110	848,771	921,704	6.91	8.59
SWITZERLAND	35,695	73,876	116,438	139,665	178,871	1.34	28.07
EAST/MED EUR	**261,793**	**378,704**	**373,476**	**357,900**	**407,296**	**3.05**	**13.80**
CYPRUS	88,446	103,118	90,845	94,033	104,376	0.78	11.00

TURKEY

1. ARRIVALS OF NON-RESIDENT TOURISTS AT NATIONAL BORDERS, BY NATIONALITY

	1999	2000	2001	2002	2003	Market share 03	% change 03-02
ISRAEL	173,347	275,586	282,631	263,867	302,920	2.27	14.80
OTHER EUROPE	**59,601**	**74,335**	**44,741**	**46,735**	**54,936**	**0.41**	**17.55**
OTHER EUROPE	59,601	74,335	44,741	46,735	54,936	0.41	17.55
MIDDLE EAST	**198,723**	**242,352**	**262,894**	**303,860**	**359,281**	**2.69**	**18.24**
MIDDLE EAST	**198,723**	**242,352**	**262,894**	**303,860**	**359,281**	**2.69**	**18.24**
BAHRAIN	1,864	489	2,293	4,567	4,122	0.03	-9.74
IRAQ	17,589	20,757	16,370	14,261	24,725	0.19	73.37
JORDAN	18,017	22,185	26,883	33,099	37,365	0.28	12.89
KUWAIT	3,702	1,294	5,298	6,972	8,164	0.06	17.10
LEBANON	13,832	15,920	21,610	30,903	34,710	0.26	12.32
LIBYA	9,025	24,002	31,462	29,959	27,882	0.21	-6.93
OMAN	301	101	490	1,204	1,298	0.01	7.81
QATAR	256	103	603	824	1,209	0.01	46.72
SAUDI ARABIA	13,802	15,283	20,450	25,593	23,244	0.17	-9.18
SYRIA	101,505	121,124	108,813	125,711	153,787	1.15	22.33
UNTD ARAB EM	2,029	1,825	3,358	4,964	6,717	0.05	35.31
EGYPT	15,607	18,569	21,937	21,155	29,667	0.22	40.24
YEMEN	1,194	700	1,413	1,809	2,138	0.02	18.19
OT MIDD EAST			1,914	2,839	4,253	0.03	49.81
SOUTH ASIA	**366,621**	**397,348**	**342,218**	**450,787**	**522,054**	**3.91**	**15.81**
SOUTH ASIA	**366,621**	**397,348**	**342,218**	**450,787**	**522,054**	**3.91**	**15.81**
BANGLADESH	709	275	727	858	2,050	0.02	138.93
INDIA	6,829	8,702	7,499	9,626	12,756	0.10	32.52
IRAN	351,852	380,704	326,931	432,083	497,189	3.73	15.07
PAKISTAN	7,231	7,667	7,061	8,220	10,059	0.08	22.37
REG.NOT SPEC	**8,920**	**10,884**	**11,444**	**10,564**	**13,673**	**0.10**	**29.43**
NOT SPECIFIE	**8,920**	**10,884**	**11,444**	**10,564**	**13,673**	**0.10**	**29.43**
OTH.WORLD	8,920	10,884	11,444	10,564	13,673	0.10	29.43

Source: World Tourism Organization (WTO)

TURKEY

2. ARRIVALS OF NON-RESIDENT VISITORS AT NATIONAL BORDERS, BY NATIONALITY

	1999	2000	2001	2002	2003	Market share 03	% change 03-02
TOTAL (*)	**7,487,285**	**10,428,153**	**11,618,969**	**13,256,028**	**14,029,558**	**100.00**	**5.84**
AFRICA	**92,605**	**112,015**	**125,684**	**134,029**	**122,912**	**0.88**	**-8.29**
NORTH AFRICA	**62,691**	**86,672**	**98,629**	**107,597**	**104,569**	**0.75**	**-2.81**
ALGERIA	21,852	33,421	39,904	41,473	42,140	0.30	1.61
MOROCCO	9,813	11,635	11,788	12,643	13,794	0.10	9.10
SUDAN	1,446	1,924	1,976	2,210	1,917	0.01	-13.26
TUNISIA	29,580	39,692	44,961	51,271	46,718	0.33	-8.88
SOUTHERN AFR		**6,048**	**17,484**	**16,168**	**8,494**	**0.06**	**-47.46**
SOUTH AFRICA		6,048	17,484	16,168	8,494	0.06	-47.46
OTHER AFRICA	**29,914**	**19,295**	**9,571**	**10,264**	**9,849**	**0.07**	**-4.04**
OTHER AFRICA	29,914	19,295	9,571	10,264	9,849	0.07	-4.04
AMERICAS	**483,821**	**632,168**	**550,731**	**323,759**	**304,088**	**2.17**	**-6.08**
CENTRAL AMER	**5,170**	**5,270**	**8,104**	**2,143**	**1,721**	**0.01**	**-19.69**
ALL CENT AME	5,170	5,270	8,104	2,143	1,721	0.01	-19.69
NORTH AMER	**453,051**	**592,580**	**509,823**	**299,665**	**278,463**	**1.98**	**-7.08**
CANADA	44,958	56,598	56,951	38,999	42,019	0.30	7.74
MEXICO	9,178	18,437	20,906	11,297	12,163	0.09	7.67
USA	395,006	515,090	429,563	247,629	222,918	1.59	-9.98
OT.NORTH.AME	3,909	2,455	2,403	1,740	1,363	0.01	-21.67
SOUTH AMER	**25,600**	**34,318**	**32,804**	**21,951**	**23,904**	**0.17**	**8.90**
ARGENTINA	10,244	12,235	9,395	2,890	6,509	0.05	125.22
BRAZIL	6,820	11,924	10,515	8,332	7,346	0.05	-11.83
CHILE	2,734	4,262	3,632	3,315	3,070	0.02	-7.39
COLOMBIA	1,769	1,420	2,479	2,259	1,797	0.01	-20.45
VENEZUELA	1,144	1,225	2,398	1,832	1,460	0.01	-20.31
OTH SOUTH AM	2,889	3,252	4,385	3,323	3,722	0.03	12.01
EAST AS/PACI	**191,145**	**262,760**	**273,981**	**297,779**	**265,150**	**1.89**	**-10.96**
N/EAST ASIA	**93,756**	**133,295**	**142,369**	**169,039**	**141,836**	**1.01**	**-16.09**
CHINA	11,047	21,570	25,295	31,951	27,557	0.20	-13.75
JAPAN	67,987	89,459	87,800	94,514	67,874	0.48	-28.19
KOREA REP.	14,722	22,266	29,274	42,574	46,405	0.33	9.00
S/EAST ASIA	**21,683**	**34,941**	**39,830**	**39,202**	**36,330**	**0.26**	**-7.33**
INDONESIA		2,984	7,315	9,609	5,928	0.04	-38.31
MALAYSIA	3,803	8,869	9,164	8,159	6,975	0.05	-14.51
PHILIPPINES	12,496	16,193	14,294	13,123	15,100	0.11	15.07
SINGAPORE	5,384	6,217	6,008	5,068	5,915	0.04	16.71
THAILAND		678	3,049	3,243	2,412	0.02	-25.62
AUSTRALASIA	**56,322**	**71,804**	**72,340**	**71,455**	**67,125**	**0.48**	**-6.06**
AUSTRALIA	46,075	58,295	58,661	58,678	56,854	0.41	-3.11
NEW ZEALAND	10,247	13,509	13,679	12,777	10,271	0.07	-19.61
OT.EAST AS/P	**19,384**	**22,720**	**19,442**	**18,083**	**19,859**	**0.14**	**9.82**
OTHER ASIA	19,064	21,878	19,216	17,628	19,572	0.14	11.03
OTH OCEANIA	320	842	226	455	287		-36.92

TURKEY

2. ARRIVALS OF NON-RESIDENT VISITORS AT NATIONAL BORDERS, BY NATIONALITY

	1999	2000	2001	2002	2003	Market share 03	% change 03-02
EUROPE	**6,127,865**	**8,746,246**	**10,047,401**	**11,731,327**	**12,438,301**	**88.66**	**6.03**
C/E EUROPE	**1,926,086**	**2,256,311**	**2,419,563**	**2,974,370**	**3,536,498**	**25.21**	**18.90**
AZERBAIJAN	128,028	179,788	177,612	163,133	193,410	1.38	18.56
ARMENIA	19,038	17,518	7,064	17,530	23,118	0.16	31.88
BULGARIA	259,075	381,697	540,452	834,073	1,006,612	7.17	20.69
BELARUS	7,418	9,614	17,163	36,371	43,746	0.31	20.28
CZECH RP/SVK	40,691						
CZECH REP		49,421	51,818	63,223	48,768	0.35	-22.86
GEORGIA	181,324	179,651	164,058	161,375	167,911	1.20	4.05
HUNGARY	25,032	36,762	38,194	51,336	48,216	0.34	-6.08
KAZAKHSTAN	30,793	38,920	37,885	43,793	65,092	0.46	48.64
KYRGYZSTAN	5,451	8,751	7,890	10,379	13,796	0.10	32.92
REP MOLDOVA	77,867	64,686	46,061	46,091	55,385	0.39	20.16
POLAND	66,209	118,174	150,916	150,949	102,347	0.73	-32.20
ROMANIA	483,184	265,175	180,911	180,203	185,174	1.32	2.76
RUSSIAN FED	438,719	676,958	757,446	946,511	1,281,407	9.13	35.38
SLOVAKIA		21,972	27,233	33,507	24,127	0.17	-27.99
TAJIKISTAN	787	1,100	1,252	1,526	3,559	0.03	133.22
TURKMENISTAN	7,376	10,979	14,999	21,317	15,785	0.11	-25.95
UKRAINE	140,850	174,034	177,245	192,661	238,962	1.70	24.03
UZBEKISTAN	14,244	21,111	21,364	20,392	19,083	0.14	-6.42
NORTHERN EUR	**1,146,395**	**1,331,245**	**1,377,011**	**1,635,710**	**1,658,843**	**11.82**	**1.41**
DENMARK	83,459	100,967	126,034	164,979	154,350	1.10	-6.44
FINLAND	39,946	53,440	64,283	80,739	59,753	0.43	-25.99
ICELAND	5,994	3,354	4,110	1,273	1,355	0.01	6.44
IRELAND	37,995	42,121	48,635	53,036	58,913	0.42	11.08
NORWAY	56,685	67,517	87,704	94,528	88,863	0.63	-5.99
SWEDEN	107,427	148,561	200,709	203,648	204,205	1.46	0.27
UK	814,889	915,285	845,536	1,037,507	1,091,404	7.78	5.19
SOUTHERN EUR	**510,122**	**859,534**	**960,933**	**992,602**	**1,138,346**	**8.11**	**14.68**
ALBANIA	27,315	29,739	26,107	29,221	32,439	0.23	11.01
BOSNIA HERZG		28,620	28,223	32,490	34,642	0.25	6.62
CROATIA		11,968	13,031	14,826	15,291	0.11	3.14
GREECE	146,871	218,670	197,258	280,033	393,517	2.80	40.53
ITALY	79,029	218,785	315,286	210,657	236,931	1.69	12.47
PORTUGAL	7,678	13,305	18,382	16,559	12,185	0.09	-26.41
SLOVENIA		8,029	7,515	10,889	15,701	0.11	44.19
SPAIN	35,453	93,105	116,067	88,811	92,326	0.66	3.96
TFYROM		108,904	113,546	120,989	119,305	0.85	-1.39
YUGOSLAV SFR	213,776						
SERBIA,MTNEG		128,409	125,518	188,127	186,009	1.33	-1.13
WESTERN EUR	**2,192,150**	**3,828,263**	**4,841,920**	**5,715,854**	**5,623,353**	**40.08**	**-1.62**
AUSTRIA	129,465	320,582	360,363	377,036	379,830	2.71	0.74
BELGIUM	149,622	256,881	310,296	313,585	308,118	2.20	-1.74
FRANCE	270,280	449,545	524,170	522,740	470,582	3.35	-9.98
GERMANY	1,388,787	2,277,502	2,884,051	3,481,671	3,332,451	23.75	-4.29
LUXEMBOURG	1,105	2,017	3,527	4,172	3,432	0.02	-17.74
NETHERLANDS	214,163	440,290	632,975	873,278	940,098	6.70	7.65
SWITZERLAND	38,728	81,446	126,538	143,372	188,842	1.35	31.71
EAST/MED EUR	**290,743**	**415,554**	**401,841**	**364,406**	**425,590**	**3.03**	**16.79**
CYPRUS	89,272	103,250	91,237	94,143	104,438	0.74	10.94
ISRAEL	201,471	312,304	310,604	270,263	321,152	2.29	18.83

2. ARRIVALS OF NON-RESIDENT VISITORS AT NATIONAL BORDERS, BY NATIONALITY

	1999	2000	2001	2002	2003	Market share 03	% change 03-02
OTHER EUROPE	**62,369**	**55,339**	**46,133**	**48,385**	**55,671**	**0.40**	**15.06**
OTHER EUROPE	62,369	55,339	46,133	48,385	55,671	0.40	15.06
MIDDLE EAST	**212,633**	**262,447**	**265,303**	**306,947**	**362,333**	**2.58**	**18.04**
MIDDLE EAST	**212,633**	**262,447**	**265,303**	**306,947**	**362,333**	**2.58**	**18.04**
BAHRAIN	1,908	489	2,337	4,569	4,133	0.03	-9.54
IRAQ	17,591	20,759	16,378	15,765	24,727	0.18	56.85
JORDAN	18,024	22,220	26,914	33,130	37,449	0.27	13.04
KUWAIT	3,727	1,311	5,325	6,989	8,210	0.06	17.47
LEBANON	14,424	16,690	22,334	31,298	35,285	0.25	12.74
LIBYA	9,125	24,042	31,473	29,970	28,185	0.20	-5.96
OMAN	315	104	495	1,206	1,298	0.01	7.63
QATAR	256	108	609	824	1,210	0.01	46.84
SAUDI ARABIA	13,890	15,521	20,612	25,657	23,676	0.17	-7.72
SYRIA	102,444	122,376	109,697	126,323	154,447	1.10	22.26
UNTD ARAB EM	2,032	1,825	3,398	4,977	6,717	0.05	34.96
EGYPT	26,672	31,772	22,396	21,583	30,556	0.22	41.57
YEMEN	1,196	705	1,416	1,810	2,141	0.02	18.29
OT MIDD EAST	1,029	4,525	1,919	2,846	4,299	0.03	51.05
SOUTH ASIA	**370,293**	**401,633**	**344,425**	**451,623**	**523,101**	**3.73**	**15.83**
SOUTH ASIA	**370,293**	**401,633**	**344,425**	**451,623**	**523,101**	**3.73**	**15.83**
BANGLADESH	709	292	781	866	2,055	0.01	137.30
INDIA	10,332	12,551	9,230	10,122	13,667	0.10	35.02
IRAN	351,937	380,877	327,146	432,282	497,282	3.54	15.04
PAKISTAN	7,315	7,913	7,268	8,353	10,097	0.07	20.88
REG.NOT SPEC	**8,923**	**10,884**	**11,444**	**10,564**	**13,673**	**0.10**	**29.43**
NOT SPECIFIE	**8,923**	**10,884**	**11,444**	**10,564**	**13,673**	**0.10**	**29.43**
OTH.WORLD	8,923	10,884	11,444	10,564	13,673	0.10	29.43

Source: World Tourism Organization (WTO)

TURKEY

3. ARRIVALS OF NON-RESIDENT TOURISTS IN HOTELS AND SIMILAR ESTABLISHMENTS, BY NATIONALITY

	1999	2000	2001	2002	2003	Market share 03	% change 03-02
TOTAL (*)	**4,805,157**	**6,788,706**	**8,769,351**	**9,859,459**	**8,983,199**	**100.00**	**-8.89**
AFRICA				**35,528**	**25,505**	**0.28**	**-28.21**
NORTH AFRICA				**24,583**	**18,255**	**0.20**	**-25.74**
ALGERIA				12,502	5,938	0.07	-52.50
MOROCCO				2,903	3,987	0.04	37.34
SUDAN				718	1,051	0.01	46.38
TUNISIA				8,460	7,279	0.08	-13.96
SOUTHERN AFR				**9,641**	**6,023**	**0.07**	**-37.53**
SOUTH AFRICA				9,641	6,023	0.07	-37.53
OTHER AFRICA				**1,304**	**1,227**	**0.01**	**-5.90**
OTHER AFRICA				1,304	1,227	0.01	-5.90
AMERICAS	**501,942**	**440,732**	**438,341**	**381,698**	**231,566**	**2.58**	**-39.33**
CENTRAL AMER				**178**	**106**		**-40.45**
ALL CENT AME				178	106		-40.45
NORTH AMER	**501,942**	**440,732**	**438,341**	**348,196**	**220,131**	**2.45**	**-36.78**
CANADA	23,885	19,059	23,886	36,446	14,453	0.16	-60.34
MEXICO				7,247	6,264	0.07	-13.56
USA	478,057	421,673	414,455	303,797	198,528	2.21	-34.65
OT.NORTH.AME				706	886	0.01	25.50
SOUTH AMER				**33,324**	**11,329**	**0.13**	**-66.00**
ARGENTINA				24,773	6,117	0.07	-75.31
BRAZIL				4,292	2,849	0.03	-33.62
CHILE				1,363	844	0.01	-38.08
COLOMBIA				467	356		-23.77
VENEZUELA				552	270		-51.09
OTH SOUTH AM				1,877	893	0.01	-52.42
EAST AS/PACI	**317,647**	**332,867**	**424,233**	**524,576**	**391,934**	**4.36**	**-25.29**
N/EAST ASIA	**288,473**	**301,649**	**374,036**	**419,305**	**331,306**	**3.69**	**-20.99**
CHINA				23,670	21,538	0.24	-9.01
JAPAN	288,473	301,649	374,036	332,168	233,847	2.60	-29.60
KOREA REP.				63,467	75,921	0.85	19.62
S/EAST ASIA				**24,960**	**14,362**	**0.16**	**-42.46**
INDONESIA				1,079	373		-65.43
MALAYSIA				6,871	4,771	0.05	-30.56
PHILIPPINES				1,904	3,536	0.04	85.71
SINGAPORE				14,037	5,249	0.06	-62.61
THAILAND				1,069	433		-59.49
AUSTRALASIA	**29,174**	**31,218**	**50,197**	**77,060**	**44,970**	**0.50**	**-41.64**
AUSTRALIA	29,174	31,218	50,197	69,543	41,829	0.47	-39.85
NEW ZEALAND				7,517	3,141	0.03	-58.21
OT.EAST AS/P				**3,251**	**1,296**	**0.01**	**-60.14**
OTHER ASIA				2,547	1,173	0.01	-53.95
ALL OCEANIA				704	123		-82.53

3. ARRIVALS OF NON-RESIDENT TOURISTS IN HOTELS AND SIMILAR ESTABLISHMENTS, BY NATIONALITY

	1999	2000	2001	2002	2003	Market share 03	% change 03-02
EUROPE	**3,122,219**	**4,910,398**	**6,816,617**	**8,425,209**	**7,912,376**	**88.08**	**-6.09**
C/E EUROPE	**579,703**	**915,703**	**1,074,262**	**1,477,550**	**1,603,975**	**17.86**	**8.56**
BULGARIA	24,813	25,806	37,088	65,690	53,805	0.60	-18.09
CZECH REP				44,641	29,833	0.33	-33.17
HUNGARY	8,785	9,002	10,644	31,016	21,970	0.24	-29.17
POLAND	18,736	61,706	69,186	77,222	129,778	1.44	68.06
ROMANIA	42,481	53,202	43,602	58,076	56,776	0.63	-2.24
CIS	484,888	765,987	913,742	1,200,905	1,311,813	14.60	9.24
NORTHERN EUR	**403,549**	**374,047**	**588,034**	**689,585**	**624,030**	**6.95**	**-9.51**
ICELAND				3,189	1,561	0.02	-51.05
IRELAND				52,894	75,388	0.84	42.53
UK	333,629	335,786	460,035	459,013	406,644	4.53	-11.41
SCANDINAVIA	69,920	38,261	127,999	174,489	140,437	1.56	-19.52
SOUTHERN EUR	**222,127**	**464,857**	**683,777**	**735,810**	**595,257**	**6.63**	**-19.10**
ALBANIA				10,842	15,279	0.17	40.92
GREECE	23,938	73,857	80,789	108,818	124,318	1.38	14.24
ITALY	100,097	202,981	372,006	293,648	182,975	2.04	-37.69
PORTUGAL				18,551	11,407	0.13	-38.51
SPAIN	69,098	150,880	189,339	186,582	163,857	1.82	-12.18
YUGOSLAV SFR	28,994	37,139	41,643	117,369	97,421	1.08	-17.00
WESTERN EUR	**1,916,840**	**3,155,791**	**4,470,544**	**5,244,075**	**4,834,032**	**53.81**	**-7.82**
AUSTRIA	77,098	251,355	212,001	256,600	227,714	2.53	-11.26
FRANCE	397,758	552,636	644,210	593,557	437,108	4.87	-26.36
GERMANY	1,137,851	1,815,514	2,796,780	3,312,540	3,147,411	35.04	-4.98
SWITZERLAND	33,006	43,540	69,850	145,632	155,304	1.73	6.64
BENELUX	271,127	492,746	747,703	935,746	866,495	9.65	-7.40
EAST/MED EUR				**259,867**	**247,865**	**2.76**	**-4.62**
CYPRUS				17,602	21,691	0.24	23.23
ISRAEL				242,265	226,174	2.52	-6.64
OTHER EUROPE				**18,322**	**7,217**	**0.08**	**-60.61**
OTHER EUROPE				18,322	7,217	0.08	-60.61
MIDDLE EAST	**105,118**	**94,939**	**141,866**	**223,860**	**214,991**	**2.39**	**-3.96**
MIDDLE EAST	**105,118**	**94,939**	**141,866**	**223,860**	**214,991**	**2.39**	**-3.96**
BAHRAIN				2,107	2,258	0.03	7.17
IRAQ	9,478	9,725	10,159	12,504	13,974	0.16	11.76
JORDAN	11,221	8,605	15,162	20,462	20,301	0.23	-0.79
KUWAIT	4,270	4,164	6,264	7,415	9,182	0.10	23.83
LEBANON	17,488	14,624	23,760	52,077	34,455	0.38	-33.84
LIBYA	5,591	13,859	16,451	13,641	11,636	0.13	-14.70
OMAN				407	472	0.01	15.97
QATAR				480	826	0.01	72.08
SAUDI ARABIA	27,663	16,288	28,008	41,779	44,649	0.50	6.87
SYRIA	13,378	15,868	26,630	35,309	32,566	0.36	-7.77
UNTD ARAB EM				11,069	18,106	0.20	63.57
EGYPT	16,029	11,806	15,432	17,395	19,164	0.21	10.17
YEMEN				582	838	0.01	43.99
OT MIDD EAST				8,633	6,564	0.07	-23.97

3. ARRIVALS OF NON-RESIDENT TOURISTS IN HOTELS AND SIMILAR ESTABLISHMENTS, BY NATIONALITY

	1999	2000	2001	2002	2003	Market share 03	% change 03-02
SOUTH ASIA	**59,985**	**61,884**	**84,900**	**114,857**	**106,882**	**1.19**	**-6.94**
SOUTH ASIA	**59,985**	**61,884**	**84,900**	**114,857**	**106,882**	**1.19**	**-6.94**
BANGLADESH				544	742	0.01	36.40
INDIA				4,998	6,893	0.08	37.92
IRAN	54,312	58,282	81,138	104,956	94,735	1.05	-9.74
PAKISTAN	5,673	3,602	3,762	4,359	4,512	0.05	3.51
REG.NOT SPEC	**698,246**	**947,886**	**863,394**	**153,731**	**99,945**	**1.11**	**-34.99**
NOT SPECIFIE	**698,246**	**947,886**	**863,394**	**153,731**	**99,945**	**1.11**	**-34.99**
OTH.WORLD	698,246	947,886	863,394	153,731	99,945	1.11	-34.99

Source: World Tourism Organization (WTO)

4. ARRIVALS OF NON-RESIDENT TOURISTS IN ALL TYPES OF ACCOMMODATION ESTABLISHMENTS, BY NATIONALITY

	1999	2000	2001	2002	2003	Market share 03	% change 03-02
TOTAL (*)	**4,822,190**	**6,804,076**	**8,778,165**	**9,871,594**	**8,991,456**	**100.00**	**-8.92**
AFRICA		**6,286**	**21,433**	**35,530**	**25,506**	**0.28**	**-28.21**
NORTH AFRICA		**5,654**	**14,496**	**24,583**	**18,255**	**0.20**	**-25.74**
ALGERIA		1,399	3,525	12,502	5,938	0.07	-52.50
MOROCCO		47	791	2,903	3,987	0.04	37.34
SUDAN		38	867	718	1,051	0.01	46.38
TUNISIA		4,170	9,313	8,460	7,279	0.08	-13.96
SOUTHERN AFR		**272**	**5,483**	**9,643**	**6,024**	**0.07**	**-37.53**
SOUTH AFRICA		272	5,483	9,643	6,024	0.07	-37.53
OTHER AFRICA		**360**	**1,454**	**1,304**	**1,227**	**0.01**	**-5.90**
OTHER AFRICA		360	1,454	1,304	1,227	0.01	-5.90
AMERICAS	**503,274**	**444,480**	**454,293**	**382,266**	**231,898**	**2.58**	**-39.34**
CENTRAL AMER		**296**	**242**	**178**	**106**		**-40.45**
ALL CENT AME		296	242	178	106		-40.45
NORTH AMER	**503,274**	**442,072**	**444,046**	**348,679**	**220,463**	**2.45**	**-36.77**
CANADA	23,908	19,064	23,886	36,456	14,453	0.16	-60.35
MEXICO		150	4,676	7,247	6,387	0.07	-11.87
USA	479,366	422,112	414,524	304,270	198,737	2.21	-34.68
OT.NORTH.AME		746	960	706	886	0.01	25.50
SOUTH AMER		**2,112**	**10,005**	**33,409**	**11,329**	**0.13**	**-66.09**
ARGENTINA		1,759	4,211	24,855	6,117	0.07	-75.39
BRAZIL		117	2,600	4,295	2,849	0.03	-33.67
CHILE			567	1,363	844	0.01	-38.08
COLOMBIA		188	1,072	467	356		-23.77
VENEZUELA		7	539	552	270		-51.09
OTH SOUTH AM		41	1,016	1,877	893	0.01	-52.42
EAST AS/PACI	**318,073**	**343,392**	**502,451**	**524,613**	**391,959**	**4.36**	**-25.29**
N/EAST ASIA	**288,480**	**306,963**	**427,501**	**419,324**	**331,306**	**3.68**	**-20.99**
CHINA		2,694	15,709	23,670	21,538	0.24	-9.01
JAPAN	288,480	301,775	374,157	332,174	233,847	2.60	-29.60
KOREA REP.		2,494	37,635	63,480	75,921	0.84	19.60
S/EAST ASIA		**2,021**	**20,241**	**24,961**	**14,362**	**0.16**	**-42.46**
INDONESIA		15	526	1,079	373		-65.43
MALAYSIA		1,156	7,510	6,871	4,771	0.05	-30.56
PHILIPPINES		47	1,058	1,904	3,536	0.04	85.71
SINGAPORE		529	10,607	14,038	5,249	0.06	-62.61
THAILAND		274	540	1,069	433		-59.49
AUSTRALASIA	**29,593**	**34,397**	**54,212**	**77,077**	**44,995**	**0.50**	**-41.62**
AUSTRALIA	29,593	31,790	50,599	69,556	41,852	0.47	-39.83
NEW ZEALAND		2,607	3,613	7,521	3,143	0.03	-58.21
OT.EAST AS/P		**11**	**497**	**3,251**	**1,296**	**0.01**	**-60.14**
OTHER ASIA			426	2,547	1,173	0.01	-53.95
ALL OCEANIA		11	71	704	123		-82.53

4. ARRIVALS OF NON-RESIDENT TOURISTS IN ALL TYPES OF ACCOMMODATION ESTABLISHMENTS, BY NATIONALITY

	1999	2000	2001	2002	2003	Market share 03	% change 03-02
EUROPE	**3,134,661**	**5,648,711**	**7,324,539**	**8,436,556**	**7,919,946**	**88.08**	**-6.12**
C/E EUROPE	**581,153**	**918,501**	**1,091,541**	**1,478,515**	**1,604,478**	**17.84**	**8.52**
BULGARIA	25,056	25,843	37,088	65,718	53,806	0.60	-18.13
CZECH REP		2,617	16,874	44,754	29,913	0.33	-33.16
HUNGARY	8,987	9,007	10,649	31,173	22,014	0.24	-29.38
POLAND	19,070	61,805	69,313	77,306	129,787	1.44	67.89
ROMANIA	42,586	53,209	43,637	58,241	56,778	0.63	-2.51
CIS	485,454	766,020	913,980	1,201,323	1,312,180	14.59	9.23
NORTHERN EUR	**405,233**	**440,197**	**663,567**	**690,037**	**624,255**	**6.94**	**-9.53**
ICELAND		438	1,326	3,189	1,561	0.02	-51.05
IRELAND		3,075	73,140	52,898	75,388	0.84	42.52
UK	334,630	342,338	460,732	459,181	406,735	4.52	-11.42
SCANDINAVIA	70,603	94,346	128,369	174,769	140,571	1.56	-19.57
SOUTHERN EUR	**222,894**	**475,142**	**720,492**	**736,543**	**595,690**	**6.63**	**-19.12**
ALBANIA		72	4,292	10,844	15,279	0.17	40.90
GREECE	24,013	73,873	80,800	108,824	124,318	1.38	14.24
ITALY	100,522	203,333	372,229	294,090	183,296	2.04	-37.67
PORTUGAL		9,070	31,518	18,557	11,509	0.13	-37.98
SPAIN	69,130	150,983	189,412	186,613	163,857	1.82	-12.19
YUGOSLAV SFR	29,229	37,811	42,241	117,615	97,431	1.08	-17.16
WESTERN EUR	**1,925,381**	**3,161,526**	**4,476,040**	**5,253,263**	**4,840,431**	**53.83**	**-7.86**
AUSTRIA	77,786	251,630	212,354	256,859	227,724	2.53	-11.34
FRANCE	403,373	553,831	645,109	593,993	440,041	4.89	-25.92
GERMANY	1,139,858	1,818,480	2,799,478	3,320,142	3,149,203	35.02	-5.15
SWITZERLAND	33,018	43,555	69,939	145,711	155,434	1.73	6.67
BENELUX	271,346	494,030	749,160	936,558	868,029	9.65	-7.32
EAST/MED EUR		**134,754**	**242,150**	**259,876**	**247,875**	**2.76**	**-4.62**
CYPRUS		10,490	15,739	17,602	21,691	0.24	23.23
ISRAEL		124,264	226,411	242,274	226,184	2.52	-6.64
OTHER EUROPE		**518,591**	**130,749**	**18,322**	**7,217**	**0.08**	**-60.61**
OTHER EUROPE		518,591	130,749	18,322	7,217	0.08	-60.61
MIDDLE EAST	**106,103**	**98,948**	**159,732**	**223,866**	**215,135**	**2.39**	**-3.90**
MIDDLE EAST	**106,103**	**98,948**	**159,732**	**223,866**	**215,135**	**2.39**	**-3.90**
BAHRAIN		28	1,545	2,107	2,258	0.03	7.17
IRAQ	9,478	9,741	10,159	12,504	13,974	0.16	11.76
JORDAN	11,305	8,605	15,162	20,462	20,301	0.23	-0.79
KUWAIT	4,320	4,175	6,264	7,415	9,182	0.10	23.83
LEBANON	17,837	14,631	23,760	52,079	34,455	0.38	-33.84
LIBYA	5,591	13,859	16,451	13,641	11,636	0.13	-14.70
OMAN		9	3,955	407	472	0.01	15.97
QATAR		6	157	480	826	0.01	72.08
SAUDI ARABIA	27,738	16,292	28,008	41,783	44,670	0.50	6.91
SYRIA	13,805	15,926	26,630	35,309	32,566	0.36	-7.77
UNTD ARAB EM		2,952	4,345	11,069	18,106	0.20	63.57
EGYPT	16,029	11,806	15,432	17,395	19,287	0.21	10.88
YEMEN		7	290	582	838	0.01	43.99
OT MIDD EAST		911	7,574	8,633	6,564	0.07	-23.97

4. ARRIVALS OF NON-RESIDENT TOURISTS IN ALL TYPES OF ACCOMMODATION ESTABLISHMENTS, BY NATIONALITY

	1999	2000	2001	2002	2003	Market share 03	% change 03-02
SOUTH ASIA	**60,153**	**62,096**	**87,652**	**115,032**	**107,067**	**1.19**	**-6.92**
SOUTH ASIA	**60,153**	**62,096**	**87,652**	**115,032**	**107,067**	**1.19**	**-6.92**
BANGLADESH		15	589	585	742	0.01	26.84
INDIA		157	2,162	5,132	6,893	0.08	34.31
IRAN	54,480	58,296	81,139	104,956	94,740	1.05	-9.73
PAKISTAN	5,673	3,628	3,762	4,359	4,692	0.05	7.64
REG.NOT SPEC	**699,926**	**200,163**	**228,065**	**153,731**	**99,945**	**1.11**	**-34.99**
NOT SPECIFIE	**699,926**	**200,163**	**228,065**	**153,731**	**99,945**	**1.11**	**-34.99**
OTH.WORLD	699,926	200,163	228,065	153,731	99,945	1.11	-34.99

Source: World Tourism Organization (WTO)

5. OVERNIGHT STAYS OF NON-RESIDENT TOURISTS IN HOTELS AND SIMILAR ESTABLISHMENTS, BY NATIONALITY

		1999	2000	2001	2002	2003	Market share 03	% change 03-02
TOTAL	(*)	**20,358,222**	**28,377,334**	**36,307,368**	**43,224,611**	**40,818,839**	**100.00**	**-5.57**
AFRICA					**109,022**	**72,239**	**0.18**	**-33.74**
NORTH AFRICA					**68,682**	**55,718**	**0.14**	**-18.88**
ALGERIA					36,199	18,822	0.05	-48.00
MOROCCO					7,992	9,804	0.02	22.67
SUDAN					1,908	2,961	0.01	55.19
TUNISIA					22,583	24,131	0.06	6.85
SOUTHERN AFR					**34,568**	**13,611**	**0.03**	**-60.63**
SOUTH AFRICA					34,568	13,611	0.03	-60.63
OTHER AFRICA					**5,772**	**2,910**	**0.01**	**-49.58**
OTHER AFRICA					5,772	2,910	0.01	-49.58
AMERICAS		**1,343,884**	**875,040**	**908,193**	**1,002,342**	**664,387**	**1.63**	**-33.72**
CENTRAL AMER					**294**	**167**		**-43.20**
ALL CENT AME					294	167		-43.20
NORTH AMER		**1,343,884**	**875,040**	**908,193**	**907,952**	**634,266**	**1.55**	**-30.14**
CANADA		63,262	40,435	55,077	82,540	36,100	0.09	-56.26
MEXICO					17,373	13,533	0.03	-22.10
USA		1,280,622	834,605	853,116	805,804	582,668	1.43	-27.69
OT.NORTH.AME					2,235	1,965		-12.08
SOUTH AMER					**94,096**	**29,954**	**0.07**	**-68.17**
ARGENTINA					69,073	16,974	0.04	-75.43
BRAZIL					15,290	6,933	0.02	-54.66
CHILE					2,741	2,428	0.01	-11.42
COLOMBIA					1,710	1,123		-34.33
VENEZUELA					1,410	935		-33.69
OTH SOUTH AM					3,872	1,561		-59.68
EAST AS/PACI		**695,559**	**519,181**	**624,253**	**925,914**	**670,110**	**1.64**	**-27.63**
N/EAST ASIA		**611,057**	**396,969**	**502,335**	**606,045**	**489,849**	**1.20**	**-19.17**
CHINA					46,270	42,927	0.11	-7.22
JAPAN		611,057	396,969	502,335	460,711	334,053	0.82	-27.49
KOREA REP.					99,064	112,869	0.28	13.94
S/EAST ASIA					**49,270**	**29,037**	**0.07**	**-41.07**
INDONESIA					1,956	973		-50.26
MALAYSIA					15,328	8,983	0.02	-41.39
PHILIPPINES					5,358	9,029	0.02	68.51
SINGAPORE					24,452	9,218	0.02	-62.30
THAILAND					2,176	834		-61.67
AUSTRALASIA		**84,502**	**122,212**	**121,918**	**263,203**	**148,713**	**0.36**	**-43.50**
AUSTRALIA		84,502	122,212	121,918	248,222	141,071	0.35	-43.17
NEW ZEALAND					14,981	7,642	0.02	-48.99
OT.EAST AS/P					**7,396**	**2,511**	**0.01**	**-66.05**
OTHER ASIA					6,007	2,226	0.01	-62.94
ALL OCEANIA					1,389	285		-79.48

TURKEY

5. OVERNIGHT STAYS OF NON-RESIDENT TOURISTS IN HOTELS AND SIMILAR ESTABLISHMENTS, BY NATIONALITY

	1999	2000	2001	2002	2003	Market share 03	% change 03-02
EUROPE	**15,755,117**	**23,679,826**	**31,893,967**	**39,909,628**	**38,229,461**	**93.66**	**-4.21**
C/E EUROPE	**2,604,053**	**3,677,627**	**4,210,161**	**6,274,021**	**7,509,465**	**18.40**	**19.69**
BULGARIA	76,927	65,692	91,557	188,152	162,941	0.40	-13.40
CZECH REP				223,087	184,081	0.45	-17.48
HUNGARY	34,179	32,360	42,485	115,243	95,608	0.23	-17.04
POLAND	67,154	245,369	281,292	327,378	256,764	0.63	-21.57
ROMANIA	139,741	163,498	139,301	182,677	173,623	0.43	-4.96
CIS	2,286,052	3,170,708	3,655,526	5,237,484	6,636,448	16.26	26.71
NORTHERN EUR	**2,021,519**	**1,984,190**	**3,046,385**	**3,439,295**	**3,201,007**	**7.84**	**-6.93**
ICELAND				6,262	3,998	0.01	-36.15
IRELAND				188,743	280,965	0.69	48.86
UK	1,693,964	1,832,062	2,401,193	2,314,599	2,238,953	5.49	-3.27
SCANDINAVIA	327,555	152,128	645,192	929,691	677,091	1.66	-27.17
SOUTHERN EUR	**667,830**	**1,085,683**	**1,553,391**	**1,953,309**	**1,687,633**	**4.13**	**-13.60**
ALBANIA				31,241	41,736	0.10	33.59
GREECE	64,727	146,648	161,177	238,240	292,947	0.72	22.96
ITALY	325,702	516,167	877,665	819,279	480,726	1.18	-41.32
PORTUGAL				39,758	26,332	0.06	-33.77
SPAIN	188,850	321,524	367,653	414,057	386,339	0.95	-6.69
YUGOSLAV SFR	88,551	101,344	146,896	410,734	459,553	1.13	11.89
WESTERN EUR	**10,461,715**	**16,932,326**	**23,084,030**	**27,415,171**	**25,004,581**	**61.26**	**-8.79**
AUSTRIA	556,194	1,303,197	1,164,326	1,689,332	1,427,588	3.50	-15.49
FRANCE	1,552,349	1,890,049	2,242,522	2,370,769	1,511,173	3.70	-36.26
GERMANY	6,886,384	10,934,445	15,313,178	17,788,271	16,283,624	39.89	-8.46
SWITZERLAND	104,716	240,704	396,639	684,540	623,512	1.53	-8.92
BENELUX	1,362,072	2,563,931	3,967,365	4,882,259	5,158,684	12.64	5.66
EAST/MED EUR				**742,519**	**787,189**	**1.93**	**6.02**
CYPRUS				38,025	46,997	0.12	23.60
ISRAEL				704,494	740,192	1.81	5.07
OTHER EUROPE				**85,313**	**39,586**	**0.10**	**-53.60**
OTHER EUROPE				85,313	39,586	0.10	-53.60
MIDDLE EAST	**320,057**	**233,976**	**368,533**	**601,135**	**615,695**	**1.51**	**2.42**
MIDDLE EAST	**320,057**	**233,976**	**368,533**	**601,135**	**615,695**	**1.51**	**2.42**
BAHRAIN				7,387	6,165	0.02	-16.54
IRAQ	29,341	19,520	24,284	40,492	48,162	0.12	18.94
JORDAN	36,085	20,435	37,066	57,475	65,842	0.16	14.56
KUWAIT	14,654	10,374	14,703	20,885	24,726	0.06	18.39
LEBANON	47,534	32,428	51,067	97,608	88,193	0.22	-9.65
LIBYA	19,785	44,132	53,443	46,112	32,470	0.08	-29.58
OMAN				985	1,187		20.51
QATAR				1,472	2,423	0.01	64.61
SAUDI ARABIA	80,046	37,098	71,814	134,618	119,461	0.29	-11.26
SYRIA	35,431	31,921	65,747	85,491	79,519	0.19	-6.99
UNTD ARAB EM				32,837	64,724	0.16	97.11
EGYPT	57,181	38,068	50,409	59,053	62,802	0.15	6.35
YEMEN				1,433	2,191	0.01	52.90
OT MIDD EAST				15,287	17,830	0.04	16.64

5. OVERNIGHT STAYS OF NON-RESIDENT TOURISTS IN HOTELS AND SIMILAR ESTABLISHMENTS, BY NATIONALITY

	1999	2000	2001	2002	2003	Market share 03	% change 03-02
SOUTH ASIA	**155,801**	**157,215**	**255,200**	**339,592**	**314,812**	**0.77**	**-7.30**
SOUTH ASIA	**155,801**	**157,215**	**255,200**	**339,592**	**314,812**	**0.77**	**-7.30**
BANGLADESH				1,397	2,614	0.01	87.12
INDIA				14,621	21,408	0.05	46.42
IRAN	138,839	148,340	247,134	313,215	278,994	0.68	-10.93
PAKISTAN	16,962	8,875	8,066	10,359	11,796	0.03	13.87
REG.NOT SPEC	**2,087,804**	**2,912,096**	**2,257,222**	**336,978**	**252,135**	**0.62**	**-25.18**
NOT SPECIFIE	**2,087,804**	**2,912,096**	**2,257,222**	**336,978**	**252,135**	**0.62**	**-25.18**
OTH.WORLD	2,087,804	2,912,096	2,257,222	336,978	252,135	0.62	-25.18

Source: World Tourism Organization (WTO)

6. OVERNIGHT STAYS OF NON-RESIDENT TOURISTS IN ALL TYPES OF ACCOMMODATION ESTABLISHMENTS, BY NATIONALITY

	1999	2000	2001	2002	2003	Market share 03	% change 03-02
TOTAL (*)	**20,434,883**	**28,510,906**	**36,368,500**	**43,312,498**	**40,866,002**	**100.00**	**-5.65**
AFRICA		**13,694**	**53,128**	**109,024**	**72,242**	**0.18**	**-33.74**
NORTH AFRICA		**11,678**	**36,767**	**68,682**	**55,718**	**0.14**	**-18.88**
ALGERIA		2,292	8,722	36,199	18,822	0.05	-48.00
MOROCCO		131	2,534	7,992	9,804	0.02	22.67
SUDAN		66	2,024	1,908	2,961	0.01	55.19
TUNISIA		9,189	23,487	22,583	24,131	0.06	6.85
SOUTHERN AFR		**654**	**10,548**	**34,570**	**13,614**	**0.03**	**-60.62**
SOUTH AFRICA		654	10,548	34,570	13,614	0.03	-60.62
OTHER AFRICA		**1,362**	**5,813**	**5,772**	**2,910**	**0.01**	**-49.58**
OTHER AFRICA		1,362	5,813	5,772	2,910	0.01	-49.58
AMERICAS	**1,347,862**	**884,715**	**964,901**	**1,010,626**	**669,497**	**1.64**	**-33.75**
CENTRAL AMER		**694**	**455**	**294**	**167**		**-43.20**
ALL CENT AME		694	455	294	167		-43.20
NORTH AMER	**1,347,862**	**879,953**	**922,538**	**915,235**	**639,376**	**1.56**	**-30.14**
CANADA	63,327	40,440	55,077	82,566	36,100	0.09	-56.28
MEXICO		246	10,559	17,373	15,273	0.04	-12.09
USA	1,284,535	837,685	853,246	813,061	586,038	1.43	-27.92
OT.NORTH.AME		1,582	3,656	2,235	1,965		-12.08
SOUTH AMER		**4,068**	**41,908**	**95,097**	**29,954**	**0.07**	**-68.50**
ARGENTINA		3,050	28,805	70,061	16,974	0.04	-75.77
BRAZIL		701	6,459	15,303	6,933	0.02	-54.70
CHILE			1,342	2,741	2,428	0.01	-11.42
COLOMBIA		188	1,547	1,710	1,123		-34.33
VENEZUELA		42	1,271	1,410	935		-33.69
OTH SOUTH AM		87	2,484	3,872	1,561		-59.68
EAST AS/PACI	**696,608**	**553,757**	**762,837**	**925,986**	**670,440**	**1.64**	**-27.60**
N/EAST ASIA	**611,089**	**411,759**	**588,414**	**606,082**	**489,849**	**1.20**	**-19.18**
CHINA		11,063	30,145	46,270	42,927	0.11	-7.22
JAPAN	611,089	397,176	502,533	460,720	334,053	0.82	-27.49
KOREA REP.		3,520	55,736	99,092	112,869	0.28	13.90
S/EAST ASIA		**3,188**	**38,275**	**49,274**	**29,037**	**0.07**	**-41.07**
INDONESIA		15	1,041	1,956	973		-50.26
MALAYSIA		1,761	16,947	15,328	8,983	0.02	-41.39
PHILIPPINES		99	2,659	5,358	9,029	0.02	68.51
SINGAPORE		1,039	16,690	24,456	9,218	0.02	-62.31
THAILAND		274	938	2,176	834		-61.67
AUSTRALASIA	**85,519**	**138,769**	**134,872**	**263,234**	**149,043**	**0.36**	**-43.38**
AUSTRALIA	85,519	133,397	127,694	248,244	141,395	0.35	-43.04
NEW ZEALAND		5,372	7,178	14,990	7,648	0.02	-48.98
OT.EAST AS/P		**41**	**1,276**	**7,396**	**2,511**	**0.01**	**-66.05**
OTHER ASIA			956	6,007	2,226	0.01	-62.94
ALL OCEANIA		41	320	1,389	285		-79.48

6. OVERNIGHT STAYS OF NON-RESIDENT TOURISTS IN ALL TYPES OF ACCOMMODATION ESTABLISHMENTS, BY NATIONALITY

	1999	2000	2001	2002	2003	Market share 03	% change 03-02
EUROPE	**15,808,271**	**26,143,491**	**33,441,912**	**39,984,737**	**38,267,172**	**93.64**	**-4.30**
C/E EUROPE	**2,613,966**	**3,690,764**	**4,302,842**	**6,285,833**	**7,511,460**	**18.38**	**19.50**
BULGARIA	77,924	65,799	91,557	188,271	162,942	0.40	-13.45
CZECH REP		12,520	90,417	223,456	184,712	0.45	-17.34
HUNGARY	34,790	32,368	42,520	115,533	95,656	0.23	-17.20
POLAND	68,421	245,547	281,993	327,570	256,796	0.63	-21.61
ROMANIA	140,412	163,505	139,474	183,854	173,625	0.42	-5.56
CIS	2,292,419	3,171,025	3,656,881	5,247,149	6,637,729	16.24	26.50
NORTHERN EUR	**2,031,240**	**2,393,183**	**3,248,517**	**3,444,547**	**3,203,371**	**7.84**	**-7.00**
ICELAND		1,318	2,726	6,262	3,998	0.01	-36.15
IRELAND		7,331	195,360	188,752	280,965	0.69	48.85
UK	1,696,916	1,901,226	2,401,984	2,315,991	2,240,123	5.48	-3.28
SCANDINAVIA	334,324	483,308	648,447	933,542	678,285	1.66	-27.34
SOUTHERN EUR	**670,920**	**1,119,179**	**1,645,778**	**1,958,412**	**1,689,753**	**4.13**	**-13.72**
ALBANIA		555	18,544	31,247	41,736	0.10	33.57
GREECE	64,929	146,671	161,188	238,256	292,947	0.72	22.95
ITALY	327,838	518,216	878,307	822,933	482,628	1.18	-41.35
PORTUGAL		16,689	61,385	39,770	26,519	0.06	-33.32
SPAIN	189,002	321,747	367,798	414,530	386,339	0.95	-6.80
YUGOSLAV SFR	89,151	115,301	158,556	411,676	459,584	1.12	11.64
WESTERN EUR	**10,492,145**	**16,963,077**	**23,119,223**	**27,468,096**	**25,035,710**	**61.26**	**-8.86**
AUSTRIA	559,827	1,305,879	1,166,829	1,690,622	1,427,612	3.49	-15.56
FRANCE	1,567,120	1,892,704	2,247,792	2,374,963	1,520,130	3.72	-35.99
GERMANY	6,897,299	10,955,494	15,335,059	17,830,614	16,301,447	39.89	-8.58
SWITZERLAND	104,895	240,742	397,263	685,049	623,799	1.53	-8.94
BENELUX	1,363,004	2,568,258	3,972,280	4,886,848	5,162,722	12.63	5.65
EAST/MED EUR		**416,470**	**664,464**	**742,536**	**787,292**	**1.93**	**6.03**
CYPRUS		22,775	33,849	38,025	46,997	0.12	23.60
ISRAEL		393,695	630,615	704,511	740,295	1.81	5.08
OTHER EUROPE		**1,560,818**	**461,088**	**85,313**	**39,586**	**0.10**	**-53.60**
OTHER EUROPE		1,560,818	461,088	85,313	39,586	0.10	-53.60
MIDDLE EAST	**322,581**	**245,307**	**403,817**	**601,150**	**617,898**	**1.51**	**2.79**
MIDDLE EAST	**322,581**	**245,307**	**403,817**	**601,150**	**617,898**	**1.51**	**2.79**
BAHRAIN		114	5,268	7,387	6,165	0.02	-16.54
IRAQ	29,341	19,536	24,284	40,492	48,162	0.12	18.94
JORDAN	36,323	20,435	37,066	57,475	65,842	0.16	14.56
KUWAIT	14,753	10,386	14,703	20,885	24,726	0.06	18.39
LEBANON	48,499	32,435	51,067	97,610	88,193	0.22	-9.65
LIBYA	19,785	44,132	53,443	46,112	32,470	0.08	-29.58
OMAN		9	4,355	985	1,187		20.51
QATAR		6	371	1,472	2,423	0.01	64.61
SAUDI ARABIA	80,230	37,103	71,814	134,631	119,564	0.29	-11.19
SYRIA	36,469	31,979	65,747	85,491	79,519	0.19	-6.99
UNTD ARAB EM		10,148	11,359	32,837	64,724	0.16	97.11
EGYPT	57,181	38,068	50,409	59,053	64,902	0.16	9.90
YEMEN		45	745	1,433	2,191	0.01	52.90
OT MIDD EAST		911	13,186	15,287	17,830	0.04	16.64

TURKEY

6. OVERNIGHT STAYS OF NON-RESIDENT TOURISTS IN ALL TYPES OF ACCOMMODATION ESTABLISHMENTS, BY NATIONALITY

	1999	2000	2001	2002	2003	Market share 03	% change 03-02
SOUTH ASIA	**157,054**	**157,618**	**262,823**	**343,997**	**316,618**	**0.77**	**-7.96**
SOUTH ASIA	**157,054**	**157,618**	**262,823**	**343,997**	**316,618**	**0.77**	**-7.96**
BANGLADESH		41	2,437	2,344	2,614	0.01	11.52
INDIA		322	5,185	18,079	21,408	0.05	18.41
IRAN	140,092	148,354	247,135	313,215	279,004	0.68	-10.92
PAKISTAN	16,962	8,901	8,066	10,359	13,592	0.03	31.21
REG.NOT SPEC	**2,102,507**	**512,324**	**479,082**	**336,978**	**252,135**	**0.62**	**-25.18**
NOT SPECIFIE	**2,102,507**	**512,324**	**479,082**	**336,978**	**252,135**	**0.62**	**-25.18**
OTH.WORLD	2,102,507	512,324	479,082	336,978	252,135	0.62	-25.18

Source: World Tourism Organization (WTO)

TURKS AND CAICOS ISLANDS

1. ARRIVALS OF NON-RESIDENT TOURISTS AT NATIONAL BORDERS, BY COUNTRY OF RESIDENCE

	1999	2000	2001	2002	2003	Market share 03	% change 03-02
TOTAL	120,898	152,291	165,920	154,961			
AMERICAS	98,316	136,211	148,025	140,349			
CARIBBEAN	4,777	6,921	6,790	5,017			
ANTIGUA,BARB	7	22	26	27			
BAHAMAS	1,862	2,189	2,405	1,955			
BARBADOS	155	159	171	129			
BERMUDA		133	94	92			
BR.VIRGIN IS		51	25	12			
CAYMAN IS		245	213	228			
CUBA		5	24	24			
DOMINICA	3	17	4	2			
DOMINICAN RP		976	354	266			
GRENADA	2	10	10				
GUADELOUPE		4	9	5			
HAITI		1,100	846	345			
JAMAICA	830	1,191	1,936	1,482			
MARTINIQUE		8	7	5			
MONTSERRAT	4	23		5			
ARUBA		4	12	4			
BONAIRE			1	1			
CURACAO		2	5				
PUERTO RICO		135	93	101			
ST.KITTS NEV		18	13	7			
ANGUILLA	1	22	18	7			
ST.LUCIA	98	64	65	42			
SAINT MAARTE		8	7	3			
ST.VINCENT,G	1	18	37	25			
TRINIDAD TBG	22	158	186	156			
US.VIRGIN IS		22	24	12			
OTH CARIBBE	1,792	337	205	82			
CENTRAL AMER	6	17	28	20			
BELIZE	6	17	28	20			
NORTH AMER	93,500	128,108	140,407	134,722			
CANADA	9,949	15,597	15,282	14,775			
USA	83,551	112,511	125,125	119,947			
SOUTH AMER	33	1,165	800	590			
ARGENTINA		564	405	172			
BRAZIL		147	73	87			
GUYANA	33	121	77	62			
VENEZUELA		77	62	74			
OTH SOUTH AM		256	183	195			
EAST AS/PACI		113	57	35			
N/EAST ASIA		113	57	35			
JAPAN		113	57	35			
EUROPE	11,498	11,829	11,086	10,634			
NORTHERN EUR	3,841	5,077	6,563	6,898			
DENMARK	65	17		21			

TURKS AND CAICOS ISLANDS

1. ARRIVALS OF NON-RESIDENT TOURISTS AT NATIONAL BORDERS, BY COUNTRY OF RESIDENCE

	1999	2000	2001	2002	2003	Market share 03	% change 03-02
IRELAND		83		67			
NORWAY	41	88		32			
SWEDEN	113	123	56	136			
UK	3,622	4,766	6,507	6,642			
SOUTHERN EUR	**2,235**	**2,366**	**1,843**	**1,161**			
GREECE		25		9			
ITALY	2,141	2,188	1,724	1,082			
PORTUGAL	4	49		18			
SPAIN	90	104	119	52			
WESTERN EUR	**5,422**	**4,182**	**2,250**	**2,479**			
AUSTRIA	288	365		104			
BELGIUM	138	181	154	119			
FRANCE	1,828	1,752	1,268	1,569			
GERMANY	2,757	1,427	476	357			
LUXEMBOURG	8	20		10			
NETHERLANDS	24	71	37				
SWITZERLAND	379	366	315	320			
OTHER EUROPE		**204**	**430**	**96**			
OTHER EUROPE		204	430	96			
REG.NOT SPEC	**11,084**	**4,138**	**6,752**	**3,943**			
NOT SPECIFIE	**11,084**	**4,138**	**6,752**	**3,943**			
OTH.WORLD	11,084	4,138	6,752	3,943			

Source: World Tourism Organization (WTO)

TUVALU

1. ARRIVALS OF NON-RESIDENT TOURISTS AT NATIONAL BORDERS, BY NATIONALITY

	1999	2000	2001	2002	2003	Market share 03	% change 03-02
TOTAL	**1,098**	**1,079**	**1,140**	**1,313**	**1,377**	**100.00**	**4.87**
AMERICAS	**50**	**59**	**65**	**92**	**130**	**9.44**	**41.30**
NORTH AMER	**50**	**59**	**65**	**92**	**130**	**9.44**	**41.30**
CANADA	4	6	10	14	17	1.23	21.43
USA	46	53	55	78	113	8.21	44.87
EAST AS/PACI	**957**	**922**	**957**	**1,075**	**1,101**	**79.96**	**2.42**
N/EAST ASIA	**236**	**222**	**189**	**152**	**109**	**7.92**	**-28.29**
JAPAN	236	222	189	152	109	7.92	-28.29
AUSTRALASIA	**231**	**249**	**305**	**362**	**352**	**25.56**	**-2.76**
AUSTRALIA	165	161	165	187	207	15.03	10.70
NEW ZEALAND	66	88	140	175	145	10.53	-17.14
MELANESIA				**336**	**336**	**24.40**	
FIJI				336	336	24.40	
MICRONESIA					**162**	**11.76**	
KIRIBATI					162	11.76	
OT.EAST AS/P	**490**	**451**	**463**	**225**	**142**	**10.31**	**-36.89**
OTHER ASIA	98	35	47	68	58	4.21	-14.71
ALL OCEANIA	392	416	416	157	84	6.10	-46.50
EUROPE	**73**	**62**	**102**	**108**	**97**	**7.04**	**-10.19**
NORTHERN EUR	**14**	**23**	**31**	**34**	**46**	**3.34**	**35.29**
UK	14	23	31	34	46	3.34	35.29
WESTERN EUR	**40**	**18**	**25**	**39**	**28**	**2.03**	**-28.21**
FRANCE	9	5	21	13	16	1.16	23.08
GERMANY	31	13	4	26	12	0.87	-53.85
OTHER EUROPE	**19**	**21**	**46**	**35**	**23**	**1.67**	**-34.29**
OTHER EUROPE	19	21	46	35	23	1.67	-34.29
REG.NOT SPEC	**18**	**36**	**16**	**38**	**49**	**3.56**	**28.95**
NOT SPECIFIE	**18**	**36**	**16**	**38**	**49**	**3.56**	**28.95**
OTH.WORLD	18	36	16	38	49	3.56	28.95

Source: World Tourism Organization (WTO)

UGANDA

1. ARRIVALS OF NON-RESIDENT TOURISTS AT NATIONAL BORDERS, BY COUNTRY OF RESIDENCE

	1999	2000	2001	2002	2003	Market share 03	% change 03-02
TOTAL	**189,347**	**192,755**	**205,287**	**254,212**	**304,656**	**100.00**	**19.84**
AFRICA	**116,207**	**131,687**	**149,907**	**192,278**	**233,043**	**76.49**	**21.20**
EAST AFRICA	**97,944**	**112,616**	**122,741**	**158,039**	**196,006**	**64.34**	**24.02**
ETHIOPIA	1,704	1,300	1,348	1,509	1,811	0.59	20.01
KENYA	68,167	60,900	64,933	80,516	113,681	37.31	41.19
RWANDA	7,293	36,041	39,597	52,431	50,107	16.45	-4.43
TANZANIA	20,780	14,375	16,863	23,583	30,407	9.98	28.94
CENTRAL AFR	**7,552**	**7,957**	**5,974**	**7,586**	**5,890**	**1.93**	**-22.36**
DEM.R.CONGO	7,552	7,957	5,974	7,586	5,890	1.93	-22.36
NORTH AFRICA	**931**	**760**	**2,994**	**3,969**	**5,606**	**1.84**	**41.24**
SUDAN	931	760	2,994	3,969	5,606	1.84	41.24
OTHER AFRICA	**9,780**	**10,354**	**18,198**	**22,684**	**25,541**	**8.38**	**12.59**
OTHER AFRICA	9,780	10,354	18,198	22,684	25,541	8.38	12.59
AMERICAS	**12,898**	**11,947**	**12,922**	**14,785**	**16,409**	**5.39**	**10.98**
NORTH AMER	**12,341**	**11,646**	**12,420**	**14,139**	**15,683**	**5.15**	**10.92**
CANADA	2,539	2,053	1,870	2,216	2,507	0.82	13.13
USA	9,802	9,593	10,550	11,923	13,176	4.32	10.51
OTHER AMERIC	**557**	**301**	**502**	**646**	**726**	**0.24**	**12.38**
OTH AMERICA	557	301	502	646	726	0.24	12.38
EAST AS/PACI	**6,123**	**4,899**	**4,757**	**4,188**	**4,845**	**1.59**	**15.69**
N/EAST ASIA	**2,189**	**1,718**	**1,564**	**1,616**	**1,842**	**0.60**	**13.99**
CHINA	1,127	945	1,025	1,036	1,181	0.39	14.00
JAPAN	1,062	773	539	580	661	0.22	13.97
AUSTRALASIA	**2,678**	**2,069**	**1,325**	**1,325**	**1,555**	**0.51**	**17.36**
AUSTRALIA	1,916	1,550	1,068	1,100	1,349	0.44	22.64
NEW ZEALAND	762	519	257	225	206	0.07	-8.44
OT.EAST AS/P	**1,256**	**1,112**	**1,868**	**1,247**	**1,448**	**0.48**	**16.12**
OTHER ASIA	1,256	1,112	1,868	1,247	1,448	0.48	16.12
EUROPE	**43,133**	**36,050**	**30,395**	**33,850**	**39,207**	**12.87**	**15.83**
C/E EUROPE	**270**	**167**	**278**	**312**	**349**	**0.11**	**11.86**
CZECH RP/SVK	49	28	43	39	63	0.02	61.54
RUSSIAN FED	221	139	235	273	286	0.09	4.76
NORTHERN EUR	**29,124**	**24,706**	**18,011**	**20,711**	**23,277**	**7.64**	**12.39**
DENMARK	2,299	1,654	1,401	1,499	1,642	0.54	9.54
FINLAND	204	178	133	227	224	0.07	-1.32
IRELAND	765	707	700	700	863	0.28	23.29
NORWAY	8,642	6,717	894	1,480	1,528	0.50	3.24
SWEDEN	1,470	1,496	1,257	1,637	1,844	0.61	12.65
UK	15,744	13,954	13,626	15,168	17,176	5.64	13.24
SOUTHERN EUR	**2,192**	**1,604**	**2,150**	**1,842**	**2,009**	**0.66**	**9.07**
ITALY	2,128	1,560	2,080	1,735	1,924	0.63	10.89

UGANDA

1. ARRIVALS OF NON-RESIDENT TOURISTS AT NATIONAL BORDERS, BY COUNTRY OF RESIDENCE

	1999	2000	2001	2002	2003	Market share 03	% change 03-02
SERBIA,MTNEG	64	44	70	107	85	0.03	-20.56
WESTERN EUR	**10,324**	**8,606**	**9,042**	**9,888**	**12,246**	**4.02**	**23.85**
AUSTRIA	442	249	168	262	349	0.11	33.21
BELGIUM	1,649	1,446	1,407	1,438	1,748	0.57	21.56
FRANCE	1,650	1,320	1,351	1,353	3,022	0.99	123.36
GERMANY	3,304	2,497	2,920	3,280	3,519	1.16	7.29
NETHERLANDS	2,278	2,203	2,111	2,339	2,474	0.81	5.77
SWITZERLAND	1,001	891	1,085	1,216	1,134	0.37	-6.74
OTHER EUROPE	**1,223**	**967**	**914**	**1,097**	**1,326**	**0.44**	**20.88**
OTHER EUROPE	1,223	967	914	1,097	1,326	0.44	20.88
MIDDLE EAST	**3,183**	**2,032**	**1,792**	**1,836**	**1,976**	**0.65**	**7.63**
MIDDLE EAST	**3,183**	**2,032**	**1,792**	**1,836**	**1,976**	**0.65**	**7.63**
EGYPT	773	553	546	609	583	0.19	-4.27
OT MIDD EAST	2,410	1,479	1,246	1,227	1,393	0.46	13.53
SOUTH ASIA	**7,048**	**5,538**	**5,514**	**6,439**	**7,647**	**2.51**	**18.76**
SOUTH ASIA	**7,048**	**5,538**	**5,514**	**6,439**	**7,647**	**2.51**	**18.76**
INDIA	6,206	4,810	4,588	5,708	6,623	2.17	16.03
PAKISTAN	842	728	926	731	1,024	0.34	40.08
REG.NOT SPEC	**755**	**602**		**836**	**1,529**	**0.50**	**82.89**
NOT SPECIFIE	**755**	**602**		**836**	**1,529**	**0.50**	**82.89**
OTH.WORLD	755	602		836	1,529	0.50	82.89

Source: World Tourism Organization (WTO)

UKRAINE

1. ARRIVALS OF NON-RESIDENT TOURISTS AT NATIONAL BORDERS, BY COUNTRY OF RESIDENCE

	1999	2000	2001	2002	2003	Market share 03	% change 03-02
TOTAL	**4,232,358**	**6,430,940**	**9,174,165**	**10,516,665**	**12,513,883**	**100.00**	**18.99**
AFRICA	**6,928**	**15,296**	**5,227**	**4,748**	**12,367**	**0.10**	**160.47**
EAST AFRICA	**427**	**2,047**	**619**	**340**	**5,251**	**0.04**	**1,444.41**
BURUNDI	10	146	12	20	6		-70.00
ETHIOPIA	86	364	179	108	1,800	0.01	1.566.67
ERITREA			2	6	16		166.67
KENYA	36	264	20	22	69		213.64
MADAGASCAR	2	146	25	9	10		11.11
MALAWI			20		1		
MAURITIUS	190	352	301	62	197		217.74
MOZAMBIQUE	13	152	4	2	2		
RWANDA	6	177	9	6	2,885	0.02	*********
SOMALIA	14	182	15	47	88		87.23
ZIMBABWE	12		3	15	33		120.00
UGANDA	15	1		16	114		612.50
TANZANIA	27	255	29	27	18		-33.33
ZAMBIA	16	8			5		
OTH.EAST.AFR					7		
CENTRAL AFR	**219**	**800**	**278**	**297**	**2,469**	**0.02**	**731.31**
ANGOLA	54	196	86	78	2,204	0.02	2.725.64
CAMEROON	64	241	52	83	117		40.96
CHAD	7	172	4	8	16		100.00
CONGO	87	191	125	108	102		-5.56
DEM.R.CONGO			2				
SAO TOME PRN	1		9	3	1		-66.67
OTH MID.AFRI	6			17	29		70.59
NORTH AFRICA	**4,236**	**5,453**	**2,958**	**2,775**	**3,082**	**0.02**	**11.06**
ALGERIA	437	809	531	650	339		-47.85
MOROCCO	1,230	1,361	744	800	1,316	0.01	64.50
SUDAN	352	771	422	332	274		-17.47
TUNISIA	2,217	2,512	1,261	993	1,153	0.01	16.11
SOUTHERN AFR	**694**	**4,313**	**542**	**491**	**715**	**0.01**	**45.62**
SOUTH AFRICA	691	4,299	542	485	702	0.01	44.74
OTH.SOUTH.AF	3	14		6	13		116.67
WEST AFRICA	**1,352**	**2,683**	**830**	**845**	**850**	**0.01**	**0.59**
CAPE VERDE	14	6	6	5	29		480.00
BENIN	19	161	63	80	16		-80.00
GHANA	117	509	189	159	76		-52.20
GUINEA	56	227	63	62	16		-74.19
LIBERIA	9	31	26	122	154		26.23
MALI	14	236	11	13	20		53.85
MAURITANIA	40	178	16	10	28		180.00
NIGERIA	289	531	287	254	393		54.72
GUINEABISSAU	21	184	45	42	8		-80.95
SENEGAL	23	209	50	35	17		-51.43
SIERRA LEONE	697	5	13	1	19		1.800.00
TOGO	33	213	34	24	20		-16.67
BURKINA FASO	19	193	27	31	12		-61.29
OTH.WEST.AFR	1			7	42		500.00

UKRAINE

1. ARRIVALS OF NON-RESIDENT TOURISTS AT NATIONAL BORDERS, BY COUNTRY OF RESIDENCE

	1999	2000	2001	2002	2003	Market share 03	% change 03-02
AMERICAS	**70,158**	**70,542**	**64,096**	**52,632**	**83,451**	**0.67**	**58.56**
CARIBBEAN	**2,991**	**2,877**	**594**	**694**	**1,655**	**0.01**	**138.47**
ANTIGUA,BARB		2	119		462		
BAHAMAS	958	1,212	9	33	47		42.42
BERMUDA	1				22		
BR.VIRGIN IS	1,327	40			419		
CAYMAN IS	2				21		
CUBA	502	711	399	426	513		20.42
DOMINICAN RP	5		12	9	30		233.33
JAMAICA	17	194	20	11	41		272.73
ARUBA	28						
ST.LUCIA	2	146	2	176	1		-99.43
ST.VINCENT,G	137	239	16	35	77		120.00
TRINIDAD TBG	6	165	17	4	4		
OTH CARIBBE	6	168			18		
CENTRAL AMER	**439**	**1,094**	**814**	**1,359**	**1,148**	**0.01**	**-15.53**
BELIZE	17	203	626	1,145	9		-99.21
COSTA RICA	32	261	58	38	43		13.16
EL SALVADOR	48	185	39	14	42		200.00
GUATEMALA	3	3	23	4	11		175.00
HONDURAS	234	5	5	7	28		300.00
NICARAGUA	12	237	4	5	556		*********
PANAMA	93	200	59	146	459		214.38
NORTH AMER	**64,562**	**62,013**	**60,080**	**48,140**	**78,392**	**0.63**	**62.84**
CANADA	9,953	8,474	10,078	9,567	11,530	0.09	20.52
GREENLAND		2	1				
MEXICO	585	642	1,056	203	523		157.64
USA	54,024	52,895	48,945	38,370	66,339	0.53	72.89
SOUTH AMER	**2,166**	**4,558**	**2,608**	**2,439**	**2,256**	**0.02**	**-7.50**
ARGENTINA	627	1,122	787	681	588		-13.66
BOLIVIA	87	250	49	41	270		558.54
BRAZIL	630	1,241	1,070	1,119	685	0.01	-38.78
CHILE	164	364	230	95	94		-1.05
COLOMBIA	124	229	76	81	104		28.40
ECUADOR	83	383	129	119	76		-36.13
GUYANA	25	5	3		4		
PARAGUAY	32	22	4	4	4		
PERU	176	385	137	179	251		40.22
URUGUAY	119	238	19	18	26		44.44
VENEZUELA	99	319	104	90	136		51.11
OTH SOUTH AM				12	18		50.00
EAST AS/PACI	**23,979**	**26,625**	**17,107**	**21,900**	**26,362**	**0.21**	**20.37**
N/EAST ASIA	**13,292**	**14,874**	**8,617**	**13,500**	**17,520**	**0.14**	**29.78**
CHINA	7,508	5,153	4,261	8,451	8,332	0.07	-1.41
TAIWAN(P.C.)	211	4,063	72	80	230		187.50
HK,CHINA	12	3	5	26	158		507.69
JAPAN	3,102	2,384	1,725	2,109	4,526	0.04	114.60
KOREA D P RP	220	562	689	236	163		-30.93
KOREA REP.	1,326	1,263	254	1,137	3,304	0.03	190.59
MONGOLIA	913	1,446	1,611	1,461	806	0.01	-44.83

UKRAINE

1. ARRIVALS OF NON-RESIDENT TOURISTS AT NATIONAL BORDERS, BY COUNTRY OF RESIDENCE

	1999	2000	2001	2002	2003	Market share 03	% change 03-02
OT NORTH AS					1		
S/EAST ASIA	**7,275**	**8,178**	**3,429**	**3,686**	**6,305**	**0.05**	**71.05**
BRUNEI DARSM				6	4		-33.33
MYANMAR	1	13	1	19	49		157.89
CAMBODIA	5	141	173	51	96		88.24
INDONESIA	93	203	163	142	359		152.82
LAO P.DEM.R.	108	5	2		36		
MALAYSIA	114	370	197	637	1,723	0.01	170.49
PHILIPPINES	680	544	319	398	1,509	0.01	279.15
SINGAPORE	81	608	81	95	176		85.26
VIET NAM	5,523	5,640	2,293	2,173	2,125	0.02	-2.21
THAILAND	670	598	200	165	228		38.18
OTH S/E ASIA		56					
AUSTRALASIA	**3,402**	**3,534**	**5,057**	**4,714**	**2,518**	**0.02**	**-46.58**
AUSTRALIA	3,051	2,388	4,671	4,440	2,189	0.02	-50.70
NEW ZEALAND	351	1,146	386	274	329		20.07
MELANESIA			**3**		**19**		
FIJI			3		19		
OT.EAST AS/P	**10**	**39**	**1**				
OEAP	10	39	1				
EUROPE	**4,098,338**	**6,283,415**	**9,061,051**	**10,408,714**	**12,345,396**	**98.65**	**18.61**
C/E EUROPE	**3,866,611**	**6,048,961**	**8,781,741**	**10,065,891**	**11,974,308**	**95.69**	**18.96**
AZERBAIJAN	22,853	22,714	10,337	10,445	13,510	0.11	29.34
ARMENIA	19,801	15,423	10,845	16,475	21,640	0.17	31.35
BULGARIA	19,941	17,477	14,075	13,573	12,817	0.10	-5.57
BELARUS	548,360	954,083	752,716	1,045,093	1,595,369	12.75	52.65
CZECH REP	59,852	38,908	18,127	15,579	17,503	0.14	12.35
ESTONIA	9,590	8,912	9,670	9,751	10,199	0.08	4.59
GEORGIA	24,468	23,407	12,191	15,687	18,335	0.15	16.88
HUNGARY	506,437	502,206	357,228	776,241	1,181,959	9.45	52.27
KAZAKHSTAN	4,529	8,709	8,603	18,625	20,658	0.17	10.92
KYRGYZSTAN	1,778	2,184	1,850	3,871	11,687	0.09	201.91
LATVIA	22,403	24,034	23,524	23,787	19,414	0.16	-18.38
LITHUANIA	21,616	20,503	23,678	26,098	30,058	0.24	15.17
REP MOLDOVA	1,051,704	2,186,313	2,194,146	2,259,446	2,556,999	20.43	13.17
POLAND	184,653	282,987	366,886	555,998	1,239,195	9.90	122.88
ROMANIA	31,871	54,339	53,703	43,195	68,102	0.54	57.66
RUSSIAN FED	1,222,374	1,788,080	4,857,618	5,170,280	5,026,201	40.16	-2.79
SLOVAKIA	84,525	69,886	42,952	42,529	105,056	0.84	147.02
TAJIKISTAN	1,147	3,040	2,508	3,053	2,052	0.02	-32.79
TURKMENISTAN	3,253	2,481	1,995	2,775	4,594	0.04	65.55
UZBEKISTAN	25,456	23,275	19,089	13,390	18,960	0.15	41.60
NORTHERN EUR	**38,016**	**40,803**	**45,305**	**52,701**	**48,611**	**0.39**	**-7.76**
DENMARK	4,619	4,826	5,768	7,687	4,846	0.04	-36.96
FINLAND	2,688	3,366	2,310	1,737	2,922	0.02	68.22
ICELAND	392	196	58	45	152		237.78
IRELAND	857	1,413	1,013	1,282	1,637	0.01	27.69
NORWAY	1,621	2,695	1,840	2,794	3,187	0.03	14.07
SWEDEN	4,838	5,916	4,120	4,283	6,606	0.05	54.24
UK	23,001	22,391	30,196	34,873	29,261	0.23	-16.09
SOUTHERN EUR	**39,251**	**33,953**	**36,931**	**42,384**	**60,806**	**0.49**	**43.46**

UKRAINE

1. ARRIVALS OF NON-RESIDENT TOURISTS AT NATIONAL BORDERS, BY COUNTRY OF RESIDENCE

	1999	2000	2001	2002	2003	Market share 03	% change 03-02
ALBANIA	241	394	252	346	356		2.89
ANDORRA	22	177	7	8	6		-25.00
BOSNIA HERZG	412	780	559	571	532		-6.83
CROATIA	2,195	2,565	1,376	1,363	1,814	0.01	33.09
GREECE	8,192	6,093	8,430	9,665	10,553	0.08	9.19
HOLY SEE			148	155	33		-78.71
ITALY	15,087	9,572	14,146	19,031	30,444	0.24	59.97
MALTA	47	133	158	186	740	0.01	297.85
PORTUGAL	298	757	797	649	1,281	0.01	97.38
SAN MARINO	6	2	1	14	31		121.43
SLOVENIA	3,415	3,588	2,165	1,464	1,951	0.02	33.27
SPAIN	3,837	4,278	4,858	4,828	6,766	0.05	40.14
TFYROM	1,002	943	1,030	722	1,092	0.01	51.25
SERBIA,MTNEG	4,497	4,671	3,004	3,382	5,207	0.04	53.96
WESTERN EUR	**103,329**	**104,781**	**122,392**	**141,613**	**188,003**	**1.50**	**32.76**
AUSTRIA	8,846	9,727	13,405	13,446	11,966	0.10	-11.01
BELGIUM	5,306	3,881	2,784	2,627	5,606	0.04	113.40
FRANCE	15,633	15,759	16,139	16,636	25,396	0.20	52.66
GERMANY	59,288	62,448	77,905	94,986	118,513	0.95	24.77
LIECHTENSTEN	16	229	26	103	54		-47.57
LUXEMBOURG	196	410	232	260	504		93.85
MONACO	1	4		78	937	0.01	1.101.28
NETHERLANDS	9,614	5,811	6,920	8,287	18,235	0.15	120.04
SWITZERLAND	4,429	6,512	4,981	5,190	6,792	0.05	30.87
EAST/MED EUR	**51,131**	**54,917**	**74,682**	**106,125**	**73,668**	**0.59**	**-30.58**
CYPRUS	825	1,264	2,197	3,045	1,823	0.01	-40.13
ISRAEL	36,008	36,943	57,416	80,813	39,995	0.32	-50.51
TURKEY	14,298	16,710	15,069	22,267	31,850	0.25	43.04
MIDDLE EAST	**14,195**	**18,436**	**13,399**	**14,777**	**18,720**	**0.15**	**26.68**
MIDDLE EAST	**14,195**	**18,436**	**13,399**	**14,777**	**18,720**	**0.15**	**26.68**
BAHRAIN	44	229	57	46	89		93.48
PALESTINE				726	505		-30.44
IRAQ	204	837	240	196	111		-43.37
JORDAN	3,225	3,583	2,691	2,910	3,078	0.02	5.77
KUWAIT	253	767	363	235	271		15.32
LEBANON	3,128	2,179	2,569	3,149	4,298	0.03	36.49
LIBYA	807	1,284	1,034	1,318	2,259	0.02	71.40
OMAN	51	413	48	40	38		-5.00
QATAR	21	208	11	10	32		220.00
SAUDI ARABIA	153	383	151	133	289		117.29
SYRIA	3,199	4,043	4,415	3,632	5,367	0.04	47.77
UNTD ARAB EM	1,078	1,331	272	231	342		48.05
EGYPT	989	1,394	1,421	2,053	1,902	0.02	-7.36
YEMEN	103	325	127	98	139		41.84
OT MIDD EAST	940	1,460					
SOUTH ASIA	**10,774**	**11,363**	**7,453**	**9,866**	**13,978**	**0.11**	**41.68**
SOUTH ASIA	**10,774**	**11,363**	**7,453**	**9,866**	**13,978**	**0.11**	**41.68**
AFGHANISTAN	1,547	2,043	933	595	407		-31.60
BANGLADESH	798	1,177	413	412	235		-42.96
SRI LANKA	714	1,067	408	378	221		-41.53
INDIA	3,548	3,301	2,622	4,103	6,249	0.05	52.30

UKRAINE

1. ARRIVALS OF NON-RESIDENT TOURISTS AT NATIONAL BORDERS, BY COUNTRY OF RESIDENCE

	1999	2000	2001	2002	2003	Market share 03	% change 03-02
IRAN	2,949	2,167	2,275	3,222	5,824	0.05	80.76
MALDIVES	12	158	32	6	5		-16.67
NEPAL	63	211	68	63	66		4.76
PAKISTAN	1,142	1,239	702	1,087	971	0.01	-10.67
OTH STH ASIA	1						
REG.NOT SPEC	**7,986**	**5,263**	**5,832**	**4,028**	**13,609**	**0.11**	**237.86**
NOT SPECIFIE	**7,986**	**5,263**	**5,832**	**4,028**	**13,609**	**0.11**	**237.86**
OTH.WORLD	7,986	5,263	5,832	4,028	13,609	0.11	237.86

Source: World Tourism Organization (WTO)

3. ARRIVALS OF NON-RESIDENT TOURISTS IN HOTELS AND SIMILAR ESTABLISHMENTS, BY NATIONALITY

	1999	2000	2001	2002	2003	Market share 03	% change 03-02
TOTAL	**3,392,614**	**3,906,545**	**4,133,531**	**5,445,367**	**5,871,023**	**100.00**	**7.82**
AFRICA	**153,899**	**173,601**	**218,162**	**310,722**	**306,872**	**5.23**	**-1.24**
EAST AFRICA	**9,532**	**9,443**					
SOMALIA	9,532	9,443					
NORTH AFRICA	**17,660**	**18,841**	**21,740**	**31,211**	**35,347**	**0.60**	**13.25**
SUDAN	17,660	18,841	21,740	31,211	35,347	0.60	13.25
OTHER AFRICA	**126,707**	**145,317**	**196,422**	**279,511**	**271,525**	**4.62**	**-2.86**
OTHER AFRICA	126,707	145,317	196,422	279,511	271,525	4.62	-2.86
AMERICAS	**130,280**	**139,474**	**149,802**	**238,749**	**254,362**	**4.33**	**6.54**
NORTH AMER	**118,824**	**128,406**	**135,635**	**218,990**	**230,413**	**3.92**	**5.22**
CANADA	24,322	27,859	36,742	95,878	55,297	0.94	-42.33
USA	94,502	100,547	98,893	123,112	175,116	2.98	42.24
OTHER AMERIC	**11,456**	**11,068**	**14,167**	**19,759**	**23,949**	**0.41**	**21.21**
OTH AMERICA	11,456	11,068	14,167	19,759	23,949	0.41	21.21
EAST AS/PACI	**247,673**	**263,609**	**284,878**	**395,061**	**427,506**	**7.28**	**8.21**
N/EAST ASIA	**27,132**	**28,079**	**26,624**	**32,876**	**37,549**	**0.64**	**14.21**
JAPAN	27,132	28,079	26,624	32,876	37,549	0.64	14.21
OT.EAST AS/P	**220,541**	**235,530**	**258,254**	**362,185**	**389,957**	**6.64**	**7.67**
OTHER ASIA	190,015	199,529	212,882	293,751	305,550	5.20	4.02
ALL OCEANIA	30,526	36,001	45,372	68,434	84,407	1.44	23.34
EUROPE	**1,016,869**	**1,076,813**	**1,115,373**	**1,468,015**	**1,584,792**	**26.99**	**7.95**
C/E EUROPE	**232,081**	**228,785**	**205,126**	**267,655**	**324,484**	**5.53**	**21.23**
RUSSIAN FED	232,081	228,785	205,126	267,655	324,484	5.53	21.23
NORTHERN EUR	**293,025**	**337,865**	**384,443**	**491,604**	**496,147**	**8.45**	**0.92**
UK	293,025	337,865	384,443	491,604	496,147	8.45	0.92
WESTERN EUR	**238,255**	**258,491**	**292,924**	**364,574**	**371,334**	**6.32**	**1.85**
FRANCE	65,755	60,955	69,620	90,735	98,624	1.68	8.69
GERMANY	147,736	171,519	194,079	236,660	235,147	4.01	-0.64
NETHERLANDS	24,764	26,017	29,225	37,179	37,563	0.64	1.03
OTHER EUROPE	**253,508**	**251,672**	**232,880**	**344,182**	**392,827**	**6.69**	**14.13**
OTHER EUROPE	253,508	251,672	232,880	344,182	392,827	6.69	14.13
MIDDLE EAST	**923,248**	**1,088,753**	**1,220,738**	**1,556,533**	**1,583,258**	**26.97**	**1.72**
MIDDLE EAST	**923,248**	**1,088,753**	**1,220,738**	**1,556,533**	**1,583,258**	**26.97**	**1.72**
PALESTINE	10,583	11,004	11,759	15,042	13,946	0.24	-7.29
IRAQ	11,233	13,137	13,623	18,521	18,401	0.31	-0.65
JORDAN	48,569	55,344	58,844	73,140	76,553	1.30	4.67
LEBANON	46,842	55,790	61,133	74,225	83,137	1.42	12.01
SYRIA	36,622	43,341	44,177	53,836	60,104	1.02	11.64
EGYPT	85,259	94,058	96,002	111,822	121,221	2.06	8.41

UNITED ARAB EMIRATES

3. ARRIVALS OF NON-RESIDENT TOURISTS IN HOTELS AND SIMILAR ESTABLISHMENTS, BY NATIONALITY

	1999	2000	2001	2002	2003	Market share 03	% change 03-02
YEMEN	27,381	33,557	39,474	47,383	36,912	0.63	-22.10
OT MIDD EAST	656,759	782,522	895,726	1,162,564	1,172,984	19.98	0.90
SOUTH ASIA	**500,985**	**568,453**	**590,378**	**807,094**	**921,698**	**15.70**	**14.20**
SOUTH ASIA	**500,985**	**568,453**	**590,378**	**807,094**	**921,698**	**15.70**	**14.20**
BANGLADESH	31,647	42,038	32,787	45,987	45,580	0.78	-0.89
INDIA	216,219	235,493	246,335	336,046	357,941	6.10	6.52
IRAN	137,678	154,861	194,140	270,350	334,453	5.70	23.71
PAKISTAN	115,441	136,061	117,116	154,711	183,724	3.13	18.75
REG.NOT SPEC	**419,660**	**595,842**	**554,200**	**669,193**	**792,535**	**13.50**	**18.43**
NOT SPECIFIE	**419,660**	**595,842**	**554,200**	**669,193**	**792,535**	**13.50**	**18.43**
N RESID ABRO (*)	419,660	595,842	554,200	669,193	792,535	13.50	18.43

Source: World Tourism Organization (WTO)

UNITED ARAB EMIRATES

5. OVERNIGHT STAYS OF NON-RESIDENT TOURISTS IN HOTELS AND SIMILAR ESTABLISHMENTS, BY NATIONALITY

	1999	2000	2001	2002	2003	Market share 03	% change 03-02
TOTAL	**8,554,043**	**10,313,499**	**10,126,372**	**12,359,593**	**14,191,984**	**100.00**	**14.83**
AFRICA	**474,742**	**579,354**	**642,681**	**806,365**	**872,745**	**6.15**	**8.23**
EAST AFRICA	**29,020**	**26,669**					
SOMALIA	29,020	26,669					
NORTH AFRICA	**50,833**	**60,120**	**58,690**	**73,597**	**84,742**	**0.60**	**15.14**
SUDAN	50,833	60,120	58,690	73,597	84,742	0.60	15.14
OTHER AFRICA	**394,889**	**492,565**	**583,991**	**732,768**	**788,003**	**5.55**	**7.54**
OTHER AFRICA	394,889	492,565	583,991	732,768	788,003	5.55	7.54
AMERICAS	**306,640**	**372,269**	**386,446**	**524,020**	**602,103**	**4.24**	**14.90**
NORTH AMER	**279,085**	**339,900**	**343,999**	**472,341**	**536,106**	**3.78**	**13.50**
CANADA	61,870	74,991	87,030	180,558	134,588	0.95	-25.46
USA	217,215	264,909	256,969	291,783	401,518	2.83	37.61
OTHER AMERIC	**27,555**	**32,369**	**42,447**	**51,679**	**65,997**	**0.47**	**27.71**
OTH AMERICA	27,555	32,369	42,447	51,679	65,997	0.47	27.71
EAST AS/PACI	**560,503**	**631,997**	**610,373**	**824,890**	**956,483**	**6.74**	**15.95**
N/EAST ASIA	**66,714**	**80,844**	**73,112**	**82,536**	**102,956**	**0.73**	**24.74**
JAPAN	66,714	80,844	73,112	82,536	102,956	0.73	24.74
OT.EAST AS/P	**493,789**	**551,153**	**537,261**	**742,354**	**853,527**	**6.01**	**14.98**
OTHER ASIA	426,848	467,520	444,260	612,347	685,930	4.83	12.02
ALL OCEANIA	66,941	83,633	93,001	130,007	167,597	1.18	28.91
EUROPE	**3,222,013**	**3,933,469**	**3,746,942**	**4,399,671**	**4,826,954**	**34.01**	**9.71**
C/E EUROPE	**932,256**	**1,001,440**	**812,138**	**910,063**	**1,054,744**	**7.43**	**15.90**
RUSSIAN FED	932,256	1,001,440	812,138	910,063	1,054,744	7.43	15.90
NORTHERN EUR	**789,560**	**1,065,594**	**1,193,125**	**1,451,979**	**1,574,331**	**11.09**	**8.43**
UK	789,560	1,065,594	1,193,125	1,451,979	1,574,331	11.09	8.43
WESTERN EUR	**726,132**	**969,406**	**983,243**	**1,018,541**	**1,065,598**	**7.51**	**4.62**
FRANCE	179,228	188,120	197,384	236,050	249,386	1.76	5.65
GERMANY	479,797	699,553	692,954	673,823	699,367	4.93	3.79
NETHERLANDS	67,107	81,733	92,905	108,668	116,845	0.82	7.52
OTHER EUROPE	**774,065**	**897,029**	**758,436**	**1,019,088**	**1,132,281**	**7.98**	**11.11**
OTHER EUROPE	774,065	897,029	758,436	1,019,088	1,132,281	7.98	11.11
MIDDLE EAST	**2,057,963**	**2,453,001**	**2,488,015**	**2,941,737**	**3,345,105**	**23.57**	**13.71**
MIDDLE EAST	**2,057,963**	**2,453,001**	**2,488,015**	**2,941,737**	**3,345,105**	**23.57**	**13.71**
PALESTINE	23,990	25,352	26,243	29,928	29,346	0.21	-1.94
IRAQ	39,226	41,155	40,356	48,319	50,513	0.36	4.54
JORDAN	131,181	140,433	134,253	158,968	175,979	1.24	10.70
LEBANON	134,609	155,527	151,959	165,598	195,412	1.38	18.00
SYRIA	94,274	108,880	101,492	121,456	136,658	0.96	12.52
EGYPT	201,548	251,983	240,782	254,026	296,319	2.09	16.65

UNITED ARAB EMIRATES

5. OVERNIGHT STAYS OF NON-RESIDENT TOURISTS IN HOTELS AND SIMILAR ESTABLISHMENTS, BY NATIONALITY

	1999	2000	2001	2002	2003	Market share 03	% change 03-02
YEMEN	64,096	77,109	90,347	99,859	79,599	0.56	-20.29
OT MIDD EAST	1,369,039	1,652,562	1,702,583	2,063,583	2,381,279	16.78	15.40
SOUTH ASIA	**1,139,435**	**1,309,404**	**1,276,429**	**1,690,591**	**2,106,343**	**14.84**	**24.59**
SOUTH ASIA	**1,139,435**	**1,309,404**	**1,276,429**	**1,690,591**	**2,106,343**	**14.84**	**24.59**
BANGLADESH	59,195	75,713	65,236	92,326	89,090	0.63	-3.50
INDIA	495,317	543,871	549,867	717,049	819,990	5.78	14.36
IRAN	339,324	403,941	427,391	580,214	816,580	5.75	40.74
PAKISTAN	245,599	285,879	233,935	301,002	380,683	2.68	26.47
REG.NOT SPEC	**792,747**	**1,034,005**	**975,486**	**1,172,319**	**1,482,251**	**10.44**	**26.44**
NOT SPECIFIE	**792,747**	**1,034,005**	**975,486**	**1,172,319**	**1,482,251**	**10.44**	**26.44**
N RESID ABRO (*)	792,747	1,034,005	975,486	1,172,319	1,482,251	10.44	26.44

Source: World Tourism Organization (WTO)

UNITED KINGDOM

2. ARRIVALS OF NON-RESIDENT VISITORS AT NATIONAL BORDERS, BY COUNTRY OF RESIDENCE

	1999	2000	2001	2002	2003	Market share 03	% change 03-02
TOTAL	**25,396,000**	**25,211,000**	**22,835,000**	**24,181,000**	**24,715,000**	**100.00**	**2.21**
AFRICA	**588,000**	**618,000**	**630,000**	**631,000**	**569,000**	**2.30**	**-9.83**
EAST AFRICA	**113,000**	**127,000**	**105,000**	**127,000**	**107,000**	**0.43**	**-15.75**
ZIMBABWE	28,000	31,000	26,000	28,000	17,000	0.07	-39.29
OTH.EAST.AFR	85,000	96,000	79,000	99,000	90,000	0.36	-9.09
NORTH AFRICA	**32,000**	**35,000**	**50,000**	**42,000**	**33,000**	**0.13**	**-21.43**
ALL NORT AFR	32,000	35,000	50,000	42,000	33,000	0.13	-21.43
SOUTHERN AFR	**300,000**	**304,000**	**319,000**	**276,000**	**266,000**	**1.08**	**-3.62**
SOUTH AFRICA	300,000	304,000	319,000	276,000	266,000	1.08	-3.62
WEST AFRICA	**121,000**	**130,000**	**134,000**	**158,000**	**139,000**	**0.56**	**-12.03**
NIGERIA	87,000	92,000	92,000	111,000	102,000	0.41	-8.11
OTH.WEST.AFR	34,000	38,000	42,000	47,000	37,000	0.15	-21.28
OTHER AFRICA	**22,000**	**22,000**	**22,000**	**28,000**	**24,000**	**0.10**	**-14.29**
OTHER AFRICA	22,000	22,000	22,000	28,000	24,000	0.10	-14.29
AMERICAS	**5,000,000**	**5,287,000**	**4,582,000**	**4,619,000**	**4,326,000**	**17.50**	**-6.34**
CARIBBEAN	**104,000**	**105,000**	**98,000**	**109,000**	**90,000**	**0.36**	**-17.43**
ALL CO CARIB	104,000	105,000	98,000	109,000	90,000	0.36	-17.43
NORTH AMER	**4,654,000**	**4,938,000**	**4,290,000**	**4,342,000**	**4,074,000**	**16.48**	**-6.17**
CANADA	660,000	772,000	647,000	660,000	652,000	2.64	-1.21
MEXICO	55,000	69,000	63,000	71,000	76,000	0.31	7.04
USA	3,939,000	4,097,000	3,580,000	3,611,000	3,346,000	13.54	-7.34
SOUTH AMER	**184,000**	**187,000**	**150,000**	**119,000**	**108,000**	**0.44**	**-9.24**
ARGENTINA	69,000	73,000	61,000	19,000	29,000	0.12	52.63
BRAZIL	99,000	98,000	69,000	83,000	70,000	0.28	-15.66
VENEZUELA	16,000	16,000	20,000	17,000	9,000	0.04	-47.06
OTHER AMERIC	**58,000**	**57,000**	**44,000**	**49,000**	**54,000**	**0.22**	**10.20**
OTH AMERICA	58,000	57,000	44,000	49,000	54,000	0.22	10.20
EAST AS/PACI	**2,062,000**	**2,256,000**	**1,834,000**	**1,854,000**	**1,809,000**	**7.32**	**-2.43**
N/EAST ASIA	**806,000**	**934,000**	**688,000**	**721,000**	**660,000**	**2.67**	**-8.46**
CHINA	46,000	41,000	58,000	64,000	68,000	0.28	6.25
TAIWAN(P.C.)	47,000	42,000	37,000	39,000	38,000	0.15	-2.56
HK,CHINA	150,000	183,000	146,000	158,000	131,000	0.53	-17.09
JAPAN	495,000	557,000	366,000	368,000	314,000	1.27	-14.67
KOREA REP.	68,000	111,000	81,000	92,000	109,000	0.44	18.48
S/EAST ASIA	**240,000**	**259,000**	**214,000**	**205,000**	**200,000**	**0.81**	**-2.44**
MALAYSIA	75,000	92,000	78,000	80,000	74,000	0.30	-7.50
SINGAPORE	113,000	123,000	86,000	84,000	79,000	0.32	-5.95
THAILAND	52,000	44,000	50,000	41,000	47,000	0.19	14.63
AUSTRALASIA	**921,000**	**951,000**	**845,000**	**839,000**	**867,000**	**3.51**	**3.34**
AUSTRALIA	728,000	777,000	694,000	702,000	723,000	2.93	2.99
NEW ZEALAND	193,000	174,000	151,000	137,000	144,000	0.58	5.11
OT.EAST AS/P	**95,000**	**112,000**	**87,000**	**89,000**	**82,000**	**0.33**	**-7.87**
OTHER ASIA	95,000	112,000	87,000	89,000	82,000	0.33	-7.87

UNITED KINGDOM

2. ARRIVALS OF NON-RESIDENT VISITORS AT NATIONAL BORDERS, BY COUNTRY OF RESIDENCE

	1999	2000	2001	2002	2003	Market share 03	% change 03-02
EUROPE	**17,046,000**	**16,307,000**	**15,060,000**	**16,409,000**	**17,371,000**	**70.29**	**5.86**
C/E EUROPE	**734,000**	**709,000**	**741,000**	**778,000**	**1,017,000**	**4.11**	**30.72**
CZECH REP	135,000	132,000	115,000	122,000	202,000	0.82	65.57
HUNGARY	93,000	102,000	104,000	132,000	111,000	0.45	-15.91
POLAND	220,000	180,000	225,000	188,000	325,000	1.31	72.87
RUSSIAN FED	112,000	100,000	108,000	117,000	138,000	0.56	17.95
OTH C/E EUR	174,000	195,000	189,000	219,000	241,000	0.98	10.05
NORTHERN EUR	**3,846,000**	**3,766,000**	**3,504,000**	**3,956,000**	**4,064,000**	**16.44**	**2.73**
DENMARK	458,000	421,000	394,000	431,000	425,000	1.72	-1.39
FINLAND	137,000	154,000	100,000	121,000	122,000	0.49	0.83
ICELAND	41,000	47,000	41,000	38,000	63,000	0.25	65.79
IRELAND	2,075,000	2,087,000	2,039,000	2,439,000	2,488,000	10.07	2.01
NORWAY	507,000	455,000	403,000	397,000	433,000	1.75	9.07
SWEDEN	628,000	602,000	527,000	530,000	533,000	2.16	0.57
SOUTHERN EUR	**2,435,000**	**2,329,000**	**2,217,000**	**2,465,000**	**2,894,000**	**11.71**	**17.40**
GIBRALTAR	23,000	24,000	24,000	32,000	22,000	0.09	-31.25
GREECE	202,000	224,000	185,000	169,000	185,000	0.75	9.47
ITALY	1,076,000	949,000	857,000	977,000	1,168,000	4.73	19.55
MALTA	57,000	49,000	46,000	36,000	50,000	0.20	38.89
PORTUGAL	174,000	174,000	172,000	170,000	193,000	0.78	13.53
SPAIN	829,000	849,000	856,000	1,010,000	1,206,000	4.88	19.41
YUGOSLAV SFR	74,000	60,000	77,000	71,000	70,000	0.28	-1.41
WESTERN EUR	**9,622,000**	**9,139,000**	**8,248,000**	**8,874,000**	**9,038,000**	**36.57**	**1.85**
AUSTRIA	242,000	227,000	191,000	219,000	263,000	1.06	20.09
BELGIUM	1,077,000	997,000	916,000	966,000	936,000	3.79	-3.11
FRANCE	3,223,000	3,087,000	2,852,000	3,077,000	3,073,000	12.43	-0.13
GERMANY	2,794,000	2,758,000	2,309,000	2,556,000	2,611,000	10.56	2.15
LUXEMBOURG	53,000	51,000	55,000	44,000	42,000	0.17	-4.55
NETHERLANDS	1,617,000	1,440,000	1,411,000	1,419,000	1,549,000	6.27	9.16
SWITZERLAND	616,000	579,000	514,000	593,000	564,000	2.28	-4.89
EAST/MED EUR	**409,000**	**364,000**	**350,000**	**336,000**	**358,000**	**1.45**	**6.55**
CYPRUS	76,000	66,000	76,000	80,000	104,000	0.42	30.00
ISRAEL	230,000	220,000	205,000	191,000	162,000	0.66	-15.18
TURKEY	103,000	78,000	69,000	65,000	92,000	0.37	41.54
MIDDLE EAST	**409,000**	**429,000**	**403,000**	**360,000**	**346,000**	**1.40**	**-3.89**
MIDDLE EAST	**409,000**	**429,000**	**403,000**	**360,000**	**346,000**	**1.40**	**-3.89**
SAUDI ARABIA	112,000	107,000	90,000	78,000	63,000	0.25	-19.23
UNTD ARAB EM	99,000	119,000	112,000	109,000	113,000	0.46	3.67
EGYPT	49,000	52,000	48,000	32,000	41,000	0.17	28.13
OT MIDD EAST	149,000	151,000	153,000	141,000	129,000	0.52	-8.51
SOUTH ASIA	**291,000**	**314,000**	**326,000**	**308,000**	**294,000**	**1.19**	**-4.55**
SOUTH ASIA	**291,000**	**314,000**	**326,000**	**308,000**	**294,000**	**1.19**	**-4.55**
BANGLADESH	16,000	16,000	19,000	18,000	12,000	0.05	-33.33
INDIA	183,000	206,000	189,000	205,000	199,000	0.81	-2.93
IRAN	17,000	17,000	22,000	23,000	26,000	0.11	13.04
PAKISTAN	75,000	75,000	96,000	62,000	57,000	0.23	-8.06

6. OVERNIGHT STAYS OF NON-RESIDENT TOURISTS IN ALL TYPES OF ACCOMMODATION ESTABLISHMENTS, BY COUNTRY OF RESIDENCE

	1999	2000	2001	2002	2003	Market share 03	% change 03-02
TOTAL	**211,735,000**	**203,762,000**	**189,513,000**	**199,283,000**	**203,431,000**	**100.00**	**2.08**
AFRICA	**11,172,000**	**9,879,000**	**11,357,000**	**12,163,000**	**11,119,000**	**5.47**	**-8.58**
EAST AFRICA	**2,864,000**	**2,379,000**	**2,078,000**	**2,880,000**	**2,390,000**	**1.17**	**-17.01**
ZIMBABWE	937,000	577,000	588,000	536,000	622,000	0.31	16.04
OTH.EAST.AFR	1,927,000	1,802,000	1,490,000	2,344,000	1,768,000	0.87	-24.57
NORTH AFRICA	**781,000**	**454,000**	**886,000**	**865,000**	**873,000**	**0.43**	**0.92**
ALL NORT AFR	781,000	454,000	886,000	865,000	873,000	0.43	0.92
SOUTHERN AFR	**4,971,000**	**4,381,000**	**5,482,000**	**5,100,000**	**4,668,000**	**2.29**	**-8.47**
SOUTH AFRICA	4,971,000	4,381,000	5,482,000	5,100,000	4,668,000	2.29	-8.47
WEST AFRICA	**2,020,000**	**2,393,000**	**2,572,000**	**2,939,000**	**2,813,000**	**1.38**	**-4.29**
NIGERIA	1,335,000	1,488,000	1,274,000	1,746,000	1,776,000	0.87	1.72
OTH.WEST.AFR	685,000	905,000	1,298,000	1,193,000	1,037,000	0.51	-13.08
OTHER AFRICA	**536,000**	**272,000**	**339,000**	**379,000**	**375,000**	**0.18**	**-1.06**
OTHER AFRICA	536,000	272,000	339,000	379,000	375,000	0.18	-1.06
AMERICAS	**46,383,000**	**48,238,000**	**42,315,000**	**43,645,000**	**41,921,000**	**20.61**	**-3.95**
CARIBBEAN	**1,903,000**	**2,125,000**	**2,012,000**	**2,458,000**	**2,583,000**	**1.27**	**5.09**
ALL CO CARIB	1,903,000	2,125,000	2,012,000	2,458,000	2,583,000	1.27	5.09
NORTH AMER	**40,336,000**	**43,031,000**	**36,481,000**	**38,341,000**	**36,024,000**	**17.71**	**-6.04**
CANADA	8,930,000	8,885,000	7,395,000	7,810,000	7,351,000	3.61	-5.88
MEXICO	398,000	923,000	623,000	794,000	537,000	0.26	-32.37
USA	31,008,000	33,223,000	28,463,000	29,737,000	28,136,000	13.83	-5.38
SOUTH AMER	**2,992,000**	**2,348,000**	**2,491,000**	**1,886,000**	**2,666,000**	**1.31**	**41.36**
ARGENTINA	806,000	1,100,000	742,000	507,000	382,000	0.19	-24.65
BRAZIL	2,012,000	1,147,000	1,358,000	1,159,000	1,744,000	0.86	50.47
VENEZUELA	174,000	101,000	391,000	220,000	540,000	0.27	145.45
OTHER AMERIC	**1,152,000**	**734,000**	**1,331,000**	**960,000**	**648,000**	**0.32**	**-32.50**
OTH AMERICA	1,152,000	734,000	1,331,000	960,000	648,000	0.32	-32.50
EAST AS/PACI	**28,697,000**	**31,154,000**	**29,806,000**	**28,687,000**	**30,888,000**	**15.18**	**7.67**
N/EAST ASIA	**9,436,000**	**10,701,000**	**9,556,000**	**8,950,000**	**9,986,000**	**4.91**	**11.58**
CHINA	835,000	1,077,000	1,730,000	1,216,000	1,770,000	0.87	45.56
TAIWAN(P.C.)	727,000	694,000	453,000	1,029,000	1,955,000	0.96	89.99
HK,CHINA	1,526,000	1,984,000	2,298,000	1,804,000	1,466,000	0.72	-18.74
JAPAN	5,735,000	6,084,000	3,502,000	3,931,000	3,406,000	1.67	-13.36
KOREA REP.	613,000	862,000	1,573,000	970,000	1,389,000	0.68	43.20
S/EAST ASIA	**3,002,000**	**2,873,000**	**2,853,000**	**3,228,000**	**3,289,000**	**1.62**	**1.89**
MALAYSIA	1,061,000	1,299,000	939,000	1,683,000	1,694,000	0.83	0.65
SINGAPORE	1,082,000	971,000	877,000	906,000	981,000	0.48	8.28
THAILAND	859,000	603,000	1,037,000	639,000	614,000	0.30	-3.91
AUSTRALASIA	**14,766,000**	**15,666,000**	**15,689,000**	**14,436,000**	**15,534,000**	**7.64**	**7.61**
AUSTRALIA	11,201,000	12,170,000	12,914,000	11,678,000	13,125,000	6.45	12.39
NEW ZEALAND	3,565,000	3,496,000	2,775,000	2,758,000	2,409,000	1.18	-12.65
OT.EAST AS/P	**1,493,000**	**1,914,000**	**1,708,000**	**2,073,000**	**2,079,000**	**1.02**	**0.29**

6. OVERNIGHT STAYS OF NON-RESIDENT TOURISTS IN ALL TYPES OF ACCOMMODATION ESTABLISHMENTS, BY COUNTRY OF RESIDENCE

	1999	2000	2001	2002	2003	Market share 03	% change 03-02
OTHER ASIA	1,493,000	1,914,000	1,708,000	2,073,000	2,079,000	1.02	0.29
EUROPE	**112,682,000**	**100,565,000**	**93,437,000**	**101,739,000**	**105,831,000**	**52.02**	**4.02**
C/E EUROPE	**8,832,000**	**8,281,000**	**8,639,000**	**9,583,000**	**16,999,000**	**8.36**	**77.39**
CZECH REP	1,396,000	1,277,000	987,000	770,000	1,940,000	0.95	151.95
HUNGARY	570,000	677,000	881,000	985,000	1,709,000	0.84	73.50
POLAND	2,213,000	2,059,000	2,865,000	3,870,000	7,993,000	3.93	106.54
RUSSIAN FED	1,419,000	1,424,000	1,688,000	1,395,000	1,548,000	0.76	10.97
OTH C/E EUR	3,234,000	2,844,000	2,218,000	2,563,000	3,809,000	1.87	48.61
NORTHERN EUR	**18,750,000**	**18,081,000**	**16,626,000**	**18,433,000**	**17,875,000**	**8.79**	**-3.03**
DENMARK	2,713,000	2,496,000	2,097,000	2,558,000	1,944,000	0.96	-24.00
FINLAND	872,000	1,150,000	912,000	958,000	795,000	0.39	-17.01
ICELAND	185,000	217,000	234,000	445,000	407,000	0.20	-8.54
IRELAND	8,080,000	7,847,000	8,077,000	9,927,000	9,675,000	4.76	-2.54
NORWAY	2,358,000	2,542,000	2,107,000	1,829,000	1,948,000	0.96	6.51
SWEDEN	4,542,000	3,829,000	3,199,000	2,716,000	3,106,000	1.53	14.36
SOUTHERN EUR	**26,523,000**	**21,537,000**	**19,520,000**	**21,091,000**	**22,582,000**	**11.10**	**7.07**
GREECE	2,735,000	2,823,000	1,618,000	2,015,000	1,715,000	0.84	-14.89
ITALY	11,791,000	8,073,000	7,186,000	7,749,000	8,048,000	3.96	3.86
PORTUGAL	1,311,000	1,105,000	1,381,000	1,439,000	1,206,000	0.59	-16.19
SPAIN	8,983,000	8,624,000	8,562,000	9,348,000	10,957,000	5.39	17.21
YUGOSLAV SFR	1,703,000	912,000	773,000	540,000	656,000	0.32	21.48
WESTERN EUR	**53,447,000**	**47,448,000**	**44,119,000**	**48,448,000**	**44,378,000**	**21.81**	**-8.40**
AUSTRIA	1,960,000	1,812,000	1,268,000	1,761,000	1,813,000	0.89	2.95
BELGIUM	3,345,000	2,695,000	2,721,000	2,999,000	2,667,000	1.31	-11.07
FRANCE	18,105,000	16,196,000	16,274,000	17,735,000	13,765,000	6.77	-22.39
GERMANY	18,744,000	17,120,000	14,182,000	15,392,000	15,435,000	7.59	0.28
LUXEMBOURG	234,000	206,000	216,000	167,000	152,000	0.07	-8.98
NETHERLANDS	7,140,000	5,931,000	5,859,000	6,276,000	7,032,000	3.46	12.05
SWITZERLAND	3,919,000	3,488,000	3,599,000	4,118,000	3,514,000	1.73	-14.67
EAST/MED EUR	**3,270,000**	**3,067,000**	**2,882,000**	**2,298,000**	**2,168,000**	**1.07**	**-5.66**
ISRAEL	1,617,000	1,704,000	1,622,000	1,452,000	1,166,000	0.57	-19.70
TURKEY	1,653,000	1,363,000	1,260,000	846,000	1,002,000	0.49	18.44
OTHER EUROPE	**1,860,000**	**2,151,000**	**1,651,000**	**1,886,000**	**1,829,000**	**0.90**	**-3.02**
OTHER EUROPE	1,860,000	2,151,000	1,651,000	1,886,000	1,829,000	0.90	-3.02
MIDDLE EAST	**6,496,000**	**6,697,000**	**6,006,000**	**6,063,000**	**5,523,000**	**2.71**	**-8.91**
MIDDLE EAST	**6,496,000**	**6,697,000**	**6,006,000**	**6,063,000**	**5,523,000**	**2.71**	**-8.91**
SAUDI ARABIA	1,752,000	1,717,000	1,400,000	1,325,000	1,209,000	0.59	-8.75
UNTD ARAB EM				1,831,000	1,626,000	0.80	-11.20
EGYPT	734,000	732,000	714,000	536,000	614,000	0.30	14.55
OT MIDD EAST	4,010,000	4,248,000	3,892,000	2,371,000	2,074,000	1.02	-12.53
SOUTH ASIA	**6,305,000**	**7,229,000**	**6,592,000**	**6,986,000**	**8,149,000**	**4.01**	**16.65**
SOUTH ASIA	**6,305,000**	**7,229,000**	**6,592,000**	**6,986,000**	**8,149,000**	**4.01**	**16.65**
BANGLADESH	251,000	205,000	313,000	206,000	382,000	0.19	85.44
INDIA	3,640,000	4,118,000	3,924,000	4,753,000	5,054,000	2.48	6.33
IRAN	569,000	579,000	459,000	445,000	972,000	0.48	118.43

6. OVERNIGHT STAYS OF NON-RESIDENT TOURISTS IN ALL TYPES OF ACCOMMODATION ESTABLISHMENTS, BY COUNTRY OF RESIDENCE

	1999	2000	2001	2002	2003	Market share 03	% change 03-02
PAKISTAN	1,845,000	2,327,000	1,896,000	1,582,000	1,741,000	0.86	10.05

Source: World Tourism Organization (WTO)

UNITED REPUBLIC OF TANZANIA

2. ARRIVALS OF NON-RESIDENT VISITORS AT NATIONAL BORDERS, BY COUNTRY OF RESIDENCE

	1999	2000	2001	2002	2003	Market share 03	% chang 03-02
TOTAL	**627,417**	**501,669**	**525,122**	**575,296**	**576,198**	**100.00**	**0.**
AFRICA	**262,559**	**201,934**	**213,013**	**249,601**	**267,940**	**46.50**	**7.**
EAST AFRICA	**215,237**	**164,097**	**178,577**	**200,295**	**216,086**	**37.50**	**7.**
BURUNDI	28,329	14,651	5,869	6,951	11,907	2.07	71.
COMOROS	1,118	894	1,482	2,656	1,346	0.23	-49.
ETHIOPIA	3,095	2,474	1,099	1,628	1,465	0.25	-10.
ERITREA	180	144	205	241	125	0.02	-48.
DJIBOUTI	12	9	31	423	176	0.03	-58.
KENYA	106,297	84,993	102,235	112,036	119,406	20.72	6.
MADAGASCAR			241	717	332	0.06	-53.
MALAWI	14,421	11,531	16,573	17,531	14,267	2.48	-18.
MAURITIUS	208	166	315	1,021	781	0.14	-23.
MOZAMBIQUE	7,776	6,215	4,543	1,149	3,340	0.58	190.
RWANDA	12,196	9,752	6,016	4,090	12,061	2.09	194.
SEYCHELLES	298	238	149	618	204	0.04	-66.
SOMALIA	2,863	2,290	389	1,040	1,547	0.27	48.
ZIMBABWE	4,197	3,356	4,523	8,480	3,795	0.66	-55.
UGANDA	26,307	21,035	25,330	28,618	34,664	6.02	21.
ZAMBIA	7,940	6,349	9,577	13,096	10,670	1.85	-18.
CENTRAL AFR	**11,675**	**9,335**	**9,071**	**15,369**	**8,972**	**1.56**	**-41.**
ANGOLA	1,389	1,110	390	261	386	0.07	47.
CAMEROON	2,321	1,856	372	1,009	806	0.14	-20.
CENT.AFR.REP	4	3	12	18	363	0.06	1.916.
CHAD	35	28	27	20	27		35.
CONGO	7,877	6,299	276	377	140	0.02	-62.
DEM.R.CONGO	20	16	7,837	12,784	6,850	1.19	-46.
GABON	29	23	157	900	400	0.07	-55.
NORTH AFRICA	**452**	**362**	**1,519**	**1,955**	**674**	**0.12**	**-65.**
ALGERIA	74	60	234	52	81	0.01	55.
MOROCCO	82	66	49	74	66	0.01	-10.
SUDAN			921	1,493	442	0.08	-70.
TUNISIA	296	236	315	336	85	0.01	-74.
SOUTHERN AFR	**23,095**	**18,466**	**20,071**	**25,369**	**37,099**	**6.44**	**46.**
BOTSWANA	2,178	1,741	1,173	781	632	0.11	-19.
LESOTHO	272	218	282	519	288	0.05	-44.
NAMIBIA	838	670	380	845	598	0.10	-29.
SOUTH AFRICA	18,732	14,977	17,568	22,916	35,071	6.09	53.
SWAZILAND	1,075	860	668	308	510	0.09	65.
WEST AFRICA	**12,100**	**9,674**	**3,775**	**6,613**	**5,109**	**0.89**	**-22.**
CAPE VERDE	31	25	10	10	4		-60.
BENIN	1,052	841	458	410	406	0.07	-0.
GAMBIA	276	221	266	190	219	0.04	15.
GHANA	2,920	2,335	623	1,993	1,303	0.23	-34.
GUINEA	165	132	101	183	199	0.03	8.
COTE IVOIRE			119	578	306	0.05	-47.
LIBERIA	65	52	54	111	95	0.02	-14.
MALI	748	598	254	206	158	0.03	-23.
MAURITANIA	1,586	1,268	204	234	124	0.02	-47.
NIGER	53	42	41	84	86	0.01	2.
NIGERIA	1,044	835	693	1,428	1,214	0.21	-14.
GUINEABISSAU					1		

UNITED REPUBLIC OF TANZANIA

2. ARRIVALS OF NON-RESIDENT VISITORS AT NATIONAL BORDERS, BY COUNTRY OF RESIDENCE

	1999	2000	2001	2002	2003	Market share 03	% change 03-02
SENEGAL	1,463	1,170	301	394	496	0.09	25.89
SIERRA LEONE	2,313	1,849	301	211	193	0.03	-8.53
TOGO	296	236	211	186	173	0.03	-6.99
BURKINA FASO	88	70	139	395	132	0.02	-66.58
AMERICAS	**61,908**	**49,001**	**45,544**	**59,077**	**49,781**	**8.64**	**-15.74**
CARIBBEAN	**2,666**	**2,132**	**3,027**	**974**	**532**	**0.09**	**-45.38**
ANTIGUA,BARB	2	2	12	16	43	0.01	168.75
BAHAMAS			18	2			
BARBADOS	24	19	37	24			
CUBA	108	86	30	183	39	0.01	-78.69
DOMINICA			114	51	18		-64.71
GRENADA				24			
HAITI	16	13	178	31	36	0.01	16.13
JAMAICA	2,462	1,968	2,397	538	283	0.05	-47.40
ST.LUCIA					16		
TRINIDAD TBG	54	44	241	105	97	0.02	-7.62
CENTRAL AMER	**66**	**53**	**257**	**644**	**465**	**0.08**	**-27.80**
COSTA RICA	22	17	87	353	132	0.02	-62.61
EL SALVADOR	16	13	12	4	79	0.01	1.875.00
GUATEMALA	10	8	12		46	0.01	
HONDURAS	2	2	107	32	5		-84.38
NICARAGUA	2	2	27	227	31	0.01	-86.34
PANAMA	14	11	12	28	172	0.03	514.29
NORTH AMER	**53,653**	**42,899**	**38,338**	**50,994**	**47,429**	**8.23**	**-6.99**
CANADA	11,702	9,357	6,782	12,042	10,354	1.80	-14.02
MEXICO	603	482	750	793	656	0.11	-17.28
USA	41,348	33,060	30,806	38,159	36,419	6.32	-4.56
SOUTH AMER	**5,523**	**3,917**	**3,922**	**6,465**	**1,355**	**0.24**	**-79.04**
ARGENTINA	593	475	740	281	199	0.03	-29.18
BOLIVIA	3	2	24	50	14		-72.00
BRAZIL	237	189	523	4,476	408	0.07	-90.88
CHILE	137	110	207	142	99	0.02	-30.28
COLOMBIA	2,848	2,277	1,323	523	320	0.06	-38.81
ECUADOR	266	213	57	47	31	0.01	-34.04
GUYANA	121	97	401	44	36	0.01	-18.18
PARAGUAY			20	25	3		-88.00
PERU	1,261	509	420	125	141	0.02	12.80
SURINAME					43	0.01	
URUGUAY	22	17	42	160	32	0.01	-80.00
VENEZUELA	35	28	165	592	29	0.01	-95.10
EAST AS/PACI	**47,898**	**38,299**	**46,605**	**30,087**	**27,208**	**4.72**	**-9.57**
N/EAST ASIA	**18,603**	**14,874**	**16,372**	**11,919**	**12,949**	**2.25**	**8.64**
CHINA	7,084	5,664	5,002	3,163	4,007	0.70	26.68
TAIWAN(P.C.)	47	38	221	470	221	0.04	-52.98
HK,CHINA			30	281	22		-92.17
JAPAN	7,529	6,020	7,822	5,574	5,936	1.03	6.49
KOREA D P RP					59	0.01	
KOREA REP.	3,943	3,152	3,285	2,428	2,690	0.47	10.79
MONGOLIA			12	3	14		366.67

UNITED REPUBLIC OF TANZANIA

2. ARRIVALS OF NON-RESIDENT VISITORS AT NATIONAL BORDERS, BY COUNTRY OF RESIDENCE

	1999	2000	2001	2002	2003	Market share 03	% change 03-02
S/EAST ASIA	**8,668**	**6,931**	**10,538**	**4,221**	**2,228**	**0.39**	**-47.22**
BRUNEI DARSM					170	0.03	
MYANMAR	2	2	13	214	20		-90.65
CAMBODIA	4	3	30	28	102	0.02	264.29
INDONESIA	3,488	2,789	4,788	734	322	0.06	-56.13
MALAYSIA	840	672	2,002	926	366	0.06	-60.48
PHILIPPINES	3,537	2,828	2,072	1,058	655	0.11	-38.09
SINGAPORE	163	130	534	589	217	0.04	-63.16
VIET NAM	25	20	53	51	19		-62.75
THAILAND	609	487	1,046	621	357	0.06	-42.51
AUSTRALASIA	**20,594**	**16,467**	**19,672**	**13,748**	**11,989**	**2.08**	**-12.79**
AUSTRALIA	10,470	8,372	11,755	9,715	9,698	1.68	-0.17
NEW ZEALAND	10,124	8,095	7,917	4,033	2,291	0.40	-43.19
MELANESIA	**33**	**27**	**23**	**199**	**42**	**0.01**	**-78.89**
FIJI	33	27	23	199	42	0.01	-78.89
EUROPE	**186,311**	**157,470**	**162,225**	**191,982**	**191,025**	**33.15**	**-0.50**
C/E EUROPE	**2,357**	**1,885**	**3,904**	**5,679**	**6,850**	**1.19**	**20.62**
AZERBAIJAN					57	0.01	
ARMENIA			12	16	28		75.00
BULGARIA	92	74	44	352	1,220	0.21	246.59
BELARUS			18	447	39	0.01	-91.28
CZECH REP	437	349	473	672	539	0.09	-19.79
ESTONIA			30	56	22		-60.71
HUNGARY	181	144	197	359	389	0.07	8.36
KAZAKHSTAN	6	5	12	3	36	0.01	1.100.00
LATVIA			74	250	117	0.02	-53.20
LITHUANIA			35	84	61	0.01	-27.38
POLAND			1,109	1,382	2,181	0.38	57.81
ROMANIA	196	157	95	150	425	0.07	183.33
RUSSIAN FED	781	625	1,453	1,404	1,385	0.24	-1.35
SLOVAKIA	278	222	35	79	44	0.01	-44.30
UKRAINE	386	309	305	422	307	0.05	-27.25
UZBEKISTAN			12	3			
NORTHERN EUR	**87,086**	**70,129**	**71,814**	**68,792**	**71,226**	**12.36**	**3.54**
DENMARK	8	506	2,853	5,524	5,210	0.90	-5.68
FINLAND	5,662	4,527	4,985	2,630	4,163	0.72	58.29
ICELAND	4	3	79	469	35	0.01	-92.54
IRELAND	7,915	6,328	4,689	3,508	4,145	0.72	18.16
NORWAY	10,265	8,205	8,473	4,984	5,590	0.97	12.16
SWEDEN	20,071	16,049	16,610	8,408	8,427	1.46	0.23
UK	43,161	34,511	34,125	43,269	43,656	7.58	0.89
SOUTHERN EUR	**19,910**	**15,921**	**18,625**	**42,474**	**38,127**	**6.62**	**-10.23**
ALBANIA			18	10	25		150.00
ANDORRA			12	10	7		-30.00
BOSNIA HERZG	850	680	141	56	15		-73.21
CROATIA	76	61	99	190	139	0.02	-26.84
GREECE	8	6	848	410	775	0.13	89.02
HOLY SEE					14		
ITALY	7,213	5,768	8,035	23,459	24,675	4.28	5.18
MALTA			30	52	84	0.01	61.54
PORTUGAL	1,248	998	873	1,486	2,288	0.40	53.97

UNITED REPUBLIC OF TANZANIA

2. ARRIVALS OF NON-RESIDENT VISITORS AT NATIONAL BORDERS, BY COUNTRY OF RESIDENCE

	1999	2000	2001	2002	2003	Market share 03	% change 03-02
SAN MARINO			12	20	43	0.01	115.00
SLOVENIA	278	222	179	464	176	0.03	-62.07
SPAIN	10,055	8,040	8,295	16,054	9,565	1.66	-40.42
TFYROM			12	66	46	0.01	-30.30
SERBIA,MTNEG	182	146	71	197	275	0.05	39.59
WESTERN EUR	**74,815**	**67,821**	**65,935**	**71,278**	**73,169**	**12.70**	**2.65**
AUSTRIA	3,024	2,418	2,499	3,101	2,908	0.50	-6.22
BELGIUM	10,772	8,613	8,537	6,203	6,497	1.13	4.74
FRANCE	21,493	17,186	16,990	22,059	22,103	3.84	0.20
GERMANY	28,272	22,606	21,190	17,855	19,222	3.34	7.66
LIECHTENSTEN					8		
LUXEMBOURG	43	34	98	127	100	0.02	-21.26
MONACO			15	73	76	0.01	4.11
NETHERLANDS	564	8,451	10,514	15,891	15,272	2.65	-3.90
SWITZERLAND	10,647	8,513	6,092	5,969	6,983	1.21	16.99
EAST/MED EUR	**2,143**	**1,714**	**1,947**	**3,759**	**1,653**	**0.29**	**-56.03**
CYPRUS	163	130	42	84	104	0.02	23.81
ISRAEL	999	799	1,623	3,360	1,188	0.21	-64.64
TURKEY	981	785	282	315	361	0.06	14.60
MIDDLE EAST	**37,944**	**30,339**	**29,675**	**16,682**	**13,742**	**2.38**	**-17.62**
MIDDLE EAST	**37,944**	**30,339**	**29,675**	**16,682**	**13,742**	**2.38**	**-17.62**
BAHRAIN			16	308	118	0.02	-61.69
PALESTINE			20	10	280	0.05	2,700.00
IRAQ	180	144	187	330	559	0.10	69.39
JORDAN	1,494	1,195	911	405	302	0.05	-25.43
KUWAIT	1,992	1,593	2,436	449	947	0.16	110.91
LEBANON			463	505	387	0.07	-23.37
LIBYA	239	191	390	169	163	0.03	-3.55
OMAN	10,901	8,717	9,966	7,728	5,225	0.91	-32.39
QATAR					34	0.01	
SAUDI ARABIA	778	622	435	384	249	0.04	-35.16
SYRIA	43	34	72	700	263	0.05	-62.43
UNTD ARAB EM	5,551	4,438	4,448	1,425	884	0.15	-37.96
EGYPT	8,095	6,472	4,594	1,120	1,145	0.20	2.23
YEMEN	8,671	6,933	5,737	3,149	3,186	0.55	1.17
SOUTH ASIA	**30,797**	**24,626**	**28,060**	**27,867**	**26,502**	**4.60**	**-4.90**
SOUTH ASIA	**30,797**	**24,626**	**28,060**	**27,867**	**26,502**	**4.60**	**-4.90**
BANGLADESH	1,696	1,356	1,320	141	277	0.05	96.45
SRI LANKA	705	564	567	3,670	1,695	0.29	-53.81
INDIA	23,567	18,844	24,068	21,973	22,215	3.86	1.10
IRAN	2,601	2,080	599	385	272	0.05	-29.35
NEPAL	27	22	203	165	362	0.06	119.39
PAKISTAN	2,201	1,760	1,303	1,533	1,681	0.29	9.65

Source: World Tourism Organization (WTO)

UNITED STATES

1. ARRIVALS OF NON-RESIDENT TOURISTS AT NATIONAL BORDERS, BY COUNTRY OF RESIDENCE

	1999	2000	2001	2002	2003	Market share 03	% change 03-02
TOTAL (*)	**48,504,187**	**51,218,701**	**46,906,868**	**43,524,707**	**41,212,213**	**100.00**	**-5.31**
AFRICA	**273,762**	**295,090**	**286,783**	**241,011**	**236,067**	**0.57**	**-2.05**
EAST AFRICA	**44,979**	**46,725**	**53,101**	**43,257**	**39,674**	**0.10**	**-8.28**
BURUNDI	129	308	475	289	181		-37.37
COMOROS	13	23	22	19	10		-47.37
ETHIOPIA	5,282	5,177	5,382	4,749	5,582	0.01	17.54
ERITREA	826	407	599	1,025	1,034		0.88
DJIBOUTI	339	403	236	127	191		50.39
KENYA	13,720	14,229	20,651	17,275	13,913	0.03	-19.46
MADAGASCAR	610	708	678	500	499		-0.20
MALAWI	1,155	1,365	1,332	1,212	1,098		-9.41
MAURITIUS	1,731	1,899	1,577	846	701		-17.14
MOZAMBIQUE	791	987	918	710	623		-12.25
REUNION	400	331	202	81	174		114.81
RWANDA	723	776	682	657	674		2.59
SEYCHELLES	401	419	420	266	246		-7.52
SOMALIA	96	105	78	23	22		-4.35
ZIMBABWE	7,420	8,080	6,832	5,457	5,223	0.01	-4.29
UGANDA	3,976	3,885	3,632	3,326	3,215	0.01	-3.34
TANZANIA	4,275	4,286	4,972	3,530	3,506	0.01	-0.68
ZAMBIA	3,092	3,337	4,413	3,165	2,782	0.01	-12.10
CENTRAL AFR	**9,521**	**9,995**	**11,714**	**10,973**	**10,550**	**0.03**	**-3.85**
ANGOLA	2,891	3,146	3,207	2,912	2,781	0.01	-4.50
CAMEROON	3,137	3,124	4,279	5,003	5,214	0.01	4.22
CENT.AFR.REP	117	159	228	169	47		-72.19
CHAD	225	240	229	229	230		0.44
CONGO	1,355	1,604	2,273	1,432	1,111		-22.42
DEM.R.CONGO	101	111	119	81	76		-6.17
EQ.GUINEA	114	150	133	83	78		-6.02
GABON	1,509	1,404	1,197	1,031	980		-4.95
SAO TOME PRN	72	57	49	33	33		
NORTH AFRICA	**31,760**	**33,342**	**27,291**	**17,294**	**16,179**	**0.04**	**-6.45**
ALGERIA	2,719	3,294	3,268	1,988	1,631		-17.96
MOROCCO	19,487	19,079	17,106	12,464	11,857	0.03	-4.87
WESTN.SAHARA		1	1	1	1		
SUDAN	1,014	1,479	1,659	852	670		-21.36
TUNISIA	8,540	9,489	5,257	1,989	2,020		1.56
SOUTHERN AFR	**111,146**	**120,332**	**98,951**	**77,381**	**75,206**	**0.18**	**-2.81**
BOTSWANA	2,160	2,391	2,490	2,116	1,873		-11.48
LESOTHO	329	326	248	272	201		-26.10
NAMIBIA	1,081	1,144	1,021	883	912		3.28
SOUTH AFRICA	107,258	116,113	94,882	73,910	72,029	0.17	-2.54
SWAZILAND	318	358	310	200	191		-4.50
WEST AFRICA	**76,356**	**84,696**	**95,726**	**92,106**	**94,458**	**0.23**	**2.55**
CAPE VERDE	3,587	3,906	4,958	1,744	1,211		-30.56
BENIN	779	741	670	669	698		4.33
GAMBIA	1,832	2,966	2,336	3,382	2,910	0.01	-13.96
GHANA	14,118	16,073	17,184	18,957	20,760	0.05	9.51
GUINEA	3,474	4,184	4,334	3,589	3,958	0.01	10.28
COTE IVOIRE	6,284	5,226	5,127	2,514	1,649		-34.41
LIBERIA	2,376	3,823	2,367	1,400	848		-39.43

UNITED STATES

1. ARRIVALS OF NON-RESIDENT TOURISTS AT NATIONAL BORDERS, BY COUNTRY OF RESIDENCE

	1999	2000	2001	2002	2003	Market share 03	% change 03-02
MALI	2,108	4,015	3,845	2,743	2,705	0.01	-1.39
MAURITANIA	534	707	776	558	564		1.08
NIGER	1,054	1,433	2,118	4,930	1,720		-65.11
NIGERIA	29,734	27,124	37,406	40,128	46,938	0.11	16.97
GUINEABISSAU	118	71	64	30	15		-50.00
SENEGAL	7,874	11,185	10,395	7,762	6,830	0.02	-12.01
SIERRA LEONE	464	706	697	765	882		15.29
TOGO	1,056	1,590	2,250	1,801	1,695		-5.89
BURKINA FASO	964	946	1,199	1,134	1,075		-5.20
AMERICAS	**28,759,665**	**30,338,382**	**29,577,703**	**27,979,856**	**26,362,298**	**63.97**	**-5.78**
CARIBBEAN	**1,257,625**	**1,331,297**	**1,201,811**	**1,052,576**	**998,266**	**2.42**	**-5.16**
ANTIGUA,BARB	24,162	24,918	20,207	16,317	16,479	0.04	0.99
BAHAMAS	282,286	293,911	293,022	262,469	253,229	0.61	-3.52
BARBADOS	60,002	57,071	46,494	41,934	41,558	0.10	-0.90
BERMUDA	7,366	7,474	7,107	6,227	13,382	0.03	114.90
BR.VIRGIN IS	25,100	29,708	23,745	14,497	14,748	0.04	1.73
CAYMAN IS	52,276	52,922	46,252	35,069	37,160	0.09	5.96
CUBA	5,613	48,614	31,425	26,880	18,543	0.04	-31.02
DOMINICA	16,120	16,174	14,221	17,271	6,792	0.02	-60.67
DOMINICAN RP	200,817	197,298	171,568	153,586	153,019	0.37	-0.37
GRENADA	10,192	10,412	8,656	7,161	7,509	0.02	4.86
GUADELOUPE	11,177	10,253	7,448	6,290	6,019	0.01	-4.31
HAITI	72,726	72,190	65,169	59,444	59,756	0.14	0.52
JAMAICA	233,547	242,903	229,003	183,903	159,484	0.39	-13.28
MARTINIQUE	12,594	9,912	7,500	6,021	5,902	0.01	-1.98
MONTSERRAT	998	1,027	727	650	696		7.08
NETH.ANTILES	67,282	60,042	52,378	58,043	54,170	0.13	-6.67
ST.KITTS NEV	11,596	12,084	10,183	7,917	7,897	0.02	-0.25
ANGUILLA	5,185	5,177	4,121	3,050	3,451	0.01	13.15
ST.LUCIA	17,693	18,100	14,941	12,530	12,007	0.03	-4.17
ST.VINCENT,G	6,900	7,291	5,931	4,992	4,928	0.01	-1.28
TRINIDAD TBG	117,396	137,689	127,102	118,336	111,820	0.27	-5.51
TURKS,CAICOS	16,597	16,127	14,611	9,989	9,717	0.02	-2.72
CENTRAL AMER	**730,813**	**821,614**	**770,803**	**704,050**	**655,841**	**1.59**	**-6.85**
BELIZE	27,005	30,352	28,682	22,327	22,074	0.05	-1.13
COSTA RICA	160,781	176,056	143,434	124,993	112,880	0.27	-9.69
EL SALVADOR	152,787	184,574	207,890	197,159	177,240	0.43	-10.10
GUATEMALA	163,095	185,677	171,955	162,367	151,891	0.37	-6.45
HONDURAS	81,998	90,714	87,645	85,322	82,099	0.20	-3.78
NICARAGUA	45,649	46,892	43,483	36,387	37,244	0.09	2.36
PANAMA	99,498	107,349	87,714	75,495	72,413	0.18	-4.08
NORTH AMER	**24,038,000**	**25,244,000**	**25,074,000**	**24,408,000**	**23,186,000**	**56.26**	**-5.01**
CANADA	14,110,000	14,648,000	13,507,000	12,968,000	12,660,000	30.72	-2.38
MEXICO	9,928,000	10,596,000	11,567,000	11,440,000	10,526,000	25.54	-7.99
SOUTH AMER	**2,733,227**	**2,941,471**	**2,531,089**	**1,815,230**	**1,522,191**	**3.69**	**-16.14**
ARGENTINA	501,660	533,936	434,011	164,658	150,719	0.37	-8.47
BOLIVIA	37,718	49,135	34,943	25,011	22,307	0.05	-10.81
BRAZIL	665,013	737,245	551,406	405,094	348,945	0.85	-13.86
CHILE	181,234	192,361	150,350	115,359	95,389	0.23	-17.31
COLOMBIA	415,724	417,065	371,747	321,439	280,259	0.68	-12.81
ECUADOR	118,759	129,938	147,527	139,094	119,737	0.29	-13.92
FALKLAND IS	73	113	99	106	94		-11.32

UNITED STATES

1. ARRIVALS OF NON-RESIDENT TOURISTS AT NATIONAL BORDERS, BY COUNTRY OF RESIDENCE

	1999	2000	2001	2002	2003	Market share 03	% change 03-02
FR.GUIANA	276	158	168	94	102		8.51
GUYANA	18,465	17,435	16,955	19,358	15,991	0.04	-17.39
PARAGUAY	18,870	18,714	16,405	12,069	9,754	0.02	-19.18
PERU	159,276	192,062	186,008	164,482	154,324	0.37	-6.18
SURINAME	6,528	7,039	5,832	5,237	5,346	0.01	2.08
URUGUAY	57,406	69,607	60,346	47,316	34,801	0.08	-26.45
VENEZUELA	552,225	576,663	555,292	395,913	284,423	0.69	-28.16
EAST AS/PACI	**7,301,839**	**7,921,004**	**6,535,276**	**5,888,710**	**5,192,366**	**12.60**	**-11.83**
N/EAST ASIA	**6,166,371**	**6,637,369**	**5,463,511**	**4,917,373**	**4,299,930**	**10.43**	**-12.56**
CHINA	191,175	249,441	232,416	225,565	157,326	0.38	-30.25
TAIWAN(P.C.)	453,299	457,302	357,064	288,032	238,999	0.58	-17.02
HK,CHINA	192,911	203,300	170,267	135,409	114,112	0.28	-15.73
JAPAN	4,826,077	5,061,377	4,082,661	3,627,264	3,169,682	7.69	-12.62
KOREA D P RP	40	28	16	29	29		
KOREA REP.	498,643	661,844	617,892	638,697	617,573	1.50	-3.31
MACAU, CHINA	4,226	4,077	3,195	2,377	2,209	0.01	-7.07
S/EAST ASIA	**468,235**	**552,372**	**485,456**	**442,246**	**367,837**	**0.89**	**-16.83**
BRUNEI DARSM	1,380	1,230	943	762	702		-7.87
MYANMAR	1,208	1,357	1,301	1,461	829		-43.26
CAMBODIA	636	2,319	3,304	2,575	3,115	0.01	20.97
INDONESIA	62,634	71,390	59,672	45,811	40,744	0.10	-11.06
LAO P.DEM.R.	636	1,045	1,608	1,190	955		-19.75
MALAYSIA	59,785	74,507	52,396	40,750	34,274	0.08	-15.89
PHILIPPINES	144,678	168,053	180,549	173,203	134,338	0.33	-22.44
TIMOR-LESTE				27	8		-70.37
SINGAPORE	118,476	136,439	99,010	97,259	87,525	0.21	-10.01
VIET NAM	4,417	9,061	12,928	12,360	9,463	0.02	-23.44
THAILAND	74,385	86,971	73,745	66,848	55,884	0.14	-16.40
AUSTRALASIA	**643,615**	**711,571**	**570,150**	**516,710**	**512,912**	**1.24**	**-0.74**
AUSTRALIA	483,157	539,559	425,934	407,130	405,698	0.98	-0.35
NEW ZEALAND	160,458	172,012	144,216	109,580	107,214	0.26	-2.16
MELANESIA	**13,719**	**10,535**	**8,761**	**6,178**	**5,238**	**0.01**	**-15.22**
SOLOMON IS	433	128	148	159	99		-37.74
FIJI	7,370	6,817	5,789	4,112	3,408	0.01	-17.12
NEW CALEDNIA	3,609	1,759	1,476	1,025	961		-6.24
VANUATU	640	495	414	214	184		-14.02
PAPUA N.GUIN	1,667	1,336	934	668	586		-12.28
MICRONESIA	**1,432**	**1,139**	**731**	**580**	**583**		**0.52**
CHRISTMAS IS	32	21	17	14	15		7.14
COCOS IS	4	3	4	11	3		-72.73
KIRIBATI	714	639	578	516	547		6.01
NAURU	682	476	132	39	18		-53.85
POLYNESIA	**8,467**	**8,018**	**6,667**	**5,623**	**5,866**	**0.01**	**4.32**
COOK IS	566	542	342	244	456		86.89
FR.POLYNESIA	3,761	3,373	2,293	2,176	2,434	0.01	11.86
NIUE	58	10	18	11	6		-45.45
PITCAIRN	2	1		2			
TONGA	2,897	2,719	2,746	2,112	1,713		-18.89
TUVALU	59	57	60	41	23		-43.90
WALLIS FUT.I	201	110	101	31	26		-16.13
SAMOA	923	1,206	1,107	1,006	1,208		20.08

UNITED STATES

1. ARRIVALS OF NON-RESIDENT TOURISTS AT NATIONAL BORDERS, BY COUNTRY OF RESIDENCE

	1999	2000	2001	2002	2003	Market share 03	% change 03-02
EUROPE	**11,634,166**	**12,052,331**	**9,906,957**	**8,964,202**	**8,981,711**	**21.79**	**0.20**
C/E EUROPE	**401,409**	**427,655**	**392,498**	**360,881**	**349,781**	**0.85**	**-3.08**
AZERBAIJAN	1,713	1,951	1,562	1,322	1,508		14.07
ARMENIA	8,654	8,663	6,634	4,453	3,244	0.01	-27.15
BULGARIA	11,690	11,418	11,996	13,858	13,868	0.03	0.07
BELARUS	4,617	4,444	4,338	4,451	5,033	0.01	13.08
CZECH RP/SVK	11,601	11,590	9,971	16,473	7,535	0.02	-54.26
CZECH REP	42,442	43,758	39,018	26,209	33,174	0.08	26.57
ESTONIA	6,497	6,745	5,894	5,630	5,569	0.01	-1.08
GEORGIA	5,099	2,173	2,153	2,618	3,106	0.01	18.64
HUNGARY	53,030	59,174	45,311	35,001	31,984	0.08	-8.62
KAZAKHSTAN	3,038	3,311	3,608	3,602	3,355	0.01	-6.86
KYRGYZSTAN	803	906	796	765	600		-21.57
LATVIA	5,957	7,161	6,218	5,870	5,280	0.01	-10.05
LITHUANIA	5,615	9,122	11,484	9,482	7,539	0.02	-20.49
REP MOLDOVA	1,209	1,625	1,159	1,177	1,427		21.24
POLAND	104,624	116,277	108,244	108,707	107,892	0.26	-0.75
ROMANIA	25,529	27,418	28,261	26,440	25,058	0.06	-5.23
RUSSIAN FED	81,378	76,739	70,348	64,228	62,330	0.15	-2.96
SLOVAKIA	12,093	13,235	12,498	12,235	10,677	0.03	-12.73
TAJIKISTAN	214	213	298	295	250		-15.25
TURKMENISTAN	159	194	342	185	176		-4.86
UKRAINE	10,966	14,477	14,923	12,169	15,098	0.04	24.07
USSR(former)	311	252	209	177	171		-3.39
UZBEKISTAN	4,170	6,809	7,233	5,534	4,907	0.01	-11.33
NORTHERN EUR	**5,223,005**	**5,728,668**	**4,947,947**	**4,595,440**	**4,729,636**	**11.48**	**2.92**
DENMARK	146,479	149,211	126,345	118,716	125,435	0.30	5.66
FINLAND	90,622	93,649	72,864	64,860	67,761	0.16	4.47
ICELAND	27,491	27,682	20,868	18,692	21,389	0.05	14.43
IRELAND	246,394	285,697	276,806	259,687	254,320	0.62	-2.07
NORWAY	145,601	147,540	123,268	112,593	113,233	0.27	0.57
SWEDEN	314,258	321,881	230,538	204,156	211,386	0.51	3.54
UK	4,252,160	4,703,008	4,097,258	3,816,736	3,936,112	9.55	3.13
SOUTHERN EUR	**1,180,351**	**1,181,262**	**932,504**	**822,594**	**830,396**	**2.01**	**0.95**
ALBANIA	2,732	5,737	4,453	4,405	4,101	0.01	-6.90
ANDORRA	1,378	1,235	954	777	800		2.96
BOSNIA HERZG	4,019	5,430	4,755	4,068	4,154	0.01	2.11
CROATIA	10,701	11,244	10,073	9,676	9,685	0.02	0.09
GIBRALTAR	1,133	1,363	929	690	841		21.88
GREECE	57,879	61,361	49,371	44,839	40,993	0.10	-8.58
HOLY SEE	22	28	19	8	13		62.50
ITALY	626,217	612,357	472,348	406,160	408,633	0.99	0.61
MALTA	8,792	8,437	6,679	4,482	4,080	0.01	-8.97
PORTUGAL	79,413	86,333	67,222	56,012	54,572	0.13	-2.57
SAN MARINO	905	794	503	281	284		1.07
SLOVENIA	15,379	14,886	10,980	7,300	9,420	0.02	29.04
SPAIN	362,848	361,177	291,052	269,520	284,031	0.69	5.38
TFYROM	3,094	2,841	2,960	3,404	3,119	0.01	-8.37
SERBIA,MTNEG	5,839	8,039	10,206	10,972	5,670	0.01	-48.32
WESTERN EUR	**4,446,309**	**4,270,968**	**3,235,462**	**2,834,150**	**2,738,152**	**6.64**	**-3.39**
AUSTRIA	194,230	175,533	123,295	97,930	99,924	0.24	2.04
BELGIUM	248,821	249,957	181,693	159,052	151,069	0.37	-5.02
FRANCE	1,059,014	1,087,087	875,854	734,260	688,887	1.67	-6.18

UNITED STATES

1. ARRIVALS OF NON-RESIDENT TOURISTS AT NATIONAL BORDERS, BY COUNTRY OF RESIDENCE

	1999	2000	2001	2002	2003	Market share 03	% change 03-02
GERMANY	1,984,627	1,786,045	1,313,756	1,189,856	1,180,212	2.86	-0.81
LIECHTENSTEN	2,163	2,011	1,653	1,248	1,099		-11.94
LUXEMBOURG	19,368	16,385	12,093	9,646	9,522	0.02	-1.29
MONACO	5,641	5,622	4,550	3,851	3,707	0.01	-3.74
NETHERLANDS	526,819	553,297	411,742	384,367	373,690	0.91	-2.78
SWITZERLAND	405,626	395,031	310,826	253,940	230,042	0.56	-9.41
EAST/MED EUR	**383,092**	**443,778**	**398,546**	**351,137**	**333,746**	**0.81**	**-4.95**
CYPRUS	11,485	12,152	10,893	9,378	9,485	0.02	1.14
ISRAEL	283,306	325,199	305,431	263,097	249,034	0.60	-5.35
TURKEY	88,301	106,427	82,222	78,662	75,227	0.18	-4.37
MIDDLE EAST	**234,082**	**249,260**	**237,357**	**126,613**	**110,111**	**0.27**	**-13.03**
MIDDLE EAST	**234,082**	**249,260**	**237,357**	**126,613**	**110,111**	**0.27**	**-13.03**
BAHRAIN	6,373	6,735	6,256	3,802	3,745	0.01	-1.50
IRAQ	361	537	949	541	442		-18.30
JORDAN	14,809	17,327	18,490	12,339	11,798	0.03	-4.38
KUWAIT	23,758	23,930	22,834	14,204	13,775	0.03	-3.02
LEBANON	15,099	18,599	19,401	14,517	12,981	0.03	-10.58
LIBYA	271	297	283	212	199		-6.13
OMAN	5,116	5,396	5,051	3,468	2,911	0.01	-16.06
QATAR	5,328	5,860	5,730	2,842	2,698	0.01	-5.07
SAUDI ARABIA	72,891	75,320	69,755	25,588	18,727	0.05	-26.81
SYRIA	7,640	8,470	8,237	5,194	3,843	0.01	-26.01
UNTD ARAB EM	37,635	40,039	37,518	19,080	18,353	0.04	-3.81
EGYPT	42,777	44,612	41,438	24,315	20,225	0.05	-16.82
YEMEN	1,858	1,995	1,259	445	388		-12.81
OT MIDD EAST	166	143	156	66	26		-60.61
SOUTH ASIA	**300,673**	**362,634**	**362,792**	**324,315**	**329,660**	**0.80**	**1.65**
SOUTH ASIA	**300,673**	**362,634**	**362,792**	**324,315**	**329,660**	**0.80**	**1.65**
AFGHANISTAN	158	129	125	135	227		68.15
BANGLADESH	11,380	12,724	12,218	9,585	8,434	0.02	-12.01
BHUTAN	168	150	230	154	188		22.08
SRI LANKA	8,392	9,898	8,730	6,613	7,622	0.02	15.26
INDIA	228,072	274,202	269,674	257,271	272,161	0.66	5.79
IRAN	8,453	9,364	8,536	4,996	3,454	0.01	-30.86
MALDIVES	104	124	97	72	82		13.89
NEPAL	3,620	4,101	5,450	6,047	6,270	0.02	3.69
PAKISTAN	40,326	51,942	57,732	39,442	31,222	0.08	-20.84

Source: World Tourism Organization (WTO)

UNITED STATES VIRGIN ISLANDS

3. ARRIVALS OF NON-RESIDENT TOURISTS IN HOTELS AND SIMILAR ESTABLISHMENTS, BY NATIONALITY

	1999	2000	2001	2002	2003	Market share 03	% change 03-02
TOTAL	**483,734**	**607,342**	**597,437**	**585,684**	**623,723**	**100.00**	**6.49**
AFRICA	**323**	**179**	**170**	**828**	**132**	**0.02**	**-84.06**
OTHER AFRICA	**323**	**179**	**170**	**828**	**132**	**0.02**	**-84.06**
ALL AFRICA	323	179	170	828	132	0.02	-84.06
AMERICAS	**452,307**	**533,421**	**540,598**	**494,324**	**531,271**	**85.18**	**7.47**
CARIBBEAN	**32,967**	**32,040**	**27,121**	**26,893**	**28,632**	**4.59**	**6.47**
BAHAMAS	193	299	285	110	112	0.02	1.82
BARBADOS	262	388	356	247	325	0.05	31.58
BR.VIRGIN IS	5,195	3,847	3,068	3,289	2,928	0.47	-10.98
DOMINICAN RP	57	68	184	90	50	0.01	-44.44
JAMAICA	277	266	219	218	147	0.02	-32.57
PUERTO RICO	25,269	24,324	21,212	21,859	23,639	3.79	8.14
TRINIDAD TBG	144	142	236	207	145	0.02	-29.95
OTH CARIBBE	1,570	2,706	1,561	873	1,286	0.21	47.31
CENTRAL AMER	**319**	**205**	**192**	**192**	**238**	**0.04**	**23.96**
COSTA RICA	102	51	64	81	125	0.02	54.32
EL SALVADOR	4			2	1		-50.00
GUATEMALA	41	17	34	6			
HONDURAS	8	5		1	6		500.00
NICARAGUA					1		
PANAMA	164	126	94	77	103	0.02	33.77
OT CENT AMER		6		25	2		-92.00
NORTH AMER	**416,830**	**499,318**	**511,627**	**466,279**	**501,413**	**80.39**	**7.53**
CANADA	4,934	4,373	4,022	4,372	4,809	0.77	10.00
MEXICO	239	135	177	169	247	0.04	46.15
USA	411,657	494,810	507,428	461,738	496,357	79.58	7.50
SOUTH AMER	**2,191**	**1,858**	**1,658**	**960**	**988**	**0.16**	**2.92**
ARGENTINA	1,001	908	713	232	171	0.03	-26.29
BOLIVIA	134	9	15	51	87	0.01	70.59
BRAZIL	474	334	347	266	226	0.04	-15.04
CHILE	264	140	169	96	89	0.01	-7.29
COLOMBIA	35	46	63	54	146	0.02	170.37
ECUADOR	1	12	8	12	1		-91.67
GUYANA	3	3	18	6	21		250.00
PARAGUAY				3			
PERU	46	15	32	20	35	0.01	75.00
URUGUAY	27	9	25	49	10		-79.59
VENEZUELA	199	367	268	162	198	0.03	22.22
OTH SOUTH AM	7	15		9	4		-55.56
EAST AS/PACI	**785**	**798**	**389**	**333**	**365**	**0.06**	**9.61**
N/EAST ASIA	**454**	**484**	**249**	**204**	**186**	**0.03**	**-8.82**
TAIWAN(P.C.)		32	18	13	60	0.01	361.54
JAPAN	454	452	231	191	126	0.02	-34.03
AUSTRALASIA	**331**	**314**	**140**	**129**	**179**	**0.03**	**38.76**
AUSTRALIA	245	187	126	109	176	0.03	61.47

UNITED STATES VIRGIN ISLANDS

3. ARRIVALS OF NON-RESIDENT TOURISTS IN HOTELS AND SIMILAR ESTABLISHMENTS, BY NATIONALITY

	1999	2000	2001	2002	2003	Market share 03	% change 03-02
NEW ZEALAND	86	127	14	20	3		-85.00
EUROPE	**19,469**	**12,450**	**8,708**	**6,144**	**7,756**	**1.24**	**26.24**
NORTHERN EUR	**14,361**	**8,094**	**5,760**	**3,341**	**4,158**	**0.67**	**24.45**
DENMARK	10,452	4,281	2,146	1,282	2,082	0.33	62.40
FINLAND	103	130	46	42	68	0.01	61.90
NORWAY	360	375	146	113	117	0.02	3.54
SWEDEN	362	307	175	98	143	0.02	45.92
UK	3,084	3,001	3,247	1,806	1,748	0.28	-3.21
SOUTHERN EUR	**2,084**	**1,671**	**1,284**	**1,150**	**1,470**	**0.24**	**27.83**
GREECE	43	93	149	68	135	0.02	98.53
ITALY	1,679	1,283	882	895	1,042	0.17	16.42
PORTUGAL	37	31	33	11	30		172.73
SPAIN	325	264	220	176	263	0.04	49.43
WESTERN EUR	**2,641**	**2,304**	**1,474**	**1,547**	**1,895**	**0.30**	**22.50**
AUSTRIA	272	125	57	58	69	0.01	18.97
FRANCE	690	731	511	414	440	0.07	6.28
GERMANY	1,184	900	532	763	744	0.12	-2.49
NETHERLANDS	86	127	14	20	213	0.03	965.00
SWITZERLAND	409	421	360	292	429	0.07	46.92
OTHER EUROPE	**383**	**381**	**190**	**106**	**233**	**0.04**	**119.81**
OTHER EUROPE	383	381	190	106	233	0.04	119.81
REG.NOT SPEC	**10,850**	**60,494**	**47,572**	**84,055**	**84,199**	**13.50**	**0.17**
NOT SPECIFIE	**10,850**	**60,494**	**47,572**	**84,055**	**84,199**	**13.50**	**0.17**
OTH.WORLD	10,850	60,494	47,572	84,055	84,199	13.50	0.17

Source: World Tourism Organization (WTO)

2. ARRIVALS OF NON-RESIDENT VISITORS AT NATIONAL BORDERS, BY NATIONALITY

	1999	2000	2001	2002	2003	Market share 03	% change 03-02
TOTAL	**2,273,164**	**2,235,887**	**2,136,446**	**1,353,872**	**1,508,055**	**100.00**	**11.39**
AMERICAS	**1,759,517**	**1,758,399**	**1,708,380**	**1,030,738**	**1,159,580**	**76.89**	**12.50**
NORTH AMER		**41,609**	**40,700**	**34,961**	**49,667**	**3.29**	**42.06**
CANADA		3,019	3,304	2,835	3,409	0.23	20.25
MEXICO		6,384	6,674	6,317	10,567	0.70	67.28
USA		32,206	30,722	25,809	35,691	2.37	38.29
SOUTH AMER	**1,729,482**	**1,706,397**	**1,660,033**	**981,181**	**1,084,704**	**71.93**	**10.55**
ARGENTINA	1,532,725	1,510,386	1,478,561	813,304	866,570	57.46	6.55
BOLIVIA		1,973	1,870	1,803	2,442	0.16	35.44
BRAZIL	153,740	140,905	121,882	118,400	151,383	10.04	27.86
CHILE	22,498	22,080	26,358	18,690	32,751	2.17	75.23
PARAGUAY	20,519	21,185	20,654	18,015	17,716	1.17	-1.66
PERU		6,452	7,266	8,460	10,749	0.71	27.06
VENEZUELA		3,416	3,442	2,509	3,093	0.21	23.28
OTHER AMERIC	**30,035**	**10,393**	**7,647**	**14,596**	**25,209**	**1.67**	**72.71**
OTH AMERICA	30,035	10,393	7,647	14,596	25,209	1.67	72.71
EAST AS/PACI		**6,515**	**5,531**	**5,618**	**6,230**	**0.41**	**10.89**
N/EAST ASIA		**3,929**	**3,112**	**3,321**	**2,833**	**0.19**	**-14.69**
JAPAN		2,483	2,170	1,871	1,847	0.12	-1.28
OT NORTH AS		1,446	942	1,450	986	0.07	-32.00
AUSTRALASIA		**2,276**	**2,167**	**2,087**	**2,665**	**0.18**	**27.70**
AUSTRALIA		1,454	1,524	1,630	2,063	0.14	26.56
NEW ZEALAND		822	643	457	602	0.04	31.73
OT.EAST AS/P		**310**	**252**	**210**	**732**	**0.05**	**248.57**
OEAP		310	252	210	732	0.05	248.57
EUROPE	**86,167**	**85,039**	**70,009**	**56,159**	**73,230**	**4.86**	**30.40**
NORTHERN EUR		**12,071**	**12,201**	**9,877**	**13,454**	**0.89**	**36.22**
DENMARK		683	654	540	813	0.05	50.56
FINLAND		513	444	358	761	0.05	112.57
IRELAND		668	696	641	1,045	0.07	63.03
NORWAY		749	670	594	956	0.06	60.94
SWEDEN		1,733	1,596	1,269	1,699	0.11	33.88
UK		7,725	8,141	6,475	8,180	0.54	26.33
SOUTHERN EUR		**32,308**	**26,646**	**21,765**	**28,341**	**1.88**	**30.21**
GREECE		539	418	376	584	0.04	55.32
ITALY		10,957	9,007	7,549	9,607	0.64	27.26
PORTUGAL		1,575	1,252	893	1,456	0.10	63.05
SPAIN		19,237	15,969	12,947	16,694	1.11	28.94
WESTERN EUR		**29,820**	**27,165**	**21,902**	**26,309**	**1.74**	**20.12**
AUSTRIA		1,195	1,241	883	1,302	0.09	47.45
BELGIUM		1,442	1,286	1,117	1,344	0.09	20.32
FRANCE		10,404	9,452	7,517	9,095	0.60	20.99
GERMANY		10,396	9,454	7,981	9,584	0.64	20.09
LUXEMBOURG		34	45	22	26		18.18
NETHERLANDS		3,244	2,891	1,964	2,180	0.14	11.00

URUGUAY

2. ARRIVALS OF NON-RESIDENT VISITORS AT NATIONAL BORDERS, BY NATIONALITY

	1999	2000	2001	2002	2003	Market share 03	% change 03-02
SWITZERLAND		3,105	2,796	2,418	2,778	0.18	14.89
EAST/MED EUR		**2,292**	**2,372**	**2,000**	**2,325**	**0.15**	**16.25**
ISRAEL		2,292	2,372	2,000	2,325	0.15	16.25
OTHER EUROPE	**86,167**	**8,548**	**1,625**	**615**	**2,801**	**0.19**	**355.45**
OTHER EUROPE		8,548	1,625	615	2,801	0.19	355.45
ALL EUROPE	86,167						
MIDDLE EAST		**201**	**2,627**	**170**	**131**	**0.01**	**-22.94**
MIDDLE EAST		**201**	**2,627**	**170**	**131**	**0.01**	**-22.94**
ALL MID EAST		201	2,627	170	131	0.01	-22.94
REG.NOT SPEC	**427,480**	**385,733**	**349,899**	**261,187**	**268,884**	**17.83**	**2.95**
NOT SPECIFIE	**427,480**	**385,733**	**349,899**	**261,187**	**268,884**	**17.83**	**2.95**
OTH.WORLD	42,620	23,189	2,172	2,679	4,067	0.27	51.81
N RESID ABRO	384,860	362,544	347,727	258,508	264,817	17.56	2.44

Source: World Tourism Organization (WTO)

UZBEKISTAN

1. ARRIVALS OF NON-RESIDENT TOURISTS AT NATIONAL BORDERS, BY COUNTRY OF RESIDENCE

	1999	2000	2001	2002	2003	Market share 03	% change 03-02
TOTAL	**486,800**	**301,900**	**344,900**	**331,500**	**231,000**	**100.00**	**-30.32**
AFRICA			**1,000**	**1,000**	**1,000**	**0.43**	
OTHER AFRICA			**1,000**	**1,000**	**1,000**	**0.43**	
ALL AFRICA			1,000	1,000	1,000	0.43	
AMERICAS	**8,500**	**6,000**	**10,000**	**4,100**	**2,000**	**0.87**	**-51.22**
OTHER AMERIC	**8,500**	**6,000**	**10,000**	**4,100**	**2,000**	**0.87**	**-51.22**
ALL AMERICAS	8,500	6,000	10,000	4,100	2,000	0.87	-51.22
EAST AS/PACI	**301,800**	**195,900**	**192,900**	**195,100**	**145,000**	**62.77**	**-25.68**
OT.EAST AS/P	**301,800**	**195,900**	**192,900**	**195,100**	**145,000**	**62.77**	**-25.68**
ALL ASIA	301,800	195,900	192,900	195,100	145,000	62.77	-25.68
EUROPE	**145,000**	**72,000**	**109,000**	**99,800**	**51,000**	**22.08**	**-48.90**
OTHER EUROPE	**145,000**	**72,000**	**109,000**	**99,800**	**51,000**	**22.08**	**-48.90**
ALL EUROPE	145,000	72,000	109,000	99,800	51,000	22.08	-48.90
MIDDLE EAST	**23,500**	**21,000**	**24,000**	**23,500**	**24,000**	**10.39**	**2.13**
MIDDLE EAST	**23,500**	**21,000**	**24,000**	**23,500**	**24,000**	**10.39**	**2.13**
ALL MID EAST	23,500	21,000	24,000	23,500	24,000	10.39	2.13
SOUTH ASIA	**8,000**	**7,000**	**8,000**	**8,000**	**8,000**	**3.46**	
SOUTH ASIA	**8,000**	**7,000**	**8,000**	**8,000**	**8,000**	**3.46**	
ALL STH ASIA	8,000	7,000	8,000	8,000	8,000	3.46	

Source: World Tourism Organization (WTO)

VANUATU

1. ARRIVALS OF NON-RESIDENT TOURISTS AT NATIONAL BORDERS, BY COUNTRY OF RESIDENCE

	1999	2000	2001	2002	2003	Market share 03	% change 03-02
TOTAL	**50,746**	**57,591**	**53,300**	**49,461**	**50,400**	**100.00**	**1.90**
AMERICAS	**1,343**	**1,547**	**1,413**	**1,438**	**1,625**	**3.22**	**13.00**
NORTH AMER	**1,343**	**1,547**	**1,413**	**1,438**	**1,625**	**3.22**	**13.00**
ALL NORTH AM	1,343	1,547	1,413	1,438	1,625	3.22	13.00
EAST AS/PACI	**45,525**	**51,803**	**48,234**	**44,256**	**44,876**	**89.04**	**1.40**
N/EAST ASIA	**915**	**811**	**834**	**731**	**571**	**1.13**	**-21.89**
JAPAN	915	811	834	731	571	1.13	-21.89
AUSTRALASIA	**37,256**	**44,829**	**41,179**	**36,993**	**37,221**	**73.85**	**0.62**
AUSTRALIA	30,769	36,805	33,667	29,730	29,492	58.52	-0.80
NEW ZEALAND	6,487	8,024	7,512	7,263	7,729	15.34	6.42
MELANESIA	**5,037**	**4,124**	**4,039**	**4,704**	**5,050**	**10.02**	**7.36**
NEW CALEDNIA	5,037	4,124	4,039	4,704	5,050	10.02	7.36
OT.EAST AS/P	**2,317**	**2,039**	**2,182**	**1,828**	**2,034**	**4.04**	**11.27**
OTH OCEANIA	2,317	2,039	2,182	1,828	2,034	4.04	11.27
EUROPE	**3,063**	**3,401**	**2,683**	**2,948**	**3,003**	**5.96**	**1.87**
OTHER EUROPE	**3,063**	**3,401**	**2,683**	**2,948**	**3,003**	**5.96**	**1.87**
ALL EUROPE	3,063	3,401	2,683	2,948	3,003	5.96	1.87
REG.NOT SPEC	**815**	**840**	**970**	**819**	**896**	**1.78**	**9.40**
NOT SPECIFIE	**815**	**840**	**970**	**819**	**896**	**1.78**	**9.40**
OTH.WORLD	815	840	970	819	896	1.78	9.40

Source: World Tourism Organization (WTO)

VENEZUELA

1. ARRIVALS OF NON-RESIDENT TOURISTS AT NATIONAL BORDERS, BY NATIONALITY

	1999	2000	2001	2002	2003	Market share 03	% change 03-02
TOTAL	**586,900**	**469,047**	**584,399**	**431,677**	**336,974**	**100.00**	**-21.94**
AFRICA	**860**	**380**	**819**	**518**	**438**	**0.13**	**-15.44**
EAST AFRICA	**48**	**14**					
BURUNDI	17	3					
ETHIOPIA	2						
KENYA	1	3					
RWANDA	27	8					
ZIMBABWE	1						
CENTRAL AFR	**13**	**5**					
CAMEROON	9	5					
DEM.R.CONGO	4						
NORTH AFRICA	**88**	**117**					
ALGERIA		16					
MOROCCO	87	98					
TUNISIA	1	3					
SOUTHERN AFR	**666**	**208**					
BOTSWANA		11					
SOUTH AFRICA	401	194					
OTH.SOUTH.AF	265	3					
WEST AFRICA	**45**	**36**					
MALI		3					
MAURITANIA	2	3					
NIGERIA	34	30					
SENEGAL	9						
OTHER AFRICA			**819**	**518**	**438**	**0.13**	**-15.44**
ALL AFRICA			819	518	438	0.13	-15.44
AMERICAS	**296,212**	**172,071**	**280,101**	**185,276**	**154,334**	**45.80**	**-16.70**
CARIBBEAN	**13,441**	**12,760**	**15,849**	**11,728**	**9,137**	**2.71**	**-22.09**
ANTIGUA,BARB	1	5					
BAHAMAS	1	5					
BARBADOS	3,529	3,201	3,993	2,948	2,300	0.68	-21.98
CUBA	777	545	1,085	669	581	0.17	-13.15
DOMINICAN RP	2,502	1,339	2,323	1,501	1,267	0.38	-15.59
GRENADA	626	665					
HAITI	148	117					
JAMAICA	149	95					
NETH.ANTILES		226					
ARUBA		5					
PUERTO RICO	88	46					
ST.KITTS NEV	7						
ST.LUCIA	95						
ST.VINCENT,G	112	166					
TRINIDAD TBG	5,406	6,345	6,960	5,454	4,113	1.22	-24.59
OTH CARIBBE			1,488	1,156	876	0.26	-24.22
CENTRAL AMER	**5,219**	**2,628**	**4,656**	**2,983**	**2,531**	**0.75**	**-15.15**
BELIZE	9	8					
COSTA RICA	2,719	1,691	2,504	1,717	1,398	0.41	-18.58
EL SALVADOR	270	106					

VENEZUELA

1. ARRIVALS OF NON-RESIDENT TOURISTS AT NATIONAL BORDERS, BY NATIONALITY

	1999	2000	2001	2002	2003	Market share 03	% change 03-02
GUATEMALA	425	237					
HONDURAS	155	27					
NICARAGUA	255	76					
PANAMA	1,386	483	1,201	690	627	0.19	-9.13
OT CENT AMER			951	576	506	0.15	-12.15
NORTH AMER	**170,308**	**119,738**	**167,847**	**117,835**	**94,746**	**28.12**	**-19.59**
CANADA	27,191	38,045	32,982	29,106	20,588	6.11	-29.27
MEXICO	14,572	7,569	13,730	8,722	7,447	2.21	-14.62
USA	128,545	74,124	121,135	80,007	66,711	19.80	-16.62
SOUTH AMER	**107,244**	**36,945**	**91,749**	**52,730**	**47,920**	**14.22**	**-9.12**
ARGENTINA	30,553	9,538	27,396	15,133	14,108	4.19	-6.77
BOLIVIA	1,392	589					
BRAZIL	20,213	7,984	18,909	11,022	9,929	2.95	-9.92
CHILE	16,198	4,234	12,340	6,786	6,345	1.88	-6.50
COLOMBIA	24,543	8,902	20,029	11,855	10,576	3.14	-10.79
ECUADOR	2,599	992	2,321	1,357	1,222	0.36	-9.95
GUYANA	319	583					
PARAGUAY	648	134					
PERU	6,443	2,577	5,037	3,120	2,707	0.80	-13.24
SURINAME	76	256					
URUGUAY	4,260	1,156	3,459	1,892	1,773	0.53	-6.29
OTH SOUTH AM			2,258	1,565	1,260	0.37	-19.49
EAST AS/PACI	**5,069**	**3,286**	**6,835**	**3,756**	**3,201**	**0.95**	**-14.78**
N/EAST ASIA	**4,010**	**2,407**	**4,969**	**3,015**	**2,646**	**0.79**	**-12.24**
CHINA	872	474	1,180	676	615	0.18	-9.02
TAIWAN(P.C.)	21	68					
HK,CHINA	17	38					
JAPAN	2,768	1,663	3,448	2,090	1,835	0.54	-12.20
KOREA REP.	331	164					
MONGOLIA	1						
OT NORTH AS			341	249	196	0.06	-21.29
S/EAST ASIA	**446**	**208**	**316**	**215**	**176**	**0.05**	**-18.14**
INDONESIA	1	3					
MALAYSIA	72	38					
PHILIPPINES	318	93					
SINGAPORE	49	55					
THAILAND	6	19					
ALL S/E ASIA			316	215	176	0.05	-18.14
AUSTRALASIA	**613**	**671**	**617**	**526**	**379**	**0.11**	**-27.95**
AUSTRALIA	283	469					
NEW ZEALAND	330	202					
AUST/N.ZLND			617	526	379	0.11	-27.95
OT.EAST AS/P			**933**				
OEAP			933				
EUROPE	**277,014**	**288,037**	**290,914**	**237,250**	**175,159**	**51.98**	**-26.17**
C/E EUROPE	**1,876**	**2,231**	**1,854**	**1,613**	**1,156**	**0.34**	**-28.33**
BULGARIA	42	172					
CZECH REP	279	300	296	248	182	0.05	-26.61
ESTONIA		22					

VENEZUELA

1. ARRIVALS OF NON-RESIDENT TOURISTS AT NATIONAL BORDERS, BY NATIONALITY

	1999	2000	2001	2002	2003	Market share 03	% change 03-02
HUNGARY	118	204					
LATVIA	9	5					
LITHUANIA	8	55					
POLAND	807	1,022	836	773	536	0.16	-30.66
ROMANIA	76	63					
RUSSIAN FED	527	374	465	348	271	0.08	-22.13
UKRAINE	10	14					
OTH C/E EUR			257	244	167	0.05	-31.56
NORTHERN EUR	**39,407**	**50,480**	**51,199**	**41,661**	**30,793**	**9.14**	**-26.09**
DENMARK	4,871	10,645	10,434	8,636	6,325	1.88	-26.76
FINLAND	1,131	414					
ICELAND	22						
IRELAND	462	412					
NORWAY	2,687	3,002	3,359	2,607	1,977	0.59	-24.17
SWEDEN	2,865	2,699	3,812	2,666	2,149	0.64	-19.39
UK	27,369	33,308	32,299	26,880	19,624	5.82	-26.99
OTH NORT EUR			1,295	872	718	0.21	-17.66
SOUTHERN EUR	**84,281**	**38,107**	**63,340**	**41,566**	**34,787**	**10.32**	**-16.31**
ALBANIA		3					
ANDORRA	26						
BOSNIA HERZG	9	14					
CROATIA	36	55					
GREECE	507	197					
ITALY	48,277	19,681	37,421	23,396	20,166	5.98	-13.81
PORTUGAL	5,712	3,288	5,390	3,558	2,967	0.88	-16.61
SPAIN	29,628	14,803	20,060	14,288	11,389	3.38	-20.29
TFYROM		11					
SERBIA,MTNEG	86	55					
OT SOUTH EUR			469	324	265	0.08	-18.21
WESTERN EUR	**150,224**	**196,497**	**173,248**	**151,603**	**107,740**	**31.97**	**-28.93**
AUSTRIA	6,209	4,442	6,341	4,419	3,566	1.06	-19.30
BELGIUM	8,684	15,779	11,798	11,300	7,660	2.27	-32.21
FRANCE	25,617	20,417	24,792	18,526	14,362	4.26	-22.48
GERMANY	52,783	80,286	67,168	60,426	42,320	12.56	-29.96
LIECHTENSTEN	1	3					
LUXEMBOURG	140	213					
MONACO		3					
NETHERLANDS	49,667	71,310	56,341	52,310	36,039	10.69	-31.10
SWITZERLAND	7,123	4,044	6,497	4,320	3,588	1.06	-16.94
OTH WEST EUR			311	302	205	0.06	-32.12
EAST/MED EUR	**1,226**	**722**	**1,058**	**621**	**551**	**0.16**	**-11.27**
CYPRUS	9						
ISRAEL	1,042	477	1,058	621	551	0.16	-11.27
TURKEY	175	245					
OTHER EUROPE			**215**	**186**	**132**	**0.04**	**-29.03**
OTHER EUROPE			215	186	132	0.04	-29.03
MIDDLE EAST	**519**	**462**	**643**	**432**	**371**	**0.11**	**-14.12**
MIDDLE EAST	**519**	**462**	**643**	**432**	**371**	**0.11**	**-14.12**
PALESTINE		3					
IRAQ	103	125					
JORDAN	26	11					

VENEZUELA

1. ARRIVALS OF NON-RESIDENT TOURISTS AT NATIONAL BORDERS, BY NATIONALITY

	1999	2000	2001	2002	2003	Market share 03	% change 03-02
LEBANON	175	155					
LIBYA	26	8					
SAUDI ARABIA		5					
SYRIA	154	128					
EGYPT	35	27					
ALL MID EAST			643	432	371	0.11	-14.12
SOUTH ASIA	**686**	**256**	**468**	**302**	**270**	**0.08**	**-10.60**
SOUTH ASIA	**686**	**256**	**468**	**302**	**270**	**0.08**	**-10.60**
AFGHANISTAN		5					
INDIA	615	218					
IRAN	3	22					
MALDIVES	43						
PAKISTAN	25	11					
ALL STH ASIA			468	302	270	0.08	-10.60
REG.NOT SPEC	**6,540**	**4,555**	**4,619**	**4,143**	**3,201**	**0.95**	**-22.74**
NOT SPECIFIE	**6,540**	**4,555**	**4,619**	**4,143**	**3,201**	**0.95**	**-22.74**
OTH.WORLD	6,540	4,555	4,619	4,143	3,201	0.95	-22.74

Source: World Tourism Organization (WTO)

VIET NAM

2. ARRIVALS OF NON-RESIDENT VISITORS AT NATIONAL BORDERS, BY NATIONALITY

	1999	2000	2001	2002	2003	Market share 03	% change 03-02
TOTAL	**1,781,754**	**2,140,000**					
AFRICA	**4,599**	**1,707**					
SOUTHERN AFR	**595**	**646**					
SOUTH AFRICA	560	646					
OTH.SOUTH.AF	35						
OTHER AFRICA	**4,004**	**1,061**					
OTHER AFRICA	4,004	1,061					
AMERICAS	**54,524**	**79,185**					
NORTH AMER	**52,768**	**77,430**					
CANADA	9,776	13,993					
USA	42,667	63,007					
OT.NORTH.AME	325	430					
OTHER AMERIC	**1,756**	**1,755**					
OTH AMERICA	1,756	1,755					
EAST AS/PACI	**1,013,856**	**1,352,942**					
N/EAST ASIA	**816,400**	**1,055,395**					
CHINA	483,953	620,059					
TAIWAN(P.C.)	170,501	210,134					
HK,CHINA	8,022	21,246					
JAPAN	110,569	150,550					
KOREA REP.	43,131	53,245					
OT NORTH AS	224	161					
S/EAST ASIA	**166,156**	**253,723**					
CAMBODIA	74,056	124,083					
INDONESIA	3,544	7,048					
LAO P.DEM.R.	19,548	27,390					
MALAYSIA	15,936	20,334					
PHILIPPINES	6,127	18,530					
SINGAPORE	26,829	29,031					
THAILAND	19,256	26,110					
OTH S/E ASIA	860	1,197					
AUSTRALASIA	**31,300**	**43,824**					
AUSTRALIA	27,202	39,035					
NEW ZEALAND	4,098	4,789					
EUROPE	**200,472**	**234,388**					
C/E EUROPE	**7,504**	**8,981**					
RUSSIAN FED	4,169	5,957					
OTH C/E EUR	3,335	3,024					
NORTHERN EUR	**65,460**	**79,191**					
DENMARK	8,479	8,701					
SWEDEN	7,501	8,023					
UK	40,765	53,536					
OTH NORT EUR	8,715	8,931					

2. ARRIVALS OF NON-RESIDENT VISITORS AT NATIONAL BORDERS, BY NATIONALITY

	1999	2000	2001	2002	2003	Market share 03	% change 03-02
SOUTHERN EUR	**13,368**	**16,171**					
ITALY	8,463	9,787					
OT SOUTH EUR	4,905	6,384					
WESTERN EUR	**114,050**	**128,207**					
FRANCE	68,816	71,085					
GERMANY	14,408	25,279					
SWITZERLAND	9,873	10,249					
OTH WEST EUR	20,953	21,594					
OTHER EUROPE	**90**	**1,838**					
OTHER EUROPE	90	1,838					
SOUTH ASIA	**6,428**	**6,632**					
SOUTH ASIA	**6,428**	**6,632**					
SRI LANKA	604	665					
INDIA	4,600	4,805					
PAKISTAN	466	552					
OTH STH ASIA	758	610					
REG.NOT SPEC	**501,875**	**465,146**					
NOT SPECIFIE	**501,875**	**465,146**					
OTH.WORLD	220,183	188,663					
N RESID ABRO	281,692	276,483					

Source: World Tourism Organization (WTO)

VIET NAM

2. ARRIVALS OF NON-RESIDENT VISITORS AT NATIONAL BORDERS, BY COUNTRY OF RESIDENCE

	1999	2000	2001	2002	2003	Market share 03	% change 03-02
TOTAL	**1,781,754**	**2,140,000**	**2,330,050**	**2,627,988**	**2,428,735**	**100.00**	**-7.58**
AFRICA	**4,599**	**1,707**					
SOUTHERN AFR	**595**	**646**					
SOUTH AFRICA	560	646					
OTH.SOUTH.AF	35						
OTHER AFRICA	**4,004**	**1,061**					
OTHER AFRICA	4,004	1,061					
AMERICAS	**243,549**	**241,708**	**266,433**	**303,519**	**258,991**	**10.66**	**-14.67**
NORTH AMER	**241,793**	**239,917**	**266,433**	**303,519**	**258,991**	**10.66**	**-14.67**
CANADA	31,091	30,845	35,963	43,552	40,063	1.65	-8.01
USA	210,377	208,642	230,470	259,967	218,928	9.01	-15.79
OT.NORTH.AME	325	430					
OTHER AMERIC	**1,756**	**1,791**					
OTH AMERICA	1,756	1,791					
EAST AS/PACI	**1,059,357**	**1,398,885**	**1,484,799**	**1,694,624**	**1,669,541**	**68.74**	**-1.48**
N/EAST ASIA	**824,265**	**1,067,376**	**1,152,934**	**1,320,286**	**1,241,095**	**51.10**	**-6.00**
CHINA	484,102	626,476	672,846	724,385	693,423	28.55	-4.27
TAIWAN(P.C.)	173,920	212,370	200,061	211,072	207,866	8.56	-1.52
HK,CHINA	9,172	22,170					
JAPAN	113,514	152,755	204,860	279,769	209,730	8.64	-25.03
KOREA REP.	43,333	53,452	75,167	105,060	130,076	5.36	23.81
OT NORTH AS	224	153					
S/EAST ASIA	**167,281**	**255,338**	**240,883**	**269,448**	**327,050**	**13.47**	**21.38**
BRUNEI DARSM	306	359	415	434	592	0.02	36.41
MYANMAR	554	839	1,837	1,131	1,369	0.06	21.04
CAMBODIA	74,366	124,557	76,620	69,538	84,256	3.47	21.17
INDONESIA	3,563	7,061	11,116	13,456	16,799	0.69	24.84
LAO P.DEM.R.	19,577	27,918	40,696	37,237	75,396	3.10	102.48
MALAYSIA	16,008	20,378	26,265	46,086	48,662	2.00	5.59
PHILIPPINES	6,509	18,760	20,035	25,306	22,983	0.95	-9.18
SINGAPORE	26,988	29,100	32,110	35,261	36,870	1.52	4.56
THAILAND	19,410	26,366	31,789	40,999	40,123	1.65	-2.14
AUSTRALASIA	**67,811**	**73,447**	**90,982**	**104,890**	**101,396**	**4.17**	**-3.33**
AUSTRALIA	63,056	68,162	84,085	96,624	93,292	3.84	-3.45
NEW ZEALAND	4,755	5,285	6,897	8,266	8,104	0.33	-1.96
OT.EAST AS/P		**2,724**					
OTHER ASIA		2,724					
EUROPE	**241,537**	**271,183**	**307,722**	**343,360**	**293,636**	**12.09**	**-14.48**
C/E EUROPE	**8,009**	**9,475**	**8,092**	**7,964**	**8,604**	**0.35**	**8.04**
RUSSIAN FED	4,208	6,017	8,092	7,964	8,604	0.35	8.04
OTH C/E EUR	3,801	3,458					
NORTHERN EUR	**74,926**	**87,216**	**97,815**	**108,676**	**98,095**	**4.04**	**-9.74**
DENMARK	10,016	9,785	10,780	11,815	10,432	0.43	-11.71

VIET NAM

2. ARRIVALS OF NON-RESIDENT VISITORS AT NATIONAL BORDERS, BY COUNTRY OF RESIDENCE

	1999	2000	2001	2002	2003	Market share 03	% change 03-02
FINLAND	3,468	2,771	3,565	4,149	4,312	0.18	3.93
NORWAY	6,262	6,425	7,920	8,586	7,404	0.30	-13.77
SWEDEN	8,994	9,347	10,877	14,444	12,599	0.52	-12.77
UK	43,863	56,355	64,673	69,682	63,348	2.61	-9.09
OTH NORT EUR	2,323	2,533					
SOUTHERN EUR	**13,765**	**16,577**	**20,116**	**22,527**	**14,827**	**0.61**	**-34.18**
ITALY	8,819	10,138	11,608	12,221	8,976	0.37	-26.55
PORTUGAL	3,840	5,577	7,406	10,306	5,851	0.24	-43.23
OT SOUTH EUR	1,106	862	1,102				
WESTERN EUR	**144,747**	**156,077**	**181,699**	**204,193**	**172,110**	**7.09**	**-15.71**
AUSTRIA	3,446	4,011	4,570	4,476	4,387	0.18	-1.99
BELGIUM	8,158	8,556	8,944	10,325	9,017	0.37	-12.67
FRANCE	86,026	86,492	99,700	111,546	86,791	3.57	-22.19
GERMANY	21,719	32,058	39,096	46,327	44,609	1.84	-3.71
NETHERLANDS	12,994	12,347	15,592	18,125	16,079	0.66	-11.29
SWITZERLAND	12,187	12,337	13,797	13,394	11,227	0.46	-16.18
OTH WEST EUR	217	276					
OTHER EUROPE	**90**	**1,838**					
OTHER EUROPE	90	1,838					
SOUTH ASIA	**6,428**	**6,639**	**8,086**				
SOUTH ASIA	**6,428**	**6,639**	**8,086**				
SRI LANKA	604	665	658				
INDIA	4,600	4,812	5,844				
PAKISTAN	466	552	637				
OTH STH ASIA	758	610	947				
REG.NOT SPEC	**226,284**	**219,878**	**263,010**	**286,485**	**206,567**	**8.51**	**-27.90**
NOT SPECIFIE	**226,284**	**219,878**	**263,010**	**286,485**	**206,567**	**8.51**	**-27.90**
OTH.WORLD	226,284	219,878	263,010	286,485	206,567	8.51	-27.90

Source: World Tourism Organization (WTO)

YEMEN

3. ARRIVALS OF NON-RESIDENT TOURISTS IN HOTELS AND SIMILAR ESTABLISHMENTS, BY NATIONALITY

	1999	2000	2001	2002	2003	Market share 03	% change 03-02
TOTAL	**58,370**	**72,836**	**75,579**	**98,020**	**154,667**	**100.00**	**57.79**
AFRICA	**4,312**	**5,658**	**4,867**	**3,045**	**8,627**	**5.58**	**183.32**
NORTH AFRICA	**2,310**	**2,288**	**2,009**	**1,472**	**1,875**	**1.21**	**27.38**
SUDAN	2,310	2,288	2,009	1,472	1,875	1.21	27.38
OTHER AFRICA	**2,002**	**3,370**	**2,858**	**1,573**	**6,752**	**4.37**	**329.24**
OTHER AFRICA	2,002	3,370	2,858	1,573	6,752	4.37	329.24
AMERICAS	**6,732**	**8,161**	**2,879**	**4,429**	**12,932**	**8.36**	**191.98**
NORTH AMER	**5,932**	**5,702**	**2,466**	**3,527**	**3,860**	**2.50**	**9.44**
USA	5,932	5,702	2,466	3,527	3,860	2.50	9.44
OTHER AMERIC	**800**	**2,459**	**413**	**902**	**9,072**	**5.87**	**905.76**
OTH AMERICA	800	2,459	413	902	9,072	5.87	905.76
EAST AS/PACI	**4,862**	**8,788**	**6,209**	**11,303**	**16,666**	**10.78**	**47.45**
N/EAST ASIA	**1,316**	**1,240**	**683**	**1,262**	**628**	**0.41**	**-50.24**
JAPAN	1,316	1,240	683	1,262	628	0.41	-50.24
AUSTRALASIA	**418**	**446**	**446**	**468**	**377**	**0.24**	**-19.44**
AUSTRALIA	418	446	446	468	377	0.24	-19.44
OT.EAST AS/P	**3,128**	**7,102**	**5,080**	**9,573**	**15,661**	**10.13**	**63.60**
OTHER ASIA	3,128	7,102	5,080	9,573	15,661	10.13	63.60
EUROPE	**22,201**	**24,825**	**26,920**	**15,828**	**13,033**	**8.43**	**-17.66**
NORTHERN EUR	**2,759**	**4,342**	**1,468**	**1,951**	**4,640**	**3.00**	**137.83**
UK	2,759	4,342	1,468	1,951	4,640	3.00	137.83
SOUTHERN EUR	**2,572**	**4,748**	**7,136**	**2,352**	**1,731**	**1.12**	**-26.40**
ITALY	2,572	4,748	7,136	2,352	1,731	1.12	-26.40
WESTERN EUR	**11,654**	**10,245**	**12,310**	**6,911**	**3,776**	**2.44**	**-45.36**
FRANCE	4,500	4,535	4,653	2,792	1,882	1.22	-32.59
GERMANY	5,810	4,194	5,721	2,772	1,894	1.22	-31.67
NETHERLANDS	976	1,014	1,317	693			
SWITZERLAND	368	502	619	654			
OTHER EUROPE	**5,216**	**5,490**	**6,006**	**4,614**	**2,886**	**1.87**	**-37.45**
OTHER EUROPE	5,216	5,490	6,006	4,614	2,886	1.87	-37.45
MIDDLE EAST	**20,263**	**25,404**	**34,704**	**63,415**	**103,409**	**66.86**	**63.07**
MIDDLE EAST	**20,263**	**25,404**	**34,704**	**63,415**	**103,409**	**66.86**	**63.07**
IRAQ	2,250	2,543	3,988	1,691	2,846	1.84	68.30
JORDAN	2,744	2,352	2,569	2,385	2,689	1.74	12.75
SAUDI ARABIA	7,533	9,842	14,404	38,254	59,669	38.58	55.98
SYRIA	1,574	2,278	3,040	3,727	6,780	4.38	81.92
EGYPT	2,632	3,355	2,517	2,509	3,677	2.38	46.55
OT MIDD EAST	3,530	5,034	8,186	14,849	27,748	17.94	86.87

YEMEN

5. OVERNIGHT STAYS OF NON-RESIDENT TOURISTS IN HOTELS AND SIMILAR ESTABLISHMENTS, BY NATIONALITY

	1999	2000	2001	2002	2003	Market share 03	% change 03-02
TOTAL		**473,434**	**224,156**	**588,120**	**928,002**	**100.00**	**57.79**
AFRICA		**21,815**	**13,255**	**38,658**	**51,762**	**5.58**	**33.90**
NORTH AFRICA		**10,657**	**6,147**	**7,933**	**11,250**	**1.21**	**41.81**
SUDAN		10,657	6,147	7,933	11,250	1.21	41.81
OTHER AFRICA		**11,158**	**7,108**	**30,725**	**40,512**	**4.37**	**31.85**
OTHER AFRICA		11,158	7,108	30,725	40,512	4.37	31.85
AMERICAS		**50,253**	**14,626**	**61,486**	**77,592**	**8.36**	**26.19**
NORTH AMER		**40,038**	**13,252**	**36,734**	**23,160**	**2.50**	**-36.95**
USA		40,038	13,252	36,734	23,160	2.50	-36.95
OTHER AMERIC		**10,215**	**1,374**	**24,752**	**54,432**	**5.87**	**119.91**
OTH AMERICA		10,215	1,374	24,752	54,432	5.87	119.91
EAST AS/PACI		**53,424**	**20,623**	**87,989**	**95,796**	**10.32**	**8.87**
N/EAST ASIA		**7,303**	**2,174**	**3,996**	**3,768**	**0.41**	**-5.71**
JAPAN		7,303	2,174	3,996	3,768	0.41	-5.71
AUSTRALASIA		**2,382**	**1,149**	**981**	**2,262**	**0.24**	**130.58**
AUSTRALIA		2,382	1,149	981	2,262	0.24	130.58
OT.EAST AS/P		**43,739**	**17,300**	**83,012**	**89,766**	**9.67**	**8.14**
OTHER ASIA		43,739	17,300	83,012	89,766	9.67	8.14
EUROPE		**191,227**	**90,232**	**113,246**	**82,398**	**8.88**	**-27.24**
NORTHERN EUR		**30,587**	**5,749**	**30,336**	**27,840**	**3.00**	**-8.23**
UK		30,587	5,749	30,336	27,840	3.00	-8.23
SOUTHERN EUR		**38,140**	**21,239**	**8,531**	**10,386**	**1.12**	**21.74**
ITALY		38,140	21,239	8,531	10,386	1.12	21.74
WESTERN EUR		**85,970**	**43,193**	**26,652**	**22,656**	**2.44**	**-14.99**
FRANCE		36,923	14,821	9,614	11,292	1.22	17.45
GERMANY		36,529	19,794	11,970	11,364	1.22	-5.06
NETHERLANDS		8,920	6,214	2,546			
SWITZERLAND		3,598	2,364	2,522			
OTHER EUROPE		**36,530**	**20,051**	**47,727**	**21,516**	**2.32**	**-54.92**
OTHER EUROPE		36,530	20,051	47,727	21,516	2.32	-54.92
MIDDLE EAST		**156,715**	**85,420**	**286,741**	**620,454**	**66.86**	**116.38**
MIDDLE EAST		**156,715**	**85,420**	**286,741**	**620,454**	**66.86**	**116.38**
IRAQ		17,610	10,932	28,287	17,076	1.84	-39.63
JORDAN		16,127	5,805	32,299	16,134	1.74	-50.05
SAUDI ARABIA		55,718	30,967	85,167	358,014	38.58	320.37
SYRIA		8,974	7,296	32,455	40,680	4.38	25.34
EGYPT		21,352	7,741	34,514	22,062	2.38	-36.08
OT MIDD EAST		36,934	22,679	74,019	166,488	17.94	124.93

ZAMBIA

1. ARRIVALS OF NON-RESIDENT TOURISTS AT NATIONAL BORDERS, BY COUNTRY OF RESIDENCE

	1999	2000	2001	2002	2003	Market share 03	% change 03-02
TOTAL (*)	**404,247**	**457,419**	**491,991**	**565,073**	**577,515**	**100.00**	**2.20**
AFRICA	**301,942**	**294,479**	**316,736**	**363,783**	**371,791**	**64.38**	**2.20**
EAST AFRICA	**144,676**	**148,652**	**159,887**	**183,640**	**187,683**	**32.50**	**2.20**
KENYA	3,002	2,113	2,273	2,611	2,668	0.46	2.18
ZIMBABWE	119,108	116,461	125,263	143,872	147,040	25.46	2.20
TANZANIA	19,188	27,308	29,372	33,735	34,478	5.97	2.20
OTH.EAST.AFR	3,378	2,770	2,979	3,422	3,497	0.61	2.19
CENTRAL AFR	**30,634**	**43,056**	**46,310**	**53,190**	**54,361**	**9.41**	**2.20**
ALL MID AFRI	30,634	43,056	46,310	53,190	54,361	9.41	2.20
NORTH AFRICA	**1,346**	**529**	**569**	**654**	**668**	**0.12**	**2.14**
ALL NORT AFR	1,346	529	569	654	668	0.12	2.14
SOUTHERN AFR	**123,952**	**101,111**	**108,754**	**124,902**	**127,652**	**22.10**	**2.20**
SOUTH AFRICA	74,157	70,899	76,258	87,578	89,506	15.50	2.20
OTH.SOUTH.AF	49,795	30,212	32,496	37,324	38,146	6.61	2.20
WEST AFRICA	**1,334**	**1,131**	**1,216**	**1,397**	**1,427**	**0.25**	**2.15**
ALL.WEST.AFR	1,334	1,131	1,216	1,397	1,427	0.25	2.15
AMERICAS	**15,121**	**27,469**	**29,546**	**33,935**	**34,683**	**6.01**	**2.20**
NORTH AMER	**13,521**	**25,036**	**26,929**	**30,929**	**31,611**	**5.47**	**2.21**
CANADA	3,735	7,524	8,093	9,295	9,500	1.64	2.21
USA	9,786	17,512	18,836	21,634	22,111	3.83	2.20
OTHER AMERIC	**1,600**	**2,433**	**2,617**	**3,006**	**3,072**	**0.53**	**2.20**
OTH AMERICA	1,600	2,433	2,617	3,006	3,072	0.53	2.20
EAST AS/PACI	**17,451**	**27,709**	**29,803**	**34,230**	**34,985**	**6.06**	**2.21**
N/EAST ASIA	**1,381**	**2,266**	**2,437**	**2,799**	**2,861**	**0.50**	**2.22**
JAPAN	1,381	2,266	2,437	2,799	2,861	0.50	2.22
AUSTRALASIA	**12,480**	**19,748**	**21,241**	**24,396**	**24,934**	**4.32**	**2.21**
AUSTRALIA	8,627	15,791	16,985	19,508	19,938	3.45	2.20
NEW ZEALAND	3,853	3,957	4,256	4,888	4,996	0.87	2.21
OT.EAST AS/P	**3,590**	**5,695**	**6,125**	**7,035**	**7,190**	**1.24**	**2.20**
OTHER ASIA	3,590	5,695	6,125	7,035	7,190	1.24	2.20
EUROPE	**67,253**	**105,409**	**113,375**	**130,218**	**133,085**	**23.04**	**2.20**
NORTHERN EUR	**45,073**	**67,013**	**72,077**	**82,784**	**84,607**	**14.65**	**2.20**
DENMARK	2,958	4,077	4,385	5,036	5,147	0.89	2.20
SWEDEN	2,961	3,667	3,944	4,530	4,630	0.80	2.21
UK	34,123	51,459	55,348	63,570	64,970	11.25	2.20
SCANDINAVIA	5,031	7,810	8,400	9,648	9,860	1.71	2.20
SOUTHERN EUR	**2,350**	**2,396**	**2,577**	**2,960**	**3,025**	**0.52**	**2.20**
ITALY	2,350	2,396	2,577	2,960	3,025	0.52	2.20
WESTERN EUR	**10,019**	**7,665**	**8,244**	**9,469**	**9,677**	**1.68**	**2.20**
FRANCE	3,723	3,208	3,450	3,963	4,050	0.70	2.20
GERMANY	6,296	4,457	4,794	5,506	5,627	0.97	2.20

ZAMBIA

1. ARRIVALS OF NON-RESIDENT TOURISTS AT NATIONAL BORDERS, BY COUNTRY OF RESIDENCE

	1999	2000	2001	2002	2003	Market share 03	% change 03-02
OTHER EUROPE	**9,811**	**28,335**	**30,477**	**35,005**	**35,776**	**6.19**	**2.20**
OTHER EUROPE	9,811	28,335	30,477	35,005	35,776	6.19	2.20
SOUTH ASIA	**2,480**	**2,353**	**2,531**	**2,907**	**2,971**	**0.51**	**2.20**
SOUTH ASIA	**2,480**	**2,353**	**2,531**	**2,907**	**2,971**	**0.51**	**2.20**
INDIA	2,480	2,353	2,531	2,907	2,971	0.51	2.20

Source: World Tourism Organization (WTO)

ZIMBABWE

1. ARRIVALS OF NON-RESIDENT TOURISTS AT NATIONAL BORDERS, BY COUNTRY OF RESIDENCE

	1999	2000	2001	2002	2003	Market share 03	% change 03-02
TOTAL (*)	**2,100,520**	**1,868,412**	**2,067,864**				
AFRICA	**1,508,326**	**1,403,774**	**1,593,558**				
EAST AFRICA	**845,854**	**508,105**	**936,023**				
MOZAMBIQUE	206,572	111,970	187,373				
ZAMBIA	598,759	365,695	720,678				
OTH.EAST.AFR	40,523	30,440	27,972				
SOUTHERN AFR	**550,318**	**812,370**	**617,769**				
ALL STH AFRI	550,318	812,370	617,769				
OTHER AFRICA	**112,154**	**83,299**	**39,766**				
OTHER AFRICA	112,154	83,299	39,766				
AMERICAS	**114,865**	**116,128**	**110,106**				
NORTH AMER	**100,291**	**78,592**	**90,204**				
CANADA,USA	100,291	78,592	90,204				
OTHER AMERIC	**14,574**	**37,536**	**19,902**				
OTH AMERICA	14,574	37,536	19,902				
EAST AS/PACI	**99,952**	**79,530**	**102,129**				
AUSTRALASIA	**64,984**	**56,053**	**76,123**				
AUST/N.ZLND	64,984	56,053	76,123				
OT.EAST AS/P	**34,968**	**23,477**	**26,006**				
ALL ASIA	34,968	23,477	26,006				
EUROPE	**377,377**	**268,980**	**262,071**				
NORTHERN EUR	**189,436**	**135,643**	**155,199**				
UK/IRELAND	189,436	135,643	155,199				
WESTERN EUR	**129,608**	**68,080**	**67,671**				
GERMANY	65,391	32,971	32,241				
NETHERLANDS	39,491	23,311	23,630				
SWITZERLAND	24,726	11,798	11,800				
OTHER EUROPE	**58,333**	**65,257**	**39,201**				
OTHER EUROPE	58,333	65,257	39,201				

Source: World Tourism Organization (WTO)

ZIMBABWE

2. ARRIVALS OF NON-RESIDENT VISITORS AT NATIONAL BORDERS, BY COUNTRY OF RESIDENCE

	1999	2000	2001	2002	2003	Market share 03	% change 03-02
TOTAL	**2,249,615**	**1,966,582**	**2,217,429**	**2,041,202**	**2,256,205**	**100.00**	**10.53**
AFRICA	**1,652,605**	**1,496,802**	**1,737,186**	**1,760,097**	**1,942,052**	**86.08**	**10.34**
EAST AFRICA	**933,978**	**563,818**	**1,007,190**	**494,598**	**706,445**	**31.31**	**42.83**
KENYA					12,311	0.55	
MALAWI					71,968	3.19	
MAURITIUS					3,580	0.16	
MOZAMBIQUE	215,948	117,735	191,392	242,154	295,103	13.08	21.87
UGANDA					3,363	0.15	
TANZANIA					6,166	0.27	
ZAMBIA	676,696	409,532	786,839	224,302	313,954	13.92	39.97
OTH.EAST.AFR	41,334	36,551	28,959	28,142			
CENTRAL AFR					**38,974**	**1.73**	
ANGOLA					19,630	0.87	
DEM.R.CONGO					19,344	0.86	
SOUTHERN AFR	**598,051**	**848,963**	**675,500**	**1,183,064**	**1,141,128**	**50.58**	**-3.54**
BOTSWANA					242,750	10.76	
LESOTHO					6,065	0.27	
NAMIBIA					5,880	0.26	
SOUTH AFRICA					882,726	39.12	
SWAZILAND					3,707	0.16	
ALL STH AFRI	598,051	848,963	675,500	1,183,064			
WEST AFRICA					**6,770**	**0.30**	
GHANA					1,059	0.05	
NIGERIA					5,711	0.25	
OTHER AFRICA	**120,576**	**84,021**	**54,496**	**82,435**	**48,735**	**2.16**	**-40.88**
OTHER AFRICA	120,576	84,021	54,496	82,435	48,735	2.16	-40.88
AMERICAS	**116,109**	**117,532**	**111,727**	**65,194**	**61,181**	**2.71**	**-6.16**
CARIBBEAN					**415**	**0.02**	
ALL CO CARIB					415	0.02	
NORTH AMER	**101,445**	**79,941**	**91,714**	**55,180**	**55,160**	**2.44**	**-0.04**
CANADA					7,375	0.33	
MEXICO					588	0.03	
USA					47,197	2.09	
CANADA,USA	101,445	79,941	91,714	55,180			
SOUTH AMER					**1,687**	**0.07**	
ARGENTINA					617	0.03	
BRAZIL					1,070	0.05	
OTHER AMERIC	**14,664**	**37,591**	**20,013**	**10,014**	**3,919**	**0.17**	**-60.86**
OTH AMERICA	14,664	37,591	20,013	10,014	3,919	0.17	-60.86
EAST AS/PACI	**100,788**	**80,678**	**103,280**	**65,916**	**68,414**	**3.03**	**3.79**
N/EAST ASIA					**24,307**	**1.08**	
HK,CHINA					8,199	0.36	
JAPAN					9,648	0.43	
KOREA REP.					6,460	0.29	

ZIMBABWE

2. ARRIVALS OF NON-RESIDENT VISITORS AT NATIONAL BORDERS, BY COUNTRY OF RESIDENCE

	1999	2000	2001	2002	2003	Market share 03	% change 03-02
S/EAST ASIA					**1,446**	**0.06**	
MALAYSIA					1,134	0.05	
SINGAPORE					312	0.01	
AUSTRALASIA	**65,281**	**56,631**	**76,519**	**36,841**	**40,141**	**1.78**	**8.96**
AUSTRALIA					25,054	1.11	
NEW ZEALAND					15,087	0.67	
AUST/N.ZLND	65,281	56,631	76,519	36,841			
OT.EAST AS/P	**35,507**	**24,047**	**26,761**	**29,075**	**2,520**	**0.11**	**-91.33**
OTHER ASIA					1,970	0.09	
ALL ASIA	35,507	24,047	26,761	29,075			
OTH OCEANIA					550	0.02	
EUROPE	**380,113**	**271,570**	**265,236**	**149,995**	**169,938**	**7.53**	**13.30**
NORTHERN EUR	**190,642**	**136,808**	**156,519**	**77,262**	**68,896**	**3.05**	**-10.83**
UK					58,354	2.59	
UK/IRELAND	190,642	136,808	156,519	77,262			
SCANDINAVIA					10,542	0.47	
SOUTHERN EUR					**33,971**	**1.51**	
ITALY					18,682	0.83	
PORTUGAL					11,398	0.51	
SPAIN					3,891	0.17	
WESTERN EUR	**130,416**	**68,608**	**68,425**	**44,455**	**61,541**	**2.73**	**38.43**
AUSTRIA					1,922	0.09	
FRANCE					12,504	0.55	
GERMANY	66,084	33,379	32,694	21,333	25,902	1.15	21.42
NETHERLANDS	39,606	23,430	23,925	17,465			
SWITZERLAND	24,726	11,799	11,806	5,657	8,285	0.37	46.46
BENELUX					12,928	0.57	
OTHER EUROPE	**59,055**	**66,154**	**40,292**	**28,278**	**5,530**	**0.25**	**-80.44**
OTHER EUROPE	59,055	66,154	40,292	28,278	5,530	0.25	-80.44
MIDDLE EAST					**2,209**	**0.10**	
MIDDLE EAST					**2,209**	**0.10**	
EGYPT					1,552	0.07	
OT MIDD EAST					657	0.03	
SOUTH ASIA					**12,411**	**0.55**	
SOUTH ASIA					**12,411**	**0.55**	
INDIA					10,424	0.46	
PAKISTAN					1,987	0.09	

Source: World Tourism Organization (WTO)

NOTES: 1999 - 2003

1. ARRIVALS OF NON-RESIDENT TOURISTS AT NATIONAL BORDERS, BY NATIONALITY

MALDIVES	**TOTAL**	ARRIVALS BY AIR.
MARSHALL ISLANDS	**TOTAL**	AIR ARRIVALS.
MYANMAR	**TOTAL**	INCLUDING TOURIST ARRIVALS THROUGH BORDER ENTRY POINTS TO YANGON.
NEPAL	**GREECE**	INCLUDING CYPRUS.
NIGER	**TOTAL**	AIR ARRIVALS.
NORWAY	**TOTAL**	FIGURES ARE BASED ON "THE GUEST SURVEY" CARRIED OUT BY "INSTITUTE OF TRANSPORT ECONOMICS".
PAKISTAN	**TOTAL**	2003: PROVISIONAL DATA.
PARAGUAY	**TOTAL**	EXCLUDING NATIONALS RESIDING ABROAD AND CREW MEMBERS. 2000: INBOUND AND OUTBOUND TOURISM SURVEY - CENTRAL BANK OF PARAGUAY. 2001-2003: E/D CARDS IN THE "SILVIO PETIROSSI" AIRPORT AND PASSENGER COUNTS AT THE NATIONAL BORDER CROSSINGS - NATIONAL POLICE AND SENATUR.
PERU	**TOTAL**	2003: PROVISIONAL DATA.
PORTUGAL	**TOTAL**	EXCLUDING ARRIVALS OF NATIONALS RESIDING ABROAD. INCLUDING ARRIVALS FROM ABROAD TO INSULAR POSSESSIONS OF MADEIRA AND THE AZORES.
SAINT MAARTEN	**TOTAL**	ARRIVALS AT PRINCESS JULIANA INTERNATIONAL AIRPORT; INCLUDING VISITORS TO ST. MAARTEN (THE FRENCH SIDE OF THE ISLAND).
	FRANCE	INCLUDING RESIDENTS OF THE FRENCH WEST INDIES.
SRI LANKA	**TOTAL**	EXCLUDING NATIONALS RESIDING ABROAD.
THAILAND	**TOTAL**	INCLUDING NATIONALS RESIDING ABROAD.
TUNISIA	**TOTAL**	EXCLUDING NATIONALS RESIDING ABROAD.

NOTES: 1999 - 2003

1. ARRIVALS OF NON-RESIDENT TOURISTS AT NATIONAL BORDERS, BY COUNTRY OF RESIDENCE

MALAWI	**TOTAL**	2003: PROVISIONAL DATA.
MALAYSIA	**TOTAL**	INCLUDES SINGAPORE RESIDENTS CROSSING THE FRONTIER BY ROAD THROUGH JOHORE CAUSEWAY.
MARTINIQUE	**TOTAL**	INCLUDING FRENCH OVERSEAS DEPARTMENTS AND TERRITORIES.
MEXICO	**TOTAL**	INCLUDING NATIONALS RESIDING ABROAD. 2003: PRELIMINARY DATA.
MICRONESIA (FEDERATED STATES OF)	**TOTAL**	ARRIVALS IN THE STATES OF KOSRAE, CHUUK, POHNPEI AND YAP.
MONTSERRAT	**TOTAL**	AIR ARRIVALS. INCLUDING NATIONALS RESIDING ABROAD.
NEPAL	**GREECE**	INCLUDING CYPRUS.
NEW CALEDONIA	**ALL CO CARIB**	MARTINIQUE, GUADELOUPE AND GUYANA.
	REUNION	2001: INCLUDING MAYOTTE.
	TOTAL	INCLUDING NATIONALS RESIDING ABROAD.
NIUE	**TOTAL**	ARRIVALS BY AIR, INCLUDING NIUANS RESIDING USUALLY IN NEW ZEALAND.
PALAU	**TOTAL**	AIR ARRIVALS (PALAU INTERNATIONAL AIRPORT).
PHILIPPINES	**N RESID ABRO**	PHILIPPINE PASSPORT HOLDERS PERMANENTLY RESIDING ABROAD; EXCLUDES OVERSEAS FILIPINO WORKERS.
PORTUGAL	**TOTAL**	EXCLUDING ARRIVALS OF NATIONALS RESIDING ABROAD. INCLUDING ARRIVALS FROM ABROAD TO INSULAR POSSESSIONS OF MADEIRA AND THE AZORES.
PUERTO RICO	**TOTAL**	ARRIVALS BY AIR. FISCAL YEAR JULY TO JUNE. 2003: PRELIMINARY DATA. SOURCE: "JUNTA DE PLANIFICACION DE PUERTO RICO".
RWANDA	**TOTAL**	2001: JANUARY-NOVEMBER.
SAINT EUSTATIUS	**TOTAL**	EXCLUDING NETHERLANDS ANTILLEAN RESIDENTS.
SAINT KITTS AND NEVIS	**TOTAL**	AIR ARRIVALS.
SAINT LUCIA	**TOTAL**	EXCLUDING NATIONALS RESIDING ABROAD. 2003: PROVISIONAL DATA.
SAINT VINCENT AND THE GRENADINES	**TOTAL**	ARRIVALS BY AIR.
SIERRA LEONE	**TOTAL**	ARRIVALS BY AIR.
SOUTH AFRICA	**CHINA**	INCLUDING HONG KONG, CHINA.
	TOTAL	EXCLUDING ARRIVALS BY WORK AND CONTRACT WORKERS.
SRI LANKA	**TOTAL**	EXCLUDING NATIONALS RESIDING ABROAD.
SWEDEN	**TOTAL**	DATA ACCORDING TO A NEW SURVEY, IBIS, INCOMING VISITORS TO SWEDEN. SOURCE: SWEDISH TOURIST AUTHORITY AND STATISTICS SWEDEN.
THAILAND	**TOTAL**	INCLUDING NATIONALS RESIDING ABROAD.
TONGA	**TOTAL**	ARRIVALS BY AIR.
TRINIDAD AND TOBAGO	**TOTAL**	ARRIVALS BY AIR.
UNITED STATES	**TOTAL**	DATA INCLUDE MEXICANS STAYING ONE NIGHT OR LONGER IN THE UNITED STATES.
ZAMBIA	**TOTAL**	2001-2003: PROVISIONAL DATA.
ZIMBABWE	**TOTAL**	EXCLUDING IN TRANSIT PASSENGERS.

2. ARRIVALS OF NON-RESIDENT VISITORS AT NATIONAL BORDERS, BY NATIONALITY

MACAU, CHINA	**TOTAL**	INCLUDING ARRIVALS BY SEA, LAND AND BY AIR. INCLUDED STATELESS AND CHINESE PEOPLE WHO DO NOT HAVE PERMANENT RESIDENCY IN HONG KONG, CHINA.
REPUBLIC OF MOLDOVA	**TOTAL**	VISITORS WHO ENJOYED THE SERVICES OF THE ECONOMIC AGENTS OFFICIALLY REGISTERED UNDER TOURISM ACTIVITY AND ACCOMMODATION (EXCLUDING THE REGIONS OF THE LEFT BANK OF THE DNIESTR AND THE MUNICIPALITY OF BENDER).
SINGAPORE	**TOTAL**	EXCLUDING MALAYSIAN CITIZENS ARRIVING BY LAND.
SYRIAN ARAB REPUBLIC	**TOTAL**	EXCLUDING ARRIVALS OF NATIONALS RESIDING ABROAD.
TURKEY	**TOTAL**	TRAVELLERS, INCLUDING TEMPORARY IMMIGRANTS, DIPLOMATS, CONSULAR REPRESENTATIVES AND MEMBERS OF THE ARMED FORCES. EXCLUDING ARRIVALS OF CREW MEMBERS, TRANSIT PASSENGERS AND NATIONALS OF THE COUNTRY RESIDING ABROAD.

2. ARRIVALS OF NON-RESIDENT VISITORS AT NATIONAL BORDERS, BY COUNTRY OF RESIDENCE

NEW ZEALAND	**TOTAL**	DATA REGARDING TO SHORT TERM MOVEMENTS ARE COMPILED FROM A RANDOM SAMPLE OF PASSENGER DECLARATIONS. INCLUDING NATIONALS RESIDING ABROAD. SOURCE: STATISTICS NEW ZEALAND, EXTERNAL MIGRATION.
PALESTINE	**TOTAL**	2001-2003: ARRIVALS TO THE WEST BANK ONLY. EXCLUDING JERUSALEM AND THE GAZA STRIP DUE TO THE LACK OF CONTROL ON THE BORDERS OF THESE REGIONS.
PANAMA	**TOTAL**	TOTAL NUMBER OF VISITORS BROKEN DOWN BY PERMANENT RESIDENCE WHO ARRIVED IN PANAMA AT TOCUMEN INTERNATIONAL AIRPORT AND PASO CANOA BORDER POST. 2003: PRELIMINARY DATA.
SAINT EUSTATIUS	**TOTAL**	AIR ARRIVALS.
	NETH.ANTILES	INCLUDES RESIDENTS OF ST. EUSTATIUS.
SAINT VINCENT AND THE GRENADINES	**TOTAL**	ARRIVALS BY AIR.
SINGAPORE	**TOTAL**	EXCLUDING MALAYSIAN CITIZENS ARRIVING BY LAND.
SOUTH AFRICA	**TOTAL**	EXCLUDING NATIONALS RESIDING ABROAD. INCLUDING ARRIVALS BY PURPOSE OF HOLIDAY, BUSINESS, STUDY, WORK, TRANSIT, BORDER TRAFFIC AND CONTRACT WORKERS.

3. ARRIVALS OF NON-RESIDENT TOURISTS IN HOTELS AND SIMILAR ESTABLISHMENTS, BY NATIONALITY

MALTA	TOTAL	2003: DATA BASED ON DEPARTURES (INBOUND TOURISM TRAVEL SURVEY).
MOROCCO	TOTAL	ARRIVALS IN CLASSIFIED HOTELS, HOLIDAY VILLAGES AND TOURIST RESIDENCES.
PERU	TOTAL	2003: PROVISIONAL DATA.
TURKEY	TOTAL	ARRIVALS AT LICENSED ESTABLISHMENTS INCLUDING: HOTELS, MOTELS, BOARDING HOUSES, INNS, APARTMENT HOTELS, HOLIDAY VILLAGES, SPA HOTELS AND SPECIAL HOTELS. RESULTS OF A MONTHLY SURVEY CARRIED OUT AMONG ACCOMMODATION ESTABLISHMENTS LICENSED BY THE MINISTRY OF TOURISM.
UNITED ARAB EMIRATES	N RESID ABRO	INCLUDING DOMESTIC TOURISM.

3. ARRIVALS OF NON-RESIDENT TOURISTS IN HOTELS AND SIMILAR ESTABLISHMENTS, BY COUNTRY OF RESIDENCE

NETHERLANDS	**TOTAL**	HOTELS AND BOARDING HOUSES.
PHILIPPINES	**TOTAL**	AIR ARRIVALS.
	N RESID ABRO	PHILIPPINE PASSPORT HOLDERS PERMANENTLY RESIDING ABROAD; EXCLUDES OVERSEAS FILIPINO WORKERS.
POLAND	**TOTAL**	1999: OCTOBER-SEPTEMBER. 2000-2003: JANUARY-DECEMBER.
PUERTO RICO	**OTH.WORLD**	INCLUDING CREW MEMBERS.
	TOTAL	FISCAL YEAR JULY TO JUNE. HOTELS REGISTERED BY THE "COMPAÑIA DE TURISMO DE PUERTO RICO".
	US.VIRGIN IS	FOR YEARS PREVIOUS TO FISCAL YEAR 2001, AGREGATED DATA OF TOURISTS COMING FROM MINOR ANTILLES WHO SPECIFIED THEIR COUNTRY OF ORIGIN ARE INCLUDED.
	OTH CARIBBE	AS FROM FISCAL YEAR 2001, AGGREGATED DATA OF TOURISTS COMING FROM MINOR ANTILLES WHO DID NOT SPECIFY THEIR COUNTRY OF ORIGIN ARE INCLUDED.
QATAR	**TOTAL**	ARRIVALS AT HOTELS ONLY.
ROMANIA	**ALL AFRICA**	INCLUDING EGYPT.
	ALL CENT AME	INCLUDING MEXICO.
SPAIN	**TOTAL**	ARRIVALS AT HOTELS AND "HOSTALES" (ACCOMMODATION ESTABLISHMENTS PROVIDING LIMITED SERVICES).
SWAZILAND	**TOTAL**	ARRIVALS IN HOTELS ONLY.
SWITZERLAND	**ALL NORT AFR**	ALGERIA, LIBYA, MOROCCO AND TUNISIA.
TOGO	**BURKINA FASO**	INCLUDING MALI AND NIGER.

4. ARRIVALS OF NON-RESIDENT TOURISTS IN ALL TYPES OF ACCOMMODATION ESTABLISHMENTS, BY NATIONALITY

MALTA	**TOTAL**	2003: DATA BASED ON DEPARTURES (INBOUND TOURISM TRAVEL SURVEY).
SLOVAKIA	**TOTAL**	2000: EXCLUDING ARRIVALS IN PRIVATE ACCOMMODATION = 7,086.
TURKEY	**TOTAL**	RESULTS OF A MONTHLY SURVEY CARRIED OUT AMONG ACCOMMODATION ESTABLISHMENTS LICENSED BY THE MINISTRY OF TOURISM.

4. ARRIVALS OF NON-RESIDENT TOURISTS IN ALL TYPES OF ACCOMMODATION ESTABLISHMENTS, BY COUNTRY OF RESIDENCE

PHILIPPINES	**TOTAL**	AIR ARRIVALS.
	N RESID ABRO	PHILIPPINE PASSPORT HOLDERS PERMANENTLY RESIDING ABROAD; EXCLUDES OVERSEAS FILIPINO WORKERS.
POLAND	**TOTAL**	1999: OCTOBER-SEPTEMBER. 2000-2003: JANUARY-DECEMBER.
PORTUGAL	**TOTAL**	INCLUDING ARRIVALS AT ACCOMMODATION ESTABLISHMENTS IN MADEIRA AND THE AZORES.
ROMANIA	**ALL AFRICA**	INCLUDING EGYPT.
	ALL CENT AME	INCLUDING MEXICO.
SPAIN	**TOTAL**	2000: ARRIVALS AT HOTELS, "HOSTALES", CAMPING AND TOURISM APARTMENTS. 2001-2003: ARRIVALS AT HOTELS, "HOSTALES", CAMPING, TOURISM APARTMENTS AND RURAL DWELLINGS.

5. OVERNIGHT STAYS OF NON-RESIDENT TOURISTS IN HOTELS AND SIMILAR ESTABLISHMENTS, BY NATIONALITY

MADAGASCAR	**TOTAL**	ALL STAR-ESTABLISHMENTS (REGISTERED AND NON-REGISTERED).
MALTA	**TOTAL**	2003: DATA BASED ON DEPARTURES (INBOUND TOURISM TRAVEL SURVEY).
MOROCCO	**TOTAL**	OVERNIGHT STAYS IN CLASSIFIED AND UNCLASSIFIED HOTELS, HOLIDAY VILLAGES AND TOURIST RESIDENCES.
NORWAY	**TOTAL**	NIGHTS IN REGISTERED ESTABLISHMENTS. FIGURES RELATE TO ESTABLISHMENTS WITH 20 OR MORE BEDS.
PERU	**TOTAL**	2003: PROVISIONAL DATA.
TURKEY	**TOTAL**	CLASSIFIED HOTELS, MOTELS, BOARDING HOUSES, INNS, APARTMENT HOTELS, HOLIDAY VILLAGES, SPA HOTELS AND SPECIAL HOTELS. RESULTS OF A MONTHLY SURVEY CARRIED OUT AMONG ACCOMMODATION ESTABLISHMENTS LICENSED BY THE MINISTRY OF TOURISM.
UNITED ARAB EMIRATES	**N RESID ABRO**	INCLUDING DOMESTIC TOURISM.

NOTES: 1999 - 2003

5. OVERNIGHT STAYS OF NON-RESIDENT TOURISTS IN HOTELS AND SIMILAR ESTABLISHMENTS, BY COUNTRY OF RESIDENCE

NETHERLANDS	**TOTAL**	HOTELS AND BOARDING HOUSES.
NEW CALEDONIA	**TOTAL**	IT REFERS TO HOTELS IN NOUMEA.
POLAND	**TOTAL**	1999: OCTOBER-SEPTEMBER. 2000-2003: JANUARY-DECEMBER.
PORTUGAL	**TOTAL**	OVERNIGHT STAYS IN HOTELS, APARTHOTELS, MOTELS, INNS, BOARDING HOUSES, POUSADAS, HOLIDAY VILLAGES AND TOURIST APARTMENTS. INCLUDING OVERNIGHTS STAYS IN ESTABLISHMENTS IN MADEIRA AND THE AZORES.
QATAR	**TOTAL**	NIGHTS IN HOTELS ONLY.
ROMANIA	**ALL AFRICA**	INCLUDING EGYPT.
	ALL CENT AME	INCLUDING MEXICO.
SPAIN	**TOTAL**	NIGHTS IN HOTELS AND "HOSTALES" (ACCOMMODATION ESTABLISHMENTS PROVIDING LIMITED SERVICES).
SWEDEN	**TOTAL**	NIGHTS IN HOTELS ONLY.
SWITZERLAND	**ALL NORT AFR**	ALGERIA, LIBYA, MOROCCO AND TUNISIA.
TOGO	**BURKINA FASO**	INCLUDING MALI AND NIGER.

6. OVERNIGHT STAYS OF NON-RESIDENT TOURISTS IN ALL TYPES OF ACCOMMODATION ESTABLISHMENTS, BY NATIONALITY

MALTA	**TOTAL**	2003: DATA BASED ON DEPARTURES (INBOUND TOURISM TRAVEL SURVEY).
SLOVAKIA	**TOTAL**	2000: EXCLUDING NIGHTS IN PRIVATE ACCOMMODATION = 38,934.
TURKEY	**TOTAL**	RESULTS OF A MONTHLY SURVEY CARRIED OUT AMONG ACCOMMODATION ESTABLISHMENTS LICENSED BY THE MINISTRY OF TOURISM.

6. OVERNIGHT STAYS OF NON-RESIDENT TOURISTS IN ALL TYPES OF ACCOMMODATION ESTABLISHMENTS, BY COUNTRY OF RESIDENCE

MALAWI	**TOTAL**	2003: PROVISIONAL DATA.
NETHERLANDS	**TOTAL**	EXCLUDING OVERNIGHT STAYS AT FIXED PITCHES (HIRED ON A YEARLY OR SEASONAL BASIS).
PORTUGAL	**TOTAL**	INCLUDES OVERNIGHT STAYS IN ACCOMMODATION ESTABLISHMENTS IN MADEIRA AND THE AZORES.
ROMANIA	**ALL AFRICA**	INCLUDING EGYPT.
	ALL CENT AME	INCLUDING MEXICO.
SPAIN	**TOTAL**	2000: NIGHTS IN HOTELS, "HOSTALES", CAMPING AND TOURISM APARTMENTS. 2001-2003: NIGHTS IN HOTELS, "HOSTALES", CAMPING, TOURISM APARTMENTS AND RURAL DWELLINGS.

NOTES: 1999 - 2003

1. ARRIVÉES DE TOURISTES NON RÉSIDENTS AUX FRONTIÈRES NATIONALES, PAR NATIONALITÉ

ILES MARSHALL	**TOTAL**	ARRIVEES PAR VOIE AERIENNE.
MALDIVES	**TOTAL**	ARRIVEES PAR VOIE AERIENNE.
MYANMAR	**TOTAL**	COMPRENANT LES ARRIVEES DE TOURISTES AUX POSTES-FRONTIERES DE YANGON.
NEPAL	**GRECE**	Y COMPRIS CHYPRE.
NIGER	**TOTAL**	ARRIVEES PAR VOIE AERIENNE.
NORVEGE	**TOTAL**	LES CHIFFRES SE FONDENT SUR "L'ENQUETE AUPRES DE LA CLIENTELE" DE L'INSTITUT D'ECONOMIE DES TRANSPORTS.
PAKISTAN	**TOTAL**	2003: DONNEES PROVISOIRES.
PARAGUAY	**TOTAL**	A L'EXCLUSION DES NATIONAUX RESIDANT A L'ETRANGER ET DES MEMBRES DES EQUIPAGES. 2000: ENQUETE SUR LE TOURISME RECEPTEUR ET SUR LE TOURISME EMETTEUR - BANQUE CENTRALE DU PARAGUAY. 2001-2003: CARTES D'EMBARQUEMENT ET DE DEBARQUEMENT A L'AEROPORT SILVIO PETIROSSI ET COMPTAGES DES PASSAGERS LORS DU FRANCHISSEMENT DES FRONTIERES NATIONALES - POLICE NATIONALE ET SENATUR.
PEROU	**TOTAL**	2003: DONNEES PROVISOIRES.
PORTUGAL	**TOTAL**	SONT EXCLUDES LES ARRIVEES DE NATIONAUX RESIDANT A L'ETRANGER. SONT INCLUSES LES ARRIVEES EN PROVENANCE DE L'ETRANGER AUX POSSESSIONS INSULAIRES DE MADEIRE ET DES ACORES.
SAINT-MARTIN	**TOTAL**	ARRIVEES A L'AEROPORT INTERNATIONAL "PRINCESS JULIANA"; Y COMPRIS LES VISITEURS A ST. MARTIN (PARTIE FRANCAISE DE L'ILE).
	FRANCE	Y COMPRIS LES RESIDENTS DES ANTILLES FRANÇAISES.
SRI LANKA	**TOTAL**	A L'EXCLUSION DES NATIONAUX RESIDANT A L'ETRANGER.
THAILANDE	**TOTAL**	Y COMPRIS LES NATIONAUX RESIDANT A L'ETRANGER.
TUNISIE	**TOTAL**	A L'EXCLUSION DES NATIONAUX RESIDANT A L'ETRANGER.

NOTES: 1999 - 2003

1. ARRIVÉES DE TOURISTES NON RÉSIDENTS AUX FRONTIÈRES NATIONALES, PAR PAYS DE RÉSIDENCE

AFRIQUE DU SUD	CHINE	Y COMPRIS HONG-KONG, CHINE.
	TOTAL	A L'EXCLUSION DES ARRIVEES PAR TRAVAIL ET LES TRAVAILLEURS CONTRACTUELS.
ETATS-UNIS	TOTAL	LES DONNES COMPRENNENT LES MEXICAINS QUI PASSENT UNE OU PLUSIEURS NUITS AUX ETATS-UNIS.
MALAISIE	TOTAL	Y COMPRIS LES RESIDENTS DE SINGAPOUR TRAVERSANT LA FRONTIERE PAR VOIE TERRESTRE A TRAVERS LE JOHORE CAUSEWAY.
MALAWI	TOTAL	2003: DONNEES PROVISOIRES.
MARTINIQUE	TOTAL	Y COMPRIS LES DEPARTEMENTS ET TERRITOIRES FRANÇAIS D'OUTREMER .
MEXIQUE	TOTAL	Y COMPRIS LES NATIONAUX RESIDANT A L'ETRANGER. 2003: DONNEES PRELIMINAIRES.
MICRONESIE (ETATS FEDERES DE)	TOTAL	ARRIVEES DANS LES ETATS DE KOSRAE, CHUUK, POHNPEI ET YAP.
MONTSERRAT	TOTAL	ARRIVEES PAR VOIE AERIENNE. Y COMPRIS LES NATIONAUX RESIDANT A L'ETRANGER.
NEPAL	GRECE	Y COMPRIS CHYPRE.
NIOUE	TOTAL	ARRIVEES PAR VOIE AERIENNE, Y COMPRIS LES NATIONAUX DE NIUE RESIDANT HABITUELLEMENT EN NOUVELLE-ZELANDE.
NOUVELLE-CALEDONIE	T.CARAIBES	MARTINIQUE, GUADELOUPE ET GUYANE.
	TOTAL	Y COMPRIS LES NATIONAUX RESIDANT A L'ETRANGER.
	REUNION	2001: Y COMPRIS MAYOTTE.
PALAOS	TOTAL	ARRIVEES PAR VOIE AERIENNE (AEROPORT INTERNATIONAL DE PALAU).
PHILIPPINES	N RESID ETRA	TITULAIRES D'UN PASSEPORT PHILIPPIN RESIDANT EN PERMANENCE A L'ETRANGER; TRAVAILLEURS PHILIPPINS EXCLUS.
PORTO RICO	TOTAL	ARRIVEES PAR VOIE AERIENNE. ANNEE FISCALE DE JUILLIET A JUIN. 2003: DONNEES PRELIMINAIRES. SOURCE: "JUNTA DE PLANIFICACION DE PUERTO RICO".
PORTUGAL	TOTAL	SONT EXCLUDES LES ARRIVEES DE NATIONAUX RESIDANT A L'ETRANGER. SONT INCLUSES LES ARRIVEES EN PROVENANCE DE L'ETRANGER AUX POSSESSIONS INSULAIRES DE MADEIRE ET DES ACORES.
RWANDA	TOTAL	2001: JANVIER-NOVEMBRE.
SAINTE-LUCIE	TOTAL	A L'EXCLUSION DES NATIONAUX RESIDANT A L'ETRANGER. 2003: DONNEES PROVISOIRES.
SAINT-EUSTACHE	TOTAL	A L'EXCLUSION DES RESIDENTS DES ANTILLES NEERLANDAISES.
SAINT-KITTS-ET-NEVIS	TOTAL	ARRIVEES PAR VOIE AERIENNE.
SAINT-VINCENT-ET-LES-GRENADINES	TOTAL	ARRIVEES PAR VOIE AERIENNE.
SIERRA LEONE	TOTAL	ARRIVEES PAR VOIE AERIENNE.
SRI LANKA	TOTAL	A L'EXCLUSION DES NATIONAUX RESIDANT A L'ETRANGER.
SUEDE	TOTAL	DONNEES REPOSANT SUR UNE NOUVELLE ENQUETE (IBIS) AUPRES DES VISITEURS DU TOURISME RECEPTEUR. SOURCE: "SWEDISH TOURIST AUTHORITY" ET "STATISTICS SWEDEN".
THAILANDE	TOTAL	Y COMPRIS LES NATIONAUX RESIDANT A L'ETRANGER.
TONGA	TOTAL	ARRIVEES PAR VOIE AERIENNE.
TRINITE-ET-TOBAGO	TOTAL	ARRIVEES PAR VOIE AERIENNE.

NOTES: 1999 - 2003

1. ARRIVÉES DE TOURISTES NON RÉSIDENTS AUX FRONTIÈRES NATIONALES, PAR PAYS DE RÉSIDENCE

ZAMBIE	**TOTAL**	2001-2003: DONNEES PROVISOIRES.
ZIMBABWE	**TOTAL**	A L'EXCLUSION DES PASSAGERS EN TRANSIT.

2. ARRIVÉES DE VISITEURS NON RÉSIDENTS AUX FRONTIÈRES NATIONALES, PAR NATIONALITÉ

MACAO, CHINE	**TOTAL**	Y COMPRIS LES ARRIVEES PAR MER, TERRE ET AIR. Y COMPRIS LES APATRIDES ET LES CHINOIS QUI NE RESIDENT PAS DE MANIERE PERMANENTE A HONG-KONG, CHINE.
REPUBLIQUE ARABE SYRIENNE	**TOTAL**	A L'EXCLUSION DES ARRIVEES DE NATIONAUX RESIDANT A L'ETRANGER.
REPUBLIQUE DE MOLDOVA	**TOTAL**	VISITEURS QUI ONT BENEFICIE DES SERVICES DES AGENTS ECONOMIQUES OFFICIELLEMENT ENREGISTRES AVEC LE TYPE D'ACTIVITE TOURISME ET DES UNITES D'HEBERGEMENT QUI LEUR APPARTIENNENT (A L'EXCEPTION DES REGIONS DE LA PARTIE GAUCHE DU DNIESTR ET DE LA MUNICIPALITE DE BENDER).
SINGAPOUR	**TOTAL**	A L'EXCLUSION DES ARRIVEES DE MALAISIENS PAR VOIE TERRESTRE.
TURQUIE	**TOTAL**	VOYAGEURS, Y COMPRIS LES IMMIGRANTS TEMPORAIRES, DIPLOMATES, REPRESENTANT CONSULAIRES ET MEMBRES DES FORCES ARMEES. SONT EXCLUES LES ARRIVEES DES MEMBRES DES EQUIPAGES, DES PASSAGERS EN TRANSIT ET DES NATIONAUX RESIDANT A L'ETRANGER.

2. ARRIVÉES DE VISITEURS NON RÉSIDENTS AUX FRONTIÈRES NATIONALES, PAR PAYS DE RÉSIDENCE

AFRIQUE DU SUD	**TOTAL**	A L'EXCLUSION DES NATIONAUX RESIDANT A L'ETRANGER. Y COMPRIS LES ARRIVEES PAR MOTIF DE VACANCES, AFFAIRES, ETUDES, TRAVAIL, TRANSIT, TRAFIC FRONTALIER ET TRAVAILLEURS CONTRACTUELS.
NOUVELLE-ZELANDE	**TOTAL**	LES DONNEES RELATIVES AUX MOUVEMENTS DE COURTE DUREE SONT OBTENUES A PARTIR D'UN ECHANTILLON ALEATOIRE DE DECLARATIONS DES PASSAGERS. Y COMPRIS LES NATIONAUX RESIDANT A L'ETRANGER. SOURCE: STATISTIQUES DE LA NOUVELLE ZELANDE, IMMIGRATION.
PALESTINE	**TOTAL**	2001-2003: UNIQUEMENT ARRIVEES EN CISJORDANIE. JERUSALEM ET LA BANDE DE GAZA SONT EXCLUS EN RAISON DU MANQUE DE CONTROLE AUX FRONTIERES DANS CES ZONES.
PANAMA	**TOTAL**	NOMBRE TOTAL DE VISITEURS ARRIVEES AU PANAMA PAR L'AEROPORT INTERNATIONAL DE TOCUMEN ET LE POSTE FRONTIERE DE PASO CANOA, CLASSES SELON LEUR RESIDENCE PERMANENTE. 2003: DONNEES PRELIMINAIRES.
SAINT-EUSTACHE	**TOTAL**	ARRIVEES PAR VOIE AERIENNE.
	ANTILLES NEE	Y COMPRIS LES RESIDENTS DE SAINT-EUSTACHE.
SAINT-VINCENT-ET-LES-GRENADINES	**TOTAL**	ARRIVEES PAR VOIE AERIENNE.
SINGAPOUR	**TOTAL**	A L'EXCLUSION DES ARRIVEES DE MALAISIENS PAR VOIE TERRESTRE.

3. ARRIVÉES DE TOURISTES NON RÉSIDENTS DANS LES HÔTELS ET ÉTABLISSEMENTS ASSIMILÉS, PAR NATIONALITÉ

EMIRATS ARABES UNIS	**N RESID ETRA**	Y COMPRIS LE TOURISME INTERNE.
MALTE	**TOTAL**	2003: DONNEES TIREES DES DEPARTS ("INBOUND TOURISM TRAVEL SURVEY").
MAROC	**TOTAL**	ARRIVEES DANS LES HOTELS HOMOLOGUES, VILLAGES DE VACANCES ET RESIDENCES TOURISTIQUES.
PEROU	**TOTAL**	2003: DONNEES PROVISOIRES.
TURQUIE	**TOTAL**	ARRIVEES DANS LES ETABLISSEMENTS HOMOLOGUES Y COMPRIS: HOTELS, MOTELS, PENSIONS, AUBERGES, HOTELS-APPARTEMENTS, VILLAGES DE VACANCES, HOTELS STATIONS THERMALES ET HOTELS SPECIAUX. RESULTATS DE L'ENQUETE MENSUELLE REALISEE AUPRES DES ETABLISSEMENTS D'HEBERGEMENT CLASSES PAR LE MINISTERE DU TOURISME.

3. ARRIVÉES DE TOURISTES NON RÉSIDENTS DANS LES HÔTELS ET ÉTABLISSEMENTS ASSIMILÉS, PAR PAYS DE RÉSIDENCE

ESPAGNE	**TOTAL**	ARRIVEES DANS LES HOTELS ET LES "HOSTALES" (ETABLISSEMENTS D'HEBERGEMENT OFFRANT DES SERVICES LIMITES).
PAYS-BAS	**TOTAL**	HOTELS ET PENSIONS.
PHILIPPINES	**TOTAL**	ARRIVEES PAR VOIE AERIENNE.
	N RESID ETRA	TITULAIRES D'UN PASSEPORT PHILIPPIN RESIDANT EN PERMANENCE A L'ETRANGER; TRAVAILLEURS PHILIPPINS EXCLUS.
POLOGNE	**TOTAL**	1999: OCTOBRE-SEPTEMBRE. 2000-2003: JANVIER-DECEMBRE.
PORTO RICO	**AUT.MONDE**	Y COMPRIS LES MEMBRES DES EQUIPAGES.
	TOTAL	ANNEE FISCALE DE JUILLIET A JUIN. HOTELS ENREGISTRES PAR LA "COMPAÑIA DE TURISMO DE PUERTO RICO".
	IL.VIERG.AM	POUR LES ANNEES ANTERIEURES A L'ANNEE FISCALE 2001, DES DONNEES AGREGEES DES TOURISTES EN PROVENANCE DES PETITES ANTILLES QUI ONT SPECIFIE LEUR PAYS D'ORIGINE SONT INCLUES.
	AUT CARAIBES	A PARTIR DE L'ANNEE FISCALE 2001, DONNEES AGREGEES DES TOURISTES EN PROVENANCE DES PETITES ANTILLES QUI N'ONT PAS SPECIFIE LEUR PAYS D'ORIGINE SON INCLUES.
QATAR	**TOTAL**	ARRIVEES DANS LES HOTELS UNIQUEMENT.
ROUMANIE	**TOUTES AFRIC**	Y COMPRIS L'EGYPTE.
	T.AMER.CENTR	Y COMPRIS LE MEXIQUE.
SUISSE	**T.AFR.NORD**	ALGERIE, LIBYE, MAROC ET TUNISIE.
SWAZILAND	**TOTAL**	ARRIVEES DANS LES HOTELS UNIQUEMENT.
TOGO	**BURKINA FASO**	Y COMPRIS LE MALI ET LE NIGER.

NOTES: 1999 - 2003

4. ARRIVÉES DE TOURISTES NON RÉSIDENTS DANS TOUS LES TYPES D'ÉTABLISSEMENTS D'HÉBERGEMENT, PAR NATIONALITÉ

MALTE	**TOTAL**	2003: DONNEES TIREES DES DEPARTS ("INBOUND TOURISM TRAVEL SURVEY").
SLOVAQUIE	**TOTAL**	2000: A L'EXCLUSION DES ARRIVEES DANS L'HEBERGEMENT PRIVE = 7.086.
TURQUIE	**TOTAL**	RESULTATS DE L'ENQUETE MENSUELLE REALISEE AUPRES DES ETABLISSEMENTS D'HEBERGEMENT CLASSES PAR LE MINISTERE DU TOURISME.

4. ARRIVÉES DE TOURISTES NON RÉSIDENTS DANS TOUS LES TYPES D'ÉTABLISSEMENTS D'HÉBERGEMENT, PAR PAYS DE RÉSIDENCE

ESPAGNE	**TOTAL**	2000: ARRIVEES DANS HOTELS, "HOSTALES", CAMPING ET APPARTEMENTS TOURISTIQUES. 2001-2003: ARRIVEES DANS HOTELS, "HOSTALES", CAMPING, APPARTEMENTS TOURISTIQUES ET LOGEMENTS RURAUX.
PHILIPPINES	**TOTAL**	ARRIVEES PAR VOIE AERIENNE.
	N RESID ETRA	TITULAIRES D'UN PASSEPORT PHILIPPIN RESIDANT EN PERMANENCE A L'ETRANGER; TRAVAILLEURS PHILIPPINS EXCLUS.
POLOGNE	**TOTAL**	1999: OCTOBRE-SEPTEMBRE. 2000-2003: JANVIER-DECEMBRE.
PORTUGAL	**TOTAL**	Y COMPRIS LES ARRIVEES DANS LES ETABLISSEMENTS D'HEBERGEMENT A MADERE ET AUX ACORES.
ROUMANIE	**TOUTES AFRIC**	Y COMPRIS L'EGYPTE.
	T.AMER.CENTR	Y COMPRIS LE MEXIQUE.

5. NUITÉES DE TOURISTES NON RÉSIDENTS DANS LES HÔTELS ET ÉTABLISSEMENTS ASSIMILÉS, PAR NATIONALITÉ

EMIRATS ARABES UNIS	**N RESID ETRA**	Y COMPRIS LE TOURISME INTERNE.
MADAGASCAR	**TOTAL**	ETABLISSEMENTS DE CLASSE ETOILE (CLASSES ET NON CLASSES).
MALTE	**TOTAL**	2003: DONNEES TIREES DES DEPARTS ("INBOUND TOURISM TRAVEL SURVEY").
MAROC	**TOTAL**	NUITEES DANS LES HOTELS HOMOLOGUES ET NON HOMOLOGUES, VILLAGES DE VACANCES ET RESIDENCES TOURISTIQUES.
NORVEGE	**TOTAL**	NUITEES DANS LES ETABLISSEMENTS HOMOLOGUES. LES DONNEES NE COUVRENT QUE LES ETABLISSEMENTS AVEC UNE CAPACITE D'AU MOINS 20 LITS.
PEROU	**TOTAL**	2003: DONNEES PROVISOIRES.
TURQUIE	**TOTAL**	HOTELS CLASSES, MOTELS, PENSIONS DE FAMILLES, AUBERGUES, APARTHOTELS, VILLAES DE VACANCES, STATIONS THERMALES ET HOTELS SPECIAUX. RESULTATS DE L'ENQUETE MENSUELLE REALISEE AUPRES DES ETABLISSEMENTS D'HEBERGEMENT CLASSES PAR LE MINISTERE DU TOURISME.

5. NUITÉES DE TOURISTES NON RÉSIDENTS DANS LES HÔTELS ET ÉTABLISSEMENTS ASSIMILÉS, PAR PAYS DE RÉSIDENCE

ESPAGNE	**TOTAL**	NUITEES DANS LES HOTELS ET LES "HOSTALES" (ETABLISSEMENTS D'HEBERGEMENT OFFRANT DES SERVICES LIMITES).
NOUVELLE-CALEDONIE	**TOTAL**	IL S'AGIT DES HOTELS DE NOUMEA.
PAYS-BAS	**TOTAL**	HOTELS ET PENSIONS.
POLOGNE	**TOTAL**	1999: OCTOBRE-SEPTEMBRE. 2000-2003: JANVIER-DECEMBRE.
PORTUGAL	**TOTAL**	NUITEES DANS LES HOTELS, APARTHOTELS, MOTELS, AUBERGES, PENSIONS, POUSADAS, VILLAGES DE VACANCES ET APPARTEMENTS TOURISTIQUES. Y COMPRIS LES NUITEES DANS LES ETABLISSEMENTS A MADERE ET AUX AÇORES.
QATAR	**TOTAL**	NUITEES DANS LES HOTELS UNIQUEMENT.
ROUMANIE	**TOUTES AFRIC**	Y COMPRIS L'EGYPTE.
	T.AMER.CENTR	Y COMPRIS LE MEXIQUE.
SUEDE	**TOTAL**	NUITEES DANS LES HOTELS UNIQUEMENT.
SUISSE	**T.AFR.NORD**	ALGERIE, LIBYE, MAROC ET TUNISIE.
TOGO	**BURKINA FASO**	Y COMPRIS LE MALI ET LE NIGER.

6. NUITÉES DE TOURISTES NON RÉSIDENTS DANS TOUS LES TYPES D'ÉTABLISSEMENTS D'HÉBERGEMENT, PAR NATIONALITÉ

MALTE	**TOTAL**	2003: DONNEES TIREES DES DEPARTS ("INBOUND TOURISM TRAVEL SURVEY").
SLOVAQUIE	**TOTAL**	2000: A L'EXCLUSION DES NUITEES DANS L'HEBERGEMENT PRIVE = 38.934.
TURQUIE	**TOTAL**	RESULTATS DE L'ENQUETE MENSUELLE REALISEE AUPRES DES ETABLISSEMENTS D'HEBERGEMENT CLASSES PAR LE MINISTERE DU TOURISME.

6. NUITÉES DE TOURISTES NON RÉSIDENTS DANS TOUS LES TYPES D'ÉTABLISSEMENTS D'HÉBERGEMENT, PAR PAYS DE RÉSIDENCE

ESPAGNE	**TOTAL**	2000: NUITEES DANS HOTELS, "HOSTALES", CAMPING ET APPARTEMENTS TOURISTIQUES. 2001-2003: NUITEES DANS HOTELS, "HOSTALES", CAMPING, APPARTEMENTS TOURISTIQUES ET LOGEMENTS RURAUX.
MALAWI	**TOTAL**	2003: DONNEES PROVISOIRES.
PAYS-BAS	**TOTAL**	A L'EXCLUSION DES NUITEES DANS DES INSTALLATIONS FIXES (LOUEES SUR UNE BASE ANNUELLE OU SAISONIERE).
PORTUGAL	**TOTAL**	Y COMPRIS LES NUITEES DANS LES ETABLISSEMENTS D'HEBERGEMENT A MADERE ET AUX AÇORES.
ROUMANIE	**TOUTES AFRIC**	Y COMPRIS L'EGYPTE.
	T.AMER.CENTR	Y COMPRIS LE MEXIQUE.

1. LLEGADAS DE TURISTAS NO RESIDENTES EN LAS FRONTERAS NACIONALES, POR NACIONALIDAD

ISLAS MARSHALL	TOTAL	LLEGADAS POR VIA AEREA.
MALDIVAS	TOTAL	LLEGADAS POR VIA AEREA.
MYANMAR	TOTAL	INCLUIDAS LAS LLEGADAS DE TURISTAS A TRAVES DE LOS PUNTOS DE ENTRADA FRONTERIZOS A YANGON.
NEPAL	GRECIA	INCLUIDO CHIPRE.
NIGER	TOTAL	LLEGADAS POR VIA AEREA.
NORUEGA	TOTAL	LAS CIFRAS SE BASAN EN "THE GUEST SURVEY", UN ESTUDIO REALIZADO POR EL "INSTITUTE OF TRANSPORT ECONOMICS".
PAKISTAN	TOTAL	2003: DATOS PROVISIONALES.
PARAGUAY	TOTAL	EXCLUIDOS LOS NACIONALES RESIDENTES EN EL EXTRANJERO Y LOS MIEMBROS DE TRIPULACIONES. 2000: ENCUESTA SOBRE TURISMO RECEPTOR Y EMISOR - BANCO CENTRAL DEL PARAGUAY. 2001-2003: TARJETAS E/D EN EL AEROPUERTO SILVIO PETIROSSI Y PLANILLAS DE PASAJEROS EN LOS PUESTOS TERRESTRES - POLICIA NACIONAL Y SENATUR.
PERU	TOTAL	2003: DATOS PRELIMINARES.
PORTUGAL	TOTAL	EXCLUIDAS LAS LLEGADAS DE NACIONALES RESIDENTES EN EL EXTRANJERO. INCLUIDAS LAS LLEGADAS PROCEDENTES DEL EXTRANJERO A LAS POSESIONES INSULARES DE MADEIRA Y DE LAS AZORES.
SAN MARTIN	TOTAL	LLEGADAS AL AEROPUERTO INTERNACIONAL "PRINCESS JULIANA"; INCLUIDOS LOS VISITANTES A SAN MARTIN (PARTE FRANCESA DE LA ISLA).
	FRANCIA	INCLUIDOS LOS RESIDENTES DE LAS ANTILLAS FRANCESAS.
SRI LANKA	TOTAL	EXCLUIDOS LOS NACIONALES RESIDENTES EN EL EXTRANJERO.
TAILANDIA	TOTAL	INCLUIDOS LOS NACIONALES RESIDENTES EN EL EXTRANJERO.
TUNEZ	TOTAL	EXCLUIDOS LOS NACIONALES RESIDENTES EN EL EXTRANJERO.

NOTAS: 1999 - 2003

1. LLEGADAS DE TURISTAS NO RESIDENTES EN LAS FRONTERAS NACIONALES, POR PAÍS DE RESIDENCIA

ESTADOS UNIDOS	**TOTAL**	LOS DATOS COMPRENDEN A LOS MEXICANOS QUE PASAN UNA O MAS NOCHES EN LOS ESTADOS UNIDOS.
FILIPINAS	**N RESID EXTR**	TITULARES DE PASAPORTES FILIPINOS QUE RESIDEN PERMANENTEMENTE EN EL EXTRANJERO; ESTAN EXCLUIDOS LOS TRABAJADORES FILIPINOS.
MALASIA	**TOTAL**	INCLUDIOS RESIDENTES DE SINGAPUR QUE ATRAVIESAN LA FRONTERA POR VIA TERRESTRE A TRAVES DE JOHORE CAUSEWAY.
MALAWI	**TOTAL**	2003: DATOS PROVISIONALES.
MARTINICA	**TOTAL**	INCLUIDOS LOS DEPARTAMENTOS Y TERRITORIOS FRANCESES DE ULTRAMAR.
MEXICO	**TOTAL**	INCLUIDOS LOS NACIONALES RESIDENTES EN EL EXTRANJERO. 2003: DATOS PRELIMINARES.
MICRONESIA (ESTADOS FEDERADOS DE)	**TOTAL**	LLEGADAS EN LOS ESTADOS DE KOSRAE, CHUUK, POHNPEI Y YAP.
MONTSERRAT	**TOTAL**	LLEGADAS POR VIA AEREA. INCLUIDOS LOS NACIONALES RESIDENTES EN EL EXTRANJERO.
NEPAL	**GRECIA**	INCLUIDO CHIPRE.
NIUE	**TOTAL**	LLEGADAS POR VIA AEREA, INCLUIDOS LOS NACIONALES DE NIUE QUE RESIDEN HABITUALMENTE EN NUEVA ZELANDA.
NUEVA CALEDONIA	**TODOS CARIBE**	MARTINICA, GUADALUPE Y GUYANA.
	TOTAL	INCLUIDOS LOS NACIONALES RESIDENTES EN EL EXTRANJERO.
	REUNION	2001: INCLUIDO MAYOTTE.
PALAU	**TOTAL**	LLEGADAS POR VIA AEREA (AEROPUERTO INTERNACIONAL DE PALAU).
PORTUGAL	**TOTAL**	EXCLUIDAS LAS LLEGADAS DE NACIONALES RESIDENTES EN EL EXTRANJERO. INCLUIDAS LAS LLEGADAS PROCEDENTES DEL EXTRANJERO A LAS POSESIONES INSULARES DE MADEIRA Y DE LAS AZORES.
PUERTO RICO	**TOTAL**	LLEGADAS POR VIA AEREA. AÑO FISCAL DE JULIO A JUNIO. 2003: DATOS PRELIMINARES. FUENTE: JUNTA DE PLANIFICACION DE PUERTO RICO.
RWANDA	**TOTAL**	2001: ENERO-NOVIEMBRE.
SAINT KITTS Y NEVIS	**TOTAL**	LLEGADAS POR VIA AEREA.
SAN EUSTAQUIO	**TOTAL**	EXCLUIDOS LOS RESIDENTES DE LAS ANTILLAS NEERLANDESAS.
SAN VICENTE Y LAS GRANADINAS	**TOTAL**	LLEGADAS POR VIA AEREA.
SANTA LUCIA	**TOTAL**	EXCLUIDOS LOS NACIONALES RESIDENTES EN EL EXTRANJERO. 2003: DATOS PROVISIONALES.
SIERRA LEONA	**TOTAL**	LLEGADAS POR VIA AEREA.
SRI LANKA	**TOTAL**	EXCLUIDOS LOS NACIONALES RESIDENTES EN EL EXTRANJERO.
SUDAFRICA	**CHINA**	INCLUYE HONG KONG, CHINA.
	TOTAL	EXCLUIDAS LAS LLEGADAS POR TRABAJO Y LOS TRABAJADORES CON CONTRATO.
SUECIA	**TOTAL**	DATOS SEGUN UNA NUEVA ENCUESTA, IBIS, VISITANTES LLEGADOS A SUECIA. FUENTE: AUTORIDAD DE TURISMO DE SUECIA Y ESTADISTICAS DE SUECIA.
TAILANDIA	**TOTAL**	INCLUIDOS LOS NACIONALES RESIDENTES EN EL EXTRANJERO.
TONGA	**TOTAL**	LLEGADAS POR VIA AEREA.
TRINIDAD Y TABAGO	**TOTAL**	LLEGADAS POR VIA AEREA.

NOTAS: 1999 - 2003

1. LLEGADAS DE TURISTAS NO RESIDENTES EN LAS FRONTERAS NACIONALES, POR PAÍS DE RESIDENCIA

ZAMBIA	TOTAL	2001-2003: DATOS PROVISIONALES.
ZIMBABWE	TOTAL	EXCLUIDOS LOS PASAJEROS EN TRANSITO.

2. LLEGADAS DE VISITANTES NO RESIDENTES EN LAS FRONTERAS NACIONALES, POR NACIONALIDAD

MACAO, CHINA	**TOTAL**	INCLUIDAS LAS LLEGADAS POR MAR, TIERRA Y AIRE. INCLUYE APATRIDAS Y PERSONAS DE ORIGEN CHINO QUE NO RESIDEN DE FORMA PERMANENTE EN HONG KONG, CHINA.
REPUBLICA ARABE SIRIA	**TOTAL**	EXCLUIDAS LAS LLEGADAS DE NACIONALES RESIDENTES EN EL EXTRANJERO.
REPUBLICA DE MOLDOVA	**TOTAL**	VISITANTES QUE SE BENEFICIARON DE LOS SERVICIOS DE LOS AGENTES ECONOMICOS REGISTRADOS OFICIALMENTE EN LA ACTIVIDAD TURISTICA Y EN EL ALOJAMIENTO (EXCLUIDAS LAS REGIONES DEL MARGEN IZQUIERDO DEL DNIESTR Y LA MUNICIPALIDAD DE BENDER).
SINGAPUR	**TOTAL**	EXCLUIDAS LLEGADAS DE LOS MALASIOS POR VIA TERRESTRE.
TURQUIA	**TOTAL**	VIAJEROS, INCLUIDOS INMIGRANTES TEMPOREROS, DIPLOMATICOS, REPRESENTANTES CONSULARES Y MIEMBROS DE LAS FUERZAS ARMADAS. EXCLUIDAS LAS LLEGADAS DE MIEMBROS DE TRIPULACIONES, DE PASAJEROS EN TRANSITO Y DE NACIONALES DEL PAIS RESIDENTES EN EL EXTRANJERO.

2. LLEGADAS DE VISITANTES NO RESIDENTES EN LAS FRONTERAS NACIONALES, POR PAÍS DE RESIDENCIA

NUEVA ZELANDIA	**TOTAL**	LOS DATOS RELATIVOS A LOS MOVIMIENTOS DE CORTA DURACION SE OBTIENEN DE UNA MUESTRA ALEATORIA DE DECLARACIONES DE LOS PASAJEROS. INCLUIDOS LOS NACIONALES RESIDENTES EN EL EXTRANJERO. FUENTE: ESTADISTICAS NUEVA ZELANDIA, INMIGRACION.
PALESTINA	**TOTAL**	2001-2003: LLEGADAS A CISJORDANIA UNICAMENTE. EXCLUIDOS JERUSALEN Y LA FRANJA DE GAZA DEBIDO A LA FALTA DE CONTROL EN LAS FRONTERAS DE DICHAS ZONAS.
PANAMA	**TOTAL**	TOTAL DE VISITANTES INGRESADOS A PANAMA, POR EL AEROPUERTO INTERNACIONAL DE TOCUMEN Y LA FRONTERA DE PASO CANOA SEGUN DOMICILIO PERMANENTE. 2003: DATOS PRELIMINARES.
SAN EUSTAQUIO	**TOTAL**	LLEGADAS POR VIA AEREA.
	ANTILLAS NEE	INCLUIDOS LOS RESIDENTES DE SAN EUSTAQUIO.
SAN VICENTE Y LAS GRANADINAS	**TOTAL**	LLEGADAS POR VIA AEREA.
SINGAPUR	**TOTAL**	EXCLUIDAS LLEGADAS DE LOS MALASIOS POR VIA TERRESTRE.
SUDAFRICA	**TOTAL**	EXCLUIDOS LOS NACIONALES RESIDENTES EN EL EXTRANJERO. INCLUIDAS LAS LLEGADAS POR MOTIVO DE VACACIONES, NEGOCIOS, ESTUDIOS, TRABAJO, TRANSITO, TRAFICO FRONTERIZO Y TRABAJADORES CON CONTRATO.

3. LLEGADAS DE TURISTAS NO RESIDENTES A LOS HOTELES Y ESTABLECIMIENTOS ASIMILADOS, POR NACIONALIDAD

EMIRATOS ARABES UNIDOS	**N RESID EXTR**	INCLUIDO EL TURISMO INTERNO.
MALTA	**TOTAL**	2003: DATOS PROCEDENTES DE LAS SALIDAS ("INBOUND TOURISM TRAVEL SURVEY").
MARRUECOS	**TOTAL**	LLEGADAS EN HOTELES HOMOLOGADOS, CIUDADES DE VACACIONES Y RESIDENCIAS TURISTICAS.
PERU	**TOTAL**	2003: DATOS PRELIMINARES.
TURQUIA	**TOTAL**	LLEGADAS A LOS ESTABLECIMIENTOS HOMOLOGADOS INCLUIDOS: HOTELES, MOTELES, PENSIONES, ALBERGUES, APARTAHOTELES, CIUDADES DE VACACIONES, ESTACIONES TERMALES Y HOTELES ESPECIALES. RESULTADOS DE LA ENCUESTA MENSUAL REALIZADA EN CIERTOS ESTABLECIMIENTOS DE ALOJAMIENTO CLASIFICADOS POR EL MINISTERIO DE TURISMO.

3. LLEGADAS DE TURISTAS NO RESIDENTES A LOS HOTELES Y ESTABLECIMIENTOS ASIMILADOS, POR PAÍS DE RESIDENCIA

ESPAÑA	**TOTAL**	LLEGADAS A HOTELES Y HOSTALES.
FILIPINAS	**TOTAL**	LLEGADAS POR VIA AEREA.
	N RESID EXTR	TITULARES DE PASAPORTES FILIPINOS QUE RESIDEN PERMANENTEMENTE EN EL EXTRANJERO; ESTAN EXCLUIDOS LOS TRABAJADORES FILIPINOS.
PAISES BAJOS	**TOTAL**	HOTELES Y PENSIONES.
POLONIA	**TOTAL**	1999: OCTUBRE-SEPTIEMBRE. 2000-2003: ENERO-DICIEMBRE.
PUERTO RICO	**OTR.MUNDO**	INCLUYE A LOS MIEMBROS DE LAS TRIPULACIONES.
	TOTAL	AÑO FISCAL DE JULIO A JUNIO. HOTELES ENDOSADOS POR LA COMPAÑIA DE TURISMO DE PUERTO RICO.
	IS.VIRG.AMER	PARA LOS AÑOS ANTERIORES AL FISCAL 2001, SE INCLUYEN CIFRAS AGREGADAS DE LOS TURISTAS PROCEDENTES DE LAS ANTILLAS MENORES QUE ESPECIFICARON SU PAIS DE PROCEDENCIA.
	OTROS CARIBE	A PARTIR DEL AÑO FISCAL 2001, SE INCLUYEN CIFRAS AGREGADAS DE LOS TURISTAS PROCEDENTES DE LAS ANTILLAS MENORES QUE NO ESPECIFICARON SU PAIS DE PROCEDENCIA.
QATAR	**TOTAL**	LLEGADAS A LOS HOTELES UNICAMENTE.
RUMANIA	**TODOS AFRICA**	INCLUIDO EGIPTO.
	T.AMER.CENTR	INCLUIDO MEXICO.
SUIZA	**T.AFR.NORTE**	ARGELIA, LIBIA, MARRUECOS Y TUNEZ.
SWAZILANDIA	**TOTAL**	LLEGADAS EN HOTELES UNICAMENTE.
TOGO	**BURKINA FASO**	INCLUIDOS MALI Y NIGER.

4. LLEGADAS DE TURISTAS NO RESIDENTES EN TODO TIPO DE ESTABLECIMIENTOS DE ALOJAMIENTO, POR NACIONALIDAD

ESLOVAQUIA	**TOTAL**	2000: EXCLUIDAS LAS LLEGADAS EN ALOJAMIENTO PRIVADO = 7.086.
MALTA	**TOTAL**	2003: DATOS PROCEDENTES DE LAS SALIDAS ("INBOUND TOURISM TRAVEL SURVEY").
TURQUIA	**TOTAL**	RESULTADOS DE LA ENCUESTA MENSUAL REALIZADA EN CIERTOS ESTABLECIMIENTOS DE ALOJAMIENTO CLASIFICADOS POR EL MINISTERIO DE TURISMO.

4. LLEGADAS DE TURISTAS NO RESIDENTES EN TODO TIPO DE ESTABLECIMIENTOS DE ALOJAMIENTO, POR PAÍS DE RESIDENCIA

ESPAÑA	**TOTAL**	2000: LLEGADAS EN HOTELES, HOSTALES, CAMPING Y APARTAMENTOS TURISTICOS. 2001-2003: LLEGADAS EN HOTELES, HOSTALES, CAMPING, APARTAMENTOS TURISTICOS Y ALOJAMIENTOS/CASAS RURALES.
FILIPINAS	**TOTAL**	LLEGADAS POR VIA AEREA.
	N RESID EXTR	TITULARES DE PASAPORTES FILIPINOS QUE RESIDEN PERMANENTEMENTE EN EL EXTRANJERO; ESTAN EXCLUIDOS LOS TRABAJADORES FILIPINOS.
POLONIA	**TOTAL**	1999: OCTUBRE-SEPTIEMBRE. 2000-2003: ENERO-DICIEMBRE.
PORTUGAL	**TOTAL**	INCLUIDAS LAS LLEGADAS A LOS ESTABLECIMIENTOS DE ALOJAMIENTO DE MADEIRA Y DE LAS AZORES.
RUMANIA	**TODOS AFRICA**	INCLUIDO EGIPTO.
	T.AMER.CENTR	INCLUIDO MEXICO.

5. PERNOCTACIONES DE TURISTAS NO RESIDENTES EN HOTELES Y ESTABLECIMIENTOS ASIMILADOS, POR NACIONALIDAD

EMIRATOS ARABES UNIDOS	**N RESID EXTR**	INCLUIDO EL TURISMO INTERNO.
MADAGASCAR	**TOTAL**	TODOS LOS ESTABLECIMIENTOS CATEGORIZADOS POR ESTRELLAS (HOMOLOGADOS Y NO HOMOLOGADOS).
MALTA	**TOTAL**	2003: DATOS PROCEDENTES DE LAS SALIDAS ("INBOUND TOURISM TRAVEL SURVEY").
MARRUECOS	**TOTAL**	PERNOCTACIONES EN HOTELES HOMOLOGADOS Y NO HOMOLOGADOS, CIUDADES DE VACACIONES Y RESIDENCIAS TURISTICAS.
NORUEGA	**TOTAL**	PERNOCTACIONES EN LOS ESTABLECIMIENTOS HOMOLOGADOS. LOS DATOS CUBREN SOLAMENTE LOS ESTABLECIMIENTOS CON UNA CAPACIDAD DE 20 O MAS CAMAS.
PERU	**TOTAL**	2003: DATOS PRELIMINARES.
TURQUIA	**TOTAL**	HOTELES HOMOLOGADOS, MOTELES, PENSIONES, ALBERGUES, APARTHOTELES, CIUDADES DE VACACIONES, ESTACIONES TERMALES Y HOTELES ESPECIALES. RESULTADOS DE LA ENCUESTA MENSUAL REALIZADA EN CIERTOS ESTABLECIMIENTOS DE ALOJAMIENTO CLASIFICADOS POR EL MINISTERIO DE TURISMO.

5. PERNOCTACIONES DE TURISTAS NO RESIDENTES EN HOTELES Y ESTABLECIMIENTOS ASIMILADOS, POR PAÍS DE RESIDENCIA

ESPAÑA	**TOTAL**	PERNOCTACIONES EN HOTELES Y HOSTALES.
NUEVA CALEDONIA	**TOTAL**	CORRESPONDE A LOS HOTELES DE NOUMEA.
PAISES BAJOS	**TOTAL**	HOTELES Y PENSIONES.
POLONIA	**TOTAL**	1999: OCTUBRE-SEPTIEMBRE. 2000-2003: ENERO-DICIEMBRE.
PORTUGAL	**TOTAL**	PERNOCTACIONES EN LOS HOTELES, APARTHOTELES, MOTELES, ALBERGUES, PENSIONES, POSADAS, CIUDADES DE VACACIONES Y APARTAMENTOS TURISTICOS. INCLUIDAS LAS PERNOCTACIONES EN LOS ESTABLECIMIENTOS DE MADEIRA Y DE LAS AZORES.
QATAR	**TOTAL**	PERNOCTACIONES EN LOS HOTELES UNICAMENTE.
RUMANIA	**TODOS AFRICA**	INCLUIDO EGIPTO.
	T.AMER.CENTR	INCLUIDO MEXICO.
SUECIA	**TOTAL**	PERNOCTACIONES EN LOS HOTELES UNICAMENTE.
SUIZA	**T.AFR.NORTE**	ARGELIA, LIBIA, MARRUECOS Y TUNEZ.
TOGO	**BURKINA FASO**	INCLUIDOS MALI Y NIGER.

6. PERNOCTACIONES DE TURISTAS NO RESIDENTES EN TODO TIPO DE ESTABLECIMIENTOS DE ALOJAMIENTO, POR NACIONALIDAD

ESLOVAQUIA	**TOTAL**	2000: EXCLUIDAS LAS PERNOCTACIONES EN ALOJAMIENTO PRIVADO = 38.934.
MALTA	**TOTAL**	2003: DATOS PROCEDENTES DE LAS SALIDAS ("INBOUND TOURISM TRAVEL SURVEY").
TURQUIA	**TOTAL**	RESULTADOS DE LA ENCUESTA MENSUAL REALIZADA EN CIERTOS ESTABLECIMIENTOS DE ALOJAMIENTO CLASIFICADOS POR EL MINISTERIO DE TURISMO.

6. PERNOCTACIONES DE TURISTAS NO RESIDENTES EN TODO TIPO DE ESTABLECIMIENTOS DE ALOJAMIENTO, POR PAÍS DE RESIDENCIA

ESPAÑA	**TOTAL**	2000: PERNOCTACIONES EN HOTELES, HOSTALES, CAMPING Y APARTAMENTOS TURISTICOS. 2001-2003: PERNOCTACIONES EN HOTELES, HOSTALES, CAMPING, APARTAMENTOS TURISTICOS Y ALOJAMIENTOS/CASAS RURALES.
MALAWI	**TOTAL**	2003: DATOS PROVISIONALES.
PAISES BAJOS	**TOTAL**	EXCLUIDAS LAS PERNOCTACIONES EN INSTALACIONES FIJAS (ALQUILADAS ANUALMENTE O POR TEMPORADA).
PORTUGAL	**TOTAL**	INCLUIDAS LAS PERNOCTACIONES EN LOS ESTABLECIMIENTOS DE ALOJAMIENTO DE MADEIRA Y DE LAS AZORES.
RUMANIA	**TODOS AFRICA**	INCLUIDO EGIPTO.
	T.AMER.CENTR	INCLUIDO MEXICO.